Strategy

Strategy

Theory, Practice, Implementation

Professor Dave Mackay, Dr Mikko Arevuo,
and Professor Maureen Meadows

Second edition

OXFORD
UNIVERSITY PRESS

Great Clarendon Street, Oxford, OX2 6DP,
United Kingdom

Oxford University Press is a department of the University of Oxford.
It furthers the University's objective of excellence in research, scholarship,
and education by publishing worldwide. Oxford is a registered trade mark of
Oxford University Press in the UK and in certain other countries

Published in the United States of America by Oxford University Press
198 Madison Avenue, New York, NY 10016, United States of America

British Library Cataloguing in Publication Data
Data available

Library of Congress Control Number: 2022947990

ISBN 978–0–19–284539–9

Printed in the UK by
Bell & Bain Ltd., Glasgow

ABOUT THE AUTHORS

Dave Mackay is Professor of Strategy and Digital Transformation at the Strathclyde Business School at the University of Strathclyde. Previously, he held business management roles in multinational, small and medium-sized enterprises and entrepreneurial start-up organizations in the United Kingdom. He has a continuing research interest in developing understanding of effective strategic management and organizational leadership practices, technologies, and knowledge. As a practitioner, Dave has engaged with a wide range of private, public, and charitable organizations, supporting their strategy work and development of implementable, practical outcomes. Dave has taught and consulted internationally in locations including the United States, India, Hong Kong, Malaysia, Singapore, Oman, Bahrain, Jordan, and the United Arab Emirates.

Mikko Arevuo is Senior Lecturer in Strategic Management at Cranfield School of Management, Cranfield University. Prior to moving into academia, he was a senior business practitioner in global financial services. His research and teaching interests are in strategy as guided emergence and senior management and group decision-making processes. Mikko has consulted widely in the public and private sectors, including Fortune 500 companies and policymakers as a facilitator providing evidence-based tools and frameworks to support strategic decision-making processes. A native of Finland, Mikko earned his BA in Economics and Political Science from University of Michigan, Ann Arbor, and his MBA and PhD from Cranfield University. Mikko is a member of the Society of Professional Economists, Fellow of the Royal Society of Arts, and Senior Fellow of Advance HE (Higher Education Academy).

Maureen Meadows is Professor of Strategic Management at the Centre for Business in Society at Coventry University. Formerly with the Open University Business School and Warwick Business School, Maureen's research interests include the use of strategy tools such as scenario planning and visioning by senior managers and the post-merger integration phase following mergers and acquisitions deals. With a background in mathematics, statistics, and operational research, Maureen has many years' experience of working with 'big data' and customer analytics, both as a practitioner in the financial services sector and as an academic. She has published on the progress and problems experienced by organizations working on strategic projects such as market segmentation, relationship marketing, and customer relationship management.

ACKNOWLEDGEMENTS

The authoring process has been a most rewarding journey for us. In keeping with custom, we would like to acknowledge and thank people who have given us their time, shared their wisdom, and supported us during the writing process. First and foremost, we would like to thank each of the strategy practitioners who gave the author team his or her time. Your invaluable contribution makes this book different from other strategic management texts and allows the reader to learn from your experience.

We have been supported throughout the writing process by a magnificent team at Oxford University Press. In particular, we would like to thank the book's Commissioning Editor, Nicola Hartley, and Content Development Editor, Daisy Pemble. We are grateful for the excellent editorial support, encouragement, guidance, and organization provided throughout a disrupted period for us all. Also, we owe a debt of gratitude to Jon Crowe and the wider team at Oxford University Press for the professional services and positive scholarly environment they have provided. From start to finish, it has been a pleasure to be associated with OUP.

To the many anonymous academic colleagues who provided reviews and insights into updated versions of the chapters, we cannot thank you enough for your guiding, constructive feedback. We hope you can detect how your inputs have shaped and improved the finished article.

To our colleagues, friends, and families, we thank you for bearing with us as we put many other aspects of life on pause to complete the project. For our closest families, we have a few specific things to say.

From Dave: To Jen, Jack, and Matthew, with thanks for your continual support and infinite patience in evenings, weekends, and holidays in the face of the seemingly endless promises of 'I'll just be a few more minutes'—made it in the end!

From Mikko: I am forever indebted to and in awe of the most important people in my life, my wife Erika and my children Max and Eva. Your love, support, and unwavering belief in me kept me going and enduring to the end.

From Maureen: To Matthew, Tom, and Joe, whose love, patience, and support make everything possible!

Mikko, Dave, and Maureen, September 2022

Academic Editorial Review Panellists

We are grateful to the members of the strategy academic community who generously contributed their expertise, advice, and time to reviewing and improving the text of this volume. Thank you for helping shape the text in multiple ways!

Dr Michael Mathews, University of Exeter

Dr Hans Andersson, Linköping University

Dr Maeve McArdle, Dundalk Institute of Technology

Mr. Edward J. Collins, University of Reading

Dr Mark Crowder, Manchester Metropolitan University

Mr Neil Young, De Montfort University

Dr Andrew Wild, University of Nottingham

Professor Ian Finlayson, Chichester University

Dr Arve Pettersen, Norwegian University of Science and Technology

Dr Maksym Koghut, University of Kent

Dr Chris Corker, University of York

Professor Henrik Dellestrand, Uppsala University

Dr Sathyajit Gubbi, Groningen University

Dr Niklas Hallberg, Lund University

Dr Francesca Pallotti, University of Greenwich

Professor Paul Hughes, De Montfort University

Mr Garry Carr, Leeds Beckett University

Dr Josh Morton, University of Leeds

Dr Mariya Eranova, Royal Holloway University

Dr Azhdar Karami, Bangor University

Mr Richard Howarth, Nottingham Trent University

Dr Folajimi Ashiru, Coventry University

Practitioner Editorial Review Panellists

To the diverse range of individuals who have contributed their implementation wisdom and Practitioner Insights, we appreciate you sharing your unique perspectives on strategy in practice. We thank you for adding a further dimension to the learning potential for readers. In order of appearance in the book:

Marianne Meehan, Entrepreneur, Strategy Consultant, and Business Mentor

Kirsty Lloyd Williams, Head of Strategy Validation, abrdn

Professor Bernie Bulkin, OBE, Professor of Chemistry, former Chief Scientist and senior executive at BP, venture capitalist, and radio broadcaster and columnist

Aileen McLeod, Director of Business Planning and Commercial, SSEN

Dr Ibrahim Saif, CEO, the Jordan Strategy Forum

David McGinley, CEO, Cammell Laird

Gordon Ramsay, Plant leader, P&G

Dick Howeson, CEO, uTalk

Kylie Jamieson, Senior Manager, Beaconfield Partners

Kieran Phelan, Global Sustainability and Compliance Director, William Grant & Sons

Ned Phillips, Founder and CEO, Bambu

Fazeela Gopalani, Head of Middle East, ACCA

Kathryn Kerle, Independent non-executive director

Nada Khorchid, CEO, Lead for Impact

Leslie Rance, Partner, MindofaFox

Fiona Logan, CEO, Insights

PREFACE

Thanks for picking up the second edition of *Strategy: Theory, Practice, Implementation*! In the crowded market for strategy textbooks, we appreciate that you have identified with our aim of helping students to think, communicate, and act like strategists.

Our approach to writing this book has emerged from our shared experiences in teaching, consulting, researching, and leading strategy work in different settings. In particular, we noticed a gap between the formal theoretical approaches to strategy typically taught at undergraduate and postgraduate levels and the practices and processes of strategy adopted by organizational practitioners. It may be that those we were working with had internalized previously studied theoretical frameworks or that, through practice and experience, they have developed an ability to think strategically without making an explicit reference to theoretical constructs in their work. Our feeling, though, was that there was a missing 'middle ground', in which the realities of addressing strategic issues and opportunities could be connected with the theories that can help frame, explain, and resolve strategy challenges in an effective way.

Responding to strategic problems, issues, and opportunities always involves decision-making. However, in practice, the assumptions of rationality and decision-making conditions that we know from economics often bear little resemblance to what takes place on the ground. Strategists commonly have to operate in complex, dynamic environments, making decisions with limited information under conditions of uncertainty and ambiguity. In such situations, the optimal way forward may not be knowable, and decisions may be subject to managerial biases and political motivations. Rather than rational derivation of clear plans, strategy becomes a continuing process of negotiation, (re)action, interpretation, and learning. How this is continually enacted by practitioners—over time, in context, using practices, tools, and activities—is the focus of this book.

In adopting this view of strategy, we believe this book has several distinct features. First, what people do and experience in strategy are a recurring focus in each chapter to set a platform for learning about how strategy happens in a range of settings and situations. We believe this is a key aspect of developing knowledge, skills, and behaviours in strategy that enhance student employability—graduate practical abilities are high on the agenda for most potential employers! Further, there is a burgeoning body of strategy process and practice theory with which we wanted to connect, share, and exemplify.

To meet our aim of developing students' abilities to think, talk, and act as effective strategy practitioners, we have shaped the latest strategy theory into a 'process–practice' framework which draws all elements of the book together. To bring the process–practice framework to life, we have covered classic strategy topics that will allow you to deepen your knowledge of scholarly thought and discuss and collaborate with students and practitioners of strategy from around the world. Equally, we've embraced topics of high relevance to contemporary strategy, such as the opportunities and threats associated with trends in digital transformation and platform innovation, sustainable development and growth, and internationalization and globalization. We've included a diverse set of case examples from all manner of industries and from all continents and from public-sector and third-sector organizations alongside private firms large and small. For each case, we've asked a range of questions to test and extend your thinking on what people actually do in strategy and how theory can be used to interrogate practice.

A further distinctive feature of the book is the extent to which we have placed the practitioner at the centre of the strategy-making and strategic decision-making processes. In each chapter, in addition to theory and case examples, we include a 'practitioner perspective'—an unvarnished view of how strategy is implemented in practice from an experienced individual's unique history. There is a written summary in each chapter and an accompanying video interview on the book website. The practitioners have a wide range of backgrounds and identities, and we have represented their views exactly as they expressed them. Whilst we have tried to select practitioners with an interest in the topic addressed in each chapter, they all also offer general insights about their own theories-in-use of strategy practice. This extensive engagement with practitioners is a unique feature of this book. Emphasizing human action in strategic management draws widely from the work of some of the greatest minds of management, economics, psychology, managerial cognition, behavioural and evolutionary economics, decision-making, and strategizing activities and practices literature. We are excited about the potential of these practitioner resources to support learning for students that have yet to gain strategy experience or those looking to broaden their perspectives as to what really happens in strategy practice. For colleagues designing strategy modules, we are equally looking forward to learning about—and possibly collaborating on—innovative teaching and pedagogical applications of these resources to meet the needs and interests of the modern strategy student.

We have also developed what we believe are the most comprehensive method guides available for the application of mainstream theories of strategy and common strategy tools (and also a few lesser-known approaches too!). We have engaged with methods or theories in such a way that you should be able to interpret, explain, or do the work of strategy differently as an outcome of reading each chapter. We had previously found ourselves drawing such guides out for students at all levels during courses without a reference text to support them. These guides should allow you to build confidence and capabilities in application of well-established views of strategy as a platform to then engaging with more specialized and nuanced considerations in the field. All the method guides reported in the chapters we have used in consultancy practice, teaching, and even for our own companies or business activities. However, we have tried to write them in such a way that they are a non-prescriptive starting point for undertaking strategy work. Our wish is that students and teachers can creatively 'make the tools their own' according to personal preference and the needs of the situations you face.

Indeed, throughout the book, we have attempted to engage with strategy as a 'situated' activity. For us, this means that how strategy is best understood, approached, and enacted will depend on the history and circumstances of those involved. Thus, we have written about how strategy 'might be' rather than what strategy 'is', in order that the student can engage in or the tutor can facilitate learning about strategy that embodies their own interests and experiences. To support this personal engagement with the subject, we present a wide range of relevant theories and how they might be useful in practice, case examples to provoke inquiry and reflection, and practitioner perspectives as examples of how others grapple with the subject matter. We start the book by offering multiple interpretations of what strategy might mean, whilst resisting firm commitment to any particular definition, and conclude by describing multiple ways in which you can continue your own unique life-long learning journey about strategy-in-practice through reflection. For colleagues, whilst we lean towards pedagogies that help students build deep process and practice understanding, we've endeavoured to write in an open way that means you can adopt chapter combinations and interpretations of the text that fit the needs of your teaching philosophy.

We hope you enjoy using the book, exploring the online resources, and, of course, trying to apply the learning. Good luck in your journey to think, talk, and act like a strategist!

The Author Team, September 2022

GUIDE TO THE BOOK

 LEARNING OBJECTIVES

○ A list of clear outcomes, using key terms from the chapter, indicates what you can expect to learn. You can use this list to navigate the chapter content, making your learning experience focused and efficient.

 TOOLBOX

○ Key concepts, theories, frameworks, and models are highlighted in this feature and accompanied by short annotations to help you build your knowledge of strategic tools. This very practical feature also provides a handy revision resource for later study.

 OPENING CASE STUDY

Based on a range of small, medium, and large organizations across a variety of sectors and geographies, this feature opens each chapter to set the scene. Carefully placed questions for discussion accompany the opening case, asking you to identify the key themes and critically consider the strategy discussed as you progress through the chapter.

 CASE EXAMPLES

Shorter case vignettes within the chapter focus on key concepts and also cover a vast range of organizations. The case examples allow you to pause and consider how the illustration relates to the concepts discussed and, through further questions for discussion, help check your developing understanding of the topic or encourage you to discuss and debate with classmates.

PRACTITIONER INSIGHTS

Based on first-hand interviews with exceptional strategy experts from across the globe, practitioner insights provide you with unique insight into how the strategic tools and concepts discussed within the chapter are applied in the real world. These in-chapter interviews are accompanied by online video interviews with each practitioner.

CHAPTER SUMMARY

○ Chapter summaries provide a brief outline of the important concepts to take away, helping you to consolidate your learning before you move on. They also contextualize each subject area within the bigger picture of the process–practice model of strategy.

END-OF-CHAPTER QUESTIONS

1. Recall questions and application questions enable you to remind yourself of the key points of the chapter and then apply your knowledge to practise deeper strategic thinking.

2. Here, you are encouraged to put yourself in the position of a professional, pick organizations you are interested in, and consider how you would think, talk, and act like a strategist in those scenarios.

FURTHER READING

Seminal and cutting-edge research is listed, along with brief annotations of each, to support you in reading beyond the chapter and to facilitate easy navigation of the key academic perspectives in the field. Research insights and additional further reading references are provided online to further broaden your academic reading.

GUIDE TO THE ONLINE RESOURCES

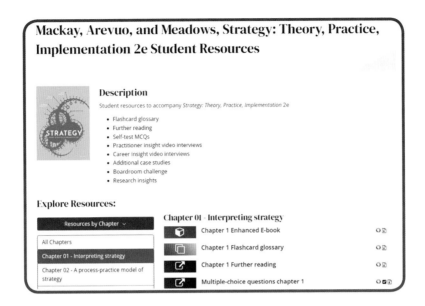

www.oup.com/he/mackay2e

For students

Enhanced e-book

An interactive version of the text includes selected online resources at your fingertips to enhance the learning experience. The enhanced e-book enables on-the-go assessment, video viewing, and further reading and research, all in one place.

Practitioner insights

Uniquely filmed for this text, practitioner insight videos award students with an exciting glimpse into the world of professionals from a diverse range of organizations. Sixteen outstanding strategists talk about their experiences throughout their career in relation to the corresponding chapter topic. These videos offer deeper insight into the tools they use in their day-to-day working life and offer students the chance to examine the implementation of strategy theory in the professional world. Practitioner insights also provide a chance to appreciate how studying strategy will help support future careers, following in the footsteps of experts.

Research insights

Abstracts for key pieces of research to accompany each chapter serve to broaden your perspective of the academic field, accompanied by author insights into how each paper can support your study. The research insights help support you to become the most well-rounded strategy graduates of the future, ensuring that the practice of strategy is balanced with academic rigour.

Career insights

A bespoke video of each practitioner offers employability guidance, including skills you can develop throughout your course, and also outside your course, in order to best prepare you for your career.

Additional case studies

Sixteen additional case studies from organizations around the world broaden students' learning even further. These case studies include companies spanning five continents, including Deliveroo, Uniqlo, and BritBox, and are accompanied with learning outcomes, questions for discussion, and multimedia ancillary material.

Student assessment

Multiple-choice and multiple-response questions enable you to check your understanding as you progress through the chapters. Feedback sends you back to the particular section of the chapter to pinpoint the gaps in your knowledge quickly and easily and allow you to revisit the topic according to your needs.

Further reading

Additional further reading recommendations ensure that you are well informed as you refine your own strategic thinking beyond the text.

Flashcard glossary

Key terms and phrases are provided in a flashcard glossary to quickly test understanding.

For lecturers

Teaching notes for in-chapter opening cases and case examples

Teaching ideas for class work use the opening case studies and case examples in each chapter. Potential approaches to the questions for discussion that accompany each opening case and case example in the book are also included.

PowerPoint teaching slides

PowerPoint slides for lecturers support teaching by providing all the tables and figures in a presentation-style suite of slides.

Teaching notes to accompany additional case studies

Teaching notes and suggested approaches to answering the questions for discussion in class accompany each additional online case study.

Test bank

Additional assessment is provided in the tutor test bank.

Boardroom challenge, including teaching notes

A designed workshop exercise, including teaching notes, through which class delivery colleagues can challenge students to integrate and apply their learning towards addressing a practical organizational strategy issue. This could be used in a range of teaching situations such as group role play exercises or action learning simulations.

CONTENTS

DETAILED CONTENTS

OPENING CASES, CASE EXAMPLES, AND PRACTITIONER INSIGHTS

FIGURES

TABLES

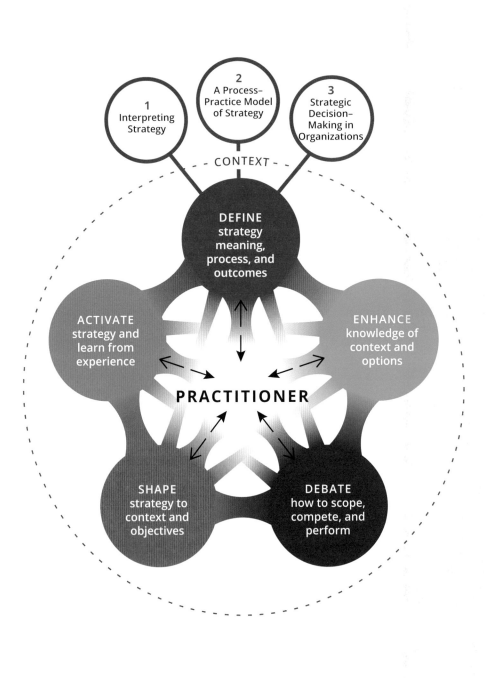

PART
ONE

Define strategy meaning, process, and outcomes

We start by addressing how you can clarify and agree what strategy means to those involved and identify appropriate approaches to strategy activity and decision-making. To build your understanding and vocabulary, in Chapter 1 we introduce a wide range of interpretations of strategy you might encounter, in Chapter 2 we examine process and practice theories and how they might be used in combination to explain activity, and in Chapter 3 we review decision-making theories of high relevance to strategy work. To support your capacity to apply these insights, Chapter 1 describes a framework of twelve complementary ways to approach discussing what strategy means to stakeholders, Chapter 2 offers frameworks for selecting categories of strategy activity that can drive progress, and Chapter 3 shows how you can adopt decision-making principles—as individuals or groups—that match the needs of any situation you face.

By the end of Part 1, you should have enhanced abilities to think, talk, and act like a practitioner, defining strategy meaning, approaches, and outcomes.

CHAPTER ONE

Interpreting Strategy

CONTENTS

LEARNING OBJECTIVES

By the end of this chapter, you should be able to:

○ Explain how strategy can be interpreted in multiple ways

○ Evaluate the challenges and benefits of agreeing a shared understanding of strategy with key stakeholders

○ Critically assess the usefulness of strategy in different organizational situations and from different stakeholder perspectives

○ Appreciate the value of strategy as a mechanism for coordinating organizational effort and decision-making

○ Reconcile how strategy is interpreted within and between stakeholder groups

TOOLBOX

○ **12Ps of strategy**
A framework that highlights different ways in which strategy might be interpreted; provides a method to discuss and explore what strategy means to stakeholders in different settings.

○ **Strategy scoping method**
An approach to structured discussion and clarification of a shared meaning of strategy between stakeholders in any given context.

Access the online resources to watch a short video clip where Marianne Meehan shares her top career tips.

1

1.1 **Introduction**

Strategy is a mainstay in the management of organizational, civic, and personal life. It is rare to find an organization that doesn't have a strategy, either explicitly or implicitly. At a country level, industrial strategies abound for growing economies, boosting productivity, and addressing global change. For example, companies vie to help us develop personal financial strategies to save for later life, and the role of political strategies in determining the outcome of elections and influencing public opinion is becoming increasingly important.

Yet, for all its widespread usage, the meaning of the term 'strategy' is hard to pin down. As we will explore, strategy can be interpreted in many ways according to the experience and perspective of individuals. The academics, consultants, gurus, and practitioners jostling to advise organizations rarely agree on the definition or even the nature of strategy. If you ask 10 people what they mean by strategy, you will likely receive 10 different explanations! According to historian Sir Lawrence Freedman (2013: ch. 1), **strategy** defies precise definition yet is the best word we have to describe efforts to:

> *'maintain a balance between ends, ways and means'; 'identifying objectives and the resources and methods available for meeting such objectives' within the context of the 'drama and challenge' of the 'inherent unpredictability of human affairs'.*

This lack of clear definition of strategy presents us with a fundamental issue. When working with others in the development and implementation of strategy, how can we be sure that we hold compatible views about what strategy means? And how can we know we are working towards the same outcomes if we understand strategy differently?

Relatedly, there are varied opinions as to the value of strategy. Strategy theoretically provides us with a way of coordinating activities, priorities, and decisions across groups of individuals towards achieving shared long-term aims. However, these outcomes assume that when presented with a strategy, all individuals will be ready, willing, and able to interpret that strategy consistently and enact it without error. When the volatility, uncertainty, ambiguity, and complexity (VUCA) of our ever-changing context is factored in (see Millar et al. 2018), the question arises as to how valuable strategy might be for individuals, organizations, institutions, or nations.

Given these challenges, to explain how strategy can benefit an organization, we will focus on examining strategy practice—what is actually done—and strategy process—how activities relating to strategy occur in context and over time. To do so requires us to consider the role of people—their knowledge, abilities, and behaviours—and the way in which the flow of strategy work might occur. As Henry Mintzberg (Mintzberg and Hunsicker 1988: 73) notes, 'to manage strategy is to craft thought and action, control and learning, stability and change'.

Our intention here is to create a reference text which enables the application of what we know about strategy from research to how it might occur in practice. For students in a classroom setting, the book will give insights about how to think, talk, and act like a strategist. You will be able to build your skills in undertaking meaningful strategy analysis and recommendations when faced with real-world situations.

In this opening chapter, we review what strategy might mean to **stakeholders**—those individuals or groups affected by and with the power to influence strategy. By building awareness of possible interpretations of strategy, you will be equipped to discuss strategy with others regardless of their perspective. Stakeholder views can then be reconciled through collective conversation to express a shared meaning of strategy in context. In being able to lead this sort of 'strategy scoping' work in your future career, you become able to move from telling others what strategy 'is'—its meaning, form, function, and outputs—to enabling a group to agree and activate strategy work in a way that fits their needs.

To aid you in this task, after introducing a range of concepts and interpretations of strategy, we introduce a strategy scoping method (see the Tool Box for an explanation of this) that can help you initiate strategy conversations and shared meaning making. By the conclusion of this chapter, you should be aware of a range of ways in which strategy might be understood, discussed, or enacted.

1.2 Strategy in modern organizations

Entire books have been written about the history of strategy and the development of approaches to strategy in different parts of the world (for instance, Freedman (2013) and Jullien (2004)). Indeed, writing on strategy dates back millennia with early treatises such as the *Art of War*, attributed to the Chinese military strategist Sun Tzu some 2,500 years ago and *How to Survive under Siege*, written by the Greek writer Aeneas Tacticus around 2,400 years ago.

To set the scene for examining current interpretations of strategy, we will review how the usage of strategy has evolved in modern organizations (see Whittington (2019) for a review of modern developments or Mackay and Zundel (2017) for an examination of contrasting deployments of strategy and tactics). We will focus on describing the changing ways in which strategy has been part of organizational life in recent decades. Thereafter, we review the benefits that different 'types' of strategy are expected to bring to an organization.

Evolving use of strategy

Strategy as a focus of management and consultancy interest in modern business life came to the fore in the 1960s. Prior to this, annual financial reviews and **budgeting** activities were the main long-range planning activities in an organization.

According to Pettigrew et al. (2006), the rise of strategy as an expected part of managerial life has its foundations in academic and consultancy practice from the United States. Work by US academics such as Alfred Chandler, Kenneth Andrews, and Igor Ansoff did much to establish the modern usage of strategy in organizations. In the 1960s, on both sides of the Atlantic, specific ideas of strategy started to enter business school teaching and research, a trend which increasingly gathered pace until a focus on strategy emerged as a stand-alone discipline from business **policy** in the late 1970s.

In early incarnations of strategy, it was associated with the **formulation** of **rational plans**, policies, and **organizational designs** intended to deliver long-term business performance. This concept of strategy was catalysed by the emergence of US consultancy firms—such as McKinsey and the Boston Consulting Group—specializing in developing tools, terminology, and managerial support for rational analytical strategy work. These consultancy firms rapidly grew outside

1

the United States, exporting the emerging concept of strategy as an elaborately planned procedure around the world.

Through the 1970s and 1980s, the academic and practitioner strategy communities turned more towards the ideas of industrial economics and organization (I/O), as exemplified by the work of Michael Porter (1980, 1984) in developing further tools and concepts. These ideas stemmed originally from industrial economists grappling with a concern of how large organizations achieve monopoly positions. Porter's key insight was to turn this concern on its head, arguing that in competitive environments the strategies employed by such organizations can form the bases of competitive strategy. This brought into focus the idea of competitive advantage, the capacity to outperform competitors, which was based on the relationship between industry structure, organizations' conduct, and superior financial performance. Strategy became associated with the analysis of environmental conditions and the adoption of a defensive and profitable market 'position' in which the organization might outperform its competitors—known as the 'market-based' view (MBV) of strategy.

The market-based view was augmented in the 1980s by the 'resource-based' view (RBV), becoming the dominant research focus in the 1990s. Finding its roots in the work of the American-born British economist Edith Penrose (1959), from an RBV perspective, competitive advantage is understood to arise from possessing distinctive bundles of resources that can be used to create outcomes valued by customers. In essence, organizations that have resources which are relatively rare, difficult to imitate, and can be used to create outcomes valued by customers will have an advantage over their competitors lacking such resources. According to the RBV, strategy is about identifying unique value-creating resources—which are difficult to replicate and at the organization's disposal—and organizing effectively to exploit them and deliver superior performance. An overview of the MBV and the RBV is presented in Table 1.1. In Chapters 5 and 6, we examine in depth how these influential views of strategy can be put into practice.

TABLE 1.1 **Brief comparison of market-based and resource-based views**

	Market-based view	**Resource-based view**
Means	Organizational conduct in the external environment can create competitive advantage	Configuration of distinctive and ordinary resources can create competitive advantage
Also known as	The 'outside-in' approach—making decisions based on external factors	The 'inside-out' approach—organizing internal factors to create external value
Important concepts	Macro trends Industry structure Market position Competitor activities Organizational conduct	Resource base Configuration/bundles Distinctiveness Capabilities Value creation
Benefits	Generates deep insights about the current and future external context	Helps better exploit what the organization already has available
Limitations	Based on assumption that market position is a matter of choice—not always possible to react to external context in an ideal way	Having resources and being able to organize to exploit them does not necessarily create benefits—value is determined by external factors

Source: authors.

In one sense, the MBV and the RBV are complementary as it is beneficial to understand both the **external context** and the **resource base** of the organization during strategy work. Equally, the MBV and the RBV both examine the world from a 'rational' perspective and thus have shared limitations. Through the 1970s and 1980s, widespread adoption of these economics-grounded works into MBA teaching and **consultancy** practice meant that strategy as a rational business planning activity became further promoted in management language and literature.

A significant limitation of analytical planning approaches typified by the RBV and MBV is that human aspects of strategy are marginalized (Bartlett and Ghoshal 1994). By underplaying the role of **agency** (the ability of humans to be creative and exhibit independently minded choice), purely analytical theories of strategy don't necessarily match practice (see Franco-Santos et al. 2017). In reaction to this missing human factor, academic enquiry into 'process' aspects of how strategy is made and managed in practice emerged in the mid-1980s. To varying degrees, **process studies** address how human factors, such as errors, learning, culture, habit, power, and politics, play a role in how strategy happens. Process studies examine how, over time, strategy happens through the activities and approaches of fallible human beings operating within a complex and ever-changing world (e.g. MacKay and Chia 2013). As Mintzberg and Waters (1985) observe, what is realized through strategy is a product of deliberate and emergent activity. This means that strategy is a combination of what is planned, how those involved decide to act, and what the changing context enables.

Through the 1990s and 2000s, strategy theory and practice turned towards investigating how strategy might enable organizations to cope with competitive challenges and disruption arising from increasing **globalization** and accelerating technological advances (Kerr 2016). Consequently, topics such as **internationalization**, innovation, and **collaboration** have become increasingly intertwined with the strategy literature. Strategy studies and consultancy practice increasingly focused on how organizations might predict and cope with evolving contexts, preparing for the future by developing capacities for adaptability, **agility**, and entrepreneurship. Strategy as a practice that can be learned and improved through coaching, training, study, and **reflection** also emerged as a topic of significant interest.

Strategy theory and practice continue to evolve. At the time of writing, a focus on language, methods, and concepts of strategic resilience and sustainability permeate strategy journals and consultancy offerings. The possibilities and practicalities of engaging a wide range of stakeholders in an inclusive way through **open strategy** approaches is emerging as an important contemporary trend (Splitter et al. 2021). Topics such as **big data** (the vast volumes of information available to organizations), **digitalization** (taking action to benefit from digital technology), and **sustainability** (competing within the ecological limits of our planet) are at the fore for strategic managers in many organizations (e.g. Loonam et al. 2018). We address these contemporary themes throughout the book.

As you learn to think, talk, and act as a strategist, you will encounter concepts and theories arising from each of the time periods described. Knowing the context in which the tool or theory was developed will help you to understand both how to use it and its limitations or benefits. Older tools and theories are still in use as new developments in the field have tended to add to rather than replace the pool of methods and concepts used in strategy (Vuorinen et al. 2018). Thus, strategy is a field of interest with multiple, competing interpretations of the central concept and methods (Seidl 2007). As you study strategy, becoming conversant with a wide variety

1

of tools and theories will increase your capacity to engage with stakeholders of all backgrounds and perspectives in undertaking strategy work.

It is also worth noting that as the field has developed, strategy has been subject to recurring criticisms (see Farjoun 2007; Barnett 2016). Strategy literature and consultancy advice is often observed to be overly positive in outlook. The potential for failure, and the practical limitations and consequences of strategy approaches, are frequently understated—putting pressure on practitioners to achieve ideal outcomes that may not be possible. As a subject area, strategy is regularly identified as being subject to fads and fashions as previous methods are discarded for the latest solution or remedy that rewards originators and innovators. Over time, cynicism and change weariness about the latest and greatest way of making strategy takes hold. And where it doesn't, slavish adherence to single ways of making, managing, or researching strategy limit the possibilities of strategy effectiveness. We will attempt to address this matter by offering critical summaries of bodies of strategy literature, highlighting limitations of concepts and theories, and exemplifying practical challenges with case illustrations and possible alternative perspectives. You can play your part too by engaging with the questions throughout and challenging your thinking at the ends of chapters about what strategy means and how useful it might be in practice.

CASE EXAMPLE 1.1 ALIBABA: AN E-COMMERCE GIANT

Alibaba is a giant of e-commerce in China and an increasing presence in global internet trading activities. Founded in 1998 in Hangzhou, China, by Jack Ma and 18 collaborators, from humble beginnings Alibaba has experienced rapid **growth**.

Like Uber with ride-hailing and Airbnb with accommodation services, Alibaba is an internet platform company that facilitates trade. Alibaba provides a virtual marketplace for safe, reliable, and direct transactions between customers and businesses of any size or type from over 190 countries. On its basic service, there is no charge to businesses selling on Alibaba's platform—in 2021, 8,119 billion yuan ($1.22 Trillion) of trade occurred this way. Instead, the Alibaba.com site makes money by selling targeted advertising space, exploiting Alibaba's data analytics capabilities and customer information. To maximize its revenue from advertisers, growing and maintaining the biggest user base possible is an important focus for the organization.

The Alibaba Group also operates a range of companies supporting user needs on the platform which do charge for their services. Additional Alibaba Group commercial offerings include secure payments, financial services, distribution, and cloud computing services. In combination, this eco-system of companies creates conditions in which it is easy for all different types of users to transact.

Alibaba Group sums up its **mission** as to 'make it easy to do business anywhere' by allowing businesses to 'transform the way they market, sell and operate' through the provision of 'fundamental technology infrastructure and marketing reach'. Over the past 20 years, the effective **implementation** of this mission has richly rewarded Alibaba's owners and investors. In June 2017, Alibaba became the most valuable Asian company and was placed within the top 10 most valuable Fortune 500 firms. In December 2021, Alibaba reported consolidated revenues of 649.01 billion yuan, an increase of 22% from 2020. This revenue was generated from an active user base of 1.28bn buyers—76% of whom were located in China. Key growth areas include Alibaba's cloud computing services, operating in over

Consumers ramped up their online shopping activities during the COVID-19 pandemic *Source*: Sergei Elagin/Shutterstock.com.

25 countries and a domestic Chinese market anticipated to grow by 500% by 2025; and a 68% increase in revenue from innovation initiatives.

Alibaba benefited from 'super-charged growth' during the COVID-19 pandemic as many consumers ramped up their online shopping activities. This included a staggering 74% year-on-year revenue increase in the quarter to March 2021 for its Chinese retail operations. As consumer behaviours continue to evolve, online competition grows, global economic challenges emerge, and pandemic restrictions ease, the business now faces an unusual challenge of managing investor and business expectations about 'only' aspiring to grow at pre-pandemic rates.

It is impossible to know for sure whether Alibaba will achieve its aim of existing for at least 102 years (a number picked to enable the claim of existing within the twentieth, twenty-first, and twenty-second centuries!). Closer-term goals include to serve 2 billion global consumers, enable 10 million businesses to be profitable and create 100 million jobs by 2036. Focus areas include continuing to invest in technology and sustainable infrastructure, seeking **diversification** in service provision, exploring international opportunities to reach new consumers, and searching for external organizations with which to partner or add to the Group. Survival and growth in the long term, even for a giant of e-commerce like Alibaba, depends upon such initiatives delivering results.

Questions for discussion

Based on this case study and considering the modern development of strategy:

1. How would you describe Alibaba's strategy?

2. What do you think different stakeholders—employees, **shareholders**, customers, trading partners—want from Alibaba's strategy?

3. What factors will influence what is 'in' the strategy at Alibaba?

4. How important is flexibility of strategy to a company like Alibaba? Explain your answer.

Sources

Alibaba.com (2022). https://www.alibabagroup.com/en/about/overview (last accessed 9 August 2022)

Cheung, M.-C. (2021). Despite revenue crackdowns, Alibaba posts strong retail revenue growth. *eMarketer* (6 August), https://www.emarketer.com/content/despite-covid-government-crackdowns-alibaba-posts-strong-retail-revenue-growth (last accessed 9 August 2022)

Huang, Z. (2022). Tencent, Alibaba look like utilities after $1 trillion drubbing. *BloombergUK* (16 May) https://www.bloomberg.com/news/articles/2022-05-16/tencent-alibaba-look-like-utilities-after-1-trillion-drubbing (last accessed 9 August 2022)

Over the past 60 years, strategy in organizational life has evolved into a complex field which the strategist must navigate. However, this challenging set of circumstances is also a major source of opportunity for you as a student or practitioner of strategy. Throughout this book, we will cover many of the themes, theories, and methods that have accrued over the years in strategy academia and practice. With awareness of the rich options available for how to engage with strategy, you will be able to progress your own capabilities in thinking, talking, and (in your future careers) acting as a strategist in an effective and flexible way.

1.3 **Expectations of strategy in organizations**

We have discussed how the use of the term 'strategy' has evolved. But what does strategy mean in the context of organizations today? And in what ways does strategy benefit an organization? To provide a grounding for examining interpretations of strategy in the following section, we first explain the different types and anticipated benefits of strategy you may encounter. Being aware of these common categories and expectations will help you interpret the strategy literature and engage in debate about what strategy might mean.

Organizational strategy

Our focus is on strategy theory and practice as it might be applied in organizations. Arguably, the core long-term aim of any organization is to survive (Poulis and Poulis 2016) and preferably to thrive. This survival can happen when, over the long term, the organization is able to create value for stakeholders in a way which is less than the cost of doing so. Adapting the high-level description of strategy from the chapter introduction:

> *Organizational strategy is about maintaining a balance between ends, ways, and means of surviving and thriving—providing a framework for making choices and trade-offs; and identifying resources, methods, actions, and value-creating objectives that sustain the organization over time within an ever-changing context.*

When we describe organizational strategy, we refer to ongoing efforts to act and react in a way that secures organizational survival. Whilst growth is often a key additional aim (i.e. survive and grow), it is worth noting that not every organization seeks to grow. For many owner–managers of 'lifestyle' businesses (where the organization exists to suit the owner's needs), growth would change the nature and purpose of their organization (Kammerlander and Ganter 2015). Organizational strategy, then, is closely related to organizational purpose—a guiding sense of the long-term vision, mission, values, and intentions of an organization. Many public and third-sector organizations, for instance, do not pursue a growth agenda either, instead seeking to deliver a specific mandate within the context of the resources available to them. Organizational strategy is no less valuable in these non-profit-focused settings.

Corporate, business, and functional strategy types

There are many ways in which types of organizational strategy can be explained and discussed. Three important types of strategy are corporate, business, and functional strategy.

Corporate strategy addresses the question of 'where to operate'—identifying the industrial sectors and locations in which an organization will focus its energy and efforts. Corporate strategy can be used to articulate the intended scope of the whole organization. With this scope, an appropriate organizational structure can be implemented and reporting lines, finance/resource flows, and physical locations identified. Referring to Case Example 1.1, Alibaba's decision to expand internationally (geographical scope) is a corporate strategy decision, as was its decision to enter cloud computing services (sectoral scope).

Business strategy addresses the question of 'how to meet customer needs' to gain an advantage over competitors in selected geographies and sectors. For example, Alibaba's decision to provide its main platform free of charge to users for the basic service but to charge advertisers to reach customers is a business strategy decision intended to give the organization a competitive advantage. Jack Ma, the ex-CEO of Alibaba, identifies this business strategy decision as one of the key reasons why Alibaba was able to effectively drive eBay (who charged a transaction fee to customers) from the Chinese market in 2004 (c.f. MacKay et al. 2020). This term applies beyond 'businesses' to public- or third-sector organizations too as they compete for resources, funding, and attention whilst fulfilling a societal need (e.g. Hansen and Jacobsen 2016).

Functional strategy addresses the question of 'how to operate' in order to deliver an optimal contribution to corporate and business strategy from functions such as human resources, finance, and operations. Functional strategy balances efficiency gains from standardized working with a need for effective delivery of local functional needs determined by where and how an organization is in operation. For example, rather than standardize on one way of working, decisions about how to staff, locate, and invest in infrastructure for the high-growth cloud computing services division of Alibaba might be different from how the same decisions are taken in the heavily regulated financial services division.

The commonality between these categories is that strategy is about reading the organizational **situation** and identifying the 'best' options for purposeful action that might move towards specific desired outcomes. This purposeful action offers the promise of **efficacy**—achieving desired outcomes—and **efficiency**—achieving those outcomes with minimal use of resources.

The terms 'corporate', 'business', and 'functional strategy' provide useful ways of talking about complementary aspects of organizational strategy. When we discuss corporate strategy, our attention is directed towards the product markets and geographical locations in which the organization has the best fit and the best way in which to structure the organization to reach those markets and locations. Within those markets, business strategy challenges us to find the most effective and cost-efficient ways to fulfil customer needs. And functional strategy organizes resources in order to best deliver business and corporate strategy aims.

Whilst each type of strategy can be planned separately, better overall outcomes might be realized when they are considered as part of an organizational strategy system (Figure 1.1). This means that corporate, business, and functional strategy are related, each creating possibilities and limitations for the rest of the system (Sull et al. 2018a). For example, a change in corporate strategy may require an amendment to functional strategy or a change in functional strategy may open up new possibilities for business strategy, etc. Being aware of this system can help you to understand organizational strategy in a holistic way. Equally, it enables you to critique the coherence of organizational strategy. If business strategy intentions are to move in a direction not supported by functional strategy, it is highly likely that business strategy initiatives will fail. Challenging the extent to which corporate, business, and functional strategies align is an important step when evaluating organizational strategy.

Anticipated benefits of organizational strategy

To produce and maintain organizational strategy takes (often significant) effort and attention from a wide range of stakeholders. Why would an organization incur this cost? Quite simply, organizational strategy is anticipated to provide performance benefits that outweigh the **costs**

FIGURE 1.1 Components of organizational strategy. *Source*: authors.

involved. Specifically, organizational strategy would seem to offer the potential for enhanced managerial decision-making, **resource deployment**, stakeholder management, and coordinated action (Grant 2003). In turn, enhanced **business performance** enables the organization to survive, grow (if that is an aim), and prosper.

Managerial decision-making

Strategy can act as a set of boundaries which guide managerial decision-making. Imagine that the retail giant Amazon is presented with the opportunity to purchase a logistics firm in Spain, an innovative digital marketing firm in China, or a highly profitable manufacturer of oil and gas products in Brazil. Which of these, if any, should Amazon pursue? Organizational strategy provides a decision-making mechanism and frame of reference with which to evaluate and, if required, choose between available options (see Chapter 3).

Resource deployment

Strategy provides a blueprint for the deployment of organizational resources. Once decisions are made about where and how to operate, resources can then be deployed in a focused way to try to deliver those decisions. For example, Alibaba's continuing investment of financial resources in cloud computing capacity makes sense as a means by which to consolidate its existing market position, support platform operations, and prepare to compete in the high levels of anticipated market expansion.

Stakeholder management

Strategy acts as a **social** and a political tool to manage and engage stakeholders. Having a strategy allows communication, **engagement**, and the building of shared meaning about its current and future activities with all those who might have a stake in the organization (e.g. employees, suppliers, local community, investors, customers, etc.). Having a clear, articulated strategy creates a sense that the organization is competent and well managed. A published strategy might also be required to unlock funding for organizations of all sizes and types. For example, the strategic vision, **plan**, and developing resource base of Relativity Space has been crucial for generating sufficient investor confidence to raise over $1bn of funding prior to launching its first rocket (see Case Example 2.1 in Chapter 2).

CASE EXAMPLE 1.2 **STRATEGIC JOURNEY OF DBS**

DBS is an award-winning banking and financial services group headquartered and listed in Singapore, with a presence in 18 countries including China, India, Indonesia, and Taiwan. In 2021, DBS employed over 33,000 people serving 11.8 million customers and 340,000 institutional clients, generating a turnover of $14.3 Bn Singapore dollars (SGD) and a net profit of $6.8 Bn SGD, up 44% on 2020. A track record of financial performance at this level earned DBS 'AA-' and 'Aa1' credit ratings, amongst the highest in the world for comparable organizations.

The international finance trade publication *Euromoney* named DBS as the 'World's Best Bank 2021', commenting that DBS was 'not just surviving a [global pandemic] crisis but using it as a chance to innovate and to be a better bank. As well as fortitude and profitability, it showed opportunism and smart thinking, all underpinned by its digital leadership.' DBS also picked up multiple **industry** and national awards for digital innovation, cybersecurity, and sustainable banking achievements.

The organization's current success is built on a long-term process of strategic renewal and performance improvement under the stewardship of CEO Piyush Gupta, guided by an experienced, diverse board. Gupta joined DBS from rivals Citibank in 2009, proposing to transform the organization to be fit for an envisioned digital future in the banking sector (c.f. Sia et al. (2021) for a detailed description of the journey).

In the first five years of this transformation process, the principal focus was on establishing a 'nimble' enterprise architecture. This required the creation of a set of agile technical and operational teams to drive 'value through technology' in all areas of the business. Lean initiatives were deployed to streamline and improve the bank's key processes. Reliable infrastructure, a flexible core banking system, and mobile and internet banking capabilities were installed across international operations. And customer experience and innovation 'councils' were instigated to drive a change of employee mindset in how to create value through banking.

From 2014 to 2018, the strategy pivoted towards becoming 'an ambidextrous organisation' capable of delivering core services whilst pushing the boundaries of innovation in banking and finance across the whole group. Embracing digital technologies and adopting new ways of working were crucial aspects of this phase of strategic renewal. Building on their adaptable infrastructure, DBS invested in harnessing the power of cloud computing for efficient, scalable services, collaborating with key partners such as Microsoft and AWS to accelerate results. DBS also invited collaboration from a wide range of fintech organizations, launching the world's largest API* platform hosted by a bank. Digital practices, such as the use of data analytics to drive customer innovation, quickly became an established part of everyday work across the bank. Internationally, DBS's Digibank initiative in India created a 'paperless, signatureless, and branchless' operation, recognized as 'the safest bank in Asia' and demonstrating how digital entrepreneurship could translate to profitable market share in a traditional sector.

During this phase of transformation, DBS leaders noted that they were employing more software engineers than bankers. Consequently, DBS started to compare itself during strategic analysis to technology firms such as Google, Apple, and Netflix rather than to traditional rivals. Imagining itself as a 'software company', DBS leaders started exploring how to 'create

*API—Application Programming Interface, a software programme that allows two applications, such as a banking system and a customer mobile app, to talk to each other.

Continued

1

a 26,000-person start-up' in which employees embraced **entrepreneurial** qualities of agility, customer-focus, continual experimentation, and risk-taking.

Since 2019, DBS has sought to exploit its 'digital core' in delivering diversification and growth in a sustainable way. The combination of digital technology, entrepreneurial employees, and vast amounts of customer data have been used to explore new 'marketplaces' in cars, electricity, and property, taking DBS 'beyond banking' in Singapore. Annual reports present a strategic intent to innovate services to 'make banking joyful' for its customers, remain at the forefront of technology in banking, and adopt flexible work practices in line with post-pandemic employee expectations. Initiatives proposed for 2022 and beyond include major investment in digital money and decentralized finance technologies, increasing DBS's international footprint, promoting green and ethical investing, and delivering social impact through charitable work, employee activism, and support for **social enterprises**.

These initiatives are expected to sustain the competitive advantages of DBS in the short-to-medium term. Beyond that, the promise of the CEO and the Chairman to stakeholders is 'looking further out, given that **technological changes** could fundamentally reshape the financial system, we must do what we can to be ahead of the curve'.

Questions for discussion

1. Describe the corporate and business strategies of DBS. To what extent are they evolving?

2. Does it make sense for DBS to compare itself to technology firms rather than banks in strategic analysis? Explain your answer.

3. How have employees influenced or been influenced by DBS's strategy during transformation?

4. Critique the **suitability** of the current strategic initiatives for DBS. What initiatives would you continue, amend, or add if you were CEO and why?

Sources

DBS Group Holdings Ltd (2022). *DBS Annual Report 2021*, https://www.dbs.com/iwov-resources/images/investors/annual-report/dbs-annual-report-2021.pdf (last accessed 9 August 2022).

Sia, S.K., Weill, P., and Zhang, N. (2021). Designing a future-ready enterprise: The digital transformation of DBS Bank. *California Management Review*, **63**(3), 35–57.

Coordinated action

Strategy enables collaborative working between different functions, divisions, and locations of an organization. Through organizational strategy, it is in all stakeholders' interests that the best overall organizational performance is achieved. This can require optimal contribution, rather than maximized performance, from organizational 'components' such as divisions, business units, and teams. As described in Case Example 1.2, a transformative strategy has been crucial to the coordinated, effective renewal of DBS as a global digital leader in the banking and finance sector.

These are high-level general benefits of organizational strategy. Throughout the book, we have included many examples of further benefits to an organization or individuals engaged in specific strategy activities.

1.4 **Interpretations of strategy**

How strategy is understood by stakeholders in any given situation will be a key consideration for you as either a participant in or a leader of strategy activity. However, as identified earlier in this chapter, the field of strategy has evolved over the years to include many competing methods, concepts, and **interpretations** (Arend 2016).

So, how can strategy be understood in any given situation? How can we navigate through such a wide variety of interpretations? Mintzberg et al. (2009) note that whilst it is human nature to search for *the* definition of 'strategy', strategy—in their view—requires at least five different definitions—plan, pattern, perspective, position, and ploy. As shown in Figure 1.2, we have extended these interpretations to propose 12 possible components of strategy, based on our practical experience and themes we have detected in the academic and practitioner literature.

The 12 components describe what strategy can mean to different people but not necessarily what it means to any individual, nor what is relevant to any group of people in any given situation.

These interpretations are not mutually exclusive categories but rather strands of thinking that might be woven together into a customized view of strategy. For example, a colleague may hold a view that strategy is about defining *purpose* and setting an actionable *plan* for delivery through a clear organizational strategy *process*. This colleague may believe, with conviction, that this is how everyone understands strategy! They also may not have considered or be aware of further possible interpretations. As a student of strategy, being aware of a range of possible interpretations will increase your ability to engage stakeholders from different backgrounds and adapt your approach to strategy to suit the specific needs of a situation (Jalonen et al. 2018).

Each interpretation of strategy can be associated with a form of output and potential benefits to the organization. Also, each interpretation is subject to limitations in practice, of which it is helpful to be mindful. Further, certain conditions are required to be in place for each interpretation of strategy work to be undertaken effectively.

It is worth bearing in mind that despite differences in available interpretations, there are a number of high-level points of agreement in strategy **theory** and practice (Mintzberg et al. 2009: 15), namely, strategy (a), concerns both organization and environment; (b), is typically a complex matter; (c), affects the long-term welfare of the organization; (d), involves issues of content (what is agreed) and process (how it is agreed); (e), is not purely deliberate; (f), exists on different levels; and (g), involves a range of thought processes.

In the following sections, we describe and explain each of the interpretations of strategy. Building on Case Example 1.2, we will draw on extracts from strategy work in DBS's 2021 annual report to illustrate how you might encounter each perspective in practice. In addition, we have provided supporting references and further reading for each of the Ps in the online resources, should you wish to dig further into any of the interpretations. For further detailed examples of

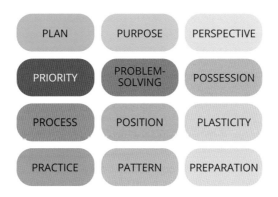

FIGURE 1.2 Interpretations of strategy. *Source*: authors.

1

how the perspectives appear in practice, you can refer to the 'practitioner insights' section at the end of each chapter (see also the practitioner videos in the *online resources*).

You will be able to use your knowledge of the 12Ps to analyse theories, concepts, and practitioner insights in the rest of the book, deepening your knowledge of how strategy might be understood in different settings. This approach should allow you to learn about and prepare to engage with strategy in practice, even if you have yet to acquire any practical experience yourself.

 Access the online resources to watch a short video clip where Marianne Meehan discusses stakeholders and defining 'strategy'.

Strategy as a plan

When asking students or practitioners 'What does strategy mean?', a common response is that strategy is a plan or roadmap for how to deliver target objectives with available resources. When subsequently asked 'Is every plan a strategy?', the answer is 'No'. Whilst strategy typically carries an implication—in part—of planning, strategy is also more than a simple plan. A strategic plan appears to be distinguished from daily plans of an operational nature by its all-encompassing (holistic) nature, a time horizon that is longer than regular operational considerations, and a foundation in a non-routine consideration of often complex circumstances (Arend et al. 2017).

As described in Table 1.2, strategy as a plan can act as a coordinating mechanism to guide the prescribed activities of individuals and teams towards common objectives. Those objectives need

TABLE 1.2 **Strategy as a plan**

Strategy as . . .	Plan
Interpretation	A deliberate course of action towards desired objectives
Function for the organization	Acts as a coordinating mechanism or guide to map out a path from where an individual/organization is today to where they/it want(s) to be in future
What is needed to work with this interpretation in practice	An articulation of what the end-points/objectives are In order to make a plan, you need to know where you are going There needs to be a sense of the constraints and resources available
Benefits	+ A commonly understood definition of strategy that is easy to discuss + Provides a way to coordinate action across a wide range of interests/people + Can track progress towards outcomes
Limitations	– Can quickly become outdated as circumstances change – Can act as an inhibitor of innovation and valuable opportunism – Gives a false sense of certainty/security
Might be expressed as . . .	'Our strategy lays out a clear road map for the next three years and the initiatives we will deliver to grow as a business'
When you are likely to encounter this interpretation	Within an organization or as a consultant; in any formal strategy exercise, some sort of plan is normally expected as part of the outputs

Source: authors.

to be defined in order that this organizing effect can be achieved and relevant activities identified and initiated. Plans need not be in any particular format or even written down, but those leading strategy work must anticipate the expectations of stakeholders that there will be some component of strategy work that is planned. Strategic planning can also be a key mechanism for assuring external stakeholders, such as investors, that the organization is well-run (e.g. Baginski et al. 2017).

Examples of strategy as a plan from DBS are shown in Figure 1.3. The format of strategic plans can be highly varied in terms of timescale, topic, categories, formats, and information embedded in the plan.

Material matters	What are the risks?	Where do we see the opportunities?	What are we doing about it?
Macroeconomic, geopolitical, and tail risks	Rising inflation driven by the gradual reopening of economies, impending interest rate hikes by central banks, and limited scope for fresh fiscal stimulus may lead to lower economic growth and increased vulnerability in the SME segment.	Higher interest rates will drive more fund-raising activities as corporates seek to lock in lower rates and hedge against existing floating rate loans. In addition, the gradual reopening of economies will lead to more trade and travel. These open up opportunities for our capital markets, treasury, syndication, trade, and retail businesses.	Our business franchise and balance sheet strength enabled us to swiftly capture regional opportunities as economies recovered. Business momentum was sustained throughout the year. Additionally, we had conservatively built up allowance reserves at the onset of the pandemic in 2020, which enabled us to benefit from asset quality improvements in 2021.

We continued to invest in our log-term growth strategy. We acquired a 13per cent stake in Shenzhen Rural-Commercial Bank and established a securities joint venture in China while expanding on our digital capabilities in our core banking business.

Read more in the 'Letter from Chairman and CEO' on pages 8–11 and 'CFO statement' on pages 20–27. |
| **Digital transformation** | The pandemic has accelerated investments in digital transformation across all industries and increased the technological capabilities of all players. Customers are also becoming increasingly digitally-savvy, driving demand for digital innovations that offer greater convenience and an enhanced banking experience. | Our investments in new technologies and our digital transformation over the last nine years have enabled us to offer a differentiated experience to our customers by making banking joyful.

Banks that are able to deliver a seamless and differentiated experience will gain a greater wallet share of revenue. | We have pivoted to managing through journeys for our critical customer processes by organizing horizontally across units and leveraging on data-driven operating models. This encourages greater accountability across teams and breaks silo thinking, enabling the bank to deliver a differentiated customer experience.

Read more in 'CIO statement' on pages 36–37, and 'Our 2021 priorities' on pages 28–33. |
| **Mastering data and artificial intelligence (AI)** | As banks rise to the challenge of meeting consumer demand for banking experiences that are intuitive, they will need to re-architect legacy technology and their data stack.

Inability to manage this transition and derive benefits from AI technologies will result in loss of competitiveness and market share. | A clear strategy for data and AI delivered in our business operating model will help drive greater economic value through: (i) increased personalization and improved experiences in customer and employee journeys, (ii) greater operational efficiencies and lower costs through higher automation, (iii) improved risk decisioning with new AI/ machine-learning models that leverage existing and new data sets, and (iv) more rapid innovation of new products/services. | We have make AI central to our core strategy and incorporated AI technologies into our management and operation processes.

We have developed ALAN, an AI protocol platform, and integrated it with ADA, our data platform. These platforms enable our data scientists to shorten the cycle time required to build compliant AI models, and accelerate deployment of the models to improve our operations and decision-making, to deliver a differentiated customer experience.

Read more in 'CIO statement' on pages 36–37. |

FIGURE 1.3 Strategy as a plan: Coordinating actions to deliver long-term aims.

Source: DBS Group Holdings Ltd (2022). *Annual Report 2021*, p. 72, https://www.dbs.com/annualreports/2021/files/media/dbs-annual-report-2021.pdf (last accessed 9 August 2022).

1 Strategy as a sense of collective purpose

In contrast with the calculations and rationality of planning, an interpretation of strategy as purpose communicates that strategy is about developing a sense of shared mission amongst the varied stakeholders associated with an organization (Ackermann and Eden 2011a). Strategy as purpose concerns the development of a long-term vision and sense of mission grounded in the intrinsic values of an organization. As described in Table 1.3, this interpretation of strategy appeals to the human need to do meaningful work (Birkinshaw et al. 2014). An interest in defining strategy as purpose is very often found in top management teams and during boardroom discussions (Bartlett and Ghoshal 1994). Once formulated, the purpose of the organization can be raised in strategy conversations at all different levels as a reference point for decision-making.

When a convincing long-term vision is articulated that aligns with the values of an organization and its purpose, it can provide a motivating and unifying effect for employees and stakeholders

TABLE 1.3 **Strategy as purpose**

Strategy as . . .	Purpose
Interpretation	A guiding sense of the long-term vision, mission, values, and intentions of an individual or organization
Function for the organization	Provides a motivating and unifying sense of direction for the whole organization based around a shared set of values, which can be translated into meaningful ambitions at all levels of the organization
What is needed to work with this interpretation in practice	Understanding of the intrinsic values of the organization; agreement as to the markets, products, structure, and operating approach that will be adopted by the organization; and an ability to combine these insights into a meaningful narrative that connects with hearts and minds
Benefits	+ Gives a broad framework to unite effort whilst enabling local creativity/innovation + Provides a motivating sense of meaning with which individuals can identify + Is less susceptible to being rendered irrelevant by changing circumstances
Limitations	– If words don't match actions, can be a source of inertia and resistance – Hard to achieve in larger organizations in an effective, authentic way – Difficult to change/alter, restricting leadership options and decision-making
Might be expressed as . . .	'Our strategy defines who we are as an organization—our aims and shared values—that guide everything we do'
When you are likely to encounter this interpretation	This is typically an interest of senior leaders across private-, public-, and third-sector organizations; appears in 'high-level', 'long-term' strategy conversations concerning the whole organization

Source: authors.

across all levels (Quinn and Thakor 2018). Following the disruption of the pandemic to established work routines, a Gartner study (Wiles 2022) observes a powerful trend of employees seeking meaningful work and expecting their organization to create an environment that resonates with their own values. An articulated, authentic organizational purpose therefore seems to be an increasingly important part of strategy work that will impact employee recruitment, retention, engagement, and effectiveness.

The long-term vision and sense of mission may act as a guiding framework, providing a reference point against which objectives can be set in the short, medium, and long term for individuals and teams.

For example, the 2021 DBS annual report summary states:

We are focused on leveraging digital technology to reimagine banking to provide our customers a full range of services in consumer banking, wealth management and institutional banking. We also see a purpose beyond banking and are committed to supporting our customers, employees and the community towards a sustainable future.

(p. 3)

These comments are consistent with a statement of strategic purpose that DBS has expressed for several years—'Transform the business—Make Banking Joyful.'

In the Chairman's statement, he elaborates:

At the time of writing, the world seems ready to open up and we are learning to live with Covid-19. At the same time, geopolitics is casting some shadows, and the macroeconomic policy pathways are uncertain. In such an environment, we have to continue to be watchful and nimble. We take heart that our business pipeline is robust. [. . .] while 2021 was our best-ever year, we will continue to re-position ourselves as a bank of the future.

(p. 11)

These statements, written in an optimistic tone, emphasize the high-level intentions of DBS to remain a nimble digital leader that benefits its stakeholders despite an uncertain operating environment. From the recognized position of strength, a continuing commitment to change and diversification is also signalled without limiting any approaches.

Strategy as a holistic perspective

A **strategic perspective** implies a long-term holistic view of circumstances, enabling decisions and actions that yield maximum advantage as described in Table 1.4. Individuals and organizations might be referred to as being strategic, implying an ability to look beyond the immediate and obvious when interpreting a situation. By being aware of the totality of their circumstances and the potential short-, medium-, and long-term consequences of their actions, strategic individuals or groups seem able to make decisions that create advantageous outcomes in the long run (Felin and Zenger 2018). Labelling an idea or message as a 'strategic' perspective can also be a communicative tool that, rightly or wrongly, is more likely to command an audiences' attention than so-called operational views.

1

TABLE 1.4 **Strategy as a holistic perspective**

Strategy as . . .	Perspective
Interpretation	A capacity to take a holistic, long-term view of circumstances—beyond the immediate and obvious—towards maximal advantage
Function for the organization	Enables thinking about the consequences and broader implications of actions, interactions, and trends affecting an individual or group
What is needed to work with this interpretation in practice	The capacity to think beyond the short-term, close at hand, immediate demands or options in any given situation; requires an openness to the ideas and actions of others, the trajectories of events, and contextual drivers
Benefits	+ Aids decision-making for long-term benefit of the individual or organization + Helps avoid knee-jerk reactions that consume resource and limit future options + Can be inspirational to others/supportive of strategic leadership
Limitations	– Without like-minded peers, strategic thinking can breed frustration/conflict – Organizational life doesn't always allow time for reflection/strategic thought – Being labelled strategic can encourage arrogance or false confidence in leaders
Might be expressed as . . .	Individuals or groups being referred to as 'strategic thinkers' that can see the whole organizational situation—current and possible futures—in a way that colleagues struggle to achieve
When you are likely to encounter this interpretation	This sort of evaluation of personal capability appears in organizational recruitment and selection processes for promotion, involvement in strategy, or commissioning of external advice

Source: authors.

A commonly used example of this is the expert chess player thinking through the combinations and permutations of acting on any of the options available to them (e.g. Graber 2009). They may appear to incur short-term losses that don't make sense to an untrained eye but which prove to be decisions that deliver victory by positioning the whole game board to their long-term advantage. However, Teece et al. (2016) point out that chess is a 'closed' system where the rules are well established, and the metaphor for **strategic thinking** underplays the extent to which dynamism and unexpected events must be accommodated. Therefore, adopting a strategic perspective means being able to influence opponents' actions towards one's own long-term gain and an ability to cope with immersion in complex and dynamic circumstances plus an openness to new thoughts, ideas, and actions (Powell 2017).

The DBS annual report 2021 includes several 'strategic perspective' statements, including from the CEO, Chairman, Chief Risk Officer, and Chief Financial Officer. These statements reflect on the short-, medium-, and long-term opportunities and challenges for the organization. Individually, these statements explain a key aspect of overall organizational performance, intended action and environmental factors underpinning decision-making. Together, the statements cohere into a rounded evaluation of the whole business situation.

Strategy as prioritization

Strategy can be interpreted as a form of collective focus and prioritization of effort. Faced with conflicting demands on the use of limited resources, choices must be made on a regular basis by managers as to what to do and what not to do in pursuit of organizational results (Sull et al. 2018b). An interpretation of strategy as prioritization is that managers and their teams have a shared sense of focus for their efforts, emotions, resources, and time (see Table 1.5). The intention of this focus is to give the greatest return on resource investment in terms of beneficial organizational outcomes.

To adopt strategy as prioritization means to be aware of options for action and use of resources and to be selective in the options that are identified for implementation. Knowing what not to do is as important as addressing specific interests (Collis 2016). This interpretation of strategy has at its heart the concept of capacity management. Strategy as prioritization is a recognition that organizational performance is a function of available capabilities and finite resources. As an illustration using financial resources, imagine that our organization has £1

TABLE 1.5 **Strategy as prioritization**

Strategy as . . .	Priority
Interpretation	Where energy, efforts, emotions, and resources are focused
Function for the organization	Concentrate the allocation of resources and effort on those initiatives that will give biggest payback to the organization and address the most pressing challenges
What is needed to work with this interpretation in practice	An awareness of the options for action and the resources at disposal, the relative value of opportunities facing the organization and the risks posed by current challenges, and a means of selecting the options to prioritize to realize the best outcomes for the organization
Benefits	+ Strategy can be made that is realistic and impactful, even with limited resources + Helps to clarify what 'not to do' and thus enables coherent decision-making + Connects strategy with action that makes sense given the current context
Limitations	– May focus on immediate needs at the expense of long-term investment – Can be highly political as those involved want their interests prioritized – Needs to be regularly revised to reflect shifting organizational context
Might be expressed as . . .	'We will focus our efforts and resources on these three strategic priorities—all other activities will have to wait until these are achieved'
When you are likely to encounter this interpretation	This is often a concern for those making functional strategies or heading up organizational units as they attempt to convert high-level ambitions into local plans, with limited resources, that deliver maximum return on effort

Source: authors.

1

million, and we have the skills to follow two investment opportunities of £500,000 and £700,000. Both are possible but, because of limited finances, pursuing one option will mean that the other cannot be achieved. Therefore, we must make a choice as to which option to prioritize. When there is more opportunity than our resource capacity can support, deciding how to allocate our resources is the process of prioritization. Having a shared sense of clear strategic priorities can guide employees and coordinate activity without prescribing exactly how they need to do their work (Gulati 2018).

For example, DBS highlights four high-level priority areas of focus for the business in 2022 and beyond—(a) transform the way we work, (b) scale our business, (c) ignite new opportunities, (d) build a sustainable franchise. Each strategic priority is associated with a set of initiatives, resources, and investments that can be explained and tracked in relation to their contribution towards the priorities (DBS Group Holdings Ltd 2022: 28–33).

Strategy as a problem-solving mechanism

Strategy is sometimes described as a mechanism for organizational-level problem-solving. The sorts of challenges that face an organization, potentially threatening its survival, will often fit the definition of a **wicked problem**. Wicked problems are over-determined, meaning that they are complex, subject to a system of influences, and don't seem to have any easy or obvious solution. For example, delivering fully sustainable operations is a wicked problem for multinational consumer goods firms that move large volumes of people, materials, and products across borders. Conventional approaches to problem-solving won't adequately address wicked problems (McMillan and Overall 2016). As described in Table 1.6, strategy activity can be approached in a way that stabilizes the conditions for decision-making and implementation of policy towards coping better with wicked problems (Wright et al. 2019).

Strategy as problem-solving requires first a diagnostic phase in which, as far as is possible, the nature of the challenges facing the organization are described and defined through data collection and analysis. Second, as the challenges become clearer, organizational policy is agreed for how to respond to the specific nature of the challenge facing the organization. This will likely require debate and consensus agreement between stakeholders based on limited data. Finally, once organizational policy is agreed (for instance, setting a policy in relation to a disruptive new technology), a coherent set of actions to implement the policy across organizational teams and functions is agreed to cope with or mitigate wicked problems (Daviter 2017).

An example of strategy as problem-solving can be seen in how DBS's strategy addresses the 'wicked problem' of sustainability.

For a few years now, DBS has focused on advancing the sustainability agenda through responsible banking, responsible business practices and creating impact beyond banking. More recently, we established a Board Sustainability Committee to provide greater governance and oversight into climate-related risks and opportunities, as well as our broader environmental, social and governance effort.

(DBS Group Holdings Ltd 2022: 10)

Further highlighted initiatives include adding $100M SGD for community and social projects, moving towards sustainable investing, improving the carbon performance of infrastructure, and joining alliances to influence policy and practice internationally. In so doing, DBS isn't seeking to

TABLE 1.6 **Strategy as problem-solving**

Strategy as . . .	Problem-solving
Interpretation	A mechanism by which to solve problems and address challenges threatening the sustainability of an organization and the attainment of its goals
Function for the organization	As either a one-off event or a continuing process, strategy fulfils an organizational function of solving problems with limited information and uncertainty about the direction of unfolding circumstances
What is needed to work with this interpretation in practice	A diagnosis which describes and defines the nature of the challenges facing the organization, an agreed policy for how best to respond to the specific nature of the challenges, and a coherent set of actions to implement the policy
Benefits	+ Brings a clarity of expected response to uncertainty about the future + Can build coping skills and organizational resilience + Connects data analytics, intuition, governance, and performance interests
Limitations	– Strategic problems tend to be 'wicked'—complex, uncertain, and without easy/obvious solutions – 'Paralysis by analysis'—can over-analyse options and responses – 'Best-guess' data analysis can create false certainty about the future
Might be expressed as . . .	'Our strategy prepares us to continue to deliver on the expectations of our shareholders, employees, customers, and communities in these challenging times'
When you are likely to encounter this interpretation	When in a context that is perceived as volatile, uncertain, ambiguous, changing, or under threat of disruption, strategy is often discussed by management teams as a means of finding solutions to threats to organizational sustainability

Source: authors.

resolve social and environmental problems on its own but rather to act in stakeholder's long-term interests, mitigate sustainability risks, and seek to create appropriate business opportunities that contribute to the greater good.

Strategy as an organizational possession

If many in organizational life are asked 'What is your strategy?', they will refer to the content of a polished piece of media such as a document, a web page, a poster on the wall, a reference card carried in the pocket, etc. In this way, strategy can be understood as a possession, something the organization has, which is evidenced by a collection of artefacts and materials communicating a coherent message (see Table 1.7).

Strategy as a set of possessions recognizes the importance of the content and format of strategy communication to the impact that strategy work might have on organizational stakeholders (Dameron et al. 2015). For strategy to act as a coordinating mechanism and decision-making aid, unambiguous information needs to be communicated through strategy media in an appealing

1

TABLE 1.7 **Strategy as a possession**

Strategy as . . .	Possession
Interpretation	A collection of artefacts, materials, and 'things' that can be used for the benefit of the organization
Function for the organization	Creates the potential for strategy to be shared, for the clarification of what is meant by strategy, and for evidence that strategy work has been completed
What is needed to work with this interpretation in practice	Agreed content with which to populate the artefacts, agreed formats and designs for the artefacts, and production and distribution mechanisms to turn them into reality
Benefits	+ Provides a visible, tangible reminder of identity and mission to employees + Gives an impression to external stakeholders of a well-run organization + Legitimizes and coordinates the work of strategic managers
Limitations	– Having fixed artefacts can encourage inertia/avoidance of strategy renewal – Artefacts don't deliver performance outcomes – Hard to create artefacts which are meaningful across stakeholder groups
Might be expressed as . . .	'Our strategy masterplan document is laid out on our website and is summarized in the annual report and on cue cards distributed to all employees'
When you are likely to encounter this interpretation	External and internal communications professionals often own the 'artefacts' of strategy, to be used to influence stakeholder views

Source: authors.

way. It is unlikely that one medium or method of communication will suffice to best meet the needs of different stakeholders and the nature of various strategic messages. Therefore, the creation of a range of appropriate artefacts and possessions—which communicate consistent messages in different ways—is often required in large-scale strategy dissemination efforts (Arnaud et al. 2016). Online methods, including social media, are now a particular concern to those working in strategy communication (Plesner and Gulbrandsen 2015).

For example, DBS engages stakeholders extensively through a broad presence on social media platforms, internal communications platforms, a website, mobile and internet banking, a press/media relations function, advertising, government relations, trade associations, and engagement with sectoral publications. These engagement mechanisms may serve primarily operational or commercial aims. They also provide points of connection through which strategic messages (such as 'make banking joyful') or strategic artefacts (such as the annual report or press releases) can be disseminated to relevant audiences. In these ways, the materials of 'strategy as a possession' can influence what stakeholders say, think, and do in relation to DBS.

 Access the online resources to watch a short video clip where Marianne Meehan discusses communication.

Strategy as an organizational process

Thinking of strategy as an organizational process brings attention to the continuing social and political interactions and **organizational learning** that shape strategy content and action over time (see Table 1.8). Strategy can be considered a social process as the content of strategy emerges through conversations and debates between organizational stakeholders (Dobusch et al. 2019). Strategy can also be considered a **political process**, as vested interests participate in those interactions, seeking to influence others towards their point of view (Conroy et al. 2017).

How strategy interactions occur over time through formal designed exchanges will directly influence how strategy content is decided, communicated, and enacted in the organization. Open processes, involving a diverse range of stakeholders in new dynamics of strategy work, are increasingly expected as a sign of engaged and inclusive leadership (Brielmaier and Friesl 2021). Equally, informal dialogue through everyday interactions will also impact how strategy is

TABLE 1.8 **Strategy as an organizational process**

Strategy as . . .	Process
Interpretation	Continuing social and political interactions and activities that shape strategy content and how it is communicated, enacted, and revised
Function for the organization	Acts as a mechanism to gather insights and build commitment throughout the organization and maintain the relevance of strategy through incorporation of learning and new insights on a continuing basis
What is needed to work with this interpretation in practice	A design of process—customized to suit local, organizational, and cultural conditions—that enables all required contributions to the development and maintenance of organizational strategy The process needs to be owned, communicated, and facilitated. How this is done will be different in each organization according to what is meant by the term 'strategy'
Benefits	+ Inclusive process can create momentum, understanding, and commitment + Provides a means to make use of diverse sources of organizational wisdom + Can minimize time and effort to establish and maintain strategy
Limitations	– Needs customized design, effective **facilitation**, and executive sponsorship – Inclusivity opens potential for mischief-making in strategy work – May generate insights and outcomes that are unpalatable for those in power
Might be expressed as . . .	'Facilitated by the policy group, the strategy review and formulation process happen on six-monthly cycles, with implementation meetings every month to track progress'
When you are likely to encounter this interpretation	Strategy 'owners'—those responsible for strategy outputs for their area/organization—will be concerned with process External consultants/facilitators often have their own designs of process, methods, and tools that they offer to clients for strategy work

Source: authors.

1

realized in the organization. Understanding the nature and extent of formal and informal strategy conversations and activities can help you, in a future strategy role, to purposefully manage strategy as a process (Vilà and Canales 2008).

Strategy process can be interpreted as the mechanism that gathers and transforms organizational inputs into options and decisions about the long-term future of the organization. Interactions with stakeholders can also provide a means of building commitment to strategy outcomes. The extent to which this is possible depends on involvement of key stakeholders in the process (Ackermann and Eden 2011b). Ongoing strategy processes also enable the renewal of strategy content, based on what has been learned from taking action or monitoring the shifting organizational context.

For example, in DBS, the strategic **risk management** priorities and initiatives represented in the organizational strategy are constantly reviewed by the Board and senior management team through 'a robust process' (p. 34), informed by the efforts, data and insights of the risk function and local risk committees monitoring the shifting internal and external contexts (p. 79). Strategic decisions can be made or updated at any moment should circumstances change, such as were necessary at the onset of the COVID-19 pandemic.

And DBS's investment in agile enterprise architecture was in part to enable responsiveness to opportunities in the business environment, supported by tightly intertwined business and functional **IT strategy** processes (Sia et al. 2021: 39).

Strategy as a target market position

When considering how value is created by the organization, strategy can be interpreted as a desired state or position in the mind of relevant stakeholders (Markides 2000). If value means 'relative worth', the value of products or services of an organization will be compared with those of competitors in the minds of customers. As a desired market position, it then follows that strategy will be how an organization attempts to be perceived by customers as having products or services that are more valuable than those of competitors (Chew and Osborne 2009). What constitutes value will depend on the target audience. This may mean **utility** of the offering (i.e. some products/services offer greater functionality than others), it may be the image or reputation of the product or service, it may be the price/perceived value for money, etc.

Strategy as a desired position has roots in the modern industrial economics and organization-based development of strategy theory described in section 1.1. It also aligns well with concepts of **marketing strategy** in which strategy considers adjusting pricing, product design, placement, and promotional activities in order to best reach customers according to what they value (e.g. Guo et al. 2018). Whatever the definition of value adopted, strategy as position refers to the **organizational conduct** required to achieve a desired perceived state in the minds of stakeholders based on the space it attempts to occupy in a competitive environment (see Table 1.9).

 Access the online resources to watch a short video clip where Marianne Meehan discusses the external environment.

An example of strategy as position is the statement of strategic intent to 'make banking joyful' and a seamless, no-hassle part of customer and consumer life through digital capabilities, products, and services superior to those of competitors. This positioning statement is a key

TABLE 1.9 **Strategy as position**

Strategy as . . .	Position
Interpretation	A state occupied in the mind of relevant stakeholders
Function for the organization	Enables an explanation of how an individual or organization will create value for stakeholders in relation to the activities of competitors
What is needed to work with this interpretation in practice	An understanding of what is achievable with existing resources and external environmental realities such as industry-structural and macro-environmental factors A keen understanding of competitor activities and what customers value are also needed
Benefits	+ Focuses attention on creating customer value as a driver of performance + Brings awareness of competitor activity as a determinant of performance + Connects well with brand- and marketing-led organizational visions
Limitations	– Factors determining position are not all within organizational control – Tends to focus within existing markets, perhaps missing disruptive new sectors – Can breed complacency/arrogance when leading position achieved
Might be expressed as . . .	'We offer the most profitable "super-premium" brand in our sector in Western Europe, the Middle East, and North America'
When you are likely to encounter this interpretation	Those with commercial management aspects of their job roles, such as sales, marketing, branding, and general management, will likely address strategy as a position in their conversations/activities

Source: authors.

marketing message which features prominently in DBS communications, annual reports, and strategic announcements. How an external view of DBS as the 'most joyful bank' will be delivered can be explained by the organization's 'transform the business' priority and its many initiatives to maintain digital leadership and stay at the forefront of new technology applications in banking.

Strategy as plasticity

Strategy as **plasticity** describes an approach to strategy synonymous with agility, entrepreneurship, and opportunism (Table 1.10). As circumstances change for an individual or organization, strategy can be a way of coordinating activities that enables the best to be made of the situation (Isenberg 1987). Strategy as plasticity describes an entrepreneurial capacity to sense and seize opportunity as presented by circumstances, moulding priorities and activities on a continuing basis according to the wisdom and expertise of those making decisions (Munro 2010). By staying attuned to their evolving circumstances and remaining open to new possibilities, opportunities and threats can be managed in as short a time as possible.

Strategy as plasticity aligns with the concept of the agile organization, in which 'small, entrepreneurial groups are designed to stay close to customers and adapt quickly to changing conditions' (Rigby et al. 2018: 90). By maintaining loose reporting **structures**, simple decision criteria, flexible

TABLE 1.10 **Strategy as plasticity**

Strategy as . . .	Plasticity
Interpretation	A means to opportunistically handle or gain advantage from a situation
Function for the organization	A way of operating which allows the individual or organization to cope with or capitalize on unfolding circumstances
What is needed to work with this interpretation in practice	An entrepreneurial capacity to recognize opportunities and the best way of seizing those opportunities for an organization or individual Agility and flexibility of individual or organizational **practice** is also required
Benefits	+ High connectivity with context allows opportunities to be sensed and seized + Fosters organizational capacity for flexibility and agility that enables survival + Encourages high relevance and efficacy of decision-making and resource use
Limitations	– Very hard to execute on an ongoing basis in large firms without a destabilizing effect – Incompatible with predictability focus of performance management **cultures** – Requires flexible operating **systems** and mindset throughout the whole organization
Might be expressed as . . .	'We are a fluid and adaptable organization, willing to take calculated risks and always on the lookout for the next opportunity'
When you are likely to encounter this interpretation	This strategic mode of operating is often seen as a defining characteristic of entrepreneurial individuals or organizations; also found to varying degrees in some national cultures (e.g. wayfinding, nomadic life, the American dream)

Source: authors.

resources, and adaptable processes and procedures, agile teams can react swiftly to unexpected, localized opportunities in order to maximize gains for the organization (Denning 2018).

As an expression of strategy as plasticity, a differentiating factor and source of value creation identified by DBS about the organization is their nimbleness and agility.

> **Nimbleness and agility**
>
> *We are of a 'goldilocks' size—big enough to have meaningful scale yet nimble enough to quickly act on opportunities [. . .] This allows us to embed customer centricity, drive agility and increase internal collaboration by embracing experimentation, entrepreneurship and innovation.*
>
> (DBS Group Holdings Ltd 2022: 66)

Organizational priorities in digital technology investment, employee training and work design, and external partnering all contribute to preserving these dynamic strategic capabilities.

Strategy as a practice

Interpreted as a practice, strategy arises from what people do rather than something an organization has (Johnson et al. 2008). As a continuing accomplishment emerging from human effort, the nature of strategy work depends on factors such as the personal characteristics of all of those contributing to and involved in strategy inside and outside the organization (Breene et al. 2007), embedded ways of working that have evolved over time, and **methods** available to formulate ideas and attempt to implement them (MacKay et al. 2020). Underpinning this human effort is the experience and wisdom of **practitioners**, their specific practices, the **flow** of knowledge and information through relationships, and the biases and limitations of how those involved think (Johnson et al. 2003). We explore this perspective in depth in Chapter 2.

Strategy as a practice helpfully provides insight as to how strategy can be better achieved through education and organizational design work (see Table 1.11). As an activity people do, there is potential to modify the way strategy is understood and enacted over time through learning and development for practitioners. Further, by considering the full set of strategy practices used or available within an organization, adjustments to team composition and strategy **process** design might help organizational strategy to be conducted in more effective ways (e.g. Lee 2019).

For example, as part of both risk and sustainability strategy practice, DBS put in place a committee structure and organizational design, in the form of a Group Sustainability Council and a Climate Steering Committee, to ensure that a number of relevant strategic management activities take place within the Group. They also established a Board Sustainability Committee to

TABLE 1.11 **Strategy as a practice**

Strategy as . . .	Practice
Interpretation	An activity people do rather than something organizations have
Function for the organization	Recognizes that strategy relies on human effort and that effort is shaped by the experience and wisdom, knowledge flows, human connections, and the ways of thinking of the people involved
What is needed to work with this interpretation in practice	Awareness of the preferred/dominant activities and practices, the range of experiences, and the ways of thinking of the people/team involved in strategy work; an ability to minimize the downsides of established practice whilst playing to the individual's/team's strengths during strategy activities
Benefits	+ Capacity for effective strategy can be developed through HR and organizational design work and learning and development activity + A focus on diversity of experience brings strength and depth to strategy work + Encourages criticality of strategy practices and outcomes, reducing arrogance
Limitations	– Engrained practices can be harmful/suboptimal for strategy work – Strategy practice that is at odds with **organizational culture** is likely to fail – Strategy is vulnerable to the biases and limited capacities of people
Might be expressed as . . .	'Our strategy draws on the strengths of our diverse senior management team, bringing a long history of organizational leadership and strategic management experience in our chosen sectors'
When you are likely to encounter this interpretation	Consultants, educators, academics, and human resource professionals will often have a view on effective strategy practices and how they might be recruited, nurtured, and enhanced in an organization

Source: authors.

'provide greater governance and oversight into climate-related risks and opportunities, as well as [our] broader ESG efforts' (DBS Group Holdings Ltd 2022: 35).

This sustainability strategy practice directed organizational activity in the preceding year that resulted in over 100,000 hours of volunteerism by staff, $20.5bn SGD of ethical investment, and 58 external awards being received for sustainability and purpose-driven efforts (DBS Group Holdings Ltd 2022: 3). In these ways, strategic sustainability practices help to realize business opportunities and positive outcomes in response to unavoidable 'wicked problems' (as described in 'Strategy as a problem-solving mechanism').

Strategy as a pattern in a stream of activity

The management scholar Henry Mintzberg famously described strategy as 'a pattern in a stream of activities'. This interpretation of strategy highlights the importance of recognizing culture when articulating strategy. Like the perspective of strategy as a practice, this can include the management team culture, their established ways of working, and their approach to engaging with others (Groysberg et al. 2018). However, this perspective goes further, also incorporating the norms, **routines**, and patterned ways of working in an organization as part of what might be referred to as strategy and strategic change (Beynon-Davies et al. 2016) (see Table 1.12).

The implication of this view of strategy is that an effective culture—where effective means able to contribute to the delivery of organizational objectives—might be a source of competitive advantage (see Wu et al. 2019). As we will explore in Chapter 4, no individual has full control over culture; it is very hard to replicate; and changing culture, even if possible in an intended way, is a long-term endeavour. Therefore, if an established way of working in an organization creates valuable outcomes, competitors may not be able to replicate or imitate the effect of that culture. Also, this perspective highlights the folly of deliberately **strategizing** in a way that is out of alignment with culture—as the management guru Peter Drucker proclaimed, 'culture eats strategy for breakfast'. Strategy as a pattern in a stream of activity challenges the strategic management team to utilize cultural norms and habitual activity productively as a basis for planning and delivering strategic initiatives (Powell 2017).

The direction of travel since 2009 for DBS has been towards digital leadership and continual transformation to stay 'ahead of the curve'. Consequently, a growth mindset culture (where learning from challenges and change informs new activities) is a valuable emergent aspect of work activity in DBS that the organization also aims to foster. By nurturing this growth mindset culture better than any competitor, DBS can aspire to strategic digital leadership initiatives and distinctive outcomes grounded in superior entrepreneurial and agile capabilities.

Strategy as preparation for the future

As preparation for the future, strategy can be interpreted as a mechanism for identifying and taking action today that builds options and capabilities that will enable an organization to respond to opportunities and challenges in the future (Birkinshaw et al. 2016). Adopting this view, strategy and strategic management methods enable management teams to look beyond short-term performance pressures and build capability for sustaining the organization in the long term (Bungay 2019). A major responsibility for a strategic management team is to prepare the

TABLE 1.12 **Strategy as a pattern in a stream of activity**

Strategy as . . .	Pattern
Interpretation	Recurring aspects of an individual or organization's activity
Function for the organization	Draws attention to the cultural norms and habitual activity which, if tapped, could constitute a powerful resource for competitive advantage
What is needed to work with this interpretation in practice	A deep sense of how work happens within an organization and its setting, developed through immersion in that context; an ability to work through rather than against natural patterns of behaviour
Benefits	+ Cultural norms that generate customer value can be a source of sustainable competitive advantage + Aligning with norms reduces resistance to strategy implementation efforts + Aligning with culture reduces the variables the strategist must consider
Limitations	– Often have to 'live' in the organization to grasp intangible aspects of culture – Culture may vary in emphases in different parts of an organization – Strategy based on culture may harm an organization if it doesn't fit with evolving competitive realities
Might be expressed as . . .	'Our proud history and expertise in this industry is at the core of our strategy and the foundation upon which we build for the future'
When you are likely to encounter this interpretation	Culture may be considered in varying degrees during strategy-making, but the fit between strategy and culture inevitably comes to the fore in 'implementation' work

Source: authors.

organization adequately to meet future competitive and operating requirements (Schoemaker et al. 2018). This is particularly challenging given that the future is very difficult to predict! So what are these requirements, and what action needs to be taken now to be ready in the future? How do we 'future-proof' strategy and, by extension, the organization?

For strategy to be an organizational mechanism for preparing for the future, it requires a set of methods and mentalities to be available for strategy work (see Table 1.13). First, there must exist systems for both environmental scanning and the monitoring of external trends and internal review of available resources and capabilities. These systems must make **data** available wherever relevant in the organization as an input to strategy work. With this data available, methods are required to enable management teams to step away from operational life and interrogate, debate, and decide on future organizational needs.

With the insights from these strategic conversations, adequate **change management** capabilities must be available to implement actions that build resources and capabilities as required. These sensing, seizing, and reconfiguring mechanisms (Teece 2007) describe the dynamic capability of the organization—'the organizational capacity to purposefully create, extend or modify its resource base' (Helfat et al. 2007: 4) (see Chapter 6). Dynamic capability enables adaptability

1

TABLE 1.13 **Strategy as preparation for the future**

Strategy as . . .	Preparation
Interpretation	A way of anticipating possible future challenges and preparing now to be ready to meet those challenges
Function for the organization	Defines and guides learning processes that read internal and external trends and anticipate possible future scenarios
	Builds organizational resilience through taking actions today that nurture the resources and capabilities required to meet future challenges
What is needed to work with this interpretation in practice	Management tools and systems for environmental scanning and internal monitoring; agreed strategic management methods to enable management teams to interrogate, debate, and decide on future organizational needs; change management capabilities to develop resources and capabilities as required; and flexibility to respond to needs as they arise
Benefits	+ Fosters managerial vigilance and constant re-evaluation of strategic needs
	+ Generates valuable shared management learning that informs action
	+ Enables necessary capabilities that fit the organization to be built and maintained
Limitations	– Requires a significant investment of management time
	– Foresight can be unsettling if not accompanied by action planning
	– Can give a false sense of confidence about 'knowing' the future perfectly
Might be expressed as . . .	'By asking ourselves "What if?" and connecting with all manner of external data sources, we develop strategic insights and contingency plans that provide assurance of our continuing success as an organization'
When you are likely to encounter this interpretation	Management teams in industries with long planning horizons (such as energy and defence) and civil servants considering national interests will often be interested in this perspective
	Further, management teams sensing likely disruption in their industry will also be interested in this view

Source: authors.

and flexibility triggered by managerial judgement and attention as organizational leaders continually evaluate how best to prepare for the future (Zeng and Mackay 2019).

In the DBS annual report, strategic initiatives, achievements, and objectives are highlighted to create a 'diverse and future-ready workforce'. At a board level, a nominating committee is responsible for maintaining a diversity of expertise and perspective in the top leadership team to minimize blind spots in current and future business strategies.

More widely, the annual report notes strategic investments towards achieving a diverse and capable workforce ready to meet the ever-changing demands of preserving DBS's digital leadership in banking. DBS's 'Women-in-Technology' and 'Hack2Hire-Her' initiatives have increased their number of female technologists; as well as this, many of their technologists 'have been upskilled through learning gamification to support the rapidly increasing demand for cloud technologies' (DBS Group Holdings Ltd 2022: 37).

1.5 **Reconciling views of strategy**

We've outlined twelve different ways in which stakeholders may think about strategy individually or collectively. Varying degrees of emphasis may be placed on each interpretation of strategy in any given situation. For example, what strategy means to the board of a multinational corporation might be significantly different from what strategy means to the managers of a production facility at one of the same organization's subsidiary locations.

With this inherent variability in understanding of what strategy means, undertaking a scoping conversation can set a solid foundation for effective interactions between participants in strategy work, engage stakeholders, and surface what is important (Bencherki et al. 2021). The 12Ps can act as a prompt to share individual views, discuss similarities and differences in interpretation, and agree a shared sense of **scope** for any strategy activities. It is important to repeat this type of conversation when moving between stakeholder groups involved in strategy. An applied example of a scoping method can be found in the online resources, and the question at the end of Case Example 1.3 challenges you to apply 12Ps thinking.

From our experience of working with a wide variety of stakeholders in many different settings, it is vital to invest time in discussing what strategy means at the outset with a group of participants in strategy activity. Doing so can help participants bond, feel heard and valued, understand how and why they are involved, and collaborate more effectively. It can also help those facilitating strategy work to deliver outcomes that meet organizational and stakeholder needs and manage group interactions in a productive way. Being able to draw on the varying perspectives and implications of each of the 12Ps will enhance your effectiveness as a participant in or leader of strategy work.

CASE EXAMPLE 1.3 **PURPOSE-DRIVEN PROFITABILITY AT ANGEL CITY FC**

Angel City FC is a Los-Angeles-based women's football team that joined the US National Women's Soccer League (NSWL) in April 2022. The club was founded in 2020 by actor and activist Natalie Portman, gaming entrepreneur Julie Uhrman, and technology venture capitalists Kara Nortman and Alexis Ohanian. The team's inaugural match, a 2–1 victory over the North Carolina Courage at the Banc of California Stadium, was watched by a sell-out crowd of 22,000 fans.

The idea for Angel City FC arose in 2019 when Portman started following the US Women's National Team's fight for equal pay with the men's team, noting also that female footballers have little post-playing earning potential or retirement funds, unlike their male counterparts. As a co-founder of Time's Up, a gender equality advocacy organization, Portman decided to create a team that would exemplify an alternative model for women's football. 'Watching my son idolize players like Megan Rapinoe and Alex Morgan the same way he did Lionel Messi or Karim Benzema, I realized that amplifying female athletes could rapidly shift culture', Portman commented.

Source: © Angel City FC.

Continued

1

The founders recognized that to create an exemplar of a professional club environment in which women could play, feel safe, and be celebrated, significant investment was required. So, from inception, Angel City raised capital like an entrepreneurial start-up, with funding rounds attracting many stars along the way. Investors were expected to buy into **purpose** as well as **profit** motives and to be available to participate in development activities. It proved a compelling proposition, attracting over 100 investors, two-thirds of whom are women, including movie stars America Ferrera, Eva Longoria, and Uzo Aduba; retired football legends Julie Foudy and Mia Hamm; and sporting greats Serena Williams and Billie-Jean King.

According to Uhrman, the 'glamour exists solely to advance the club's goals and values'. The positive publicity and associated funding enabled an immediately competitive team set-up to be established. Eni Aluko, who won 102 caps for England, joined as sporting director and experienced coach Freya Coombe was brought in to lead the team. Thereafter, two-time World Cup-winning striker Christen Press—a native Angeleno—was recruited as a star player around which to build the team and fan base. The rest of the squad was assembled from local emerging talent and international recruits alongside a draft of existing US-based players.

From day one, all involved with the club have been strongly vocal about its **values** of community and female empowerment. In March 2022, Uhrman announced that Angel City had earned $35m in sponsorship, the highest figure in the NWSL, 10% of which has been invested back into community projects. Initiatives undertaken have included creating a career transition fund for retired players; investment in local school facilities, providing equipment for emerging players and teams, and handing out thousands of meals to homeless people.

The founders of Angel city have expressed determination to avoid being one of the estimated 90% of sports team globally that fail to make money. As Uhrman notes, 'We lead with passion and **purpose** to drive to profitability—that is how we make decisions every single day.'

It seems that the timing was opportune for the launch of the club. Los Angeles didn't have a women's professional football team, and the initial strong commercial performance suggests that this was an untapped market need. More widely, the global sports market is expected to be worth $800bn by 2030, one-third of which will be from women's sports. As a sign of the growing fan base for the women's game, the best attended European fixture—men's or women's—in the season 2021/22 was in the Women's Champions League, when 91,553 fans watched Barcelona take on Real Madrid.

Noting 'vast untapped opportunities', FIFA—the governing body for football—is investing heavily in infrastructure, education, and resources to grow female participation in football around the world to 60 million players by 2026. Global **sponsors** such as Visa are supporting the development of the women's game too. Others are expected to follow this lead, for as noted by the *Financial Times*, with the rapid growth in interest in ethical investing, questions will be soon asked of any organization that doesn't distribute sponsorship activities equally between men and women's sports.

The rise of popularity of the female game is coinciding with broader consumer behaviour changes. Angela Ruggiero of Sports Innovation Lab—a sporting industry analytics start-up—notes that fans now expect clubs to produce story-based content around players, distributed on multiple conventional and social media platforms, where they can also experience quality engagement with their favourite players. These interactions are enabling a 'community-based monetization model' as online exchanges can be mined through data science methods to help teams and leagues understand their fans, serve their needs, and improve commercial performance.

This sort of model has been adopted since formation by Angel City, drawing on the skills inherent in the founder owner group to build a sporting community ecosystem as part of the start-up strategy. The long-term aims of Angel FC of becoming a global brand and a platform for equality and societal impact also seem well matched to circumstances. 'We've been building Angel City FC with the idea that we want to entertain the world', comments Uhrman. 'We come from Los Angeles, we're all storytellers, so we take on that challenge as a given for what we want to accomplish.'

There remain many institutional challenges to overcome in order to grow the women's game in a fair and sustainable way, including a need for increased consideration of female biomechanics in equipment design; the reform of male-dominated league and country association governance structures; and addressing the wide gender-based wage and prize money inequalities that exist. However, the example being created by Angel City FC is showing that Portman's dream of 'making women's soccer as valued as male soccer throughout the world' is an achievable one.

Questions for discussion

1. Using the 12Ps framework to guide your comments, describe the organizational strategy of Angel FC.

2. Which strategic initiatives seem most important for the long-term viability of Angel FC as a business?

3. If you were part of the founder group of Angel FC, what would be your strategic priorities?

Sources

Bloomberg Quicktake (2021). The business case for women's sport, https://www.youtube.com/watch?app=desktop&v=O5bafHWooWk (last accessed 9 August 2022).

Downey, S. (2022). Angel City FC writing their own story. *The Guardian* (13 April), https://www.theguardian.com/football/2022/apr/13/moving-the-goalposts-angel-city-fc (last accessed 9 August 2022).

Elder, A. (2022). Natalie Portman wanted to shift football culture. So she founded Angel City FC. *The Guardian* (18 March), https://www.theguardian.com/football/2022/mar/18/natalie-portman-wanted-to-shift-football-culture-so-she-founded-angel-city-fc (last accessed 9 August 2022).

Financial Times (2022). The business case for women's football, https://www.youtube.com/watch?v=9vr67bt-mt6U (last accessed 9 August 2022).

Guardian Sport (2022). Angel City FC win fairytale NWSL debut before 22,000 fans, https://www.theguardian.com/football/gallery/2022/apr/30/angel-city-fc-first-nwsl-game-north-carolina-courage (last accessed 9 August 2022).

PRACTITIONER INSIGHT **MARIANNE MEEHAN, ENTREPRENEUR, STRATEGY CONSULTANT, AND BUSINESS MENTOR**

Marianne Meehan is an entrepreneur, strategy consultant, and business mentor. She has held operational, general management, and directorship roles in high-growth organizations across a range of **sectors** in the United Kingdom, Europe, and the United States. She currently supports a portfolio of clients in the development and implementation of strategy. Marianne shares her views on the nature of strategy in practice.

'What does strategy mean to you?'

For me, strategy is about setting objectives for three to five years and then figuring out plans for how to deliver those desired outcomes. Strategy requires **vision** and planning but, most importantly, a focus on how implementation will happen. At its core, strategy must be about action. Without a shared commitment to some sort of future work together, there is no implementation and no delivery of outcomes. I realize that strategy can mean different things to different people. Doing an MBA helped me deepen and reframe my view of strategy. Knowledge of different theories helped me develop my own strategy practices and an ability to relate to different strategy 'requirements'. Central what I do now is an appreciation that effective strategy practice is, at its heart, tailored to the needs of the situation at any moment in time.

In terms of practice, I would advise anyone seeking to undertake work to think about:

- **Engagement**—work in a way that draws others in, for their ideas, energy, and commitment;

- **Implementation**—always push towards answering 'So what are we going to do?' when considering problems, opportunities, or options for the future;

- **Be realistic**—deal as much as you can in an unvarnished view of the world. Take multiple data sources and opinions into account to better understand the way the world is, rather than how you'd like it to be, when undertaking strategy development or planning for implementation.

Continued

1

Career path that now informs strategy perspectives

My first role was for a firm of accountants, in which I picked up basic accountancy and finance skills, seeing academic learning come to life. When I reflect back, that first role nurtured my interest in operations, processes, and strategy implementation. I then joined a small company called Water at Work in 1995. The firm provided 19-litre bottles of water and cooler machines to companies in the United Kingdom. It was a new concept in the UK market at the time—the founder saw the opportunity to import the idea from the United States. I was there for 10 years over a period of high growth. When I joined, we had 2,000 customers and 20 employees—10 years later, there were 600 employees serving 120,000 customers! It was an incredible learning experience. There was significant organic growth and we also grew through acquisition. In 1997, we were bought by a Canadian company called Sparkling Spring Water Group—a move that brought cash and resources to grow. Danone acquired Sparkling Spring Water Group in 2003 and entered into a joint venture with Eden Springs in 2004.

I left Eden Springs in 2005 to take up a Chief Financial Officer role running a Family Office for a high-net-worth family setting up an office in the Netherlands and Connecticut, United States. The main aspects of the role were to manage the family assets, develop the investment portfolio, identify and integrate other business investments, and manage all operational aspects for the family members. In 2007, we acquired a Canadian company that designed and manufactured capital equipment—I was given the task of leading the strategic change process and operations transformation. The project was a success, after which I came back to the United Kingdom in 2010 to do an MBA specializing in strategy. After graduating, I took up the newly created role of MBA Operations Director for three years before setting up my own consultancy business. I have a passion for strategy and am supporting a continuing portfolio of 10 clients on a range of projects to deliver strategic enhancement. Further, in 2015, a colleague I met through the MBA and I opened up the award-winning Tribe Yoga Studios in Edinburgh—we now have three facilities (including a spin studio) and are thinking strategically about where to go next!

'How was strategy perceived or viewed in these different environments?'

In Water at Work, there was no formal strategy—we were just doing whatever seemed necessary to grow at breakneck speed, manage cash, and survive. A strategy evolved when we connected with bigger organizations. But initially, the strategy corresponded to whatever could be accommodated in the budget–financial planning cycle. There was no concrete long-term plan, and we didn't have a formal shared view of where we were going together.

The Family Office was very different—the head had an eye for opportunity. He developed a long-term strategy focused on return on investment. He built a highly diverse portfolio through projects that (a) were interesting and (b) had high possible returns. He had many options as he was often approached by acquisition prospects because of his wealth. He took a long-term patient approach rather than quarterly-focused decisions about returns on investment. In that business, strategy was a continuing process—effective management of what we had in hand but continual readiness to react to opportunities. We had protocols that we used to keep us fit for the future. The overarching corporate strategy guided all activity; then we had specific business strategies for different work streams and, by asking 'How do we make that happen?', functional strategies were developed to deliver operational outcomes. Within the parameters of the owner's strategic vision, we all knew how to work with each other—there was trust, high understanding, positive relationships, consistent ways of working, support for each other, recognition, and reward.

As a consultant, I've noticed that strategy as a possession is vital to keeping people engaged. Documents and materials—plans, visions, writeups—are brought out time and time again to help everyone pay attention, track progress, and think in a focused way. I've found that strategy can be a scary or confusing prospect at all levels of an organization—clear and simple documentation during a strategy episode is vital to demystifying, learning, and building a shared sense of meaning. Strategy 'possessions' can give a sense of achievement and a key reference resource and are an important sign of tangible contribution as a consultant.

Across all my roles, I've found that strategy work can help surface and resolve problems that matter—enabling improvements to be realized that engage employees as it improves their lives. To allow this to happen, the practices of senior leaders in relation to strategy are crucial. If they choose to overwrite what colleagues suggest, engagement potential is harmed and the reputation of 'strategy' as a type of work is damaged. If you invite people to contribute, you have to listen to what they say and take it seriously. Otherwise, don't invite them.

When we started up the business, I used a combination of my experiences to lead development of the objectives and a vision for the company through workshop sessions. The business owners set the initial view, and then we got the whole team together in Dublin and invited participation in setting implementation priorities and plans. We use the strategy to this day and continue to update it when we feel it is necessary, such as when we have achieved an objective or we want to do something significant and new.

 Access the online resources to watch a short video clip where Marianne Meehan talks more about her career.

CHAPTER SUMMARY

In this chapter, we addressed the following learning outcomes:

○ **Explain how strategy can be interpreted in multiple ways.**
Strategy was described at a high level as the balancing of ways, means, and objectives for an individual or organization. However, strategy has been shown to be a contested term that resists precise definition. Instead, there are multiple possible interpretations of strategy that different stakeholders may adopt to varying degrees according to their personal views and understanding of the needs of a situation.

○ **Evaluate the challenges and benefits of agreeing a shared understanding of strategy with key stakeholders.**
A key challenge that the strategist faces is to work with the stakeholders involved to build agreement about what strategy means and set an appropriate scope of strategy work/target outcomes. Doing this well increases the likelihood of buy-in to the process and outcomes, and also the quality of strategy work as a wider range of inputs are gathered to highly relevant activities.

○ **Critically assess the usefulness of strategy in different organizational situations and from different stakeholder perspectives.**
Possible interpretations of strategy have accrued over the past 60 years with different intellectual and practical heritages. For example, early academic thoughts on strategy as a rational plan grounded in **analytical methods** are now complemented by process and practice theories which connect with the human aspects of making and managing strategy. With limitations and within practical constraints, each interpretation of strategy has the potential to contribute to how a group of stakeholders work together on organizational strategy. It is valuable for you to be aware of possible interpretations of strategy and to be able to guide the scoping of strategy work effectively.

○ **Appreciate the value of strategy as a mechanism for coordinating organizational effort and decision-making.**
Organizational strategy can add value as a mechanism that guides decision-making, resource allocation, stakeholder management, and coordinated actions. This mechanism will rarely be most effective when it produces fixed outcomes on a one-off basis. It will

work best when it is kept relevant through continuing managerial attention and incorporation of new learning and insights from the evolving organizational context.

○ **Reconcile how strategy is interpreted within and between stakeholder groups.**
A simple conversational approach to reconciling varied stakeholder views of strategy based on the 12P framework is proposed. Through questions that relate to established strategy interpretations, structured dialogue between stakeholders can reveal the extent to which a shared understanding of strategy is held. If what is meant by strategy is surfaced and resolved at the start of strategy work, then target outcomes can be identified and stakeholder perspectives effectively managed. A scoping method to create a customized definition of strategy according to stakeholder needs is shared in the online resources.

? END-OF-CHAPTER QUESTIONS

Recall questions

1. How has the concept of strategy developed over the twentieth century, and how does this developmental path influence how it is understood today?

2. What might we mean by organizational strategy?

3. What are the main differences between corporate, business, and functional strategies?

4. What benefits might organizational strategy yield?

5. Summarize the range of possible interpretations of strategy covered in this chapter. What are they and what do they mean?

6. Why might we choose to start a strategy process by scoping a strategy with those involved?

Application questions

A) Imagine you have been assigned to lead a strategy team within a business unit of a multinational corporation. What actions would you take initially to build stakeholder engagement in the strategy process? Draft a short plan of action with explanatory comments as to why each action should be undertaken.

B) Ask five people who have a connection with strategy (either leading, participating in, or implementing strategy work) the question, 'What does strategy mean to you?' Use the scoping method to explore their interpretation in detail and map their responses onto a diagram (in which the emphases of their responses can be compared).

C) Pick two or three organizations that are of interest to you and explore how strategy is described and used in their externally facing media (website, advertising, annual report, etc.). Note which interpretations of strategy are evident in their media and also the messages which seem to be portrayed by the styling of their media (strategy as a possession). Reflecting on the organizations' contexts and histories, suggest some explanations for the similarities and differences between the organizations' approaches.

ONLINE RESOURCES

www.oup.com/he/mackay2e

In addition to the video interviews already highlighted, the book's online resources include the following features for this chapter, specifically:

- *links to further reading material* to broaden your knowledge of key issues discussed in this chapter;

- *self-test multiple-choice questions* to test your understanding of the material covered in each section of the chapter; and

- *a flashcard glossary* to help you recall and test your understanding of key terms.

FURTHER READING

Strategy: A History by Sir Lawrence Freedman

Freedman, L. (2013). *Strategy: A History*. Oxford: Oxford University Press.

This extensive text traces the history of the development and use of strategy. It is an engaging, well-written book that takes the reader from the roots of strategy in ancient civilizations, through military applications and developments, up to the modern incarnations and interpretations of strategy used in organizational life today. It will be helpful to students looking to understand strategy beyond functional methodological interpretations.

A Treatise on Efficacy by Françoise Jullien (trans. Janet Lloyd)

Jullien, F. (2004). *A Treatise on Efficacy: Between Western and Chinese Thinking*, trans. J. Lloyd. Honolulu, HI: University of Hawaii Press.

Françoise Jullien's text compares and contrasts interpretations of strategy as originating in Ancient Greek and Chinese thought. Our modern usage of strategy—in the business press and academic life—seems strongly linked to Ancient Greek teachings and influences. As laid out in this book, there is much to learn from the processual thinking and philosophies of Ancient Chinese thought on strategy, which offers different ideas as to what it means to be strategic. This book presents these two ancient influences side by side, challenging us to ask how we can be more effective in our strategy work. It will be of use to those struggling to make strategy more impactful and to understand how we can manage strategy as a process, through people, in a complex and ever unfolding world.

Strategy Safari by Henry Mintzberg, Bruce Ahlstrand, and Joseph Lampel

Mintzberg, H., Ahlstrand, B., and Lampel, J. (2009). *Strategy Safari: Your Complete Guide through the Wilds of Strategic Management*. Harlow: Prentice Hall.

Strategy Safari is a popular text that offers a review of academic perspectives available in the strategy literature. It makes a neat complement to the different practice-focused interpretations raised in this chapter. Mintzberg and colleagues offer insights as to how a range of schools of thought in strategy—such as design, culture, power, planning, cognition—have developed and how associated research might be used separately and in combination. It will be of use to those seeking to understand how academic perspectives of strategy have emerged over the years and why there are different 'tribes' or types of strategy academic.

1

Good Strategy/Bad Strategy by Richard Rumelt

Rumelt, R.P. (2011). *Good Strategy/Bad Strategy: The Difference and Why It Matters*. London: Profile Books.

Richard Rumelt has been a highly influential US strategy academic over the past 30 years. He offers his insights as to what makes a 'good' strategy and how it might add value to strategic managers and organizations. He writes about the importance of having a core or kernel idea of strategy around which all other interpretations and actions can be developed in a coherent way. It will be helpful to those looking for ideas about how strategy can be used as a problem-solving mechanism and to further understand the importance of strategy as priority.

Opening Strategy by Richard Whittington

Whittington, R. (2019) *Opening Strategy*. Oxford: Oxford University Press.

Richard Whittington's detailed review of the emergence of contemporary views of strategy provides a valuable complement to Freedman's historical text. The author traces in detail the development of modern streams of understanding and practice in strategy and sets an agenda for the current movement in 'open strategy'. This will be useful for students seeking to research or develop inclusive, engaged strategy approaches with a wide range of stakeholders, informed by a keen sense of how strategy might be understood in the modern context.

REFERENCES

Ackermann, F. and Eden, C. (2011a). *Making Strategy: Mapping Out Strategic Success*. London: Sage.

Ackermann, F. and Eden, C. (2011b). Strategic management of stakeholders: Theory and practice. *Long Range Planning*, **44**(3), 179–96.

Arend, R.J. (2016). Divide and conquer, or the disintegration of strategic management: It's time to celebrate. *Strategic Organization*, **14**(2), 156–66.

Arend, R.J., Zhao, Y.L., Song, M., and Im, S. (2017). Strategic planning as a complex and enabling managerial tool. *Strategic Management Journal*, **38**(8), 1741–52.

Arnaud, N., Mills, C.E., Legrand, C., and Maton, E. (2016). Materializing strategy in mundane tools: The key to coupling global strategy and local strategy practice? *British Journal of Management*, **27**(1), 38–57.

Baginski, S.P., Bozzolan, S., Marra, A., and Mazzola, P. (2017). Strategy, valuation, and forecast accuracy: Evidence from Italian Strategic Plan disclosures. *European Accounting Review*, **26**(2), 341–78.

Barnett, M.L. (2016). Strategist, organize thyself. *Strategic Organization*, **14**(2), 146–55.

Bartlett, C.A. and Ghoshal, S. (1994). Changing the role of top management: Beyond strategy to purpose. *Harvard Business Review*, **72**(6), 79–88.

Bencherki, N., Sergi, V., Cooren, F., and Vásquez, C. (2021). How strategy comes to matter: Strategizing as the communicative materialization of matters of concern. *Strategic Organization*, **19**(4), 608–35.

Beynon-Davies, P., Jones, P., and White, G.R.T. (2016). Business patterns and strategic change. *Strategic Change*, **25**(6), 675–91.

Birkinshaw, J., Foss, N.J., and Lindenberg, S. (2014). Combining purpose with profits. *MIT Sloan Management Review*, **55**(3), 49–56.

Birkinshaw, J., Zimmermann, A., and Raisch, S. (2016). How do firms adapt to discontinuous change? *California Management Review*, **58**, 36–58.

Breene, R.T.S., Nunes, P.F., and Shill, W.E. (2007). The chief strategy officer. *Harvard Business Review*, **85**(10), 84–93.

Bloomberg Quicktake (2021). The business case for women's sport, https://www.youtube.com/watch?app=desktop&v=O5bafHWooWk (last accessed 9 August 2022).

Brielmaier, C. and Friesl, M. (2021). Pulled in all directions: Open strategy participation as an attention contest. *Strategic Organization*, https://doi.org/10.1177/14761270211034515.

Bungay, S. (2019). 5 myths about strategy. *Harvard Business Review* Digital *Articles* (19 April), https://hbr.org/2019/04/5-myths-about-strategy (last accessed 2 October 2022).

Cheung, M.-C. (2021). Despite COVID and government crackdowns, Alibaba posts strong retail revenue growth. *eMarketer* (6 August), https://www.emarketer.com/content/despite-covid-government-crackdowns-alibaba-posts-strong-retail-revenue-growth (last accessed 9 August 2022).

Chew, C. and Osborne, S.P. (2009). Exploring strategic positioning in the UK charitable sector: Emerging evidence from charitable organizations that provide public services. *British Journal of Management*, **20**(1), 90–105.

Collis, D. (2016). Lean strategy. *Harvard Business Review*, **94**(3), 62–8.

Conroy, K.M., Collings, D.G., and Clancy, J. (2017). Regional headquarters' dual agency role: Micro-political strategies of alignment and self-interest. *British Journal of Management*, **28**(3), 390–406.

Cummings, S. (1993). Brief case: The first strategists. *Long Range Planning*, **26**(3), 133–5.

Dameron, S., Lê, J.K., and LeBaron, C. (2015). Materializing strategy and strategizing materials: Why matter matters. *British Journal of Management*, **26**, S1–12.

Daviter, F. (2017). Coping, taming, or solving: alternative approaches to the governance of wicked problems. *Policy Studies*, **38**(6), 571–88.

DBS Group Holdings Ltd (2022). *Annual Report 2021*, https://www.dbs.com/iwov-resources/images/investors/annual-report/dbs-annual-report-2021.pdf (last accessed 9 August 2022).

Denning, S. (2018). The emergence of Agile people management. *Strategy and Leadership*, **46**(4), 3–10.

Dobusch, L., Dobusch, L., and Müller-Seitz, G. (2019). Closing for the benefit of openness? The case of Wikimedia's open strategy process. *Organization Studies*, **40**(3), 343–70.

Downey, S. (2022). Angel City FC writing their own story. *The Guardian* (13 April), https://www.theguardian.com/football/2022/apr/13/moving-the-goalposts-angel-city-fc (last accessed 9 August 2022).

Elder, A. (2022). Natalie Portman wanted to shift football culture. So she founded Angel City FC. *The Guardian* (18 March), https://www.theguardian.com/football/2022/mar/18/natalie-portman-wanted-to-shift-football-culture-so-she-founded-angel-city-fc (last accessed 9 August 2022).

Farjoun, M. (2007). The end of strategy? *Strategic Organization*, **5**(3), 197–210.

Felin, T. and Zenger, T. (2018). What sets breakthrough strategies apart: Innovative strategies depend more on novel, well-reasoned theories than on well-crunched numbers. *MIT Sloan Management Review*, **59**(2), 86–8.

Financial Times (2022). The business case for women's football, https://www.youtube.com/watch?v=9vr67btmt6U (last accessed 9 August 2022).

Franco-Santos, M., Nalick, M., Rivera-Torres, P., and Gomez-Mejia, L. (2017). Governance and wellbeing in academia: Negative consequences of applying an agency theory logic in higher education. *British Journal of Management*, **28**(4), 711–30.

Freedman, L. (2013). *Strategy: A History*. Oxford: Oxford University Press.

Graber, R.S. (2009). Business lessons from chess: A discussion of parallels between chess strategy and business strategy. *Academy of Educational Leadership Journal*, **13**(1), 79–85.

Grant, R.M. (2003). Strategic planning in a turbulent environment: Evidence from the oil majors. *Strategic Management Journal*, **24**(6), 491–517.

Groysberg, B., Lee, J., Price, J., and Cheng, J.Y.-J. (2018). The leader's guide to corporate culture. *Harvard Business Review*, **96**(1), 44–52.

Gulati, R. (2018). Structure that's not stifling. *Harvard Business Review*, **96**(3), 68–79.

Guardian Sport (2022). Angel City FC win fairytale NWSL debut before 22,000 fans, https://www.theguardian.com/football/gallery/2022/apr/30/angel-city-fc-first-nwsl-game-north-carolina-courage (last accessed 9 August 2022).

Guo, C., Wang, Y.J., Hao, A.W., and Saran, A. (2018). Strategic positioning, timing of entry, and new product performance in business-to-business markets. Do market-oriented firms make better decisions? *Journal of Business-to-Business Marketing*, **25**(1), 51–64.

1

Hansen, J.R. and Jacobsen, C.B. (2016). Changing strategy processes and strategy content in public sector organizations? A longitudinal case study of NPM reforms' influence on strategic management. *British Journal of Management*, **27**(2), 373–89.

Helfat, C.E., Finklestein, S., Mitchell, W., et al. (2007). *Dynamic Capabilities: Understanding Strategic Change in Organisations*. Oxford: Blackwell.

Huang, Z. (2022). Tencent, Alibaba look like utilities after $1 trillion drubbing. *BloombergUK* (16 May), https://www.bloomberg.com/news/articles/2022-05-16/tencent-alibaba-look-like-utilities-after-1-trillion-drubbing (last accessed 9 August 2022).

Isenberg, D.J. (1987). The tactics of strategic opportunism. *Harvard Business Review*, **65**(2), 92–7.

Jalonen, K., Schildt, H., and Vaara, E. (2018). Strategic concepts as micro-level tools in strategic sensemaking. *Strategic Management Journal*, **39**(10), 2794–826.

Johnson, G., Melin, L., and Whittington, R. (2003). Micro strategy and strategizing: Towards an activity-based view. *Journal of Management Studies*, **40**(1), 3–22.

Johnson, G., Langley, A., Melin, L., and Whittington, R. (2008). *Strategy as Practice: Research Directions and Resources*. Cambridge: Cambridge University Press.

Jullien, F. (2004). *A Treatise on Efficacy: Between Western and Chinese Thinking*, trans J. Lloyd. Honolulu, HI: University of Hawaii Press.

Kammerlander, N. and Ganter, M. (2015). An attention-based view of family firm adaptation to discontinuous technological change: Exploring the role of family CEOs' noneconomic goals. *Journal of Product Innovation Management*, **32**(3), 361–83.

Kerr, W.R. (2016). Harnessing the best of globalization. *MIT Sloan Management Review*, **58**(1), 58–67.

Lee, Y.W. (2019). Enhancing shared value and sustainability practices of global firms: The case of Samsung Electronics. *Strategic Change*, **28**(2), 139–45.

Loonam, J., Eaves, S., Kumar, V., and Parry, G. (2018). Towards digital transformation: Lessons learned from traditional organizations. *Strategic Change*, **27**(2), 101–9.

MacKay, B., Chia, R., and Nair, A.K. (2020). Strategy-in-practices: A process philosophical approach to understanding strategy emergence and organizational outcomes. *Human Relations*, https://doi.org/10.1177/0018726720929397.

Mackay, D. and Zundel, M. (2017). Recovering the divide: A review of strategy and tactics in business and management. *International Journal of Management Reviews*, **19**(2), 175–94.

MacKay, R.B. and Chia, R. (2013). Choice, chance, and unintended consequences in strategic change: A process understanding of the rise and fall of Northco Automotive. *Academy of Management Journal*, **56**(1), 208–30.

Markides, C.C. (2000). *All the Right Moves: A Guide to Crafting Breakthrough Strategy*. Boston, MA: Harvard Business School Press.

McMillan, C., and Overall, J. (2016). Wicked problems: Turning strategic management problems upside down. *Journal of Business Strategy*, **37**(1), 34–43.

Millar, C.C.J.M., Groth, O., and Mahon, J.F. (2018). Management Innovation in a VUCA World: Challenges and Recommendations. *California Management Review*, **61**(1), 5–14.

Mintzberg, H. and Hunsicker, J.Q. (1988). Crafting strategy. *McKinsey Quarterly* 3, 71–90.

Mintzberg, H. and Waters, J.A. (1985). Of strategies, deliberate and emergent. *Strategic Management Journal*, **6**(3), 257–72.

Mintzberg, H., Ahlstrand, B., and Lampel, J. (2009). *Strategy Safari: Your Complete Guide through the Wilds of Strategic Management*. Harlow: Prentice Hall.

Munro, I. (2010). Nomadic strategies in the network society: From Lawrence of Arabia to Linux. *Scandinavian Journal of Management*, **26**(2), 215–23.

Penrose, E. (1959). *The Theory of the Growth of the Firm*. Oxford: Basil Blackwell.

Pettigrew, A., Thomas, H., and Whittington, R. (2006). Strategic management: The strengths and limitations of a field. In: Pettigrew, A., Thomas, H., and Whittington, R. (eds), *Handbook of Strategy and Management*. London: Sage, pp. 1–30.

Plesner, U. and Gulbrandsen, I.T. (2015). Strategy and new media: A research agenda. *Strategic Organization*, **13**(2), 153–62.

Porter, M.E. (1980). *Competitive Strategy: Techniques for Analyzing Industries and Competitors*. New York: Free Press.

Porter, M.E. (1984). *Competitive Advantage: Creating and Sustaining Superior Performance*. New York: Free Press.

Poulis, K. and Poulis, E. (2016). Problematizing fit and survival: Transforming the law of requisite variety through complexity misalignment. *Academy of Management Review*, **41**(3), 503–27.

Powell, T.C. (2017). Strategy as diligence: Putting behavioural strategy into practice. *California Management Review*, **59**(3), 162–90.

Quinn, R.E. and Thakor, A.V. (2018). Creating a purpose-driven organization. *Harvard Business Review*, **96**(4), 78–85.

Rigby, D.K., Sutherland, J., and Noble, A. (2018). Agile at scale. *Harvard Business Review*, **96**(3), 88–96.

Rumelt, R.P. (2011). *Good Strategy/Bad Strategy: The Difference and Why It Matters*. London: Profile Books.

Schoemaker, P.J.H., Heaton, S., and Teece, D. (2018). Innovation, dynamic capabilities, and leadership. *California Management Review*, **61**(1), 15–42.

Seidl, D. (2007). General strategy concepts and the ecology of strategy discourses: A systemic-discursive perspective. *Organization Studies*, **28**(2), 197–218.

Sia, S.K., Weill, P., and Zhang, N. (2021). Designing a future-ready enterprise: The digital transformation of DBS Bank. *California Management Review*, **63**(3), 35–57.

Splitter, V., Jarzabkowski, P., and Seidl, D. (2021). Middle managers' struggle over their subject position in open strategy processes. *Journal of Management Studies*, https://doi.org/10.1111/joms.12776.

Sull, D., Turconi, S., Sull, C., and Yoder, J. (2018a). Four logics of corporate strategy. *MIT Sloan Management Review*, **59**(2), 38–44.

Sull, D., Turconi, S., Sull, C., and Yoder, J. (2018b). How to develop strategy for execution. *MIT Sloan Management Review*, **59**(2), 47.

Teece, D., Peteraf, M., and Leih, S. (2016). Dynamic capabilities and organizational agility: Risk, uncertainty and strategy in the innovation economy. *California Management Review*, **58**(4), 13–35.

Teece, D.J. (2007). Explicating dynamic capabilities: The nature and microfoundations of (sustainable) enterprise performance. *Strategic Management Journal*, **28**(13), 1319–50.

Vilà, J. and Canales, J.I. (2008). Can strategic planning make strategy more relevant and build commitment over time? The case of RACC. *Long Range Planning*, **41**(3), 273–90.

Vuorinen, T., Hakala, H., Kohtamäki, M., and Uusitalo, K. (2018). Mapping the landscape of strategy tools: A review on strategy tools published in leading journals within the past 25 years. *Long Range Planning*, **51**(4), 586–605.

Whittington, R. (2019). *Opening Strategy*. Oxford: Oxford University Press.

Wiles, J. (2022). Employees seek personal value and purpose at work (13 January), https://www.gartner.com/en/articles/employees-seek-personal-value-and-purpose-at-work-be-prepared-to-deliver (last accessed 9 August 2022).

Wright, G., Cairns, G., O'Brien, F.A., and Goodwin, P. (2019). Scenario analysis to support decision making in addressing wicked problems: Pitfalls and potential. *European Journal of Operational Research*, **278**(1), 3–19.

Wu, L.-F., Huang, I.-C., Huang, W.-C., and Du, P.-L. (2019). Aligning organizational culture and operations strategy to improve innovation outcomes: An integrated perspective in organizational management. *Journal of Organizational Change Management*, **32**(2), 224–50.

Zeng, J. and Mackay, D. (2019). The influence of managerial attention on the deployment of dynamic capability: A case study of internet platform firms in China. *Industrial and Corporate Change*, **28**(5), 1173–92.

CHAPTER TWO

A Process–Practice Model of Strategy

CONTENTS

LEARNING OBJECTIVES

2

By the end of this chapter, you should be able to:

○ Explain how strategy can be understood from a process–practice view

○ Explain what is meant by practice, practitioners, practices, tools, activity, and process in the context of strategy work

○ Evaluate the usefulness of the attention-based view as an aid to understanding what people do in relation to strategy

○ Critically assess the limitations of adopting rigid approaches to strategy

○ Articulate how the strategy process–practice framework can guide your learning about how to think, talk, and act as a strategy practitioner

TOOLBOX

○ **Combinatory model of strategy as process and practice**
A model that illustrates how strategy—as a continuous stream of activity—occurs over time and in context through an interplay of strategy formulation and implementation efforts.

○ **Attention-based view**
A set of concepts and theoretical contributions that help explain how organizations behave, adapt to changing environments, develop capabilities, and strategize according to how decision-makers' attention is informed and directed, a valuable complement to the process–practice framework.

○ **Strategy process–practice framework**
A guiding framework that can be used as a checklist and reference point for learning how to think, talk, and act like a strategist, in line with understanding of strategy as process and practice.

Access the online resources to watch a short video clip where Kirsty Lloyd-Williams shares her top career tips.

OPENING CASE STUDY THE FUTURE IS MULTI-PLANETARY AT RELATIVITY SPACE

2

'Putting a million people on Mars in our lifetime is a real possibility' according to Tim Ellis, co-founder of Relativity Space. This view arises from the potential of a technology known as 3D printing. 3D printing is an 'additive manufacturing' method in which thousands of thin layers of a raw material, fed through a robotic printing head, are fused into the shape and thickness of a digital design. 3D printing has been in development for over 25 years and is now showing transformative potential across industries as material science progresses and complementary digital technologies evolve (c.f. Ben-Ner and Siemsen 2017; Unruh 2018).

In 2015, Tim Ellis and Jordan Noone left their respective roles with Blue Origin and SpaceX to form Relativity Space. Their aim was to disrupt the 60-year-old space industry, using 3D metal printing as a core production process to build rockets 'in days rather than years'. It was the co-founders' belief, based on insights from their nascent space industry careers, that it was an achievable dream to pursue even though the necessary 3D-printing technology didn't exist at the required scale.

When forming the company, Ellis cold-emailed Mark Cuban, a billionaire technology investor, outlining their vision and asking for seed money. Cuban responded positively, buying into the potential, and providing the funds needed to kick-start development. From its Californian base, Relativity Space commenced designing the 3D printers, control software, and production system to build and test rockets able to travel to space. As of March 2022, it had over 700 employees and had taken over an ex-Boeing production facility with a view to scaling up production.

In its initial years, Relativity Space succeeded in developing the world's largest 3D metal printers, known as the Stargate printers. By demonstrating milestone achievements in technological progress, Relativity Space was able to attract a diverse range of investors that funded the next set of developments. Even before the launch of its first rocket, Terran 1, Relativity Space had raised over $1.3bn in funding and become the second most valuable privately owned space company in the world.

Additive manufacturing capabilities set Relativity Space apart from its competitors. It estimates that its rockets take 60 days and one-third of the cost to produce versus the 18-month lead time and expense of conventional manufacturing methods. Costs are held low by use of automation, minimization of capital expenditure, simple **supply chains**, and avoidance of material waste. These performance advantages arise mainly from the efficiencies of the core technology—95% of the components in the 35m-tall Terran 1 are made by 3D printing. Further, 3D printing can create single-piece components with complex geometries that require multiple methods, materials, and assemblies from a conventional 'subtractive manufacturing' approach. Consequently, Relativity Space estimates that the Terran 1 has 100 times fewer components than a conventionally built rocket.

The production system also incorporates machine learning as a driver of performance improvement, with artificial intelligence controlling printing operations whilst giving real-time quality assurance and product integrity testing. The company notes, 'as a vertically integrated technology platform, Relativity is at the forefront of an inevitable shift toward software-defined manufacturing. By fusing 3D printing, artificial intelligence, and autonomous robotics, we are pioneering the factory of the future.'

Relativity Space seems well positioned to respond to growth in the space industry, which it is estimated will be worth over US$1tn in annual revenue by 2040, up from US$350bn in 2020. It also seems to be ready to respond to competitive moves as

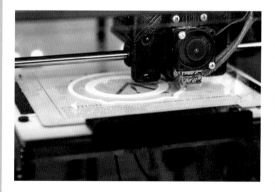

A 3D printer. *Source*: Lutz Peter/Pixabay.com.

the founder of SpaceX, Elon Musk, estimates that a major fall in the cost of launching rockets into space within the next two to three years will define the industry. Relativity Space is also developing a larger, reusable rocket design called the Terran R, with a target launch date of 2024. This should further reduce costs, improve sustainability performance, and increase capacity to meet the growing demand for rocket payloads from governments, companies, and space tourists.

A key business question for Relativity Space is if and how to diversify. Ellis has hinted at his interest in deploying Relativity's technology to disrupt conventional aerospace, creating more effective and efficient aircraft designs that today's production methods can't support. Further, there are myriad industrial and consumer products which now seem ready for disruptive innovation by those with 3D-printing mastery. And is there potential for Relativity Space to become the leading platform provider of 3D-printing technology to other manufacturers? Whatever path the company chooses to follow, it seems that the journey of this technology-based innovator is only just beginning.

Questions for discussion

Imagine you are the CEO of Relativity Space:

1. What external trends, factors, and opportunities do you think that you will have to address in your strategy work over the next three to five years?

2. What stakeholders are likely to (a) have an influence on your strategy and (b) want to be participants in your strategy work?

3. How realistic is it for you to set and stick exactly to a five-year strategy plan for Relativity Space? Explain your answer.

4. What sort of activities would you carry out in order to make and manage strategy effectively for Relativity Space?

Sources

Anderson, M. (2022). 3D-printing start-up Relativity Space is the world's second most valuable space company—and has big plans to unseat SpaceX as the ruler of a booming industry (8 March), https://www.businessinsider.com/relativity-space-startup-3d-print-rockets-colonize-mars-spacex-2022-3 (last accessed 9 August 2022).

Ben-Ner, A. and Siemsen, E. (2017). Decentralization and localization of production: The organizational and economic consequences of additive manufacturing (3D printing). *California Management Review*, 59(2), 5–23.

Farooqui, J.B. (2022). Space investing: world's first 3D-printed rocket is set to launch (17 February), https://www.proactiveinvestors.co.uk/companies/news/974428/space-investing-world-s-first-3d-printed-rocket-is-set-to-launch-974428.html (last accessed 9 August 2022).

Fast Company, https://www.fastcompany.com/90724476/most-innovative-companies-space-2022 (last accessed 9 August 2022).

Fortson, D. (2022). Tim Ellis: The space nerd 3D-printing a rocket to Mars. *Sunday Times* (27 February), https://www.thetimes.co.uk/article/tim-ellis-the-space-nerd-3d-printing-a-rocket-to-mars-gzgj2x9wx (last accessed 9 August 2022).

Relativity Space, https://www.relativityspace.com (last accessed 9 August 2022).

Unruh, G. (2018). Circular economy, 3D printing, and the biosphere rules. *California Management Review*, 60(3), 95–111.

2.1 **Introduction**

In this chapter, we focus on what people actually do in relation to strategy over time and in context. We explore how strategy can be understood as a continuing accomplishment of practitioner activity. Henry Mintzberg (1987: 66) highlights the practical value of being able to 'craft strategy', drawing on 'skill, dedication and mastery of detail [. . .] a feeling of intimacy and harmony with the materials at hand'. Using the image of a potter artfully shaping an output from clay, working and reworking materials, Mintzberg describes the practice of strategy as a continual effort in which 'formulation and implementation merge into a fluid process of learning through which creative strategies emerge'.

In line with a crafting metaphor, we introduce a dynamic 'process–practice' framework of strategy. This framework accommodates the interpretations of strategy highlighted in Chapter 1. Drawing on the latest theorizing about how strategy occurs over time in context, the process–practice framework should help you understand and explain:

- the central importance of practitioners and what they do in strategy;

- how you can cope when strategy ideas don't work out as planned in reality;

- the ways in which strategy can be considered as a continual stream of activity;

- how we can revise our practices to be effective according to our evolving situation;

- how different theories, data sources, and interpretations can be incorporated into collective strategy practices.

Being able to think in terms of a flexible process–practice framework is beneficial as strategy activity rarely, if ever, occurs in an orderly repeatable fashion. It is on this issue that linear **prescriptive models** of strategy fail. If strategy activity occurs in a fixed way, regardless of the situation, contextual factors are likely to diminish the efficiency and effectiveness of practitioner efforts. As an alternative, a process–practice framework highlights how practitioners can draw upon a range of learned and improvised **practices** to meet the changing strategy requirements of an organization over time. Through awareness and practice of different types of strategy activity, you can improve your ability to craft strategy according to your circumstances. You can also learn how to reflect on experience, read situations, and adapt your practices over time to improve your effectiveness as a strategy practitioner.

We will explore how the process–practice framework can help you work with strategy as a 'fluid process' without any artificial divide between formulation and implementation activities. This is a valuable insight to learn as, in an organizational setting, you are likely to encounter a divided view of strategy formulation and implementation. Formulation is typically seen as the responsibility of only a select few individuals such as the top team or a strategy function. Conventional thinking dictates that this small group of leaders formulates strategy as a guiding vision or masterplan and then roll out its ideas for implementation to the rest of the organization. The communication of strategy—through 'town hall' meetings, email newsletters, **performance management** systems, etc.—aligns the rest of the organization, with each team or individual receiving their part to play. Implementation then follows, guided and tracked by performance management systems and scorecards.

There is no doubt that the ideas and activities of senior leaders are crucial in strategy work. However, a portrayal of strategy where senior leaders' calculated plans are implemented by compliant employees through neat, controlled tactics seems at odds with the realities of organizational life (Mackay and Zundel 2017). Reviewing the literature on strategy failure, Candido and Santos (2015) find that many factors might influence the extent to which strategy can be defined and realized. Whilst it is not possible to define an exact failure rate for strategy, it can be concluded that no matter the intelligence or focus of senior leaders involved, strategic success for an organization is never assured.

A review of strategy implementation failure by Sull et al. (2015) highlights recurring issues across organizational strategy approaches that seem to impact effectiveness, namely:

(i) an emphasis on installing top-down 'alignment' of strategy rather than lateral coordination and agreement;

(ii)   sticking rigidly to strategy plans rather than acting opportunistically within a set of shared principles;

(iii) investing time in one-way communication rather than building shared meaning and understanding of strategy;

(iv) performance management cultures that reward 'more of the same' behaviours rather than measured risk-taking in pursuit of change and innovation;

(v)   concentrating strategy responsibility and involvement in a few leaders rather than distributing it across the organization.

How can strategy work be approached in a way that increases the likelihood of valuable outcomes being realized? Reversing the issues described by Sull et al. (2015), we can attempt strategy activity in a way that builds coordination, cooperation, and engagement; encourages alertness, reflection, and responsiveness; enables the seizing of unanticipated opportunities; builds shared meaning-making of strategy across stakeholders; rewards and recognizes appropriate risk-taking and novelty; and spreads the responsibility for strategy-making and management throughout the organization. Through such an approach, any fixed separation between strategy formulation and implementation activities dissolves.

To address strategy in this way doesn't mean ignoring established methods and approaches such as creating strategy plans and targets, using environmental analysis and business information, communicating through emails, 'town hall' meetings, and involving the top team. Instead, these activities are used to the extent that they are productive in each situation, augmented by any additional practices and stakeholder involvement required at that moment in time.

In this chapter, we examine how effective strategy approaches can be identified through a process–practice framework. We start by describing recent theorizing of strategy process and practice concepts. Drawing on these ideas, we then present a framework of strategy practice with a process dimension that incorporates the influence of context, time, and flow. We explain how the framework relates to the chapters in the remainder of the book. We conclude with a strategy professional, Kirsty Lloyd-Williams, sharing her views about how dynamic and inclusive processes and practices of strategy can allow us to cope and thrive in an ever-shifting world.

 Access the online resources to watch a short video clip where Kirsty Lloyd-Williams shares her views on inclusivity in strategy.

2.2 A process–practice framework of strategy

In this section, we introduce key concepts and a process–practice framework that help explain what people might do, over time and in context, in relation to strategy. Our definitions are informed by the **strategy-as-practice (SaP)** view. In contrast with the economics heritage of popular mainstream strategy perspectives (see Chapter 1), SaP has its roots in a sociological perspective of strategy. According to Gerry Johnson and colleagues (Johnson et al. 2008: 3), we shouldn't think of strategy as something an organization 'has', such as a market position or plan. Instead, we should consider strategy as 'something that people do [. . .] strategy is an activity'.

To learn about strategy from an SaP perspective is to ask questions about how strategy is done, who does it, and what they use to do it (Jarzabkowski et al. 2016). A SaP perspective puts emphasis on understanding strategy from 'the bottom up' through 'the day-to-day activities of organizational life which relate to strategic outcomes' (Johnson et al. 2003: 14). We can do this through a focus on activity, the people involved, the materials and **tools** they use, novel and routine ways of working, common habitual approaches, and the influence of interactions of individuals, organizations, and institutions over time.

Key definitions

Practice

Underpinning SaP is a definition of *practice as the 'on-going stream of activity' that constitutes organizational life* (Jarzabkowski 2003: 24). As a matter of organizational relevance, SaP can be considered as 'a situated, socially accomplished flow of organizational activity' (Jarzabkowski 2005: 7). The elements of this definition are instructive. 'Situated' means that the strategy **activity** undertaken occurs within context at a moment in time that will, in part, shape what is done. 'Socially accomplished' means that strategy results from the actions and interactions of practitioners. 'Flow' indicates that strategy is an ongoing concern that is always moving and shifting.

In Relativity Space, practice describes the totality of continuing actions and interactions between colleagues in different functions and divisions and their engagements with external parties such as customers and investors. This practice encompasses the delivery of daily operations and attainment of organizational outcomes such as component production and materials ordering. Strategy, as practice, describes the stream of activity and decisions within Relativity Space that relates to strategic outcomes. This might include how to develop organizational capability for building new designs of rockets, how to win new funding and meet investor expectations, how best to diversify business activity, etc. Over time, the focus of strategy practice will evolve as the organization and its context change.

Practitioners

Practitioners are those individuals and groups of individuals whose efforts and activities contribute to strategy (Paroutis and Pettigrew 2007). We may also refer to practitioners as actors as they are actively involved in the accomplishment of strategy on an ongoing basis.

The characteristics of practitioners—their history, education, experience, skills, connections, relationships, knowledge, biases, hidden agendas, etc.—influence how they think, make decisions, and act in any given situation and thus the way in which they play a part in strategy activities (Adner and Helfat 2003). Practitioners might be internal staff, such as the senior management team, department heads, functional representatives, and operators. Practitioners can also be external to the organization, such as consultants, advisers, government officials, etc.

Practitioners influence strategy through the action they take, in which they allocate their time, attention, and effort towards trying to accomplish some manner of outcome. Tim Ellis and the senior management team are practitioners who will have a recurring involvement in strategy practice in Relativity Space. How Ellis and his team focus their attention, and draw on their experience and know-how will shape formal strategy activities. Equally, investors, prospective customers, and industrial partners are all examples of other actors that may be involved in strategy practice at different moments.

Practices

Practices describe the ways of working adopted by practitioners when trying to accomplish a type of task. For example, we can use **communication practices** to share or receive information. Communication practices cover a wide range of acting including writing, texting, gesturing, speaking, listening, reading, etc. (Ocasio et al. 2018). In relation to strategy, practices refer to 'regular, shared and legitimate ways of doing strategy work' (Burgelman et al. 2018: 542). Strategy practices describe all the ways of working that we know and might draw on towards achieving strategy-related outcomes such as practices for debating the scope of strategy, practices for gathering and analysing strategic data, etc.

The format of practices can vary widely. Practices may be solo activities or involve interacting with others; practices might draw on physical supporting materials or theories and concepts to shape ways of thinking and talking. We may undertake practices consciously or automatically, depending on our familiarity with circumstances. We can deploy practices according to our preferences, skills, and understanding of the needs of a situation. As summarized by Jarzabkowski and Spee (2009: 82), practices are 'complex bundle[s] involving social, material and embodied ways of doing that are interrelated and not always articulated or conscious to the actor involved in doing'.

In the Relativity Space example, strategic practices include hosting investor events, negotiating cost advantageous supplier contracts, and prioritizing investment in the development of proprietary technology.

Activity

Activity is that which is actually done by practitioners. As we direct individual and organizational resources towards action and interaction daily, we are said to undertake activity. Organizational activity is the aggregation of what individual practitioners from inside and outside the organization do, in context, towards some matter of collective interest.

Strategic activity refers to work done towards attaining some sort of strategy-related outcome. According to Jarzabkowski (2003: 24), we use our practices, in routine or creative ways, on a continuing basis as part of strategy work. To help us build an understanding of organizational strategy, it can be helpful to examine 'episodes' in the ongoing stream of strategic activity. An 'episode' is a time period, with a defined start and end point, within which a set of activity involving practitioners, practices, context, and outcomes can be examined. To consider a strategizing episode means to focus attention on the strategic activity that occurred within a defined time period.

A pivotal moment for Relativity Space was when Ellis and Noone succeeded in convincing Mark Cuban to back—financially and reputationally—their nascent business idea. We could examine the subsequent strategizing episode in which the co-owners decided to focus intensely on developing the Stargate 3D printers. The aim was to create the innovative technology required for rocket production in the long term whilst persuading additional financiers that the company was viable and worth immediate investment. This approach led to valuable outcomes for Relativity Space, enabling capability growth and further technological development as per its strategic objectives. How strategizing happens now in Relativity Space will likely be different to how it occurred during this episode as the internal and external contexts of the organization have evolved. To build an understanding of strategy activity by examining this episode, we must therefore be mindful of what was done and the circumstances in which it occurred.

2

Tools

During strategy activity and as part of their strategy practices, practitioners may draw on strategy tools. *Tools describe the techniques, methods, models, and frameworks which support interactions and decision-making in strategy activity* (Clark 1997). Examples of strategy tools with academic roots are **PESTEL**, 5 Forces, SWOT, etc., which we will examine in later sections (see Vuorinen et al. (2018) for a review of the usage of research-led tools in strategy).

Tools can also include common technologies such as PowerPoint, which, depending on how they are used, can have a significant influence on how strategy interactions and decisions occur (Knight et al. 2018). Further, as Jalonen et al. (2018) describe, the concepts and terms that we use when talking about strategy with others can also be considered tools as they help us to progress shared thinking and decide on actions to take. Whilst we can opt to use existing tools, practitioners might also create new phrases, words, or tools of strategy to address local needs and interests (Burke and Wolf 2021). See Case Example 2.1 for an illustration from NHS England of how a range of strategy tools can be proposed at an organizational level for deployment according to local needs in an organizational sub-unit.

Strategy tools 'provide a common language for strategic conversations between managers across hierarchical, functional, and geographic boundaries' (Jarzabkowski and Kaplan 2015: 544). To better suit the situational needs of strategic activity, tools may be deployed in creative ways by practitioners beyond their formal designed scope. The actual boundaries and possibilities of strategy tools are known as **affordances**—all the possible ways in which a user might use a tool or object in everyday strategy activity (Demir 2015). As you seek to use tools effectively, being mindful of affordances can help you create '**tools-in-use**' that bring people together, spur creativity, provide legitimacy, incorporate local suggestions, and drive action in strategy practice (Giraudeau 2008). The adaption of strategy tools to suit local needs and situations can also reflect the social norms, politics, and culture of an organization, helping acceptance and engagement with strategy outcomes (Spee and Jarzabkowski 2009: 224).

Throughout this book, we will challenge you to think of how you might creatively use the mainstream strategy tools that we introduce to give maximum benefit in different situations you might face. We will also ask you to think about the possible influences—beneficial and negative—on strategy activity that your selection and modification of strategy tools might have.

Strategy tools are not covered in the Relativity Space case, but the scaled-up metal 3D-printing technology developed by the company give us an example of affordances. The Stargate printers were designed as the core additive manufacturing technological platforms for the business. The designed aim of the technology has been achieved, but additional potential to use 3D printing for different product lines, or as the basis for different business models, has been created. The affordances of the Stargate 3D printers provide Relativity Space with options to diversify its client base and sources of income.

Context

Context—the circumstances which form the setting for strategy activity to occur—matters in our understanding of strategy as it influences what practitioners decide and do in relation to strategy (Mahoney and McGahan 2007).

For ease of analysis, context is often described in terms of internal and external circumstances. Internal context refers to the cultural and historical context of an organization; its size and structure; the resources accrued over time; and existing strategic objectives, initiatives, and vision. In Chapters 4 and 6, we will consider how these elements of each organization's unique internal context can be better understood.

External context refers to the competitive and institutional settings in which an organization is embedded. The competitive setting refers to the nature, extent, and dynamics of relationships of entities with which an organization vies for its continuing existence (c.f. Jarzabkowski and Bednarek 2018). The broader institutional environment in which organizations are embedded is 'a dynamic and self-renewing system, framed by state, international, and nongovernmental forces and populated by corporations large and small, interest groups, and individuals striving to have their voices heard' (Doh et al. 2012: 36).

As we will explore in section 2.3, knowing, responding to, and exploiting the internal and external contexts is vital to making appropriate strategy decisions (Frynas et al. 2018: 88). Context also matters in terms of 'fit'—the extent to which there is a match between what external circumstances demand and what an organization does. As Markides (2000: 194) comments, 'the right strategy for any firm must account for its unique evolution as well as the evolution of its industry'—a holistic view of context can help support strategy decisions and activity that ensures continuing fit. We can also learn much about strategic potential, processes, and activities by observing the socio-cultural practices embedded in an organization (MacKay et al. 2020).

The internal context for Relativity Space includes factors such as available funding, growing employee base, proprietary 3D-printing technology, expanded locations, and diverse investment community. The external context includes the growing demand for rocket payload from different types of customers, changing competitors and competitive dynamics, possible regulatory changes, and potential new markets in which the organization can compete using 3D-printing methods. Strategic decision-making and activity are situated in these dynamic and ever-evolving contexts.

Process

Process refers to the flow of events, experiences, and activities over time that are shaped by and form the context of strategy work. A processual perspective offers a valuable analytical lens for examining the nature and implications of how strategy happens in context over time. Processual understanding is infused into the holistic 'strategic perspective' described in Chapter 1. Practitioners that continually observe, interpret, and respond to the realities of unfolding circumstances can be said to exhibit a processual perspective (Chia and Holt 2009). Being able to adapt to and anticipate the flow of events, risks, possibilities, and unexpected occurrences is a valuable capability for strategy practitioners that can impact on long-term organizational performance. Strategic ideas and activities that seem appropriate at one time can prove disastrous at a later juncture as events intervene (MacKay and Chia 2013).

A processual perspective further helps us to understand strategy as a continuing accomplishment of practitioner activity. Tsoukas and Chia (2002) explain this process view of strategy through the metaphor of a tightrope walker. From a distance, the tightrope walker looks to be standing still, whereas up close the walker is continually expending energy in making many small movements to stay in balance on the tightrope. The implication of this process view is that in organizational life, even appearing to stay the same requires energy, effort, and activity. Strategy process might then be understood as the continuing, coordinated activities of

2

CASE EXAMPLE 2.1 FOSTERING STRATEGY PRACTICES IN NHS ENGLAND

The National Health Service (NHS) is the publicly funded health-care provider within each of the nations of the United Kingdom. The NHS in England is divided into organizational units known as trusts, which serve a health-care specialism or geographical territory.

In a 2013 report, the sector regulator noted that the ability of NHS Trusts to 'develop and implement strategic and operational plans is critical if they are to deliver effective and sustainable responses to current and future challenges'. The report defined strategic planning as:

the process of developing an organization's purpose, aims and objectives, including the allocation of related resources and responsibilities, drawing on robust evidence and setting challenging but feasible timescales for achieving goals [. . .] Carrying out strategic planning at relevant points in the development of an organization will guide it through decision-making about service provision and resource allocation, and help executives and non-executives to govern effectively.

However, based on field research in 30 trusts, the regulator found that there were many instances of a lack of strategy capabilities and effective strategic practices in trust leadership teams. In response, the regulator recommended an initiative to develop 'the guidance, tools and support that [health] organizations need to strengthen their internal processes and capacity for [strategic] planning'. A toolkit developed in collaboration with the consultancy firm PWC to support all NHS providers in developing clear and well-thought-out strategies was published free to use in 2014.

A strategy framework was proposed in a toolkit format based on seven categories of strategy practice, as illustrated in Figure 2.1. Underpinning the model is a definition of strategy as 'a set of choices designed to work together to deliver the long-term goals of an organization in the face of uncertainty'. Each category of practice is intended to provide guidance for trust leadership teams in their strategy work. The framework guidance notes point out that, without being prescriptive, the tools can be adapted according to the specific needs of a trust's situation.

Frame: establish the scope of the strategy development process by identifying the important strategic choices and decisions to be made and the criteria for making them.

Diagnose: understand current performance in detail at an overall and functional level.

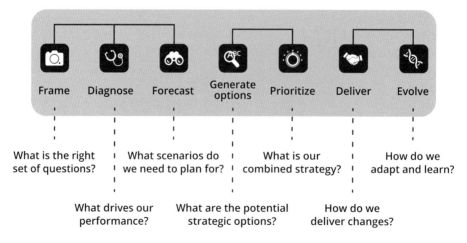

FIGURE 2.1 NHS trust strategy practices toolkit. *Source*: Strategy development toolkit, p. 3, https://assets.publishing.service.gov.uk/government/uploads/system/uploads/attachment_data/file/456099/Monitor_TDA_developing_strategy_flyer_FINAL.pdf (last accessed 10 August 2022).

Forecast: create a view of what the future might look like, including trends and technologies that may affect the organization.

Generate options: explore alternative ideas for acting to improve current services or introduce new ways of working that help to improve strategic performance.

Prioritize: choose which strategic initiatives to pursue and check that they make sense as a coherent system.

Deliver: allocate resources and define the activities, milestones, measurements, and key performance indicators as to how strategy will be realized.

Evolve: monitor outcomes of activities, re-evaluating the strategy regularly or when unexpected changes occur, and recommit to or refresh existing direction as required.

The toolkit was developed based on researching effective strategy practices within health-care organizations from within the United Kingdom and internationally, as well as strategy practices deemed to be effective in a business setting. The toolkit was piloted with five trusts to prove and refine the guidance offered for a 'health' setting.

The development director at the regulator commented that the use of the pilot toolkit:

depends on the organization's stage of development—not every Trust would seek to use every tool. The idea of the guide is that you can dip into the section that is most applicable to you. We'll refine it based on feedback over time. It's not prescriptive, it's not regulatory, it's there for Trusts to use on an ongoing basis as they see fit.

Directors from the various trusts involved in the pilot of the toolkit commented that:

'In trying the tools, we realised that some of our strategic planning has been too rigid, perhaps too focused on investments, whereas we need an approach that is much more dynamic that can reflect changes in the local health economy and our expectations as to what our role should be nationally within the NHS. We've learnt from the framework and have applied aspects to decision-making already.'

'The practices in the toolkit worked well in board discussions as an enabler of constructive challenge to assumptions and decisions. Importantly,

the framework provides a means to ensure that functional strategies are in alignment and tied in to organizational strategy needs.'

'The use of refined practices helps keep a focus on patients and their needs "as all too often in strategy development, it can become abstract and you can lose sight of what you are really trying to deliver".'

'Mindful strategy practices will keep you focused on needs of all stakeholders—such as clinicians, patients, suppliers and local communities—and will lead strategists to engage them in discussions to understand operational reality, generate options and make good decisions.'

Questions for discussion

1. What do you imagine might trigger strategizing episodes for NHS trust leaders? With whom do they need to work?

2. Drawing on the definitions of process, practice, practices, and practitioners, comment on the possible advantages and disadvantages of proposing a strategy practices toolkit for an organization such as an NHS trust.

3. To what extent might the categories of practices in the toolkit be applicable to any organization? In guidance documentation, how important is it to keep the practices generic or make them specific to a health-care organization? Explain your answer.

Sources

Gov.uk, https://www.gov.uk/government/organisations/monitor (last accessed 9 August 2022).

Gov.uk (2015). Strategy development: A toolkit for NHS providers (25 August), https://www.gov.uk/government/publications/strategy-development-a-toolkit-for-nhs-providers (last accessed 9 August 2022).

Monitor (2013). Meeting the needs of patients: Improving strategic planning in NHS foundation trusts, https://assets.publishing.service.gov.uk/government/uploads/system/uploads/attachment_data/file/286327/Meeting_the_needs_of_patients_-_Improving_strategic_planning_in_NHS_foundation_trusts.pdf (last accessed 9 August 2022).

Monitor (2014) Developing strategy: What every trust board member should know, https://assets.publishing.service.gov.uk/government/uploads/system/uploads/attachment_data/file/363273/Monitor_-_Developing_Strategy_-_a_guide_for_board_members.pdf (last accessed 9 August 2022).

2

stakeholders—from small daily actions to milestone events—that create ideas, artefacts, plans, priorities, etc. sustaining or changing the organization to the benefit of those involved with it.

In the Relativity Space example, from a process perspective, strategy will reflect the potential of evolving organizational capabilities in the context of changing customer demands, competitor moves, and regulatory constraints. As strategic investment decisions channel resources into technological developments, daily activities in the organization also create short-term strategic outcomes (e.g. tangible evidence of new technologies to attract investors) alongside learning and unanticipated outcomes (e.g. technological breakthroughs from experimentation) that shape future possibilities. Observing, interpreting, and acting on the flow of events—internal and external, daily and long term—describes strategy process as an ongoing accomplishment with the potential to deliver a more superior organizational performance than any fixed plan, set at any moment in time, might achieve.

A process perspective links to what is known as 'strong process theorizing' (Langley et al. 2013), underpinned by a philosophical view emphasizing flow and dynamism (MacKay et al. 2020). It is broader than the term 'strategy processes' commonly used by practitioners to describe the designed mechanisms, methods, and activity steps of strategy. We will examine many examples of strategy processes in this text, such as processes for strategic decision-making, analysing the external environment, making strategy at different levels, etc. A process perspective recognizes the value of understanding these designed strategy processes as part but not all of what matters in how strategy happens (see also Van de Ven (1992) for commentary on how process might feature in strategy research).

From across these definitions, we can summarize that from a process–practice view of strategy:

- strategy is accomplished ongoing, in context, through the activities of practitioners;
- strategy practices are ways of working that practitioners draw upon in routine or creative ways as they attempt to act strategically;
- strategy practices often draw on the use of tools, the design of which can be creatively adapted to suit local needs, to help undertake strategy activity in an effective way;
- strategic outcomes, once achieved, will be temporary—practitioners can seek to maintain desired outcomes through continuing activity;
- strategy as a process is never 'complete' as events and experiences continue to unfold around and through us over time.

 Access the online resources to watch a short video clip where Kirsty Lloyd-Williams discusses the changing ways in which strategy is made and managed.

2.3 Dynamic frameworks of strategy

With a set of concepts defined that explain pieces of the strategy jigsaw, how can we draw these definitions together into a usable framework? In this section, we first describe an established theoretical perspective—the attention-based view—which explains how decision-makers behave in relation to strategy. We then introduce a complementary set of dynamic frameworks which integrate process and practice considerations.

Attention-based view of strategy

The **attention-based view (ABV)** is a set of concepts and theoretical contributions that help explain how organizations behave, adapt to changing environments, develop capabilities, and make strategy according to how the limited attention of decision-makers is informed and directed. Influenced by the work of Cyert and March (1963) and Simon (1947) on behavioural theories of the firm, William Ocasio is a key proponent of the ABV.

According to Ocasio (1997: 189), attention 'encompass(es) the noticing, encoding, interpreting, and focusing of time and effort by organizational decision-makers on both (a) issues: the available repertoire of categories for making sense of the environment: problems, opportunities, and threats; and (b) answers: the available repertoire of action alternatives: proposals, routines, projects, programs, and procedures'.

What are known as **attentional structures**—communication channels, knowledge flows, organizational procedures, and opportunities for interaction with others—influence how information reaches decision-makers' attention about the issues and answers relevant to their current context (Barnett 2008). Based on their processing of information received, decision-makers will advocate strategic initiatives that Ocasio (1997: 201) describes as organizational moves: 'the myriad of actions undertaken by the firm and its decision-makers in response to or in anticipation of changes in its external and internal environment'. With whom, and how, strategy practitioners communicate will have a significant influence on what is prioritized in organizational strategy (Bencherki et al. 2021).

The ABV is useful to us in building an understanding of strategy activities over time. What managers do—what they discuss and focus on—is driven by the information they receive, their personal backgrounds and experience, and the situation/context of the organization (Gebauer 2009). As we develop our insights about how strategy activity occurs, it is helpful to consider how information is brought to the attention of decision-makers through strategy practices, tools, and interactions. Joseph and Wilson (2018) suggest that **attentional design**—using tools and procedures to deliberately channel the attention of decision-makers—will have a major influence on how strategic choices are made. Ocasio et al. (2018) note that this may be through simple actions such as considering the language used in communications such as strategic planning documents. For example, adding the term 'strategic' can divert executive attention towards considering material, decisions, or resources (Gond et al. 2018). Strategy tools can equally increase the scope of information reaching decision-makers; for example, environmental scanning and debate involving a diverse range of stakeholders can be used to influence strategic decision-makers' attention (Galbreath 2018).

The personal characteristics of practitioners can play a part in the focus of their attention. For example, the emotions of managers at different levels in Nokia played a role in the organization's fall from grace. When negative signals started emerging from the market about Nokia's products and offerings, research uncovered that senior managers feared shareholders' reactions, just as middle managers feared peers' reactions. This led to a biasing of information shared within the organization and ultimately to decision-makers paying attention to the 'wrong' things (Vuori and Huy 2016).

2

However, according to Ocasio (1997), practitioners will vary their focus of attention depending on the situations they face, and their decisions and activities will be more influenced by the context in which they are operating than their individual characteristics. Thus, from an ABV, the influence of context on the direction of attention (known as **situated attention**) is a crucial factor to consider when seeking to understand what decision-makers focus on and what they do (Ferreira 2017).

Strategy as process and practice

Burgelman et al. (2018: 541) propose the integration of process and practice concepts and perspectives, as defined in this chapter so far, through the model shown in Figure 2.2.

In this model, strategy is crafted through a continual interplay of strategizing episodes and efforts to convert strategy ideas and initiatives into reality. Strategizing episodes refer to deliberate strategy-making efforts such as board meetings or strategy workshops. Strategizing may occur on a scheduled basis, as part of habitual organizational practice. Equally, as indicated by the ABV, strategizing may be triggered by the identification of what decision-makers consider to be significant external events (Martin 2014). Decisions arising from strategizing episodes lead to organizational moves in which practitioner activities, attention, and resources attempt strategic initiatives to deliver desired outcomes. However, the strategic outcomes realized through organizational moves are a product of practitioner activity and contextual forces. Insights arising from the strategic outcomes achieved plus new information about the internal and external context then inform the next strategizing episode. Those with formal responsibility for strategy

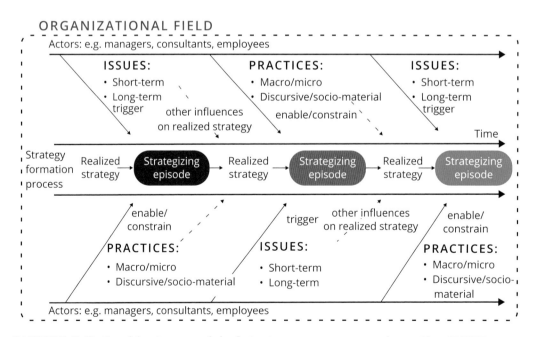

FIGURE 2.2 Combinatory model of strategy as process and practice (SAPP).
Source: reproduced with permission from Burgelman, R. et al. (2018). Strategy processes and practices: Dialogues and intersections. *Strategic Management Journal*, **39**(3), 531–58, https://doi.org/10.1002/smj.2741. © John Wiley & Sons, Ltd.

need to be able to explain strategic initiatives in terms of historical decisions, current context, and future possibilities (Sasaki et al. 2020).

Process dynamics—meaning the continuing interplay of strategizing, practitioner activity, and realized outcomes—as summarized in Figure 2.3, can explain how strategy is crafted over time (Gond et al. 2018). Figures 2.2 and 2.3 reflect the view that strategy practitioners must be aware of the effects of time, the flow of events, and the possibilities of the current context when deciding what to do and how to do it. Tracking how the context is unfolding can allow for timely intervention through strategy practices such that an advantage (albeit temporary) can be realized (Hansen and Jacobsen 2016). Over time, learning can be gained about how strategy activity occurs or could be improved by reflecting on intentions and outcomes exhibited across cycles of strategy work (Hengst et al. 2020).

The interplay of strategizing, activity, and outcomes in Figure 2.3 also explains how conducting practical experiments in highly uncertain environments can improve the quality of strategic decision-making (Pettus et al. 2018). By taking limited strategic action, observing the realized outcomes, and reflecting on the insights gained, new learning can be used to inform a subsequent round of strategizing. (Ashkenas 2013).

Process–practice framework of strategy

Building on the combinatory model, we propose a process–practice framework of strategy as shown in Figure 2.4 as a guiding reference to further explain what people do, over time and in context, in relation to strategy. At the centre of the framework are practitioners—the people involved in the 'doing' of strategy. Throughout the book, we will retain a focus on building understanding of how practitioners—individually and collectively—think, talk, and act as they engage in strategy activity. As a current or future practitioner, we will ask you to play your part

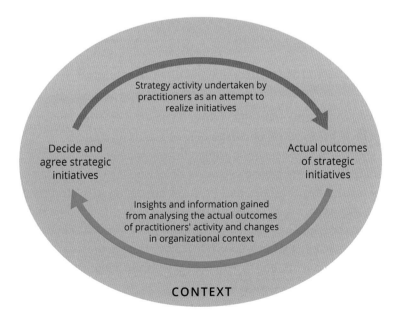

FIGURE 2.3 Interplay of strategizing, practitioner activity, and realized outcomes. *Source*: authors.

2

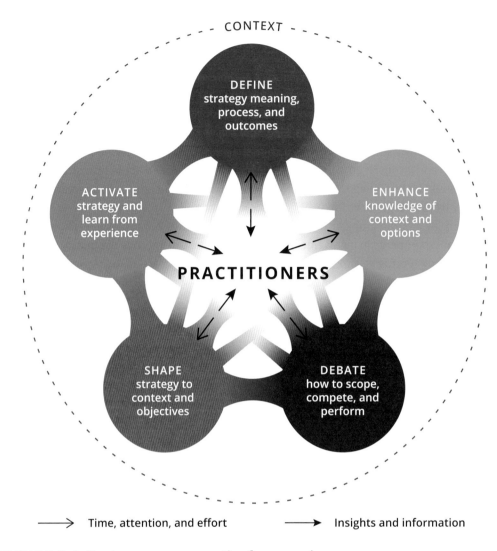

FIGURE 2.4 Strategy process–practice framework. *Source*: authors.

too—by continually challenging yourself to reflect on how the theories, concepts, methods, and examples might be of use to you in understanding or practising strategy.

The middle layer of the model shows categories of strategy practices. We propose these categories to enable you to discuss and explore ways of working that you will encounter as you participate in or lead strategizing episodes. Practices are deployed in strategy activity as practitioners allocate their time, attention, and resources to trying to do something, in turn being able to observe the consequences of their actions and gather feedback information. The outer layer of the model indicates that practitioners deploy strategy practices within context—the unfolding circumstances, events, and experiences in which strategy activity occurs over time.

Categories of practices

We have identified five main categories of strategy practices that will be explored throughout the book as shown in Figure 2.4. These categories are described by their intended outcome/contribution to strategy activity.

Define strategy meaning, approach, and outcomes: ways of working intended to establish what strategy means to stakeholders in the current context, agreeing an approach and target outcomes for strategy work, including who to involve and how in making decisions.

Enhance knowledge of context and options: practices concerning collection and analysis of data about strategy options, opportunities, and constraints arising from organizational context, environmental trends and resources, capabilities, and organizational activities.

Debate how to scope, compete and perform: practices that review the sectors and locations in which the organization could or should operate, how it competes, and how to organize and deploy resources for optimal performance.

Shape strategy to context and objectives: practices that evaluate and refine strategy ways, means, and objectives according to collaboration, innovation, and growth needs; influences of digitalization and possibilities of disruption; internationalization considerations; and sustainability attitudes, obligations, and opportunities.

Activate strategy and learn from experience: ways of leading the planning and organizing of strategizing episodes and strategic change, engaging stakeholders and building momentum for the whole organization, and continually improving understanding of how to make and manage strategy in practice.

Regulating flow

The flow of activity in strategy is underpinned by the knowledge and insights of practitioners and their interpretation of the needs, possibilities, and constraints of the context. We represent the flow of the strategy process by a two-way relationship between practitioners and practices. As explained in Figure 2.2, practitioners, consciously or unconsciously, deploy practices during strategy activity. At the same time, practitioners receive new information about the effectiveness and impact of their practices, in context, from participating in or observing strategy activity. This information may be ignored, encourage continuing activity, provoke a change in practice or type of activity, or bring activity to a stop. In effect, practitioners regulate the flow of strategy activity and decide how, if at all, practices should be deployed. Figure 2.5 further explains how the elements of the process–practice framework interface. As we will discuss in Chapter 14, traditionally, strategizing was viewed as the domain of practitioners at the top of the organization only. In this book, we explore an alternative view that strategy emerges from the collective processes and practices of a wide spectrum of organizational stakeholders (including those at the top). Through case examples and interviews, we will illustrate how a process–practice view sheds new light on the realities and usefulness of strategy to organizational practitioners in an ever-changing world.

Responsiveness to situational needs

It is possible that practitioners might address a strategic issue by collectively deploying strategy practices in a logical sequence from 'Define Strategy' round to 'Activate Strategy'. Most consultants and strategy process designers will attempt to instigate this sort of orderly collaborative working in strategy. This is an example of what we defined as 'designed strategy processes' earlier in the chapter. However, the deployment of strategy practices happens in a far more varied and reactive manner in reality.

According to their appraisal of the needs of a situation, practitioners might turn their attention and efforts towards any type of strategy practice. When practitioner attention is focused on

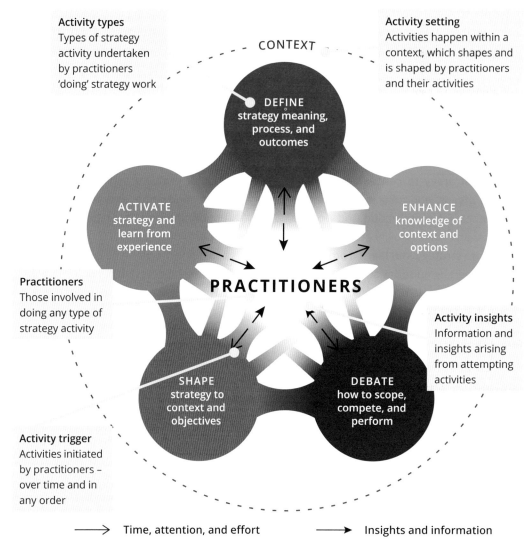

Activity types
Types of strategy activity undertaken by practitioners 'doing' strategy work

Activity setting
Activities happen within a context, which shapes and is shaped by practitioners and their activities

CONTEXT

DEFINE strategy meaning, process, and outcomes

ACTIVATE strategy and learn from experience

ENHANCE knowledge of context and options

PRACTITIONERS

Practitioners
Those involved in doing any type of strategy activity

Activity insights
Information and insights arising from attempting activities

SHAPE strategy to context and objectives

DEBATE how to scope, compete, and perform

Activity trigger
Activities initiated by practitioners – over time and in any order

⟶ Time, attention, and effort ⟶ Insights and information

FIGURE 2.5 Process–practice model explained. *Source*: authors.

a strategizing episode, information flows to practitioners which, as they interpret it, influences what they do next. This information may relate to the usefulness of their practices, the reality and needs of the context in which strategy activity is occurring, or both.

As new information from immersion in strategy activity is digested, insights that guide next steps can be gleaned (we discuss further this capacity for responsiveness in terms of reflection-in-practice in the online resources). When practitioners perceive that their activities have led to intended outcomes and that their interpretation of the context is accurate and complete, their working theories about what needs to be done are reinforced. However, when the outcomes of activity differ from expectations and/or changes in the operating context are detected, practitioners may trigger the deployment of alternative strategy practices in response (see Table 2.1).

In effect, practitioners are constantly deciding whether to continue with or revise the strategy activity they plan to do next, based on their reading of the organizational context and realities (Denning 2019).

TABLE 2.1 **Insight from learning from doing and contextual awareness**

Responsive practices	Strategizing triggered by learning by doing	Strategizing triggered by contextual awareness
Define strategy meaning, approach, and outcomes	'We need to clarify the parameters of our strategy activity'	'Our prior agreements for strategic focus could be refined to better fit the circumstances we are facing'
Enhance knowledge of context and options	'We need to build a shared understanding of our current and possible future context and the options we have available to us for taking action'	'We need to understand better how the possibilities, constraints, opportunities, and threats in our operating context have changed and the implications of trajectories of change'
Debate how to scope, compete, and perform	'We need to agree on our scope and form, how we compete, and how we organize to optimize performance'	'At an organizational level, we need to revise what we are currently doing and/or how we are doing it to avoid performance issues in a shifting context'
Shape strategy to context and objectives	'We need to prioritize and enact initiatives which make sense for us as an organization, given the specific context in which we are operating'	'We need to review our prior decisions about priority actions and resource deployments as they may no longer be optimal, given the changing context'
Activate strategy and learn from experience	'We need to find optimal ways of carrying out the focused use of resources and change projects corresponding to our strategic decisions'	'The difference between anticipated and actual strategy implementation results suggest that we need to re-evaluate our assumptions about context and related decisions and resource usage'

Source: authors.

In the NHS example, this tendency is recognized in the comments from the director at the regulator that strategy practitioners should 'dip into the section [of the guide] that is most applicable to you' and that not every trust will need to use every tool during their strategy work. This is an example of strategy as a 'situated' activity. Practitioner interpretations of the specific context and how it changes over time influence the practices used during strategy activity. Responsiveness and flexibility in practices give practitioners the ability to cope when strategy outcomes are not realized as planned. If practitioners can increase their knowledge of possible practices and improve their ability to read strategic situations, their context-sensitive deployment of practices will likely deliver more effective strategy outcomes than any prescriptive approach. This responsiveness in approach is valuable as it is normal for continuing strategy activities to require re-evaluation as practitioners disagree about what needs to be done in the context of new insights and a changing organizational context (Kaplan and Orlikowski 2013).

Facilitating strategy activity

Responsive approaches from practitioners does not mean that strategy decisions, directions, and objectives are written anew every time something changes for the organization. Rather, the process–practice models shown in Figures 2.3–2.5 describe a continuing interplay between the plans and ideals of strategy formulation and the realities of implementation practice and changing circumstances as sensed by practitioners. This interplay enables formal strategy plans, visions, possessions, and priorities to be incrementally adjusted in order to remain fitting to the organizational context. In between formal updates of strategy work, the skills and capacities of strategy practitioners are required to realize outcomes in the best way possible within the constraints of the situation.

It is possible and often necessary to plot a high-level roadmap and timetable for strategy whilst at the same time engaging in continually revised strategy practices grounded in practitioner wisdom and insights. It would be naive to ignore the pressure on most senior management teams to run a visible and logical strategy process. Equally, senior management teams and organizational leaders will be evaluated on the results that they deliver over time. Therefore, remaining open to revisiting strategy thinking and practices on a continuing basis, driven by learning from doing and awareness of contextual changes, appears vital to ensuring organizational performance in the long run. This way of engaging in strategy work can be termed as planned **emergence**—'where preparation meets opportunism' (King 2008: 362).

As you develop your own strategy experience and capabilities, you will typically have to navigate between formal published strategy plans and the realities faced by those having to take action in context over time. To become a successful strategist, you will need to develop your capacity to manage the tensions between the ideas of strategy theory and the realities of strategy practice. We can think of this as 'facilitating' strategy—where facilitation means enabling strategy process to flow in an effective way. Facilitation is required for both the (re)formulation of strategy plans and the effective deployment of those plans in practice. The process–practice framework in Figure 2.5 can give you a useful checklist to think through when building your repertoire of strategy practices that enable you to facilitate strategy in practice.

2.4 Applying the process–practice framework

Learning how to think, talk, and act like a strategist

In this section, we offer some suggestions as to how you can use this book to maximum effect. When the world changes around an organization, and change, innovation, and strategy become vital for organizational survival, 'how leaders think, speak, and act becomes paramount' (Schoemaker et al. 2018: 35). Our aim in this book is to equip you with the know-how of language, tools, and theories that will enable you to deal with the formalities and realities of strategy in your future career. By so doing, you will enhance your ability to think, talk, and act like a strategist. The knowledge of strategic practices you acquire might help you to grow and improve your personal practice as well as the effectiveness of group decision-making and project work with which you are involved. Case Example 2.2 illustrates how the strategic outlook and approach adopted by the founders of a high-end sportswear start-up shaped organizational effectiveness and influenced growth over time.

CASE EXAMPLE 2.2 **EXPONENTIAL ENTREPRENEURIAL GROWTH AT CASTORE**

A sportswear brand with a premium focus, Castore has achieved rapid expansion in recent years. Trading in over 50 countries, Castore provides high-end consumer sportswear and has supply partnerships with a diverse client base including England Cricket, USA Rugby, GB Taekwondo, Manu Samoa Rugby, McLaren F1, Team Bahrain Victorious cycling, and professional football clubs such as Newcastle United, Bayer Leverkusen, and Glasgow Rangers.

Castore was launched in August 2016 by brothers Phil and Tom Beahon. Both ex-professional sportsmen, the brothers shared a vision of creating a premium alternative to established mass-market sportwear brands. The business launched from their flat in Liverpool and was funded by family loans and a Virgin Money start-up scheme. Growth has been rapid—in 2020, turnover was $49.6M, rising to an estimated $120M in 2021. Now headquartered in Manchester, England, Castore continues to attract investment and partnerships whilst delivering revenue growth and job creation.

Reflecting on the journey so far, the Beahons note that their experience of the pressurized, results-driven sporting world informs their business approach. They both decided against pursuing 'average' sporting careers in order to attempt to create an exceptional brand—'We wanted to be really successful at what we did, and not be mediocre', comments Phil.

In the build-up to starting Castore, both brothers worked in corporate finance for retail consumer clients. They were inspired by the rise of premium brands such as Rapha Cycling and the continuing performance of premium ladies' sportswear brands Sweaty Betty and Lululemon. When planning the launch of Castore, they conducted primary market research in and around London's high-end gyms and sports venues. They observed recurring customer disappointment in sportswear products that retained odour, lost shape after a few washes, and didn't fit properly. They also noted that customers' buying habits were shifting to online options with a focus on quality, durability, excellent customer service, and speedy delivery. They concluded that there was potential for a premium men's sportswear alternative to mass market brands such as Nike, Adidas, and Under Armour.

Recognizing the hyper-competitive nature of the sportswear market, Phil commented, 'we were never going to survive unless we had the very best

McLaren F1 is one of Castore's high-end clients. *Source*: John Bezosky/Unsplash.com.

Continued

2

product, and we wanted to show the consumer our product was better than anything else that was out there, and to tell them why they should spend £95 on a gym t-shirt'.

They spent 'every penny' of their start-up fund on research and development. Initial **product development** results were sufficiently promising to attract first-round investment of £750K. This included backing from experienced consumer fashion professionals, adding experienced human capital to their growing business finance and brand assets.

To differentiate on product quality, and justify a premium price, a focus was placed on identifying designs and production methods exploiting unique technical fabrics. Key to Castore's efforts was recruiting an ex-Rapha Cycling product designer with materials expertise and extensive industry contacts. Through this colleague, Castore was able to access cutting-edge fabrics in the specialist textile markets of Italy, Portugal, and Switzerland. Advanced materials remain a key point of differentiation in the Castore value proposition. Tom estimates that where Nike will spend 20c on a metre of fabric, Castore spends £12–£14.

In March 2019, Castore became the official kit supplier to former World number 1 tennis player Andy Murray. The deal took two years to conclude and involved Murray investing in the business. Drawing on input from the player, the partnership has created a line of men's tennis wear products made from sustainable materials and has raised global awareness of the Castore brand.

As it has grown digital sales, Castore has also experimented with retail space, including launching a marquee store on King's Road in London. Generating revenue, providing brand visibility and customer insights, Phil deems the experiment a success, commenting 'We have all our online data where our customers are based, and Chelsea is a big customer base. [. . .] We get fantastic traffic, the average transaction value is far higher in store than online, and we are miles above budget.'

The brand has continued to diversify partnerships, investors, focal sports, and locations, and now provides premium ladies' sportswear lines. As Castore scales up, the brothers have identified several strategic challenges to be addressed, including dealing with the implications of Brexit, maintaining seamless digital and physical operations, and staying consumer relevant through investment in innovation.

As for the future, the brothers comment:

This is a long-term plan—we are not trying to build it as quickly as possible and then have nothing to say for it in the end. We want to build a brand that will truly compete on the world stage. [. . .] In terms of the time it's taken, the business has grown quickly, which is fantastic, but we are thinking about what is coming up—and how can we get there. I think that's probably a character trait that most successful entrepreneurs have.

Questions for discussion

1. What factors and experiences have shaped the Beahon brothers' ability to think, talk, and act like strategists and business leaders?

2. When deciding to launch Castore, market research identified a gap for a premium offering in the men's sportswear market and implications for how the business should operate. Describe how their market research translated into a strategic approach to business growth.

3. What assets/resources seem important in shaping how Castore has developed? Explain your choices.

4. What external or internal factors—and issues and opportunities—might trigger strategizing episodes for the Castore leadership team in the next few years?

Sources

Castore, https://castore.com (last accessed 9 August 2022).

Houghton, T. (2022). Castore: All you need to know about the sports fashion brand backed by Andy Murray and Asda's billionaire owners (28 April), https://www.business-live.co.uk/enterprise/ex-athlete-brothers-who-signed-17471670 (last accessed 9 August 2022).

In Opinion (2022). The mindblowing growth of Castore (16 March), https://cashnsport.com/the-mindblowing-growth-of-castore (last accessed 9 August 2022).

 Access the online resources to watch a short video clip where Kirsty Lloyd-Williams discusses the strategic challenges faced by the finance industry in recent years.

Think like a strategist

The theory that we will lay out in each of the chapters will build comprehension of the concepts, language, and possibilities of strategy in a wide range of practical situations that you are likely to encounter. Better understanding of strategy theory will give you new ways to order your thoughts, direct your attention, understand organizational contexts, and read the flow of situations from a strategic perspective. Parts 1 and 3 will equip you to be able to comprehend the major theories and perspectives by which strategy is understood. Part 2 will enable you to understand strategy analysis and evaluation methodologies and how you can deploy tools to help you better understand the context and options for strategy. Part 4 will provide you with knowledge of nuanced strategy theory and contemporary considerations that most practitioners involved in strategy activity will have to face. Part 5 will give you insights into how the activation and realization of strategy can be approached and improved through leading specific and whole-organization change initiatives, design of strategizing activities, and learning and reflection.

Talk like a strategist

Much of strategy activity involves interacting with others through discursive practices of debate and discussion (Garbuio et al. 2015). To prepare you for this, we will provide many examples of how practitioners talk and write about strategy. All chapters conclude with practitioner insights, in which we share practitioners' views in their own words to give you examples of strategy 'talk'. In addition, in all sections, we share case examples and illustrations of how strategy has been interpreted and reported in real organizational settings. Through these examples you will be able to pick up insights that enable you to discuss strategy in a credible and meaningful way. Through development of a strategy vocabulary and exposure to dialogue that is generally applicable across strategy settings, you will be in a strong position to engage practitioners in strategy-related discussions. You will also be able to think about how you can forge your own identity as a strategist through your use of strategy language and discourse (Mantere and Whittington 2021). A crucial skill in leading strategy activity is being able to ask constructive questions in order to challenge the thinking and direct the attention of other practitioners (Kahneman et al. 2019). Sometimes this is with a broad 'public' audience, sometimes it is privately with a limited number of peers (Whittle et al. 2021). Both are influential in driving business performance over time through strategy. By working through the cases in each chapter, you should be able to enhance your capacity to question others productively as part of strategy activity.

Act like a strategist

To support you in learning to act like a strategist, we have included method guides, worked examples, and application advice from our own experiences as strategy practitioners. We have focused on fundamental guides in the main text for all readers and included a range of extended guides in the online resources for those who want to build deeper insights. The main method guides can be found in Part 2, where we present ways in which you can approach analytical aspects of strategy-making. Throughout the other parts, we have included method guides wherever relevant to ensure that the reader is always able to do something new or differently as a result of engaging with the section.

2

As your capacity to think, talk, and act like a strategist grows, so too will your ability to engage with the process–practice framework. The better able you are to think like a strategist, the more you will be able to read context and information flows. The better able you are to talk like a strategist, the more comprehensively you will be able to engage others in defining, debating, and shaping discursive practices and to constructively challenge their engagement in strategy with effective questioning. And the better able you are to act like a strategist, the more effectively you will be able to analyse situations and design, lead, and learn from strategic activity.

Engaging with the process–practice framework in this book

This textbook is organized according to the different categories of strategy practices identified in the process–practice framework (see Figure 2.6). As you adopt your own approach to learning about strategy, the book is constructed in a manner that reflects the

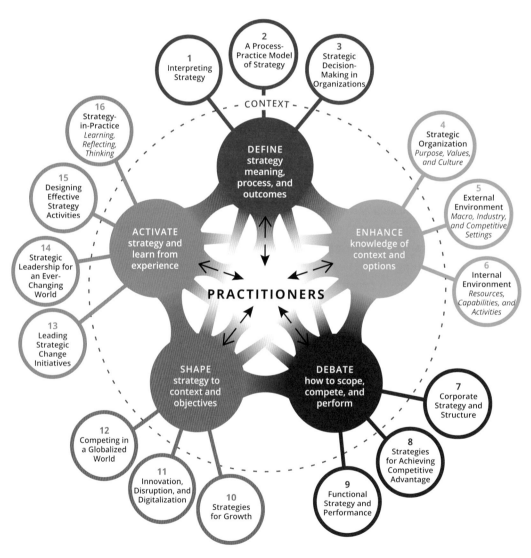

FIGURE 2.6 Process–practice framework of strategy chapter map. *Source*: authors.

process–practice framework. Chapters can be read in any order that interests you and should still make sense.

In Part 1, we examine how to define strategy meaning, approach, and outcomes. We have already explored how strategy can be interpreted and how we can build a shared meaning of strategy through a scoping exercise. The process–practice framework (Figure 2.5) and the combinatory model (Figure 2.2) give us two complementary ways of building our understanding of strategy activity and practices. In Chapter 3, we consider the process–practice model from a decision-making perspective, shedding light on how strategizing episodes and strategic decisions punctuate organizational life.

In Part 2, we cover methods that might be used to collect and analyse data that better informs practitioners about the organizational context. Data can inform our view of the historical context and matters of internal importance such as the culture, values, objectives, and purpose of the organization. And understanding the sustainability of our organizations has never been more important. Data might raise our understanding of the institutional, market, and competitive contexts in which the organization is embedded or the resource and capability context—including current activities and possible future activities. According to the focus of your strategy work, exploring some or all of these types of contextual data will aid identification of options for strategic action and strategic decision-making.

In Part 3, we review different types of strategy conversation that may occur—examining the sorts of concepts, theories, and mental framings that practitioners might adopt to have different types of strategizing episodes. Corporate strategy concerns the scope and structure of the organization; business strategy examines how the organization chooses to compete in its chosen markets; and functional strategy, implementation, and performance examines how projects or business units are organized and executed to deliver optimal results for the whole organization.

In Part 4, we consider contemporary influences that might need to be examined by practitioners refining strategy options to suit context. For many organizations, growth—through mergers and acquisitions, collaborations, or innovative means—is a target outcome for those making strategy. Increasingly, organizations will experience market disruption, discontinuous change, and impacts of digitalization; there are few organizations that are not affected by international options and flow of goods.

Finally, in Part 5, the plans and agreements of strategy decision-making processes need to be enacted. How strategic change is managed and led and how outcomes can be negotiated through social and political processes of strategy are key topics for you to understand. In an ever-changing world, we explore the importance and whole-organization effects of processes and practices of strategic leadership that are adaptive, engaging, purpose-driven, and responsible. Through online chapters, we further explore how strategy activities and strategizing episodes are designed to increase the likelihood of successful outcomes. And as we describe strategy as a continuing accomplishment, enacted by practitioners, it is also possible, through reflection and discussion, to identify points of learning and improvement that will enhance future strategy performance.

2

PRACTITIONER INSIGHT **KIRSTY LLOYD WILLIAMS, HEAD OF STRATEGY VALIDATION, ABRDN**

Kirsty Lloyd Williams is a business strategy and transformational change leader in Financial Services. Kirsty currently leads the strategy validation team at abrdn, a global investment firm, having previously held a variety of strategy roles in Standard Life Aberdeen and senior corporate change positions in Halifax Bank of Scotland (HBOS) and Lloyds Banking Group (LBG). Kirsty volunteers with Edinburgh Council social impact programmes and has worked with several primary schools on initiatives to ease 'in-work' poverty issues. Kirsty is passionate about cultural buy-in and the understanding of strategies whilst maximizing individual and group participation for implementation success.

Kirsty shares her views on strategy, change, and inclusivity.

'Can you tell us about your role?'

As a global investment firm, part of what abrdn does is to provide tools and platforms that help advisers—wealth managers or financial advisers who manage savings and/or investments on behalf of someone else—to deliver valuable services to their clients. My role is head of strategy validation for the adviser business, ensuring alignment of our priorities and initiatives to the overall goals for abrdn. This involves engaging with a diverse range of colleagues in making effective strategic choices within the ever-changing context of regulator guidance, market dynamics, cost targets, and resource availability. A central part of my role is continually supporting the executive team in making or affirming strategic decisions about where and when to focus attention, resources, and effort to deliver business performance. This strategic management process is crucial to achieving priorities for clients, colleagues, and the wider business.

'What have been the strategic challenges in the finance industry in recent years?'

The pandemic has significantly impacted on the way we work and our client and customer attitudes to savings. The markets remain volatile after several years of disruption, inflation is increasing, and after

15 years of relative stability, it feels like the basis of the sector is fundamentally changing. People are more cautious with their money, taking fewer risks with investments and adopting more defensive attitudes to their futures. In financial services, this has triggered a shift from active to passive management of funds. This means our advisory and wealth clients' priorities are changing too.

A competitive challenge within financial services, especially the adviser business, is that there is not much differentiation between competitors based on stand-alone tools, platforms, and prices, which are increasingly homogeneous. This makes attracting and retaining clients and customers a challenge for all financial services firms. The main point of differentiation now seems to be on 'ease of doing business', and competitive edge can come from offering accessible, seamless services for your customers, clients, and advisers. The effective design and deployment of a platform—relevant technology in combination with the services of our colleagues—is crucial to our continuing success.

We are continually evolving our business to maintain this edge, such as with the recent acquisition of two complementary fintech firms. The first, Finimize, provides insights about trends in the financial markets through regular, easily digestible insight summaries and explanations of activities. The second, 'Interactive Investor', is a direct-to-consumer investment platform that enables individuals to actively manage their own funds. These options that abrdn now provide allow a wider range of customers to take more control of managing their finances in an accessible, digital way.

Other challenges relate to shifting stakeholder perspectives in the sector. Increasingly, transparency in sustainability and ethical investment practices are at the forefront of industry conversations. The regulatory authorities—understandably keen to protect pensions and investments—are tightening their requirements. Technology providers are constantly innovating, creating new possibilities which require a continual effort from financial-sector organizations to keep informed. And cost-of-living-related challenges are impacting the profile of innovative offerings that customers might find appealing.

The last sectoral point I would highlight is a challenge and an opportunity—the gender representation gap. In financial services, there is an acknowledged gap of gender diversity in senior positions. Progress has been slow in addressing this issue and, compared to other sectors, this gap is more pronounced in financial services. However, the pandemic has created an opportunity to accelerate change. With an opening up of flexible ways of working, more opportunity has been created for equal participation and recognition at all organizational levels. As the pressure rises to get back into the office, we need to preserve a work environment where everyone is enabled to use their talents to contribute to their fullest ability.

'In what ways is how strategy is made and managed changing in your opinion?'

In my opinion, the time frame of strategy has changed. In previous times, we might have set five-to-ten-year strategic objectives that would remain fixed, with only delivery initiatives changing on shorter time frames. I would say that our planning approach is more agile, moving towards a rolling two-to-three-year horizon now. This change in approach significantly improves our agility and responsiveness, which assures business performance in dynamic times and uncertain circumstances. It doesn't mean we don't do longer-term transformational programmes; we just approach them as a series of coherent, shorter-term initiatives that can be addressed individually whilst achieving the same cumulative effect.

A general effect of the pandemic was to invoke **crisis management** approaches across sectors and organizations. In terms of strategy, this meant an increased level of direction from those leading the business to ensure continuity and survival in unprecedented times. As the pandemic recedes, I expect some tensions to arise in organizations where top-down approaches remain, as employees increasingly look for inclusion, openness, and a voice in defining the future and purpose of their employer. I think this pressure will eventually become irresistible and phase out remnants of crisis-mode strategizing.

In abrdn, our strategy validation process, methods, and prioritization approaches allow us to scan the industry landscape, understand the context and priorities across all areas of the business, and identify the options and initiatives most likely to drive business performance. In recent years, we've made great strides in changing how strategic decisions are articulated in a modern and relatable language so that our colleagues have a clear understanding of what we are trying to achieve. And recognizing the upside of new digital ways of working and inclusion, we are embracing new channels for how we listen to the ideas of all our talented colleagues, to the benefit of strategic effectiveness.

'What are your views on inclusivity in strategy?'

For me, inclusivity is vital to achieving strategy outcomes effectively through a passionate workforce with shared understanding and belief in the organizational aims. As you make or manage strategy, there is a need to satisfy and empower colleagues right across the workforce. Experience shows that working in a siloed or exclusionary way achieves maybe 30% of our potential. Effort invested to appropriately include everyone can drive those outputs towards 100%. In short, it doesn't make business sense to ignore or fail to maximize the talents and capabilities of anyone in your workforce. In strategy, it is so important to have an inclusive cross-section of stakeholders involved in each moment to get a diverse range of inputs and valuable options. Any team at any level lacking that diversity is unlikely to come up with the best ideas.

 Access the online resources to watch a short video clip where Kirsty Lloyd-Williams talks more about her career.

CHAPTER SUMMARY

In this chapter we addressed the following learning outcomes:

○ **Explain how strategy can be understood from a process–practice view.**

From a process–practice view, strategy is understood as a continuing accomplishment of practitioner activity over time and in context. Even strategies that advocate no change will still require effort if the status quo is to be maintained. What is crucial from this view is that strategy is something people do. This puts a focus on understanding practitioners—their characteristics, decisions, and actions—in order to understand how strategy happens. Avoiding false separation between strategy formulation and implementation practices will increase the potential for effective attainment of strategy outcomes.

○ **Explain what is meant by practice, practitioners, practices, activity, and process in the context of strategy work.**

We defined key concepts from a strategy-as-practice (SaP) perspective (a sociological take on strategy).

Practice: an 'ongoing stream of activity' that constitutes organizational life;

Practitioners: the individuals and groups of individuals whose efforts and activities contribute to strategy;

Practices: the ways of working adopted by practitioners when trying to accomplish a type of task;

Tools: the techniques, methods, models, and frameworks which support interactions and decision-making in strategy activity;

Activity: that which is actually done by practitioners;

Process: the continual unfolding of events, experiences, and activities over time;

Strategy practice: the ongoing stream of strategy-related activity in an organization—arising from practitioners drawing on practices over time and in context.

○ **Evaluate the usefulness of the attention-based view as an aid to understanding what people do in relation to strategy.**

The attention-based view (ABV) was introduced as a set of concepts and theoretical contributions that help to explain how organizations behave, adapt to changing environments, develop capabilities, and strategize according to how decision-makers' attention is informed and directed. By understanding and purposefully designing attentional structures (ways of flowing information to decision-makers), we can improve the quality of insights on which decision-makers base their selection of strategic initiatives to match the needs of the context they face.

○ **Critically assess the limitations of adopting rigid approaches to strategy.**

We noted that strategy activity rarely, if ever, plays out in a linear fashion. We noted that those designing strategy activities—such as consultants or organizational leaders—will propose an orderly arrangement of strategy practices. However, it was suggested that flexibility and responsiveness of approach to strategy work is crucial to being effective within a shifting context over time.

○ Articulate how the strategy process–practice framework can guide your learning about how to think, talk, and act as a strategy practitioner.

We noted that the better able you are to think like a strategist, the more you will be able to read context and information flows. The better able you are to talk like a strategist, the more comprehensively you will be able to engage others in defining, debating, and shaping discursive practices. And the better able you are to act like a strategist, the more effectively you will be able to analyse situations and design, lead, and learn from strategic activity. As you develop these capacities, you will grow as a strategy practitioner who is able to craft strategy in context over time through responsive and intelligent deployment of practices.

? END-OF-CHAPTER QUESTIONS

Recall questions

1. What are some of the main issues associated with separating strategy formulation and implementation activities and responsibilities?

2. Define what is meant by the terms 'practices', 'practitioners', and 'activity'. How do these terms relate to 'process' and 'practice' as defined in this chapter?

3. What does it mean when we describe strategy as a 'situated' activity?

4. Describe the five different types of practices identified in the process–practice framework.

5. What is meant by 'facilitating strategy'?

Application questions

A) Think of a situation in which you have either made a personal strategy (such as a career strategy) or been part of an organizational strategy (as part of a job role or as a member of a club or society). Recall the activities that were involved and try to write them down in the order that they happened. Try to write the activities for the time period from when you first started thinking about the strategy through to the delivery of results. Place the activities you have written down into the categories of the process–practice framework. How linear is the process (i.e. does it flow neatly from defining parameters to activating the strategy)? Can you identify activities for each of the categories? Why do you think the activities played out the way that they did? What would you do differently if you were involved in that strategy process again?

⟨ ONLINE RESOURCES

www.oup.com/he/mackay2e

2

In addition to the video interviews already highlighted, the book's **online resources** include the following features for this chapter, specifically:

– *links to further reading material* to broaden your knowledge of key issues discussed in this chapter;

– *self-test multiple-choice questions* to test your understanding of the material covered in each section of the chapter; and *a flashcard glossary* to help you recall and test your understanding of key terms.

FURTHER READING

'Strategy processes and practices' by Robert A. Burgelman et al.

Burgelman, R.A., Floyd, S.W., Laamanen, T. et al. (2018). Strategy processes and practices: Dialogues and intersections. *Strategic Management Journal*, **39**(3), 531–58.

This article provides a useful resource to further explore and deepen insights into the process–practice framework. The authors draw together many insights, literature references, and a model, which is presented in Figure 2.2 in this chapter. You may wish to refer to this article for further academic references in support of viewing strategy process as a phenomenon which occurs in context over time, enabled and constrained by the practices of those involved.

'Making connections: Harnessing the diversity of strategy-as-practice research' by Marko Kohtamäki et al.

Kohtamäki, M., Whittington, R., Vaara, E., and Rabetino, R. (2021). Making connections: Harnessing the diversity of strategy-as-practice research. *International Journal of Management Reviews*, **24**(2), 210–32.

This literature review article offers a useful map of the strategy-as-practice literature as it has developed over the past 20 years. It gives the student looking for project ideas and strategy research inspiration helpful background on trends, gaps, and contributions that might be made. It explains further the key concepts of this chapter, including process–practice perspectives.

'Suggestions for studying strategy process' by Andrew H. Van de Ven

Van de Ven, A.H. (1992). Suggestions for studying strategy process: A research note. *Strategic Management Journal*, **13**, 169.

This classic paper provides insights into how strategy process might be interpreted: as a way of building explanations of causality (if X happens, then Y will follow); as a set of concepts that refer to the actions of individuals or organizations (strategy is a kind of work that people or groups do); or as a sequence of events that describe how change happens over time (as a flow of activity). These different expressions of how strategy process is understood will help you connect with and interpret the different schools of thought 'out there' in the strategy academic literature focusing on strategy process studies.

Strategy without Design by Robert C.H. Chia and Robin Holt

Chia, R.C.H. and Holt, R. (2009). *Strategy without Design: The Silent Efficacy of Indirect Action*. Cambridge: Cambridge University Press.

This book was co-authored by the 'practitioner insights' contributor for this chapter. The book provides deep insights as to how strategy might be understood from a 'strong process' philosophy. We asked Robert to summarize the key message of the book; his response was: 'Build strategy from the bottom up through small acts and modest adjustments. Don't try grand schemes—they don't work! Only when you have a solid foundation of practical insight are you able to build. Don't be tempted to do otherwise, there is too much impatience for quick answers.'

REFERENCES

Adner, R. and Helfat, C.E. (2003). Corporate effects and dynamic managerial capabilities. *Strategic Management Journal*, **24**(10), 1011–25.

Anderson, M. (2022). 3D-printing start-up Relativity Space is the world's second most valuable space company—and has big plans to unseat SpaceX as the ruler of a booming industry (8 March), https://www.businessinsider.com/relativity-space-startup-3d-print-rockets-colonize-mars-spacex-2022-3 (last accessed 9 August 2022).

Ashkenas, R. (2013). Four tips for better strategic planning. *Harvard Business Review Digital Articles* (1 October), https://hbr.org/2013/10/four-tips-for-better-strategic-planning (last accessed 3 October 2022).

Barnett, M.L. (2008). An attention-based view of real options reasoning. *Academy of Management Review*, **33**(3), 606–28.

Bencherki, N., Sergi, V., Cooren, F., and Vásquez, C. (2021). How strategy comes to matter: Strategizing as the communicative materialization of matters of concern. *Strategic Organization*, **19**(4), 608–635.

Ben-Ner, A. and Siemsen, E. (2017). Decentralization and localization of production: The organizational and economic consequences of additive manufacturing (3D printing). *California Management Review*, **59**(2), 5–23.

Burgelman, R.A., Floyd, S.W., Laamanen, T. et al. (2018). Strategy processes and practices: Dialogues and intersections. *Strategic Management Journal*, **39**(3), 531–58.

Burke, G.T. and Wolf, C. (2021). The process affordances of strategy toolmaking when addressing wicked problems. *Journal of Management Studies*, **58**(2), 359–88.

Candido, C.J.F. and Santos, S.P. (2015). Strategy implementation: What is the failure rate? *Journal of Management & Organization*, **21**(2), 237–62.

Chia, R.C.H. and Holt, R. (2009). *Strategy without Design: The Silent Efficacy of Indirect Action*. Cambridge: Cambridge University Press.

Clark, D.N. (1997). Strategic management tool usage: A comparative study. *Strategic Change*, **6**, 417–27.

Cyert, R.M. and March, J.G. (1963). *A Behavioral Theory of the Firm*. Englewood Cliffs, NJ: Prentice Hall.

Demir, R. (2015). Strategic activity as bundled affordances. *British Journal of Management*, **26**, S125–41.

Denning, S. (2019). The ten stages of the Agile transformation journey. *Strategy & Leadership*, **47**(1), 3–10.

Doh, J.P., Lawton, T.C., and Rajwani, T. (2012). Advancing nonmarket strategy research: Institutional perspectives in a changing world. *Academy of Management Perspectives*, **26**(3), 22–39.

Farooqui, J.B. (2022). Space investing: world's first 3D-printed rock is set to launch (17 February), https://www.proactiveinvestors.co.uk/companies/news/974428/space-investing-world-s-first-3d-printed-rocket-is-set-to-launch-974428.html (last accessed 9 August 2022).

Ferreira, L.C. (2017). Sense and sensibility: Testing an attention-based view of organizational responses to social issues. *Business Ethics: A European Review*, **26**(4), 443–56.

Fortson, D. (2022). Tim Ellis: The space nerd 3D-printing a rocket to Mars. *Sunday Times* (27 February), https://www.thetimes.co.uk/article/tim-ellis-the-space-nerd-3d-printing-a-rocket-to-mars-gzgj2x9wx (last accessed 9 August 2022).

Frynas, J.G., Mol, M.J., and Mellahi, K. (2018). Management innovation made in China: Haier's Rendanheyi. *California Management Review*, **61**(1), 71–93.

Galbreath, J. (2018). Do boards of directors influence corporate sustainable development? An attention-based analysis. *Business Strategy & the Environment*, **27**(6), 742–56.

Garbuio, M., Lovallo, D., and Sibony, O. (2015). Evidence doesn't argue for itself: The value of disinterested dialogue in strategic decision-making. *Long Range Planning*, **48**(6), 361–80.

Gebauer, H. (2009). An attention-based view on service orientation in the business strategy of manufacturing companies. *Journal of Managerial Psychology*, **24**(1), 79–98.

Giraudeau, M. (2008). The drafts of strategy: Opening up plans and their uses. *Long Range Planning*, **41**(3), 291–310.

Gond, J.-P., Cabantous, L., and Krikorian, F. (2018). How do things become strategic? 'Strategifying' corporate social responsibility. *Strategic Organization*, **16**(3), 241–72.

Gov.uk (2015). Strategy development: A toolkit for NHS providers (25 August), https://www.gov.uk/government/publications/strategy-development-a-toolkit-for-nhs-providers (last accessed 9 August 2022).

Hansen, J.R. and Jacobsen, C.B. (2016). Changing strategy processes and strategy content in public sector organizations? A longitudinal case study of NPM Reforms' influence on strategic management. *British Journal of Management*, **27**(2), 373–89.

Hengst, I.-A., Jarzabkowski, P., Hoegl, M., and Muethel, M. (2020). Toward a process theory of making sustainability strategies legitimate in action. *Academy of Management Journal*, **63**(1), 246–71.

Houghton, T. (2015). Castore: All you need to know about the sports fashion brand backed by Andy Murray and Asda's billionaire owners (28 April), https://www.business-live.co.uk/enterprise/ex-athlete-brothers-who-signed-17471670 (last accessed 9 August 2022).

In Opinion (2022). The mindblowing growth of Castore (16 March), https://cashnsport.com/the-mindblowing-growth-of-castore (last accessed 9 August 2022).

Jalonen, K., Schildt, H., and Vaara, E. (2018). Strategic concepts as micro-level tools in strategic sensemaking. *Strategic Management Journal*, **39**(10), 2794–826.

Jarzabkowski, P. (2003). Strategic practices: An activity theory perspective on continuity and change. *Journal of Management Studies*, **40**(1), 23–55.

Jarzabkowski, P. (2005). *Strategy as Practice: An Activity-Based Approach*. London: Sage Publications.

Jarzabkowski, P. and Bednarek, R. (2018). Toward a social practice theory of relational competing. *Strategic Management Journal*, **39**(3), 794–829.

Jarzabkowski, P. and Kaplan, S. (2015). Strategy tools-in-use: A framework for understanding 'technologies of rationality' in practice. *Strategic Management Journal*, **36**(4), 537–58.

Jarzabkowski, P. and Spee, P.A. (2009). Strategy-as-practice: A review and future directions for the field. *International Journal of Management Reviews*, **11**(1), 69–95.

Jarzabkowski, P., Kaplan, S., Seidl, D., and Whittington, R. (2016). If you aren't talking about practices, don't call it a practice-based view: Rejoinder to Bromiley and Rau in *Strategic Organization*. *Strategic Organization*, **14**(3), 270–4.

Johnson, G., Melin, L., and Whittington, R. (2003). Micro strategy and strategizing: Towards an activity-based view. *Journal of Management Studies*, **40**(1), 3–22.

Johnson, G., Langley, A., Melin, L., and Whittington, R. (2008). *Strategy as Practice: Research Directions and Resources*. Cambridge: Cambridge University Press.

Joseph, J. and Wilson, A.J. (2018). The growth of the firm: An attention-based view. *Strategic Management Journal*, **39**(6), 1779–1800.

Kahneman, D., Lovallo, D.A.N., and Sibony, O. (2019). A structured approach to strategic decisions: Reducing errors in judgment requires a disciplined process. *MIT Sloan Management Review*, **60**(3), 67–73.

Kaplan, S. and Orlikowski, W.J. (2013). Temporal work in strategy making. *Organization Science*, **24**(4), 965–95.

King, B.L. (2008). Strategizing at leading venture capital firms: Of planning, opportunism, and deliberate emergence. *Long Range Planning*, **41**(3), 345–66.

Knight, E., Paroutis, S., and Heracleous, L. (2018). The power of PowerPoint: A visual perspective on meaning making in strategy. *Strategic Management Journal*, **39**(3), 894–921.

Kohtamäki, M., Whittington, R., Vaara, E., and Rabetino, R. (2021). Making connections: Harnessing the diversity of strategy-as-practice research. *International Journal of Management Reviews*, **24**(2), 210–32.

Langley, A., Smallman, C., Tsoukas, H., and Van de Ven, A.H. (2013). Process studies of change in organization and management: Unveiling temporality, activity, and flow. *Academy of Management Journal*, **56**(1), 1–13.

MacKay, B., Chia, R., and Nair, A.K. (2020). Strategy-in-practices: A process philosophical approach to understanding strategy emergence and organizational outcomes. *Human Relations*, **74**(9), 1337–69.

Mackay, D. and Zundel, M. (2017). Recovering the divide: A review of strategy and tactics in business and management. *International Journal of Management Reviews*, **19**(2), 175–94.

2

MacKay, R.B. and Chia, R. (2013). Choice, chance, and unintended consequences in strategic change: A process understanding of the rise and fall of Northco Automotive. *Academy of Management Journal*, **56**(1), 208–30.

Mahoney, J.T. and McGahan, A.M. (2007). The field of strategic management within the evolving science of strategic organization. *Strategic Organization*, **5**(1), 79–99.

Mantere, S. and Whittington, R. (2021). Becoming a strategist: The roles of strategy discourse and ontological security in managerial identity work. *Strategic Organization*, **19**(4), 553–578.

Markides, C.C. (2000). *All the Right Moves: A Guide to Crafting Breakthrough Strategy*. Boston, MA: Harvard Business School Press.

Martin, R.L. (2014). The big lie of strategic planning. *Harvard Business Review*, **92**(1/2), 78–84.

Mintzberg, H. (1987). Crafting strategy. *Harvard Business Review*, **65**(4), 66–75.

Monitor (2013). Meeting the needs of patients: Improving strategic planning in NHS foundation trusts, https://assets.publishing.service.gov.uk/government/uploads/system/uploads/attachment_data/file/286327/Meeting_the_needs_of_patients_-_Improving_strategic_planning_in_NHS_foundation_trusts.pdf (last accessed 9 August 2022).

Monitor (2014). Developing strategy: What every trust board member should know, https://assets.publishing.service.gov.uk/government/uploads/system/uploads/attachment_data/file/363273/Monitor_-_Developing_Strategy_-_a_guide_for_board_members.pdf (last accessed 9 August 2022).

Ocasio, W. (1997). Towards an attention-based view of the firm. *Strategic Management Journal*, **18**(S1), 187–206.

Ocasio, W., Laamanen, T., and Vaara, E. (2018). Communication and attention dynamics: An attention-based view of strategic change. *Strategic Management Journal*, **39**(1), 155–67.

Paroutis, S. and Pettigrew, A. (2007). Strategizing in the multi-business firm: Strategy teams at multiple levels and over time. *Human Relations*, **60**(1), 99–135.

Pettus, M.L., Kor, Y.Y., Mahoney, J.T., and Michael, S.C. (2018). Sequencing and timing of strategic responses after industry disruption: Evidence from post-deregulation competition in the US railroad industry. *Strategic Organization*, **16**(4), 373–400.

Sasaki, I., Kotlar, J., Ravasi, D., and Vaara, E. (2020). Dealing with revered past: Historical identity statements and strategic change in Japanese family firms. *Strategic Management Journal*, **41**(3), 590–623.

Schoemaker, P.J.H., Heaton, S., and Teece, D. (2018). Innovation, dynamic capabilities, and leadership. *California Management Review*, **61**(1), 15–42.

Simon, H.A. (1947). *Administrative Behavior: A Study of Decision-Making Processes in Administrative Organizations*. Chicago, IL: Macmillan.

Spee, A.P. and Jarzabkowski, P. (2009). Strategy tools as boundary objects. *Strategic Organization*, **7**(2), 223–32.

Sull, D., Homkes, R., and Sull, C. (2015). Why strategy execution unravels—and what to do about it. *Harvard Business Review*, **93**(3), 57–66.

Tsoukas, H. and Chia, R. (2002). On organizational becoming: Rethinking organizational change. *Organization Science*, **13**(5), 567–82.

Unruh, G. (2018). Circular economy, 3D printing, and the biosphere rules. *California Management Review*, **60**(3), 95–111.

Van de Ven, A.H. (1992). Suggestions for studying strategy process: A research note. *Strategic Management Journal*, **13**, 169–88.

Vuori, T.O. and Huy, Q.N. (2016). Distributed attention and shared emotions in the innovation process. *Administrative Science Quarterly*, **61**(1), 9–51.

Vuorinen, T., Hakala, H., Kohtamäki, M., and Uusitalo, K. (2018). Mapping the landscape of strategy tools: A review on strategy tools published in leading journals within the past 25 years. *Long Range Planning*, **51**(4), 586–605.

Whittle, A., Gilchrist, A., Mueller, F., and Lenney, P. (2021). The art of stage-craft: A dramaturgical perspective on strategic change. *Strategic Organization*, **19**(4), 636–66.

CHAPTER THREE

Strategic Decision-Making in Organizations

CONTENTS

LEARNING OBJECTIVES

3

By the end of this chapter, you should be able to:

○ Distinguish strategic decisions from routine decisions

○ Evaluate the impact of common heuristics and biases on organizational decision-making

○ Analyse the differences between rational and cognitive approaches to decision-making in organizations

○ Apply practical decision-making tools in group decision-making

○ Examine the tools and techniques available for managers to improve the quality of their decision-making processes

TOOLBOX

○ **Devil's advocacy**
A decision-making technique designed to overcome groupthink (a practice of thinking or making decisions as a group in a way that discourages creativity or joint and several responsibility). One or more people in the group takes the 'devil's advocate' role and works to point out all the flaws and risks with an option under consideration.

○ **Dialectical enquiry**
A group decision-making technique that attempts to overcome groupthink. Groups using this technique divide into two camps—those advocating for an idea and those advocating against it. Both sides highlight the advantages of their assigned decision and outline the disadvantages of the opposing idea.

○ **Scenario planning**
A forecasting tool that can be used to consider multiple future scenarios and outcomes that result from strategic decisions.

○ **Causal mapping**
Cognitive mapping in which the links between nodes represent causality or influence as understood by strategists. Causal mapping is used as a tool to aid systematic strategic thinking and decision-making.

○ **Mediating assessment protocol (MAP)**
A process that breaks down a complex judgement into multiple fact-based assessments which aim to ensure that each fact is relevant to the decision and is evaluated independently of the other facts.

 Access the online resources to watch a short video clip where Professor Bernie Bulkin OBE shares his top career tips.

OPENING CASE STUDY TO LEND OR NOT TO LEND?

First National Bank (FNB) in Kitchener (Canada) specializes in commercial real estate loans and writes, on average, over $1 billion in new loans every year, primarily to local developers and private investors. To secure a loan from FNB, a borrower must provide certain documents before their contract-to-buy expires. If these requirements are not fulfilled, the bank can refuse the approval of the loan.

The painstaking process of securing a commercial real estate loan is normally made up of two stages: competitive bidding followed by closing. During the bidding stage, the buyer solicits quotes from lenders. Then the lenders bid by sending a letter of intent, offering a loan at a stated rate of interest. The final loan itself is dependent on completion of due diligence paperwork and approvals. Finally, the buyer chooses an offer and signs the letter of intent. To confirm the offer, the buyer pays 0.25–0.5% of the loan value to the lender (the bank) as a non-refundable deposit.

During the closing stage, to finalize the loan agreement, the legal documents and approvals are completed. According to FNB's due diligence, the documents required are financial statements from the buyer, copies of leases from the seller, and bonded property appraisals, among other documents. The approvals come from two FNB representatives: the vice president, who manages the bank's loan portfolio, and FNB's risk manager, who reports directly to corporate headquarters.

Therefore, to successfully close on a property, the buyer needs to coordinate a complex three-way deal between the seller, the buyer, and the lender. All three parties must cooperate in the preparation of several required documents, and typically the closing process takes around four to six weeks but is limited by an expiration date in the contract-to-buy between the seller and the buyer.

Within this process, the skilled negotiation and execution of commercial real estate loans is carried out by the business development managers at FNB. They meet prospective borrowers, determine an appropriate interest rate for the size and risk of the transaction, secure preliminary approvals,

prepare the letter of intent, and then process the loan through the closing process.

One of the senior business development managers at the Kitchener branch of FNB is John Hamond. He specializes in loans over $1 million and single-handedly writes more than $100 million of new business each year, making him one of the most experienced and highest-grossing business development managers at the branch. His success is largely thanks to his ability to establish solid working relationships both within the company and outside FNB, in addition to his reputation for consistently successfully closing transactions.

In November 2018, Hamond began working on a loan for the Kitchener Group, a privately held company that was new to commercial real estate. Although the loan was relatively small, at $1 million, FNB saw this opportunity as potentially very lucrative in terms of future business from Kitchener. To put that into perspective, of the appraised value of the $3 million property, Kitchener only planned to borrow $900,000. To add pressure for this deal, FNB was bidding against a former colleague, which made Hamond's manager, the vice president of commercial banking, especially keen to win the bidding war. Kitchener Group was becoming a strategically important prospective client for FNB.

By December 2018, the Kitchener Group had made a successful offer on a property and entered a contract-to-buy with the seller; a month later, Kitchener invited lenders to bid on the loan and several submitted aggressive bids. By February 2019, FNB had submitted a relatively low bid, but Hamond had to lower it even more on Kitchener's request. Another month down the line, Kitchener signed a letter of intent with FNB. Kitchener then asked FNB to accelerate the closing process, according to the looming deadline for their contract-to-buy, which expired on 29 March 2019, leaving less than half the usual time for closing. To try and close the deal, Hamond agreed to work closely with the Kitchener Group's attorney, Paul Talley, who, like the Kitchener Group, was new to commercial real estate transactions.

Hamond sped up the FNB approvals as agreed and sent the draft loan agreement to Talley on

14 March 2019. Talley returned the draft loan agreement on 21 March 2019. Talley was finding it difficult to procure some of the due diligence documents and asked for leeway. Hamond agreed to be as flexible as possible.

Talley submitted a set of due diligence documents on 28 March 2019, one day before the expiration of the Kitchener Group's contract-to-buy. But the set of documents was incomplete. As we know, if a client does not provide all key documents, despite months of skilled negotiation and careful execution, the bank's risk manager may be forced to refuse the approval of the million-dollar real estate loan. In this case, Talley had not provided any tenant acknowledgements—documents procured by the seller from his tenants stating that the tenants do in fact have leases. Hamond contacted the FNB risk manager who, in line with protocol, said that the loan would indeed be rejected if it lacked tenant acknowledgements.

On Friday 29 March 2019, Talley and Hamond spent the morning frantically contacting their clients to procure tenant acknowledgements to salvage the deal. Unfortunately, they only managed to acquire one barely legible faxed tenant acknowledgement, which they knew was insufficient. Despite this, Talley wanted Hamond to seek approval of the loan with the paperwork they had and offered to provide FNB with a document guaranteeing that, within the month, Kitchener would produce the missing tenant acknowledgements. On this basis, he asked for FNB to release the money so that the closing could be agreed.

By now it was 1:00 p.m. on Friday 29 March 2019. The Kitchener Group's contract-to-buy would expire at the end of business that day . . .

Questions for discussion

Imagine you are in John Hamond's position as a senior business development manager.

1. Could you find a way to complete the transaction? What steps could you take?

2. Should you walk away from the transaction? Why/why not?

3. What, if anything, could you have done differently had you been John Hamond?

Source

Adapted from: Harrison, M. (2007). John Hamond at First National Bank, Daniel Webster College. Case from The Case Centre, Cranfield, UK.

3.1 **Introduction**

Rigorous analysis can usefully underpin strategy, but analysis itself does not lead to action. Agreed strategies must be put into practice, and this involves managerial judgement and decision-making that set the course of action for an organization.

As outlined in the dynamic frameworks of strategy in Chapter 2, decision-making is a crucial recurring feature of strategy practice. In addition to featuring as a core aspect of strategy work, decisions made about how to approach implementation, how to learn from realized outcomes, and where to focus managerial attention are highly influential on the form and effectiveness of strategy activity. As such, we will now examine the role of decision-making on strategy process and practices in detail.

Decision-making is relatively easy if we assume that human beings are fully rational, relevant information is freely available, and the decision outcomes are predictable and the risks quantifiable. Hence, when we are confronted with a problem that requires us to choose between alternatives, we consider the nature and the impact of the options that are available to us in order to find a solution. We analyse the options we have come up with and then select the one that seems the most effective and optimal solution to the problem. Powerful advanced data analytics and intelligent algorithms have been developed to help us in decision-making with the aim of reducing uncertainty and risk. However, if decision-making was as simple as theory implies, and if managerial judgement could be left to mathematical modelling and algorithms, why, in real life, do organizations keep making decisions that don't work out as planned?

The aim of this chapter is to help you to appreciate the complexity of strategic decision-making and consider how it can be improved. Sound strategic decision-making and strong strategic performance are intrinsically linked. No individual or organization can achieve perfect decision outcomes all the time. Nevertheless, as part of strategizing, strategy practitioners are regularly tasked with making decisions in volatile, uncertain, and ambiguous environments in a way that benefits the organization and its stakeholders. These decisions must consider the plurality of human effort and activity as a collective organizational phenomenon as well as incorporating the cognitive processes of individual decision-makers and decision-making groups. In this chapter, we consider the many decision-making traps that lurk in the minds of decision-makers and decision-making groups in the form of **cognitive biases** and variability of judgements called **noise** that can lead to inconsistent decision-making. Research into biases in decision-making has its roots in **prospect theory**. We also outline some of the frameworks and tools that practitioners can use to improve their decision-making processes and the quality of the decision outcomes. Finally, we outline the challenges of making decisions in groups and the role of **strategic leaders** in organizational decision-making.

3.2 Routine decisions and strategic decisions

Before we consider decision-making processes and how they can be improved, it is important that we define the types of decisions in which we are interested. We all make thousands of decisions every day. Most of them are routine, such as what we are going to wear for work or what food we are going to have for lunch. Similarly, organizations make routine decisions, such as placing a replenishment order for stationery from their office supplies provider or sales managers approving sales force travel expenditure. Most routine managerial decisions are governed by some type of decision-making guidelines or policies that require limited managerial time and effort. Indeed, algorithms are increasingly used to make previously time-consuming decisions more routine. For example, the assessment of consumer loans, credit cards, car loans, and even mortgages by financial institutions are now managed using algorithms which require limited human judgemental intervention.

Most strategic problems do not have simple solutions as they occur in the conditions of volatility, uncertainty, complexity, and ambiguity that require managerial judgement, and it is often the errors in these judgement calls that can produce poor decision outcomes (Schoemaker et al. 2018). In fact, it is estimated that half of all business decisions end in failure (Nutt 2002). McKinsey, a global strategic management consulting firm, found in a survey that 60% of senior executives thought that bad strategic decision outcomes were about as frequent as good ones, and 12% thought that good decision outcomes were altogether infrequent (McKinsey Global Survey Results 2009). Subsequent research of 800 board members by McKinsey revealed that their top aspiration for improving organizational performance was to reduce biases in decision-making and build processes to avoid decision-making traps

(Baer et al. 2017). Poor decisions can even result in disaster, for example, investment bank Lehman Brothers' monumental mistakes in their investment strategies that triggered the global financial crises of 2007–08 and oil giant BP's decision-making flaws that led to the Deepwater Horizon drilling rig disaster in 2010.

Moreover, in contrast with routine decisions, strategic decisions have an organization-wide impact. Mintzberg et al. (1976) define strategic decisions as large, expensive, and precedent-setting decisions that are made under conditions of ambiguity and uncertainty about the final decision outcome. Once a strategic decision is made and implemented, it is difficult to reverse as both financial and human resources have been committed to the decision, at least in the short term, and subsequent decisions are based on these strategic decisions.

According to Nutt and Wilson (2010), strategic decisions have the following characteristics:

- they deal with complex problems which are hard to define;
- the outcomes are risky and shrouded in uncertainty and ambiguity;
- they require an understanding of the problem before a viable solution can be formulated;
- they rarely have one best solution, but rather a series of possible solutions;
- they involve trade-offs and the setting of organizational priorities as scarce resources must be allocated to a possible solution to the problem;
- they are influenced by competing political interests that may bias decision-makers towards a solution that aligns with their preferences;
- they are often connected with other organizational problems, which warrant additional decision-making, especially once the original strategic decision is being implemented in the organization.

As this list suggests, treating strategic decision-making as a simple and singular decision between two known alternatives does not fully capture the complexity of strategic decision problems. Although we have mechanisms to assess risk through probability theory, dealing with strategic decision problems is much more difficult when the information we gather to support a decision and the actual decision outcomes are uncertain and ambiguous. We do not live in a perfect world where the future is knowable and where the outcomes of our decisions unfold in a predictable way. Think about the decision involving the proposed high-speed rail link investment between London and the North of England, known as HS2. The first phase of this project is conservatively estimated to cost close to £60 billion and the link will not be ready until 2026 at the earliest, with subsequent links being planned to be introduced in 2032–33. The magnitude of this strategic decision does not impact only one organization, or even multiple organizations, but the United Kingdom as a whole as this investment would need to be prioritized over other worthy projects by the current as well as future governments.

Critics of the HS2 project have questioned the assumption that for several decades, or even longer, people will still conduct business and live their lives in a way that requires faster travel links between London and the North. Such a high degree of uncertainty about the future of the UK economy and the way people will conduct their affairs in the future makes decision-making more of an art than a science. The best a strategist can do under such circumstances is to focus on the quality of the decision-making processes and accept that it is impossible to predict the outcome of the decision.

3

Not all strategic decisions are identical, although they share some common characteristics, as highlighted by Nutt and Wilson (2010). In the Opening Case Study of this chapter, John Hamond faced a strategic decision as he considered the prospective client as strategically important to his bank as to himself as a star business development manager. He needed to decide whether to pursue the business potential of the Kitchener Group or to stop spending his time on this small transaction and move on to more lucrative business opportunities. The timeframe for the outcomes of Hamond's decision could be considered in years in terms of how Kitchener Group would service the loan over its duration and whether the client would present more opportunities for Hamond's bank. In contrast, the decision that the UK government ministers had to make regarding the HS2 investment was of a totally different magnitude, and the impact of that decision would be felt by the whole economy for decades to come with a much greater degree of uncertainty and ambiguity.

Therefore, strategic decisions require a great deal of judgement that has far-reaching consequences not only for the decision-makers but also for the organizations and stakeholders that are affected by these decisions. Moreover, as the future is unknowable, strategists need to make decisions based on what they anticipate might happen in the future. Whilst strategic decision-makers can strive to optimize the quality of their decision-making process and the information available to them, they often have to decide when 'there is no right answer—just the best response at the time' (McKay 2020: 15).

3.3 How do we make strategic decisions?

Before we take a closer look at how decision-making processes can be improved, we start our discussion by first asking what specifically constitutes strategic decision-making. Let's first consider the following two scenarios:

1. You are about to finish your business degree from a well-known university. Your grades are good and you expect to receive several offers from leading consulting firms.

What steps will you take to select the right job?

2. You work in the corporate acquisition department of a large multinational technology firm. Your company is interested in acquiring a promising start-up in a growing financial technology (fintech) industry.

Which firm, if any, will you advise the company to acquire?

Although these two scenarios have vastly different contexts, each constitutes a problem with several alternative solutions, each requiring a decision to be made and a strategic action to be taken. As you read this section, keep these two scenarios in mind and think about how you would approach the decision problems outlined.

Let's first consider the steps to take when applying a 'rational' decision-making process to these two scenarios. The 'rational' decision-making model has its origins in economics. It assumes that humans are what economists call 'homo economicus' or 'economic man', persons who make rational decisions in order to achieve their most preferred, optimum outcome, given the constraints upon choice (Black et al. 2017). The 'rational' decision-making model prescribes us to apply the following six steps to each scenario (Bazerman and Moore 2008).

Six-step rational decision-making model

1. Define the problem.

2. Identify decision criteria.

3. Weigh the criteria.

4. Generate alternatives.

5. Rate each alternative on each criterion.

6. Compute the optimal decision.

Source: Bazerman and Moore (2008).

Once a decision-maker has defined the problem (Step 1), they need to identify the decision criteria that will be important in solving the problem (Step 2). During Step 2, the decision-maker must determine what is relevant in making the decision, which brings the decision-maker's interests, values, and personal preferences into the process. In Step 3, the decision-maker weighs the previously identified criteria in order to give them the correct priority in the decision. The decision-maker generates possible alternatives (Step 4) which could succeed in resolving the problem. No attempt is made in this step to appraise these alternatives, only to list them. In Step 5, the decision-maker must critically analyse and evaluate each alternative. The strengths and weaknesses of each option become evident as they are compared with the criteria and weightings established in Steps 2 and 3. In the final step (Step 6), each alternative is ranked according to its weighted criteria and the alternative with the highest score is selected. Assuming that you are fully rational, that you have all the relevant information available, and that you are able to assign objective weightings to each alternative, then making the 'right' decision in the two scenarios mentioned earlier would be a rather simple, mechanistic exercise.

Although arguably we should approach decision-making as rationally as possible, there are limitations to the rational model. Considering the rational decision-making model, let's go through each of the six steps and identify the difficulties strategists may come across when applying this model in practice.

Define the problem

Practitioners often unintentionally act without a thorough understanding of the problem to be solved, which can lead to them attempting to solve the wrong problem. For instance, managers could erroneously believe that a firm's poor sales performance is due to the underperforming sales force rather than the quality of a product. Extending the example of Nokia introduced in Chapter 1, having invested significant amounts of money on developing Nokia's mobile communications platform, Symbian, senior managers blamed the rapidly falling sales on problems with the physical attributes of the Nokia phones and on marketing, while refusing to believe that the problem was the very operating platform in which they had made strategic investments. Accurate judgement is needed to identify and define the problem. Managers can easily go wrong by defining the problem in terms of a proposed solution, missing a bigger problem, or diagnosing the problem in terms of its symptoms.

3

Identify the decision criteria

Most decisions require us to accomplish more than one objective. When selecting a job, we consider the reputation of the organization, the type of work we want to do, the distance from our home, the salary, opportunities for advancement, and so on. A rational decision-maker will be able to identify all relevant criteria in the decision-making process and organize them in priority order of importance, but in reality, this is almost impossible to determine objectively. For example, what one person thinks is relevant another may not and vice versa. Organizations frequently confront this problem in budgeting decisions. As resources are finite, not every worthy activity can be accommodated, and trade-offs are necessary. Hence, budgeting decisions may become influenced by non-quantifiable considerations, such as organizational politics and power, rather than return on investment analysis.

Weigh the criteria

Rational decision-makers will know the relative value they place on each of the criteria that were identified in Step 2 of the rational decision-making model. For example, when selecting a possible new employer, they can accurately assign a weighting to the reputation of the firm, a different weighting to the opportunities for advancement, etc. The weighting is based on the value the decision-maker places on each of the criteria, which may be quantifiable in monetary terms or whatever scoring criteria are being used by the decision-maker. Again, it is doubtful whether we can make such a calculation objectively.

Generate alternatives

This step requires the decision-maker to define the possible course of action. Decision-makers often spend too much time seeking alternatives and collecting ever more information to evaluate the options. This can create a barrier to effective decision-making. An optimal search for alternative solutions should continue only until the cost of the search outweighs the value of added information to be used in considering the alternative solutions. Very few of us are able to ascertain this break-even point where the cost of the search equals the benefit gained.

Rate each alternative on each criterion

This is often the most difficult step in the decision-making process as it typically requires the decision-maker trying to anticipate future events. In rational decision-making, potential consequences of each identified alternative should be considered and anticipated. But, as Henry Mintzberg observed (Mintzberg et al. 1976), the future is unknowable. As such, any decision-maker's ability to anticipate the future with any degree of accuracy should be considered limited.

Compute the optimal decision

A rational decision-maker would develop a criterion to evaluate the alternatives in order to make the most optimal decision. This would entail multiplying the ratings for each alternative by the weight for each criterion and then choosing the solution with the highest sum of the weighted ratings. But, as we have seen, there are limitations to the degree of rationality which can be achieved in developing objectively defined criteria and a rating system for the criteria. Although the mathematical calculation is relatively simple, the result is false if the component parts of the calculation are not accurate.

We have seen that a rational decision-making model assumes that practitioners approach the decision-making task in an orderly fashion and that full rationality is achievable, including the availability of all information that is relevant for the decision. Despite its limitations, the six-step list provides a useful set of considerations for thinking about what an optimal decision-making process might look like.

3.4 Bounds of human rationality

The rational decision-making model describes how a decision *should* be made, but it fails to describe how a decision *is* made in practice. So, what are the boundaries that prevent us from applying this rational model? Two main factors that constrain our ability to engage in purely rational decision-making are the bounds to our rationality and the uncertainty surrounding strategic decisions that can unfold far in the future. All strategic decisions feature evaluative human judgement, and making tough calls requires people to distil vast amounts of complex and ambiguous information into a decision. As human judgement is unreliable, all evaluations are susceptible to errors (Kahneman et al. 2019). Recent research (Kahneman et al. 2016) has shown that humans are unreliable decision-makers, and their judgements can be greatly influenced by biases as well as by irrelevant factors, noise, to the decision problem such as their current mood, the time since their last meal, and even the weather. In this section, we discuss the limitations of rational decision-making.

Nobel laureate Herbert Simon suggested that all human judgement is bounded (or limited) in its rationality, and we can better understand decision-making by describing and explaining actual decisions rather than by focusing on what should be done rationally in decision-making processes (March and Simon 1958). While Simon's framework of '**bounded rationality**' views people as attempting to make rational decisions, it acknowledges that there are limitations that prevent us from making rational decisions as prescribed by the rational decision-making model. These informational limitations include:

- a lack of important details that would help to define the problem;
- a lack of clarity in the relevant decision criteria;
- uncertainty and ambiguity about the decision outcome due to the long time frame.

There are also several limitations in the following individual abilities:

- the amount of information decision-makers can hold in their memory;
- their level of intelligence;
- errors in how the decision problem is perceived, which can inhibit the decision-maker's ability to calculate the optimal choice accurately from a number of alternatives.

Finally, Eisenhardt and Zbaracki (1992) propose politics and power as additional limitations that hinder optimum decision-making. Decision-makers may hold different and often conflicting goals in organizations (see Case Example 3.1). This makes decision-making a political process, and the final decision reflects the preference of the most powerful decision-maker or a coalition.

If human judgement is so unreliable, why not replace this decision-making with algorithms? Artificial intelligence (AI) promises to achieve better predictions and decisions from large quantities of data by spotting causal relationships and patterns that no human could detect. It is known that algorithms are more accurate in making predictions than those made by experts and that machine learning-based decision-making is noise-free. Unlike humans, an algorithm will always produce the same output from any given input, free from any external interference. Algorithms are about 10–15% better than human judgement alone (Michelman 2017). A simple example of a highly accurate algorithm is a university admissions algorithm which models student performance in the United States. A combination of test scores, grade point averages, etc. are assigned an equal weighting, which significantly outperforms admissions experts in predicting student performance.

However, there are many situations where the use of algorithms is not practical such as when inputs to a decision are idiosyncratic, hard to code in a consistent format, or when decisions involve multiple dimensions or depend on a negotiation with another party (Kahneman et al. 2016, 2021). Other organizational considerations, such as replacing employees with machines, can be too painful a process that may prevent a wider application of machine learning. Furthermore, Dietvorst et al.'s 2015 research revealed that, if decision-makers know that a specific forecast goal is hard to achieve and the previous use of an algorithm in forecasting did not fully meet the expected forecast goal in the past, decision-makers revert to using human judgement.

All of these limitations might prevent practitioners from making the sort of optimal decision assumed by the rational model. The decisions taken in light of these limitations typically overlook the full range of possible consequences, and decision-makers often forgo the best solution in favour of one that is acceptable or reasonable (Bazerman and Moore 2008). Such decision-making is referred to by Simon as **satisficing**—rather than examining all possible alternatives, people simply search until a satisfactory solution is found which will suffice because it achieves an acceptable—but not necessarily an optimum—level of performance.

CASE EXAMPLE 3.1 **WHERE WILL THE AXE FALL?**

A department within a well-known university was faced with a major strategic problem: it had to find savings that would inevitably include redundancies across academic and administrative staff departments. Student numbers of the university's degree programmes had declined steadily over the previous three years.

The university's board of governors and trustees had become increasingly concerned about the university's finances. At a recent board meeting, it had been agreed that every faculty, including this one, would need to implement permanent savings of £2 million by the end of the following academic year.

The principal of the department was tasked with forming a working group to identify savings at the university. It consisted of four academic departments as well as departments for academic quality, information systems and administration, and library and information services. The working group consisted of the heads of all departments and academic union representatives.

The atmosphere at the first working group meeting was tense, but everyone agreed that the university had to implement the cost-savings programme and that collectively they would find the required £2 million of savings. It was agreed that all department heads would consult with their staff and present their cost reduction plans at the next meeting.

At the next meeting, it became obvious that the cost reduction plans would not add up to the required amount of savings. The department heads for finance and economics and human resource management had sent their cost-savings projections in advance, and the principal noticed that their proposed savings were marginal at best. At the meeting, the head of academic quality argued that her department could not afford any savings as the department was short-staffed already. Furthermore, academic quality was a top priority for the university in order to maintain its reputation as a top-quality teaching and research institution. She suggested that the main brunt of the savings should be borne by specialist academic departments as the specialist programmes had seen the greatest reduction in student numbers.

In the absence of the two department heads whose degree programmes were identified by the head of academic quality, the other heads of academic departments objected strenuously. They argued that the academic staff were the lifeline of any university and that job cuts would cause irreparable reputational damage to the university as a whole and to the departments in question, which were well known for high-quality research output. The academic heads were insistent that any reduction in academic staff would result in large class sizes that would damage student satisfaction, and the loss of teaching and research staff would damage the school's standing in international league tables. Any cuts should come from administrative support services, which could be streamlined by reducing unproductive and needless bureaucracy, including over-zealous quality **control systems**.

At this point, the union representatives stated that they did not agree with any cost savings through staff cuts. They felt that, in comparison with other universities, this department was too top heavy. Any cost savings through staff cuts would stretch the already hard-working staff across academic and administrative departments beyond breaking point. Instead, the axe should fall on the university's management layers as there were many managers who did not contribute to teaching, research, or the day-to-day operation of the university.

The meeting ended in deadlock. No future meeting date was set as all department heads insisted that they had given their best cost-savings projections. The total of proposed savings, which included some early retirement of pension-aged staff and a reduction in contractor and visiting academic staff, amounted to £800,000, which was £1.2 million short of the set target.

Questions for discussion

1. Apply the rational decision-making model to this decision problem.

2. Identify what the participants of the meeting think would limit the rationality of the decision-making process and outcome.

3. Consider how the principal could explore other solutions to this strategic problem.

Details of the case have been written in a way that hides the identity of the organization. However, the decision problem is real.

Source

Mikko Arevuo.

Later in this chapter, we will look at various tools that are available to practitioners to improve the quality of their decision-making processes and develop capabilities in dealing with the uncertainty that surrounds complex decision problems. Although the future is inherently uncertain, there are tools that enable managers to collectively make sense of the decision problems by sharing diverse views and developing shared courses of action.

3.5 **Managerial heuristics**

Bounded human rationality and our satisficing behaviour in decision-making mean that, although we wish to think that we are rational, we do not behave according to the prescriptive rational decision-making model. These concepts help us to realize that we make decisions with

3

imperfect information and that the behaviours, political agendas, and preferences of others may not allow us to make optimal decisions. But is our judgement and decision-making biased? And if so, in what ways? Case Example 3.2 illustrates how biases can creep into our decision-making.

Where finding an optimal solution to a problem is impossible or impractical, heuristic methods can be used to speed up the process of finding a satisfactory solution. Heuristics, or rules of thumb, are often mental shortcuts that ease the cognitive burden of making a decision. Examples of heuristics include the use of a rule of thumb, an educated guess, an intuitive judgement or gut feeling, or common sense. In this section, we consider several heuristics that are common in managerial decision-making.

System One and System Two thinking

According to cognitive scientists (Kahneman et al. 1982), humans possess two modes of thinking: intuitive and reflective. In intuitive thinking, impressions, associations, feelings, intentions, and the urgency for action flow effortlessly without us having to assess our actions. This type of intuitive thinking, where initial observations made within the first few seconds create a lasting impression of the observed by the observer, is referred to as thin-slicing (Ambady and Rosenthal 1992). Intuitive thinking produces a constant representation of the world around us that allows us to do things almost automatically and simultaneously such as walking, noticing things around us, and thinking at the same time. This is known as System One thinking. It leads to action; it is effortless, and it leads us to do things and form opinions.

In contrast, System Two thinking is slow, deliberate, and requires effort. This type of reflective thinking is activated when we are faced with problems where the stakes are high, when we detect an obvious error that requires us to correct our actions, or when we must follow certain rules (such as the prescriptive model of 'rational' decision-making). But because System Two thinking requires a concerted effort, our effortless System One thinking tends to be the dominant force in decision-making. We need to make a conscious effort to fight against the impulses of the System One thinking that offers us instantaneous solutions to problems or pushes us to form opinions without any further consideration.

System One thinking is part of our biological make-up—the 'flight or fight' reflex. It is good at making us react instantaneously when we are confronted with a problem or when we are faced with a serious threat to our immediate well-being. However, even when we are confronted with a complex analytical problem without any threat to our physical well-being, System One thinking produces an instantaneous answer to the problem—a solution that we often refer to as 'gut feeling'. Our 'gut feeling' short circuits the need to engage the System Two thinking, saving us the effort to work through the analysis. This can be a tremendous advantage for managers who have accumulated significant experience and can draw on that wisdom to come up with instantaneous solutions to problems. However, 'gut feeling' can lead us astray with disastrous consequences when it signals a solution to a problem that cannot be extrapolated from past experiences. The two systems are summarized in Table 3.1.

Tversky and Kahneman (1974) identified systematic biases that influence our judgement and decision-making which result from the powerful prevalence of System One thinking. They found that we use several simplifying strategies, or **heuristics**, when making decisions. Heuristics allow us to cope with difficult and complex environments that surround decisions. Kahneman

TABLE 3.1 **System One and System Two thinking**

System One thinking	System Two thinking
Intuitive	Reflective
Automatic	Requires a concerted effort
Produces a constant representation of the world around us Examples: Simultaneous actions, such as walking, noticing things around us, and thinking	Activated when we are faced with problems where the stakes are high Examples: When we detect an obvious error that requires us to correct our actions When we have to follow certain rules (such as the prescriptive model of 'rational' decision-making)
Leads to action: effortless and leads us to do things and form instant opinions	Slow, deliberate, and requires conscious effort

Source: authors.

(2011) has proposed a general 'law of least effort' which applies to cognitive and physical exertion. His 'law' asserts that if there are several ways of achieving the same goal, people will eventually gravitate to the least demanding course of action. In the economy of action, effort is a cost, and the acquisition of a skill is driven by the balance of benefits and costs. In other words, people will eventually opt for the easiest option, which requires the least amount of effort. However, even in complex decision-making situations, people still revert to an action that requires the least effort. Rather than having to work through a problem, our cognitive and physiological make-up lead us to make decisions using decision-making heuristics to find a short cut to the decision problem.

CASE EXAMPLE 3.2 IMPARTIALITY IN HIRING DECISIONS

Abbie Conant was a young trombone player at the beginning of her musical career. She was happy playing for the Royal Opera of Turin in Italy but had decided to apply for 11 permanent openings for orchestra jobs across Europe. She was delighted to receive one invitation for an audition from the Munich Philharmonic Orchestra. She was perplexed by the letter she received addressing her as 'Dear Herr Abbie Conant', but, in her excitement, she discounted it as typo and didn't think further about it.

The auditions were held in the Deutsches Museum in Munich as the orchestra's own cultural centre was still under construction. Abbie was one

Source: Roman Voloshyn/Shutterstock.com.

Continued

of 33 hopeful musicians competing for the principal trombonist opening. The candidates were told that they would be playing from behind a screen to the selection committee sitting on the other side. Such auditions were relatively uncommon in Europe but many orchestras in the United States had revised their audition policies in the 1970s and 1980s. This involved the use of a 'blind' audition where the musician played from behind the screen to conceal their identity from the jury. The Munich Philharmonic Orchestra had made the decision to conduct a 'blind' audition because one of the candidates was the son of someone in one of the many Munich orchestras.

Abbie was candidate number 16 and she had chosen Ferdinand David's Konzertino for Trombone, which she knew was one of the workhorse audition pieces in Germany. All went well until she missed a note by cracking a G. After finishing her recital, she returned backstage to pack up her instrument and thought that the missed note had cost her the job. But the selection committee thought otherwise. They were so impressed by the beauty of her music that the remaining 17 players waiting for their turn were sent home. Abbie was invited back to the audition room and when she stepped out from behind the screen, she was met with a confused silence.

The selection committee was expecting to see Herr Conant. Instead, they saw Frau Conant.

Questions for discussion

1. The need for blind auditions assumes that our decision-making is biased. What types of biases do you think that such auditions try to eliminate?

2. How could the concept of blind auctions be used in hiring decisions in organizations that you are familiar with?

3. What impact if any do you think that 'blind' auditions have on the composition of classical music orchestras?

Sources

Gladwell, M. (2005). *Blink, the Power of Thinking without Thinking*. New York: Back Bay Books.

Goldin, C. and Rouse, C. (1997). Orchestrating impartiality: The impact of 'blind' auditions on female musicians. Working Paper 5903, NBER Working Paper series, National Bureau of Economic Research, Cambridge, MA.

New York Times (2021). To make orchestras more diverse, end blind auditions (6 August), https://www.nytimes.com/2020/07/16/arts/music/blind-auditions-orchestras-race.html (last accessed 9 August 2022).

From the view of the rational decision-making model, blind auditions are designed to debias our decision-making. It also indicates how biases can creep into all kinds of decision-making situations. We are often not conscious of our biases and the first step is for us to understand the types of biases we are confronted with before we can develop tools to confront them in our decision-making.

 Access the online resources to watch a short video clip where Professor Bernie Bulkin OBE discusses jury service and group decision-making.

Common heuristics in managerial decision-making

There are a few heuristics that research (Bazerman and Moore 2008) has shown to apply across all peoples, genders, and cultures. Table 3.2 lists the most commonly found heuristics in managerial decision-making.

The use of heuristics that can be subject to biases may produce correct or partially correct judgements (Bazerman and Moore 2008). The use of partially correct judgements should not always be discouraged, and, arguably, it might not even be possible to discourage it entirely, as we have explored the idea in sections 3.3 and 3.4 of how people tend to use some simplifying mechanisms to make complex decisions under uncertainty and ambiguity. But we have to realize that the use of heuristics in decision-making can create serious problems, primarily

TABLE 3.2 **Common heuristics in managerial decision-making**

Heuristic	Definition	Example
Representativeness	A tendency to make judgements about a new circumstance or decision problem based on how much the new situation resembles another similar past decision situation	Numerous start-up firms have attracted venture capital funding by describing them as 'it's like Uber or Air BnB', hence playing to the potential investor's representativeness bias by associating the start-up with successful firms
Confirmation	A tendency to seek out information that validates existing views and prior commitments at the same time discounting and explaining away disconfirming evidence	A company board considered a potential acquisition based on a $3 billion valuation. Investment bankers were asked to conduct an independent valuation which came in at $1.7 billion. Instead of rejecting the acquisition or considering alternatives, the board tasked the bankers with developing other means of assessing the acquisition target value, thus bridging the gap enough to reach the deal.
Anchoring	A tendency to make judgements based on an initial assessment as an anchor, but failing to make sufficient adjustments later as new information is revealed	In the above example, the $3 billion proposed acquisition price became a reference anchor and any action that followed was a reaction to this initial valuation
Overconfidence	A tendency to allow a belief in one's own capabilities or the capabilities of one's own firm to prevent a healthy level of introspection or debate about the quality of judgements and decisions	A board chair took a position with which most directors disagreed. The chair created a challenging dynamic in forcing his view, which essentially indicated that he knew more than anyone else what was good for the firm and closing down any attempt at examination and discussion of opposing views by the other directors.

Source: adapted from KPMG LLP (2018).

because people are not aware that they rely on them in making decisions. In your study of strategy, it is important to understand that it is this unawareness that may lead practitioners to make costly mistakes by applying heuristics in inappropriate contexts, which can lead to biased decision-making.

Hot and cold reflection and reflexion

As we have mentioned, an intuitive judgement or gut feeling is a managerial heuristic often used in strategic decision-making. But to what level of success? Whilst the field of strategic management has relied largely on behavioural and cognitive assumptions about strategizing, it has tended to privilege analytical, linear, and rational approaches over emotional intuitive alternatives. The limits of knowing and learning have been assumed to be a function of the limits of the ability of the strategist or strategic systems to process information, but rational processes have been a central idea. Increasingly, as we have already seen in this chapter, researchers argue that emotion plays a central role in decision-making and intuitive judgements. The role of emotion is particularly important when considering the emphasis on analysis and dispassionate reasoning in strategy processes.

3

This is particularly critical given the prevalence of surveys that suggest that many organizational leaders rely on 'gut feel' or 'intuition' in their strategic decisions. An Economist Intelligence Unit survey, sponsored by Applied Predictive Technologies in February 2014, revealed some interesting findings. Of the 174 executives from around the world that they surveyed, the majority described themselves as 'data-driven' or 'empirical'. Only 10% of the survey respondents described themselves as 'intuitive'. Yet, when they were asked what they do when the data contradicts their gut instinct, the majority replied that they would re-analyse the data or collect more data. Only 10% said that they would follow the course of action set out by the data, and 73% said that they trust their own intuition.

These findings are not surprising when one considers, as Argyris (1991) has argued, that senior executives have often reached their step on the career ladder by exercising good judgement. They are, consequently, confident in their 'gut instincts' and, because they are generally intelligent, they are also capable of justifying and rationalizing them. For example, consider leaders who have made successful decisions that might have seemed unusual or a poor choice but were a result of gut instinct: Henry Ford doubling his worker's wages in 1914 to combat falling demand for his cars; Anita Roddick's mixing of business and environmental activism with the founding of the Body Shop; Richard Branson selling his Virgin music label to support his fledgling airline; or Steve Jobs's bet on the iPod and then the iPad. These were all decisions, to quote late Chairman and CEO of General Electric, Jack Welch, that came 'straight from the gut'. However, such emotionally involved gut-feeling judgements can also lead to significant mistakes. Think of Decca Records turning down the Beatles, former Daimler-Benz CEO Jürgen Schrempp's disastrous merger with Chrysler, Hewlett Packard's former CEO Carly Fiorina's questionable acquisition of Compaq Computer, or former Royal Bank of Scotland's CEO Fred Goodwin's decision to acquire ABNAmro just as the 2008 financial crises was unfolding.

Decision-making and judgement are not, then, just a function of the pure computational processing or cognitive abilities of people. They also have an emotional component. Many of the experiences and patterns stored in memory that form the bases for intuitive judgements and the decisions that follow have been ascribed with emotional or psychological markers. They can be positive or negative, but their importance is that they influence one's 'gut feeling'. Some scholars, such as Hodgkinson and Healey (2011), argue that the emotional dimension of judgement and decision-making, while primarily unconscious, is particularly important for dynamic capabilities such as the sensing (and shaping) of opportunities, the seizing of opportunities, and the reconfiguring of assets and structures to maintain competitiveness. What we see and how we act—our categorizations, stereotypes, and biases—are as much a function of our unconscious emotional responses as they are of our reasoning ability.

3.6 Cognitive biases and strategic decision processes

In section 3.5, we discussed several biases impacting managerial decision-making. Since strategic decisions are often shrouded in ambiguity and uncertainty, there is no reason to expect that strategists are exempt from various biases (Schwenk 1988, 1995). But what kind of biases might practitioners exhibit in their strategic decision-making? And is there any way to avoid these biases or to reduce their negative impact? In this section, we consider common biases in strategic decision-making before discussing how strategists can improve the quality of their decision-making processes to mitigate these biases.

According to Tversky and Kahneman (1974), each heuristic (representativeness, confirmation, anchoring, and overconfidence, as listed in Table 3.2) may create cognitive biases that lead decision-makers into decision traps. Hogarth (1981) has identified 29 separate biases that are likely to occur in decision-making, while Bazerman and Moore (2008) discuss 13 types of cognitive biases found in managerial decision-making. As some biases are closely related to each other, we will concentrate on the most common biases that have been identified as impacting managerial decision-making.

Lovallo and Sibony's cognitive bias typology

Lovallo and Sibony (2010) and Kahneman et al. (2011) propose an indicative typology of cognitive biases in organizations that focuses on those decisions that occur most frequently and that may have the largest impact on business decision outcomes. These researchers identify four groups of biases:

- **action-orientation**: these biases result from intuitive decision-making that enables practitioners to act rather than spend time on complex analysis;

- **interest-seeking**: these biases result from a form of self-preservation as a decision-maker will choose an alternative that is most advantageous to him or her;

- **pattern-recognition**: seasoned practitioners pride themselves on pattern-recognition skills that are the product of years of experience, giving them confidence and trust in their decision-making capabilities to extrapolate from past experiences;

- **stability-seeking**: most people prefer stability to change and consensus to confrontation, which may prevent the decisions being challenged enough before the final decision is made.

Prospect theory

Loss aversion, one of the stability-seeking biases, is a particularly destructive bias and it lies at the centre of prospect theory and behavioural economics. Prospect theory is a behavioural model developed to explain decision-making involving uncertainty and risk and its relation to perceived gains and losses of decisions (Kahneman and Tversky 1979). Prospect theory can be considered as ground-breaking research in decision-making that highlights that human judgement is fallible and subject to biases. We will discuss prospect theory in more detail before moving on to a summary of the most common biases in each of the four groups.

Prospect theory (Kahneman and Tversky 1979) describes how people choose between different options, prospects, and how they estimate the perceived likelihood of each of these options. Consider a simple investment decision. You are offered a choice between one investment with a guaranteed $900 return or an investment that has a 90% likelihood of returning $1,000 and a 10% chance of returning $0. Research shows that when dealing with gains, people are risk averse and will choose the guaranteed return ($900) over a riskier prospect (90% chance of returning $1,000). Using rational decision-making theory, the expected value of both options is $900 (for the second option the expected value is ($1,000 × 0.9) + ($0 × 0.1) = $900).

3

Now consider a slightly different investment. You are asked to choose between losing a $900 investment or making an investment where you have a 90% chance of losing $1,000. Research shows that losses are treated in the opposite manner to gains. When aiming to avoid a loss, people become risk-seeking and take a chance with the second option over a sure loss.

These types of behaviour cannot easily be explained by the expected-utility approach. In both the aforementioned situations, the expected utility of both choices is the same (±$900): the probability multiplied by the expected win. Yet, people largely prefer one option over the other. Prospect theory explains that people demonstrate certainty and loss aversion biases when they make such decisions. People tend to overweigh options that are certain and are risk averse for gains. We would rather get an assured lesser gain than take a chance of gaining more but also risk possibly gaining nothing. The opposite is true when dealing with certain losses; people engage in risk-seeking behaviour to avoid a bigger loss.

People's reaction to loss is more extreme than their reaction to gain. In financial investment decisions, even experienced investors can get caught in loss aversion traps. As losses feel more extreme than gains, investors are often unwilling to cut their losses in their investment port-folios. Rather than cutting their losses, investors allow unrealized losses to accumulate in the hope that the investment will turn around as time goes by. This is known as a **sunk cost fallacy** or escalation of commitment bias that leads people to continue with a behaviour or endeavour because of previously invested resources (time, money, or effort).

Consider the Opening Case Study, where John Hamond had to decide whether to spend more time with his prospective client. Kitchener Group, an inexperienced real estate borrower, seemed unable to produce the required documentation which would allow the transaction to be concluded. Moreover, the transaction was small, but Hamond was keen to pursue it as he was under the impression that Kitchener Group could become a major client in the future. Finding a new client with significant upside potential would serve his career well, and hence Hamond was tempted to focus on the positives of the transaction only rather than asking him-self whether Kitchener's behaviour was a reflection of the firm's management that could be-come problematic should the bank enter into a long-term lending relationship with Kitchener. Moreover, having already spent a significant amount of time on the transaction, Hamond was unwilling to move on from it as he felt that without closing the deal, he would have wasted a lot of time and effort. The decision to keep pursuing the deal, even against all odds, which mani-fests itself as unwillingness to move on and accept the loss of time spent, is an example of sunk cost fallacy and escalation of commitment bias.

Typology of managerial biases

The most common biases are (Lovallo and Sibony 2010):

- action-orientation biases;
- interest-seeking biases;
- pattern-recognition biases;
- stability-seeking biases.

Table 3.3 describes each of these common biases, alongside an example of each. Through the decisions and activities of practitioners, these biases might influence how the process dynamics of strategizing (see Figure 2.3) play out, impacting the organizational strategy outcomes realized.

TABLE 3.3 **Most common biases**

	Description	Example
Action-orientation biases		
Overoptimism	The tendency for managers to be overoptimistic about the outcome of planned actions, to overestimate the likelihood of positive events, and to underestimate the likelihood of negative ones	Overoptimistic financial projections
Overconfidence	Overestimating one's skill level relative to those of others, leading managers to overestimate their ability to affect future outcomes, take credit for past outcomes, and neglect the role of chance	Overestimate one's ability to turn a failing company around when successive management teams have failed in the past
Competitor neglect	The tendency to plan without factoring in competitive responses	The launch of aggressive promotion campaigns without fully considering competitor response
Interest-seeking biases		
Misaligned individual incentives	Incentives for managers to adopt views or to seek outcomes favourable to their unit or themselves at the expense of the overall interest of the company; these self-serving views are often held genuinely, not cynically	Misaligned performance bonus payments that may lead to self-serving behaviour
Inappropriate attachments	Emotional attachment of individuals to people or elements of the business, creating misalignment of interests	Legacy products or brands that no longer add value to the organization
Pattern-recognition bias		
Confirmation	The overweighting of evidence consistent with a favoured belief, underweighting of evidence against a favoured belief, or failure to search impartially for evidence	The decision-making process focuses mainly on gathering supporting evidence for the favoured option
Management by example	Generalizing based on examples that are particularly recent or memorable	A recent successful high-profile advertising campaign becomes a template for all future campaigns
False analogies	Relying on comparisons with situations that are not directly comparable	A business practice that works in one geographic market is assumed to work in another market location
Champion bias	The tendency to evaluate a plan or proposal based on the track record of the person presenting it, more than on the facts supporting it	Halo effect—a high performing manager will continue to perform well in whatever they want the organization to do next
Stability-seeking biases		
Anchoring and adjustment	Managers root themselves to an initial value, leading to insufficient adjustments of subsequent estimates	The initial acquisition price of an acquisition becomes the negotiating anchor regardless of whether subsequent evaluations would indicate a significantly different value

Continued

TABLE 3.3 *Continued*

	Description	Example
Loss aversion	The tendency to feel losses more acutely than gains of the same amount, making us more risk averse than a rational calculation would suggest	Unwillingness to cut losses in the hope that things will turn around; loss aversion is a particularly destructive bias that results from prospect theory, which was covered in more detail earlier in this section
Sunk-cost fallacy	Managers pay attention to historical costs that are not recoverable when considering a future course of action	Money already spent on the project may lead into an 'escalation of commitment' by committing more funds into a project that may be failing; this is closely linked to loss aversion
Status quo bias	Managers prefer the status quo in the absence of pressure to change it	Managers are unwilling to adopt to changing market conditions until it may be too late
Social biases		
Groupthink	Striving for consensus at the cost of a realistic appraisal of alternative courses of action	In a group meeting, one is not willing to express a concern or a contrary view to what is being discussed to preserve consensus
Sunflower management	Tendency for groups to align with the views of their leaders, whether expressed or assumed	Unwillingness to express a contrary view for the fear that such a view could be perceived as having a negative attitude

Source: Lovallo, D. and Sibony, O. (2010). The case for behavioural strategy. *McKinsey Quarterly on Behavioral Strategy* (January), https://www.mckinsey.com/capabilities/strategy-and-corporate-finance/our-insights/the-case-for-behavioral-strategy (last accessed 19 October 2022).

Because cognitive biases are deeply embedded into the human psyche, they are difficult to detect in our own behaviours. In fact, Kahneman (2011) states that being aware of heuristics and biases does not debias one's own behaviour. However, while we may not be able to control our own intuitions, we are able to apply rational thought to detect biases in the decision-making of others. To do this, we need to first understand the nature and context of biases and then develop processes to challenge the recommendations of others. Senior managers are often expected to review recommendations and make a final call. When reviewing recommendations, practitioners often add a rather crude safety margin for biases or errors, but they very rarely undertake a systematic review of recommendations put forward to them that challenges the assumptions and the projected outcomes of the recommended decisions.

How can practitioners detect biases in strategic decisions?

Based on research with senior executives, Kahneman et al. (2011, 2021) developed a rigorous process aimed at identifying cognitive biases which may have influenced employees putting recommendations forward for senior manager approval. The aim of the process outlined in Table 3.4 is to help managers retrace steps back in the decision process where heuristics may

TABLE 3.4 **Process for evaluating recommendations for strategic decisions**

Check	Question to ask	Action to take
1. Check for interest-seeking bias	Is there any reason to expect that the team is making a recommendation based on self-interest?	Review the proposal, paying attention for overoptimism bias
2. Check for affect heuristic and interest-seeking bias	Has the team fallen in love with their proposal?	Check the process by which the proposed recommendation was formulated
3. Check for groupthink	Were there dissenting opinions within the team?	Check whether dissenting opinions were explored adequately Solicit dissenting views if in doubt
4. Check for false analogies bias	Could the recommendation be overly influenced by analogy with a memorable success?	Ask for more analogies and rigorously analyse their similarity to the current situation
5. Check for conformation bias	Are credible alternatives included with the recommendation?	Request additional options
6. Check for availability heuristic	If this decision were to be made a year from now, what information would be required, and can it be obtained now?	Create a checklist of the data needed for an informed decision
7. Check for anchoring bias	Where do projections come from? Are there any unsubstantiated numbers, extrapolation from the past, a motivation to use some base line as an anchor?	Re-anchor with figures generated from other models or benchmarks, and request a new analysis
8. Check for champion bias	Is the team assuming that a person, organization, or particular approach that is successful in one area can be just as successful in another?	Eliminate false interferences, and ask the team to seek additional comparable examples
9. Check for sunk-cost fallacy	Is the team overly attached to a history of past decisions?	Consider the issue if you had just joined the organization with the decision-making responsibility
10. Check for overoptimism	Is the base case overly optimistic?	Has the team built a case taking an outside view Consider war-gaming the decision
11. Check for overconfidence	Is the worst-case scenario bad enough?	Have the team conduct a premortem: imagine that the worst has happened, and develop a story about the causes of the failure
12. Check for loss aversion	Is the recommending team overly cautious?	Realign incentives to share responsibility for the risk, or consider how to reduce or eliminate risk

Source: adapted from Kahneman, D., Lovallo, D., and Sibony, O. (2011). The big idea: Before you make that big decision. *Harvard Business Review* (June), 51–60.

3

have steered people or groups astray. Senior executives are often tasked with approving what has been recommended by working groups. It is at this stage that senior practitioners should offer a final challenge to the decision that has been put in front of them for approval, which is also a means of safeguarding themselves against their own biases.

Embedding these practices into formal organizational decision-making procedures ensures that managers become familiar with processes that may improve the quality of their own decision-making in situations where they have the final say in a decision. As the processes become part of the organization's way of conducting business, they are used with regularity, not just when managers are unsure of which way to call a decision. Another important reason for adopting such decision-making procedures is to safeguard against overconfidence and overoptimism biases of senior decision-makers themselves.

3.7 Group decision-making

The process for evaluating strategic decisions outlined in Table 3.4 is targeted at senior executives who may have the ultimate say in a decision. But how should we understand and improve the processes for evaluating strategic problems and identifying diverse solutions to such problems? As most strategic decision problems are worked on in groups, in this section we explore the nature of collective decision-making. We also look at how organizations can effectively use group decision-making practices to improve the overall quality of their problem identification and solution development capabilities.

In complex decision situations, groups have been shown to have better problem-solving capabilities than individuals acting alone (Daft et al. 1993; van Ginkel and van Knippenberg 2009). This may be because group members bring a variety of information, critical judgement, solution strategies, and a wide range of perspectives to the decision problem. However, groups can be subject to conflict and, just as individuals, they can be subject to cognitive biases. Conflict and biases may hinder the quality of decision outcomes and group members' decision acceptance. In this section of the chapter, we start by discussing different manifestations of conflict and go on to discuss different group biases (Arevuo 2015).

Cognitive and affective conflict

Research into group decision-making has shown that group member interaction may lead to **cognitive conflict** (Hambrick 1994; Amason 1996). Cognitive conflict arises when a number of possible solutions are suggested by different group members. These solutions compete against each other when group members debate the relative merits of each solution. We can think of cognitive conflict as a competition of ideas among the group members.

Pioneering work by Amason (1996) provided a convincing argument that cognitive conflict is beneficial in collective decision-making, and this has become widely accepted by scholars. The accepted assumption is that cognitive conflict improves decision-making quality. Therefore, this has prompted researchers to explore how to create cognitive conflict in collective decision-making situations. A great deal of research has accumulated on decision-making techniques that encourage critical interaction between decision-making group members. We will discuss some of the most common techniques in turn.

Consensus decision-making

Consensus decision-making is probably the most common group decision-making approach where the agreement of all involved is sought for a decision. Consensus decision-making is about persuasion and compromise, not necessarily about what is the best decision or what works best. Consensus is about human interaction that is rooted in emotions, jumping to conclusions, and negotiation, and it may or may not include facts and analysis to support the decision.

Consensus approach makes people feel as if they have done their jobs because they have reached an acceptable and a workable conclusion. It also distributes the blame when things go wrong: 'Not my fault. It was a group decision' or 'I had to go along with it, otherwise I would have dragged down the whole group.' Consensus is a shortcut that often falls short of right action and settles for acceptable action (Alexander 2019). This sharing of blame for bad decisions may also result in a consensus group seeking a higher-risk solution that is always an endemic problem in group decisions in general.

Groupthink is particularly prevalent in consensus decision-making. It stifles creativity, suffocates independent thinking, and settles on the ideas that are most acceptable to most of the people in the group, whether or not they're the best ideas. Committees are notorious for groupthink, as are other collections of people such as work teams, political parties, families, and boards of directors. Groupthink leads to consensus because groups of people tend to gravitate to the ideas of the people who speak up in the group, the ones who speak early and with confidence.

Alexander (2019) has put forward suggestions to help groups to improve the quality of consensus decision-making:

1. *Get the commitment of the group, especially the group leader, to find the right decision with the given information, not just settle for consensus, and ensure that the group's leader is committed to getting the best thinking from everyone, even those who are normally reluctant to speak.*

2. *Get group members to express their thoughts first, before they've been influenced by the group.*

3. *Require the group to consider all points of view, their pros and cons.*

4. *Don't reject an idea because it is unpopular.*

5. *Don't jump to conclusions. Interrogate for facts and expose assumptions to scrutiny.*

In consensus decision-making no decision is made against the will of an individual or a minority. If significant concerns remain unresolved, a proposal can be blocked and prevented from going ahead. This means that the whole group must work hard at finding solutions that address everyone's concerns rather than ignoring or overruling minority opinions.

Devil's advocacy and **dialectical enquiry** have been shown to create more cognitive conflict in decision-making groups compared with the consensus approach. Research by Schweiger et al. (1986) indicated that both dialectical enquiry and devil's advocacy led to higher-quality assumptions and decision outcomes than the consensus approach to decision-making. However, decision-makers in consensus groups expressed more satisfaction and desire to continue to work with their groups and indicated a greater level of decision acceptance than those groups who were asked to apply dialectical enquiry and devil's advocacy in their decision-making process.

 Access the online resources to watch a short video clip where Professor Bernie Bulkin OBE discusses groupthink and behaviour.

Devil's advocacy

Devil's advocacy involves a group developing a solid argument for a recommended course of action and subjecting that recommendation to an in-depth formal critique. The critique calls into question the assumptions and recommendations presented to the **devil's advocate** and attempts to show why the recommendations should *not* be adopted.

Because good recommendations based on solid assumptions will survive even the most forceful and effective criticism, this approach is likely to yield sound judgements or recommendations.

There are seven steps for groups to follow in using the devil's advocacy approach to solve strategic problems (adapted from Schweiger et al. 1986):

1. Identify a problem needing group analysis and decision-making.

2. Divide the group or team into two subgroups of equal size.

3. Assign one subgroup to play devil's advocate (DA subgroup) and the other to develop a consensus recommendation for the decision problem (CO subgroup).

4. After separating into subgroups, instruct the CO group to develop a set of recommendations and build an argument for them, supported by all the key assumptions, facts, and data that underlie them. This group writes out the recommendations, assumptions, facts, and data on a whiteboard or large piece of paper. Meanwhile, instruct the DA subgroup to prepare for their critique by discussing the case and identifying critical assumptions, data, and facts that the other group might miss. Then, bring the subgroups together.

5. Instruct the CO subgroup to present its recommendations and assumptions to the DA subgroup.

6. The DA subgroup critiques the recommendations, attempting to uncover all that is wrong with the recommendations, assumptions, facts, and data and explaining why the recommendations should not be adopted.

7. Separate the subgroups again so that the CO group revises its recommendations to answer the critiques while the DA group works to find more critiques that would strengthen the recommendation.

Repeat Steps 4 and 5 until both subgroups can accept the recommendations, assumptions, and data. Once both subgroups agree on a recommended solution, move forward and enact the recommendations.

A group may appoint a devil's advocate to argue against the prevailing ideas, position, or decision of the group. While a devil's advocate can simply play a contrary role, someone who argues against a particular idea can also stimulate discussion which can identify weak points in an argument that need to be addressed. Therefore, one could consider this approach extremely useful, albeit stressful for someone advocating alone against an accepted idea in a group. However, while devil's advocacy takes into consideration many alternatives, it is true to say that it concentrates quite heavily on the shortcomings, or negatives, of the approach to an idea.

Dialectical enquiry

Dialectical enquiry is a more balanced approach than devil's advocacy as it gives equal importance to the positives and the negatives of alternatives. Like devil's advocacy, dialectical enquiry is another approach to collective decision-making. The technique can be traced back to the dialectic school of philosophy in ancient Greece. Plato and his followers attempted to define what constitutes a truth by exploring opposite positions, called thesis and antithesis. Essentially, dialectical enquiry is a debate between two opposing sets of viewpoints. Although it stimulates programmed conflict, it is a constructive approach because it elicits the benefits and limitations of opposing sets of ideas.

Organizations that use dialectical enquiry create teams of decision-makers. Each team is instructed to generate and evaluate alternative courses of action and then recommend the best one. After hearing each team's alternative courses of action, the teams and the organization's top managers meet and select the best parts of each plan and synthesize a final plan that provides the best opportunity for success. The process can be broken down to five steps (adapted from Schweiger et al. 1986):

1. The process begins with the formation of two or more divergent groups to represent the full range of views on a specific problem. Each group is made as internally homogeneous as possible. However, the groups should be as different from one another as possible. Collectively, they cover all positions that might have an impact on the ultimate solution to a problem.

2. Each group meets separately, identifies the assumptions behind its position, and rates them on their importance and feasibility. Each group then presents a 'for' and an 'against' position to the other groups.

3. Each group debates the other groups' positions and defends its own. The goal is not to convince others but to confirm that what each group expresses as its position is not necessarily accepted by others.

4. Information that is provided by all the groups is analysed. This results in the identification of information gaps and establishes guidelines for further research on the problem.

5. An attempt is made to achieve consensus among the positions. Strategies are sought that will best meet the requirements of all positions that remain viable. This final step permits the further refinement of information needed to solve the problem.

Scenario planning

Scenario planning has been used in a variety of organizational settings to explore future uncertainty to support strategic thinking and decision-making. The scenario process often involves a variety of different stakeholder groups and participants. We will explore scenario planning further in Chapter 5 as a way of considering the strategic implications of developments in an organization's external context. As a strategic decision-making aid, the scenario planning process typically consists of three phases (Ringland 2006):

- a 'preparatory' phase, where the purpose and focus of the exercise is agreed and driving forces (e.g. via PESTEL analysis, see Chapter 5) are identified;

- a 'development' phase involving the development of the scenarios themselves;

- a 'use' phase when the scenarios are used for their intended purpose, such as developing and testing strategies.

Facilitated workshops are a common setting in scenario planning. During workshops, participants progress through the stages of the process and generate content related to each stage in the process, including developing and using the scenarios themselves (O'Brien et al. 2017).

When a group of strategists set out to use scenario planning to support their strategy practice, several key issues arise (O'Brien and Meadows 2013):

1. Participants must understand the implications of a set of scenarios for their own organization.

   Burt et al. (2006) suggest that the scenario process can move participants towards a mindset of 'our' environment to understand the implications of their own analysis. The aim of scenario analysis is not to obtain forecasts of the future but to highlight crucial uncertainties that may impact upon the strategic decisions that managers must make. Ringland (2010) notes that 'senior managers spend much of their time on current, internal issues' and that scenario planning provides a non-threatening framework for a discussion where managers can surface issues of concern and move towards a more strategic conversation. O'Brien et al. (2007) suggest the use of the SWOT tool as a framework for organizing an assessment of future opportunities and threats that emerge from an analysis of the future external environment (using scenario planning) with an assessment of the strengths and weaknesses of current resources and competencies (taking a resource-based view perspective, see Chapter 6).

2. Scenarios can be used to develop a range of possible strategic options for the organization.

   The use of multiple future scenarios is intended to enrich the 'portfolio of possible strategic initiatives' (van der Heijden 2004), leading to action, new experience, and new understanding of the business environment. Organizations need to articulate the range of options open for action. O'Brien et al. (2007) describe the use of TOWS (see Chapter 15), a tool to generate strategic options based on an analysis of the externally focused opportunities and threats arising from each future scenario combined with an assessment of the current strengths and weaknesses of internal resources and competences.

3. Scenarios can be used to evaluate strategic options.

   Harries (2003) notes that one of the major pillars of scenario planning is that it is a solid basis to test the robustness of plans of action. Put simply, organizations need to know when to act and, just as importantly, when not to act. At this option evaluation stage in the scenario planning process, the set of scenarios should be used to test potential decisions against the set of assumptions contained in the scenario stories (Chermack and van der Merwe 2003).

Causal mapping

Ackermann and Eden (2011) and Bryson et al. (2014) advocate that a visual decision-making technique based on 'causal mapping' methods might help groups to improve their strategic decision-making processes. Visual tools are particularly useful in strategy work as strategic decisions are often made collectively in group working situations.

In a **causal map**, ideas are causally linked to one another using arrows and nodes. The arrows indicate how one idea or action leads to another in a means–ends relationship. In effect, the maps are word-and-arrow diagrams where the arrows mean 'might cause', 'might lead to', or 'might result in'. Causal mapping facilitates a visual representation of many ideas, actions, and their consequences (Bryson et al. 2004). An example of a fully developed strategy map is shown in Figure 3.1. This map incorporates the collective understanding of a decision problem (our Opening Case Study 'To lend or not to lend?') by a decision-making group. The group used a whiteboard and sticky notes to develop a solution to the problem.

Note how the map has been constructed in a non-linear way with groups of clustered sticky notes. All causal maps are non-linear as they reflect how we really think, and the clustered notes reflect the critical issues in the decision problem. Although a fully developed causal map may seem disorganized, the mapping process follows a logical structure.

Mapping starts by identifying the problem. Once the problem has been identified, our attention turns to thinking about possible solutions. The critical aspect of this step is not only to identify possible solutions but also to assess their feasibility. If a possible solution cannot be

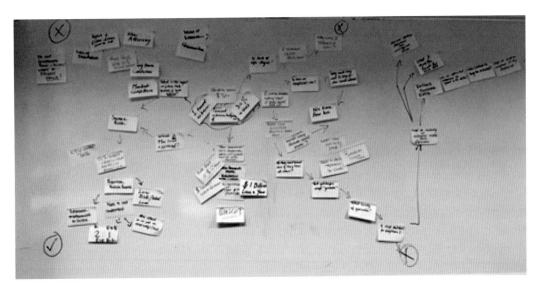

FIGURE 3.1 Causal map of the case study 'To lend or not to lend?'. *Source:* adapted from Arevuo, M., Reinmoeller, P., and Huff, A.S. (2017). How maps are made matters: Enacting artifacts in collective decision making. *Academy of Management Annual Meeting Proceedings*, **2017**(1), 1.

3

implemented for whatever reason, it should be rejected at the early stage of the discussion. An example of a possible solution to competitor threat is acquisition of the competing firm. However, if the company lacks the financial resources to execute this, acquisition as a possible solution is unfeasible and another solution to competitor threat must be found.

Once feasible solutions have been identified, the decision-makers consider the consequences of the alternative solutions. For example, if the firm has the financial resources to carry out the acquisition of the competing firm, the decision-makers should consider what consequences such an action would have on the firm more widely. For example, the acquisition could require a significant commitment of management and financial resources. If these resources were to be used for the acquisition, what would be the trade-offs and their consequences for the other operational aspects of the firm? Given the consequences of this option, is it still the best possible option in view of the resource constraints and the overall strategy of the firm? The answers to these types of question involve making all possible connections between solution options and consequences.

Causal maps that have been created in groups bring together the thinking of many people, including conflicting views, subtly different slants on the same issues, and different perspectives held by individual group members. Such group causal maps provide simplified representations of the beliefs present in the group. They may not necessarily be a representation of the reality perceived by any one individual or all the group members. Rather, a group map is a collectively constructed and shared account of a given situation by all group members (Arevuo 2015).

Group mapping could be perceived simplistically as a form of brainstorming. However, Eden and Ackerman (2010) draw a distinction between group maps and a free-flowing brainstorming of ideas. Group mapping that is used for decision-making is focused on raising issues and concerns. These are usually activities or events that can either support or challenge the decision-making aspiration of the group. In contrast with eliciting 'off-the-wall' ideas in group brainstorming sessions as the means of unleashing creativity, group mapping focuses on bringing together the current wisdom and experience of the group members as well as issues surrounding the problem situation. Therefore, group mapping is a process of engaging in a dialogue to uncover the causality between the problem and a number of potential solution outcomes, represented as a map. This process provides the means for the decision-making group to structure and merge differing perspectives that should eventually lead to a shared understanding of the issue in a holistic manner, enabling effective group decision-making such as is required in strategizing.

Increased cognitive conflict can result in affective conflict

As we have seen, the exposure of groups to various decision-making techniques can increase the level of cognitive conflict and improve the quality of the decision-making processes. This is achieved through group participants having to consider diverse alternative perspectives. However, further research suggests that although cognitive conflict may increase performance through better-quality decision-making, there is a danger that the beneficial cognitive conflict spills into a dysfunctional **affective conflict** (Parayitam and Dooley 2011). Affective conflict arises when the competition of ideas spills over into a personal conflict. The conflict is no longer limited to the competition between ideas but becomes a conflict between individuals who hold opposing views. Affective conflict, or a conflict between group members, can become destructive to the functioning of the group as a cohesive unit. Cognitive conflict has been shown to improve decision-making quality, while affective conflict has been demonstrated to have a negative impact on decision acceptance by group members as individuals become so wedded to their opinions that the group cannot make a decision on which all members agree (Parayitam and Dooley 2007, 2009). In other words, a high level of cognitive conflict may result in the best possible decision outcome in the given circumstances, but the stressful or pressurized environment created by the process of reaching the decision may also have resulted in tensions amongst the group members.

Devil's advocacy and dialectical enquiry are particularly vulnerable to the emergence of affective conflict. Decision-making group members become so attached to their own views that they perceive other group members with differing or challenging positions with hostility. If this hostility is allowed to escalate, it may result in a dysfunctional group and the group members may become unwilling to collaborate with each other in the current or any future group work situations.

Affective conflict tends to be emotional and focuses on personal incompatibilities or disputes. These disputes result from group members' personal judgements that they are not fully able to articulate to other decision-making group members. The more these personal judgements influence decisions, the more there is potential for decision-making group members to speculate and find reasons to distrust the motivation and hidden agendas of their fellow members. Hence, too much affective conflict may hinder overall group performance as the decision is not accepted by some decision-making group members regardless of the quality of the decision outcome. Research by Parayitam and Dooley (2011) indicates that too much cognitive conflict in a decision-making group may breed contempt. Therefore, they suggest that moderate levels of cognitive conflict should be maintained to ensure high-quality decision outcomes, but, in order to maintain group cohesion, managers should be mindful that cognitive conflict is positively correlated with affective conflict (Arevuo 2015). Left unchecked, affective conflict could have a detrimental influence on strategizing process dynamics.

Group decision-making biases

In addition to the cognitive biases that affect individual decision-making (discussed in section 3.6) there are several biases which pose specific challenges for group decision-making. The growing recognition of the prevalence of cognitive biases in strategic decision-making has resulted in an increased interest in how biases affect strategic thinking in collective decision-making situations.

Groups tend to make riskier decisions than individuals because risk is perceived to be shared by the group as a collective rather than borne by one individual decision-maker alone (Stoner 1968). In addition, the Abilene paradox (Harvey 1988) and 'groupthink' are two of the ever-present biases that lurk in the background in most group decision-making situations. In the Abilene paradox, a group collectively decides on a course of action that is counter to the

3

preferences of many or all the individuals in the group. It involves a common breakdown of group communication in which each member mistakenly believes that their own preferences are counter to those of the group and therefore does not raise objections. A common phrase relating to the Abilene paradox is a desire not to 'rock the boat'. This differs from *groupthink* in that the Abilene paradox is characterized by the group members 'guessing' what decision the others might prefer, without exploring options, so they may reach a decision for which nobody had any preference. As introduced earlier in this chapter, groupthink occurs within a group in which the desire for harmony or conformity results in an irrational or dysfunctional decision outcome (Janis 1972). This means that group members try to minimize conflict and reach a consensus decision without undertaking a critical evaluation of alternative viewpoints by both actively suppressing dissenting viewpoints and isolating themselves from outside influences.

Groupthink requires individuals to avoid raising controversial issues or alternative solutions, and there is a loss of individual creativity, uniqueness, and independent thinking. Dysfunctional group dynamics produce an 'illusion of invulnerability', an inflated feeling of certainty that the right decision has been made. As a result of this dysfunctional dynamic, the group can significantly overrate its own abilities in decision-making as well as significantly underrate the abilities of its opponents. This relates to our discussion about overconfidence bias in section 3.6.

So, how do groups avoid the Abilene paradox and groupthink? Nutt (2002), in his research into 'failed' decisions, has pointed out that the development of sound group decision-making processes is critical for groups to achieve meaningful decision outcomes. He considers the effective decision-making process to comprise five stages (Arevuo 2015):

1. collecting information to understand the claims calling for action;
2. establishing a direction that indicates the desired result;
3. engaging in a systematic search for ideas;
4. evaluating these ideas with the direction in mind;
5. managing the social and political barriers that can block the preferred course of action during the decision implementation stage.

We have seen how complex decision-making can be in practice. There are many decision-making traps that lurk beneath the surface. They range from our cognitive limitations and biases to group dynamics and behaviours. Therefore, the development and adoption of tools such as causal mapping to help decision-makers in eliciting multiple perspectives, provide the means for groups to produce substantive decision outcomes, and achieve agreement and decision buy-in is critical to successful strategy development and implementation.

3.8 Structured approach to strategic decisions

In this chapter, we have seen that strategic decision-making requires evaluative human judgement to distil a large amount of complex information into actionable decisions while being confronted with environmental uncertainty and information ambiguity. To accomplish this, the decision-maker can either (a) use the rational, prescriptive decision-making model to allocate quantitative scores for competing options or (b) use judgement to determine the best possible path forward.

We know that human judgement is subject to errors that stem from cognitive biases. In addition, judgement is subject to random errors—noise—that may expose the decision-maker to unhelpful factors that are irrelevant to the decision. Unreliability in human judgement has been studied for years, particularly in the context of employee-hiring decisions. Kahneman et. al. (2019, 2021) draw inspiration from this body of research and have developed a broadly applicable approach to reducing errors in strategic decision-making whenever a plan or a strategic option requires consideration and weighting of multiple dimensions of the decision. The approach is known as **Mediating assessment protocol (MAP)** and is based on the similarity between the evaluation of a strategic option and the evaluation of a job candidate. The MAP process (Kahneman et. al 2021) has three main stages:

1. **Define the mediating assessments in advance of the decision**: identification of a short list of independent mediating assessments that are critical to the evaluation of the strategic option. For example, in a corporate acquisition evaluation, in addition to financial modelling the assessments may include the quality of the target firm's management team and anticipated synergies that the acquisition is expected to capture.

2. **Use fact-based, independently made assessments**: undertake research or gather evidence on the key mediating assessments and conduct an independent evaluation/rating of the mediating assessment data.

3. **Make the decision once independent assessments are complete**: if the analysis and evaluation in Stage 2 has been truly independent, then there should be differences in the evaluation of data. Excessive coherence could indicate a problem in the independence of analysis. Discrepancies in evaluations/ratings are a positive outcome as they raise questions and debate. Diverse results will not make the decision easier, but they will make it better.

The final decision should be discussed only after each key attribute has been scored independently by each member of the decision-making group and a complete profile of the assessments has been revealed. An obvious objection to this type of decision-making is that the key assessments are not weighted, and it may seem mechanistic. However, we should not consider this as a computational approach. In fact, what this process has achieved is to delay intuition in the decision-making process. Once all the assessments have been scored and the full profile has been revealed by the process, it is time for the decision-making group to bring its judgement into the final decision. We examine further how structured processes of decision-making can be applied in strategizing activities in Chapter 15.

PRACTITIONER INSIGHT **PROFESSOR BERNIE BULKIN OBE, PROFESSOR OF CHEMISTRY, FORMER CHIEF SCIENTIST AND SENIOR EXECUTIVE AT BP, VENTURE CAPITALIST, AND RADIO BROADCASTER AND COLUMNIST**

Drawing on his varied and impressive career as Professor of Chemistry, former chief scientist and senior executive at BP, venture capitalist, and radio broadcaster and columnist, Professor Bernie Bulkin OBE shares his thoughts on management and decision-making through his life experiences. In our discussion, he tells us that not only should one focus on organizational and business activities to gain insight into many aspects of leadership and management, but also learning should be derived through a life that is well lived and keenly observed.

Many executives try to avoid jury service as serving in a trial could take them away from their business commitments for a protracted period. Professor Bulkin says that this is a mistake, not only because we have certain civic duties but also because such service presents an opportunity to learn aspects of decision-making and team-building that one would not learn on any course.

Most business teams are established for the long term, but, from time to time, diverse teams have to come together for short periods of intense work to find a solution to a problem or get a deal done. This is what a jury must do, as Professor Bulkin reflected when he found himself serving in a gang murder trial in New York City. However, unlike in business, where the final decision is made by the leader based on discussions among peers or recommendations from front-line managers, who will ultimately be accountable for it, in a jury room everyone must be in on the decision and must stand up and support the verdict. It can be quite instructive how people from all walks of life can come together and collectively reach a unanimous agreement on what constitutes a strategic decision, reflects Professor Bulkin. A verdict in a murder trial is obviously an important strategic decision as it will have far-reaching consequences for the defendant.

The testimony lasted for nine days including the final prosecution and defence statements. On the

morning of day 10, the judge addressed the jurors, explaining the need for proof beyond reasonable doubt. He also explained circumstantial evidence and under what circumstance the jury could accept it as a consideration of innocence or guilt. Finally, he moved on to discuss what, in New York State law, constituted self-defence. 'Having sat through nine days of a vast amount of testimony it was not until the very end of the proceedings that we heard this crucial bit of law on self-defence, the organizing principle according to which we had to assess the evidence', says Professor Bulkin. 'Do we sometimes do this in our meetings, in a lead-up to a decision? Do we keep back the key point until the last, perhaps to increase its impact or because we see it as a way of increasing our own impact on the group?'

The jury was dismissed to consider the evidence and the members were instructed that if they were still debating at 10 p.m. that evening they would be taken to a hotel overnight and brought back the following morning. Nine days of evidence and the judge's instructions on law were narrowed down to perhaps an hour of evidence that was relevant to the question of innocence or guilt. The majority of the jurors favoured a 'Not guilty' verdict, but some were wavering. 'At 8.30 p.m. a court police officer came to the jury room to inform us that we had to give him the names and telephone numbers of our families, given that if we had not reached a verdict within the next 90 minutes we would be sent to a hotel for the night.'

'The judge must have been very familiar with juror behaviour and knew that sending the officer in might catalyse a decision', says Professor Bulkin. So it proved, and the jury reached a unanimous

'Not guilty' verdict. Without a time limit, groups can keep debating for ever, but, as the 10 p.m. deadline loomed, the jurors in this case were motivated to get off the fence and make a decision.

When we work on important decisions, we need to be able to see the wood for the trees and focus on what is critical information for the decision—the rest is noise. Professor Bulkin says that the consideration of 'business risks' is on the agenda of every board meeting, but the evidence for ineffectual risk management in big corporations is all around us. One of the main problems is that we focus on wrong things entirely by not identifying the real underlying risks. For example, a manager might identify the failure to deliver promised growth as a major risk. In response, they might strengthen the sales force in order to deliver growth. However, this is basic management, not risk management.

Another reason where corporations fail in risk management is by not paying attention to past performance. Although past performance is not an indicator of the future in everything, it can be an indicator of a trend. Have there been two or three environmental incidents that have resulted in fines or an increasing frequency of minor incidents? An increase in the frequency of such incidents is a good indicator of a higher probability of a major incident. Boards must have the data to enable them to probe this with the management.

Finally, slick processes should not be a substitute for substantive presentation. The management has access to numerous beautiful graphics programmes for the board risk discussion agenda item. Among the papers for the board meeting there is a big foldout chart in many colours, displaying the risks. These charts are things of beauty and when they come out board members are lulled into thinking that everything is under control. 'It isn't. The thing that is under control is the use of the graphics programme.'

 Access the online resources to watch a short video clip where Professor Bernie Bulkin OBE talks more about his career.

Source

More insights on business and leadership are covered in Professor Bulkin's collection of vignettes:

Bulkin, B. (2015). *Crash Course: One Year to Become a Great Leader in a Great Company*. London: Whitefox.

 ## CHAPTER SUMMARY

In this chapter, we addressed the following learning outcomes:

○ **Distinguish strategic decisions from routine decisions.**

Most of our decisions are routine decisions that do not require much effort. In contrast, strategic decisions involve problems that do not have simple solutions. Strategic decisions are large, expensive, and precedent-setting, complex decisions that are made under conditions of volatility, ambiguity, and uncertainty of the final decision outcome. Once a strategic decision is made and implemented, it is difficult to reverse as both financial and human resources have been committed to the decision, at least in the short term.

○ **Evaluate the impact of common heuristics and biases to organizational decision-making.**

Heuristics are useful for practitioners as they can reduce the need for or totally circumvent the search for information to support a decision. However, they can result in biases that can lead into adverse consequences and decision outcomes. Human judgement is unreliable and susceptible to errors that can stem from cognitive biases or random errors.

3

○ Analyse the differences between rational and cognitive approaches to decision-making in organizations.

Rational decision-making is a multistep process for making optimal choices between alternatives. The rational decision-making process is based on logic, objectivity, and analysis over subjectivity, insight, and judgement. In contrast, cognitive decision-making models suggest that decision-making requires judgement that is bounded in its rationality, and we can better understand decision-making by describing and explaining actual decisions rather than by focusing on what should be done rationally in decision-making processes. Even if we were able to identify an optimum decision outcome, other people in our organizations may have agendas that prevent us from pursuing the optimum decision. In practice, we aim to make decisions that are based on sufficient analysis and which produce a satisfactory outcome for all key stakeholders.

○ Apply practical decision-making tools in group decision-making.

Most strategic decision-making takes place in groups. We introduced several decision-making tools that groups can use to improve the quality of their collective decision-making processes: devil's advocacy, dialectical enquiry, the Delphi method, and causal mapping. We noted that while consensus decision-making may demonstrate the highest degree of collective buy-in into a decision, collective decision-making tends to be the least creative and innovative decision-making process.

○ Examine the tools and techniques available for managers to improve the quality of their strategic decision-making processes.

As the outcomes of strategic decisions unfold in an uncertain future, the key challenge for decision-makers is to improve their strategic decision-making processes so that the decision that is made is the best possible within the limitations of bounded rationality. We identified a number of tools that decision-makers can apply to improve their decision-making processes by debiasing their decision-making and increasing the degree of cognitive conflict in collective decision-making, while at the same time reducing the potential for the emergence of affective conflict.

(?) END-OF-CHAPTER QUESTIONS

Recall questions

1. What are the key differences between routine and strategic decisions?
2. What are the characteristics of strategic decisions?
3. What are the most common heuristics and biases in managerial decision-making?
4. What is a mediating assessment protocol?

Application questions

A) You and your team are working on a problem that has far-reaching consequences for your firm. You decide to bring your team together to work on the problem. How could you organize the team to ensure that the potential solutions to the problem have been fully analysed and that all team members agree to the solution?

B) In your role as the head of the marketing department, you have the final say on the firm's decision on future advertising strategy and the budget. How would you evaluate the recommendation that has been presented to you?

C) Can you give examples of any biases you have experienced when making decisions in your personal life? In hindsight, do you feel that you made the right decision? Strategy mapping is a tool to create a visual representation of a problem. What do you think are the benefits and difficulties of using strategy maps in collective decision-making and why?

D) You have been asked to design a process for making an important strategic decision on a corporate acquisition. Using the MAP, design a step-by-step process from the first meeting where the acquisition is first discussed to the final decision.

ONLINE RESOURCES

www.oup.com/he/mackay2e

In addition to the video interviews already highlighted, the book's **online resources** include the following features for this chapter, specifically:

– *links to further reading material* to broaden your knowledge of key issues discussed in this chapter;

– *self-test multiple-choice questions* to test your understanding of the material covered in each section of the chapter; and

– *a flashcard glossary* to help you recall and test your understanding of key terms.

FURTHER READING

Visual Strategy: Strategy Mapping for Public and Non-profit Organizations by John M. Bryson, Fran Ackermann, and Colin Eden

Bryson, J.M., Ackermann, F., and Eden, C. (2014). *Visual Strategy: Strategy Mapping for Public and Non-Profit Organizations*. San Francisco, CA: John Wiley.

This is a how-to book on causal mapping. The authors show how causal mapping prevents groups of people from talking over one another and going round in circles. It helps people to speak and be heard, produce lots of ideas and understand how they fit together, make use of causal reasoning, and clarify ultimately what they want to do in terms of mission, goals, strategies, and actions.

3

'A structured approach to strategic decisions' by Daniel Kahneman, Dan Lovallo, and Olivier Sibony

Kahneman, D., Lovallo, D., and Sibony, O. (2019). A Structured Approach to Strategic Decisions. *MIT Sloan Management Review*, **60**(3), https://sloanreview.mit.edu/article/a-structured-approach-to-strategic-decisions (last accessed 19 October 2022).

The article suggests a practical and broadly applicable approach to reducing errors in strategic decision-making. This can be accomplished through the MAP, which is a structured approach to grounding strategic decisions, like interviews, on mediating assessments.

Thinking, Fast and Slow by Daniel Kahneman

Kahneman, D. (2011). *Thinking, Fast and Slow*. New York: Macmillan.

This book gives a tour of the mind and explains the two systems that drive the way we think. System 1 is fast, intuitive, and emotional; System 2 is slower, more deliberative, and more logical. The impact of overconfidence on corporate strategies, the difficulties of predicting what will make us happy in the future, the profound effect of cognitive biases on everything from playing the stock market to planning our next holiday: each of these can be understood only by knowing how the two systems shape our judgements and decisions.

'Prospect theory: An analysis of decision under risk' by Daniel Kahneman and Amos Tversky

Kahneman, D. and Tversky, A. (1979). Prospect theory: An analysis of decision under risk. *Econometrics*, **47**(2), 263–91.

This seminal article was published in the journal Econometrica and it has become that journal's most cited article of all time. In 2002, Kahneman was awarded the Nobel Prize in Economics for their work (Tversky had sadly died before the prize was awarded). It describes Kahneman and Tversky's prospect theory, an explanation of how people choose between different options and how they estimate the perceived likelihood of each of these options. Prospect theory can be considered as ground-breaking research in decision-making which highlights that human judgement is fallible and subject to biases.

'The structure of 'unstructured' decision processes' by Henry Mintzberg, Duru Raisinghani, and André Théorêt

Mintzberg, H., Raisinghani, D., and Théorêt, A. (1976). The structure of 'unstructured' decision processes. *Administrative Science Quarterly*, **21**(2), 246–75.

A field study of 25 strategic decision processes, together with a review of the related empirical literature, which suggests that a basic structure underlies these 'unstructured' processes. This structure is described in terms of 12 elements: three central phases, three sets of supporting routines, and six sets of dynamic factors. This article discusses each of these elements in turn and then proposes a general model to describe their interrelationships. The 25 strategic decision processes studied are then shown to fall into seven types of path configurations through the model.

Handbook of Decision Making edited by Paul C. Nutt and David C. Wilson

Nutt, P.C. and Wilson, D.C. (eds) (2010). *Handbook of Decision Making*. Chichester: John Wiley.

This book is an important reference text for all students of and professionals in management, organization, and decision-making. It offers a wide range of theoretical and empirical approaches to the understanding of organizational and strategic decisions. The chapters bring together a critical mass of writing on decision-making as an organizational and research activity. The book offers an appraisal of the field and suggestions for research, as well as the current status of decision-making practice and suggestions for improvement.

REFERENCES

Ackermann, F. and Eden, C. (2011). *Making Strategy: Mapping Out Strategic Success*. London: Sage.

Alexander, A. (2019). When consensus is a bad way to decide. *The Union* (10 October) https://www.theunion.com/news/twi/when-consensus-is-a-bad-way-to-decide (last accessed 9 August 2022).

Amason, A.C. (1996). Distinguishing the effects of functional and dysfunctional conflict on strategic decision-making: Resolving a paradox for top management teams. *Academy of Management Journal*, **39**, 123–48.

Ambady, N. and Rosenthal, R. (1992). Thin slices of expressive behavior as predictors of interpersonal consequences: A meta-analysis. *Psychological Bulletin*, **111**(2), 256–74.

Arevuo, M. (2015). Epistemic objects in collective decision-making: A practice perspective on the use of causal maps as situated material artifacts. PhD thesis, Cranfield School of Management, Cranfield CERES (October), https://dspace.lib.cranfield.ac.uk/bitstream/handle/1826/9879/Arevuo_M_2015.pdf?sequence=1&isAllowed=y (last accessed 9 August 2022).

Arevuo, M., Reinmoeller, P., and Huff, A.S. (2017). How maps are made matters: Enacting artifacts in collective decision making. *Academy of Management Annual Meeting Proceedings*, **2017**(1), 1.

Argyris, C. (1991). Teaching smart people how to learn. *Harvard Business Review* (May–June), 99–109.

Baer, T, Heiligtag, S., and Samandari, H. (2017) The business logic in debiasing. *McKinsey & Co.* (23 May), https://www.mckinsey.com/business-functions/risk/our-insights/the-business-logic-in-debiasing (last accessed 9 August 2022).

Bazerman, M.H. and Moore, D.A. (2008). *Judgment in Managerial Decision Making* (7th edn). New York: John Wiley.

Black, J., Hashimzade, N., and Myles, G. (2017). *Oxford Dictionary of Economics*. Oxford: Oxford University Press.

Bryson, J., Ackermann, F., Eden, C., and Finn, C. (2004). *Visible Thinking: Unlocking Causal Mapping for Practical Business Results*. Chichester: John Wiley.

Bryson, J.M., Ackermann, F., and Eden, C. (2014). *Visual Strategy: Strategy Mapping for Public and Nonprofit Organizations.* San Francisco, CA: John Wiley.

Bulkin, B. (2015). *Crash Course: One Year to Become a Great Leader in a Great Company*. London: Whitefox.

Burt, G., Wright, G., Bradfield, R., Cairns, G., and van der Heijden, K. (2006). The role of scenario planning in exploring the environment in view of the limitations of PEST and its derivatives. *International Studies of Management and Organisation*, **36**, 50–76.

Chermack, T. and van der Merwe, L. (2003). The role of constructivist learning in scenario planning. *Futures*, **35**, 445–60.

Daft, R.L., Bettenhausen, K.R., and Tyler, B.B. (1993). Implications of top managers' communication choices for strategic decisions. In: Huber, G.P. and Glick, W.H. (eds), *Organizational Change and Redesign: Ideas and Insights in Improving Performance*. Oxford: Oxford University Press.

Dietvorst, B.J., Simmons, J.P., and Massey, C. (2015). Algorithm aversion: People erroneously avoid algorithms after seeing them err. *Journal of Experimental Psychology*, **144**(1), 114–26.

Eden, C. and Ackermann, F. (2010). Decision-making in groups: Theory and practice. In: Nutt, P.C. and Wilson, D.C. (eds), *Handbook of Decision Making*. Chichester: John Wiley, pp. 231–72.

Eisenhardt, K.M. and Zbaracki, M.J. (1992). Strategic decision making. *Strategic Management Journal*, **13**, 17–37.

Gladwell, M. (2005). *Blink, the Power of Thinking without Thinking*. New York: John Back Bay Books.

Goldin, C. and Rouse, C. (1997). Orchestrating impartiality: The impact of 'blind' auditions on female musicians. Working Paper 5903, NBER Working Paper series, National Bureau of Economic Research, Cambridge, MA.

3

Hambrick, D.C. (1994). Top management groups: A conceptual integration and reconsideration of the 'group' label. In: Staw, B.M. and Cummings, L.L. (eds), *Research in Organizational Behavior*. Greenwich, CT: JAI Press, pp. 171–214.

Harries, C. (2003). Correspondence to what? What is good scenario-based decision making?. *Technological Forecasting and Social Change*, **70**(8), 797–817.

Harrison, M. (2007). John Hammond at First National Bank, Daniel Webster College. Case from The Case Centre, Cranfield, UK.

Harvey, J. (1988). The Abilene paradox: The management of agreement. *Organizational Dynamics*, Summer, 17–34.

Hines, A. (2006). Strategic foresight: The state of the art. *Futurist* (September–October), 18–21.

Hodgkinson, G. and Healey, M. (2011). Psychological foundations of dynamic capabilities: Reflexion and reflection in strategic management. *Strategic Management Journal*, **32**(13), 1500–16.

Hogarth, R.M. (1981). Beyond discrete biases: Functional and dysfunctional aspects of judgmental heuristics. *Psychological Bulletin*, **90**(2), 197–217.

Janis, I.L. (1972). *Victims of Group Think*. New York: Free Press.

Kahneman, D. (2011). *Thinking, Fast and Slow*. New York: Macmillan.

Kahneman, D. and Tversky, A. (1979). Prospect theory: An analysis of decision under risk. *Econometrica*, **47**(2), 263–91.

Kahneman, D., Slovic, P., and Tversky, A. (eds) (1982). *Judgment under Uncertainty: Heuristics and Biases*. Cambridge: Cambridge University Press.

Kahneman, D., Lovallo, D., and Sibony, O. (2011). The big idea: Before you make that big decision. *Harvard Business Review* (June), 51–60.

Kahneman, D., Rosenfield, A.M., Gandhi, L., and Blaser, T. (2016). Noise—How to overcome the high hidden cost of inconsistent decision making. *Harvard Business Review* (reprint October).

Kahneman, D., Lovallo, D., and Sibony, O. (2019). A structured approach to strategic decisions. *MIT Sloan Management Review*, **60**(3), https://sloanreview.mit.edu/article/a-structured-approach-to-strategic-decisions (last accessed 19 October 2022).

Kahneman, D., Sibony, O. and Sunstein, C. R. (2021). *Noise—A Flaw in Human Judgment*, London: William and Collins.

KPMG LLP (2018). *Women Corporate Directors*. Delaware: The Women Corporate Directors Education and Development Foundation, Inc. & KPMG LLP.

Lovallo, D. and Sibony, O. (2010). The case for behavioural strategy. *McKinsey Quarterly* (January), https://www.mckinsey.com/quarterly/the-magazine (last accessed 9 August 2022).

McKay, A. (2020). What exactly is strategic leadership? *Human Resources Magazine*, **25**(3), 14–17.

McKinsey Global Survey Results (2009). Flaws in strategic decision-making. *McKinsey Quarterly* (January), https://www.mckinsey.com/quarterly/the-magazine (last accessed 9 August 2022).

March, J.G. and Simon, H.A. (1958). *Organizations*. New York: John Wiley.

Maule, A.J. and Hodgkinson, G.P. (2002). Heuristics, biases, and strategic decision making. *Psychologist*, **15**, 68–71.

Michelman, P (2017). When people don't trust algorithms. *MIT Sloan Management Review*, **59**(1), 11–13.

Mintzberg, H., Raisinghani, D., and Théorêt, A. (1976). The structure of 'unstructured' decision processes. *Administrative Science Quarterly*, **21**(2), 246–75.

New York Times (2021). To make orchestras more divers, end blind auditions (6 August), https://www.nytimes.com/2020/07/16/arts/music/blind-auditions-orchestras-race.html (last accessed 9 August 2022).

Nutt, P.C. (2002). *Why Decisions Fail: Avoiding the Blunders and Traps that Lead to Debacles*. San Francisco, CA: Berrett-Kohler.

Nutt, P.C. and Wilson, D.C. (eds) (2010). *Handbook of Decision Making*. Chichester: John Wiley.

O'Brien, F., Meadows, M., and Murtland, M. (2007). Creating and using scenarios: Exploring alternative possible futures and their impact on strategic decisions. In: O' Brien, F. and Dyson, R.G. (eds), *Supporting Strategy: Frameworks, Methods and Models*. Chichester: Wiley, p. 406.

O'Brien, F. and Meadows, M. (2013). Scenario orientation and use to support strategy development. *Technological Forecasting and Social Change*, **80**(4), 643–56.

O'Brien, F., Meadows, M., and Griffiths, S. (2017). Serialisation and the use of Twitter: Keeping the conversation alive in public policy scenario projects. *Technological Forecasting and Social Change*, **124**, 26–40.

Parayitam, S. and Dooley, R.S. (2007). The relationship between conflict and decision outcomes: moderating effects of cognitive- and affect-based trust in strategic decision-making teams. *International Journal of Conflict Management*, **18**(1), 42–73.

Parayitam, S. and Dooley, R.S. (2009). The interplay between cognitive and affective conflict and cognition- and affect-based trust in influencing decision outcomes. *Journal of Business Research*, **62**(8), 789–96.

Parayitam, S. and Dooley, R.S. (2011). Is too much cognitive conflict in strategic decision-making teams too bad? *International Journal of Conflict Management*, **22**, 342–57.

Ringland, G. (2006). *Scenario Planning: Managing the Future* (2nd edn). Wiley: Chichester.

Ringland, G. (2010). The role of scenarios in strategic foresight. *Technological Forecasting and Social Change,* **77**(9), 1493–8.

Schoemaker, P.J.H., Heaton, S., and Teece, D. (2018). Innovation, dynamic capabilities, and leadership. *California Management Review*, **61**(1), 15–42.

Schweiger, D., Sandberg, W., and Ragan, J. (1986). Group approaches for improving strategic decision making: A comparative analysis of dialectical inquiry, devil's advocacy, and consensus. *Academy of Management Journal*, **29**(1), 51–71.

Schwenk, C.R. (1988). *Essence of Strategic Decision Making*. Lexington, MA: Lexington Books.

Schwenk, C.R. (1995). Strategic decision making. *Journal of Management*, **21**, 471–93.

Stoner, J.A.F. (1968). Risky and cautious shifts in group decisions: The influence of widely held values. *Journal of Experimental Psychology*, **4**, 442–59.

Sund, K.J., Galvan, R.J., and Huff, A.S. (eds) (2016). *Uncertainty and Strategic Decision Making*. Bingley: Emerald Group.

Tversky, A. and Kahneman, D. (1974). Judgment under uncertainty: Heuristics and biases. *Science*, **185**, 1124–31.

van Ginkel, W.P. and van Knippenberg, D. (2009). Knowledge about the distribution of information and group decision making: When and why does it work? *Organizational Behavior and Human Decision Processes*, **108**(2), 218–29.

van der Heijden, K. (2004). Can internally generated futures accelerate organizational learning? *Futures,* **36**, 145–59.

Verity, J. (2003). Scenario planning as a strategy technique. *European Business Journal*, **15**, 185–95.

3

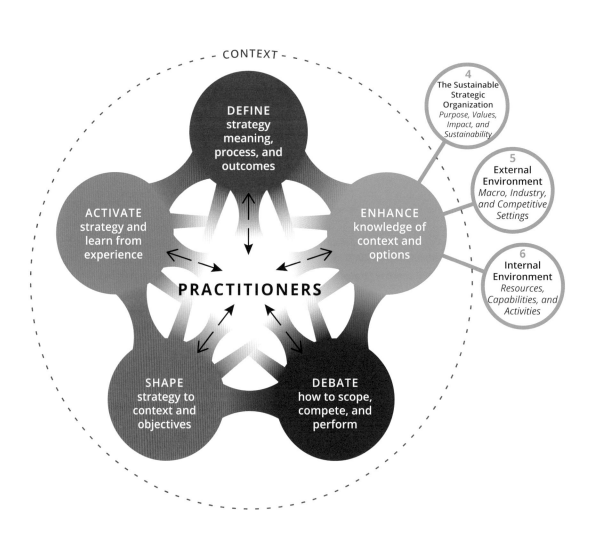

PART TWO

Enhance knowledge of context and options

Organizational activity and strategizing are embedded in societal, industrial, and competitive settings. In Part 2, we examine how the internal and external context of an organization might be investigated, analysed, and understood to inform strategizing activity. We start our discussion in Chapter 4 by considering the purpose of the organization and the values that guide its operations. In this chapter, we appraise the importance of the organization's overall purpose, corporate social responsibility, and the concepts of 'creating shared value', impact, and sustainability as key factors in organizational strategy process and outcomes. We argue that it is the amalgamation of the varied values with the purpose that form the basis of all organizational activity. In Chapter 5, we assess the nature and impact of the external context of the organization, presenting analytical frameworks to identify and assess trends, opportunities, and threats. Finally, in Chapter 6, we look inside the organization at its internal resources and capabilities. For an organization to survive and flourish in a competitive environment, it requires resources, capabilities, and processes, and an ability to renew them, to support its value-adding activities. The composition of the organization's internal resource base and architecture are critical building blocks of competitive strategy.

By the end of Part 2, you should have enhanced abilities to think, talk, and act like a strategy practitioner, investigating and enhancing knowledge of context and options.

CHAPTER FOUR

The Sustainable Strategic Organization
Purpose, Values, Impact, and Sustainability

CONTENTS

By the end of this chapter, you should be able to:

○ Evaluate how an organization's purpose, vision, mission, and values translate to deliverable performance targets and objectives

○ Critically assess the concepts of shareholder and stakeholder value maximization and examine how organizations can effectively engage with stakeholders who have conflicting interests

○ Appraise the importance of sustainability as a factor in organizational strategy processes and outcomes

○ Evaluate the relevance and possible impact of the 'triple bottom line' and 'sustainable development goals' concepts to an organization's strategy and stakeholder groups

○ Critically assesses the relative merits and limitations of approaches to sustainability strategy

TOOLBOX

○ **Mission statement development**
A framework that can be applied to develop forward-looking statements that communicate the purpose, values, and mission of the organization to both internal and external stakeholders, including the impact on wider society.

○ **Theory of shareholder and stakeholder value maximization**
An important analysis of the overall purpose of the organization: whose interests does the organization serve?

○ **Corporate social responsibility (CSR)**
A perspective in which an organization's obligations to society at large are prioritized over other business objectives to varying degrees. Applied to strategy, CSR will influence the sustainability and impact outcomes achieved by an organization.

○ **'Creating shared value' approach (CSV)**
Focuses on growing total value created for the organization and its stakeholders and splitting the benefits fairly. CSV is increasingly entering organizational strategy processes as a means of enhancing sustainability outcomes and communicating alignment of sustainability strategies to the long-term purpose and obligations of the organization.

○ **Stakeholder mapping**
An analytical framework to identify and prioritize the organization's stakeholders.

Triple bottom line (TBL)

A model of sustainable performance in which a balance is achieved within a system of objectives addressing people-, profit-, and planet-related outcomes. TBL can be used as a framework to evaluate and enhance organizational objectives and initiatives towards achieving sustainability.

Sustainable development goals (SDGs)

Proposed by the United Nations, SDGs are a framework of goals and objectives intended to influence national, local, and organizational strategies for sustainable development. Alignment of objectives with the SDGs framework can help to communicate and explain how sustainability is prioritized in organizational strategy and practice.

Access the online resources to watch a short video clip where Aileen McLeod shares her top career tips.

OPENING CASE STUDY HOW A US START-UP SEEKS TO TACKLE INEQUALITY

The US internet service market is dominated by a handful of major telecommunications companies that have long been criticized for failing to invest in rural and low-income urban neighbourhoods. Research that goes beyond what is self-reported by the major providers suggests that there are some 42 million Americans without a reliable internet connection. Underline, a start-up company that focuses on community infrastructure, is hoping to disrupt the internet service industry by building open-access fibre networks across medium-sized urban communities and break up broadband monopolies across the country.

Underline works with communities to deliver foundational intelligent infrastructure, including open-access fibre-optic networks. They are driven by a singular mission: to ensure the vibrancy of their nation through building this infrastructure in a socially equitable manner. They believe these networks are the essential foundation for ultra-fast access to information, a competitive market for content and services, job formation and reskilling for workers, distributed health-care services, new wireless solutions, and resilient modern infrastructure, including responsible energy creation.

Underline's business is motivated by the conviction that digital infrastructure plays a critical role in the health and functioning of society. According to Underline, US communities are on dangerously divergent paths that threaten the financial, social, and cultural well-being of the communities and the competitive position of the nation. Some communities experience job creation, population growth, and increasing wealth per capita, but for others, opportunity is stunted with crumbling infrastructure, shrinking workforces, high unemployment, and lower educational attainment. These communities are at risk of being permanently left behind. 'To address these inequalities, Underline seeks to deliver intelligent infrastructure—built on a foundation of open access fibre—with an ethos of community partnership and in the spirit of social justice. With an ethic of partnership and social purpose we work alongside communities to deploy critical modern infrastructure.'

In the open-access model, a city or a private company like Underline builds and maintains the physical infrastructure and invites multiple independent providers to run services on the network. The open-access model is intended to make it easier for small and start-up service companies to enter the market without facing the high costs of building their own network. The competition within the open-access architecture can then drive innovation and fast speeds at more affordable prices, giving consumers choice beyond what is currently offered by the major telecommunications giants. In addition, open access networks can facilitate economic development as new firms look to relocate to areas with more choices for reliable, high-speed internet access and existing businesses can be better served. Furthermore, these multi-purpose neutral networks can be used by local governments, city utilities, and other public institutions such as libraries and schools to upgrade their connectivity and offer a variety of new public services and 'smart city' upgrades.

Underline's first project was established in 2021 in Colorado Springs, where 10% of households have no internet access. The project allows consumers to choose between at least three full-service internet providers offering internet speeds of between 500/500 Mbps and 10/10 Gbps, along with other value-added services. For city residents, the price ranges from $49 a month to $250 a month for different levels of service. For low-income families who qualify for Underline's Opportunity Programme, the 500/500 Mbps plan is available for $30 a month.

Living the Underline values

When the COVID-19 pandemic shut down schools, one of the largest school districts in Colorado Springs had to rely on Wi-Fi buses to facilitate access to virtual classrooms for many students. This worked as a temporary solution, but as the pandemic showed no sign of easing, the school district needed to find a more permanent workaround for this issue of poor connectivity. The school district is situated in the city's urban centre, serving some 26,000 students, half of whom are non-white and over 40% of whom qualify for free school lunches. When high-speed internet needed to livestream classes costs around $100 per month for the average family, for some it comes down to the choice between an online education and putting food on the table.

School board president, Shawn Gullixson, sees the partnership with Underline as a potential 'game changer'. Not only does Underline provide affordable internet access for families in their own homes, but also it works to create a private, secure network for the school district that can be accessed remotely from anywhere.

Sustainability of the business model

The idea of an open-access network isn't new. The City of Stockholm in Sweden built one of the world's largest open-access fibre networks in the 1990s, and today it covers 90% of the city's homes and businesses. But the model is uncommon in the United States, in part because of challenges from major corporations who have a significant influence on broadband policy. It can also be difficult to sustain the business model based on how revenues are shared between the network operator and the service providers.

'Open access networks have largely been done by municipalities that were not trying to break even very quickly', says Christopher Mitchell, programme director of the Community Broadband Networks Initiative. 'The challenge for Underline is to get the returns it needs in a reasonable time period.' But Underline executives contend that the project benefits from investors who 'believe in the market and our strategy and are willing to back us on the premise that we can build a nationwide open access network'. Among Underline's backers is philanthropist Laurene Powell Jobs, whose grant-making organization the Emerson Collective seeks to advance equality. 'We bring a combination of technology and funding so that the local government is not burdened with trying to solve this problem' of the digital divide, says Underline's CEO Bob Thompson. Unlike traditional telecom investments, which promise a relatively quick return, it takes a lot longer for fibre networks to turn a profit. 'Underline is one of a few instances in which I think we see a different kind of investment mentality from investors that are putting money into telecommunications', says Christopher Mitchell, programme director for the Institute of Local Self-Reliance. 'There are more investors that look at Underline and say, "No, this is a good, long-term stable investment, where, I might not get all my money back in five years, but over the longer haul, I'm going to have good returns over a longer period of time."'

Underline is a private company with a profit motive. What is clear, however, is that the success of the firm is intricately tied in with the social and economic impact it will make in the many underserved communities across the country.

Questions for discussion

1. Critically evaluate the effectiveness and clarity of Underline's mission and values. Do they communicate what the company does? Do they inspire you?

2. How are Underline's mission and values evident in their project in Colorado Springs?

3. What are the main benefits of Underline's business model to US communities and their customers?

Continued

4. Undertake research on social enterprises, such as the Big Issue and the Eden Project in the United Kingdom, that are often set up in communities to change the world for the better. How does Underline's business model differ from those of social enterprises?

5. Do you think Underline's business model is sustainable? If yes, why? If not, why not?

Sources

BloombergUK (2020). There are far more Americans without broadband than previously thought (19 February), https://www.bloomberg.com/news/articles/2020-02-19/where-the-u-s-underestimates-the-digital-divide?sref=0IejgNtz (last accessed 10 August 2022).

BloombergUK (2021). Startup takes on Big Telecom, starting in Colorado Springs (19 October), https://www.bloomberg.com/news/articles/2021-10-19/startup-tries-new-approach-to-tackle-the-digital-divide (last accessed 10 August 2022).

Open Access, https://muninetworks.org/content/open-access (last accessed 10 August 2022).

Underline, https://underline.com (last accessed 10 August 2022).

Underline Infrastructure, https://www.talentticker.ai/company/underline-infrastructure-389917 (last accessed 10 August 2022).

4.1 **Introduction**

From a process–practice perspective, strategizing occurs within an historical context that encompasses the organization's developmental path, culture, values, objectives, and the overall direction of travel. As discussed in Chapter 2, this context can be a trigger for and an enabler or a constraint on strategy activity. In this chapter, we consider how strategists can build knowledge of internal organizational context as an aid to effective strategizing. We begin by considering how organizational purpose—a strategic factor of high importance in disrupted times—differs from an organizational direction and how purpose affects and matters to those delivering and managing strategy. We present a process model of how to work within the context of an organization's stated purpose in practice. We also evaluate two different perspectives on the question of who the organization serves: shareholders, stakeholders, or both? We then expand our discussion to consider the role of the organization in a wider societal and organizational context in terms of its stakeholders. Most organizations possess stakeholders with conflicting interests, so it is imperative that we consider the mechanisms that organizations can use to manage the various stakeholder groups that have an interest in the activities of the company.

We then move to examine the concept of sustainability, what it means, and how it influences strategy making. For some, the concept of sustainability presents a set of wicked problems for which there are no easy or practical solutions in a consumption-focused world (Dentoni et al. 2016). However, there is a growing view that sustainability is a '**megatrend**'—meaning a global shift such as globalization or digital technologies—that is reshaping the world and changing the way we live and do business (PWC 2019); sustainable approaches will increasingly impact all organizations, industries, societies, and nations (Lubin and Esty 2010). From a process–practice perspective, this means that sustainability—alongside digitalization and globalization—is a feature of the macro-context for most organizations that will increasingly trigger strategizing episodes and require practitioner attention and relevant practices, and activities for many years to come. Those organizations that build their sustainability capabilities and credentials now will be well placed to benefit from the new opportunities arising from the sustainability megatrend in the next decade (NCE 2018).

4.2 Organizational purpose

An organization's purpose affirms its existence by defining what the organization does, who it serves, and where the organization expects to be in the future. These activities and aspirations are often articulated in forward-looking vision statements about the organization's activities. Mirvis et al. (2010) consider vision as a statement of a desired future for a company that provides an intellectual framework defining a strategic direction and a conceptual map of how the organization moves from its current reality to a desired future state.

According to Ratan Tata, the retired CEO of Tata Group, the purpose of any organization is 'a spiritual and moral call for action; it is what a person or company stands for' (Tata et al. 2013). Commercial enterprises exist to make a profit, but they are also integral participants in communities and society, both locally and globally. Some state that there is a persistent myth that the ultimate purpose of a firm is to maximize shareholder value (Tata et al. 2013). However, profit maximization is not a purpose; it is an outcome that results from offering a valuable customer proposition and making a positive ethical impact in its community.

For example, consider Nestlé's purpose statement:

We strive to create products that are right for consumers and that contribute to public health and a sound environment. It's good business. We build for the long term, act with focus and combine global resources with local know-how to create value for both society and our shareholders at a meaningful scale. We do so because we believe that business should act as a force for good. We have made bold commitments to achieve net zero greenhouse gas emissions by 2050 and make 100% of our packaging recyclable or reusable by 2025. We will continue to advance our sustainability agenda and create new business opportunities by ensuring Nestlé brands speak to our purpose.

(Nestlé 2021)

Note how Nestlé's purpose statement articulates a forward-looking aspiration that inspires and motivates employees to work towards a better and healthier world. Aligned with the description of strategy as purpose in Chapter 1, this statement outlines for the organization and its employees a role through which it might contribute to society and in so doing ensures the long-term success of the firm. We will explore Nestlé in more detail in Case Example 4.1. Naturally, for any organization to survive, it has to offer products and services that customers find valuable and that will enhance their quality of life in some way. In our opening case, for example, Underline sought to enhance their customers' quality of life by bringing high-speed internet to low-income communities. Many companies do not have explicit purpose statements but instead have several other statements that describe organizational direction: vision, mission, and value statements. Kenny (2014) has produced a typology to distinguish various statements as a first step in helping organizations to produce forward-looking documents that are both motivational and achievable (see Table 4.1).

TABLE 4.1 **Kenny's typology of forward-looking statements**

Kenny's typology	Definition	Aim	Example
A vision statement	What the organization wishes to become in some years' time	To elevate thinking beyond the organization's day-to-day activities in a clear and memorable way It is usually articulated by the firm's senior management	The vision statement of the charity Save the Children is very short and therefore memorable Save the Children's vision is to create 'a world in which every child attains the right to survival, protection, development, and participation'
A **mission statement**	What are the business activities that the organization engages in (and what are those that it doesn't) now and in the future?	To provide focus for the managers and the employees	Google defines its mission statement in terms of what the company does: 'To organize the world's information and make it universally accessible and useful'
A value statement	The organization's desired culture	To act as a behavioural compass for all the employees and managers of the firm by articulating a set of principles which govern both the inward and outward conduct of all organizational participants	Disney's value statement articulates honesty integrity, respect, courage, openness, diversity, and balance as the fundamental values of the organization: 'These values are demonstrated through such traits and behaviours like making guests happy, caring about fellow cast members, working as a team, delivering quality, fostering creativity, paying attention to every detail, and having an **emotional commitment** to Disney'
A purpose statement	The heartbeat of the organization	To connect the heart of the organization with the head by putting managers and employees in customers' shoes and considering the role of the organization as a member of society	Oxfam clearly states the reason (or purpose) for the charity's existence: 'Oxfam strives to help create lasting solutions to the injustice of poverty. We are part of a global movement for change, one that empowers people to create a future that is secure, just, and free from poverty.'

Source: authors.

Many organizations do not produce separate documents for each forward-looking statement within the typology outlined in Table 4.1. Unfortunately, these forward-looking statements are often a confused mix of vision and mission and are either too general to have any practical value or too aspirational to be deliverable in practice. On the other hand, with quarterly performance pressures, especially for publicly quoted companies, the forward-looking aspirations are often overshadowed by short-term considerations and quick fixes. This can be exacerbated by the emergence of crises—such as a sharp rise in the price of global energy, which draws attention and effort away from purposeful intent to short-term coping. In terms of purpose, this is problematic as any statement produced to guide the organization should be aspirational, memorable, inspirational, and, most importantly, achievable by the organization.

Many organizations articulate purpose, vision, and mission statements in their corporate documents and websites. However, the existence of a forward-looking statement does not guarantee that the organization or its employees adhere to those recorded aspirations or whether this translates to their target audience. When managers attempt to impose a vision, employees do not take the message to heart. Employees must make the connection from the meaningfulness of their work to the company vision and mission to internalize and imbed them in their daily work (Cable and Vermeulen 2018).

There are numerous ways of measuring the success of an organization in delivering on the stated purpose, vision, and mission and adhering to its own standards set in its forward-looking statement. For example, some of the more common measurement criteria include the sustainability of the organization's profitability over an extended period, market share, brand value and customer perception, employee satisfaction surveys, etc. In addition, the social impact of most large organizations is monitored by corporate social responsibility agencies, including UN Global Compact, which monitor and help organizations adhere to and advance the universal principles of human and labour rights, environmental protection, and anti-corruption practices. It should be noted that these indicators are retrospective measurements. However, most firms conduct competitor intelligence analysis, and many branding and corporate social responsibility agencies produce annual rankings of companies on a set of criteria (such as Corporate Knights or B-Corp listings). Strategists use such rankings to evaluate their firm's performance against that of the competitors for potential reputational resource advantages (see Chapter 6 for a further explanation of reputational resources).

Some companies do not publish forward-looking vision or mission statements at all. For example, Apple Inc. does not have a mission statement on its website but instead tells people what the firm has accomplished and what 'amazing' things the firm's products can do. Rather than articulating a mission statement, Apple shows people what mission it is currently on: 'Apple designs Macs, the best personal computers in the world [. . .] Apple leads the digital music revolution [. . .] Apple is reinventing the mobile phone with its revolutionary iPhone and AppStore' (Palotta 2011). Rather than trying to predict the future of computing and the digital world, Apple chooses to emphasize its commitment to producing products and services ethically, honestly, and in full compliance with the law that allows people to do 'amazing' digital things now, regardless of how the future unfolds. Or, as Apple CEO Tim Cook states, 'We do the right thing, even when it is not easy' (https://www.apple.com/compliance, last accessed 10 August 2022).

Whatever the nature of aspirational forward-looking statements in terms of their detail, organizations must be able to develop processes and inspire employees to live up to the publicly stated or internally established standards to deliver, go on a mission, and show the world that they are doing what they have set out to accomplish.

 Access the online resources to watch a short video clip where Aileen McLeod discusses the role of purpose in strategy and governance.

4.3 **Delivering on vision, mission, and values**

We have discussed several forward-looking statements that are used to articulate an organization's purpose, vision, mission, and values. But the key questions are 'How do organizations ensure that they live up to these statements?' and 'What processes can strategists develop to help their organization live up to its values and deliver the vision and mission?' To realize the vision and mission of the organization, consistent with corresponding purpose and values, strategy practitioners might engage with goals, objectives, and initiatives, tracking progress using key performance indicators and targets. In this section, we examine what these terms mean and how they might influence the strategy process.

Goals, objectives, and initiatives

Organizations use goals, objectives, and initiatives to help them achieve their vision.

Goals

As described by Ackermann and Eden (2011), goals are the long-term aims of an organization—the 'ends' it might try to achieve. Goals can be common to all organizations in an industry; for example, all publicly listed organizations will aim to maximize shareholder return, and, increasingly, sustainability and wider societal impact are becoming embedded as essential components of long-term organizational aims. Equally, goals might be specific to a smaller number of organizations in a sector, such as 'Be a leading research institute in Canada'. Such a goal might be a high-level, long-term aim for some Canadian universities, but other universities might aspire to alternative goals, such as teaching excellence and quality of student experience.

Goals can be expressed as a 'future state' of the organization, describing a vision of how the organization aspires to be and to operate at a later point in time. The goal system should be consistent and tied to purpose and vision of the organization. Goals may have a quantitative component (e.g. 'Be the number one organization by revenue in our sector') or be wholly qualitative (e.g. 'Be renowned for our philanthropy and social impact').

Objectives

Objectives can be considered as intermediate outcomes towards achieving goals. In comparison with goals, objectives are more specific statements of future intent that are tied to the organization's mission statement. For example, an objective for the goal 'Be a leading research institute in Canada' might be 'Increase the number of *Financial Times* (FT) ranked journal articles submitted each year to 100 by 2026', and another objective might be 'Grow annual research council funding to $10 million by 2025'.

The format of these example objectives conforms to what is known as SMART criteria. SMART is an acronym that means:

Specific: target a specific area for focus of effort/resource allocation.
Measurable: be associated with an indicator of progress.
Achievable: be realistic to believe that the objective can be delivered in the current context with available resources.

Relevant: connected to the goals and current situation of the organization.

Time-related: has a defined timeframe for delivery.

Objectives are equivalent to milestones on the road to delivery of goals. Objectives might be revised on a more regular basis than goals as an organization's context unfolds.

Initiatives

Initiatives are projects to which specific organizational resources are deployed. Initiatives can be considered the specific practical means by which objectives are achieved. For example, to 'grow annual research council funding to $10 million by 2025', initiatives the organization might undertake could be:

- creating a peer review system for the internal evaluation of draft grant applications;
- retaining an external grant application writer to be made available as a resource for all draft applications more than $2.5 million in value;
- implementing a grant-writing progress tracking system.

Initiatives can be quantified in terms of an associated budget, timescale, and organizational accountability (such as a department or individual being given responsibility for making the initiative happen). Initiatives can typically be triggered, revised, or cancelled at short notice. The value of an initiative might be explained in relation to the objectives that are supported by delivering the initiative.

Key performance indicators and targets

Key performance indicators (KPIs) describe the ways in which progress towards objectives will be evaluated. For example, for the objective 'Grow annual research council funding to $10 million by 2025' listed earlier, KPIs might include 'number of research grant applications submitted every year', 'average value of research grant applications', and 'grant submission win rate'.

For each KPI, there can be an associated target to which organizational performance might aspire and against which it might be evaluated. Targets which push for performance that exceeds historical attainment levels are referred to as 'stretch targets'. For example, the targets for the research income KPIs could be as set out in Table 4.2.

Targets and KPIs provide a means of tracking the overall performance of the organization as well as progress against achieving specific goals and objectives. Targets may be accompanied by what are known as 'control limits' and 'glide paths'.

Control limits are the levels of performance that will trigger a corrective action in an organization. For example, if the average application value in Table 4.2 is tracking at $1.5 million halfway through the year, action may be required with those applying for grants to improve progress towards the target. Control limits might be high (e.g. when the rate of employee absence goes above 4%) or low (e.g. when production line efficiency drops below 85%). When control limits are breached, a managerial response will typically be required. If you are responsible for an area of organizational performance, this may mean that you must provide a root-cause analysis of any issues and propose a corrective action plan. This is equally true for operational and strategic control limits (see Marianne Meehan's Practitioner Insight in Chapter 1 for an

TABLE 4.2 **Examples of targets associated with KPIs**

KPI	Target	Rationale
Number of research grant applications submitted every year	10 applications per year	An evaluation of historical grant application activity shows the institution averaging 8–12 applications per year; therefore, this seems a realistic target
Average value of research grant applications	Average application value $2.5 million	Considering win and application rate, an average research grant value of $2.5 million is required to achieve the overall goal; reviewing prior bid activity, the range of submission goes from $1 million to $4 million, so $2.5 million is achievable
Grant submission win rate	Win rate 40%	Historical performance in this KPI has been tracking at 35%, so to aim for 40% can be considered a stretch target

Source: authors.

example of how strategic initiatives and daily operations are monitored and managed through targets and reviews).

An issue with control limits is that progress towards achieving KPIs for targets may not always be linear. For example, if the research councils in the example in Table 4.2 only accept applications every four months, the institution will deliver no applications for the first three months of the year. Therefore a 'glide path', which is a chart of anticipated progress against meeting a target based on knowledge of organizational activity and context, is used to enable more nuanced management of KPIs and targets. Glide paths should be constructed based on knowledgeable evaluation of possible progress against a target. Glide paths will be less helpful when a straight line is drawn between a starting level of performance and a desired end state. Figure 4.1 is an example of a glide path for research grant applications over a year. Rather than draw a straight

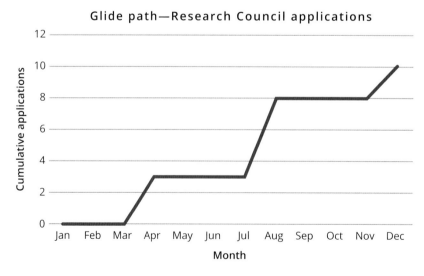

FIGURE 4.1 **Example of a glide path for a target.** *Source*: authors.

line from 0 in January to 10 in December, the anticipated number of applications reflects the timescales for submission anticipated by the authors. The horizontal lines represent months in which no submissions should be anticipated.

To the extent they are deployed in an organization, these concepts will play a role in strategizing from a process–practice perspective. Depending on the scale of the correction required, a strategizing episode might be triggered by a control limit breach or by drifting significantly off glide path on a strategic initiative. We explore the strategic role of control levers and systems further in Chapter 7.

Associated with KPIs in strategy practice is the term **'balanced scorecard'**, first proposed by Kaplan and Norton (1992). As we will discuss in Chapter 9, a balanced scorecard is a set of both leading and lagging KPIs for an organization which address performance holistically, that is, not just on financial performance. A balanced scorecard should comprise indicators selected according to the specific context and needs of the organization, as outlined in Table 4.3. Versus initial conceptualizations of what should be included in a balanced scorecard, arguably sustainability should now feature as a 'fifth column', representing purposeful attention to societal and environmental outcomes alongside financial performance (Kalendar and Vayvay, 2016).

Imagining, monitoring, and delivering organizational aims

Figure 4.2 shows how the concepts of goals, objectives, initiatives, KPIs, and targets operate in combination to imagine, monitor, and deliver organizational aims. You can see how work on specific initiatives can contribute to realizing the aims of the organization. Initiatives provide a means through which to meet objectives. Equally, objectives justify the investment of resources behind an initiative by providing target outcomes to which the initiative will contribute. Similarly, short-term objectives (e.g. one-year targets) show the paths through which longer-term goals (e.g. three to fie years, organization dependent) will be realized over time, and goals help to explain how achieving objectives will help the organization.

A single initiative can support multiple objectives, as shown in Figure 4.3. For example, an initiative to 'create a peer review system for the internal evaluation of draft grant applications' could contribute to the objective 'Grow annual research council funding to $10 million by 2025' and support another objective such as 'Double the number of multi-disciplinary committees by

TABLE 4.3 **Measures relating to the balanced scorecard**

KPI	Indicator
Financial and business performance	Running a financially viable and sustainable organization, meeting the needs of shareholders and stakeholders
Customer and commercial performance	Understanding and meeting the needs of customers, competing effectively, and generating revenue
Operations and infrastructure	Buildings, equipment, systems, and processes that create and deliver customer value and employee services
People, learning, and development	Building human capacity to meet current and future needs

Source: authors.

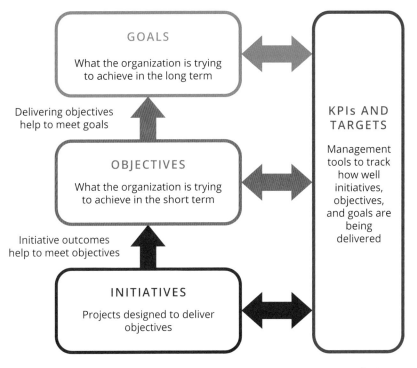

FIGURE 4.2 Imagining, monitoring, and delivering organizational aims.
Source: authors.

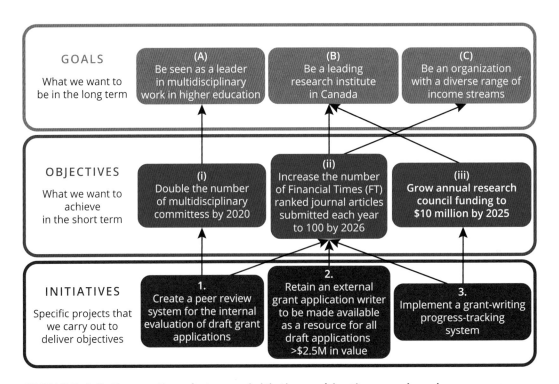

FIGURE 4.3 Connections between initiatives, objectives, and goals. *Source*: authors.

2024'. Further, objectives can relate to multiple goals. Using the same example, 'Grow annual research council funding to $10 million by 2025' will contribute to attainment of the goal 'Be a leading research institute in Canada' and 'Be an organization with a diverse range of income streams'.

When evaluating strategic initiatives and options for action, it is valuable to understand these relationships to identify the best use of organizational resources. If you can map the objectives that might be supported by the initiatives under consideration, you will be able to identify the initiatives that might give the best return on investment. You will also be able to articulate how goals are anticipated to be achieved through objectives and associated initiatives.

In your work as a strategist, you will need to prioritize deployment of resources as part of your strategy work. Having a sense of the relationships between initiatives, objectives, and goals can help you make choices about which projects to work on first to deliver most benefit to the organization. The map in Figure 4.3 could be enhanced by further examining the links between the elements (this is a simple example of a causal map described in Chapter 3). Knowing the extent of the contribution represented by each arrow or the certainty with which we can claim that an initiative will deliver on an objective could add further nuance to our decision-making.

4.4 Shareholder or stakeholder value maximization?

So far in this chapter, we have discussed the purpose of organizations and considered their role and sphere of influence more widely than solely focusing on generating revenue and profit. We then outlined the processes that strategists can apply to deliver the firm's vision. But let's go back to our explanation of an organization's purpose as an affirmation of the reason for its existence. For example, what does the organization do, who does it serve, and where does it expect to be in the future? We will now focus on one of these questions: whose interests does the firm serve?

The answer to this fundamental question is far from straightforward. For example, should firms simply serve their shareholders' interests or should they have a responsibility to their communities and to society more generally? Or is this broader societal role the responsibility of government? The debate over whether organizations should have a wider social responsibility beyond the core activities has historically been controversial. Professor Milton Friedman, a Nobel Laureate in Economics, famously stated that the only social responsibility of business is to use its resources to engage in activities designed to increase profits. Friedman's position has become known as the shareholder model of business. Friedman argued that having a wider social responsibility beyond maximizing returns to the shareholders (the owners of a business) was an immoral idea that violates the rights of the shareholders (Friedman 1970). Friedman and his University of Chicago colleagues argued that shareholders who had invested in a firm were expecting the business to engage in activities that would maximize returns for their investment and that to use corporate resources to solve non-business social problems would effectively amount to theft from shareholders. Should shareholders wish to solve wider social problems, they should do so privately through their own charitable contributions, not through contributions by the business that shareholders had invested in with the expectation of earning a return on their investment. Friedman and his colleagues also pointed out that successful firms already make a wider social contribution as a normal course of their business activities by providing employment and through taxes on their profits that are paid to both local and central governments.

The critics of this shareholder value maximization proposition are many. For example, Stout (2012) states that shareholder value thinking leads corporate managers to focus on short-term performance at the expense of long-term value creation. Jensen (2002) argues that to maximize value, corporate managers must both satisfy and enlist the support of all corporate stakeholders—customers, employees, managers, suppliers, financiers, and local communities. This wider concern for other stakeholders, beyond the narrow focus on shareholders, has become known as the stakeholder value view. According to this view, instead of striving to maximize shareholder wealth, managers should strive to balance all stakeholder interests (Freeman 1984). In contrast with the shareholder view, the stakeholder view posits that the essence of the firm is to create value for all stakeholders, not just the firm's shareholders alone.

So, are shareholder and stakeholder perspectives incompatible? Van der Linden and Freeman (2017) state that Friedman never thought that corporate managers should ignore other stakeholder interests. But his concern for stakeholder interests was limited to the extent that they were instrumental to the interest of shareholders. However, as Van der Linden and Freeman (2017) discuss, Friedman's thinking was not opposed to the stakeholder view if it is accepted that the primary responsibility of corporate managers is to create as much value as possible for stakeholders because this is how one creates as much value as possible for the shareholders. In other words, what's good for all stakeholders is good for the firm's ultimate owners—the shareholders.

In addition, we should note that it's hard to create value for all stakeholders without making a profit unless the organization is a charity or an aid organization that relies on donations and benefactors to sustain its activity (Birkinshaw et al. 2014). Therefore, the profit motive that is the cornerstone of any firm's *raison d'être* is good for the wider society. As we will see in Case Example 4.1, Nestlé's corporate purpose is to help shape a better and healthier world by inspiring people to live healthier lives. So, contributing to the wider society makes good business sense as it will also ensure the long-term success of the company. The acceptance of organizations' wider social concerns that are combined with the profit motive, two concepts of **corporate social responsibility (CSR)** and **creating shared value** have become commonplace in strategy conversations. In the next section, we discuss these two concepts as strategic initiatives.

Corporate social responsibility

Corporate social responsibility (CSR) describes the organization's attitude towards going beyond the profit motive and delivering positive social and environmental impacts (Vashchenko 2017). Initiatives undertaken through CSR programmes can generate goodwill, enhanced reputation, and legitimacy to communities in which the organization operates (Choi et al. 2018).

Freeman and Dmytriyev (2017) propose that the needs of stakeholders and the scope of CSR only partially overlap. Both CSR and stakeholder theory argue for the importance of incorporating societal interests into business activity as firms are an integral part of any society. However, whilst stakeholder theory considers responsibility to the wider society important, but only as one part among the firm's other corporate responsibilities, CSR theory prioritizes the firm's responsibility to society over other business responsibilities. Figure 4.4 illustrates the relationship between stakeholder theory and CSR.

In Figure 4.4, the inner ring represents the organization's immediate stakeholders over which it has some degree of control. The outer ring includes groups of secondary stakeholders which may exercise a powerful influence over the activities of the organization but over which the organization has little control. With an ever-growing interest in the activities of organizations by **non-governmental organizations (NGOs)**, consumer groups, and communities, there is a need to identify strategy approaches with the potential to manage and influence all stakeholders appropriately. In this regard, CSR can help, but only in a limited way, as certain stakeholders are prioritized over others, as shown in Figure 4.4.

Depending on its governance approach and values, an organization may undertake CSR initiatives for reasons ranging from pure philanthropy, to environmental concerns, to an active pursuit of enhanced value for all (Rangan et al. 2015). Whilst CSR may be core to an organization, it is not uncommon for CSR programmes to be viewed as unrelated activities detached from the overall strategy of the firm and without top management sponsorship. To make CSR initiatives impactful and sustainable, organizations must develop coherent

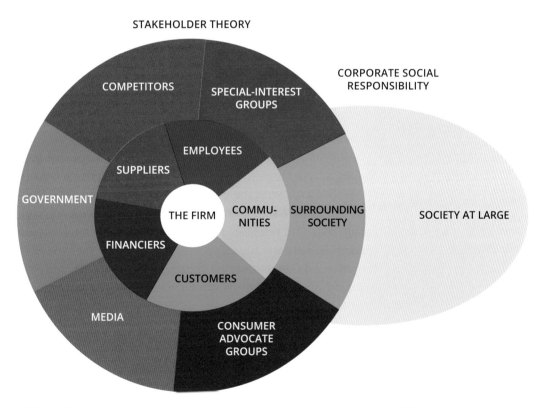

FIGURE 4.4 **Relationship between stakeholder theory and CSR.** *Source*: reproduced from Freeman, R.E. and Dmytriyev, S. (2017). Corporate social responsibility and stakeholder theory: Learning from each other. *Emerging Issues in Management*, **2**, 7–15, http://dx.doi.org/10.4468/2017.1.02freeman.dmytriyev. CC BY 4.0.

strategies that tie CSR into their business models and avoid unnecessarily compromising continuing operations (Costa et al. 2015). For this to succeed, economic issues should not be separated from social, business, ethical, and environmental factors. Crucially, profit-making and societal gain should not be perceived to be moving in opposite directions (Freeman 1984; Harris and Freeman 2008).

Creating shared value

For those involved in strategy work, how might engagement with the 'secondary' stakeholders identified in Figure 4.4 be managed through CSR as part of organizational practice and strategy? Porter and Kramer (2011) state that most firms remain stuck in a 'social responsibility' mindset in which societal issues remain on the periphery, and they are not an integral part of strategy. In response, they advocate a new business model of creating shared value (CSV) (Porter and Kramer 2011). The key principle of a CSV strategy is that it must explain how **economic value** can be created in a way that creates social value and that social value initiatives deliver economic returns—for example, investing in a wellness programme that boosts the health of employees and their families, reducing absenteeism and raising productivity.

As a management philosophy, CSV considers that the concept of value is defined as benefits relative to costs, not benefits alone. Those costs could be to the natural environment or to local communities, which are typically not considered within the boundaries of accounting conventions. Therefore, organizations increasingly need to create new business and/or operating models that consider society's needs whilst building a profitable enterprise (Pfitzer et al. 2013).

With a CSV approach, novel ways of achieving economic success which deliver societal benefits may be uncovered. If CSV thinking can be incorporated in an organization's strategy, then profitability and competitive position, which create economic value by creating social value, can be delivered. In this way, CSV is not about sharing or redistributing the value that has already been generated. Instead, it is about expanding the overall pool of value created.

For example, the Fairtrade movement aims to increase the proportion of revenue that goes to disadvantaged farmers by paying a higher price for the same crops, meaning that a redistributionist approach is taken rather than expanding the overall value being created. A CSV perspective would focus on improving crop cultivation techniques and improving efficiency, crop yields, product quality, and sustainability. This would lead to the expansion of the total revenue and profit pool, which benefits both farmers and the companies that buy from them. Studies of cocoa farmers in the Côte d'Ivoire indicate that while Fairtrade agreements may increase farmers' incomes by 10–20%, shared value investments can increase their incomes by more than 300% (Porter and Kramer 2011). The differences between CSR and CSV are highlighted in Table 4.4.

Skandia, a Swedish insurance and financial services firm, provides an example of how CSV can be applied in the service industries. In 2002, Skandia faced significant losses of up to SEK (Swedish Krona) 2.6 billion ($308 million) because of an unprecedented volume of claims against its employee long-term sick leave insurance product. Adopting a CSV mentality, it then spent several years researching how healthy organizations work and piloting initiatives that tackled the root causes of long-term absenteeism. Based on this research, Skandia piloted a 'rehab hotline' to refer at-risk employees to appropriate therapists for physiological and psychological support through career advice services.

TABLE 4.4 **Difference between corporate social responsibility and the creation of shared value**

Corporate social responsibility	Creation of shared value
Values: doing good, citizenship, philanthropy, sustainability	Values: economic and societal benefits relative to costs
Discretionary by the firm or in response to external pressure	Joint company and community value creation—integral to competing in a marketplace
Separate from profit maximization	Integral to profit maximization
Agenda is determined by external reporting to stakeholders and personal preferences	Agenda is company specific
Impact is limited by corporate CSR budget	Realigned to the entire corporate budget

Source: based on Porter and Kramer (2011: 76).

In 2009, Skandia rolled out the 'rehab' package free of charge as part of its broader occupational pension and insurance package, and employers' premiums were linked to the health status of each client firm. This innovative insurance product in a highly competitive market provided Skandia with a differentiation advantage. Moreover, major value was created for Skandia's clients as sick leave rates declined. By 2014, the percentage of sick-leavers relative to overall employees stood at 2% in Skandia's clients, compared with the national average of 7%. Skandia benefited, shareholders were rewarded, clients saw productivity improvements, and clients' employees felt significant societal benefit.

CASE EXAMPLE 4.1 **NESTLÉ IN SOCIETY**

We focus our energy and resources where unlocking the power of food can make the greatest difference to the lives of people and pets, protect and enhance the environment, and generate significant value for our shareholders and other stakeholders alike.

To do so we will continue working with our partners to:

- Enable people and families to lead healthier, happier lives by continuously improving the nutritional profile of our products.

- Build supply chain resilience by improving livelihoods and being a responsible partner to the communities directly connected to our business activities.

- Steward resources for future generations by enhancing the environmental performance of our operations and scaling up nature-based solutions to regenerate our biosphere.

- Support the development of more circular economy solutions.

(Nestlé 2021)

Nestlé is a leading nutrition, health, and wellness company with around 308,000 employees worldwide, more than 2,000 brands in 189 countries,

Continued

Nestlé's 'Good Food, Good Life' slogan reflects its position as a nutrition, health, and wellness company. *Source*: DCStockPhotography/Shutterstock.com.

and sales of CHF (Swiss francs) 84.3 billion in 2020 (Nestlé 2020). The company was ranked as the sixth leading food brand worldwide in 2021 (Statista.com).

For most of the twentieth century, Nestlé enjoyed high levels of profitability, having established factories early on in developing countries and worked with local farmers to improve infrastructure, crop yields, and productivity. However, in the early 1980s, Nestlé became subject to scrutiny that resulted in a call for a boycott by some NGOs. Nestlé was blamed by some NGOs for 'aggressive marketing techniques' of breast milk substitutes in developing countries, particularly among the poor, who did not always have access to clean drinking water—a necessity when preparing baby formula that is safe for consumption. Furthermore, in the 1990s, the entire processed food and beverage industry began to face severe challenges because of increasing health consciousness by consumers, who began switching from processed products to healthier organic alternatives. Major food companies were blamed for causing a global epidemic of obesity and diabetes, and governments stepped up their regulations to force food manufacturers to reduce the sugar and salt content in their products and improve the quality of their food labelling, often based on a variation of the traffic light system.

Considering these changes, Nestlé has started to reposition its business as a nutrition, health, and wellness company by reformulating its products, adding micronutrients, developing disease-specific nutritional supplements, and expanding into skin health. As a logical extension of this repositioning strategy, Nestlé has embraced the CSV approach to the productivity of its smallholder farmers and their communities. CSV is designed to bring business and society together in creating economic returns as part of generating value for both the shareholders and society at large. An example of Nestlé's CSV approach is the way the company sources raw materials such as cocoa, coffee, and milk from more than 680,000 farmers worldwide. In some cases, a lack of investment in the social and agricultural infrastructure in a region or country may make it difficult for farmers to supply Nestlé with high-quality crops. To address these difficulties, Nestlé provides farmers with access to the knowledge and information that they need to increase productivity and establish sustainable production systems (Kruschwitz 2013).

Every two years, Nestlé invites an independent third party to conduct a formal review of the activities and the issues that matter the most to the business and the firm's stakeholders, which is designed to support the firm's strategic decision-making. The issues of concern are evaluated to determine both the risks and opportunities for Nestlé's reputation, revenues, and costs. The most important material issues in 2019 were identified as the following:

For individuals and families: enabling healthier and happier lives

- *Offering tastier and healthier choices*
- *Inspiring people to lead healthier lives*
- *Building, sharing and applying nutritional knowledge*

For our communities: helping develop thriving, resilient communities

- *Enhancing rural development and livelihoods*
- *Respecting and promoting human rights*
- *Promoting decent employment and diversity*

For the planet: stewarding resources and the environment

- *Caring for water*
- *Acting on climate change*
- *Safeguarding the environment*

(Nestlé 2020: 38–9)

Nestlé has attempted to integrate the CSV approach throughout the firm's operations. To improve nutrition and conserve water, the company does not have a 'sustainability officer', but CSV-related objectives and activities are put into key performance indicators (KPIs) of every employee, from the shop floor to the top management team.

Through this consistent performance measurement approach, the CSV philosophy is increasingly embedded into the firm's organization culture, shaping the functional activities of the organization.

Questions for discussion

1. Apply the CSV framework described in Table 4.4 to the Nestlé case by identifying an example of how Nestlé has approached CSV against each of the five practices.

2. What activities can you detect in the Nestlé case that correspond to the profit, people, and planet aspects of the firm's activities?

3. If you were a shareholder in Nestlé, why might you approve of the CSV approach, and why might you challenge it?

4. Thinking as a strategist, why might it be in Nestlé's long-term interest to try to encourage a cultural shift towards adopting the 'Creating Shared Value' way of doing business?

Sources

Nestlé (2020). Annual review 2019, https://www.nestle.com/sites/default/files/2020-03/2019-annual-review-en.pdf (last accessed 10 August 2022).

Statista (2022a), Household penetration rate of leading food brands worldwide in 2021 (29 June), https://www.statista.com/statistics/1240461/leading-ten-food-brand-penetration-global (last accessed 10 August 2022).

Statista (2022b). Nestlé—statistics & facts (2 June), https://www.statista.com/topics/1439/nestle/#dossierContents__outerWrapper (last accessed 10 August 2022).

Stakeholder management

As we have seen, business has evolved beyond shareholder value maximization towards a view that the interests of business and society are inextricably linked. Corporations are today expected to take into consideration not only shareholders' interests but also those of other groups, organizations, and individuals that have a stake or an interest in the organization. The greater the stakeholders' understanding of the organization, and the closer the organization's ties to its stakeholders, the easier it is to create sustainable value, both for the organization and the organization's stakeholder groups, including wider society.

Stakeholders, to use a definition put forward by Freeman (1984), are any one group or individual who can affect or is affected by the achievement of an organization's purpose, principally financiers, customers, suppliers, employees, and communities. Freeman argues that stakeholders can have a significant impact on organizational performance that is beyond their role as factors of production or consumption (e.g. employees or customers). Therefore, it is important that organizational leaders identify key stakeholders and engage with them when setting strategic direction and making strategic decisions. This is particularly critical for organizations that have invited customers and suppliers to participate directly in the design of products and services through co-creation initiatives. Research indicates that stakeholders do not actively participate in co-creation unless they are allowed to generate value for themselves as well (Ramaswamy and Gouillart 2010). So, how might an organization manage its stakeholders to maximize the benefit for everyone?

Stakeholder mapping

To effectively manage stakeholders and engage them strategically, it is important for organizational leaders and strategy practitioners to understand who their key stakeholders are, where they come from, and their level of interest in and power over the organization.

Stakeholder mapping is a process that aims to identify a list of key stakeholders across the whole stakeholder spectrum. Mapping can be broken into four phases:

1. **Stakeholder identification**: listing of relevant groups, organizations, and people;
2. **Stakeholder analysis**: understanding stakeholder perspectives, interests, and power;
3. **Stakeholder map generation**: visualizing a relationship between the organization and the stakeholders;
4. **Stakeholder ranking**: ordering of stakeholder importance and their influence on the organization.

Several different frameworks for undertaking stakeholder mapping and analysis are available. The most common mapping framework, developed by Mendelow (1981, 1986), characterizes stakeholders in terms of their interest and power. This is a useful tool for understanding political priorities as stakeholder groups often have conflicting interests. For example, in Western market economies, the interests of shareholders and managers often conflict with the interests of labour unions regarding salaries. Similarly, environmental and community groups are often in conflict with natural resource extraction firms, such as in the highly politicized and emotional disagreement over the use of fracking to extract natural gas or oil from deep-rock formations (an example of disputes concerning fracking is discussed in Chapter 5).

The two dimensions of Mendelow's power–interest matrix is shown in Figure 4.5. The matrix depicts stakeholders relative to the power they hold and the extent to which they are likely to demonstrate interest in either supporting or opposing a particular strategy of the firm. The four boxes from the matrix are considered in more detail in Table 4.5.

Stakeholder mapping enables the organization to understand its stakeholders and potentially move its relationship with them beyond transactional relationships towards understanding,

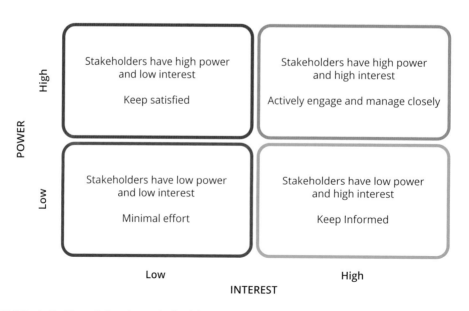

FIGURE 4.5 Mendelow's stakeholder power–interest matrix. *Source*: authors.

TABLE 4.5 **Mendelow's stakeholder matrix in more detail**

Level of stakeholder power and interest	Influence of stakeholder	Action required from the organization	Example
High interest and high power	Key players Likely to have a significant influence over the organization and may be the driver behind change or strategy implementation Likely to possess the power to stop change or a strategy going ahead if they are unsatisfied with what is being proposed	The organization will need to actively engage in consultation with this group	Shareholders Labour unions Financiers
High interest and low power	Has an interest in the organization Unlikely to have the power to influence change Can attempt to join forces with a group with power (such as the press, media, and the government, who normally do not have much interest in the day-to-day activities of an individual organization) and become a key player as a result	Keep this group informed of the organization's operations and performance	Pressure groups Other non-governmental organizations with a high interest in the organization
Low interest and high power	Has the potential to become a 'high interest and high power' stakeholder group	It is essential that this group is kept satisfied that the organization is operating within the accepted norms of the law so that they are less likely to gain interest and exercise their power	The media is unlikely to have a significant interest in day-to-day activities of the organization but may become a powerful stakeholder if the organization is discovered to have engaged in unethical activities
Low interest and low power	Unlikely to have an interest in the organization and its direction This may be due to their lack of power to influence the organization and they are likely to accept the prevailing situation and show little if any resistance to the strategy or the changes in the organization	Limited effort by the organization beyond ensuring that any contractual agreements are properly discharged	Contractors who are working in the organization on a specific assignment for a predetermined contract period

Source: authors.

engagement, and respect. The key questions that management should ask when developing a stakeholder engagement strategy are as follows (Kourdi 2015):

1. Which stakeholders are the most significant for the organization? Whose input will be valuable when strategy is being developed, and who are instrumental in its implementation?

2. How do the organization's stakeholders relate to each other, and how could these relationships be strengthened or leveraged further?

3. What do the organization's stakeholder groups value? What do they want of the organization and how effective are they at getting it?

4. How will the organization be able to strengthen and manage the stakeholder relationships?

5. How should the organization communicate with its various stakeholder groups, with what frequency, message, and communications channel?

Stakeholder management is not an easy task, especially as it is a political process with several conflicting interests. However, engaged stakeholders can be an important resource for the organization to generate sustainable advantage, earn the company a solid reputation for sound business practices in the community, and successfully fulfil the organization's purpose. From a process–practice perspective, stakeholder interactions are central to the strategizing process and process dynamics (see Figures 2.4, 2.5, and Case Example 4.2) through either involvement in activities or as triggers to episodes. Practices for engaging effectively and interdependently with stakeholders are crucial for strategic leadership, as we will discuss further in Chapter 14.

CASE EXAMPLE 4.2 GAP INC. STAKEHOLDER MAPPING

Gap's commitment to social responsibility was first articulated in 1992 when the company published one of the earliest sets of ethical sourcing principles in the garment industry. Despite 100 people operating globally to police and enforce Gap's code, which covered labour, environmental, health, and safety standards across the firm's suppliers and subcontractors in its global supply chain, Gap's local suppliers failed to implement the code's requirements.

When several serious labour and environmental protection violations were uncovered, Gap came under pressure from advocacy groups in the United States and the United Kingdom. There was much media attention surrounding protests outside Gap's head office in San Francisco for several weeks—especially when the groups protested with no clothes on. Executives realized that there was a legal problem with the way in which Gap assessed risk to ethical trade, and they identified that the level of change required to improve their risk mitigation approach to ethical trade and reassure their critics necessitated a major overhaul.

As the first step to deeper engagement with its stakeholders, Gap undertook a stakeholder mapping exercise by listing as many stakeholders as possible and then ranking them by their importance. 'We recognized that it would not be possible for us to have a strategic relationship with each of the stakeholders, so we highlighted those who we deemed to be the most key', recalled Deanna Robinson, Gap's head of monitoring and vendor development.

Prioritizing stakeholders allowed the firm to focus on developing transparent relationships with a few of the most influential organizations. 'We will never be able to engage at the same level of depth with every organization that exists', explained Daryl Knudsen, Gap's director of public policy and stakeholder engagement, 'but by engaging with organizations who themselves have extensive networks, we have managed to receive some level of input and influence from those networks.'

An external consultancy firm facilitated this mapping process at Gap. They involved participants from different function groups, including legal, public relations, government affairs, and global compliance in the stakeholder mapping process, to create a map of stakeholders that was customized and prioritized by those participating. This not only enabled Gap to ensure that employees were engaged with the new process and strategy, but it also facilitated a development opportunity for those employees to get to know who the key stakeholders were and additionally enabled the executives to better understand how the decisions they make and their relationships with stakeholders impact the lives of labourers making their clothes.

This activity meant that Gap's approach was starting to evolve from a risk-averse legalistic strategy to one based on proactive engagement which could tease out stakeholder needs, positions, and motivations. It was a significant change in the company's approach, which meant that many of the senior decision-makers were learning about stakeholder theory and discovering who their stakeholders were for the first time.

Once Gap had identified its stakeholders, the company set about getting to know them better and consulting them on improving their labour practices. There was one meeting which had important consequences for the company. Gap's executives met Lynda Yanz, of the Maquila Solidarity Network (MSN) in Toronto, Canada, which is an influential workers' rights group concerned with labour rights issues in the Americas and a key sourcing market for the company. Yanz advised that Gap should

work to engage stakeholders more holistically, and this would mean that stakeholders could communicate directly about emerging issues with corporate responsibility team members.

This meeting made one other thing clear to the executives: to improve labour conditions, they could not do this alone but needed to develop partnerships with relevant stakeholders and participate in emerging multi-stakeholder initiatives. After meeting with MSN, Gap joined two multi-stakeholder initiatives (MSIs): the New-York-based Social Accountability International in 2003 and the London-based Ethical Trading Initiative (ETI) in 2004. By joining these MSIs, executives felt that they had provided a safe platform for tackling issues with various stakeholders as well as gaining their insights and perspectives on the best ways to handle those issues raised.

Questions for discussion

1. What were the main differences between Gap's legalistic risk mitigation and stakeholder mapping approaches?

2. Gap executives admitted that they were mistaken in trying to 'go it alone' in their efforts to improve labour conditions. Why is this admission significant?

3. What groups emerged as key stakeholders in the case, why, and how did Gap address their concerns?

Sources

Smith, N.C., Ansett, S., and Erez, L. (2011). How Gap Inc. engaged with its stakeholders. *MIT Sloan Management Review* (Summer).

Smith, N.C., Ansett, S., and Erez, L. (2019). How Gap engaged with its stakeholders. In: Lenssen, G. and Smith, N. (eds), *Managing Sustainable Business*. Dordrecht: Springer.

So far in this chapter, we have discussed the purpose and values of an organization and shown how the strict focus on pure shareholder value maximization has been replaced by concern for wider stakeholder and societal issues while still maintaining the profit motive. Alongside increasing inequality linked to globalization effects that we will address in Chapter 12, sustainability is a major global issue of the twenty-first century. Already in 2010, over 75% of executives worldwide believed that sustainability was important to the financial success of their firms, but they have been, until recently, slow to take serious steps to embed it in their business practices

(Mirvis et. al. 2010). Today, the critical issue is no longer whether sustainability should occupy a strategic role in organizational activities but how to capture value from various sustainability practices (McKinsey & Co. 2021). In the remainder of this chapter, we discuss how sustainability practices shape an organization's strategy. We consider the extent to which sustainability is incorporated into strategy work or expressed through the creation of separate sustainability strategies.

Access the online resources to watch a short video clip where Aileen McLeod shares her views on the importance of stakeholder engagement in strategy work.

4.5 What does sustainability in strategy mean?

Sustainability describes the capacity of a system to continue over time. If we adopt the perspective that the sole purpose of an organization is to generate economic value for shareholders, questions of sustainability focus on the potential to deliver financial returns and expenditure on a continuing basis. Sustainability in this context means taking actions and financial decisions in the present which don't jeopardize the future capability of the organization to create economic value for shareholders (Elkington 2017). However, if we consider organizations to be part of a broader ecosystem with natural, commercial, and social dimensions, sustainability can only be achieved with a broader set of objectives. With this stakeholder view, sustainability implies understanding and managing the impact of actions taken today by an organization on the future of the financial, social, and natural environmental systems in which they are embedded (Eccles and Serafeim 2013).

   The attitude to sustainability reflected in the practices of employees and managers can be considered an attribute of an organization's culture that influences the possibilities of sustainability (Wickert and de Bakker 2019). For some organizations, a commitment to a stakeholder view of sustainability is so woven into the fabric of organizational practice and strategic decision-making that it is taken for granted. For others, sustainability is treated as a cost that needs to be managed through exceptional organizational practices and isolated strategic decision-making.

   Understanding how sustainability is viewed in an organization is a crucial piece of contextual understanding for the strategy practitioner. Attitude to sustainability will have a bearing on which strategic options are best suited to the organizational culture and sense of purpose (Geradts and Bocken 2019). Further, strategy practitioners may be called upon to produce a sustainability strategy.

Triple bottom line

A well-known conceptual model for sustainability is the **triple bottom line (TBL)** shown in Figure 4.6. The TBL proposes that systemic sustainability should be evaluated on the combined basis of economic, social, and environmental performance which delivers profit-, people-, and planet-related outcomes, respectively (Elkington 1998). At an organizational level, it is argued that the TBL delivers more value for shareholders over time as a managerial decision-making

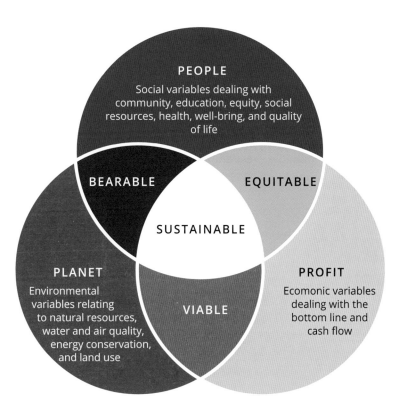

FIGURE 4.6 Triple bottom line: Balancing people, planet, and profit. *Source*: Copyright © 2019 All Rights Reserved by BNAC Environmental Solutions Inc.

framework than an exclusive focus on traditional bottom-line thinking present in financial reports and statements.

Profit focus

The **profit focus** remains a key component of the performance criteria of any private organization. For not-for-profit organizations, profit can be read as financial performance. Every organization needs to be mindful of its sources of income/funding and its cost base. Over time, an organization cannot indefinitely sustain a cost base that exceeds levels of income. Therefore, to be able to continue as a viable entity, financial sustainability must be given due consideration as part of organizational strategy (Santos and Williamson 2015). However, a profit focus doesn't preclude people or planet gains. As Kurt Kuehn, the chief financial officer of the multinational delivery firm UPS, notes, socially and environmentally beneficial initiatives that emphasize efficiency can also contribute to financial sustainability (Kuehn and McIntire 2014).

People focus

A **people focus** directs attention to organizations' impact on their stakeholders such as employees, shareholders, owners, customers, and suppliers. Each person with a 'stake' in the organization will have a sense of the fairness and **acceptability** of how the organization operates, its viability over time, and whether their individual relationship with the organization can be maintained. A people focus can result in positive outcomes for an organization. For instance, in an examination of a selection of social enterprises—businesses with a social or environmental mission—in Vietnam, Truong and Barraket (2018: 2963) found that considerate treatment of staff and their families by the employer led to reciprocal goodwill and effort from employees, which enabled the organizations to grow in a resource-constrained environment.

A positive impact on the local communities in which an organization is embedded can arise from a people focus. Caesar's Entertainment, one of the world's largest gaming companies, has won more than 50 awards for its sustainability leadership efforts to 'act responsibly with its customers, support local communities, treat employees with respect and support them in building satisfying careers' (Posner and Kiron 2013: 65).

Planet focus

A **planet focus** is about the relationship between an organization and the natural environment—how finite resources and energy are used, how waste is created and managed, and how climate change is impacted by organizational activities. The concept of natural capital—natural resources linked to location and geographical conditions (introduced in Chapter 6)—is highly relevant to the planet focus. For an organization to be considered sustainable, the land it owns and the physical environment it inhabits must be maintained to at least a minimum threshold level. Others go further and focus on planet outcomes as a key feature of their business. For instance, Bureo is a Chilean start-up that recycles discarded fishing nets into its Netplus range of affordable nets for the fishing industry, whilst reclaiming hundreds of tonnes of marine plastic pollution.

Further, all organizations are embedded in, impacted by, and have an impact on **climate**. Climate describes the patterns in weather conditions in any given area. Climate change describes a shift in weather conditions in an area over time, often with consequences for natural environmental conditions. With implications for living standards around the world, climate change is a major international concern for governments and intergovernmental organizations such as the United Nations (UN). Increasingly, environmental sustainability is a core topic for organizations to consider because of government policy and **regulation**. Consideration of how to manage organizational inputs and outputs, energy, waste, pollution, and emissions, and the relationship with the natural ecosystems and climate is becoming a mandatory feature of strategy practice. For example, Fairtrade requires the adoption of sustainable agricultural practices as part of its support for coffee farmer groups, minimizing climate impact whilst protecting the fertility of the land and future production potential (Fairtrade 2019).

Sustainability as a system

An important feature of the TBL model is that each component is interrelated: sustainability is thought of as a dynamic system requiring management of profit, people, and planet factors in a coherent way. For example, having a keen focus on the natural environment and impact on individuals and societies might create an organization with apparent high moral standing. However, if this leads to neglect of financial viability, the organization will have a short lifespan, limiting the positive impact and outcomes it might achieve. Equally, a focus on the planet as an instrumental means of enhancing profit might create a viable organization in the physical sense but not one that is sustainable in terms of relationships with local communities, politicians, and talented employees if social factors are not considered.

FIGURE 4.7 Triple bottom line at Novo Nordisk. *Source*: from Novo Nordisk, http://www. novonordisk.co.uk/about-novo-nordisk-in-uk/corporate_overview/sustainability.html (last accessed 4 October 2022).

Novo Nordisk, a Danish multinational pharmaceutical company, describes the TBL as 'how they do business' (see Figure 4.7). On their website, the company writes:

By promoting responsible and ethical business practices throughout our global value chain and continuously reducing the negative environmental impacts generated by our activities, we stimulate economic growth that is socially just and environmentally sustainable. TBL makes good business. It delivers long-term growth for our business by building trust, protecting and enhancing our licence to operate and attracting and retaining the best people.

(Novo Nordisk 2019)

Effectively, the TBL describes sustainability as a system of interlocking priorities. This system works by ensuring balance between economic viability, positive social impact, and environmental stewardship. When too much emphasis is placed on any one of these, organizational performance will not be delivered in a sustainable way. This doesn't mean instant failure for an organization that doesn't balance its priorities. Instead, it means that habits and culture that have a finite lifespan become embedded in the organization, ultimately limiting its capacity to continue operating successfully.

4.6 Sustainability as a factor of influence in strategy work

In this section, we consider how attitudes and priority initiatives arising in the international and national political and competitive environments exert pressure on organizations to engage with sustainability. We also examine how views of sustainability within ownership, leadership, and staff populations might impact on strategy. Building your understanding of the priorities and attitudes of different stakeholder groups will help you determine the ways in which sustainability concerns should be incorporated into strategy activity.

External drivers of sustainability

International community

The term 'international community' refers to collaboration between nations. Typically, this collaboration is brokered by an intergovernmental organization formed to coordinate collective agreement and initiatives on a specific topic of shared interest. Sustainability is one such key concern for the international community. For example, beyond inter-nation conflict, in the *World Economic Forum Global Risks Report* for 2022, climate action failure, extreme weather, and **biodiversity** loss are seen as the gravest threats to global stability and peace, closely followed by social cohesion erosion and livelihood crises (World Economic Forum 2022: 14). In 2018, the **Intergovernmental Panel on Climate Change (IPCC)** issued the stark warning that uncontrollable and irreversible **climate change** impacts will be reached in 2030 without significant adjustment of human activity about emissions and environmental management. The IPCC (2022) has highlighted that the loss of biodiversity should be a major cause for concern for the international community. Biodiversity describes the variety and variation in the species of life on the planet. Local and global ecosystems are finely balanced, and as species are lost because of human activity, the system can be damaged, leading to further harm to all species (including humans).

The consequences of unsustainable development threaten life and living standards around the world. Climate change may render regions uninhabitable soon—from rising sea levels destroying coastal communities to temperature increases to life-threatening levels in locations with little rainfall (such as the Middle East and Australia). As shifts in weather patterns arising from climate change destroy farming traditions and subsistence living in many, typically poor, regions of the world, the human consequences can be drastic. The health, well-being, livelihood, and ways of life of many people are placed in jeopardy.

Equally, the concept of **sustainable development** (i.e. human progress that doesn't harm future generations or the planet) promises new ways of global interaction, cooperation, and understanding whilst raising living standards. Taking the lead in the international community, in September 2015, the UN authorized 17 **sustainable development goals (SDGs)**, as illustrated in Figure 4.8 (UN 2019). Each of these goals is a high-level topic of common interest that nations

FIGURE 4.8 UN sustainable development goals. *Source*: United Nations Sustainable Development Goals. Copyright © United Nations.

from around the world might collaborate on to bring a halt to unsustainable human activity. Each of the goals has a set of specific aims and solutions proposed by the UN.

These SDGs might be relevant to the organizational strategist in several ways (Lamach 2017). Increasingly, the SDGs are featuring in organizational strategy work as an external reference benchmark to explain and justify internal sustainability initiatives. Aligning with the SDGs gives a common language to unite stakeholders in understanding how and why the organization is responding to global sustainability challenges (Schramade 2017). Aligning with the SDGs might also open access to funding initiatives, where the requirements involve showing evidence of sustainable development. Further, the SDGs are being interpreted and used to shape national governmental policy. As the laws and regulatory expectations of nation states are being aligned with SDGs, ease of doing business and commercial opportunities are increasing for organizations that embrace the SDGs in their strategy work and communications. Therefore, strategy practitioners and their organizations stand to benefit from engaging with governments and regulators in relation to sustainability (Santos and Williamson 2015).

National governments

Governments are key stakeholders for organizations in relation to sustainability. Governments contribute to international communities and so have a vested interest in the sort of initiatives described above. Organizations that align with programmes such as the sustainable development goals are likely to find routes to productive dialogue with national governments. For example, the Colombian government has established a forum to engage organizations and citizens in planning how to best implement the SDGs in the country (Mead 2019).

Further, governments have a strong interest in TBL outcomes from their industrial base and from public- and third-sector organizations. It is in a government's interest to balance the preservation of natural heritage, wildlife, infrastructure, industries, and ways of life in rural and urban communities. In effect, this is a sustainability agenda. A government will also be liable for addressing the negative impacts associated with sustainability barriers such as climate change, for instance, the cost and disruption to businesses and communities associated with flooding. As flooding arises from a combination of factors, such as climate change, mass agricultural practices, river management, and urban development, local and national governments will typically foot the bill for flooding incidents. To avoid such negative financial outcomes, a government might legislate and regulate organizational practice towards sustainable approaches.

CASE EXAMPLE 4.3 **SDGs IN IBERDROLA**

Iberdrola is a global energy firm headquartered in Spain. Owning energy-related companies in many countries, Iberdrola cites a group vision of 'creating a sustainable, greener energy future'. Shaping the group strategy and delivery of this vision is a firm commitment to the SDGs. An extract from the group's website is displayed in Figure 13.4.

In line with our activity, the Iberdrola group is focusing its efforts on supplying affordable and clean energy (goal 7) [in Figure 4.8] and fighting against climate change (goal 13). It has created a specific long-term incentive plan to achieve this. In addition, the group makes a direct contribution to guarantee clean water and sanitation

Continued

4

(goal 6), has increased its investment in R&D activities (goal 9), promotes respect to life on land (goal 15) and works to establish partnerships for the goals (goal 17). The company also makes an indirect contribution to all other sustainable development goals and has launched the first credit line with a sustainable indicator to achieve them. The group's contribution to social and economic development of the communities in which it operates and to protect the environment is articulated through its sustainable energy business model.

(Iberdrola, https://www.iberdrola.com/
sustainability/committed-sustainable-
development-goals, last accessed
4 October 2022)

Drawing on the perspectives of strategy introduced in Chapter 1, we can identify several related ways in which the SDGs have permeated group strategy in Iberdrola (see Figure 4.9):

- **Strategy as priority**: rather than attempt to do everything, Iberdrola identifies focal SDGs and goals where the greatest direct

contribution can be achieved. The SDGs identified are best aligned with the core business of the organization, bringing a realism and focus to the subsequent connection of SDGs with organizational strategy.

- **Strategy as possession**: in presenting the SDGs within their strategy work, Iberdrola re-applies the original UN artwork and terminology. This use of imagery makes the Iberdrola sustainability strategy instantly recognizable and aids stakeholder communication of what the organization is working on and why.

- **Strategy as purpose**: the articulation of the commitment to sustainability uses the SDGs to define part of the future vision of the organization. How the SDGs will connect with core business is described with reference to individual SDGs, and long-term aims of positive social and environmental impact are identified.

- **Strategy as problem-solving**: through strategy work tied to a selection of the SDGs, Iberdrola is directly tackling sustainability problems that have arisen, in part, because of

MAIN FOCUS   **DIRECT CONTRIBUTION**

INDIRECT CONTRIBUTION TO ALL OTHER SDGs

FIGURE 4.9 Iberdrola's deployment of the SDGs. *Source*: United Nations Sustainable Development Goals. Copyright © United Nations.

energy production in the past. By showing industry leadership in addressing these sectoral issues, Iberdrola might create competitive advantage and threshold competencies.

- **Strategy as preparation for the future**: Iberdrola identifies a future in which energy production must be sustainable as defined by the triple bottom line. By building capacities and creating resources to meet this future state now, including embedding sustainability within the organizational culture, Iberdrola is preparing for the future.

Regardless of the extent to which one agrees with Iberdrola's approach, sustainability can be seen to be a core concern for the business—deliberately woven into the fabric of its strategic work. For the strategists in Iberdrola, engagement with the concept of 'sustainability' will be a crucial consideration for the foreseeable future.

Questions for discussion

1. If you were a shareholder in Iberdrola, what would be your perspective on the organization's commitment to sustainability in general and engagement with the SDGs in particular?

2. If you were an employee in Iberdrola, would the organization's statements about a sustainable future be important to you? Explain your answer.

3. If you were a government official in a country in which Iberdrola operates, how might you react to Iberdrola's public commitment to addressing a targeted set of SDGs?

Because of international trends, many governments also sense opportunity in relation to sustainability. As technological solutions to environmental challenges create new industries and jobs (e.g. renewable energy from sources such as wind power and biomass), and as social initiatives build national capabilities (e.g. raising education and living standards for all citizens), an emphasis on sustainable development has the potential to contribute to many national objectives. Figure 4.10 shows the possible global benefits of engaging with sustainable development rather than 'business as usual'.

Benefits also include global reputation within the international community. In engaging with existing organizations, governments may incentivize organizational practice to evolve towards sustainable approaches through funding, tax breaks, and procurement initiatives. For example, a study of local council performance measures in New Zealand in the build-up to more stringent government sustainability laws coming into force showed an embrace of social and environmental practices by the councils. This anticipatory action was, in part, driven be a desire to maximize funding potential after the new laws were introduced (Othman et al. 2017).

Such governmental activity may be viewed as a constraint on the strategy process. Mandatory responses to local and national government sustainability policies, laws, and regulations may be understood as part of the cost of doing business. Equally, if sustainability can be incorporated into the everyday operation of the organization, government incentives and opportunities, which are withheld from competitors, may be available to the organization. In this way, organizations that go '**beyond compliance**' might create competitive advantage—doing well whilst 'doing good'. For instance, Superglass, a UK-based manufacturer of home insulation materials, has transformed its business performance by pioneering sustainability practices that push well beyond the minimum regulatory requirements.

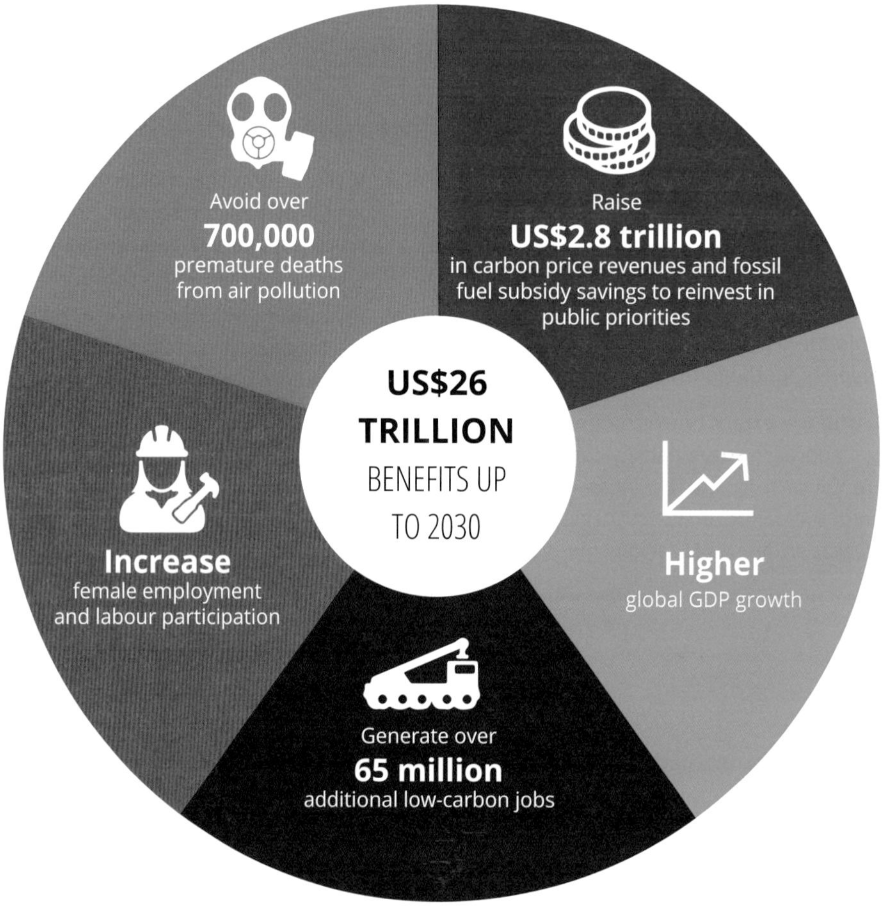

FIGURE 4.10 Anticipated global gains of sustainable development. *Source*: Global Commission on the Economy and Climate (2018). https://newclimateeconomy.report/2018/wp-content/uploads/sites/6/2018/08/18_NCE_iconwheels-05.png (last accessed 10 August 2022).

It is useful to note that there is extensive variation in practice between the attitudes of nation states to sustainability. As you examine the macro-context for an organization, *PESTEL* (political, economic, social, technological, environmental, and legislative trends—covered extensively in Chapter 5) can serve as a valuable framework through which to understand the trajectory of sustainability within a country. When conducting PESTEL analysis, how government currently legislates—and is likely to legislate in future—on sustainability might affect organizational strategy. Direct connection between the organizational aims of the TBL and the trends of the macro-environment can be found in the PESTEL framework (economic, social, and environmental). Indirectly, movement in the political, legislative, and technological aspects of macro-trends will also have a bearing on how sustainability and strategy are managed within organizations.

Non-governmental organizations and community pressures

Organizations may be subject to powerful pressures to engage with sustainability from NGOs (Hart et al. 2003). NGOs are non-profit groups organized at a local, national, or international level around a common purpose. NGOs focus on providing services and information to citizens or advocating on their behalf with government and organizations (Conley and Williams 2005). NGOs may monitor organizational activity, praising exemplars of what they deem good practice and criticizing or actively mobilizing against practice which they deem unacceptable. The actions of NGOs can affect an organization's reputation and relationship with government and limit possible options for action (Eccles and Serafeim 2013).

An example of a sustainability-related NGO is the B-Lab (https://bcorporation.uk/about-b-lab). Headquartered in Pennsylvania, B-Lab is a non-profit organization that 'serves a global movement to redefine success in business so that all companies compete not only to be the best in the world, but the best for the world, and as a result, society enjoys a shared and durable prosperity'.

B-Lab has developed an audit structure that examines the impact of an organization's practices against governance, workers, community, and environmental impact criteria. Organizations showing sufficient sustainable practices and capabilities can then be registered for **Benefit Corporation (B-Corp)** status as a public symbol of their sustainability credentials. At the start of 2022, 4,191 B-Corps of all sizes and sectors had been certified in over 50 countries (https://bcorporation.uk/directory).

B-Lab is engaging with governments, businesses, and the UN to develop a digital platform to expand the reach of B-Corp certification and the availability of free-to-use sustainability management tools as well as lobbying for legislative changes around the world that encourage sustainability-positive regulatory environments.

Community pressures can also have an influence on an organization's practices. The priorities of the local community may differ from those of the organization. Typically, local communities will be interested in preserving habitat, infrastructure, and ways of life. Organizations may be interested in deploying habitat and infrastructure to productive ends and changing ways of life for economic return. Tensions may arise in relation to specific initiatives proposed by organizations. For example, proposals to route waste streams from a production process into a river—even within legal limits for pollution—may lead to protest and disruption among community members.

Local communities may be more amenable to the activities of social enterprises that 'pursue a social mission while relying on a commercial business model' (Santos et al. 2015: 36). Social enterprises are characterized by having a clear social and/or environmental mission, generating most of the income through commercial trade, and reinvesting most profits to further the social mission (Social Enterprise 2019). When business acumen is used to ensure financial viability, social enterprises have the potential to create significant societal and environmental value (Powell et al. 2019).

Social enterprises tend to generate goodwill in the communities in which they operate through outcomes such as local job creation and meeting specific social needs. For example, Divine Chocolate is a fair-trade chocolate company co-owned by the 85,000 cocoa farmers of the KuapaKokoo cooperative in Ghana: 'As owners, they get a share in the profits, a say in the company, and a voice in the global marketplace' (Divine Chocolate 2019).

The scale of social enterprise activity is growing. A research report by Social Enterprise UK (an NGO) in 2018 found that there were over 100,000 social enterprises contributing £60 billion to the UK economy and employing two million people, considerably higher than previous estimates. We will discuss the impact of social enterprises on organizational strategy in section 4.7 later in this chapter.

Shareholder attitude

An increasing concern for owners, shareholders, and investors is the role that sustainability plays in organizational strategy. Lubin and Esty (2010) note a growing disconnect between the importance of sustainability to those setting organizational strategies and the perceived relevance of sustainability to mainstream investors. They suggest that transparent sustainability reporting and the active management of sustainability concerns—as expressed through strategy—is vital to reassuring those who own the company of its long-term prospects. Indeed, Mark Carney, the UN Special Envoy on Climate Action and Finance, former Governor of the Bank of England, has warned financial institutions that the climate crisis may render many of their assets worthless (BBC 2019).

Further, a new type of investment approach, known as sustainable investing, has emerged to meet the needs of shareholders for whom sustainability is a moral and ethical concern. UBS, a Swiss global investment and financial services firm, defines sustainable investing as 'a way to invest for the returns you expect while staying true to your values. That's whether you care about a cause, driving social change, or how a company or country conducts itself' (UBS 2019). Sustainable investing appears to be gaining traction because of increased societal awareness of sustainability and topics such as climate change and business impact (Cubas-Díaz and Martínez Sedano 2018). The SDGs are increasingly providing a useful common framework with which investors can interpret the sustainability plans and actions of organizations when they consider how to invest (Schramade 2017). Also, for institutional investors, a desire to avoid embarrassing revelations about investments in industries with conflicting values is changing shareholder attitudes.

UBS identifies three ways in which to achieve sustainable investing:

- **exclusion:** avoiding companies and industries that don't reflect your values from your investment portfolio;

- **integration:** selecting organizations that actively engage with environmental, social, and corporate governance as part of your portfolio;

- **impact:** alongside financial returns, tracking the measurable difference made to environmental and social outcomes by the companies you invest in.

Sustainability is increasingly a topic of scrutiny for shareholders of publicly listed firms seeking to attract investment and maintain share price. Morgan Stanley, an investment bank, concluded from the first three years' experience of operating a '**sustainable investment** foundation' that 'sustainability concerns will prove more than just a temporary trend and assume a prominent, and permanent, position in the dialogue between companies and investors' (Choi 2016: 62). As you consider how sustainability might influence organizational strategy, the trend towards sustainable investing implies that the owners of the firm, or funders of public- and third-sector organizations, will expect, at a minimum, strategy options, initiatives, and objectives to be able to be explained in terms of sustainability impacts and implications (Eccles and Klimenko 2019).

Competitive pressures

Competitive advantage—the potential to outperform the break-even competitor in a chosen sector—is increasingly impacted by the topic of sustainability (see Chapters 6 and 8 for an in-depth discussion of competitive advantage). Whether adopting cost-leadership, differentiation, or focus strategies, an organization's response to attitudes to sustainability within a sector will influence its competitive advantage.

The cost base of organizations adopting a cost-leadership strategy may be reduced by sustainability initiatives. Initiatives that reduce waste, such as minimizing logistics through local sourcing and reducing energy usage, can have a TBL impact whilst maintaining a focus on cost leadership; for example, Ryanair reports that its commitment to fuel-efficient jets is principally to keep costs down. Further, ensuring that minimum regulatory requirements are met in all aspects of an organization avoids any costs associated with non-compliance. For organizations that compete on differentiation, financial benefits can also arise from sustainability initiatives. For instance, 3M—a global manufacturing conglomerate—instituted the Pollution Prevention Pays (3P) initiative, which focused engineering resource on designing outsources of pollution from its production processes. Over 20 years of the initiative, 3M reported a reduction in toxic releases by 99% and greenhouse gas emissions by 72%, saving billions of dollars (Winston 2012).

For organizations deploying differentiation strategy, sustainability initiatives may offer the potential to enhance the value of offerings to customers; for example, as illustrated in Case Example 14.1, well-being multinational Natura's portfolio of sustainability initiatives enhances its differentiation advantage (Rodríguez Vilá et al. 2017). Consumers or customers concerned with climate change, such as local government tenders, may seek—and be willing to pay more for—products from organizations with green credentials and sustainable operational processes. This consumer behaviour of making purchasing decisions to express morality and values is referred to as **consumer activism**, and it has an increasingly powerful presence in brand management (Chatzidakis and Shaw 2018).

For example, in early 2019, Gillette gained a high level of publicity for aligning its traditionally stereotypically 'macho' marketing approach with evident support for the #metoo movement and disregarding the idea of toxic masculinity (*The Guardian* 2019). Sustainability is a topic which features heavily in consumer activism campaigns. Further, an overt commitment to sustainable products and ethical processes can create a sense of pride for employees (Epley and Kumar 2019) This makes the organization more attractive to talented potential employees and helps to retain that talent within an industry, as well as boosting creativity in product development (Posner and Kiron 2013).

Within an industrial sector, new niches may emerge from sustainable practice, such as Method's environmentally friendly cleaning products within the home-care sector (https://method-home.com). Equally, there is scope for disruptive innovation in relation to sustainability that might eliminate significant costs of production. For example, British Recycled Plastics (https://britishrecycledplastic.co.uk) reclaims the raw materials used to make its external furniture products, providing a lower cost base than competitors that use non-recycled equivalents, and allowing it to price its offerings keenly.

Competitive advantage is a relative measure (organization versus break-even competitor). In other words, the actions of competitors in parallel with the organization's own actions define competitive advantage. For organizations electing not to evolve towards sustainable practice, whilst others in the sector do, competitive disadvantage may arise at some point in the future. Competitive disadvantage is when an organization is unable to break even as customers are only willing to pay less than the cost of providing them with goods or services (Bowman and Ambrosini 2007). This may be the fate of organizations that fail to comply with legal standards for or keep pace with changing customer perspectives on sustainability.

For those organizations that embrace sustainability, performance aims such as revenue growth or increased profitability may arise because of incorporating sustainability into organizational strategy work. Whelan and Fink (2016) articulate that enhanced sustainability efforts are highly likely to lead to lower cost of capital, better operational performance, and high stock price. Further, given macro-trends in the international community and local and national government priorities, building a capacity for and track record in sustainability will increase the resilience, efficiency, and relevance of the organization.

Internal perspectives on sustainability

Leadership attitude

A recent survey of executives (Kiron et al. 2017) identified that a crucial factor in the success of sustainability initiatives—from individual projects, to building a culture of sustainability, to delivering triple bottom line outcomes—relies on getting buy-in from the board and making a solid business case. How leaders describe sustainability to others in the organization has a direct impact on the traction that sustainability initiatives can gather (Elkington 2017). Without collective leadership support, sustainability will likely remain on the periphery of an organization's way of working.

Within organizations, the attitude of leaders towards sustainability has a significant impact on the extent to which it is reflected as a key concern in organizational practice (Arena et al. 2018). Unilever's former CEO Paul Polman reflects on the role of leadership and management in embedding sustainability into the organization:

> Sustainability is a grand goal for multinational companies that have been focused for years on quarterly profits and shareholder value. But financial performance and sustainability are not mutually exclusive, if the very significant barriers to aligning them can be identified and surmounted with impassioned management. Once companies start on a path toward sustainability, momentum takes hold and the organizations can move forward, with the majority of their employees striving toward sustainability.

> Bhattacharya and Polman (2017: 12)

For leaders, finding ways in which to work with sustainability—and implement sustainability initiatives effectively—remains a significant challenge. As we'll explore in Chapter 14, from a process–practice perspective, collective processes of strategic leadership involving a broad coalition of stakeholders in strategizing offer potential to accelerate organizational adoption of sustainability as a way of operating. Having experience working with sustainability initiatives plays a significant role in a leader's willingness to promote sustainability in their own organization (Schaltenbrand et al. 2018). Being willing to learn, open to critical feedback, taking the first action steps despite uncertainty, and attempting to engage staff in a holistic way are identified as leadership approaches that will define the extent to which sustainability is nurtured in an organization (Elkington 2018b). Regardless of the approach adopted, ignoring sustainability as a topic of core leadership concern is not an option. Sustainability is an imperative that organizational leadership must address (Lubin and Esty 2010).

Employee attitude

Studies have found that corporate engagement with sustainability and TBL objectives over time leads to enhanced staff job satisfaction and an increase in staff behaviours that contribute to TBL outcomes (Perez et al. 2018). This may be attributable to an enhanced sense of purpose for employees and pride at working for an organization that recognizes the shared challenges of meeting SDGs (Casey and Sieber 2016). As highlighted in the 'strategy as purpose' discussion in Chapter 1, improved business performance and profitability are likely to follow from high employee engagement in developing and implementing sustainability practices.

As sustainability has gained traction as a topic of interest in the mainstream media and in published organizational strategies and corporate communications, employee awareness of sustainability has grown (Onkila et al. 2018). Further, the human resources function within an organization can play a key role in attracting prospective employees by promoting sustainability credentials as a proxy for the values of the organization and gauging the personal fit with the organization before making a recruitment choice (de Stefano et al. 2018).

A positive employee attitude towards sustainability is not a given, however, and may need to be developed through engagement work, including communication, education, and incentivization activities backed up by the availability of supporting tools and work methods (Bhattacharya 2018). The adoption of environmental management systems—operating frameworks that explain how to design and operate business processes with minimal environmental impact—encourage shared sustainable practices and make it clear to employees that sustainability is a necessary part of everyday life (Lyon and Maxwell 2011).

As an aspect of organizational culture, changing employees' attitudes to sustainability takes time and effort. Organizations that aim to build deep employee commitment and capabilities in sustainable practices should expect progress that is gauged in months and years (Spicer and Hyatt 2017). Without a commonly held attitude amongst employees that places sustainability as a core concern for the organization, it is highly unlikely that sustainable outcomes will be delivered in a significant way (Geradts and Bocken 2019). Therefore, strengthening and aligning employee attitudes to sustainability is a matter of strategic concern for organizations. Equally, understanding the existing attitude to sustainability as part of the cultural resources of the organization will help you in evaluating options for action in strategy work.

 Access the online resources to watch a short video clip where Aileen McLeod discusses how sustainability features in organizational strategy at SSEN.

4.7 Embedding sustainability in strategy

The dark side of CSR, CSV, and sustainability arguments

Management research continues to explore ways in which sustainability concerns, such as those expressed in the SDGs, might be further incorporated into organizational strategy and practice (Rosati and Faria 2019). However, this should be done in a balanced and possibly critical way to address problematic realities as well as potential upsides of sustainability trends. So, as we reflect on the possible value of CSR, CSV, and sustainability approaches to organizational strategy, it is helpful to be aware of points of criticism levelled at these concepts.

Earlier, we outlined how CSR can be used to make a positive societal contribution. Based on how CSR has been misused in practice, it has a mixed reputation. CSR programmes may be viewed with cynicism by stakeholders as 'redemption tools' or 'insurance' against reputational damage and negative press rather than sources of positive social or environmental impact (Choi et al. 2018; Freeman and Dmytriyev 2017). Others have criticized CSR for 'moral licensing', which means that doing good in the community creates a feeling of being excused for behaving at a lower standard of conduct with other stakeholders (Ormiston and Wong 2013). CSR is often seen as a 'non-core' business interest that is likely to be dropped if an organization experiences financial issues (Campbell 2007). Further, CSR may also be seen as a superficial act to pre-empt stricter regulations of business activities by the authorities (Freeman and Dmytriyev 2017).

CSV was an attempt by Porter and Kramer (2011) to repair some of the trust issues associated with CSR and capitalism in general. However, it has ended up being subject to similar criticism as CSR. Jackson and Limbrick (2019) note that CSV retains a focus on self-interest above everything else. Crane et al. (2014: 130) comment that CSV is 'unoriginal; it ignores the tensions inherent to responsible business activity; it is naive about business compliance; and it is based on a shallow conception of the corporation's role in society'. Bansal and DesJardine (2014) observe that CSV can still lead to unsustainable growth activities that borrow resources from future needs, and Dembek et al. (2016) suggest that CSV is more a management 'buzzword' than a concrete set of practices.

Further, the principles of environmental sustainability have long been plagued by the malpractice of **greenwashing**—deliberately misleading consumers about the environmental practices of a company or the environmental traits or benefits of a product or service (Parguel et al. 2011). To boost sales or avoid activist scrutiny, organizations may misuse terms such as 'eco', 'environmentally friendly', 'green', 'earth friendly', and 'sustainability' when describing their products or business practices to give a false impression of their sustainability (Chen and Chang 2013: 489). This may be particularly true for organizations seeking to build market share in new locations or sectors (Maniora 2018). The rise in social media usage has driven down more overt forms of greenwashing as organizational claims can now be rapidly checked and debunked by activist networks (Lyon and Montgomery 2013).

These criticisms seem to be at odds with organizational reality, given the many and varied examples of sustainability, CSV, and CSR practice discussed in this chapter. But the overarching issue is perhaps that practice fails to live up to theory in too many cases—giving the appearance of positive action whilst failing to deliver social or environmental impact. Bansal and DesJardine (2014) observe that a short-term focus on results in strategy is at odds with the long-term view of sustainability required to take CSV and CSR seriously. It is this lack of concrete results that prompted Elkington (2018a) to issue his product recall for the 'triple bottom line' concept. These issues might be reversed by deliberately and systematically adopting sustainability practices that have been shown to deliver organizational performance as an integral and normal part of how your organization functions (Ioannou and Serafeim 2019).

Practical lessons for integrating sustainability in strategy

To help you consider how sustainability might be embedded in organizational life and rendered a core consideration in organizational strategy, we draw on the findings of a large-scale survey of sustainability strategy practice (Kiron et al. 2017) which was conducted in collaboration with the Boston Consulting Group, a global strategy consultancy. Eight high-level lessons were identified in survey responses from 60,000 organizations globally as to how sustainability might be approached in and through strategy activity (see Table 4.6).

TABLE 4.6 **Lessons from practice in applying sustainability through strategy**

Lesson	Survey finding	Example from this chapter
1. Set your sustainability vision and ambition	90% of executives see sustainability as important, but only 60% of companies have sustainable strategy	Iberdrola's articulation of a sustainability vision linked to the SDGs
2. Focus on material issues	Companies that focus on material issues report up to 50% added profit from sustainability Those that don't focus on material issues struggle to add value from their sustainability activities	Bureo's use of reclaimed fishing net material as a sustainable basis for their business
3. Set up the right organization to achieve your ambition	Building sustainability into business units doubles an organization's chance of profiting from its sustainability activities	Underline's embedded social and environmental impacts, alongside profit, influence its national organizational structure and operating approach
4. Explore business model innovation opportunities	Nearly 50% of companies have changed their business models because of sustainability opportunities	Nestlé's adoption of a CSV model to refocus as a nutrition, health, and wellness company
5. Develop a clear business case for sustainability	While 60% of companies have a sustainability strategy, only 25% have developed a clear business case for their sustainability efforts	Angel City's profitable start-up based on a visible set of social impact initiatives and declarations of purpose (Chapter 1)
6. Get the Board of Directors on board	86% of respondents agreed that boards should play a strong role in their company's sustainability efforts but only 48% say their CEOs are engaged and fewer (30%) agreed that their sustainability efforts had strong board-level oversight	Natura's highly engaged chairman and executive team acting as advocates for sustainable practice
7. Develop a compelling sustainability value-creation story for investors	75% of executives in investment companies think sustainability performance should be considered in investment decisions, but only 60% of corporate executives think investors care about sustainability performance	UBS's commitment to ethical investing and arguments as to this being the only way forward aligning with the views of ex-Governor of the Bank of England, Mark Carney
8. Collaborate with a variety of stakeholders to drive strategic change	90% of executives believe collaboration is essential to sustainability success but only 47% say their companies collaborate strategically	Skandia working with health professionals and clients to deliver new initiatives

Source: authors.

These high-level findings can act as a checklist for you to consider strategic initiatives which might embed sustainability within an organization. Each of these could be a trigger for or practices of implementing strategizing. To do this, you could redraw this table, and fill the third column with a response to the question: 'How could we respond to this key lesson?'

The outcome of the study by Kiron et al. (2017) and further practitioner-orientated sustainability research (e.g. Geradts and Bocken 2019; Lubin and Esty 2010; Posner and Kiron 2013) seems to give a clear message that sustainability can no longer be treated as a peripheral concern in an organization. Instead, concepts of sustainability must be embedded in strategy processes, practices, and objectives, and sustainability strategy should be tightly integrated with other functional strategies of the organization. Leadership plays a crucial role in making this happen by creating clear business cases for enhanced sustainability, engagement of staff, stakeholders, collaboratives, and the communication of benefits and supportive narratives. For many organizations, transformation of structure, ways of working, systems and methods, attitudes, and even products and services may be implied by a strategic sustainability agenda. And no organization seems able to do this alone—it takes engagement, collaboration, and open innovation with an organization's value chain and external stakeholders to deliver sustainability-focused strategy.

PRACTITIONER INSIGHT **AILEEN MCLEOD, DIRECTOR OF BUSINESS PLANNING AND COMMERCIAL, SSEN**

Aileen McLeod is the Director of Business Planning and Commercial at SSEN Transmission, the owner and operator of the North of Scotland electricity transmission system. Aileen has over 20 years of experience in the utilities sector, both as the regulator and regulated. Her interests encompass corporate strategy, sustainable and purposeful business practice, regulatory economics, and the just transition.

'How does sustainability feature in organizational strategy at SSEN?'

The short answer is sustainability is in everything relating to strategy at SSEN Transmission! Sustainability is one of the core values of the business. It has been for a very long time. It's not just a value that exists on a piece of paper; it is central to how work happens in the organization on a daily basis. In our last employee survey, sustainability ranked top alongside teamwork as the core values that are the most meaningful and influence our behaviours.

How we manage carbon and climate change is at the heart of our whole organization interest in

sustainability. This is understandable given the focus of the energy sector on achieving Net Zero (which the UN define as 'cutting greenhouse gas emissions to as close to zero as possible, with any remaining emissions re-absorbed from the atmosphere, by oceans and forests'). However, sustainability as a practice has much broader effects in the organization. For example, sustainability is woven into our approach to governance in terms of how we set goals and objectives, report our progress, organize committees, make decisions, and design business processes and organizational structures. And none of it feels forced—sustainability as a value is a natural part of our organizational DNA. That, perhaps, can be traced to our roots in hydroelectric generation and being embedded in a distinct community in the North of Scotland.

It also helps that sustainability has been a focus for action in our industry for many years. In the United Kingdom, the independent Climate Change Committee that advises the government and the devolved administrations reports that emissions from the electricity supply sector are 76% below 1990 levels. The Committee observes that across the electricity sector the focus is on action without there necessarily being an overarching plan. This is probably true as each participant is focusing on driving sustainability outcomes according to specific requirements of their geographical location and needs of their customer base. But I would also note that this is different to other sectors, where there is perhaps an overarching plan but insufficient action. I suspect that this 'say–do' gap is true in many sectors nearer the start of their sustainability journey.

Our experience has been that when sustainability influences actions every day, stakeholders are able to move past cynicism and greenwashing concerns. Sustainability has to be about what people do, not just what managers, organizations, or governments say. As an organizational focus, sustainability is a vitally important, evolving topic that should be inseparable from strategy. I keep coming back to an idea that strategy is about why we are here. If you are answering that question without having sustainability as part of the answer, then your organization will increasingly struggle to remain a going concern. Sustainability is about a longer-term and bigger picture than any tactical concerns you have about short-term organizational performance. Sustainability requires you to consider your impact and consequences of activities, co-dependencies with others, and the needs of a broad range of stakeholders. In fact, I think we maybe have the framing of sustainability and strategy inverted—should strategy be a subset of sustainability, not the other way around?

'Could you share your views on the importance of stakeholder engagement in strategy work?'

I don't know how you can develop an effective, meaningful, deliverable strategy without engaging with stakeholders. If the success of your strategy ultimately depends on other parties taking action, you have to engage with them and seek their participation at the earliest opportunity. If your strategy-making is a group of senior leaders sitting in a windowless room with a set of post-its, you're wasting your time!

Stakeholders is a broad term and implies different people and groups for different organizations. Given what we do, for us it is perhaps easier to think who isn't a stakeholder! We consider a stakeholder to be someone who has to act in response to or is affected by an activity that we are undertaking in order for us to be successful. This will include amongst others current, future, and indirect employees; all of our supply chain; government, local authorities, communities, environmental agencies, consumer groups, NGOs, trade representatives, consumers of energy, and any parties connected to our network.

Where you have stakeholders with whom you can readily engage, it can be a rewarding and tangible activity to do so in order to identify issues and tensions, agreements and shared ambition, co-created action and collaboration potential. A big challenge for us, though, is what to do with harder-to-reach stakeholders, such as those that aren't yet born! What should be our proxy for the needs and interests of those stakeholders? Their views matter as the consequences of decisions and actions we are taking today will impact their lives.

We have a separate published stakeholder engagement strategy and plan. This is a common feature across the United Kingdom's regulated network utilities sector. Water companies, for example, have stakeholder strategies, as do our peers in energy networks. Although originally required by our regulator, we have found a high level of thoughtfulness in stakeholder engagement to be highly beneficial to our business performance. Having a defined stakeholder engagement strategy helps us to avoid being caught up in short-term issues of importance to some stakeholders at the cost of addressing longer-term needs. Avoiding such myopic effects (see Chapter 14), stakeholder engagement can then act as an invaluable informant, rather than a determinant, of strategy work.

'What are your views on the role of purpose in strategy and governance?'

Purpose is what we are here for and is becoming ever more important as a concept for organizational leaders as our world is increasingly interconnected. Purpose is about tangible outcomes that are for the overall benefit of the organization and its stakeholders. I believe that purpose is distinct from aspirations or visions and should demonstrated in day-to-day practice. I was thinking about the

Continued

language of mission, vision, and values, which can be useful in certain settings, and reflecting back to the start of my career. As an analyst, full of enthusiasm, I wanted to make a difference, and I remember wondering what all those words meant. What I was able to see though was what was practiced around me, including purposeful patterns in behaviours and actions. As leaders, how much time do we spend ensuring that our words about organizational purpose match our actions and the experiences of our customer and employees? When matching, purpose can be a highly valuable part of strategy and governance, bringing meaning and guidance across actions and decisions across organizational levels. But without matching actions, the words of purpose are meaningless and, at worst, destructive to organizational cohesion.

'Generally, what would you advise strategic leaders to prioritize?'

There are two things I would urge strategic leaders to consider. First, stay in touch with your organization. At the end of the day, people are people and

will do what they want and think is the right thing, not what you say. So, stay in touch with the practitioners and stakeholders around you so you can know their reality and collaborate effectively. This can be difficult in the new, hybrid ways of working.

Second, as a strategy practitioner, invest effort in foresight and forward-looking exploration that others don't have the time to do. These activities will be a waste of time if you don't share and communicate your findings, so make sure you engage others to turn your insights into relevant actions. It isn't self-indulgent to explore new ways of thinking and practice, even when day job pressures are intense; it is a crucial ongoing part of your role as a strategic leader.

 Access the online resources to watch a short video clip where Aileen McLeod talks more about her career.

Source
(Net Zero, https://www.un.org/en/climatechange/net-zero-coalition, last accessed 10 August 2022)

CHAPTER SUMMARY

In this chapter, we addressed the following learning outcomes:

○ Evaluate how an organization's purpose, vision, mission, and values translate to deliverable performance targets and objectives.
An organization's purpose is the affirmation of the reason for its existence: for example, what does the organization do, who does it serve, and where does it expect to be in the future? These questions are articulated in forward-looking statements about the organization's activities and are used to give direction to the organization's participants as well as to communicate what the organization stands for to external stakeholders.

○ Critically assess the concepts of shareholder and stakeholder value maximization and examine how firms can effectively engage with stakeholders who have conflicting interests.
Commercial enterprises exist to make a profit, but they are also an integral participant in society and global community. Modern business practice has evolved from a narrowly focused **shareholder value maximization** to wider **stakeholder value maximization**. Being a good corporate citizen makes good business sense. All organizations possess stakeholders with conflicting interests. Not all stakeholders have the same degree of power and interest in the organization's activities. Stakeholder mapping is a tool for strategists to group stakeholders based on their relative power and interest and to develop strategies to manage these diverse power and interest groups.

○ Appraise the importance of sustainability as a factor in organizational strategy processes and outcomes.

Sustainability has been shown to be an increasingly important facet of organizational strategy. Increasingly, external stakeholders seek assurances about an organization's approach to sustainability. The operating environments shaped by governments, NGOs, and communities set constraints and reward progress towards sustainable operating approaches. Sustainability is a dynamic topic, and the trends point towards it gaining in prominence as a required feature of organizational strategy.

○ Evaluate the relevance and possible impact of the triple bottom line and sustainable development goals concepts to an organization's strategy and stakeholder group.

The triple bottom line (TBL) was shown to be a system for measuring business performance that balances people, profit, and planet considerations. It is increasingly a common concept used in strategy and business management. As sustainability grows as a topic of concern for stakeholders, the TBL increases in relevance for organizational strategy. However, caution is required in ensuring that it leads to concrete action and the realization of sustainable outcomes. The sustainable development goals (SDGs) defined by the UN were shown to be a valuable common framework which sets out a sustainable development agenda that is influencing the plans and practices of nations, organizations, and individuals.

○ Critically assess the relative merits and limitations of approaches to sustainability strategy.

Corporate social responsibility (CSR) is a commonly understood term referring to how an organization understands and adapts its obligations to society through strategic initiatives. Not without benefit, CSR is also subject to significant criticism. Creating shared value (CSV) is a management philosophy which extends CSR to improve benefits for a wider range of stakeholders whilst enhancing sustainability outcomes. However, CSV arguably is subject to the same underlying issues as CSR.

? END-OF-CHAPTER QUESTIONS

Recall questions

1. List and define an organization's forward-looking statements.

2. What are the elements of a stakeholder map?

3. Define the term 'sustainability' as it might be used within the context of organizational strategy.

4. Describe and explain the difference between a financial bottom line and the TBL.

5. What are the SDGs, and how are they shaping strategy communications for some organizations?

6. What are the main similarities, differences, benefits, and deficiencies of CSR and CSV?

Application questions

A) Why do you think organizations should have clearly articulated purpose, mission, and value statements?

B) The only responsibility of a firm is to make a profit. Do you agree with this statement? If yes, why? If not, why not?

C) Think of an organization (of any type, sector, or size) you know well and evaluate its TBL performance. What could it do to improve its performance? Use any concepts or perspectives from the chapter to help you decide and draw on the practical sustainability guides in making suggestions of options for action.

D) Search online for trends in sustainability. Based on your research, nominate three trends which you think will be most influential on organizational strategy in a sector or territory that you are familiar with. Describe how an organization might gain an advantage by anticipating and preparing for the unfolding of the identified sustainability trends.

ONLINE RESOURCES

www.oup.com/he/mackay2e

In addition to the video interviews already highlighted, the book's **online resources** include the following features for this chapter, specifically:

– *links to further reading material* to broaden your knowledge of key issues discussed in this chapter;

– *self-test multiple-choice questions* to test your understanding of the material covered in each section of the chapter; and

– *a flashcard glossary* to help you recall and test your understanding of key terms.

FURTHER READING

'The social responsibility of business is to create value for stakeholders' by R. Edward Freeman and Heather Elms

Freeman, R.E. and Elms, H. (2018). The social responsibility of business is to create value for stakeholders. *MIT Sloan Management Review* (January), https://sloanreview.mit.edu/article/the-social-responsibility-of-business-is-to-create-value-for-stakeholder (last accessed 5 May 2019).

This article proposes that the stakeholder approach aims to create a new narrative about business that enables companies to make the lives of communities and people better through the creation of stakeholder value rather than simply profit to shareholders. The article suggests a recognition that if we want the outcome of business to be a more responsible form of capitalism, stakeholders are required to value business responsibility.

'Why making money is not enough' by Ratan Tata et al.

Tata, R., Hall, S.L., Sharma, A., and Sarkar, C. (2013). Why making money is not enough. *MIT Sloan Management Review* (Summer).

The authors argue that it is possible to build and lead companies that retain a deeper purpose. Ratan Tata, one of the article's authors, writes that Tata Group's founder, Jamsetji N. Tata, believed that acquiring wealth was not the primary purpose of life; he considered that his company's mission was to help the communities in which it operated. Even today, despite the growing wealth of the Tata Group, company leaders are not featured in the listings of the richest people in India or the world. This is because two-thirds of the shares of Tata Sons, the holding company of the Group, belong to the Tata Trusts, one of the largest and oldest Indian philanthropic foundations.

'Vision, mission, values: Guideposts to sustainability' by Philip Mirvis et al.

Mirvis, P., Googins, B., and Kinnicutt, S. (2010) Vision, mission, values: Guideposts to sustainability. *Organizational Dynamics*, **39**, 316–24.

Although most executives are committed to sustainability and it is incorporated into organizations' purpose and value statements, there continues to be an disconnect between short-term profit pressures and good intentions. The authors argue that as companies adopt a border and more inclusive view of corporate responsibility, they also need to develop organizational 'response-ability'. The responsibility for the management and monitoring of an organization's wider societal impact rests with the board of directors to track and report to the public how the organization is performing between high-minded statements of vision, mission, and valued and everyday ground-level activities and practices.

'How companies capture the value of sustainability' by McKinsey & Co.

McKinsey & Co. (2021). How companies capture the value of sustainability: Survey findings (28 April), https://www.mckinsey.com/capabilities/sustainability/our-insights/how-companies-capture-the-value-of-sustainability-survey-findings (last accessed 22 October 2022).

Survey results suggest that to catch up with high-performing, value-creating companies from their sustainability efforts, other companies might start by understanding which sustainability practices are most closely lined with positive financial impact. The report identifies three areas of management orientation and focus: (a) approach sustainability issues as business opportunities; (b) build organization-wide accountability for results; and (c) seek impact through collaboration across supply chain by setting new standards, promoting new technological innovation, or advocating environmental policy shifts.

'Unlocking the inclusive growth story of the 21st century: accelerating climate action in urgent times' by the New Climate Economy

The New Climate Economy (2018). Unlocking the inclusive growth story of the 21st century: accelerating climate action in urgent times, https://newclimateeconomy.report/2018 (last accessed 17 August 2022).

Briefly referenced in the chapter, this is a compelling read about the future of topics such as climate reporting, international action, crucial economic systems—clean energy, cities, food and land use, water and industry—and a 'new growth agenda' for development that is 'strong, sustainable, balanced, and inclusive'. This report is full of useful information and perspective that will help you to make sense of the sustainability megatrend.

'Solutions to fight climate change' by Solar Impulse Foundation

Solar Impulse Foundation. Solutions to fight climate change, https://solarimpulse.com (last accessed 17 August 2022)

*The Solar Impulse Foundation aims to identify 1000 **eco-innovations**, 'bringing together protection of the environment and financial viability to show that these solutions are not expensive fixes to problems, but rather opportunities for clean economic growth'. Many interesting examples of technological and business model innovations are made available through this site.*

REFERENCES

Ackermann, F. and Eden, C. (2011). *Making Strategy: Mapping Out Strategic Success.* London: Sage.

Almirall, E., Wareham, J., Ratti, C. et al. (2016). Smart cities at the crossroads: New tensions in city transformation. *California Management Review*, **59**(1), 141–52.

Arena, C., Michelon, G., and Trojanowski, G. (2018). Big egos can be green: A study of CEO hubris and environmental innovation. *British Journal of Management*, **29**(2), 316–36.

Bansal, P. and DesJardine, M. (2014). Business sustainability: It is about time. *Strategic Organization*, **12**(1), 70–8.

BBC (2019). Bank of England chief Mark Carney issues climate change warning (30 December), https://www.bbc.co.uk/news/business-50868717 (last accessed 10 August 2022).

Bhattacharya, C.B. (2018). How to make sustainability every employee's responsibility. *Harvard Business Review Digital Articles*, 2–5, https://hbr.org/2018/02/how-to-make-sustainability-every-employees-responsibility (last accessed 22 October 2022).

Bhattacharya, C.B. and Polman, P. (2017). Sustainability lessons from the front lines. *MIT Sloan Management Review*, **58**(2), 1–13.

Birkinshaw, J., Foss, N.J., and Lindenberg, S. (2014). Combining purpose with profits. *MIT Sloan Management Review* (Spring).

BloombergUK (2020). There are far more Americans without broadband than previously thought (19 February), https://www.bloomberg.com/news/articles/2020-02-19/where-the-u-s-underestimates-the-digital-divide?-sref=01ejgNtz (last accessed 10 August 2022).

BloombergUK (2021). Startup takes on Big Telecom, starting in Colorado Springs (19 October), https://www.bloomberg.com/news/articles/2021-10-19/startup-tries-new-approaches-to-tackle-the-digital-divide (last accessed 10 August 2022).

Bowman, C. and Ambrosini, V. (2007). Identifying valuable resources. *European Management Journal*, **25**(4), 320–9.

Cable, D. and Vermeulen, F. (2018). Making work meaningful: A leader's guide. *McKinsey Quarterly* (October), https://www.mckinsey.com/capabilities/people-and-organizational-performance/our-insights/making-work-meaningful-a-leaders-guide (last accessed 22 October 2022).

Campbell, J.L. (2007). Why would corporations behave in socially responsible ways? An institutional theory of corporate social responsibility. *Academy of Management Review*, **32**(37), 946–67.

Casey, D. and Sieber, S. (2016). Employees, sustainability, and motivation: Increasing employee engagement by addressing sustainability and corporate social responsibility. *Research in Hospitality Management*, **6**(1), 69–76.

Chatzidakis, A. and Shaw, D. (2018). Sustainability: Issues of scale, care, and consumption. *British Journal of Management*, **29**(2), 299–315.

Chen, Y.-S. and Chang, C.-H. (2013). Greenwash and green trust: The mediation effects of green consumer confusion and green perceived risk. *Journal of Business Ethics*, **114**(3), 489–500.

Choi, A. (2016). Morgan Stanley perspectives on sustainable investing: Acceleration and integration. *Journal of Applied Corporate Finance*, **28**(2), 62–5.

Choi, J.J., Jo, H., Kim, J., and Kim, M.S. (2018). Business groups and corporate social responsibility. *Journal of Business Ethics*, **153**(4), 931–54.

Conley, J.M. and Williams, C.A. (2005). Engage, embed, and embellish: Theory versus practice in the corporate social responsibility movement. *Journal of Corporation Law*, **31**(1), 1–38.

Costa, C., Lages, L.F., and Hortinha, P. (2015). The bright and dark side of CSR in export markets: Its impact on innovation and performance. *International Business Review*, **24**(5), 749–57.

Crane, A., Palazzo, G., Spence, L.J., and Matten, D. (2014). Contesting the value of 'creating shared value'. *California Management Review*, **56**(2), 130–51.

Cubas-Díaz, M. and Martínez Sedano, M.Á. (2018). Measures for sustainable investment decisions and business strategy: A triple bottom line approach. *Business Strategy and the Environment*, **27**(1), 16–38.

De Stefano, F., Bagdali, S., and Camuffo, A. (2018). The HR role in corporate social responsibility and sustainability: A boundary-shifting literature review. *Human Resource Management*, **57**(2), 549–66.

Dembek, K., Singh, P., and Bhakoo, V. (2016). Literature review of shared value: A theoretical concept or a management buzzword? *Journal of Business Ethics*, **137**(2), 231–67.

Dentoni, D., Bitzer, V., and Pascucci, S. (2016). Cross-sector partnerships and the co-creation of dynamic capabilities for stakeholder orientation. *Journal of Business Ethics*, **135**(1), 35–53.

Divine Chocolate (2019). About us—owned by cocoa farmers. made for chocolate lovers, http://www.divinechocolate.com/us/about-us (last accessed 20 December 2019).

Eccles, R.G. and Klimenko, S. (2019). The investor revolution. *Harvard Business Review,* **97**(3), 106–16.

Eccles, R.G. and Serafeim, G. (2013). The performance frontier. *Harvard Business Review*, **91**(5), 50–60.

Elkington, J. (1998). Accounting for the triple bottom line. *Measuring Business Excellence*, **2**(3), 18–22.

Elkington, J. (2017). The 6 ways business leaders talk about sustainability. *Harvard Business Review Digital Articles*, 2–5, https://hbr.org/2017/the-6-ways-business-leaders-talk-about-sustainability (last accessed 22 October 2022).

Elkington, J. (2018a). 25 years ago I coined the phrase 'triple bottom line.' Here's why it's time to rethink it. *Harvard Business Review Digital Articles*, 2–5, https://hbr.org/2018/06/25-years-ago-i-coined-the-phrase-triple-bottom-line-heres-why-im-giving-up-on-it (last accessed 22 October 2022).

Elkington, J. (2018b). Climate change is an overwhelming problem: here are 4 things executives can do today. *Harvard Business Review Digital Articles*, 2–5, https://hbr.org/2018/01/climate-change-is-an-overwhelming-problem-here-are-4-things-executives-can-do-today (last accessed 22 October 2022).

Epley, N. and Kumar, A. (2019). How to design an ethical organization. *Harvard Business Review*, **97**(3), 144–50.

Fairtrade (2019). Fairtrade and sustainability, http://www.fairtrade.org.uk/What-is-Fairtrade/Fairtrade-and-sustainability (last accessed 10 August 2022).

Fegade, V., Shrivatsava, R.L., and Kale, A.V. (2015). Design for remanufacturing: Methods and their approaches. *Materials Today: Proceedings*, **2**(4), 1849–58.

Freeman, R.E. (1984). *Strategic Management: A Stakeholder Approach*. Cambridge: Cambridge University Press.

Freeman, R.E. and Dmytriyev, S. (2017). Corporate social responsibility and stakeholder theory: Learning from each other. *Emerging Issues in Management*, **2**, 7–15.

Friedman, M. (1970). The social responsibility of business is to increase profits. *New York Times Magazine* (13 September), https://www.nytimes.com/1970/09/13/archives/a-friedman-doctrine-the-social-responsibility-of-business-is-to.html (last accessed 22 October 2022).

Geradts, T.H.J. and Bocken, N.M.P. (2019). Driving sustainability-oriented innovation. *MIT Sloan Management Review*, **60**(2), 9–16.

Global Commission on the Economy and Climate (2018). The new growth agenda, https://newclimateeconomy.report/2018/the-new-growth-agenda (last accessed 10 August 2022).

The Guardian (2019). Gillette MeToo ad on toxic masculinity cuts deep with men's rights activists (15 January), https://www.theguardian.com/world/2019/jan/15/gillette-metoo-ad-on-toxic-masculinity-cuts-deep-with-mens-rights-activists (last accessed 10 August 2022).

Harris, J.D. and Freeman, R.E. (2008). The impossibility of the separation thesis. *Business Ethics Quarterly*, **18**(4), 541–8.

4

Hart, S.L., Milstein, M.B., and Caggiano, J. (2003). Creating sustainable value: Executive commentary. *Academy of Management Executive*, **17**(2), 56–69.

Ioannou, I. and Serafeim, G. (2019). Yes, sustainability can be a strategy. *Harvard Business Review Digital Articles*, 2–4, https://www.ipccch/report/ar6/wg2/resources/spm-headline-statements (last accessed 22 October 2022).

IPCC (Intergovernmental Panel on Climate Change (2022). Summary for policymakers headline statements (28 February), https://www.ipcc.ch/report/ar6/wg2/resources/spm-headline-statements (last accessed 10 August 2022).

Jackson, I. and Limbrick, L. (2019). Creating shared value in an industrial conurbation: Evidence from the North Staffordshire ceramics cluster. *Strategic Change*, **28**(2), 133–8.

Jensen, M.C. (2002). Value maximization and the corporate objective function. In: Andriof, J., Waddock S., Rahman, S., and Husted, B. (eds), *Unfolding Stakeholder Thinking: Theory, Responsibility, and Engagement*. Sheffield: Greenleaf, pp. 65–184.

Kalendar, Z, and Vayvay, O (2016). The fifth pillar of the balanced scorecard: Sustainability. *Procedia—Social and Behavioral Sciences*, **235**, 76–83.

Kaplan, R.S. and Norton, D.P. (1992). The balanced scorecard—measures that drive performance. *Harvard Business Review*, **70**, 71–9.

Kenny, G. (2014). Your company's purpose is not its vision, mission, or values. *Harvard Business Review* (September).

Kiron, D., Unruh, G., Kruschwitz, N. et al. (2017). Corporate sustainability at a crossroads. *MIT Sloan Management Review* (May).

Kourdi, J. (2015). *100 Business Tools for Success: All the Management Models That Matter in 500 Words or Less.* London: Hachette UK.

Kruschwitz, N. (2013). Creating shared value at Nestlé (10 September), https://sloanreview.mit.edu/article/creating-shared-value-at-nestle (last accessed 10 August 2022).

Kuehn, K. and McIntire, L. (2014). Sustainability a CFO can love. *Harvard Business Review*, **92**(4), 66–74.

Lamach, M.W. (2017). How our company connected our strategy to sustainability goals. *Harvard Business Review Digital Articles*, 1–4, https://hbr.org/2010/05/the-sustainability-imperative (last accessed 22 October 2022).

Lee, Y.W. (2019). Enhancing shared value and sustainability practices of global firms: The case of Samsung Electronics. *Strategic Change*, **28**(2), 139–45.

Lubin, D.A. and Esty, D.C. (2010). The sustainability imperative. *Harvard Business Review* (May), 42–51.

Lyon, T.P. and Maxwell, J.W. (2011). Greenwash: Corporate environmental disclosure under threat of audit. *Journal of Economics & Management Strategy*, **20**(1), 3–41.

Lyon, T.P. and Montgomery, A.W. (2013). Tweetjacked: The impact of social media on corporate greenwash. *Journal of Business Ethics*, **118**(4), 747–57.

McKinsey & Co. (2021). How companies capture the value of sustainability: Survey findings (28 April), https://www.mckinsey.com/capabilities/sustainability/our-insights/how-companies-capture-the-value-of-sustainability-survey-findings (last accessed 22 October 2022).

Maniora, J. (2018). Mismanagement of sustainability: what business strategy makes the difference? Empirical evidence from the USA. *Journal of Business Ethics*, **152**(4), 931–47.

Mead, L. (2019). Paper describes Colombia's efforts to localize, achieve SDGs (24 January), https://sdg.iisd.org/news/paper-describes-colombias-efforts-to-localize-achieve-sdgs (last accessed 10 August 2022).

Mendelow, A. (1981). Environmental scanning: The impact of the stakeholder concept. In: *ICIS Proceedings*.

Mendelow, A. (1986). Proceedings of the Second International Conference on Information Systems, Cambridge, MA.

Mirvis, P., Googins, B., and Kinnicutt, S. (2010). Vision, mission, values. *Organizational Dynamics*, **39**(4), 316.

NCE (New Climate Economy) (2018). The 2018 Report of the Global Commission on the Economy and Climate, https://newclimateeconomy.report/2018 (last accessed 10 August 2022).

Nestlé (2020). Annual review 2019, https://www.nestle.com/sites/default/files/2020-03/2019-annual-review-en.pdf (last accessed 10 August 2022).

Nestlé (2021). Pursuing our value-creation strategy, https://www.nestle.com/aboutus/strategy (last accessed 10 August 2022).

Novo Nordisk (2019). Driving change, http://www.novonordisk.co.uk/about-novo-nordisk-in-uk/corporate_overview/sustainability.html (last accessed 10 August 2022).

Onkila, T., Mäkelä, M., and Järvenpää, M. (2018). Employee sensemaking on the importance of sustainability reporting in sustainability identity change. *Sustainable Development*, **26**(3), 217–28.

Ormiston, M.E. and Wong, E.M. (2013). License to ill: The effects of corporate social responsibility and CEO moral identity on corporate social irresponsibility. *Personnel Psychology*, **66**, 861–93.

Othman, R., Nath, N., and Laswad, F. (2017). Sustainability reporting by New Zealand's local governments. *Australian Accounting Review*, **27**(3), 315–28.

Palotta, D. (2011). A logo is not a brand (15 June), https://fbo1.typepad.com/salt_lake_city_ut_6181162/SLC_files/PDFs/A-Logo_Is_Not_A_Brand.pdf (last accessed 21 October 2022).

Parguel, B., Benoît-Moreau, F., and Larceneux, F. (2011). How sustainability ratings might deter 'greenwashing': A closer look at ethical corporate communication. *Journal of Business Ethics*, **102**(1), 15–28.

Perez, S., Fernández-Salinero, S., and Topa, G. (2018). Sustainability in organizations: Perceptions of corporate social responsibility and Spanish employees' attitudes and behaviors. *Sustainability*, **10**, 1–15.

Pfitzer, M.W., Bockstette, V., and Stamp, M. (2013). Innovating for shared value. *Harvard Business Review* (September), https://hbr.org/2013/09/innovating-for-shared-value (last accessed 22 October 2022).

Porter, M.E. and Kramer, M.R. (2011). Creating shared value. *Harvard Business Review* (January–February), https://hbr.org/2011/01/the-big-idea-creating-shared-value (last accessed 22 October 2022).

Posner, B. and Kiron, D. (2013). How Caesars Entertainment is betting on sustainability. *MIT Sloan Management Review*, **54**(4), 63–71.

Powell, M., Gillett, A., and Doherty, B. (2019). Sustainability in social enterprise: Hybrid organizing in public services. *Public Management Review*, **21**(2), 159–86.

PWC (PriceWaterhouseCoopers) (2019). Megatrends, https://www.pwc.co.uk/issues/megatrends.html (last accessed 10 August 2022).

Ramaswamy, V. and Gouillart, F. (2010). Building the co-creative enterprise. *Harvard Business Review*, **88**(10), 100–9.

Rangan, V.K., Chase, L., and Karim, S. (2015). The truth about CSR. *Harvard Business Review* (May–June).

Rodríguez Vilá, O., Bharadwaj, S., and Knowles, J. (2017). Competing on social purpose: Interaction. *Harvard Business Review*, **95**(6), 94–101.

Rosati, F. and Faria, L.G.D. (2019). Addressing the SDGs in sustainability reports: The relationship with institutional factors. *Journal of Cleaner Production*, **215**, 1312–26.

Santos, F.M., Pache, A.-C., and Birkholz, C. (2015). Making hybrids work: Aligning business models and organizational design for social enterprises. *California Management Review*, **57**(3), 36–58.

Santos, J.F.P. and Williamson, P.J. (2015). The new mission for multinationals. *MIT Sloan Management Review*, **56**(4), 45–54.

Schaltenbrand, B., Foerstl, K., Azadegan, A., and Lindeman, K. (2018). See what we want to see? The effects of managerial experience on corporate green investments. *Journal of Business Ethics*, **150**(4), 1129–50.

Schramade, W. (2017). Investing in the UN Sustainable Development Goals: Opportunities for companies and investors. *Journal of Applied Corporate Finance*, **29**(2), 87–99.

Sheth, H. and Babiak, K. (2010). Beyond the game: Perceptions and practices of corporate social responsibility in the professional sport industry. *Journal of Business Ethics*, **91**(3), 433–50.

Slaper, T.F. and Hall, T.J. (2011). The triple bottom line: What is it and how does it work?, http://www.ibrc.indiana.edu/ibr/2011/spring/article2.html (last accessed 10 August 2022).

Smith, N.C., Ansett, S., and Erez, L. (2011). How Gap Inc engaged with its stakeholders. *MIT Sloan Management Reivew* (Summer).

Smith, N.C., Ansett, S., and Erez, L. (2019). How Gap engaged with its stakeholders. In: Lenssen, G. and Smith, N. (eds), *Managing Sustainable Business*. Dordrecht: Springer.

Social Enterprise (2019). Can I register to become a social enterprise?, https://www.socialenterprise.org.uk (last accessed 26 May 2019).

Spicer, A. and Hyatt, D. (2017). Walmart's emergent low-cost sustainable product strategy. *California Management Review*, **59**(2), 116–41.

Statista (2022a). Household penetration rate of leading food brands worldwide in 2021 (29 June), https://www.statista.com/statistics/1240461/leading-ten-food-brand-penetration-global (last accessed 10 August 2022).

Statista (2022b). Nestlé—statistics & facts (2 June), https://www.statista.com/topics/1439/nestle/#dossierContents__outerWrapper (last accessed 10 August 2022).

Stout, L. (2012). *The Shareholder Value Myth: How Putting Shareholders First Harms Investors, Corporations, and the Public*. San Francisco, CA: Berrett-Koehler.

Tata, R., Hall, S.L., Sharma, A., and Sarkar, C. (2013). Why making money is not enough. *MIT Sloan Management Review* (Summer), https://sloanreview.mit.edu/article/why-making-money-is-not-enough (last accessed 22 October 2022).

Truong, A. and Barraket, J. (2018). Engaging workers in resource-poor environments: The case of social enterprise in Vietnam. *International Journal of Human Resource Management*, **29**(20), 2949–70.

UBS (2019). Sustainable investing, https://www.ubs.com/uk/en/wealth-management/sustainable-investing/education.html (last accessed 10 August 2022).

UN (United Nations) (2019). Sustainable development goals, https://www.un.org/sustainabledevelopment/sustainable-development-goals (last accessed 10 August 2022).

Van der Linden, B. and Freeman, E. (2017). Profit and other values: Thick evaluation in decision making. *Business Ethics Quarterly*, **27**(3), 353–79.

Vashchenko, M. (2017). An external perspective on CSR: What matters and what does not? *Business Ethics: A European Review,* **26**(4), 396–412.

Whelan, T. and Fink, C. (2016). The business case for sustainability. *Harvard Business Review* (October), 1–10.

Wickert, C. and de Bakker, F.G.A. (2019). How CSR managers can inspire other leaders to act on sustainability. *Harvard Business Review Digital Articles*, 2–5, https://hbr.org/2019/01/how-csr-managers-can-inspire-other-leaders-to-act-on-sustainability (last accessed 22 October 2022).

Winston, A. (2012). 3M's sustainability innovation machine. *Harvard Business Review Digital Articles*, 2–4, https://hbr.org/2012/05/3ms-sustainability-innovation (last accessed 22 October 2022).

Winston, A. (2018). Does Wall Street finally care about sustainability? *Harvard Business Review Digital Articles*, 1–5, https://hbr.org/2018/01/does-wall-street-finally-care-about-sustainability (last accessed 22 October 2022).

World Economic Forum (2022). The Global Risks Report 2022, 17th Edition Insight Report, https://www3.weforum.org/docs/WEF_The_Global_Risks_Report_2022.pdf (last accessed 10 August 2022).

4

CHAPTER FIVE

External Environment
Macro, Industry, and Competitive Settings

CONTENTS

LEARNING OBJECTIVES

By the end of this chapter, you should be able to:

○ Explain how the relationship between an organization and the context within which it is embedded impacts on strategy and competitive advantage through concepts of structure, position, conduct, and performance

○ Evaluate the non-market macro-environmental drivers shaping an organization and the ecosystem in which it resides

○ Interrogate market structures, dynamics, and trends, explaining the implications for buyers, competitors, and suppliers

○ Critically assess the direct competitive context for an organization, identifying the customer value creation and competitive characteristics most likely to enable survival and growth

○ Argue the benefits of using external environmental analysis tools

○ Agree a refined set of external environmental analytical outcomes by triangulating findings from across levels of analysis and testing ideas through scenario thinking

5

TOOLBOX

○ **Market-based view**
A theoretical perspective that helps explain how organizations can gain or sustain competitive advantage based on their position, conduct, and performance within external structures.

○ **Ecosystems view**
A theoretical perspective that considers organizations as embedded in a complex network of relationships. An ecosystem arises through the activities of all participants; it may be in an organization's best interests to act in a way that improves the ecosystem.

○ **PESTEL**
A method for analysing the macro-level trends and factors affecting an organization and its broad ecosystem; helps to build understanding of the context in which an organization is embedded.

○ **Industry analysis**
A method for analysing the current attractiveness and future potential of the organization's markets; examines forces that shape market profitability and sustainability for organizations.

○ **Strategic group analysis**
A method for identifying clusters of competitors that are following broadly similar strategies to serve similar groups of customers; enables identification of performance criteria that an organization can use to compare itself with competitors.

○ **Competitor profiling**
A method that guides evaluation of how competitors operate and how they might act/react to future strategic initiatives by your own organization.

○ **Integrative review**
A method for consolidating and improving initial insights and options generated by external analysis techniques.

○ **Scenario thinking**
A method for exploring the possible future implications of current trends and trajectories; helps you to think about what strategic initiatives might be needed today in order to be ready for future challenges.

Access the online resources to watch a short video clip where Dr Ibrahim Saif shares his top career tips.

OPENING CASE STUDY **A BUMPY RIDE FOR THE AUTOMOTIVE INDUSTRY**

Organizations in the global automotive industry are facing an external environment in flux. New opportunities and threats from the changing industrial landscape are influencing strategic decision-making processes and organizational performance for all involved in the automotive supply chain.

Globalization continues to exert an influence as automotive firms headquartered in emerging economies change their competitive approach. Chinese car manufacturers are increasing exports (e.g. Geely has been targeting Russia since 2007), while technology firms are collaborating with automotive firms in pioneering new models and features (such as Automotive Cloud, a partnership between Microsoft and VW). Further, the dynamics of competition are likely to be altered by mergers and acquisitions as established firms seek to deliver greater efficiencies and grow capacity to respond to shifting consumer tastes on a global scale. As traditional automotive organizations consolidate, the potential for suppliers, consumers, and governments to benefit from the automotive industry will be altered.

The industry is also being shaken by unprecedented disruption in the technological landscape. First, autonomous vehicles, or 'self-driving' cars, are reaching commercial launch. This new generation of vehicles promises to improve transport network efficiencies and create new freedoms for commuters in general, and for young, old, and disabled passengers in particular. Tesla expanded beta trials of its 'Full Self Driving' software in late 2020; rivals such as BMW, Ford, and Volvo are all pursuing their own ambitious programmes, with most major firms likely to follow suit soon. Autonomous vehicles have also attracted new market entrants; for example, Google and Apple may seek to disrupt the competitive dynamics of the automotive industry through autonomous vehicles. Lacking a legacy car business to defend, their cash-rich status means that they have the power to acquire a medium-scale—or even large-scale—auto manufacturer.

Many hurdles facing the commercialization of autonomous vehicles remain—including clarifying insurance and liability for accidents on an industrial scale, revisiting requirements to hold drivers' licences, and overcoming public health and safety concerns. In key markets such as the United States, lawmakers and consumers remain unconvinced about the readiness of the technology. Technology-based lawsuits are becoming more common as firms converge on superior designs of both electric and autonomous vehicles. Further, as cars become increasingly technologically enhanced, connected to the internet of things, **cyber-security** becomes an increasing risk and liability for automotive manufacturers.

The rise of electric vehicle technology is also shaping the external context. Grants from governments (e.g. in the United Kingdom) have incentivized established firms to pursue electric vehicle manufacture. In Norway, almost 65% of new passenger cars sold in 2021 were electric, and only electric vehicles will be on sale from as early as 2025. And in July 2022, the European Union agreed draft legislation banning the sale of new petrol or diesel cars by 2035.

At the intersection of electric and autonomous vehicles, Tesla is investing in 'Giga-factories' that change the economics of car production, creating politically popular, high-paying jobs and reducing production costs. This new approach may disrupt the operational set-up required by large incumbents whilst demanding new competencies in digital innovation, technology platform management, and external collaboration. New entrants, such as those selling equipment to retrofit a vehicle to be self-driving, are appearing at all stages of the supply chain, affecting incumbents beyond the main manufacturers.

Tracking changes in the external environment, and exerting favourable influence wherever possible, has never been more important for managers in the automotive industry.

The rise of electric vehicle technology is shaping the external context. *Source*: Ernest Ojeh/Unsplash.com.

Questions for discussion

1. What trends are occurring at a global level that will influence the strategy of firms in the automotive industry over the next five years?

2. What factors within the electric vehicle industry will shape how firms compete as the industry grows?

3. If Google decided to compete directly with Tesla, what main strategic initiatives might they undertake?

Sources

Auto Express (2019). Driverless cars: Everything you need to know about autonomous car revolution (13 September), http://www.autoexpress.co.uk/car-tech/85183/driver-less-cars-everything-you-need-to-know-about-autonomous-vehicles (last accessed 10 August 2022).

Automotive News Europe (2021). VW, Microsoft's partner to develop self-driving car software (11 February), https://europe.autonews.com/automakers/vw-microsoft-partner-develop-self-driving-car-software (last accessed 10 August 2022).

Evers-Hillstrom, K. (2022). Lawmakers stall over self-driving cars, *The Hill* (6 July), https://thehill.com/driving-into-the-future/3513598-lawmakers-stall-over-self-driving-cars (last accessed 10 August 2022).

The Financial Times (2022). Geely questions future in Russia despite opening for China's carmakers (24 March), https://www.ft.com/content/49d90df8-1f80-471c-a895-49914dbac3e4 (last accessed 17 October 2022).

The Financial Times (2022). What Tesla's Berlin gigafactory means for its future in China (3 April), https://www.ft.com/content/7c3d6eb3-ca0b-4475-9da5-8e304162791b (last accessed 17 October 2022).

Gov.uk. Low-emission vehicles eligible for a plug-in grant, https://www.gov.uk/plug-in-car-van-grants/what-youll-get (last accessed 17 October 2022).

The Guardian (2022a). EU's electric vehicle drive leaves supercars at the back of the grid (2 July), https://www.theguardian.com/business/2022/jul/02/eus-electric-vehicle-drive-leaves-supercars-at-the-back-of-the-grid (last accessed 10 August 2022).

The Guardian (2022b). How self-driving cars got stuck in the slow lane (27 March), https://www.theguardian.com/technology/2022/mar/27/how-self-driving-cars-got-stuck-in-the-slow-lane (last accessed 10 August 2022).

https://time.com/6133180/norway-electric-vehicles/#:~:text=Almost%20sixty%2Dfive%20percent%20of,purchased%20all%20over%20the%20country (last accessed 17 October 2022).

5.1 **Introduction**

Individuals and organizations don't exist in a vacuum. They are embedded in relationships, systems, and structures that inform and constrain their activity and which are, in turn, sustained or changed by organizational activity. In this chapter, we examine methods and theories that can build our understanding of the external context. We consider how this external context influences and is influenced by our own strategy activities—now and in the future.

We start by unpacking the market-based view (MBV), first introduced in Chapter 1, and an **ecosystems perspective**. The MBV—also known as the 'outside-in' approach—is a well-known theoretical perspective in strategy literature. An ecosystems perspective is a contemporary view of an external context in which organizations are an active part. Understanding the concepts and arguments of MBV and ecosystems perspectives will give you new ways of thinking about the nature and implications of the external context in which an organization is embedded.

We then introduce a set of methods for analysing the external context. Many methods are available to aid strategic managers' examination of relevant aspects of their external context. Directed at different levels and scales of enquiry, these methods encourage practitioners to organize data about the external environment and draw possible implications for strategy activity. We will first review a range of methods to help you sense changes in external context and to draw insights and implications from any information you discover.

- At a 'macro' level of enquiry, the *PESTEL* framework helps us to identify and analyse the priority factors and trends that affect wide groups of related organizations.
- At a 'market' level of enquiry, an industry forces framework helps us to evaluate the structure, dynamics, and profitability of groups of organizations interacting in the provision and consumption of similar products and services.
- At a 'micro' level of enquiry, competitive analysis methods generate insights about direct competitor activities and specific customer needs facing an organization.

These methods use concepts and frameworks to enable you to gather, organize, and interpret a core set of data about the external context. The use of complementary methods enables you to evaluate and possibly combine data generated by analysis. Where information from different levels of enquiry corresponds to the same external phenomena (Figure 5.1), you can compare insights arising, enhancing your ability to build a rich picture of what is happening in the external context (referred to as 'triangulation', discussed later in this chapter). For example, macro-analysis might detect a technology trend with the potential to open up a market to new entrants that currently has high barriers to entry. If close competitors are also exploring the use of this new technology, there is a set of deep insights to be derived relating to the technology trend that could influence strategy activity.

Building knowledge of how to interpret the external context is useful in strategy practice. Relating to the process–practice model (see Figure 2.5), the external context may be a source of triggers for strategizing, stakeholders and practitioners to be engaged, and resources and constraints that might impact on strategic initiatives. A need to examine the external context might be part of formal strategy activity or might arise in an ad hoc way from events encountered

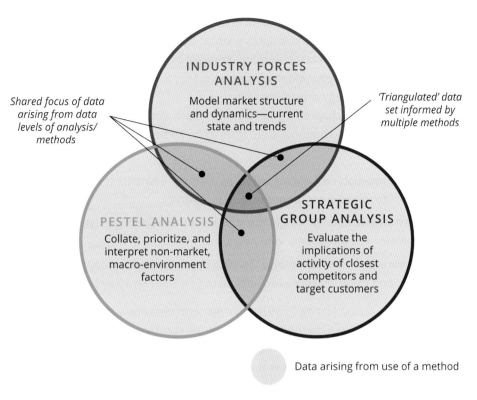

Shared focus of data arising from data levels of analysis/ methods

INDUSTRY FORCES ANALYSIS

Model market structure and dynamics—current state and trends

'Triangulated' data set informed by multiple methods

PESTEL ANALYSIS

Collate, prioritize, and interpret non-market, macro-environment factors

STRATEGIC GROUP ANALYSIS

Evaluate the implications of activity of closest competitors and target customers

Data arising from use of a method

FIGURE 5.1 **Complementary methods of analysis.** *Source*: authors.

during day-to-day operations. Theories and concepts direct our attention to aspects of our external context that we might not otherwise have considered. As we gather and organize data guided by frameworks, we become aware of changing trajectories or new factors in the external environmental. Through discussion and debate, we can establish possible implications of individual or systemic changes in the external context, maintaining our ability to respond (Morton et al. 2018). It is then up to those involved in strategy to decide whether there is a need to respond to these implications by triggering a strategizing episode. As addressed in Chapter 3, deciding to take the step from awareness to action will be a matter of judgement based on practitioner wisdom, experience, preferences, and biases. Insights from well-executed external analysis can usefully inform these decisions.

As we proceed through the chapter, it is wise to remember the practical limitations of external enquiry. Each theory and method focuses on a limited aspect of the external context and can only provide an approximation of actual events and trajectories. The way in which you choose to interpret concepts and customize analysis methods will shape the insights achieved. So too will the accuracy and comprehensiveness of information used to populate frameworks. The degree of initial understanding of practitioners—of the context and methods—influences the degree of new insight that can be achieved through external analysis. The completion of a framework is often a descriptive or organizing activity, not automatically triggering strategic activity or deep learning for all practitioners. And the external context continually unfolds, even as analysis is being conducted; it is vital that we are aware of the shelf-life of any insights arising from applying tools.

Despite these shortcomings, and by keeping these considerations in mind, we can benefit from the strategic conversations and insights enabled by analytical tools whilst minimizing the potential for false certainty and static thinking. Knowing how to interrogate the current 'state' and apparent trajectories of your external context, within the limits of methods, will improve your effectiveness as a strategy practitioner.

As you work through this chapter, if you can understand and critique the market-based view and the range of concepts and methods used to describe and evaluate the external context, you will grow your capacity to:

- **think like a strategist**: monitoring unfolding external events and effectively interpreting information into implications, priorities, and decisions;
- **talk like a strategist**: asking the right questions when considering external data and talking with shared meaning and insight with peers;
- **act like a strategist**: applying methods, leading others through analysis, recording justified implications, and using insights as an informant of further strategy practices.

This chapter focuses on explaining foundational 'generic' versions of external analysis methods. Your knowledge of these methods can usefully be combined, contrasted, and extended with theories and methods from other chapters. The methods and theories of the 'inside-out' resource-based view covered in Chapter 6 make a strong complement to the 'outside-in' approach detailed in this chapter. Further, the methods and theories of Part 4, addressing topics such as growth potential, internationalization, and digitalization, have the potential to create hybrid strategy practices and methods when combined with generic external analysis tools. We encourage you to experiment, to make your own innovative strategic approaches to 'enhancing knowledge of context and options'.

5.2 Analysing the external context

What do we mean by the external context?

The external context—or external environment—refers to all aspects of an organization's situation which exist beyond the boundaries of its direct control. For the sake of enabling 'easy' analysis, the external environment is often treated as a separate entity acting on the organization. This understanding of the organization and its environment is known as an **isolated interpretation** (Figure 5.2), and corresponds to a **structuralist approach** to strategy (Kim and Mauborgne 2009). In our experience, it is common practice in strategy analysis to conduct external environmental analysis which focuses only on the impact of the external environment on an organization.

An incomplete picture of the opportunities and threats presented by the external environment will emerge from this isolated approach to analysis. As an alternative, the organization can be thought of as a constituent part of its context, embedded in a broader system of external interactions and events. This is illustrated as an **embedded approach** to external analysis in Figure 5.2. Our practical experience of working with organizational strategy suggests that

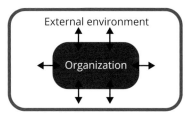

Isolated interpretation—organization separate to environment

Embedded interpretation—organization as part of environment

FIGURE 5.2 Isolated and embedded interpretations of organization external context. *Source*: authors.

different strategic insights will be developed through analysis, depending on how the relationship between an organization and its external environment is interpreted.

It is widely accepted that events occurring in the external environment will constrain and enable strategic options for an organization. However, it can also be argued that the strategic choices enacted by organizations will, in turn, shape the external environment. For example, the legislative environment acts on individuals and organizations, constraining their activity. However, organizations need not be passive recipients of legislative forces. For instance, in the United Kingdom, community groups have successfully lobbied local government to delay or ban shale gas fracking activity in their county (Nyberg et al. 2018). Through individual or collective lobbying activities, an organization can play an active part in shaping the legislative context in which it operates.

An ecosystems perspective of the external context

As described in Chapter 2, process theorists (e.g. Chia and Holt 2009) advocate an embedded interpretation of the organization–environment relationship. Further, the rise in popularity of dynamic capability theory (see Chapter 6), and the associated notion that organizations may have a capacity to proactively shape their external context, has challenged structuralist thinking and external analysis. Thus, whilst the external environment provides the context for organizational activity, it is also partly the product of previous organizational activity through relationships with other external structures. For instance, the collaborative action of German, Italian, and French automakers lobbying their respective governments has fast-tracked the preparation of autonomous vehicle-friendly domestic legislative environments. In turn, the German, Italian, and French governments led the modification of a 46-year-old United Nations (UN) automotive treaty to support autonomous vehicles globally, signed into law in 2014.

Being able to anticipate the impact of strategic actions on the external environment can help organizational decision-making processes and identify routes by which organizational activity can favourably shape the external environment. To imagine how this might happen, as an expression of an embedded perspective, the term **ecosystem** is increasingly used in strategy theory and practice to draw attention to the interconnected nature of organizational existence.

A business ecosystem refers to intentional communities of economic actors whose individual business activities share in some large measure the fate of the whole community (Moore 2006). It is rare now for an organization not to have some sort of collaboration with other organizations. As collaborative relationships multiply, a network of organizations co-creating value emerges, in which structures, relationships, and ways of working co-evolve over time. The external structures and relationships in which an organization is embedded can be described as the organization's **business ecosystem**.

Use of the ecosystems concept has grown in recent years such that it now challenges the notion of an 'industry' as the most relevant external label for organizational context (Fuller et al. 2019). As shown in Figure 5.3, in a review of the academic literature, Tsujimoto et al. (2018) identified that the notion of an ecosystem might be applied to describe all the actors attached to single industries (such as mass-market electric vehicles), related industries (all types of car

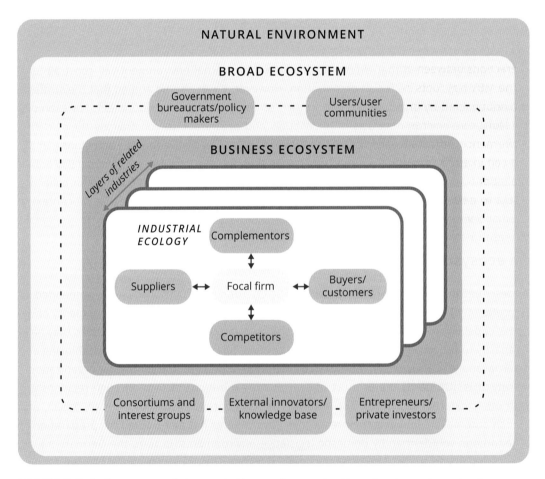

FIGURE 5.3 Ecosystem interpretations of organizational external context.
Source: adapted with permission from Tsujimoto, M. et al. (2018). A review of the ecosystem concept—towards coherent ecosystem design. *Technological Forecasting and Social Change*, **136**, 49–58, https://doi.org/10.1016/j.techfore.2017.06.032. © 2017 The Authors. Published by Elsevier Inc.

manufacturer), or broad ecosystems of 'multi-actor' networks (the business ecosystem plus further actors such as governments, consumers, and universities).

In this chapter, we explore how a focal organization can analyse the ecosystems context (see Figure 5.3) through market-level and macro-level methods, respectively. In Chapter 11, we will explore how **platform strategy**, leadership, and innovation can be approached as part of organizational strategy.

A market-based view of strategy

A focus on the external context and its importance as a determinant of organizational strategy is often referred to as a market-based view (MBV) of strategy. It is also known as an 'outside-in' perspective on strategy and organizational performance. According to the tenets of the MBV, external environmental structures provide the context for organizational activity in an industry/market. As described in seminal texts by Michael Porter (*Competitive Strategy* (1980) and *Competitive Advantage* (1984)), the choices organizations make for how they position themselves in that market will result in differential performance according to how well their conduct matches the needs of customers relative to the competitive alternatives. This structure–conduct–performance (SCP) model is at the heart of MBV thinking (Figure 5.4). In this figure, an embedded interpretation of the SCP framework is represented, showing the feedback effects and two interactions between an organization and the external environment.

The MBV has roots in industrial economics theory which holds that the position an organization adopts in the minds of its customers, relative to its competitors, will be a key determinant of its long-term success. There are practical limitations to this as a sole explanation for strategic performance. For example, it assumes that all organizations have equal access to resources and can execute repositioning activities as a matter of choice. Customers are assumed to act in a rational manner, selecting the best positioned organizations to meet their needs based on access to perfect information about market alternatives. In Chapter 3, we examined why this rationalist view rarely, if ever, fully explains decision-making. With awareness of the limitations of these underlying assumptions, tools associated with the MBV can form a useful part of a

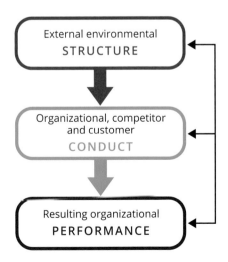

FIGURE 5.4 The structure–conduct–performance framework. *Source*: authors.

well-balanced portfolio of methods that improve strategy work without leaving you vulnerable to the limitations of any single theoretical perspective.

Knowing MBV concepts can help you be aware of external structures and relationships that might constrain and enable your strategic choices and which might be usefully influenced through the activities of your organization.

Structures

The external environment can be understood as a complex arrangement of overlapping structures. Structures refer to the enduring physical, social, and institutional settings in which an organization's activity occurs.

- **Physical environment**: the geography, terrain, and place in which the organization is located. The Scotch whisky industry, for instance, is highly impacted by geographical boundaries—producers need to operate within appropriate terrain in Scotland for their output to be considered a Scotch brand (see Chapter 10 Practitioner Insight).

- **Social environment**: the stakeholders—employees, communities, suppliers, customers, competitors, etc.—which the organization directly interacts with. For example, establishing a Tesla 'gigafactory' requires engagement with potential employees, local government, community representatives, and supplier organizations to enable successful development of the facility.

- **Institutional environment**: the intra-organizational setting for the organization—government bodies, industry sectors, customer groups, national cultures, etc.—within which the organization is embedded. Emirates Airlines, for instance, must take action within the rules and legislation of trading blocs such as the European Union (EU) as well as the Open Skies policy and the laws of the countries in which it operates. It is also required to conform with common technical and operational practices of the global airline industry.

Further instances of the above are raised by Case Example 5.1; the positioning of Arçelik, a white goods manufacturer, in its external environment has arguably made an important contribution to its competitive advantage and continuing success.

A useful binary distinction when examining the external context is between market and non-market structures (Doh et al. 2012).

- Market structures refer to the arrangement of competitors, suppliers, and customers that are interested in a type of product or service. Market structures have a direct impact on organizational competitive advantage and can be profiled by industry forces and competitive analysis methods, as described later in this chapter.

- Non-market structures refer to all other enduring aspects of the external environment—government and non-governmental organizations, local communities, the natural environment, universities, etc.—in which organizational activity takes place. The impact of non-market structures on competitive advantage for an organization can be analysed using PESTEL analysis.

Structures constitute an organizational landscape which can be mapped through strategic analysis. Ghemawat (2017) argues for mapping business landscapes—plotting different strategic choices in terms of their potential contribution to economic profitability given structures in the external context. According to Ghemawat, the aim of strategy is to find 'high points' on this land-scape where strategic choices offer high economic returns for an organization, given its context.

Relationships

Focusing on analysing structures or market/non-market factors is a convenient way of dividing up the external context. Equally, paying attention to the connectedness of these structures can yield valuable insights. Organizations exist 'in a nexus of relationships between governments, individuals, markets, and other social institutions' (Mahoney and McGahan 2007: 12). By interpreting the nature of relationships between different aspects of the external environment, you can learn about unfolding trends. For example, for energy companies, understanding of research developments in fracking technology must be accompanied by awareness of social and governmental attitudes to the environmental impact of such extractive techniques. Without understanding how governments, consumers, and researcher initiatives are developing in combination, a balanced sense of the commercial potential of fracking and related strategic options for action will not be possible.

Evaluating the implications of how the organization relates to its external environment can build arguments in support of strategic action. In aspects of the external environment which command managerial attention on a frequent basis, such as the direct competitive environment, enhanced understanding of the relationships between competitors and customer groups is vital. For instance, if an organization learns that, after a series of quality failures, a previously loyal customer no longer trusts a competitor that has been supplying them exclusively, it may represent an opportunity to be pursued. Using the methods described in Chapter 4, an organization may map its own external stakeholder relationships by thinking through 'With whom do we interact?' Further, reflecting on 'Who is interacting in our external environment, and how might it affect us?' will build up a sense of how the external context may unfold. In both cases, analysis of relationships and interactions through and beyond the boundaries of the organization can yield valuable strategic insights.

 Access the online resources to watch a short video clip where Dr Ibrahim Saif discusses the external environment.

CASE EXAMPLE 5.1 COMPETITIVE ADVANTAGE IN WHITE GOODS SUPPLY

Headquartered in Turkey, Arçelik is a manufacturer of white goods such as fridges and freezers. In 2021, it generated revenue of $6.95 billion. Around 65% of its turnover arises in international markets.

Several factors relating to Arçelik's position in the external environment have contributed to its competitive advantage and continuing success. In December 1995, Turkey became part of the European Union customs union, allowing Turkish firms to reach nearly 300 million consumers on more favourable terms of trade. Arçelik responded rapidly

Continued

to this change, becoming a leading supplier of budget appliances in Western Europe.

Arçelik has also exploited a global shift in supply chain possibilities as information technology and trade liberalization have created many opportunities for creating international production operations. To minimize production costs whilst maximizing closeness to consumers, Arçelik now operates 28 production facilities in 9 countries, employing around 40,000 staff. Given Turkey's geographic position at the East of Europe and the West of Asia, Arçelik is in a favourable location to manage the flow of goods between a wide range of production facilities and consumer markets.

Arçelik is pursuing long-term expansion in Asia's growing markets. Despite variations in local government, consumer tastes, and competitive landscapes according to country, the white goods industry is consistently in a hyper-competitive state. In response, Arçelik is taking a carefully considered range of strategic actions to target different markets in different ways, according to the needs of each country. For example, it opened a fridge factory in Thailand in 2015, it purchased a domestic white goods manufacturer in Pakistan in 2016, and it is partnering with Tata in India to sell under a local brand, Voltas, and import goods made in Turkey. In March 2019, Arçelik purchased a majority stake in Singer Bangladesh, the country's largest retailer of consumer durables. These actions are designed to maintain favourable relationships with local governments and suppliers, whilst positioning the firm as a reliable value-for-money brand which profitably meets the needs of consumers in each market it serves.

Questions for discussion

1. Explain how the physical location of Arçelik's headquarters has been of benefit to its recent success.

2. Discuss what seem to be crucial macro-environmental trends that can benefit Arçelik on a continuing basis.

3. If you were the CEO of Arçelik, what sort of external environmental data would be helpful as you review your strategy?

Sources

AA.com (Anadolu Agency) (2019). Turkey: Majority stake in singer Bangladesh for Arcelik (24 March), https://www.aa.com.tr/en/asia-pacific/turkey-majority-stake-in-singer-bangladesh-for-arcelik/1427587 (last accessed 10 August 2022).

Arçelik, https://www.arcelikglobal.com/en/company/about-us/overview(last accessed 10 August 2022).

The Economist (2017a). A Turkish maker of white goods is looking outwards (1 June), https://www.economist.com/business/2017/06/01/a-turkish-maker-of-white-goods-is-looking-outwards (last accessed 10 August 2022).

Revenue for Arçelik, https://companiesmarketcap.com/arcelik/revenue/#:~:text=Revenue%20in%202021%20(TTM)%3A,(TTM)%20is%20%241.55%20B (last accessed 10 August 2022).

S & P Global Ratings (2022). Arçelik A.S. (28 January), https://www.spglobal.com/_assets/documents/ratings/research/101085511.pdf (last accessed 10 August 2022).

Competitive advantage from a market-based view

Developing insights into the structures and relationships in the external environment can help managers to understand their competitive advantage. As we will explore in detail in Chapter 8, competitive advantage describes a firm's potential to beat its rivals in any outcome of interest (Peteraf and Barney 2003). An organization has competitive advantage if it can create more value than the marginal (break-even) competitor in a market. For private-sector organizations, competitive advantage is typically equated to profit potential. For public- and third-sector organizations, competitive advantage might be gauged by different criteria, such as the ability of the organization to access funding.

A principal aim of strategy is to enable an organization to gain or sustain competitive advantage through the planned allocation of resources and purposeful action. With competitive advantage, a firm will be able to deliver a return for its owners, or a non-private organization will be able to deliver its mandate. From an MBV, competitive advantage arises by adopting a position in external structures from which perceived benefits for customers can be created that they are willing to pay more for than the economic costs of producing those benefits. An MBV thus directs strategists' attention to the dynamics of non-market and market structures in which the organization is embedded. Strategic choices can then be made about how to maintain or adjust an organization's position in the external environment to enhance or sustain competitive advantage.

From an ecosystems perspective, competitive advantage might also arise through playing a pivotal role in a network of organizations, acting as a 'keystone'. Keystone organizations 'provide a stable and predictable set of common assets', such as Alibaba's ecommerce platform (see Chapter 1) or Android by Google, which allows other organizations to build their own offerings (Iansiti and Levien 2004). By enhancing the ecosystem, keystone organizations can enhance their own prospects of survival and success. The focus of organizational strategy broadens to consider how initiatives might develop the whole ecosystem to the benefit of all organizations. For example, should you aim to undertake initiatives that might result in 50% of a market of £10 million or initiatives that lead to 20% of a market that you've supported growing to £100 million? We will return to the idea of a keystone organization in Case Example 5.2 (as we discuss Delivery Hero and other takeaway ordering firms); and we will also explore keystone advantage in Chapter 11 as we examine a related concept—platform leadership.

Competitive advantage and the MBV can be applied not just to a whole organization but also to components of an organization. Our discussion of resources and capabilities in Chapter 6 illustrates some ways in which functions, business units, or teams might strategize. Applying the concept of competitive advantage at a business unit or team level can help you identify how a business unit or team sustains its contribution to the broader organization. You will be able to evaluate whether the work carried out by the team or business unit remains more valuable to the organization than alternative internal options (e.g. sister units) or external options (e.g. **outsourcing**).

5.3 **Developing a core data set on the external environment**

There are hundreds of tools available for conducting strategy environmental analysis (Vuorinen et al. 2018), each examining some aspect of the external context. Faced with such an array of options, where should you start building your knowledge of the external context? In this section, we discuss how a set of three methods—PESTEL, industry forces, and competitive analysis—might be used to probe the external context in complementary ways. Each method directs attention to distinct aspects of the external environment (Hambrick and Fredrickson 2001) and, using a theoretically informed structured approach, develops a set of implications specific to the focal organization. Each method is subject to inherent strengths and limitations (Table 5.1), of which you should be mindful.

When used in combination, these methods generate a foundational set of data about the external environment as a strong starting point for strategy conversations. In terms of return

TABLE 5.1 **Purpose, advantages, and limitations of a range of external analysis tools**

Method	Purpose	Advantages	Limitations
Macro-level PESTEL analysis	Identify the high-level trends in the external context that will impact on the organization's ecosystem Gain insight about how to meet these challenges in the future or attempt to influence the macro-environment	+ Can provide foresight of threats to the organization's relevance/existence + Helps identify where long-term investment and capability building should be directed + Highlights the possibilities of shaping the ecosystem in a way which is favourable to the organization + Reduces the likelihood of being caught out by blind spots in team thinking	− Significant volumes of data need to be managed and prioritized − Will yield different results according to where the boundaries for analysis are drawn − Reviews external factors in isolation: the macro-environment results from complex combinations of PESTEL factors − Does not review the market specifics of competition for an organization
Market-level **industry forces analysis**	Evaluate the attractiveness of the markets and industries in which the organization competes Direct energy and effort to markets where there will be maximum potential of returns for the organization	+ Brings order to analysis of the attractiveness of the organization's markets + Provides a means of identifying where markets need to be exited in a controlled manner + Identifies actions which might be taken to extend favourable market conditions for an organization	− Implications can be highly sensitive to where market boundaries are drawn − Does not address nuances of how market segments are serviced − Can be misleading at a high level of aggregation, and more meaningful focus on individual product or geographic markets is time-consuming
Micro-level competitive analysis	Focus on developing deep insights about the activities of direct competitors and what is valued by target customers Assess the likelihood of the organization being able to compete effectively in this context	+ Generates strategic insights of high relevance to 'daily' operations + Focuses on customer value creation, bringing attention to competitive advantage + Brings rigour and structure to analysis of direct competition, controlling for 'commonly held beliefs' about factors for competitive success in the strategy process	− Only focuses on market-segment-related insights − Does not factor in trends and future trajectories − Requires discipline in execution, as it addresses factors which many in the organization believe they already understand − May uncover politically sensitive insights about the realities of how well the organization is competing

Source: authors.

on effort, this core data set will suffice for many strategy teams. For others, who wish to conduct a nuanced analysis according to the perceived needs of the organization's situation, the core data set forms a strong platform for that work. As highlighted in our discussion of the attention-based view in Chapter 2, building diverse communication and information flows will improve the quality of insights available for those making strategic decisions.

As outlined in section 5.1, these methods can be described in terms of the level of analysis; each operates with a different scope when prompting a review of the external context. We will consider each in turn—defining the framework, considering supporting theory, reviewing its application, and highlighting its limitations. We will then review how the insights emerging from each tool can be used in combination to derive a useful external environmental core data set (Figure 5.1).

Analysing non-market factors in the macro-environment

PESTEL analysis

PESTEL is a method for examining trends in the macro-environment and how they might influence and be influenced by an organization. It brings scrutiny to the non-market structures in which organizational activities occur and in which the organization is embedded. For the strategist, PESTEL is a thought-provoking complement to the implications of market structures uncovered through industrial and competitive analysis.

PESTEL is an acronym for six macro-environmental factors which can be used to describe the broad external context:

Political: the local, national, and supra-regional political trends that shape the operating environment for the organization. This will take into consideration how the political will of powerful individuals, political parties, campaign groups, and local, national, and regional governments might have a direct or indirect impact on the operating environment for the organization. The strategist may wish to consider how they can individually or collectively find a voice in the political process. For example, President Trump's approach to business and environmental policy marked a change in direction from the Obama administration, altering the landscape of opportunities and threats for those working or trading in the United States in many industries (Wright et al. 2019).

Economic: the health and trends (often cyclical) of economic activity which have an impact on organizational activity. This addresses factors such as energy prices, interest rates, foreign exchange, national growth, etc. in the economic settings in which the organization operates. For the strategist, awareness of macro-economic conditions is a key informant of risk management and decision-making in relation to investments and capacity management. For instance, the economics of the global airline industry and the viability of many firms competing in the industry are affected by oil price fluctuations. Consequently, many airlines engage in a financial risk management activity called hedging when purchasing fuel.

Social: trends in attitudes and demographics within society which shape the products, services, and way of operating of the organization. Reviewing macro-social conditions will consider how customer needs are evolving in the long term and how employee expectations and availability are shifting. This factor raises questions about capabilities that need to be invested in now such that they can meet future customer demands in a sustainable way.

5

For example, shifting consumer attitudes towards data, technology, and openness of information has created whole new markets and industries based on social media platforms.

Technological: developments in product, process, and service-enabling technologies, and the associated possibilities and impacts on the value the organization creates and how it operates. As we will explore in Chapter 11, a central concern in strategizing is how technological developments in all walks of life might cross over to the domain of the organization. Trends in investment, research, and development activities through the knowledge base (universities, institutes, colleges, etc.), other industries, and in different geographies are all reviewed here. For the strategist, this can be an unsettling piece of analysis as the potential implications of technological progress are digested (from a game-changing opportunity, which, to be seized, requires organizational transformation, to possible extinction events for the current organizational set-up). As illustrated in the Opening Case Study, macro-level technological trends in autonomous vehicles and electric power technology are transforming the automotive industry and transportation more generally.

Environmental: a macro-review of how the changing state of the natural environment will affect the activities of all within an organization's ecosystem. Broadly, this will address the implications of climate change on the natural environment and acceptable organizational practices, regulation of environmental impact (e.g. waste, emissions, carbon footprint), and incentives and opportunities for progressive environmental practices. The environmental angle has a clear cross-over with all other PESTEL categories but is worth isolating as a recurring influential macro-factor that will shape the future operating context for industries, as examined in Chapter 4. For the strategist, this factor draws attention to an organization's sustainability agenda and how that might permeate strategy. Increasingly, organizational opportunity and competitive advantage appear to be available for those willing to embed sustainability in organizational purpose and strategizing practice.

Legislative: direction of travel and scheduled developments in the laws, legislation, and regulation affecting all stakeholders in the localities in which an organization operates. By considering the current and likely future formal parameters within which an organization operates, decisions can be made about how to optimally organize activity and how to reconfigure products/services to exploit opportunity and avoid the costs of non-compliance presented by the legislative context. For example, changes in minimum wage legislation can impact the scope of services which can be offered by charitable organizations as funding sources fail to keep pace with statutory obligations.

PESTEL is widely used as a basis for macro-environmental analysis. Variations of the acronym exist (e.g. STEP, STEEP, STEEPL), reflecting different interpretations of the scope of each of the underlying categories (e.g. some integrate the legislative category into the political category).

How to apply PESTEL

This section explains how PESTEL can be used to conduct macro-environmental analysis with maximum return on effort. It is important to remember that a perfect model of the external environment is not a feasible outcome. Instead, this analysis can be used to uncover trends in the ecosystem which might require a strategic response by the organization. The descriptions in this section, and the full worked example of PESTEL analysis (Figure 5.5), reflect the most efficient and effective applications of PESTEL we have encountered in our consultancy experience.

(A) PREPARE TEMPLATE

Create a blank table ready for population with descriptive data.

Note, only two descriptions have been included in this example. This is only for the sake of space. Include as many entries as seem relevant in practice.

Factor	Description	Priority
Political		
Economic		
Social		
Technological		
Environmental		
Legislative		

(B) ADD DESCRIPTIONS

Based on research of the macro-environmental context, add in descriptions of trends and influences that may affect the organization.

Keep these descriptions in a summary format for usability, citing headline facts and figures but reserving details for a separate explanatory document.

Factor	Descriptions	Priority
Political	Favourable policies in United States and European nations for domestic players	
	Political intervention in trading bloc terms likely as a consequence of Brexit	
Economic	Over-capacity in industry (25–30%)	
	Emergence of 'middle class' in many developing economies main growth area	
Social	Strong global demand for 'luxury' brands	
	Gen Y pushing demand for sustainable products	
Technological	Emergence of hybrid and electrical technologies	
	Autonomous vehicles nearing commercialization	
Environmental	Air pollution/emissions control part of public debate globally	
	Carbon footprint of production under scrutiny	
Legislative	European legislation governing emissions regulation tightening	
	Global legislation imminent on recyclability of material usage	

(C) PRIORITIZE DESCRIPTIONS

Informed by the research activity, debate the relative priority of all descriptive entries in the table. This prioritization will be specific to the strategy team's organization.

A visual indicator is used in this example—the more the quadrants are filled in, the higher the priority. Numbers, letters, or a simple priority/not priority categorization would also work.

Factor	Descriptions	Priority
Political	Favourable policies in United States and European nations for domestic players	
	Political intervention in trading bloc terms likely as a consequence of Brexit	
Economic	Over-capacity in industry (25–30%)	
	Emergence of 'middle class' in many developing economies main growth area	
Social	Strong global demand for 'luxury' brands	
	Gen Y pushing demand for sustainable products	
Technological	Emergence of hybrid and electrical technologies	
	Autonomous vehicles nearing commercialisation	
Environmental	Air pollution/emissions control part of public debate globally	
	Carbon footprint of production under scrutiny	
Legislative	European legislation governing emissions regulation tightening	
	Global legislation imminent on recyclability of material usage	

FIGURE 5.5 Completion of PESTEL for a global automotive firm. *Source*: authors.

Factor	Descriptions	Priority
Political	Favourable policies in United States and European nations for domestic players	
	Political intervention in trading bloc terms likely as a consequence of Brexit	
Economic	Over-capacity in industry (25–30%)	←
	Emergence of 'middle class' in many developing economies main growth area	←
Social	Strong global demand for 'luxury' brands	
	Gen Y pushing demand for sustainable products	
Technological	Emergence of hybrid and electrical technologies	←
	Autonomous vehicles nearing commercialization	←
Environmental	Air pollution/emissions control part of public debate globally	
	Carbon footprint of production under scrutiny	
Legislative	European legislation governing emissions regulation tightening	←
	Global legislation imminent on recyclability of material usage	

(D) DECIDE CUT-OFF

As a team, debate where to draw the line in evaluating strategic implications of priorities.

In this case, the top five factors are selected as the topics for developing implications and action options.

Implications	Options for Action
Over-capacity means that consolidation is highly likely—a wave of mergers and acquisitions is imminent, which the organization must prepare to defend or exploit	
If growth is going to come from the middle classes in developing economies, it is essential to maintain a strong presence in these markets	
Major technological disruption from autonomous vehicles and electrical power technology demand an investment in competences required to deal with the new landscape	
New EU laws on tighter emission control will have to be prepared for, affecting all players in the European market	

(E) DEVELOP IMPLICATIONS

Discussing the identified priorities in combination, identify implications for the future of the organization.

Where appropriate, combine factors together in drawing implications. In this example, the technological disruption from two priority factors is addressed through a single implication.

Priorities

Implications	Options for Action
Over-capacity means that consolidation is highly likely—a wave of mergers and acquisitions is imminent, which the organization must prepare to defend or exploit	Arrange and manage financial position to fend off takeovers
	Commission scanning of market for merger & acquisition targets
If growth is going to come from the middle classes in developing economies, it is essential to maintain a strong presence in these markets	Explore joint venture options in top ten growing emerging markets
	Invest in marketing intelligence for all emerging markets
Major technological disruption from autonomous vehicles and electrical power technology demand an investment in competences required to deal with the new landscape	Prioritize investment in electric vehicle R&D activity
	Source tech partner firms for AV technology
New EU laws on tighter emission control will have to be prepared for, affecting all players in the European market	Lobby for long timescales to meet new emissions standards
	Increase staffing in emissions compliance function

(F) OPTIONS FOR ACTION

For each of the implications, develop potential organizational responses under the heading "Options for action".

These options are not a commitment to follow through. Instead, they will be fed into the strategy process as options for action for consideration, supported by macro-environmental analysis.

FIGURE 5.5 *Continued*

Step 1. Agree the operating principles for the boundaries of PESTEL

Whilst PESTEL is intended to help you think about the ecosystem in which your organization exists, it is also important to define limits on the scope of that analysis. Where the line is drawn for inclusion in PESTEL analysis will influence the effort involved in conducting research. For example, imagine you are examining trends in the macro-environment for an Indian airline serving only the domestic market. Do you run PESTEL analysis for the airline industry for India, Asia, or the world?

We advise that the boundary for each PESTEL factor is set according to organizational relevance. These judgements may lead to different outcomes for each factor by each team conducting strategy. The key question to ask is, 'What macro-environmental trends might impact us in the future?' In the case of the Indian airline, global trends in aircraft technology might have to be considered as the **diffusion** of any new technology in the future will likely make it relevant to the organization. In terms of macro-social trends, however, limiting that analysis to India makes more sense, given the domestic focus of the airline.

Step 2. Create a research plan to investigate the PESTEL factors

To keep the PESTEL exercise manageable, create an initial research plan. Start by identifying the sources which might be reviewed about macro-trends, applying the 'relevance' principle from Step 1 to set appropriate limits. Possible sources include industry and academic journals; the publications of government bodies, trade associations, third-sector and non-governmental organizations; business press; and the mainstream media. Further specialist research may be available at a price or through libraries.

Step 3. Populate a table with descriptions of relevant factors

Create a table (see Figure 5.5) in which you compile the findings of your research. Keep the descriptions brief, with supporting information and sources in a separate document. Where there are options for categories into which to allocate an identified trend, select the most appropriate fit; do not duplicate the entry across more than one category. Provided that the point is captured once within the table, the framework has served its purpose.

Step 4. Prioritize the macro-trends identified based on potential future impact

PESTEL analysis will generate a multitude of possible macro-environmental influences. Not all of these will be of equal relevance or importance to the future of the organization. Prioritizing identified trends is an important act in converting PESTEL research into a useful strategy outcome.

Through debate and discussion, use your judgement to allocate a priority status to each of the macro-factors identified. This should result in a simple priority/non-priority label for each factor and a shared understanding of the supporting rationale. In the table, capture the prioritization outcomes for each of the identified trends. Prioritized trends might be highlighted in bold and/or ranking scoring displayed if appropriate. Visual indicators can also be used to good effect. See Figure 5.5 for an applied PESTEL example for a global original equipment manufacturer (OEM) in the automotive industry. These prioritized trends are sometimes referred to as key drivers—specific non-market factors which are believed to have most influence on the organization's future performance.

Step 5. Develop organizational implications for priority trends

Build your knowledge of the external context by discussing the possible organizational implications of the priority factors. To do so, debate the question, 'If this trend continues as anticipated, what does it imply for our organization in the short, medium, and long term?' A priority trend may have several implications, and each implication may be supported by more than one priority trend. You might find that the organizational implications are supported by multiple PESTEL factors. This is normal and highlights that the macro-context is only divided into separate categories for our convenience when conducting analysis. It may help to create a separate table of implications at this point (see illustration E, Figure 5.5).

Step 6. Identify options for action

If you decide that the implications might require an organizational response, the final step is to identify options for strategic initiatives/action. Listing such options is not a commitment to follow through with action. Rather, this step creates a useful input to strategic decision-making which reflects macro-environmental considerations. For example, imagine you have identified an implication of macro-trends that 'our current products are likely to become obsolete within three years'. Your corresponding options for strategic action could be 'Exit the product market within the next year', 'Invest in R&D towards creating a new generation of products', and 'Lobby for tighter regulation on emergent technology'.

Options for action might focus on how to maintain or enhance competitive advantage or keystone advantage through intelligent responses to macro-trends. Options for action might address how to attempt to shape macro-trends as well as how to react to the consequences of changes in the ecosystem. Identifying options for action helps you to avoid feeling powerless when faced with the implications of external environmental forces. Concluding your PESTEL analysis with a set of options for action keeps a focus on activity and creates a 'common currency' that can be built on by other methods of analysis.

Analysing market structure and dynamics

Next, we review a method for examining the structure and dynamics of the markets in which an organization operates. A market is defined as the individuals, organizations, and activities involved in the provision or consumption of a product or service within a defined geography. An industry can be defined as related markets which can be grouped together according to either similarity in products (e.g. the mobile computing industry) and/or geographies (e.g. Australian industry). Industry forces analysis provides a means of examining the organizational implications of how a market is structured and interacts now and in the future. Whilst this analysis can be applied to a whole industry, we will examine how it can be applied to a specific geographic or product market.

Markets vary significantly in size and characteristics. Organizations may seek to compete across a range of product or geographical markets, each with its own distinctive characteristics. Within a market, there may be many ways in which organizations seek to compete and operate. Industry forces analysis helps the strategist to decide whether the organization should continue to operate in a market and, if so, what actions might usefully shape the configuration of the market structure to the organization's advantage. Industry forces analysis should not be confused with competitive analysis (addressed in the next section on 'micro-level' analysis).

A foundation in the 'Five Forces'

Porter's framework, the 'Five Forces' (Figure 5.6), is reported (Grundy 2006) as the most common analytical framework used in market-based strategic analysis (see also his highly influential *Harvard Business Review* article—Porter 2008). Although it has been subject to extensive critique, it is a mainstay of strategy theory and practice. In defining what we mean by industry forces, we build on **Five Forces** thinking, addressing the limitations of Porter's model by adding further components.

The Five Forces framework describes and analyses the effect of market structure on profitability, and therefore attractiveness, for organizations. Five forces analysis also models the structure and dynamics of the market so that you can better understand options for remaining and influencing in a market or exiting it at the appropriate time. If the amount of possible profit in a market is a 'pie', Five Forces helps us to understand how big the pie is and how it will be divided up (Brandenburger 2002). The model prompts you to identify how the relationship between buyers, suppliers and customers, potential new market entrants, and substitute offerings shapes the profitability and appropriation of profit in a market. The meaning of each of these forces is described in Table 5.2.

The profit potential for competitors in the market will be determined by the extent to which bargaining power exists over buyers and suppliers. For example, if an organization is the only provider of a vital service in a particular market, it has very high bargaining power over its buyers (a monopoly situation). Therefore, it can set a price which contains a high profit margin as the customer doesn't have any further options—pay the price or don't get the service. This also applies in reverse for an organization in relation to its own suppliers. If an organization is the only buyer of a product or service from multiple sellers, it will have high bargaining power

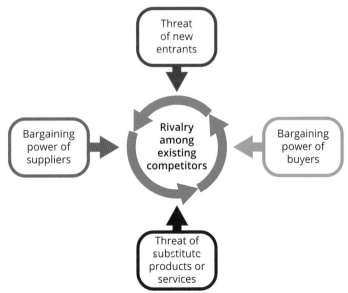

THE FIVE FORCES THAT SHAPE INDUSTRY COMPETITION

FIGURE 5.6 **The Five Forces (5F) framework.** *Source*: Porter, M.E. (2008). The five competitive forces that shape competitive strategy. *Harvard Business Review* (January), 25–41. By permission of Harvard Business Publishing.

TABLE 5.2 **Description of each of the Five Forces**

Force	Definition
Buyer power	The bargaining power and related attitudes of customers which will determine the price customers are willing to pay for the goods/services in this market. The more bargaining power customers have, the less profit for competitors.
Supplier power	The bargaining power and related attitudes of suppliers which will determine the extent to which profit can be retained by those offering goods/services in this market. The more power suppliers have to control supply and set prices for inputs to the market, the less profit there will be for competitors.
Competitive rivalry	The range, scale, similarity, and behaviour of competing organizations directly serving the market that will influence how much profitability is available in total, and how it is distributed. The more one competitor has power over rivals (through superior competitive advantage), the more of the available profit they will be able to appropriate.
Threat of new entrants	The likelihood that new competitors will enter an industry, bringing with them capacity to meet buyer demands and a desire to compete in a way that will erode profit potential for existing competitors.
Threat of substitutes	The extent to which customers may be tempted to abandon this market in favour of alternative goods and services providing comparable utility by different means. If viable substitutes are available, the price competitors can charge in this market will be limited.

Source: authors.

(a **monopsony** situation). It can then offer to pay a price that is close to cost for the supplier. Understanding the extent of bargaining power with buyers and suppliers can generate valuable insights about the potential for competitive advantage in a market.

A further force to consider in understanding market attractiveness is the extent of direct competition. The more competition in a sector, the greater the likelihood that profit potential will be reduced for an organization. Many organizations competing in a market does not mean that every competitor cannot be profitable (i.e. all organizations can hold some sort of competitive advantage in a market). For instance, competitors operating in a growing market where demand outstrips supply might all be profitable. From an ecosystems perspective, there is a logic to collaborating with competitors to grow the overall market to the benefit of all. However, where there is intense competition, overall profit will be divided amongst more players, and competitor activity can influence the behaviour of buyers and suppliers through negotiation, advertising, collaboration, etc., altering the balance of bargaining power for an organization with its buyers and suppliers. Therefore, profiling the competitive forces in a market—intensity and interactions with buyers and suppliers—provides insights for an organization about the attractiveness of the market.

There are two further factors advocated in Porter's framework which influence the buyer–supplier–competitor forces. 'Barriers to entry' is an assessment of the extent to which it is feasible for new competitors to join the market. If a market appears highly profitable, as evidenced by the success of current competitors, others may be attracted to enter that market. If there are high barriers to entry, the effort required to enter the market is prohibitive for many organizations. High barriers to entry will protect the profitability of the industry for current incumbents. Low barriers to entry will lead to a quick erosion of the profit for current players as new entrants increase the level of competition. Profiling this force can be useful in building an understanding of how competition and bargaining power aspects of the market may change in the future.

Availability of substitutes is Porter's final force. The concept refers to the availability of alternative markets through which customers can achieve sufficiently similar outcomes to the focus market. For example, bicycle hire is a substitute market to the car hire industry. They both provide the similar utility of being able to lease a mechanism for moving from A to B. However, the technology involved, the cost base, and the supply chain differ substantially, and the customer realizes the utility of the offerings by distinctive means. Thus, whilst these markets have some commonalities, the organizations operating in them are substitutes rather than direct competitors.

Understanding the extent to which substitutes might be attractive to customers will provide insights about the profitability potential of a market. The more attractive available substitutes are, the less able prices are to rise in a market without driving current customers to that substitute. In our practical experience, it is normal for the concept of substitutes to be misapplied. The common mistake is to evaluate substitutes as only marginally different direct competitors. For example, it would be an error to consider Facebook search and Google search as substitutes, rather than competing organizations. It may be true that their main product or service—the offering that made them famous—is in different markets. But in the market being evaluated (online search), they are in direct competition through similar technological means. A substitute for this market would be encyclopaedias, the availability of which is unlikely to have any impact on the structure or interactions of the online search market. Note that the reverse argument does not apply as the rise of the online search market as a substitute for encyclopaedias has significantly altered the attractiveness of that market.

Limitations of Five Forces analysis

According to Porter (Argyres and McGahan 2002), the original Five Forces model was intended to be a specific aid to decision-making. However, it has been critiqued extensively, particularly for being treated as a holistic tool of strategic evaluation, perhaps more so than any other strategic management framework (cf. Grundy 2006). Its limitations include the following:

- **Five Forces is too static**: by taking only a snapshot of the current situation, Five Forces doesn't capture the trajectory of the market. On the basis that the structures, relationships, and activities within a market may change over time, Five Forces might generate analytical insights with a short shelf-life. This challenge can be mitigated by tracing historical paths and analysing trends in industry forces. Further, reflecting on the market life cycle and any enduring structural characteristics of the market can improve your understanding of market attractiveness and appropriate options for action.

- **Five Forces insights are dependent on where the market boundaries are drawn**: considerations of the application of Five Forces to the luxury car market, or the second-hand car market, or the second-hand luxury car market will all yield different outcomes. And where should geographical boundaries be drawn to deliver the most useful outcomes for those making strategic decisions? To address this limitation, it may be necessary to create multiple models of industry forces for a focal market, re-running analysis with narrower and broader market boundaries.

- **Five Forces doesn't represent all the factors that impact on market profitability**: non-market factors such as government interests or labour union activity can impact on the structure and attractiveness of a market—these are not represented in the Five Forces. This partly explains the value of undertaking strategic analysis using complementary methods. By combining the outcomes of industry forces analysis with macro- and micro-level outcomes, a more comprehensive picture of the external environment is established.

- **Five Forces ignores the effects of non-competitive products and services that influence profitability**: Five Forces analysis focuses attention on the direct supplier, buyer, and competitor relationships in a specific market. However, just as individuals and organizations don't exist within a vacuum, nor does a market exist in isolation. Non-competitive, non-substitutable products and services from alternative markets can have a significant influence on the profitability and attractiveness of an industry (Brandenburger and Nalebuff 1996). For example, the development of a vehicle-charging infrastructure market will impact the profitability and dynamics of the Norwegian electric vehicle (EV) market. These complementary effects are not addressed in the Five Forces framework.

- **Five Forces doesn't consider the potential importance of networks on market attractiveness**: the dynamics and structure of a market may be influenced by what are known as network effects. This refers to how the customer value of a product or service is dependent on the size and availability of a relevant network. For example, if the purpose of a telephone is to enable remote conversation, the usefulness of a telephone to a customer (and the price they are willing to pay for it) will depend on how many of the customer's contacts also have telephones which are networked together. The more relevant contacts that are connected to that network, the more valuable the telephone is to the customer.

An industry forces analysis framework

To conduct valuable analysis of the market-level context, we advocate that you draw an industry forces framework (Figure 5.7) incorporating Porter's Five Forces. This challenges you to consider further factors which mitigate the limitations of Five Forces and incorporate industrial ecology thinking (Figure 5.3). Porter (2008: 86) identifies many of these additional factors, pointing out that they are not forces that determine a market's structure but rather factors that influence the Five Forces. In practice, for a strategy team seeking to conduct market-level analysis, it is less important whether a consideration is labelled a force or a factor and more important that organizational implications of a matter of relevance is addressed.

Influence of complementarities

Complementarities are offerings from a separate market—providing a different utility to customers—which will influence the dynamics of the focal market. For example, video games producers are complementors to console hardware manufacturers. They are not in active competition, nor are they substitutes, and they are not buyers or suppliers to console manufacturers. However,

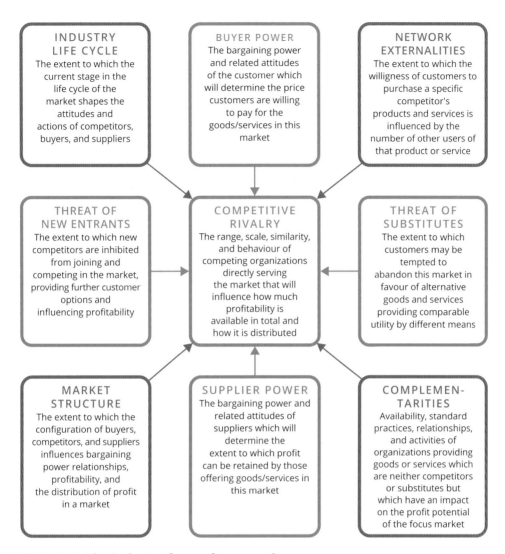

FIGURE 5.7 The industry forces framework. *Source*: authors.

the activities of video games manufacturers will be highly influential on the structure and attractiveness of the console hardware market. Without a library of available games or a pipeline of game development activity, a console is unlikely to attract much customer interest. Equally, the development of the console hardware market influences the structure and interactions of the video games market. Many commentators describe complementarities as the 'sixth force', such is their potential relevance to insightful market-level analysis.

Influence of industry life cycle

It can be useful to consider the historical development of a market when seeking to profile industry forces (Lei and Slocum 2005). Figure 5.8 depicts a typical life cycle curve for a market. As the market emerges, competition is between a limited number of innovative competitors for early adopting customers. As the interested customer base grows over time, revenues rise and potentially more competition is attracted into the market. Eventually, a stage of maturity

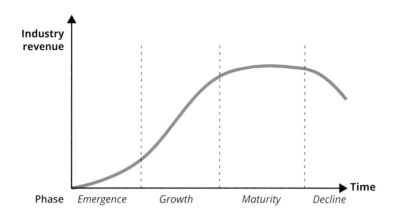

FIGURE 5.8 The industry life cycle curve. *Source*: authors.

is reached where revenues level out before the market goes into decline as the customer base moves on to alternative products and interests.

Considering the position of a market on this life cycle curve can provide a useful input to industrial forces analysis and strategic decision-making. For example, imagine an organization innovating in two new markets, A and B, both in the emergence phase. Reflecting on the 'barriers to new entry' force, how easy is it for new competitors to enter the market? Market A appears to have higher growth potential but lower barriers to entry than market B. The organization may choose to pursue market B as it is recognized that many competitors will probably join market A as it enters the growth phase, whereas competition will be more limited in market B. Alternatively, if market B had been in decline rather than emergence, the organization would choose to prioritize market A instead.

Table 5.3 shows relevant questions about and implications of **industry life cycle** positioning that you may wish to consider when undertaking industry forces analysis.

Influence of market configuration

Within industry forces analysis, the configuration of competitors, buyers, and suppliers—the market structure—can be useful to focus on during strategic conversations. The nature of the market structure (Figure 5.9) can be a major influence on the perceived attractiveness for strategic decision-makers. In a market where an organization is a monopoly or oligopoly competitor, even temporarily, actions which preserve and exploit this status will be desirable. In hyper-competitive and (near-) perfectly competitive markets, finding alternative markets with greater profit potential may be a focus of strategic conversations.

An increasingly common term used to describe market structures with high competitor, buyer, and supplier forces is 'red ocean markets'. The metaphor was first proposed by Kim and Mauborgne (2005) to illustrate the red ink accounting losses and threats to survival of organizations operating in highly competitive markets (like blood in shark-infested waters!). Kim and Mauborgne suggest that organizations should constantly be seeking the temporary monopolies of 'blue oceans'—markets for customer needs which are currently unserved (i.e. lack competition) and which hold high profit potential. The strategic mindset and methods required to pursue blue ocean market innovation are addressed in Chapter 11.

TABLE 5.3 **Interpreting industry life cycle**

Life cycle stage	Potential implications for competing organizations	Questions to consider
Emergence	Unlikely that any one standard or competitor will dominate	How can we innovate in a way that shapes this market in our favour?
	Likely scope for experimentation, innovation, and shaping market characteristics	Does this market have potential to develop and grow?
Growth	Scalability of offering and operations is required to keep pace and maintain or grow market share	How can we take action to increase our capture of market share?
	New entrants may be attracted if profit potential is high	What can we do to advantageously grow the total market size?
	Network externalities may start to show if there are buyer and supplier benefits from focusing on a single-platform/ standard offering	Can we do anything (on our own or collaborating with competitors) to deter new competitors from entering the market?
		Are any network externalities developing? What can we do to become the preferred option for buyers?
Maturity	Growth levels off and competition becomes more intense	How well do we stack up against the competition?
	Likely that industry will not attract many more entrants at this point	Are we making enough profit to justify staying in this market, or should we seek new sources of growth?
	Those with high market share and effective operations will likely seek to remain; other organizations may start seeking alternative uses of resources	Can we reduce our costs to improve our profitability, even if total market profit isn't increasing?
Decline	Organizations start to leave the market as reducing volume impacts its attractiveness as a focus of organizational resources	Should we exit this market?
		If we remain, how can we capture the market share of exiting firms?
	However, profit potential may be sustained for organizations that remain, provided that a sufficient number of competitors leave.	How should we review our prices in this declining market?
		What is the remaining lifespan of the market, and how should we plan our time in it?

Source: authors.

Influence of network externalities

Network externality—also known as the network effect—describes a situation where the market structure aligns around a dominant standard, platform, or product. This can have a profound influence on market structure and attractiveness (Chatterjee and Matzler 2019). It often leads to a monopolistic market structure, for example, Uber as a ride-hailing platform in many cities. There is a network effect as customers are attracted to the Uber platform because it has most drivers (suppliers), and drivers are attracted to the Uber platform as it has most customers. For both drivers and customers, there is less utility in using less populated platforms (i.e. the value of the platform is a function of the number of customers associated with it). Over time, this self-reinforcing dynamic (or virtuous cycle) can maintain a monopoly situation. As a result

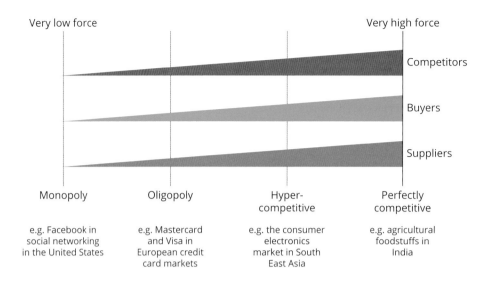

FIGURE 5.9 The impacts of differing market structures. *Source*: authors.

of network externalities, those holding the largest network in certain markets can achieve a sustainable competitive advantage, aided by customer and supplier behaviour. We explore this idea further through the concept of platform leadership discussed in Chapter 11. For markets in emergence or growth phases, it is worthwhile for the strategy team to be vigilant for any signs of network externalities during market-level analysis. Unless the organization is the beneficiary of a network externality, exiting a market early where network externality is developing can be a prudent option for strategic action.

Non-market external factors

Whilst PESTEL analysis highlights macro-trends in the external environment, it can also draw attention to non-market factors which have an influence on the attractiveness of an industry. For example, government views of a market can have a major influence on industry attractiveness. This might be represented in the original Five Forces through government-enforced legislative barriers to entry. Further though, what if a government owns a stake in one of the competing firms or decides to take a lax approach to the enforcement of intellectual property law? Awareness of how government might influence market structure, relationships, and activity can generate valuable insights about the attractiveness of an industry. Indirectly, activities in the ecosystem from institutions such as universities, governmental, and non-governmental organizations, may have an impact on the attractiveness of a market. Thus, when completing industry forces analysis, a practical step can be to check the findings from PESTEL analysis for non-market factors which may indirectly affect the attractiveness of a market.

Applying industry forces analysis

This section explains how an industry forces framework can be used to conduct market-level analysis. As with PESTEL, the aim is not to create an exact model of the markets in which an organization is operating. Instead, this analysis should deepen your awareness and enable informed decision-making of the market context of the organization.

Step 1. Define the boundaries for industry forces analysis and identify relevant iterations

Before starting to gather data, it is important to define the product market and geographical boundaries. Without identified boundaries, industry forces analysis can quickly become muddled. For many organizations, it will be necessary to conduct more than one industry forces analysis. Exactly how many times the analysis is required will be determined by their situation. For every combination of distinctive product groupings and geographic market boundaries that apply to an organization, a new industry forces analysis will be required. This can also apply to any markets (products or geographies) that an organization is considering entering.

Step 2. For each iteration, populate the industry forces framework

Seek data to populate this framework from a combination of internal expertise (if available) and external sources such as trade publications; legislation; and the websites of competitors, suppliers, and buyers. Complete two tables organizing data relating to the market factors and Five Forces categories for the agreed product and geographic market scope. Figure 5.10 is a worked example. A further format for organizing data is to make a version of Porter's diagram (Figure 5.6) with additional notes recording further factors of relevance. As long as the data is organized and represented in a clear way, you should pick an approach to organizing data that suits your preferences.

Step 3. Categorize each force based on the data collected

With a rich set of descriptive data collected and organized, the next step is to evaluate the 'force' being exerted that is shaping market competition (Table 5.2 provides a guide to interpreting the forces). For each force, note the decision (e.g. low, very high, etc.) in the table.

CASE EXAMPLE 5.2 SATISFYING THE GROWING GLOBAL APPETITE FOR ONLINE TAKEAWAY MARKETS

Despite the pressures of the COVID-19 pandemic, investors have been drawn to the profit potential of online takeaway markets across the world. For example, the market capitalization of Delivery Hero, a takeaway ordering firm headquartered in Berlin, rose by 82% in the year following its initial public offering (or IPO)—from €4.5 billion in June 2017 to 8.2 billion a year later—and has since risen to $8.87 billion (April 2022) following the challenges of COVID-19. The number of orders processed by Delivery Hero and its brands worldwide grew to around 1.3 billion in 2020.

The high valuation of these relatively new firms (such as Just Eat in the United Kingdom, Takeaway.com in the Netherlands, or DoorDash in the United States) can be partly explained by their emergence as the dominant platforms in their local markets. Food takeaway markets are characterized by a 'winner-takes-all' structure, in which, after an initial period of equal competition for consumer attention, one firm in a geographical territory will emerge as the preferred site of both consumers and suppliers during the growth phase of the industry life cycle. With most orders placed online through mobile devices, research has shown that consumers tend to install only one food-ordering app. Thus, once a firm starts to gain more consumers than its competitors, it is favoured by more suppliers (as they are concerned with maximizing their own revenue). This, in turn, attracts more consumers wanting more choice, and a virtuous cycle of growth is established for one dominant firm.

Continued

There are challenges for leading firms to maintaining this profitable position in the long term. First, online platform giants such as Amazon and Alibaba are configured to profit from mass online transactions in different contexts and are entering online takeaway markets. Second, as consumer interest in technology and health shifts, platform firms must also keep pace with consumers' lifestyle preferences. For example, how will wearable technology such as Google glass shape consumers' use of takeaway ordering in the future? Third, governments are increasingly paying attention to the takeaway ordering market. Apart from encouraging consumers to eat healthy foods, governments are scrutinizing the employment practices of platform operators using 'zero hours' contracts in their supply chain. Takeaway platform companies typically organize casual delivery workers in their thousands, treating them as independent agents. Legislation around this human resourcing approach could disrupt the profit potential of the market.

The strategic management team at Delivery Hero is discovering that an understanding of local nuance and legislation is as vital as financial resources when expanding into new markets such as Saudi Arabia and Hong Kong. To continue to grow in a global industry estimated at over $130 billion in 2022, organizations such as Delivery Hero must remain vigilant as to the specific industry forces at play in each of their target markets.

Questions for discussion

1. Referring back to the concept of a keystone organization earlier in this chapter, explain how Delivery Hero's success has been helped by '**keystone advantage**'.

2. How likely is it that Delivery Hero will be challenged by a major competitor in its home country market of Germany? Explain your answer.

3. If you were CEO of Delivery Hero, what knowledge of the external context would you value most as you develop your strategy?

Sources

Delivery Hero (2018). 12 months listed—and still hungry! Here's what happened in the first year after IPO (29 June), https://www.deliveryhero.com/blog/one-year-after-ipo (last accessed 10 August 2022).

The Economist (2017b). Food-delivery firms like Delivery Hero are thriving (6 July), https://www.economist.com/business/2017/07/06/food-delivery-firms-like-delivery-hero-are-thriving (last accessed 10 August 2022).

The Economist (2021). Why Germany is such tough food terrain for food delivery (11 December), https://www.economist.com/business/2021/12/11/why-germany-is-such-tough-terrain-for-food-delivery (last accessed 10 August 2022).

Statista (2022a). Estimated online food delivery market size worldwide from 2022 to 2027 (28 March), https://www.statista.com/statistics/1170631/online-food-delivery-market-size-worldwide (last accessed 10 August 2022).

Statista (2022b). Number of orders processed by Delivery Hero worldwide from 2013 to 2021 (23 June), https://www.statista.com/statistics/696465/delivery-hero-number-of-orders/#:~:text=The%20number%20of%20orders%20processed,approximately%201%2C304%20million%20in%202020 (last accessed 10 August 2022).

Step 4. Review the history of each force to build understanding of trends

An element of dynamism is introduced by considering the industry life cycle. Identifying how all forces are changing over time can provide a further valuable set of inputs. This activity counteracts the 'static' limitation of a single iteration of the framework.

The steps involved are:

(a) identifying a suitable length of time for review of organizational history;

(b) examining trends in the descriptive data relating to each force from the past to the present;

(c) making a set of arguments to support a claim about the direction of travel for each force.

The length of time for review, the clarity of data required to claim a trend, and the required depth of supporting arguments will be a matter of judgement and agreement, according to the organization's situation. In practice, we find that discussions of trends in industry forces analysis can benefit from insights from PESTEL analysis. In the table, the overall anticipated direction of travel and a short statement of the supporting arguments should be noted for each force (a trajectory column has also been added in Figure 5.10).

Step 5. Draw organizational implications from the findings

Next, convert the descriptive model of the forces and factors operating in the market into organizational implications. This involves asking, 'Given the current state, and direction of travel, of these industry forces and the underlying market factors, what are the implications for our organization in the short, medium, and long term?'

You may wish to ask, 'Is this a market in which we want to remain?' If analysis shows that profitability is falling, and the forces are working against any sort of recovery of profitability, an organization may consider exiting the market. This means a controlled withdrawal in a way that does minimal harm to the organization and the diversion of resources towards alternative, more valuable activities, or markets. This can be a tough call to make as organizational inertia and historical emotional attachment to a market can be hard to overcome. However, it can also be a matter of organizational survival: for example, despite an extensive history in the industry, IBM's exit from the business of manufacturing mainframes is considered a vital action in recovering from the negative effects of its Roadmap 2015 strategy.

Further issues are worth considering in discussions of industry forces. What capacity might the organization have to drive down forces that are currently 'high' and harming profitability? Can the organization contribute to keeping forces 'low' that are currently enabling industry profitability? Should you avoid taking any action in relation to industry forces? If analysis suggests that industry profitability is acceptable now and appears to be so in the future, a sensible outcome from analysis could be to 'do nothing'. This strategic inaction is quite different from thoughtless inaction. Recognizing that intervention isn't required, or might not help, or is even wasteful, and that resources are better deployed elsewhere is an entirely plausible outcome from industry forces analysis.

The agreement of implications is achieved through informed debate by the strategy team, referring to the data and arguments gathered in previous steps. Implications should be noted in the table.

Step 6. Identify options for action

As with PESTEL analysis, the final step in this analysis is to identify options for strategic action as an input to strategic decision-making. Steps 2–6 can then be repeated for all relevant market and geographical parameters identified in Step 1.

Undertaking market analysis can lead managers to a shared understanding of the markets where efforts will be focused in the future and a sense of the options available for them to manage their participation in those markets in an effective way.

 Access the online resources to watch a short video clip where Dr Ibrahim Saif discusses strategy framework and communication.

Factors of market relevance

Factor	Description
Industry life cycle	Industry in early growth phase: 2% of new vehicle registrations electric in 2017—up 80% from 2016. High levels of innovation.
Market structure	Hyper-competitive at present: fifty-five plug-in models and differentiated variants available. No platform standard established yet.
Network externalities	No network externalities in evidence yet
Complementarities	Double-digit growth of charging infrastructure market year on year. 13,000 charging points UK-wide as of Aug 2017.
Non-market contextual factors	High levels of government incentives to competitors and buyers of electric vehicles. Political pressure to reduce emissions.

Forces shaping market competition

Category	Description	Force	Trajectory
Buyer power	Charging network growing, buyers incentivized to adopt vehicles, grants widely available so demand now outstripping supply	Low	⬇
Supplier power	Supply to automotive OEMs is highly competitive; proprietary EV technology being developed and held by OEMs	Low	⬌
Competitive rivalry	13 major automotive firms offering EVs in UK; Market demand growing rapidly—supply struggling to meet demand	Mid	⬆
Threat of new entrants	Government incentives and maturing supply chain generating start-ups and further entry into EV market from existing auto industry	High	⬌
Threat of substitutes	Vast improvements in hybrid technology and 'clean' internal combustion engine; continued presence of public transport	Mid	⬆

Implications	Options for action
It is to the organization's advantage that bargaining power remains weak for buyers and suppliers, so actions should be considered to contribute to maintaining these currently low forces.	Lobby the government to keep incentive schemes in place (maintaining high adoption)
	Continue to invest in 'in-house' R&D for EV-specific components and technology
Whilst there are many competitors, the market is growing fast so it is still potentially profitable. Need to be mindful that this force is likely to intensify as new entrants continue to be attracted, and market share and profitability will come under pressure in the future.	Ramp up efforts to capture market share, building brand reputation and customer loyalty where possible during early growth phase
	Urge government to back existing players with financial incentives
Threat of substitutes suggests alternative markets will continue to keep a downward pressure on the EV market for some time to come. Not committing to EV alone could help manage the risk associated with this pressure.	Continue to invest in alternative technological options—hybrid and clean internal combustion engine (ICE—as part of R&D portfolio)

FIGURE 5.10 A worked example of applied market-level analysis. *Source*: authors.

Competitive analysis

Our final form of external analysis can be termed 'micro-level' or competitive analysis. When undertaking micro-level analysis, insights are drawn from exploring an organization's immediate relationships and interactions with customers and competitors. Anticipating the future actions, demands, and responses of external parties to which the organization is closely coupled aids strategic management conversations and decision-making at a level of detail below market-level analysis. In this section, we explain how strategic group analysis can be used as a method to examine the influences of and on the organization from direct competition and customers.

Strategic group analysis

Strategic group analysis identifies direct competitors that should be studied as part of micro-level analysis. A **strategic group** is defined as the collection of organizations adopting broadly the same strategy to service the needs of the same group of customers (Cool and Schendel 1987). Strategic groups can be identified by mapping the position of competitors in an industry against two competitive criteria (Figure 5.11).

For example, in the UK airline industry, firms such Ryanair, EasyJet, and Jet2.com form a strategic group, offering low-cost flights to a wide range of domestic and European destinations from multiple regional and international airports. They are targeting holidaymakers and price-conscious business travellers. This renders them distinctive from, for example, British Airways and KLM, which provide short-, medium-, and long-haul flights at a higher price point, targeting less cost-conscious business and holiday travellers.

If Ryanair is our focus organization, it makes sense that priority consideration is given to the actions of direct competitors, for example, EasyJet and Jet2.com. Without ignoring other strategic groups, this focus on a limited, highly relevant set of competitors enables the organization to

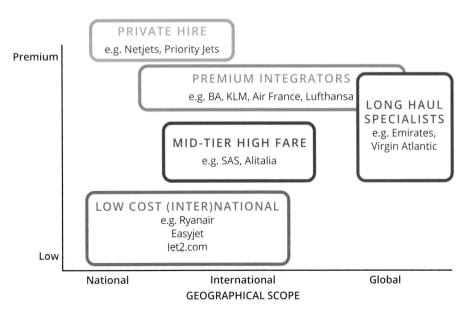

FIGURE 5.11 Strategic group analysis for the UK airline industry. *Source*: authors.

develop nuanced competitive insights. Strategic group analysis also enables an exploration of the expectations and buying criteria of the specific customer segments targeted by the organization. By building a picture of what it takes to meet the needs of target customers in a superior way to competitors, micro-level analysis can allow you to identify options for actions which can sustain or improve competitive performance.

Competitor profiling

Focusing your attention on profiling direct competitors will generate valuable insights into the likely actions and reactions of your organization's closest rivals to changing circumstances, including those instigated by your own strategic activities. This may be supported by competitive intelligence—'legal practices of gathering market information that have sometimes been associated with legal infringements and espionage' (Reinmoeller and Ansari 2016: 117).

In practice, much may be known about direct competitors by a management team through experience of the daily running of the organization. However, adopting a structured approach to **competitor profiling** can ensure well-rounded thinking and avoid blind spots. Table 5.4 illustrates a structured approach to evaluating the likely activities of competitors based on what they have done in the past, how they aspire to operate, and what they are ultimately seeking to achieve.

Considering a range of factors and indicators, the strategy team can develop a coherent, in-depth analysis of the direct competitors in their strategic group. As each competitor is reviewed using the same criteria, the strategy team will also generate insights about the commonalities of the strategic group. Identifying patterns of recurring goals, values, or routines within the strategic group will assist the identification of organizational implications.

Undertaking competitive analysis

This section explains how strategic group analysis and competitor profiling can be used to enact micro-level environmental analysis.

Step 1. Decide on the criteria for identifying strategic groups

First, select appropriate labels for axes on the strategic group chart that can be used to position industry players relative to each other. As with the industry forces analysis, it may be necessary to run this exercise more than once, preparing a selection of strategic group analysis charts to identify the closest competitors. The famous 4Ps model of marketing (McCarthy 1960) can provide a useful starting point for consideration as labels for each axis.

> **Price**: compare organizations according to the prices they charge for their products/service (e.g. low—medium—premium—super-premium prices).
> **Product**: compare organizations according to the variation in their product/service lines (e.g. single products vs multiple products, fixed products vs customizable offerings, etc.).
> **Placement**: compare the geographic range or availability of the products/services (e.g. widely available vs exclusively stocked, regional vs national vs international geographic availability).
> **Promotion**: compare the approach to communicating with customers (e.g. mass marketed vs targeted promotion).

TABLE 5.4 **Competitor profiling**

Factors	Reason for profiling	What do competitors really want?	How do competitors aspire to operate?	What have competitors traditionally done?
Strategic dimensions	These strategic factors shape competitor strategy. Understanding them will help predict competitor actions	What goals, published and unpublished, does the organization have?	What are the stated beliefs, ethics, and values of the organization that will influence decision-making and action?	What routines, capabilities, and standard practices define and constrain strategic actions?
Characteristics	Key questions to ask about the strategic dimensions	What governance and ownership structure is in place, and how will this affect strategic action?	How embedded are the stated values in the operating approach and historical actions of the competitor?	How do culture, information flow, size, maturity, leadership stability, and organizational complexity shape actions?
Top management	Pay attention to how the top management team operates. As the strategic decision-makers, they will be key in determining how the competitor acts	How are the top team compensated? How credible are they in the pursuit of organizational goals? What is their reputation for action?	What are the life experiences of the top team? To what extent do they role model and seek external advice in a manner consistent with stated organizational values?	To what extent do egos and self-justification define the top management team approaches? Are they reported as micromanagers, or is power devolved?
Strategic organization	Review the structure and scale of the competitor to evaluate how its actions might be constrained or enabled by how it is organized	What are the scale and diversity of the business, overall business priorities, market position, and competitive advantage?	Do all aspects of the business, functions, business units, and divisions share common values? How ethical is the behaviour of the competitor at all levels?	Are there any patterns in the strategic actions enacted? Is there any history of blind spots in thinking or organizational politics shaping strategic action?
Capabilities strategies	Consider the long-term commitments to growing and exploiting specific capabilities. These will shape what it can do	What is the stated intent about the capabilities on which the competitor will be based in the long term?	What key capabilities are emphasized in the long term? Does the competitor commit to investing in improvements consistent with their values?	To what extent does the organization continually invest in new capabilities and/or capability renewal?
Performance results and attitude	The way in which the organization performs, and even interprets success, will have an impact on how it competes	How well has the competitor performed in delivering profitability, growth, revenue, sustainability, and non-economic outcomes?	How well is risk managed for the benefit of all stakeholders? What is the attitude to external threats, opportunities, and use of funds?	How do performance management approaches and commitment to non-economic goals seem to influence strategic choice?

Source: authors.

According to the characteristics of the markets in which the organization competes, different dimensions of comparison will make sense. For example, in the airline example discussed earlier, price and placement are highly relevant variables for comparing firm activities. On the other hand, promotion, whilst not irrelevant, is less useful. However, in the drinks industry, promotion is a highly relevant variable with which to compare the activities of different firms.

Step 2. Map competitors onto the strategic group analysis charts, identifying clusters

Plot all competitors in the market onto the strategic group analysis chart according to how they correspond to the selected axes. The position of your own organization should also be marked. Identify clusters of firms that locate in similar positions. These clusters represent 'strategic groups'. It can be helpful for conversations following the charting activity to give a name to each cluster.

The charting activity can be repeated against alternative axes labels. Aside from checking the allocation of strategic groups, this analysis can generate further insights as to how the organization's own strategic group operates. The outcome of this step is a description of the strategic group(s)—direct competitors and target customers—in which the organization operates.

Step 3. Describe the characteristics and expectations of the customer segments targeted by the organization's strategic group

Evaluating the implications of an organization's strategic group, customer value creation is explored first. The key question to be posed is, 'What do customers value from the offerings of organizations in this group?' This requires discussion of what is valued by the customer segments served by the group. Market reports/intelligence, insights from internal expertise, and a review of competitor market-facing material are all useful. A common mistake in this step is to list strengths or achievements of the organization—focus only on what is valued by the customers served by the group.

The outcomes of this conversation should be documented in a table. An example is given in Figure 5.12, the implications of strategic group analysis for Nissan and its Leaf electric vehicle in the United Kingdom. By the end of this step, the strategy team should have a description of points of customer value for the focal strategic group.

Step 4. Identify the characteristics for competitive success

What are the commonalities in the strategic group as to how organizations make profit whilst creating value for target customers? A 'recipe' of common characteristics for creating customer value in a sustainable way can be uncovered through a review of organizational and competitor activities. It should be possible to explain any aspect of the group 'recipe' in terms of how it contributes to profitably creating value for target customers. It might be useful to consider the prompts listed in Table 5.4 to aid discussion. Findings should be noted in the analysis table under 'Common competitive characteristics'.

For example, considering budget European airlines, low-cost culture, modern aircraft, lean operations, mass customer awareness, and effective digital customer interfaces might all be common factors in this strategic group. Each of these characteristics can be explained in terms of how they contribute to the airline being able to operate profitably whilst delivering frequent low-price flights to a wide range of European destinations (what the customer seeks).

Premium

LUXURY ELECTRIC
e.g. Mercedes, BMW, Audi

'BORN ELECTRIC' SPECIALISTS
e.g. Tesla

PRICING

OPTIONS FOR THE MASSES
e.g. Nissan, Toyota, Renault, Mazda, VW

ASPIRING ELECTRIC
e.g. Volvo

Mass-market

Diverse   Focused

PRODUCT PORTFOLIO

Characteristics of customer value	Common competitive characteristics	Relative performance (5 high)
Access to government incentives/tax breaks	Compliance with government requirements	5
Range of EV vehicle that meets my needs	Reliable technical performance and >100 mile range for battery	4
The look, feel, and features of a mainstream car	Common aesthetics with mainstream product lines	3
An accessible price for purchase	Benefits of economies of scale and lean knowledge	4
Low maintenance costs	High reliability designs	4

Implications	Options for action
The organization is leading competitors in compliance with government requirements, which in turn benefits (and attracts) cost-conscious customers. This is an advantage to be protected and exploited.	Lobby the government to keep the pace of new EV-friendly legislation high
	Build superior compliance and funding access message into marketing dialogue with potential customers
Technical performance in EV technology and regular vehicle reliability and low-cost production is strong—action needs to be taken to reinforce and seek improvements in these customer-valued features.	Maintain investment in range performance technology and EV reliability R&D activity
	Create an operations team to transfer lean knowledge to EV production
There is scope to bring the look, feel, and features of the EV more in line with customers' expectations of what is involved in a mainstream car. This could ward off competitor attacks in the future.	Invest in aesthetic design teams and R&D activity to move EV beyond 'prototypical' look, feel, and features towards a mainstream design

FIGURE 5.12 A worked example of competitive analysis. *Source*: authors.

Step 5. Evaluate the organizational performance of competitors

As far as possible, an objective appraisal of the organization's performance versus strategic group competitors is required based on the common competitive characteristics noted in the previous step. Working through each competitive characteristic, the question to ask is, 'What is our performance, relative to competitors, against this competitive criterion?'

You should note, in a consistent way, the outcomes of this evaluation activity in column 3, labelled 'Relative performance'. Simple numeric scoring or qualitative descriptors (5, leading performance; 3, average; 1, lagging performance) are adequate. It is a good idea to make some short supporting notes and reserve any detailed analysis of relative performance to a separate document.

Step 6. Draw organizational implications from the findings

As with previous methods, the next activity is to convert the evaluation of relative performance in the strategic group into organizational implications. If relative performance is strong, the straightforward implication for the organization may be that it is worthwhile to continue to operate in this group. If relative performance could be improved, the effort and resources required to raise performance can be discussed. And if relative performance is poor, does it make sense for the organization to continue to operate in this group? Or should the organization attempt to reposition towards an alternative strategic group with a different set of competitive criteria? Capture the outcomes of this discussion in a separate table (see the example in Figure 5.12).

Step 7. Develop options for strategic action

Based on the organizational implications identified, options for strategic action can be derived. If the organization has decided that it will no longer compete within a strategic group, it may choose to move towards a different group or to seek a new competitive space (attempting to serve a group of customers in a novel way). This sort of repositioning requires a significant investment of transformative organizational effort. Such a bold initiative is not unheard of as a deliberate strategic manoeuvre. There was a trend in UK manufacturing organizations in the 2000s to attempt repositioning towards 'higher-value' strategic groups. As reported by the OECD (2007), 'moving up the value chain' through a process of '**servitization**', the high-value manufacturing movement involved augmenting product supply with additional services or changing the way in which customer demands were met. For example, power organizations such as Rolls Royce and Aggreko moved from the provision of physical power generation units to selling clients 'power by the hour'. Under this arrangement, the client paid for the power they received, and the responsibility for maintaining and even operating equipment was handled by the supplier for a fee.

If an organization is confident in its ability to compete within a group, the options for action will then correspond to sustaining or improving its ability to do so. This will likely mean investment and attention directed towards initiatives that consolidate performance in the defining characteristics for the group. For example, in the budget airline industry, Ryanair prioritized a campaign called 'Always getting better' to drive continuous improvement whilst protecting its low-cost efficient operating model. In parallel, it invested heavily in upgrading its digital customer interface, began advertising on television to grow customer awareness, and continued to invest in new fleet. In combination, these initiatives maintained the competitive edge for the organization versus its competitors in the UK budget airline strategic group. Any options for strategic action should be noted in the final column of the table.

5.4 Combining insights and options from external context analysis

An integrative review comparing, combining, and refining insights arising from complementary methods can deliver several benefits. First, by comparing the outcomes from each method, contradictions and tensions can be highlighted for further evaluation and debate. Second, reflective review highlights opportunities to merge related options for action into 'better' options supported by a range of arguments. Third, through discussion and reflection, you can develop narratives for sharing with others as a result of your analysis.

Integrative review of external analysis outcomes

To prepare for an integrative review, the findings arising from each method are compiled into a master table. In a reversal of previous approaches, we suggest that the first column is the options for action, the second column lists associated organizational implications, and the third column refers to supporting data from each analysis method. A partial worked example is shown in Table 5.5.

TABLE 5.5 **Integrative review: Example of an initial table of compiled insights**

Options for action	Organizational implications	Supporting data
Prioritize investment in electric vehicle R&D activity	Prepare technical competence and production capabilities for new industry era	Technology development trends—PESTEL
Continue to invest in 'in-house' R&D for EV-specific components and technology	Prevent bargaining power drifting towards the EV supply chain, and enhance ability to compete against rivals	Low supplier power and trending rise—industry forces
Invest in aesthetic design teams to move EV towards a mainstream design	Address a customer need that is currently not well served, and avoid becoming a competitive disadvantage in future	Customer value of aesthetics—competitive analysis
Continue to invest in alternative technological portfolio options— hybrid and clean ICE	Manage risk of price–performance trade-off switches for customers to **substitute** to electric vehicles	Threat of substitutes— industry forces
Maintain investment in range performance technology and EV reliability R&D activity	Keep pace with competitors and preserve strong technical performance that positions products well	Competitive performance— competitor analysis
Source tech partner firms for audio-visual (AV) technology	Prepare technical competence and production capabilities for new industry era	Technology development trends—PESTEL

Source: authors.

When compiling the table, arrange the options for action next to other options addressing the same 'theme' or topic. It doesn't matter if the options for action are in direct contradiction. For example, in preparing the table, you would locate 'Increase in-house investment in the development of electric vehicles' and 'Reduce in-house investment in the development of electric vehicles' next to each other (see dialectical enquiry in Chapter 3). In Table 5.5, findings included relate to a theme of technological developments arising from the worked examples earlier in this chapter.

With all options for action arranged in the table, you can proceed to reflect on and review the outcomes. Identical options for action can be consolidated into single entries in the table and supporting arguments compiled. If an option for action is implied by PESTEL, industry forces, and competitive analysis, you have a strong argument for giving that option priority consideration in decision-making. This does not mean that options for action implied by one piece of analysis only aren't worthy of consideration. It might be that the action option has emerged from a nuanced insight that would only be detected by one type of analysis. However, corroboration from different levels of analysis—particularly from reviewing market and non-market structures—is a signal to which you should pay attention.

You may decide to retain all options until further analysis can be conducted. Equally, where different options have arisen for a topic or theme, a **triangulation** approach can be used for creative development of new options. Triangulation is originally a navigational technique, where the selection of three landmarks can be used to orient a map and determine the map-holder's current location. In strategic analysis and business research, the process of triangulation can help to develop new options, informed by the implications of different methods (Tassabehji and Isherwood 2014). Figure 5.13 illustrates this process.

For example, imagine that PESTEL analysis suggests macro-environmental trends that will become increasingly hostile to an industry sector in the long term (implying that preparations should be started for industry exit), whereas industry forces and competitive analysis suggest that the organization is performing well and should invest in defending its currently profitable industry position. Figure 5.14 shows such an example in relation to electric vehicle technology development for a firm currently performing well with superior internal combustion engine technology. PESTEL analysis suggests that environmental pressures, changes in government and consumer attitudes, and progress in technological performance will direct the future of the

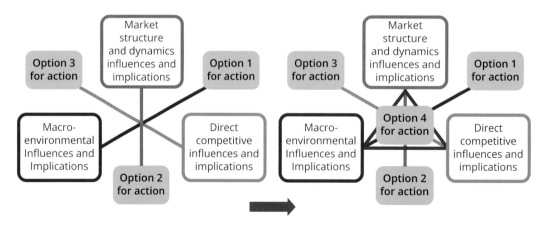

FIGURE 5.13 The development of new options through triangulation.
Source: authors.

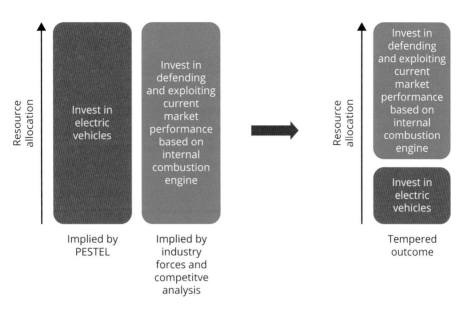

FIGURE 5.14 A worked example of option triangulation. *Source*: authors.

mass automotive industry strongly towards electrical vehicles. However, the industry forces and strategic group analysis show that there remains significant profit potential from continuing to exploit the current market performance in the short term.

Bringing the different modes of analysis together can create a tempered set of implied actions. In this automotive case, immediate investment actions to defend the industry position might still be proposed but appropriately scaled to organizational risk/opportunity posed by the potential change in long-term direction. At the same time, investing in developing capabilities and technology in electric vehicle manufacture prepares the organization for long-term change.

By the end of the integrative review process, a refined set of external analyses—descriptive models, organizational implications, and justified options for strategic action—will be available to support subsequent strategy practices. Along with a core 'internal' analysis data set (see Chapter 6), this data will feed directly into the strategic decision-making process.

Scenario thinking

A useful further method for testing external environmental analysis is scenario thinking (MacKay and McKiernan 2018). This borrows mechanisms from scenario planning—a process of modelling plausible alternative futures for a market, industry, nation, etc. Scenario planning was originally developed to help military leaders 'think the unthinkable' and plan for all eventualities as the nuclear weapons arms race unfolded. The method has been applied in the business world since the early 1980s. Notably, Shell use scenario planning to inform and validate the large capital investments that the organization is frequently required to make around the world in complex and ever-changing macro-environmental conditions (for an update, see Case Example 5.3 on scenario thinking and energy transformation at Shell). This sort of outcome is described as 'future learning' as involvement in scenario conversations helps strategists to avoid myopia and blind spots in their current thinking and possibly 'jolt' stakeholders out of outmoded ways of thinking about their strategic context (Burt et al. 2021). In these ways, scenario thinking helps those strategizing to retain flexibility to respond to future environmental change through better knowing which range of investments to make in the here and now (Grant 2003).

Access the online resources to watch a short video clip where Dr Ibrahim Saif discusses scenario planning.

Scenario planning can be a highly technical exercise, involving large teams and months of activity. However, we can borrow **scenario thinking** to run an efficient review of external environmental analysis outcomes. The aim of a scenario-thinking review is to check how well the full set of options for strategic action will prepare the organization to address plausible alternative futures (Phadnis et al. 2015). In the same way that an aerospace manufacturer tests the

---

CASE EXAMPLE 5.3 SCENARIO THINKING AND ENERGY TRANSFORMATION AT SHELL

The three energy transformation scenarios summarized below—Waves, Islands, and Sky 1.5—were developed by Shell, the oil and gas multinational, reflecting the pressures of the COVID-19 pandemic. They present three stories that explore different initial recovery responses to the crises of 2020 and how these responses develop into future pathways throughout the 2020s and beyond.

For more information, view the video: https://www.shell.com/energy-and-innovation/the-energy-future/scenarios/the-energy-transformation-scenarios/the-energy-transformation-scenarios-launch-presentation.html

In *Waves*, the initial response to the crises of 2020 is to repair the economy—wealth first. Other underlying societal and environmental pressures receive less attention initially until their relative neglect provokes backlash reactions. Then, moving quickly, but starting later than required to meet the goal of the Paris Agreement, global society achieves an energy system with net-zero emissions—late, but fast, decarbonization.

In *Islands*, governments and societies decide to focus on their own security, with a new emphasis on nationalism threatening to unravel the post-war geopolitical order. Although the normal course of equipment and infrastructure **replacement** and the deployment of cleaner technologies bring progress and eventually net-zero emissions, the world overshoots the timeline and does not achieve the goal of the Paris agreement—late and slow decarbonization.

In *Sky 1.5*, the initial response to the crises of 2020 is to focus on responding to the pandemic and related challenges to public well-being—health

first. Lessons learned from shared best practices, alignments of diverse interests, and institutional improvements help create a pathway to the health not only of people and society but also of the environment, including meeting the stretch goal of the Paris Agreement—accelerated decarbonization now.

Questions for discussion

1. Imagine you are a manager in the automotive industry.

    a. How do you think your organization should respond to the alternative futures suggested by Shell?

    b. Which of the three scenarios do you think is the most challenging for your industry and your organization, and why?

    c. Can you identify some possible actions that your organization could be taking *now* to enhance its current strategic plans and prepare for future uncertainties?

2. Imagine you are a manager in a public health organization. Answer the same three questions (a, b, and c) above.

Source

Shell (2021). The energy transformation scenarios (1 June), https://www.shell.com/promos/energy-and-innovation/download-full-report/_jcr_content.stream/1627553067906/fba2959d9759c5ae806a03acfb187f1c33409a91/energy-transformation-scenarios.pdf (last accessed 17 October 2022).

performance of prototypes in a wind-tunnel machine, this sort of review is known as strategic 'wind-tunnelling'. It provides a means by which to compensate for many of the limitations of PESTEL analysis.

Wind-tunnelling options for strategic action

To give the best return on effort for the strategy team, we recommend following a scenario-thinking approach that re-uses insights from external environmental analysis wherever possible.

Step 1. Define the parameters for the wind-tunnelling exercise

First, agree the trends from the external environment on which to construct scenarios. The strategy team can revisit the outcomes of their work in PESTEL analysis identifying key trends or drivers from the macro-environment. Select the top two trends as a starting point (the exercise can be repeated for further combination of trends). For example, in the automotive case, trend 1 could be the commercialization of autonomous vehicle technology and trend 2 could be the mass adoption of electric vehicles.

For each of these priority trends, two polar opposite futures are defined: (a) the trend happens as predicted and (b) the trend doesn't happen/occurs only in a minor way. Applied to the autonomous vehicle trend, two polar opposites could be (a) autonomous vehicles are widely adopted and (b) autonomous vehicle technology fails to be realized; for electric vehicles, the polar opposites could be (a) electric vehicles achieve mass adoption and (b) electric vehicles attract only limited adoption.

These priority trends and their associated predictability/unpredictability polarities are used to set a template for the scenario conversation. Figure 5.15 shows the template for the automotive example, with each axis corresponding to a priority trend.

The strategy team should set the timescale to be discussed, according to what makes sense, given the two axes. In the automotive example, findings in PESTEL work suggested that both widespread commercialization of AV technology and mass adoption of electric vehicles could be achieved over the next five years. Therefore, adopting this as a timescale would make sense.

2. Populate the scenario template with data from analysis

The strategy team then engages in a discussion about each of the quadrants on the grid. Each quadrant frames the range of possibilities that could emerge within the parameters defined by the two axes. All themes of interest emerging from any level of external environmental analysis should be reviewed. How these themes of interest might manifest in each of the quadrants mapped on the template is discussed and insights are noted.

For example, talent recruitment/management was a theme of interest arising from external environmental analysis in the automotive case. Consider the top left quadrant of the grid. What kind of talent is required in a future with widespread AV technology but limited adoption of electric vehicles? Traditional automotive engineers will be required, but so will many software and electronic engineers. In the top right quadrant, the nature of the automobile has shifted significantly, and software, electrical, and electronic engineers will be in high demand in the

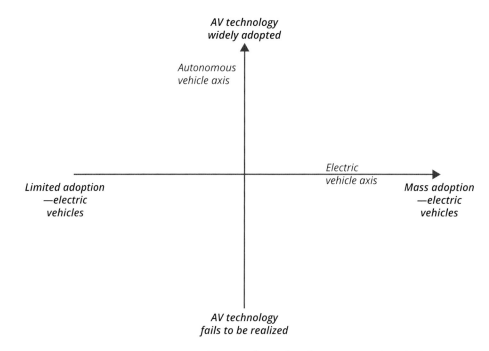

FIGURE 5.15 An example scenario template for the automotive industry.
Source: authors.

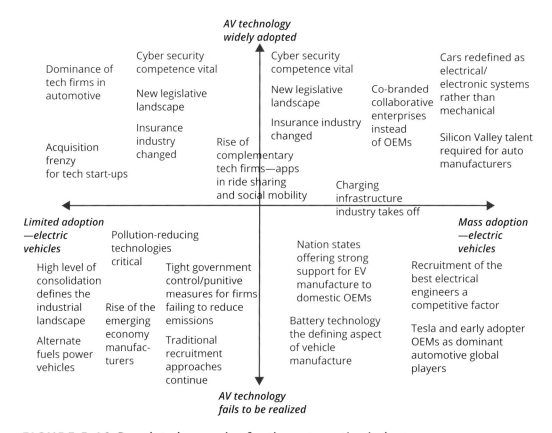

FIGURE 5.16 Populated scenarios for the automotive industry. *Source*: authors.

industry. In the bottom left quadrant, traditional talent approaches should be continued and in the bottom right, electrical engineers will be in high demand.

Figure 5.16 shows the scenario template populated for a range of themes in the automotive example.

3. Create the labels and narratives for each quadrant

Once the template is populated, a set of narratives describing the future are created by joining together the imagined future details in each quadrant. Each quadrant is also given a label which summarizes the key implication for the industry. Our experience tells us that this is a non-trivial matter. The creative act of summarizing and articulating plausible alternative futures is a key step in helping the management team to avoid myopic thinking. The automotive example is illustrated in Figure 5.17.

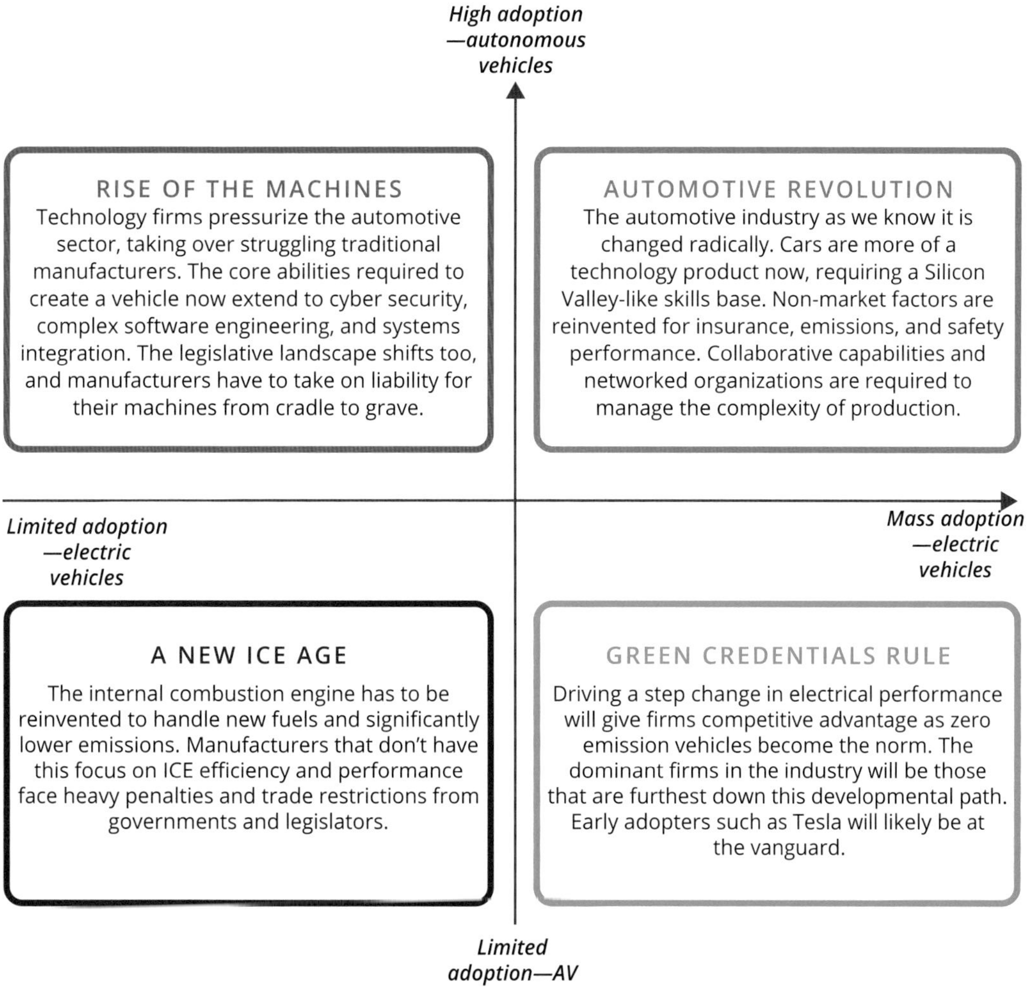

High adoption —autonomous vehicles

RISE OF THE MACHINES
Technology firms pressurize the automotive sector, taking over struggling traditional manufacturers. The core abilities required to create a vehicle now extend to cyber security, complex software engineering, and systems integration. The legislative landscape shifts too, and manufacturers have to take on liability for their machines from cradle to grave.

AUTOMOTIVE REVOLUTION
The automotive industry as we know it is changed radically. Cars are more of a technology product now, requiring a Silicon Valley-like skills base. Non-market factors are reinvented for insurance, emissions, and safety performance. Collaborative capabilities and networked organizations are required to manage the complexity of production.

Limited adoption —electric vehicles

Mass adoption —electric vehicles

A NEW ICE AGE
The internal combustion engine has to be reinvented to handle new fuels and significantly lower emissions. Manufacturers that don't have this focus on ICE efficiency and performance face heavy penalties and trade restrictions from governments and legislators.

GREEN CREDENTIALS RULE
Driving a step change in electrical performance will give firms competitive advantage as zero emission vehicles become the norm. The dominant firms in the industry will be those that are furthest down this developmental path. Early adopters such as Tesla will likely be at the vanguard.

Limited adoption—AV

FIGURE 5.17 Future narratives for the automotive industry. *Source*: authors.

PRACTITIONER INSIGHT **DR IBRAHIM SAIF, CEO, JORDAN STRATEGY FORUM**

Dr Ibrahim Saif is the CEO of the Jordan Strategy Forum (JSF). Previously, he served in Jordan as Minister of Energy and Mineral Resources and Minister of Planning and International Cooperation. Dr Saif was a senior scholar at the Carnegie Middle East Center and a consultant to the World Bank, the International Monetary Fund, and other international organizations.

'What does strategy mean to you?'

Strategy involves defining actionable steps that enable you to achieve practical targets. In various strategic leadership positions I've held, strategy activity required figuring out what we needed to do and then quickly moving into the practicalities of assigning jobs and responsibilities and getting people behind what needed to be achieved. Having a long-term vision is also important in strategy, although that can often be a shared vision with other entities. In one of my ministerial roles, setting vision for energy and mineral resources was part of my strategy remit, but this needed to connect into the direction for the country. At a national level, it was important to work in harmony with the needs and interests of multiple stakeholders and institutions, bearing in mind their own targets and influences. In Jordan, we also had to consider how our vision meshed with the vision of surrounding countries.

Strategy work can only succeed if you are constantly reconsidering your actions and keeping your targets under review. You build your strategy on certain assumptions and scenarios. For example, the cost of production—domestic or external—is a key factor influencing government policy and business activity in Jordan. But such factors can change at any moment, and your plans and initiatives needed to be reviewed accordingly. At a higher level, you may have to revisit your long-term vision when faced with significant change. It is important to shape your strategy practice accordingly when the external environment is characterized by uncertainty. You could work through an elaborate process. But any fixed long-term strategy in a volatile context would lack credibility. Instead, using targets and indicators to trigger flexible responses in your strategy initiatives is a more fruitful approach.

'How does the JSF enable its members to understand their external context?'

The JSF is a 'think tank', funded by a **consortium** of private-sector organizations that wants to create jobs, encourage competition, and raise governance standards. The vision of the JSF is to promote the **private sector** as a leading player in the national ecosystem that delivers benefit for the country. The JSF isn't dominated by any one firm. Instead, it is comprised of small, medium, and large organizations from across industries and stakeholder groups. Participants come together to debate and learn about events, trends, success stories, and cross-sectoral issues defining the business landscape. We work with representatives of trade partners, the World Bank, the International Monetary Fund, etc. to assess the business environment in Jordan and the surrounding region.

When members of the JSF meet, they value simple methods, common-sense debates, and discussion as the main mechanisms for generating insights. Discussion themes that we explore can be self-generated—members are very active in raising topics relating to the emergence of new technologies, for example. Alternatively, we might use credible sources, such as the annual World Economic Forum report on global competitiveness, to stimulate forum members to re-examine aspects of the business environment. We also engage in benchmarking and survey work. We manage a tool called the Investment Confidence Index based on data gathered from a range of stakeholders in the business environment in Jordan. We use the Index to provoke a response from our members and to encourage them to stay attuned to reality.

'What is your experience of strategy at a national level?'

When I was leading strategy planning in a ministerial role, I worked on multiple scenarios to prepare my thinking about possible futures. Jordan imports 98% of the materials required to satisfy its energy needs. Requirements at a national level are susceptible to shifts in three macro-factors in particular—energy technology development, volatility of energy prices, and variations in patterns of consumption. These factors may all be in motion at the same time. Being able to read and react quickly to systemic changes was crucial to our national strategic capability and being able to meet our national energy needs on an ongoing basis.

At a national level, there are many players who must be considered when formulating strategies, including the private sector, non-governmental organizations, citizens, and parliamentary and legislative interests. We were also very aware of regional politics and trends and a need to bear in mind what is happening with our neighbours. In government, a key aim is to create the right ecosystem between legislators, regulators, and the private sector in a transparent way. If done well, this system can deliver major contributions to national-level performance.

 Access the online resources to watch a short video clip where Dr Ibrahim Saif talks more about his career.

4. Review and, where appropriate, adjust options for strategic action based on the emergent scenarios

The final scenario conversation should use the four alternatives as a frame of reference to review the completeness of the set of options for strategic action. The questions to ask, for each scenario, are:

1. 'If this scenario were to happen, which of our current options for strategic action would be most relevant?'

2. 'Do we have any major gaps in how our options for strategic action could prepare us for dealing with this scenario?' If yes, 'How could we amend/augment our options for strategic action to help us better prepare for this scenario?'

In this way, the scenarios play a wind-tunnelling role, using plausible alternative futures to test how well the identified options for strategic action might prepare the organization to survive and grow.

 Access the online resources to watch a short video clip where Dr Ibrahim Saif discusses environmental change and crisis management.

 CHAPTER SUMMARY

In this chapter, we addressed the following learning outcomes:

○ Explain how the relationship between an organization and the external context in which it is embedded impacts on strategy and competitive advantage through concepts of structure, position, conduct, and performance.
We reviewed how the position of an organization in external environmental structures, through relationships and interactions with other organizations, will impact its

competitive advantage. Organizational performance will be influenced by the strategic conduct of the firm as choices are made about how to act in response to, and attempting to influence, external structures.

○ **Evaluate the non-market, macro-environmental drivers shaping an organization and the ecosystem in which it resides.**
PESTEL factors offer a useful framework to evaluate the forces acting on all organizations in an industry. Not all PESTEL factors will have equal influence on an organizational ecosystem—identifying the priority forces, or key drivers, allows the identification of the relevant options for strategic action.

○ **Interrogate market structures, dynamics, and trends, explaining the implications for buyers, competitors, and suppliers.**
Industry forces analysis enables a strategy team to review the attractiveness of different product or geographic markets. It augments Porter's Five Forces framework with further factors—complementarities, network externalities, market structure, industry life cycle, and non-market indirect effects. It can be used to develop organizational implications of underlying structures, dynamics, and trends for market competitors, buyers, and suppliers.

○ **Critically assess the direct competitive context for an organization, identifying the customer value creation and competitive characteristics most likely to enable survival and growth.**
Competitive analysis focuses on how the needs of target groups of customers are serviced by the closest competitors of the organization, known as the strategic group of the organization. By identifying common factors for success within the strategic group, competitive analysis enables the identification of actions that can enhance the competitive performance of the organization or seek to reposition it within a different competitive space.

○ **Argue the benefits of using combinations of external environmental analysis tools.**
Each environmental analysis tool has a specific purpose, providing the strategist with insights to a bounded aspect of the external context. All such tools have strengths and limitations. The strategist is advised to use tools from across levels of analysis to generate a balanced set of insights into the external environmental context facing the organization.

○ **Agree a refined set of external environmental analytical outcomes by triangulating findings from across levels of analysis and testing ideas through scenario thinking.**
To gain maximum benefit from using a combination of external environmental analysis tools, options for action identified across levels of analysis should be pooled and reconciled. This may involve finding new options for action through a process of triangulation. The combined and revised set of options for action can be tested and refined through the application of scenario thinking, drawing on key drivers from the macro-environment identified through PESTEL analysis. This sort of reflective practice—conducted as part of strategic conversations between organizational decision-makers—can significantly benefit efforts to craft informed, robust strategies.

? END-OF-CHAPTER QUESTIONS

Recall questions

1. What is the main difference between an isolated interpretation and an embedded interpretation of an organization and its external environment?

2. Explain what is meant by the **SCP** framework of the market-based view and its implications for organizational strategy.

3. Explain what is meant by a business ecosystem.

4. What is meant by market and non-market external environmental factors?

5. What macro-environmental factors does the acronym PESTEL stand for?

6. What are the purpose, advantages, and disadvantages of PESTEL, industry forces, and competitive analysis?

7. What does scenario planning add to the process of conducting external environmental analysis?

Application questions

A) Imagine that you are leading a strategy development team within a privately owned firm that sells one main product line into the UAE and Oman. Describe and justify the process you would advocate to the owners of the firm for conducting external environmental analysis.

B) Select an organization that is familiar to you, and develop a statement of the strategic group(s) associated with the organization. Who are the direct competitors? What do the target customers seem to value? What are the factors for success for organizations operating within that strategic group?

C) Pick an industry you know well, and work through a scenario development process for that industry based on two priority trends from the macro-environment. What outcomes were delivered by the process which would be of interest to organizations in that industry? What did you learn from conducting the process about the benefits and limitations of scenario planning?

⟳ ONLINE RESOURCES

www.oup.com/he/mackay2e

In addition to the video interviews already highlighted, the book's **online resources** include the following features for this chapter, specifically:

– *links to further reading material* to broaden your knowledge of key issues discussed in this chapter;

– *self-test multiple-choice questions* to test your understanding of the material covered in each section of the chapter; and

– *a flashcard glossary* to help you recall and test your understanding of key terms.

FURTHER READING

Competitive Strategy and *Competitive Advantage* by Michael Porter

Porter, M.E. (1980). *Competitive Strategy: Techniques for Analyzing Industries and Competitors*. New York: Free Press.
Porter, M.E. (1984). *Competitive Advantage: Creating and Sustaining Superior Performance.* New York: Free Press.

Michael Porter has been recognized as the most influential strategy author via several seminal textbooks written from a market-based view. These two books are the original source of many theories/frameworks of market-based analysis, still popular today in strategy education and consultancy practice.

Scenarios: The Art of Strategic Conversation by Kees van der Heijden

van der Heijden, K. (2008). *Scenarios: The Art of Strategic Conversation* (2nd edn). Chichester: John Wiley.

This is a well-regarded text by a leading scholar with extensive practical experience. It is helpful for any strategist seeking to know more about how to mitigate the limitations of macro-environmental analysis in practice through scenario-based strategic conversations with a team.

Strategy and the Business Landscape by Pankaj Ghemawat

Ghemawat, P. (2017). *Strategy and the Business Landscape*. London: Pearson.

Combining examples from global organizations and market-based theorizing, this text offers further insights into how a consultant might apply tools of strategic analysis with a market-based emphasis.

'The myths and realities of business ecosystems' by Jack Fuller, Mark Jacobides, and Martin Reeves

Fuller, J., Jacobides, M.G., and Reeves, M. (2019). The myths and realities of business ecosystems. *MIT Sloan Management Review* (25 February) 60(3), 2–10.

An excellent primer on the current state of business ecosystems thinking. It explains the concepts of ecosystems in comparison with alternative market arrangements, dispels multiple myths grounded in commonly held beliefs about ecosystems, and gives advice about how to start to deploy ecosystems thinking.

REFERENCES

AA.com (Anadolu Agency) (2019). Turkey: Majority stake in singer Bangladesh for Arcelik(24 March), http://www.aa.com/tr/en/asia-pacific/turkey-majority-stake-in-singer-bangladesh-for-arcelik/1427587 (last accessed 17 October 2022).

Argyres, N. and McGahan, A.M. (2002). An interview with Michael Porter. *Academy of Management Executive*, **16**(2), 43–52.

Auto Express (2019). Driverless cars: Everything you need to know about autonomous car revolution (13 September), ke-http://www.autoexpress.co.uk/car-tech/85183/driver-less-cars-everything-you-need-to-know-about-autonomous-vehicles (last accessed 10 August 2022).

Automotive News Europe (2021). VW, Microsoft's partner to develop self-driving car software (11 February), https://europe.autonews.com/automakers/vw-microsoft-partner-develop-self-driving-car-software (last accessed 10 August 2022).

Brandenburger, A. (2002). Porter's added value: High indeed! *Academy of Management Executive*, **16**(2), 58–60.

Brandenburger, A. and Nalebuff, B. (1996). *Co-Opetition*. New York: Crown Publishing Group.

Burt, G., Mackay, D., and Mendibil, K. (2021). Overcoming multi-stakeholder fragmented narratives in land use, woodland and forestry policy: The role scenario planning and 'dissociative jolts'. *Technological Forecasting and Social Change*, **166**, 1, https://doi.org/http://dx.doi.org/10.1016/j.techfore.2021.120663.

Chatterjee, S. and Matzler, K. (2019). Simple rules for a network efficiency business model: The case of Vizio. *California Management Review*, **61**(2), 84–103.

Chia, R.C.H. and Holt, R. (2009). *Strategy without Design: The Silent Efficacy of Indirect Action*. Cambridge: Cambridge University Press.

Cool, K.O. and Schendel, D. (1987). Strategic group formation and performance: The case of the US pharmaceutical industry, 1963–1982. *Management Science*, **33**(9), 1102–24.

Delivery Hero (2018). 12 months listed—and still hungry! Here's what happened in the first year after IPO (29 June), https://www.deliveryhero.com/blog/one-year-after-ipo (last accessed 10 August 2022).

Doh, J.P., Lawton, T.C., and Rajwani, T. (2012). Advancing nonmarket strategy research: Institutional perspectives in a changing world. *Academy of Management Perspectives*, **26**(3), 22–39.

The Economist (2017a). A Turkish maker of white goods is looking outwards (1 June), https://www.economist.com/business/2017/06/01/a-turkish-maker-of-white-goods-is-looking-outwards (last accessed 10 August 2022).

The Economist (2017b). Food-delivery firms like Delivery Hero are thriving (6 July), https://www.economist.com/business/2017/07/06/food-delivery-firms-like-delivery-hero-are-thriving (last accessed 10 August 2022).

The Economist (2021). Why Germany is such tough food terrain for food delivery (11 December), https://www.economist.com/business/2021/12/11/why-germany-is-such-tough-terrain-for-food-delivery (last accessed 10 August 2022).

Evers-Hillstrom, K. (2022). Lawmakers stall over self-driving cars, *The Hill* (6 July), https://thehill.com/driving-into-the-future/3513598-lawmakers-stall-over-self-driving-cars (last accessed 10 August 2022).

The Financial Times (2022). Geely questions future in Russia despite opening for China's carmakers (24 March), https://www.ft.com/content/49d90df8-1f80-471c-a895-49914dbac3e4 (last accessed 17 October 2022).

The Financial Times (2022). What Tesla's Berlin gigafactory means for its future in China (3 April), https://www.ft.com/content/7c3d6eb3-ca0b-4475-9da5-8e304162791b (last accessed 17 October August 2022).

Fuller, J., Jacobides, M.G., and Reeves, M. (2019). The myths and realities of business ecosystems. *MIT Sloan Management Review* (25 February) 60(3), 2–10.

Ghemawat, P. (2017). *Strategy and the Business Landscape*. London: Pearson.

Gov.uk. Low-emission vehicles eligible for a plug-in grant, https://www.gov.uk/plug-in-car-van-grants/what-youll-get (last accessed 17 October 2022).

Grant, R.M. (2003). Strategic planning in a turbulent environment: Evidence from the oil majors. *Strategic Management Journal*, **24**(6), 491–513.

Grundy, T. (2006). Rethinking and reinventing Michael Porter's Five Forces model. *Strategic Change*, **15**(5), 213–29.

The Guardian (2022a). EU's electric vehicle drive leaves supercars at the back of the grid (2 July), https://www.theguardian.com/business/2022/jul/02/eus-electric-vehicle-drive-leaves-supercars-at-the-back-of-the-grid (last accessed 17 October 2022).

The Guardian (2022b). How self-driving cars got stuck in the slow lane (27 March), https://www.theguardian.com/technology/2022/mar/27/how-self-driving-cars-got-stuck-in-the-slow-lane (last accessed 17 October 2022).

Hambrick, D.C. and Fredrickson, J.W. (2001). Are you sure you have a strategy? *Academy of Management Executive*, **15**(4), 48–59.

Iansiti, M. and Levien, R. (2004). Strategy as ecology. *Harvard Business Review*, **82**(3), 68–78.

Kim, W.C. and Mauborgne, R. (2005). *Blue Ocean Strategy*. Boston, MA: Harvard Business Review Press.

Kim, W.C. and Mauborgne, R. (2009). How strategy shapes structure. *Harvard Business Review* (September), 73–80.

Lei, D. and Slocum, J.W., Jr (2005). Strategic and organizational requirements for competitive advantage. *Academy of Management Executive*, **19**(1), 31–45.

MacKay, B. and McKiernan, P. (2018). *Scenario Thinking*. Cambridge: Cambridge University Press.

Mahoney, J.T. and McGahan, A.M. (2007). The field of strategic management within the evolving science of strategic organization. *Strategic Organization*, **5**(1), 79–99.

McCarthy, J. (1960). *Basic Marketing: A Managerial Approach*. Homewood, IL: Richard D. Irwin.

Moore, J.F. (2006). Business ecosystems and the view from the firm. *Antitrust Bulletin*, (Spring), **51**, 31–75.

Morton, J., Stacey, P., and Mohn, M. (2018). Building and maintaining strategic agility: An agenda and framework for executive IT leaders. *California Management Review*, **61**(1), 94–113.

Nyberg, D., Wright, C., and Kirk, J. (2018). Dash for gas: Climate change, hegemony, and the scalar politics of fracking in the UK. *British Journal of Management*, **29**(2), 235–51.

OECD (Organisation for Economic Co-operation and Development) (2007). Moving up the value chain: Staying competitive in the global economy, https://www.oecd.org/sti/ind/38558080.pdf (last accessed 10 August 2022).

Peteraf, M.A. and Barney, J.B. (2003). Unraveling the resource-based tangle. *Managerial and Decision Economics*, **24**(4), 309–23.

Phadnis, S., Caplice, C., Sheffi, Y., and Singh, M. (2015). Effect of scenario planning on field experts' judgment of long-range investment decisions. *Strategic Management Journal*, **36**(9), 1401–11.

Porter, M.E. (1980). *Competitive Strategy: Techniques for Analyzing Industries and Competitors*. New York: Free Press.

Porter, M.E. (1984). *Competitive Advantage: Creating and Sustaining Superior Performance*. New York: Free Press.

Porter, M.E. (2008). The five competitive forces that shape competitive performance. *Harvard Business Review* (January), 78–93.

Reinmoeller, P. and Ansari, S. (2016). The persistence of a stigmatized practice: A study of competitive intelligence. *British Journal of Management*, **27**(1), 116–42.

S & P Global Ratings (2022). Arçelik A.S. (28 January), https://www.spglobal.com/_assets/documents/ratings/research/101085511.pdf (last accessed 10 August 2022).

Shell (2021). The energy transformation scenarios (1 June), https://www.shell.com/promos/energy-and-innovation/download-full-report/_jcr_content.stream/1627553067906/fba2959d9759c5ae806a03acfb187f1c33409a91/energy-transformation-scenarios.pdf (last accessed 17 October 2022).

Statista (2022a). Estimated online food delivery market size worldwide from 2022 to 2027 (28 March), https://www.statista.com/statistics/1170631/online-food-delivery-market-size-worldwide (last accessed 10 August 2022).

Statista (2022b). Number of orders processed by Delivery Hero worldwide from 2013 to 2021 (23 June), https://www.statista.com/statistics/696465/delivery-hero-number-of-orders/#:~:text=The%20number%20of%20orders%20processed,approximately%201%2C304%20million%20in%202020 (last accessed 10 August 2022).

Tassabehji, R. and Isherwood, A. (2014). Management use of strategic tools for innovating during turbulent times. *Strategic Change*, **23**(1/2), 63–80.

Tsujimoto, M., Kajikawa, Y., Tomita, J., and Matsumoto, Y. (2018). A review of the ecosystem concept: Towards coherent ecosystem design. *Technological Forecasting and Social Change*, **136**, 49–58.

van der Heijden, K. (2008). *Scenarios: The Art of Strategic Conversation* (2nd edn). Chichester: John Wiley.

Vuorinen, T., Hakala, H., Kohtamäki, M., and Uusitalo, K. (2018). Mapping the landscape of strategy tools: A review on strategy tools published in leading journals within the past 25 years. *Long Range Planning*, **51**(4), 586–605.

Wright, G., Cairns, G., O'Brien, F.A., and Goodwin, P. (2019). Scenario analysis to support decision making in addressing wicked problems: Pitfalls and potential. *European Journal of Operational Research*, **278**(1), 3–19.

5

CHAPTER SIX

Internal Environment
Resources, Capabilities, and Activities

CONTENTS

By the end of this chapter, you should be able to:

○ Explain the importance of building an understanding of resources, capabilities, and activities in organizational strategy

○ Explain how an organization can compete through the deployment of distinctive resources using the ideas of the resource-based view

○ Evaluate the potential of an organization to manage its resource base over time through dynamic capabilities

○ Appraise the configuration of an organization as a set of supporting and value-adding activities

○ Critically assess the value of internally focused analytical tools in strategy work

6

TOOLBOX

○ **Resource-based view (RBV)**
A theoretical perspective that helps explain how organizations can gain or sustain competitive advantage based on the distinctive resources to which they have access and how they configure to use them; also known as the 'inside-out' perspective.

○ **Dynamic capability view (DCV)**
An extension of the resource-based view—a theoretical perspective that helps explain how organizations can purposefully create, extend, or modify their resource base over time.

○ **Resource-based inventory**
A checklist-based approach to building shared views about the current resource base for an organization; generates valuable insights through focused discussion and sets a strong foundation for more nuanced resource-based view analysis.

○ **VRIO analysis**
A framework for identifying resources which might act as a source of competitive advantage for an organization by the extent which they are **v**alued by the customer, **r**are, **i**mperfectly imitable, and can be used within the **o**rganization.

○ **Capability audit**
Working backwards from what an organization has done, this tool models the different types of capabilities and competences that are supported by the organization's resource base. It also enables discussion of how these capabilities and competences are used.

○ **Dynamic capability analysis**
Reviews the possibilities of modifying the organization's resource base to support a revised set of capabilities that meet future strategic needs.

○ **Value chain analysis**
Models an organization's direct activities that create value and indirect activities that shape the environment for value creation as the basis for identifying improvements to those activities that might boost organizational performance.

 Access the online resources to watch a short video clip where David McGinley shares his top career tips.

OPENING CASE STUDY LVMH: 'PASSIONATE ABOUT CREATIVITY'

Louis Vuitton Moët Hennessy (LVMH) is a global organization offering super-premium branded, high-quality products. The group bears the name of some of its most famous brands—Louis Vuitton fashion, Moët wines, and Hennessy spirits. However, it operates more broadly across five key sectors: wines and spirits, fashion and leather goods, perfumes and cosmetics, watches and jewellery, and selective retailing. In 2021, LVMH recorded revenues of €64.2 billion, profit from recurring operations of more than €17 billion, and operating free cash flow exceeding €13 billion, allowing it to claim a return to strong growth momentum following the severe disruption to the first half of 2020 due to the global COVID-19 pandemic.

A main contributor to the continued revenue growth of the group over recent decades has been a series of acquisitions of historically grounded luxury brands. On the LVMH website, it is noted that 'the LMVH group brings together truly exceptional Houses [of brands]. Each of them creates products that embody unique savoir-faire, a carefully preserved heritage and a dynamic engagement with modernity. These creations make the Houses ambassadors of a distinctively refined art de vivre.' Brands controlled by the group include Moët & Chandon, Krug, Veuve Clicquot, Hennessy, Louis Vuitton, Parfums Christian Dior, Givenchy, Guerlain, Benefit Cosmetics, TAG Heuer, Hublot, Zenith, and Bulgari.

Explaining the way in which the organization competes and performs, Francesco Trapani, president of Watchmaking and Jewellery at LVMH commented:

When you buy a brand watch or jewellery item, you don't just buy a product but also a dream of sorts. This dream is a result of several things. Today the story of the brand is important—this is

Louis Vuitton is one of the brands controlled by LVMH, contributing to the group's competitive advantage. *Source*: Andiko Baskoro/ Unsplash.com.

why brands are increasingly spending time and money on telling the public their history and the different stages of that history. The dream stems from both the fame of the brand and from its history. And whilst it is obvious we sell a product it is more and more important that we offer a product that is recognisable in style with a strong, innovative and high-quality character. This is why every year significant investment is made in developing new materials to launch new products. A client distinguishes between a brand with 20 years of experience and a brand with 150 years of experience. Brands with long histories gear their product launches to the past—they RE-launch products that are more interesting than mere new products.

Mr Trapani's comments embody the creativity and innovative spirit encouraged in the organization, in which brand houses are challenged to 'continually renew our offer, resolutely looking to the future whilst respecting their unique heritage'. In delivering super-premium goods on a global scale, LVMH operates a tightly controlled network of suppliers, production facilities, and distribution channels.

Quality is a pillar of LVMH's success [. . .] we embody everything that is most noble and accomplished in the world of craftsmanship, paying meticulous attention to detail and striving for perfection.

Further, to allow decision-making and brand management according to the needs of its heritage, sectoral changes, and in-country requirements:

LVMH's dynamic momentum is inspired by an entrepreneurial spirit at every level of the organization. We have been entrusted with the heritage of the exceptional entrepreneurs and creative talents who founded our Maisons [or Houses], and we have kept a decentralized organization to maintain the pragmatic agility that encourages efficiency and swift responsiveness. While LVMH may be the world leader, we have retained the spirit of a startup where entrepreneurial

challenges are intimately tied to creativity and a never-ending quest for the highest quality.

As an example of creating competitive advantage through unique resources, there are few organizations that can match the performance and effectiveness of LVMH. Its ability to continue to perform in this way seems to rely on continual dynamic reconfiguration of its resource base to exploit the heritage, distinctiveness, and customer loyalty of its brands. For this, insightful and nuanced strategic awareness of the resource base is required.

Questions for discussion

1. Why might customers purchase products from an LVMH brand? What are the implications for the pricing and revenue-generating opportunities for the group?

2. What resources seem to allow the organization to perform effectively in the super-luxury segment? How do these resources contribute to performance?

3. How would you describe the management priorities and concerns for organizational leaders in LVMH? To which factors do they pay most attention?

Sources

Interview with Mr Trapani, https://www.youtube.com/watch?v=WA1vHeMOHqQ (last accessed 23 April 2022).

LVMH, https://www.lvmh.com/group/about-lvmh/values-lvmh (last accessed 23 April 2022).

LVMH (2022). New records for LVMH in 2021 (27 January), https://www.lvmh.com/news-documents/press-releases/new-records-for-lvmh-in-2021 (last accessed 23 April 2022).

6.1 **Introduction**

What an organization has available to use—its **resources**—and what it is able to do—its capabilities—are crucial considerations in strategy as part of the internal context. The decisions and activities an organization engages in, now and in the future, will be enabled and constrained by the resources and capabilities it has at its disposal (Garbuio et al. 2015). From a process–practice perspective, developing awareness of these resources and capabilities and the implications for what is possible through strategy is a vital part of knowing the organizational context. In this chapter, we explore theories and methods that can help you build your knowledge of an organization's resources and capabilities and the options that are available to improve the effectiveness of how these are deployed through activity.

We also explore how distinctive resources might enable competitive advantage using the theory and concepts of what is known as the resource-based view (RBV). The RBV is a way of thinking that focuses on how an organization might grow and survive by exploiting distinctive **value-creating** resources at its disposal. The ideas of the RBV are extended through the **dynamic capability view (DCV)**, which explains how organizational resources can be created, modified, or divested over time. These theoretical perspectives will give you ways of thinking that are complementary to the market-based view (MBV) and ecosystems perspectives outlined in Chapter 5.

In this chapter, we explain how to interpret and work with RBV and DCV concepts to build knowledge of the 'internal' context and related options for strategic action in an organization. The RBV is often called the 'inside-out' approach as it focuses on the implications of the resources within an organization's control and how those resources can be used most effectively to meet the needs of customers or outperform competitors. The DCV brings into focus the potential to adapt resources—through learning, innovation, **reorganization**, acquisition, etc.—to ensure that it can compete and survive as its context changes.

Building knowledge of resources is crucial as each organization has access to a unique 'stock' of resources, accrued over time, which need to be managed according to situational needs (Dierickx and Cool 1989). Diversity in the resource stocks between firms means that they have the potential to undertake different activities and achieve differing levels of performance (Peteraf 1993).

However, having superior potential and converting potential into superior performance are two separate matters. The RBV draws on the thinking of Penrose (1959) in suggesting that entrepreneurial management of the resource base is crucial to continuing organizational performance. Evaluating the gap between what an organization might be able to do to its optimal advantage and what it currently does will generate valuable insights for you for resource-related strategic initiatives (Wernerfelt 1984, 1995). Further, understanding how resources are ebbing and flowing to the organization over time—deliberately or otherwise—can give a sense of future performance potential and resilience.

In terms of competitive advantage, building understanding of how well resources and capabilities are being used to create value requires a customer focus. Just as with competitor analysis, customers ultimately decide whether the activities of a for-profit organization are worth paying for or are worth continuing to fund for not-for-profit organizations. Examining how well the resources of the organization are being used to deliver outcomes valued by customers will provide highly relevant insights for organizational strategy. Further, a stakeholder focus can help to understand how the resource base is generating value against a broader set of goals, including social and environmental impacts (as described in Chapter 4).

We can also gain insight into competitive advantage through the RBV. The uniqueness and configuration of an organization's resources and capabilities in part determine its competitive advantage (Peteraf and Barney 2003). We will examine the possibilities of nurturing and exploiting distinctive resources in ways that might create and sustain competitive advantage. To aid you in this task, we will review a range of methods for conducting analysis of the resources, capabilities, and activities of the organization.

- **Resource-base profiling**: builds up a clear shared picture of what the organization currently has available in terms of resources.

- **VRIO analysis**: stands for 'valuable, rare, inimitable, and organization', the characteristics of resources which might give an organization competitive advantage.
- **Capability audit**: identifies the capabilities currently being used by the organization to undertake activities and deliver outcomes.
- **Dynamic capability analysis**: figures out how new resource configurations might be created to develop a capability profile that is fit for the future.
- **Value chain analysis**: identifies how organizational activities might be revised and improved to better create customer value and organizational performance.

The RBV has often been criticized for being too theoretical and of limited value to practitioners (e.g. Connor 2002). In this chapter, we address these criticisms by introducing you to methods which have been developed through applied research and consultancy practice underpinned by RBV and DCV theory. Using these methods in combination will allow you to build knowledge of resources and capabilities and to identify options for improving resource-based performance in the future.

As with external context analysis, we will reflect on the relative strengths and limitations of the different resource-based analysis methods. With this critical edge to our use of analytical tools, we might uncover insights about the resources, capabilities, and activities of the organization that might create valuable profit, people, and planet outcomes through organizational strategy practice.

6.2 Analysing an organization's resources, capabilities, and activities

The RBV has received sustained attention from strategy academics for over 35 years. Consequently, there are many RBV concepts, and an equally wide range of applications of those concepts are available in the literature. For clarity, before discussing the RBV we define our interpretation of a range of relevant concepts.

Key definitions

Resources describe *what the organization has* that can be used towards achieving any intended outcomes. There are many ways to classify resources—tangible, intangible, human, tradeable/non-tradeable. In this chapter, we work with categories of resources as defined in Table 6.1. These categories are intended to help you identify the resources that an organization has at its disposal. Please note, if you are reading about the RBV, many journal articles will use the term 'asset' to mean what we describe here as 'resources'. For LVMH, resources can be identified across all the different categories: reputational resources include its famous brands such as Moët & Chandon, Benefit Cosmetics, and TAG Heuer; it has extensive physical resources in the form of production facilities and high-end retail outlets; its highly trained artisanal workforce represent a skills resource; the intense focus on quality across the organization is a cultural resource, etc.

The **resource base** refers to *all the resources directly owned or available to the organization on a preferential basis*. The organization will have a set of resources that it owns outright, such as buildings, brand names, and equipment. It will also have exclusive rights to access the capacities of people through employment contracts. Further, through collaborative agreements with other organizations (e.g. suppliers, research institutes, partner firms), an organization might have access to the resources of others which is not available to all firms. The sum total of all these resources is described as the resource base of the organization (Helfat et al. 2007). In the LVMH case, the resource base describes all its wholly owned resources (brands, buildings, cash reserves, etc.) and preferentially accessed resources (the people who choose to continue to work there, the exclusive supplier network, etc.). LVMH can draw on any aspect of this resource base to try to achieve its aims on a continuing basis.

Resource stocks refers to *the current level of resources available to the organization*. Like the stocks of different types of food in a store cupboard, resource stocks describe the available capacity of different types of organizational resources. Resource stocks are a crucial consideration for those making strategy. At any given time, resource stocks might be allocated—deployed through organizational activities—or held in reserve; that is, they are available for deployment. Having a resource base that is fully committed to activities means that the organization has no capacity for additional initiatives. Equally, having a high level of resource stocks that are not deployed means that the organization is not engaging in productive activity. Both these extremes carry risks for organizational resilience and survival (Dierickx and Cool 1989). The financial resources (e.g. cash, available credit) of LVMH have allowed it to acquire a range of brands over recent years. Having

TABLE 6.1 **Categories of resources**

Category	Description	Such as . . .	For example . . .
Physical	Tangible resources that can be bought and sold on the open market	Buildings, equipment, vehicles, raw materials, IT infrastructure	Emirates' fleet of long-range aircraft
Natural	Natural resources linked to location and geographic conditions	Rich soil, water supply, clean air, minerals, renewable energy potential, location in economic zone	Highland Spring's access to naturally occurring water springs arising from its geographical location
Financial	Monetary assets and liabilities as recorded on a balance sheet	Creditors, debtors, funding, cash	Apple's accrued overseas 'cash pile'
Informational	Raw and refined data about the organization or its ecosystem	Customer data, supplier data, competitor data, organizational performance data	Fitbit's biometric user data—reportedly the largest such database in the world
Knowledge	Understanding of technical or commercial value	Intellectual property, trade secrets, trademarks, organizational learning	Dyson's vacuum cyclone technology incorporated in a wide product range
Reputational	The way in which the organization is perceived by stakeholders	Brand assets and awareness, trust, loyalty, goodwill towards organization	Coca-Cola's global brand reputation and symbols

TABLE 6.1 *Continued*

Category	Description	Such as ...	For example ...
Cultural	The norms and habitual ways of working in the organization	Shared employee attitudes and values, internal relationships, operational routines, engrained priorities	Hyundai's deeply engrained commitment to value engineering and reliability
Organizational	The structuring of resources, reporting, legal entities, and financial flows in the organization	Legal structure, stock market listing, tax registration, transfer pricing arrangements, HQ–subsidiary relations	Starbucks's organizational structure enables financial flows for tax efficiency in its global operations
Managerial	The capacities of the individuals and teams with resource allocation powers	Leadership charisma, accumulated experience of management team, decision-making biases	Jack Ma's charisma, connections, and approach to investment as key assets underpinning the growth of Alibaba
Skills	The specific expertise, talents, and abilities in the human resource base of the organization	Professional expertise, manual crafts, staff qualifications	The expertise of Tata Global Beverages staff as tea scientists, blenders, growers, distributors, and marketeers
Relational	The connections and assets available on a preferential basis through external stakeholders	Supplier base, government ties, customer relationships, network/ecosystem position, collaborations	Goldman Sachs's highly developed relationships with government and tax authorities across the world
Motivational	The drive, interest, and morale of staff to work towards organizational aims	Employee morale in functions or locations, incentive schemes, positivity of attitude to organizational strategy	Google's use of non-monetary rewards, recognition schemes, and on-site facilities to spur productivity

Source: authors.

uncommitted stocks of financial resources means that at any moment it has the potential to pursue new acquisitions. If the financial resources are already allocated to initiatives in a time period, it may be unable to pursue acquisition opportunities that arise unexpectedly.

Capabilities refers to *individual or collective potential to take action to a threshold level of performance.* Capabilities are best described as 'the ability to . . .' perform an activity to a minimum threshold of performance. For example, having 'the ability to legally drive' means that an individual can meet the minimum legal performance levels to drive on a public road. Capabilities arise from deploying resources, often in combinations described as 'bundles' (Lampel and Shamsie 2003); for example, a combination of a government-issued licence, practical driving skills, and a theoretical knowledge of road systems and car operation combine to enable a capability to legally drive. However, having the capability to drive legally doesn't imply exceptional performance and doesn't mean that the individual will choose to do so at any time. Ability to manage supplier networks, ability to execute acquisitions, and ability to communicate with consumers are all examples of capabilities at LVMH.

Competences refers to *individual or collective potential to take action to a superior level of performance*. As a subset of capabilities, competences refer to the capabilities in which the individual or organization can demonstrate superior performance (relative to the minimum required performance standard). Continuing the driving example, through advanced driver training, a safety track record, expert evaluation, etc., an individual may make a claim to be a competent legal driver. This means that, relative to other legal drivers, they exceed the minimum expected performance levels. Again, having such a competence doesn't mean that the individual will choose to use it at any given time. There are several competences in the LVMH example in which the organization consistently demonstrates superior performance, such as 'the ability to relaunch modernised yet historical brands' and 'the ability to deliver the highest standards of artisanal production on a global scale'.

Activities refer to *that which is actually done by the organization*. In Chapter 2, we defined activity in relation to the process–practice framework as 'that which is actually done by practitioners'. In discussing the RBV, we can also understand that an organization carries out activities, drawing on its resource base. Activities are often configured to connect together in an organizational process, where, over time, by design, activity outcomes feed into or trigger subsequent activities. Activities may be routine—recurring actions with familiar features between occurrences. Equally, activities may be novel, where an unfamiliar, innovative act is undertaken. Day-to-day operational activities involve the sourcing and conversion of materials into products, which are then distributed to customers around the world and sold through LVMH facilities. At the same time, entrepreneurial activities involve experimenting with the novel relaunch of heritage brands—trying out new materials and engaging customers in novel dialogue about their 'dreams'.

Activity outcomes refers to *the consequences of organizational activities.* Over time, organizational activities may result in a range of outcomes that affect stocks of resources. Activities may lead to the supply of products or services, generating inventory and revenue. Activities might result in a change in the resource base such as generating or consuming financial resources. Activities may result in informational outcomes—creating triggers for further organizational activities, strategizing episodes, or learning moments for those involved with the organization. Activity outcomes may be intentional or unintentional and known or unknown to those involved with the organization. For example, in LVMH, a main outcome of day-to-day activities is significant financial returns (profit from recurring operations of more than €17 billion being achieved in 2021). Acquisition activities result in extended reputational resources (brands with heritage) being at the organization's disposal.

Resource flows refers to *the incremental changes in resource stocks that occur over time*. As activities occur and outcomes are achieved, resources flow into and out of the resource base. Resource flows describe the changes in available organizational resource stocks occurring over time. These changes can be either an increase or a decrease in stock levels at a rate determined by circumstances. Some resource stocks will be affected by organizational activities; for example, regular financial outflows have to occur for the purchase of production materials. Others will be unaffected—using a knowledge resource such as a product recipe doesn't limit its use in future. Understanding, monitoring, and influencing resource flows may be a vital activity for the future performance of the organization (Dierickx and Cool 1989). For example, LVMH achieved operating free cash flows of more than €13 billion into its financial reserves in 2021.

An organization's resource, capability, and activity system

Consistent with the process–practice framework and the combinatory model (see Chapter 2), we propose that you consider organizational resources, capabilities, and activities as a dynamic system, as depicted in Figure 6.1. Over time, available stocks of resources in the resource base enable capabilities to perform a range of activities. When capabilities are deployed, resources are allocated to execute selected activities, and the consequences of those activities may result in flows to or from the resource base stock (Markides 2000). We will be able to discuss this further in the context of Case Example 6.1, Dangote Cement.

As we have seen from the LVMH example, the resource base contains diverse types and stock levels such as financial reserves, production facilities, a 'high-quality' culture, a 'house of brands', a skilled workforce, a global supplier network, etc. In combination, these resources create a potential to relaunch super-luxury heritage products across a wide range of products on a global scale. Activating this potential uses up resource stocks as cash, availability of staff and facilities, etc. are allocated to product relaunch activities, reducing available stocks of resources for alternative activities such as pursuing acquisition targets.

When the product relaunch activity is executed, all may happen as intended, resulting in a successful launch and beneficial flows to the resource base of more cash from sales, new intellectual property, enhanced brand and market knowledge, new product design skills, strengthened supplier relationships, etc. Equally, should activities not work out as planned, the consequences might be negative for the resource base, such as loss of cash (e.g. on a product recall), diminished brand reputation (from poor product performance), etc. The eroding effect of these negative flows on the resource base may limit the future capabilities of the firm as foundational resource stocks are depleted.

As the resource, capability, and **activity system** operates, the selection and execution of specific activities in practice will create a unique profile of resources for the organization. At any moment in time, the types and characteristics of resources within the resource base and the stock levels available for deployment will be a function of the historical path followed by the organization (Vergne and Durand 2011). Put in a different way, what an organization is capable of doing in the present is a function of what has happened in the past (Teece et al. 1997). This is known as organizational **path dependency**.

Path dependency raises several queries for those involved in strategy work. What resource stocks have we accrued in our resource base? What capabilities and activities might we deploy today in order build a valuable/relevant resource base in the future? By undertaking certain activities today, are we putting at risk, or even constraining, our capacity to act in the future? To understand how you can engage with these questions, later in this chapter we will consider the topic of dynamic capability—the capacity to purposefully create, extend, and modify the resource base of the organization (Helfat et al. 2007: 4).

A resource-based view of strategy

We can build on our definitions of resources, capabilities, and activities by considering the RBV or inside-out view of competitive advantage and organizational strategy. The RBV can provide us with theoretical insights as to how the organization is able to compete and survive (Wernerfelt 1984).

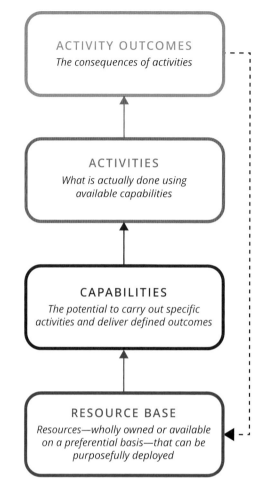

FIGURE 6.1 Resources, capabilities, and activities as a system.

Source: authors.

CASE EXAMPLE 6.1 **DANGOTE CEMENT PREPARES FOR THE FUTURE**

Aliko Dangote is Africa's richest man with a personal net worth estimated at over $14 billion. He is the founder and chairman of Dangote Cement, the largest cement producer in Africa and one of the most valuable companies on the Nigerian Stock Exchange. In addition to Dangote Cement, Mr Dangote also owns stakes in companies producing salt, sugar, pasta, and rice, as well as fertilizer, oil, and gas, all controlled through a parent company, Dangote Industries.

Originally an importer of commodities, Dangote Industries transitioned into cement manufacturing during the 1990s. Dangote Cement now has on-the-ground operations in 10 African countries and annual revenues in excess of $2.5 billion generated through the work of around 30,000 employees. A fully integrated quarry-to-customer producer, Dangote has a pan-African production capacity of 48.6 million tonnes per annum (Mta).

More factories are planned in Nigeria and throughout Africa to capitalize on major anticipated population and economic growth over the next 30 years. As countries experience increased stability and development, extensive investment in roads, buildings, urban infrastructure, and property will be required. Dangote Industries anticipate that this will drive a demand for cement that will far outweigh the current supply capacity.

Benefiting from tax holidays and investment incentives, Dangote Cement's Nigerian operations return significant financial flows to Dangote Industries. Cement is a bulky product, and Dangote Cement benefits from being in close proximity to Nigeria's substantial limestone deposits. It exports tariff free to countries in the West African trading bloc ECOWAS (the Economic Community of West African States), increasing the capacity utilization, efficiency, and profitability of its Nigerian plants. Indeed, through the activities of Dangote Cement, Nigeria has shifted from being a net importer to a net exporter of cement.

Wherever it has set up, Dangote Cement has invested heavily in large-scale plants using state-of-the-art equipment from Europe and China for high-efficiency operations. It invests in hiring a highly skilled technical workforce which operates facilities in line with recognized international quality standards, and its CEO has spoken out on the need to 'bridge Africa's skills gap'. These investments have allowed the organization to keep product costs lower and production quality higher than competitors, winning a profitable market share in its target markets. Dangote Cement also has advantages over its competitors in procurement, logistics, and distribution functions on account of the Dangote Group's size and financial strength, which allow it to achieve significant **economies of scale**.

To continue its recipe for success, Dangote Cement seeks to invest in markets where (a) limestone is naturally available, (b) government-backed investment incentives are on offer, (c) there is a large and growing population, (d) transport infrastructure is good and improving, (e) the prices of energy and fuel are low, (f) there is a 'cement deficit', (g) government policy is to invest in housing and infrastructure, and (h) existing competition uses older and smaller production plants.

Questions for discussion

1. Describe the resource base underpinning Dangote Cement's operations. Identify what you consider to be the most crucial resource combinations underpinning Dangote Cement's success. Explain your answer.

2. How are Dangote Cement, and Dangote Industries, aiming to adapt their resource base to be ready for the future?

3. Comment on Dangote's criteria for selecting new markets. To what extent does it make sense, given current organizational capabilities? Are there any long-term vulnerabilities associated with this approach?

Sources

Dangote Cement, http://www.dangotecement.com/about-us (last accessed 23 April 2022).

The Financial Times (2021). Schools must lay the foundations to bridge Africa's skills gap (12 October), https://www.ft.com/content/d0941cd2-f9bb-4e68-b539-206e32bac955 (last accessed 23 April 2022).

Forbes (2022). Aliko Dangote (10 May), https://www.forbes.com/profile/aliko-dangote (last accessed 23 April 2022).

The Guardian (2019). Concrete: The most destructive material on earth, https://www.theguardian.com/cities/2019/feb/25/concrete-the-most-destructive-material-on-earth (last accessed 23 April 2022).

The RBV is a way of thinking about how organizations use their resources to endure, and possibly succeed, over time. According to RBV theorizing, it is the difference in the resource bases of organizations—what they have, and how they use it—that is the key to explaining organizational performance differentials over time (Peteraf 1993). This contrasts with the market-based view (MBV) (see Chapter 5), in which it is assumed that all firms have equal access to equivalent resources.

At the centre of RBV theorizing is a search for resources that comply with a set of character-istics that give the organization a possible competitive edge. This crucial conceptual framework, known as the **VRIO** framework, is shown in Table 6.2.

Each characteristic in the VRIO framework is a test for whether a resource might be a source of competitive advantage for an organization. A resource that can be described by all four characteristics has the potential to be a source of sustainable competitive advantage (meaning advantage that endures despite competitor efforts). In the LVMH example at the start of the chapter, luxury brands with iconic histories are resources that meet all four VRIO criteria. The relaunched brands for Bulgari are valuable to customers to the extent that they are willing to pay a super-premium price for the associated watches and jewellery, the brand is rare as it is wholly owned by LVMH and therefore is unavailable to competitors, the history of the brand is impossible to imitate, and the brand assets are deployed through a number of products. Because the V, R, I, and O criteria are all met, the relaunched Bulgari brands create a source of sustainable competitive advantage for LVMH. We can discuss the VRIO framework further in relation to Case Example 6.2, Haier Group.

A resource that meets the V and R criteria might be a source of temporary competitive ad-vantage that is vulnerable to the activities of competitors. For example, the smartphone in-dustry was initially dominated by Blackberry (a trading name of Research-In-Motion). These products were highly valued by business customers and in short supply (rare), as other mobile manufacturers focused on fashion or mass-produced simple functionality models. Over time, however, others were able to imitate the technology of Blackberry through their own research and development (R&D) efforts, and the same mobile business computing functionality became available through mobile-enabled tablets, laptops, and wearable tech. In other words, Blackber-ry's technological resources eventually failed the 'imperfectly imitable' test. As a consequence, Blackberry's initial market dominance was eroded by firms such as Samsung and Apple.

These examples illustrate the argument made by Barney (1991) that VRIO resources, and thus sources of sustainable competitive advantage, are likely to be 'socially embedded'. This means that resources which have a history with customers, such as brands, or resources asso-ciated with organizational history, such as culture, are the most likely to pass all four VRIO cri-teria tests. If a resource can be traded on the open market, such as technological components,

TABLE 6.2 **VRIO framework**

Resource characteristic	Description
Valuable	Can be used to create outputs of value to customers that they are willing to pay for (or fund, in the case of not for profit)
Rare	In limited supply; not available to all organizations
Imperfectly imitable	It is not possible to copy or create the resource or obtain the same value from other means
Organization	Available in a format in which it can actually be used, if required, by the organization in its specific context

Source: adapted from Barney (1991, 1995).

products, or equipment, it may give a short-term advantage but will likely be vulnerable to competitor activities (Augier and Teece 2009).

If the intention of organizational strategy is to ensure survival, from the RBV it is most important to understand what the organization can do differently and the extent to which that difference is utilized (Bachmann 2002). A common error that we have found in consultancy practice is strategists describing what an organization does well—its competences—as sources of competitive advantage. What the organization does well certainly matters in terms of performance, as will be discussed later in the chapter. However, in terms of creating competitive advantage and thus the potential to do better than break-even competitors, resource difference matters more than excellence.

For example, Toyota once enjoyed a competitive advantage over US vehicle manufacturers because of its lean production systems. This advantage endured over several decades because of the cultural embeddedness of the lean approach translating into low-price, high-reliability vehicles valued by many customers that rivals could not match. However, lean production systems as a source of advantage has now eroded as rivals have caught up or new rivals have entered the market with equally strong lean production systems embedded in their organizational culture. It remains vital for Toyota to sustain excellent lean performance. To not do so would be to put the organization at a competitive disadvantage. However, the excellent lean approach of Toyota no longer sets it apart from its rivals. For Toyota, difference—and thus competitive advantage—now arises from brand and technological innovation resources.

This search for distinctive resources, or resource 'asymmetries' (Miller 2003) that are valued by the customer is at the heart of the resource-based view. Understanding where valuable resource distinctiveness can be exploited today or nurtured for the future is the central ambition of the RBV.

 Access the online resources to watch a short video clip where David McGinley discusses organizational culture and strategy implementation.

Resource bundles and complementarities

The RBV highlights that VRIO resources are rarely, if ever, deployed on their own. Instead, resources tend to be configured in 'bundles' during use (Miller and Shamsie 1996). On its own, a resource might enable a very limited range of or no capabilities. In combination with other resources, the potential for taking action can be significantly enhanced. There need be nothing special about the resources being combined to create potential for action. Equally, the value of distinctive resources might only be unlocked in the presence of 'ordinary' resources providing **complementarity**. Complementarity refers to when two separate resources enhance the qualities and usefulness of each other when present together. In the case of Dangote Cement (see Table 6.3), having highly skilled technicians enhances the output that can be achieved by modern equipment. Equally, having modern equipment will increase the productivity potential of the highly skilled staff. This is comparable to the idea of complementary firms unlocking the profit potential of an industry as discussed in Chapter 5. The example in Table 6.3 is a simple combination of two resources. In practice, it is normal to find highly complex combinations of resources in organizational life.

When undertaking resource-based analysis, it is important to understand how distinctive resources are combined with complementary resources to unlock value-creating capabilities and competitive advantage. The extent to which an organization is able to do this is described by the O criterion of VRIO (Barney 1995). If a distinctive resource cannot be made operational because of a lack of complementary resources, the distinctive resource cannot create competitive advantage. For example, a start-up firm might develop an innovative renewable energy technology that meets the VRI criteria but runs out of financial resource to commercialize it. The VRI resource was owned by the firm but was not operationalized and no competitive advantage was achieved in practice.

Understanding complementarities in relation to VRIO resources is crucial for organizations that outsource aspects of their operation. Outsourcing is when an external firm is contracted to carry out a business process for the organization rather than it being completed internally. For example, many automotive firms have outsourced the movement of parts within their assembly plants to third-party logistics firms. If complementary resources needed to realize the benefit of VRIO resources are outsourced, any issues with the outsourced service provider might directly impact on the competitive advantage of the organization (Barthelemy and Adsit 2003).

Distinctive and threshold capabilities

VRIO resources, along with complementary resources, will create **distinctive capabilities** for the organization. Distinctive capabilities refer to the potential to take value-creating actions that are not available to all competitors. For a capability to be considered distinctive, it doesn't have to be unique, just 'not common' or shared amongst competitors. When deployed effectively, distinctive capabilities may result in products and services of value to customers that generate profit for the organization.

Equally, many capabilities arising from the resource base will not be distinctive and therefore not part of a direct explanation of organizational competitive advantage. However, non-distinctive capabilities may be vital to an organization's survival, and therefore organizational strategy, because of the enabling role they play for operations. **Threshold capabilities** are capabilities that an organization is required to maintain to a minimum performance level. Threshold capabilities create the conditions in which distinctive capabilities can be exploited. For example, all chemicals manufacturers in Europe must maintain threshold capabilities in compliance with health, safety, and environmental legislation. Without these capabilities being available to the minimum required performance level, a chemicals manufacturer will not be permitted to operate. The enactment of these threshold capabilities will likely be tracked and audited against regulatory and voluntary standards (e.g. ISO14001, ISO18001, etc.). However,

TABLE 6.3 **Example of complementarity: Dangote Cement**

	Highly skilled technicians	Low-skilled technicians
Modern, high-tech equipment	Optimal performance	Moderate performance
Old, low-tech equipment	Moderate performance	Low performance

Source: authors.

as these capabilities are required of all manufacturers, they are not a source of distinctiveness, and therefore competitive advantage, for any organization. Also, the value delivered to customers is not directly linked to these capabilities.

Threshold capabilities should not be neglected when reviewing the organizational resource base. In terms of strategy, threshold capabilities will have a negative impact on organizational performance when they are not maintained and enacted to a minimum required standard. As you prepare to analyse the resource base of the organization, do not feel pressure to focus on VRIO resources only. Understanding threshold capabilities is equally important.

Analysing competences

We defined competence as the ability to achieve superior performance relative to competitors in some matter of interest. Distinctive competences are those competences which draw on distinctive resources to achieve outcomes that are prized by the customer (Ackermann and Eden 2011). For example, LVMH's ability to relaunch modernized yet historical brands delivers outcomes at a superior level of performance. As this competence is underpinned by distinctive reputational resources in the form of heritage brands, it is arguably a distinctive competence.

Distinctive competences provide potential to act in unique ways to superior performance levels in comparison to what competitors can do. As you conduct analysis of the resource base, looking for opportunities to make new resource combinations that combine competences with VRIO resources is a useful focus. For example, LVMH has a competence in creating artisanal outputs to the highest quality standards (i.e. LVMH is able to achieve these outputs in a superior way to competitors). When LVMH adds iconic brands to their portfolio, combining these brands with their artisanal production competence creates significant new sources of customer value creation, competitive advantage, and growth in sales revenue.

Competence can also aid organizational performance, and survival, through achieving threshold capabilities with efficiency. In LVMH, supply-chain management competence (above average performance for the luxury goods sector) improves the financial results of the organization. Every luxury goods manufacturer needs to move materials and finished products around the world. To lack supply-chain capabilities would be to go out of operation. However, availability of products in store is a minimum expectation of customers and is not an outcome for which they are willing to pay additional money. For LVMH, lowering costs and cash tied up in inventory holdings in the supply chain does not affect the price customers are willing to pay, meaning that the financial benefits of competence in threshold capabilities can be retained in the organization. In turn, this means that the organization has more available financial resources to invest or deploy towards other initiatives.

In the 1990s, a trend emerged in strategy consultancy towards advising on **core competences** for competitive advantage. Drawing on the influential work of Prahalad and Hamel (1990), core competences describe competences that recur throughout an organization, underpinning value creation and strategy across all aspects of operations. For example, a core competence for the budget airline Ryanair could be cost minimization. This means that all activities undertaken by the organization might incorporate a superior (versus competitors') ability to minimize the costs incurred. Where these core competences create outcomes valued by the customer (as opposed to being valued by the organization), the organization might claim core distinctive competences and sustainable competitive advantage. In this example, low-cost flights would be the outcome valued by Ryanair's customers. The theoretical proposition of core competence is that strategy work should identify core (distinctive) competences and organize operations and initiatives to best exploit and sustain the core (distinctive) competences. In practice, this can be a challenging exercise to achieve in a value-adding way during strategy work as core competences are not obvious or easily articulated for most organizations.

As you think about conducting internal analysis, you can combine analysis of capabilities and competences with competitive analysis (Chapter 5). As competitive analysis helps you to define what an organization needs to be able to do to succeed in servicing a group of customers, you can use insights about competences, and threshold and distinctive capabilities, to evaluate the performance of your organization against competitors.

Legacy issues in the resource base

A challenge in strategy work is to remain vigilant for changes in circumstances that need to be reflected in managerial thinking whilst the organization is experiencing success. As Peter Drucker suggested, success can be a curse as complacency is the biggest killer of businesses (Ashkenas 2011). In particular, it is important to continue to evaluate resources and capabilities that are considered sources of competence or competitive advantage. From a process–practice perspective, as the organizational context continues to unfold, are the resources and capabilities that were once assets now turning into liabilities?

Dorothy Leonard-Barton (1992) used the term core rigidities to describe resources which were once valuable and are still considered so in strategy work, but which are in actuality a hindrance to organizational performance. Rigidities and inertia arise when those with decision-making powers 'become emotionally attached inappropriately to the people, places, and things associated closely with the strategic status quo' (Healey and Hodgkinson 2017: 121). According to the decisions taken, the consequences of this type of emotional attachment may be fatal to the long-term survival prospects of the organization.

Kodak is an example of core rigidities leading to organizational demise. At one point in 1976, Kodak sold 95% of the world's camera film and was ranked in the top five global brands. The preceding year, Kodak had also invented a 0.01 megapixel digital camera. Over the subsequent decades, those responsible for strategic management in Kodak invested poorly in building digital photography resources and capabilities, hindered by a belief that it would harm competences, competitive advantage, and revenue in film and photo paper technologies. Despite these views, the customer and competitive environment was changing around Kodak, and digital photography was gradually destroying the mass market for photo film. By the time that the core rigidity commitment to film was acknowledged, it was too late for Kodak. On 19 January 2012, trading in Kodak's shares were suspended at 36 cents as the organization filed for bankruptcy protection. Thousands of jobs were lost and vast amounts of shareholder value destroyed (shares were trading at $90 in 1997) by a failure to embrace a technology that the company had once invented as a VRIO resource.

The same story can be found in many different industries as changes in customer interests, competitor activities, and available technology redefine the size and shapes of markets, for example, HMV in branded music sales, Nokia in mobile phones, and Barnes and Noble in bookstores.

The consequences of complacent decisions made by powerful incumbents at the peak of their success can result in once valuable resources and capabilities turning into liabilities that destroy the organization.

As you undertake analysis of the resource and capability context, including a diversity of data sources, seeking the voice of the customer and inviting critical voices alongside existing organizational narratives can improve the objectivity of your appraisal work and guard against you unwittingly or uncritically adopting legacy managerial thinking.

Dynamic capability

The RBV examines what an organization has in the present. But how can an organization purposefully adjust its resource base in order to react to or instigate change in its environment over time? And can the ability to adjust the resource base enable an organization to survive and grow? These questions are addressed by the dynamic capability perspective. In a seminal article, Teece et al. (1997) describe the dynamic capability perspective as an extension of the resource base view, incorporating evolutionary mechanisms to provide a means of explaining how some organizations can adapt and survive and how others fail. Teece et al. (1997) connect with the idea of path dependency in proposing the **paths, positions, processes (PPP) framework** for the role of dynamic capability in organizational survival (see Figure 6.2).

In the framework, processes refer to how, over time, resource stocks ebb and flow according to decisions and activities, historical paths determine an organization's current resource position, and decisions made about how to manage the resource base in the present will create possible paths/options for the organization in the future (Adner and Levinthal 2004). Dynamic

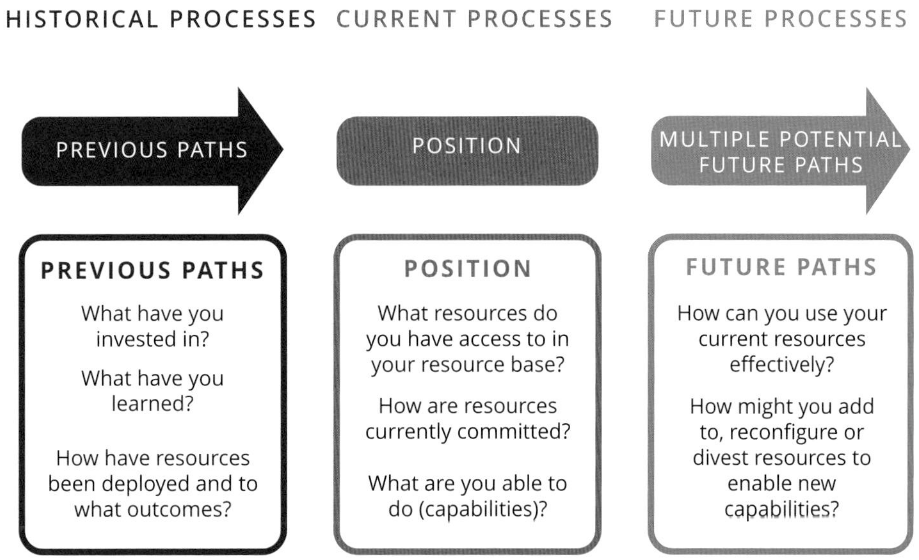

HISTORICAL PROCESSES CURRENT PROCESSES FUTURE PROCESSES

| PREVIOUS PATHS | POSITION | MULTIPLE POTENTIAL FUTURE PATHS |

PREVIOUS PATHS	**POSITION**	**FUTURE PATHS**
What have you invested in?	What resources do you have access to in your resource base?	How can you use your current resources effectively?
What have you learned?	How are resources currently committed?	How might you add to, reconfigure or divest resources to enable new capabilities?
How have resources been deployed and to what outcomes?	What are you able to do (capabilities)?	

FIGURE 6.2 Paths, positions, processes (PPP) framework. *Source*: adapted with permission from Teece, D.J., Pisano, G., and Shuen, A. (1997). Dynamic capabilities and strategic management. *Strategic Management Journal,* **18**, 509–33, https://doi.org/10.1002/(SICI)1097-0266(199708)18:7<509::AID-SMJ882>3.0.CO;2-Z. Copyright © 1997 John Wiley & Sons, Ltd.

capability gives a useful perspective for examining how organizational or even sectoral-level change occurs over time through multiple episodes of strategizing, such as the multi-decade shift in the Scotch whisky industry towards high-value, brand-led competitive approaches (MacKenzie et al. 2022). In relation to the activity system shown in Figure 6.1, historical paths describe previous cycles of the system, the resource base describes the current position, and dynamic capability is the potential to take purposeful action now in order to create a desired **resource base profile** in the future (Teece et al. 2016).

Dynamic capability can be defined as the 'organizational capacity to create, extend or modify the resource base' (Helfat et al. 2007: 4). Dynamic capability can be used to adjust the resource base in reaction to environmental changes or to modify the resource base to build new or modified capabilities for anticipated future needs (Schoemaker et al. 2018). As per the framework in Figure 6.2, with a sense of your previous paths, current position, and future options, dynamic capability would be deployed to alter the resource base in the present to be ready for future needs. **Dynamic capabilities** are the subset of organizational capabilities associated with managing or manipulating the resource base. For example, dynamic capabilities were deployed by Haier to acquire GEA—using a combination of financing, change management, and leadership capabilities to purchase and integrate the GEA resource base into the Haier resource base (Frynas et al. 2018).

Winter (2003) describes **ordinary capabilities** as the 'zero order' of the organization—the operational routines and activities that directly create value for customers through product or service provision. Dynamic capabilities are referred to as 'first order' when they are used to modify

CASE EXAMPLE 6.2 **RENDANHEYI AT HAIER**

As China's Haier Group became one of the biggest appliance makers in the world, its chairman, Zhang Ruimin, wanted to eliminate the sluggish bureaucracy that comes with size. He created a management philosophy called Rendanheyi, which translates loosely as 'employees and customers become one'. The ideology seeks to make big companies operate like a collection of start-ups, emphasizing flexibility and risk-taking—with no middle managers (Frynas et al. 2018). When Haier purchased General Electric Appliances (GEA) for $5.4 billion in 2016, Zhang thought the approach would help to revitalize a stagnant GEA— and he has since argued that Haier helped bring GEA 'back to life'.

Haier's remaking of GEA reverses a typical narrative that cash-rich Chinese companies fail when trying to assimilate Western acquisitions. Such deals include TCL's acquisition of France's Thomson Electronics, SAIC Motors' takeover of South Korea's SsangYong Motor, and Ping An Group's investment

in Fortis. 'Seventy percent of acquisitions fail, and 70 percent of that is because of culture', Zhang says. 'What we are is an example to follow.'

Rendanheyi advocates dividing monolithic business units into micro-enterprises that essentially act as start-ups with quarterly targets. Base salaries are low, with performance-based bonuses added on. 'The key tenet of the structure is that every micro-enterprise has "zero distance" to the customer', he says. Haier organizes business units around individual products instead of traditional functions such as supply chain, factory operations, and distribution. For example, everyone involved, from start to finish, in making a washing machine—from sourcing materials to manufacturing to sales—works in the same micro-enterprise. Haier is now described as 'a case study in what can be accomplished when an established company is willing to challenge bureaucracy's authoritarian structures and rule-choked practices' (Hamel and Zanini 2018: 59).

ordinary capabilities (see Figure 6.3). Dynamic capabilities do not directly create products or services, so only indirectly enable competitive advantage. However, by favourably reconfiguring the resource base, dynamic capabilities revise ordinary capabilities and create new options for action and contributing to the survival of the organization (Teece 2014).

For example, the supply chain and manufacturing processes at a shampoo production facility reflect zero-order capabilities as they produce finished goods that can be sold to customers. For efficiency gains, these zero-order processes will tend to occur in a routine way once established. The R&D capabilities that create a new variant of shampoo or the project and change management processes that introduce that variant to the production

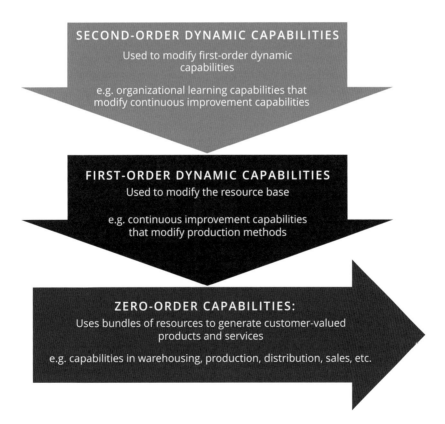

FIGURE 6.3 Orders of capabilities. *Source*: authors.

facility might be referred to as 'first-order' dynamic capabilities—changing the way in which the **zero-order capabilities** arise from the resource base. The altered zero-order capabilities then result in either revised production techniques or production of a different range of finished goods.

First-order dynamic capability can also be nurtured through organizational learning (Zollo and Winter 2002). Therefore it can be argued that learning is a 'second-order' dynamic capability; that is, learning (second order) alters dynamic capability (first order), which alters operational processes (zero order), as illustrated in Figure 6.3. Imagine that the change team of an insurance company engage in a management development programme which increases their innovation implementation skills. The programme has nurtured the team's capacity to implement innovation and thus enhanced the dynamic capability in the organizational resource base. In other words, the experience of programme learning (second order) built the team's innovation skills, enhancing the organizational capacity to intentionally modify (first order) the service operations (zero order). We can explore zero- first-, and second-order capabilities further in Case Example 6.3: data as a valuable resource at Google.

6

CASE EXAMPLE 6.3 **DATA AS A VALUABLE RESOURCE: GOOGLE DEVELOPS ITS CAPABILITIES**

Extract from: Petit, N. and Teece, D.J. (2021). Innovating Big Tech firms and competition policy: Favoring dynamic over static competition, *Industrial and Corporate Change*, **30**(5), 1168–98, https://doi.org/10.1093/icc/dtab049.

Google is an excellent example of a firm that was a successful early mover in understanding the value of collecting customer data from search and then linking it to advertising. When Google was launched 20 years ago, its key asset was its structured understanding of content on the Web; if one searched for something, there was a good chance Google could find it. At first, the customer data from this search activity were only weakly connected to the advertising industry. Google became a sub-contractor to Yahoo in 2000, the same year it launched its AdWords service. In the beginning, Google made modest profits. Now, because of its ability to connect the data assembled from customer search with the needs of a vast number of firms in many industries, Google has a very profitable business model. It has a finely detailed picture of online consumer activity, gleaned from all of the tracker cookies it puts on all of its advertisers' websites, its knowledge of individual

search history, and all of the data that Android phones send back. Google knows where device users are located, and what is located geographically proximate to the user. Google knows what websites a user just visited. Google reads Gmail emails. Google knows a lot and leverages these data with advertisers, encouraging advertisers to refine the way they present themselves, clarifying what they want, and then making the match. This structure means that when users search, they can get results that are much more likely to be useful. And the ads they give users are much more likely to be relevant and clicked on. As a result, the profit margins of Google have risen, as the company has become a superstar.

Questions for discussion

The above extract describes Google's ongoing approach to working with user data, developing its capabilities, and enhancing its business model.

1. Can you identify examples of Google's 'zero order' capabilities, perhaps relating to the collection and analysis of user data as a valuable resource?

2. Can you identify examples of Google's 'first-order' dynamic capabilities, relating to how it has modified its resource base over time?

3. Can you identify examples of Google's 'second-order' capabilities, relating to how it has modified its first order capabilities over time?

Teece (2007) further elaborates the processes underpinning dynamic capability in a sensing–seizing–reconfiguring framework. These strategic practices align with the 'preparing for the future' interpretation of strategy outlined in Chapter 1. Sensing mechanisms and processes put organizational decision-makers' data about the current and possible future resource base requirements facing an organization in context. Seizing mechanisms are decisional processes which help to determine to which insights from sensing data the organization will respond. Reconfiguring mechanisms then activate the relevant capabilities to manage flows to the resource base.

Building on Teece's sensing–seizing–transforming framework, and in line with a process–practice view, the concept of **core dynamic capabilities** can be understood as capabilities to create, extend, or modify the resource base which are continually engaged in an organization (see Figure 6.4). Core dynamic capabilities are underpinned by a constant focus of managerial

6

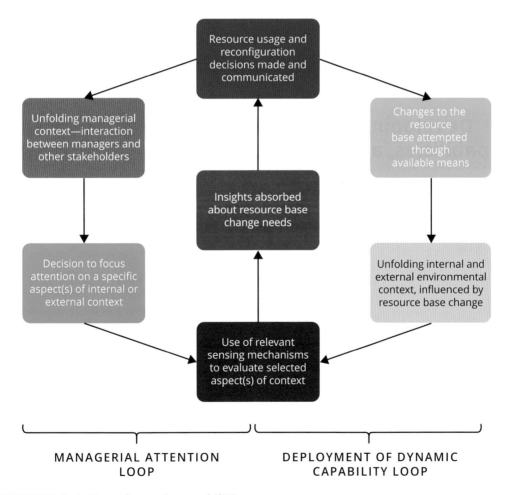

FIGURE 6.4 Core dynamic capabilities. *Source*: authors.

attention to sensing and interpreting relevant aspects of the organizational context (Zeng and Mackay 2019). For example, in LVMH, R&D processes that are continually adding new knowledge resources about materials science might be considered core dynamic capabilities. As sources of renewal in the resource base, core dynamic capabilities should be nurtured and exploited. An organization may possess dynamic capabilities which are used intermittently, if at all—referred to as contingent dynamic capabilities. Those making strategy may wish to consider if and how contingent dynamic capabilities might be deployed for the benefit of the organization.

As already described in this chapter, analysis of the resource base, distinctiveness, threshold and distinctive capabilities, competences, and core rigidities might align with the 'sensing' element of Teece's (2007) framework. In other words, collecting data and evaluating the current status of these resource base concepts is a form of dynamic capability 'sensing' activity. If missed opportunities or potential weaknesses are detected in relation to these concepts, remedial options for actions might be identified. The options for action will then feed into the option evaluation process, which aligns with dynamic capability 'seizing'. Once evaluated, any modifications arising to the resource base are implemented, which corresponds to Teece's concept of 'reconfiguration'.

Table 6.4 summarizes and illustrates the key concepts relating to 'what an organization is able to do', which we will draw on in conducting capability analysis.

 Access the online resources to watch a short video clip where David McGinley discusses research and development and the external market.

6.3 Developing insights about resources, capabilities, and activities

To put resource base theory into practice to create insights and strategy inputs about the internal context, we can deploy a set of analysis tools as listed in Table 6.5. We have selected methods which can be used by an external party, such as a student of strategy, to build knowledge of the resource base context and options for action. We illustrate the methods based on the LVMH case. These illustrations are to provide examples of how to apply the methods rather than a prescription of the level of data you need to include. How you apply the methods will be determined by the specific nature of the organization you are examining and the volume and quality of data available to you.

Resource base inventory

Creating an inventory of existing resource stocks is a valuable starting point for internal analysis. A shared view of the resource base can be derived through stakeholder dialogue and research. The typology of resources depicted in Table 6.1 provides a useful checklist to ensure that exploration of available resources is broad enough. Once a resource base inventory is created, it can form a platform for further analytical techniques.

Step 1. Uncover initial data

To answer the question, 'What does the organization have that it can use?', research the organization from multiple sources, such as the company website, news articles, and industry reports. You can often find useful information in the 'About us' and 'Media relations' sections of an organization's website. Search also for reports or interviews from current or ex-employees to gain access to insider views. Do not be concerned with the strength of any possible resource features such as 'distinctiveness', 'superior performance', or 'excellence'. Try to think broadly about what an organization has.

TABLE 6.4 **Summary of capability types**

Type	Meaning we are . . .	Illustrations from case vignettes
Threshold capability	Able to carry out an activity necessary to operate in the industry at a level of performance similar to competitors	'Able to maintain fertility of land for growing grapes' If you can't do this, then there is no possibility of competing in the wine business . . . therefore all competitors, including LVMH, have this capability
Threshold competence	Able to deliver superior operational performance in an activity required to operate in the industry	'Able to run cement production operations efficiently' Using highly skilled staff and modern equipment, Dangote can produce cement at a lower unit cost than its competitors
Distinctive capability	Able to create value for customers for which they are willing to pay us/fund us—and we continue to strive towards optimized performance	'Able to organize around customer needs' By adopting the Rendanheyi management philosophy, GEA is delivering outcomes that customers are valuing, and financial performance is improving However, this adoption is not yet at the level of the Haier group, and efforts are continuing to exploit the distinctive cultural resource of Rendanheyi
Distinctive competence	Able to create value for customers—for which they are willing to pay us/ fund us—at an optimized performance level	'Able to deliver heritage products that fulfil customer dreams' The LVMH 'houses' deliver highly valued customer outcomes—e.g. product that meets consumer expectations of perfection and individual dreams for which they are willing to pay a super-premium LVMH aims to sustain and exploit what is industry-leading, optimized performance in this area
Dynamic capability	Able to modify our resource base and adapt our capabilities when required	'Able to expand cement production operations into new territories' Dangote cement has consistently demonstrated an ability to extend its resource base through new on-the-ground operations in new countries, following a clear set of strategic guidelines whilst doing so

TABLE 6.4 *Continued*

Type	Meaning we are . . .	Illustrations from case vignettes
Core dynamic capability	Able to continually modify and adapt our resource base and capabilities	'Able to grow through acquisition' LVMH is in perpetual acquisition mode—scanning for and maintaining resource stocks to be able to respond to opportunities of extending its 'house of brands' by acquisition
Core rigidity	Maintaining a capability that was once useful but might now be a liability	Whilst part of GE, the once successful function-orientated organizing approach was stifling business performance; when a customer-centric approach was adopted on moving to Haier, the improved financial performance revealed the extent to which the 'ability to organize in a functionally optimal way' had been a core rigidity for GEA

Source: authors.

TABLE 6.5 **Resource base analysis methods**

Method	Purpose
Resource-base inventory	Agree the existing 'stocks' of organizational resources
VRIO analysis	Identify resources with the potential for creating competitive advantage from within the resource base
Capability audit	Profile the main capabilities and competences that the organization currently uses
Dynamic capability analysis	Identify how new resource configurations and capabilities can be arranged in order to meet shifting organizational needs
Value chain analysis	Identify options for enhancing the configuration of value-creating activities in the organization or its network

Source: authors.

Step 2. Capture and organize resource and capability data

As information is accumulated, capture and organize suggestions against the resource catego-ries suggested in Table 6.1. Ideas should be written as succinctly as possible without being too general. For example, rather than listing individual pieces of production machinery or writing one-word entries such as 'equipment', the facilitator might note 'cutting-edge production ma-chinery utilizing technology XYZ' as an available resource. Table 6.6 shows an example of an initial resource inventory for LVMH.

Step 3. Reflect on completeness of inventory

Once the table is initially populated, review your combined thinking with participants, and chal-lenge yourselves to answer the question, 'What resources have we missed?' If a category of resources is not deemed relevant as a response to the question, then it need not be included. There may be no further resources to add.

This initial method may lead to some straightforward strategy options being identified that are intended to address gaps in the resource profile. However, the main intention of this inventory is to form the basis of a range of subsequent analysis, exploring in greater detail the characteristics, possibilities, and implications of the organizational resource base.

VRIO analysis

The resource base inventory was prepared without any consideration of characteristics such as distinctiveness of resources. We can now use the VRIO criteria to evaluate identified resources as potential sources of competitive advantage.

Step 1. Prepare a VRIO template

Transfer the organizational resources into the left column of a table (such as Table 6.7), where the remaining columns are labelled with the VRIO category headings.

TABLE 6.6 **Illustrative resource base inventory for LVMH**

Category	Description	Resources (what the organization has that it can use)
Physical	Tangible resources that can be bought and sold on the open market	Extensive portfolio of owned locations in prime sites for luxury shopping
Natural	Natural resources linked to location and geographic conditions	Vineyards in the Champagne region
Financial	Monetary assets and liabilities as recorded on a balance sheet	Free cashflow from highly profitable operations
Informational	Raw and refined data about the organization or its ecosystem	Customer database; extensive supply chain data
Knowledge	Understanding of technical or commercial value	Materials science patents; luxury supply chain process knowledge
Reputational	Way in which the organization is perceived by stakeholders	Extensive luxury brand portfolio grounded in natural heritage
Cultural	Norms and habitual ways of working in the organization	Engrained focus on the highest level of quality and uncompromising commitment to brand values
Organizational	Structuring of resources, reporting, legal entities, and financial flows in the organization	French corporate headquarters; globally distributed separate legal entities for each brand headquarter
Managerial	Capacities of the individuals and teams with resource allocation powers	Bernard Arnault as a figurehead; highly experienced management team for each brand
Skills	Specific expertise, talents, and abilities in the human resource base of the organization	Artisanal craft skills in selected luxury sectors; brand management skills; lean production expertise
Relational	Connections with and assets available on a preferential basis through external stakeholders	Extensive supplier network supported by LVMH experts; strong government relations in key markets
Motivational	Drive, interest, and morale of staff to work towards organizational aims	Committed staff base; non-monetary recognition schemes

Source: authors.

Step 2. Evaluate each entry in the table against the VRIO criteria

For each of the resources in the table, work through the column headings, responding to the questions raised in Table 6.8.

Step 3. Identify possible sources of competitive advantage

As described earlier in this chapter, resources that are valuable and rare might be a source of temporary competitive advantage for organizations; resources that satisfy all the VRIO criteria might be a source of sustainable competitive advantage. Review the evaluation outputs in the table, highlighting the possible sources of temporary and sustainable competitive advantage.

Table 6.9 shows a sample of VRIO analysis applied to a selection of the resources identified in Table 6.6 for LVMH. The distinctive resources underpinning sustainable competitive advantage for LVMH appear to be the historically embedded super-luxury brand portfolio, the artisanal craft skills of the workforce, and selected locational resources such as vineyards in the Champagne region. Temporary advantage might arise from store locations (vulnerable to trends towards online shopping and reselling alternatives) and materials science patents (vulnerable to being superseded by competitor R&D activities).

TABLE 6.7 **VRIO template**

Resource	Valuable	Rare	Inimitable	Organization
Resource 1				
Resource 2				
...				
Resource *N*				

Source: authors.

TABLE 6.8 **VRIO evaluation prompts**

Resource characteristic	Description	Question to ask
Valuable	Can be deployed to create outputs of value to the customers	Is the customer willing to pay money for the direct output of this resource? If YES = Valuable
Rare	In limited supply; not available to all organizations	Is this resource available to only a limited subset of those competing in the sector? If YES = Rare
Imperfectly imitable	It is not possible to copy or create the resource	Is this resource impossible to substitute or copy in a way that is of equal value to the customer? If YES = Imperfectly imitable
Organization	Can be deployed effectively within the organization	Is it possible for the organization to use this resource in a purposeful way? If YES = Organization ready

Source: authors.

The challenge with this method is to remain focused on distinctiveness rather than excellent performance. For example, lean production expertise might be highly valuable to LVMH in maximizing profitability by reducing operating costs. However, this doesn't translate into an output for which the customer is willing to pay more. Therefore, lean production expertise doesn't meet the V of the VRIO criteria.

Step 4. Identify options for actions to create, protect, or exploit VRIO resources

With insights generated about possible sources of temporary or sustainable competitive advantage identified, possible options for action can be identified. Table 6.10 shows an example of a range of options for how possible sources of competitive advantage might be protected or exploited within LVMH.

This is a quick and easy method of challenging strategizing participants to think about the competitive advantage potential in the resource base. However, it does have some significant limitations. First, by focusing on individual resources, the effect of complementarities and resource combinations is lost. This matters as competitive advantage might arise from capabilities created from combinations of resources. Second, this analysis focuses on what the organization currently has or has access to in the resource base. What the organization could be in the future is not addressed. This 'present focus' may limit creative and entrepreneurial thinking. Third, examining distinctive resources doesn't necessarily cover how competences can deliver strategically important operational performance gains. The following methods—with a focus on current and potential capabilities—enable us to mitigate these issues.

TABLE 6.9 **Extract from VRIO analysis for LVMH**

Resource	Valuable	Rare	Inimitable	Organization
Vineyards in the Champagne region	Yes	Yes	Yes	Yes
Extensive luxury brand portfolio grounded in natural heritage	Yes	Yes	Yes	Yes
Artisanal craft skills in selected luxury sectors	Yes	Yes	Yes	Yes
Extensive property portfolio in prime sites for luxury shopping	Yes	Yes	No	Yes
Material science patents	Yes	Yes	No	Yes
Free cash flow from highly profitable operations	No	No	No	Yes
Extensive customer database of wealthy clients	No	Yes	Yes	Yes
Extensive supply chain data	No	No	No	Yes
. . .	. . .	. . .	. . .	. . .
Engrained focus on the highest level of quality	Yes	No	No	Yes
Non-monetary recognition schemes	No	No	No	Yes

Source: authors.

TABLE 6.10 **Options for action to create, protect, or exploit competitive advantage**

Resource	Option for action to create, protect, or exploit competitive advantage
Extensive property portfolio in prime sites for luxury shopping	Use legal action to prevent reselling of LVMH products Build online presence but refrain from online selling
Vineyards in the Champagne region	Lobby to protect 'Champagne' label status as only being created by grapes from the Champagne region
Materials science patents	Continue to invest in materials science R&D
	Explore ways to exploit materials science patents across product categories
Extensive luxury brand portfolio grounded in natural heritage	Continually search for acquisition opportunities for super-luxury brands with established histories
Artisanal craft skills in selected luxury sectors	Invest extensively in apprenticeship training schemes in all product categories

Source: authors.

Capabilities audit

To develop a sense of how resources are used in combination, we can conduct a **capabilities audit**. Informed by the outcomes achieved by the organization in the recent past or what it is currently delivering, we can identify the strengths and development opportunities of the organization's capability profile. We can use emerging insights from a capabilities audit as an input to strategic decision-making. This method also provides a foundation for dynamic capability analysis, exploring creative ways in which to manage the resource base.

Step 1. Collate information about the activity outcomes achieved by the organization

To build an evidence base for auditing capabilities, we use the concepts of the activity system (from Figure 6.1) in reverse, starting with activity outcomes, to drive our research activities. Consider the outcomes that an organization currently achieves or has achieved in its recent history. What products and services does it offer? What business results has it achieved? What adjustments to its resource base has it made, such as new partnerships, new international locations, updated technology, new hires, etc.?

Compile a list of any outcomes you identify in either a table or a shared location. Figure 6.5 shows a free-form record of quantitative and qualitative, current and recent outcomes identified from analysing the 2018 summary statement to shareholders for LVMH.

Step 2. Identify how activity outcomes were achieved

The information in Figure 6.5 is helpful as identifying capabilities is a subjective task. By starting with what we know the organization has actually done (activity outcomes), we can then turn our focus to the activities that delivered the outcome. These activities represent the 'doing' of capabilities—relating capabilities to activities and outcomes helps you discuss and agree capabilities with colleagues.

Once a set of outcomes has been collated, respond to the question, 'What activities did the organization do to achieve these outcomes?' Consider each outcome in turn and note the

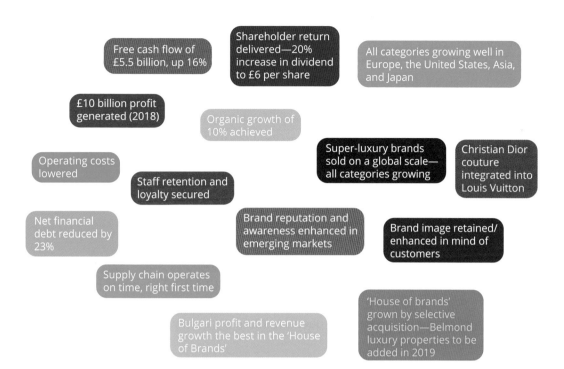

FIGURE 6.5 Example activity outcomes from LVMH. *Source*: authors.

activities through which the outcome was achieved and the underlying capabilities that enabled the activities. Table 6.11 shows a selection of capabilities identified for LVMH.

It is natural when you start this exercise to identify capabilities that are high level or generically worded. Challenge yourself to break these down further as it will help further

TABLE 6.11 **Example capabilities for LVMH**

Ability to:
Manage each brand according to the needs of its specific heritage
Acquire super-premium brands across luxury sectors
Influence and inspire a luxury brand organization consistently
Apply latest material standards to historical products
Consistently take decisions and actions that preserve brand quality and integrity
Maintain drive and commitment of staff to sustaining super-luxury standards
Benefit from corporate scale whilst preserving individual brand identity
Raise funds to back major acquisitions
Maintain the fertility of land for cultivating grapes
Maintain perfect retail availability of quality assured products
Operate global product supply network with minimal disruption

Source: authors.

analysis as to how we can build the capability base for the future. For example, 'Ability to lower operating costs' is a generic high-level capability. This might be broken down further into capabilities such as 'Ability to implement lean thinking in production', 'Ability to manage a just-in-time global supply chain', or 'Ability to sustain a quality culture focused on zero defects', etc.

You might also find that different outcomes are achieved through the same capability. For example, the capability 'Ability to flow financial resources throughout the group' might support several outcomes such as 'Belmond luxury properties acquired', 'Dividend improved for shareholders', and 'Net debt reduced by 23%'. Only record the capability once in your list. However, it is also helpful to make a note of where a capability delivers multiple outcomes for future discussion.

Step 3. Organize the capabilities into categories

Organize the capabilities you have identified according to categories as per Table 6.12.

In this example, no core rigidities were revealed for LVMH from the initial data sources reviewed. This may change with further research or upon interviewing insiders. Review the categorized list of capabilities and ask the question, 'Given the activity outcomes identified, what capabilities have we missed?'

Step 4. Draw implications and options for action

Once you have a completed list, discuss implications for what the organization might do in future with existing capabilities. Use the category headings to help you think about the possibilities. For example, if the organization has an extensive set of threshold competences, how might these be deployed to deliver enhanced organizational performance?

TABLE 6.12 **Types of capability: Illustrations from LVMH**

Type	Illustrations from LVMH case example: Ability to . . .
Threshold capability	Sustain the fertility of the land for grape growing Maintain retail availability of products
Threshold competence	Integrate lean thinking into artisan-orientated production Benefit from corporate scale whilst preserving individual brand identity
Distinctive capability	Manage a global network of super-luxury retail outlets Take business decisions that preserve brand integrity
Distinctive competence	Deliver heritage products that fulfil customer dreams Manage brands according to the needs of specific categories
Dynamic capability	Research and apply materials science to heritage products Arrange funding to support acquisitions
Core dynamic capability	Grow through acquisition

Source: authors.

Dynamic capability analysis

The data developed through the capability audit approach can be used as the basis for **dynamic capability analysis**. Using this method, you can explore how the resource base might be purposefully modified to enhance the set of capabilities available to the organization.

Step 1. Evaluate the existing profile of capabilities

Starting with the capabilities identified for each type (such as in Table 6.12), consider capabilities that you think the organization would benefit from:

(a) adding to the portfolio;

(b) revising to increase range or performance potential;

(c) extending into new applications;

(d) retiring from the portfolio.

In a table template such as Table 6.13, make a note of any adjustments to the capability profile that, in your view, might benefit the organization.

TABLE 6.13 **Dynamic capability analysis**

Capability change	Target capabilities	Resource base change	Dynamic capability needed	Appraisal of existing dynamic capability (DC)
Add	Ability to serve the luxury foods market with a heritage brand	Add a 'luxury food company' to the house of brands	Acquisition	Acquisition DC available
Modify	Ability to apply sustainable materials science to heritage brands	Add 'sustainability' expertise to R&D base Licence sustainable materials database	Talent recruitment Innovation management Procurement	Talent management and procurement DCs available Investment in training required to adequately develop innovation management DC
Extend	Ability to apply lean thinking to operation of luxury retail outlets	Add 'lean retail' knowledge Hire 'lean retail' human resource	Talent recruitment Change management	Talent recruitment DC available Change management DC requires external input to add domain expertise
Remove	Ability to supply luxury lifestyle magazines	Sell luxury lifestyle magazine brands	Divestiture	Not present seek to contract external experts to manage sale

Source: authors.

Step 2. Identify resource base changes to enable revised capability profile

Identify the adjustments to the resource profile that would be required to deliver the revised capability profile. To help you identify what might need to be done, look back at the resource base inventory. Think about the types of resource stocks and also the extent to which they are currently committed. It may be necessary to create additional capacity of existing stocks in order to enable capability revisions. Additional capacity might also be made available by divesting current resources or retiring existing capabilities to free up allocated resource stocks.

Step 3. Evaluate the adequacy of existing dynamic capabilities

Evaluate whether the organization has adequate dynamic capabilities to deliver the required resource base changes. To do so, work through the adjustment in resources identified in Table 6.13. Against each resource, identify the dynamic capabilities from Table 6.13 that will be deployed to deliver the change. If the required first-order dynamic capability isn't available in the organization, either identify the second-order dynamic capability that will be used to develop the first-order dynamic capability or reconsider whether to pursue the resource base change.

Step 4. Draw implications and options for action

To complete the analysis, consider the possible implications of the deployment of dynamic capabilities in terms of future capabilities for the organization. Consider how a revised capability profile could enhance the exploitation of distinctive resources and/or enhance organizational performance.

Resource and capability analysis is challenging to complete in a way that reflects reality when you are an outsider to an organization. However, without expecting perfection, conducting such an analysis will still generate valuable contextual insights; you will learn methods that prepare you to conduct such an analysis once you are on the inside of an organization. Being able to conduct this sort of analysis will greatly increase your ability to contribute to strategic decision-making conversations.

Value chain analysis

The final method we consider, known as **value chain analysis**, complements resource and capability analysis by focusing on strategic activities. Value chain analysis examines the configuration of activities in an organization, searching for alternative arrangements that improve business performance (Kaplan and Norton 2008). As the title suggests, the focus of analysis is on how activities add value, or relative worth, to stakeholders as part of a sequence or chain. It is important to understand what value means to the stakeholders of the organization under review as it may differ in different situations (Kornberger 2017). Relating to meeting customer needs, where the chain of activities can be ordered more effectively or efficiently, customer service and organizational performance can be improved. Relating to creation of value in line with broader stakeholder needs (as described in Chapter 4 as the 'creating shared value' approach), improvements to social and environmental impact might also be identified through value chain analysis.

First proposed by Michael Porter (1985) in his seminal book on competitive advantage, value chain is a strategy tool that is widely taught on management programmes. In his initial text, Porter described different categories of value chain activity and exemplified the concept with an example of a white goods manufacturer. He identified two main types of activity—primary and support. Primary activities correspond to zero-order capabilities (see Figure 6.3) and the sequence of operational activities through which products and services are directly created. Support activities are those organizational activities that create the conditions in which primary activities occur. Within primary and support activities, Porter identified a series of organizing categories as explained in Table 6.14.

Step 1. Set the boundaries for your analysis

As with other forms of strategy analysis, you need to set appropriate boundaries for modelling value-creating activities. For example, it may be more appropriate to create several value chain analyses for different divisions of a multinational rather than trying to create a single analysis for the whole organization. Once your boundary has been selected, ensure that all participants in the analytical process are following the same parameters.

Step 2. Identify support and primary activities

List the primary and support activities that the organization currently undertakes in either table or diagram format. Remember to focus on activities—that which is done—rather than resources—what the organization has. It can be helpful here to refer to resource and capability analysis for coherence and relevant activities. Table 6.15 shows a summary version of this task for LVMH (the tighter the boundaries, the more detailed and useful the value chain will be).

TABLE 6.14 **Value chain organizing**

Category	Description
Support	
Firm infrastructure	Activities governing, managing, and arranging the environment in which all other activities occur
Human resources management	Activities organizing human resources: hiring, firing, remunerating, developing employees, etc.
Technology development	Activities developing systems, products, technologies, and knowledge used by the organization
Procurement	Activities purchasing or arranging inputs and resources to be used by the organization
Primary	
Inbound logistics	Activities associated with receiving and storing inputs to operational processes
Operations	Activities through which raw inputs are transformed into more valuable outputs using resources
Outbound logistics	Activities associated with collecting, storing, and distributing operational outputs to customers
Marketing and sales	Activities through which customers become aware of and purchase operational outputs
Services	Activities through which the post-sale value of operational outputs is maintained or enhanced

Source: authors.

TABLE 6.15 **Value chain analysis for LVMH**

Component	Content
Firm infrastructure	Group leadership by Bernard Arnault, brand governance by industry expert managers, maintenance of super-premium stores
Human resource management	Deployment of talent management programmes, value systems, brand education for employees
Technology development	R&D activities exploring heritage-based product development technologies, implementation of lean production systems
Procurement	Execution of mergers and acquisitions (M&A) processes, maintenance of super-premium material sourcing/procurement systems, rigorous management of high-quality supply chain
Inbound logistics	Coordination with global supply network, material conformance processes
Operations	Craft-based production processes, staffed by artisans, manual operations, 100% inspection regime
Outbound logistics	Non-internet distribution through wholly owned network of luxury stores
Marketing and sales	Celebrity endorsements, active limitation of product supply, implementation of destroy remnants policy, exclusive event sponsorship
Services	No-questions-asked after-care, integrated portfolio for major clients

Source: authors.

For organizations which combine services and manufacturing, or only provide services, it will be necessary to modify the definitions/categories in the direct operation to better suit the nature of the customer offering. This is particularly true for third-sector or public-sector organizations. It is good practice to redefine the descriptions of the organizing categories to suit the nature of the organization, whilst not forgetting to examine primary and support activities.

For service organizations, inbound logistics can be understood as receiving customer requests. For example, call-handling systems in an insurance contact centre could be considered as part of inbound logistics services and outbound logistics could describe activities in which call outcomes are communicated to the customer by email and text.

Step 3. Evaluate the current configuration of the value chain

Work through each nominated activity in each of the organizing categories and challenge the extent to which primary activities are required to create value or support activities are necessary to allowing the direct operation to function properly. If activities are not required to sustain customer value creation, they might be considered for elimination to boost operational performance and to free up resource stocks. As highlighted, you can also consider value in terms of social and environmental impact and seek ways in which to alter value chain activities to improve performance against people and planet outcomes.

If activities are confirmed as being required, work through the activities and identify whether those activities might be modified or outsourced to a third party to boost performance and/ or enhance customer value creation. Further, any potential vulnerabilities in activities that are identified from this scrutiny might be captured for an action response.

Step 4. Draw implications and options for action

Based on the analysis of activities, draw implications on the potential benefits and risks of modifying the value chain. This may include the identification of value-adding activities that are critical to defend/maintain in house so that they can be protected and customer value creation potential preserved. For many organizations, the direct operation is finely tuned, and many of the benefits of value chain will be yielded by analysing support activities.

PRACTITIONER INSIGHT **DAVID MCGINLEY, CEO, CAMMELL LAIRD**

David McGinley is chief executive officer for Cammell Laird, shipbuilding and engineering firm, working across marine, industrial services, and energy sectors (https://www.cammell-laird.co.uk). At the start of his career, David served in the British Royal Navy for 24 years, rising to the rank of warrant officer. In his subsequent civilian career, David has held senior positions with several organizations, including business development director and director of Commercial Port Operations for Babcock Marine. David is a past president of the UK Shipbuilders and Ship Repairers Association and is also a Council member of the Society of Maritime Industries. David shares his views on resources, capabilities, and strategy.

leadership have a responsibility to set organizational expectations and ensure that we adhere to our obligations. Through these behaviours and towards fully delivering a client brief, we are then able to make effective use of our technical facilities.

'If capabilities are "what an individual or organization can do", what capabilities matter most to your organization?'

'If resources are "what an organization has that it can use", what are the crucial resources for Cammell Laird for the long term?'

Crucial resources for us are our people, facilities, and reputation. Reputation is paramount in our industry, where clients rely on us to complete safety-critical work on complex equipment. We have worked hard to develop a reputation for delivering on time with zero defects in a fully Health and Safety Executive-compliant manner. Our reputation is a key reason why clients continue to entrust us with their critical assets. We rely on our people to deliver on our commitments to our clients in the manner they expect. Our technical staff are highly trained experts who work in a systematic, safe manner, whilst always seeking innovative ways to meet client needs. Our client-facing commercial staff must be able to communicate transparently and manage stakeholders effectively, setting the highest standards in ethical conduct during all phases of relationship management. Those in positions of

As you might expect, our capabilities in servicing client needs arise from combinations of our critical resources of people, facilities, and reputation. We are able to have effective working relationships with clients because of our trusted reputation. We have advanced technical capabilities in engineering, ship repair, conversion, and fabrication that we can match to client needs. Our workforce capabilities arise from the skills and experience of our staff, channelled through comprehensive organizational systems (which comply with a range of internationally recognized ISO standards) to make sure that we work in a safe, consistent way. As a leadership team, we work hard to build a positive, forward-looking culture that ties these capabilities together into an organization that clients want to work with.

To protect and grow our capabilities, we invest heavily in training and succession planning. Training-wise, we are always looking to improve our work systems and capabilities in safe, efficient operations, often through partnering with local education providers. We are also permanently engaged in recruiting

Continued

6

into our workforce—with an average workforce age of 54, this is a crucial task for us. We are trying to ensure a future talent pipeline through a portfolio of activities. We have invested significantly in apprenticeships across every site to create a local supply of the technical skills we need. We hire graduate managers to bring external perspectives and business function knowledge. Having a blend of apprenticeship- and degree-trained individuals is important for us. And we will support any staff member looking to better themselves through education and progress through the business, without forcing anyone to do so. Finally, we are continually investing in our technical facilities to ensure that we can deliver all the client asks of us in a safe, reliable, and profitable manner.

'How do you ensure that Cammell Laird's resource and capability base is kept relevant to the strategic needs of the organization in the future?'

I receive many internal reviews and industry reports as inputs to strategic decision-making. At present, fluctuations in oil prices and the difficult political climate associated with Brexit are impacting our industry and business. In addition, personally I try to be 'present' in the business as much as possible to help me decide what to do. Any time I'm at a site, I'll do a walk-around myself. I like to take the chance to talk to people informally and listen to what they have to say. I also organize regular breakfast meetings with a cross-section of staff. I give them some views as to what is happening, but then I stop talking and ask their opinions. We also have formal suggestion schemes for technical and business process improvements. When solutions work, those who originated the ideas receive a financial reward. Opening up multiple channels for social interaction at all levels is so important to knowing the reality of what needs adjusted in the organization.

'What does strategy mean to you?'

Strategy is how you live your life in a high-level arc towards end goals of some sort. If your goals are achievable, how you get there is a strategy. If they aren't achievable, then you don't have a strategy. It is your responsibility as a business leader to define a path that people can follow. You need to ground your aims and plans in reality without stifling aspiration. If you want a business to perform, then you have to look at its capabilities, determine what it can do, and set your strategy accordingly.

You can be specific with interim targets without being too fixed on strategy. For me, it is best to use strategy as a set of boundaries within which you can manoeuvre as an organization. You use initiatives and activities to move you forward but you have to be prepared to change as circumstances change around you. There are many outside influences into which you have no input to which you might need to respond.

To make this work, as a leader, I think that you need to feel a deep connection to the business and your staff. If you don't nurture people so they can feel that they can fail and learn, then you won't push on as a collective—communications falter, colleagues go into themselves, and you will underachieve. For me, it is just as crucial to never deny issues or problems as it is to recognize and celebrate successes. We are all human at the end of the day. To appropriate a famous saying, by successfully working well, together, we increase the ability for us all to 'live long and prosper'.

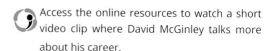 Access the online resources to watch a short video clip where David McGinley talks more about his career.

CHAPTER SUMMARY

In this chapter, we addressed the following learning outcomes:

○ Explain the importance of building an understanding of resources, capabilities, and activities in organizational strategy.

Understanding the interplay of resources, capabilities, and activities is valuable in organizational strategy. Resources are defined as what an organization has that it can use. Capabilities are defined as what the organization can do to a minimal performance threshold. Available capabilities emanate from bundles of available resources. When capabilities are deployed, we can refer to this as organizational activity. Activity results in outcomes that affect the organizational context (customers, competitors, local communities, etc.). Activity can also result in incremental changes to the resource base; for example, selling a product generates cash, which tops up financial resources. The consumption and replenishment of resource stocks are referred to as flows.

○ Explain how an organization can compete through the deployment of distinctive resources using concepts and ideas of the resource-based view.

From a resource-based view, competitive advantage arises from the possession of resources that meet the VRIO—valuable, rare, inimitable, and organization—criteria. Competitive advantage from VRIO is only a potential. For competitive advantage to lead to organizational performance, VRIO resources need to be deployed—typically in bundles with complementary resources—in a way that creates differential performance from competitors and at a cost that is less than the customer is willing to pay.

○ Evaluate the potential of an organization to manage its resource base over time through dynamic capability.

Dynamic capability describes the capacity to purposefully create, extend, or modify the resource base of the organization. For an organization to have dynamic capability, capacities must exist to sense the possibilities of resource base change, decide which resource base change opportunities to seize, and reconfigure the resource base in response. Dynamic capability emanates from the resource base—what an organization has achieved in the past can give a strong indication as to what it can do in the present. Analysing the knowledge, processes, capabilities, and capacities in the resource base will enable the strategist to evaluate the potential for purposeful resource base change over time.

○ Appraise the configuration of an organization as a set of supporting and value-adding activities.

If value means 'relative worth' (i.e. a product or service that the customer is willing to pay for), then analysis of the activities that create value can be important for the strategist. Customer willingness to pay can be understood as arising from a series of activities which, to varying degrees, add value. Value chain analysis examines the activities in an organization which might create value directly (primary activities) or shape an environment in which value can be created (support activities). Enhancing primary or supporting activities through improvement, outsourcing, or reconfiguration actions, or the elimination of non-value-adding activities, can improve the performance of the organization.

○ Critically assess the value of internally focused analytical tools in strategy work.

As with all tools and perspectives, RBV has the potential to add value to our thinking, depending on how we use it. It is also subject to limitations. In the academic literature, RBV is criticized for being too static, having limited predictive power, being of limited use to managers, having a grounding in circular logic, and being subject to confusion from causal ambiguity. In this chapter, we have proposed methods that might mitigate some of these effects and enable valuable insights for strategists through the application of RBV thinking. We encourage students and practitioners to try the methods for themselves and judge the value of the RBV on the usefulness of the insights gathered.

6

? END-OF-CHAPTER QUESTIONS

Recall questions

1. Define resources, capabilities, competences, and activities. Explain how these concepts operate together in an organization using the terms 'stocks' and 'flows'.

2. Describe the key components of the resource base framework commonly referred to as VRIO. Explain how each component contributes to competitive advantage.

3. What is meant by dynamic capability? How might dynamic capability be useful to an organization?

4. Explain the potential value of threshold capabilities to an organization.

5. Explain the difference between primary and support activities, and explain how each of these categories are used in value chain analysis.

Application questions

A) Select an organization that is familiar to you and complete a resource and capability audit based on available information. What seem to be the main sources of competitive advantage from a resource base view? What dynamic capability does the organization appear to have? How could the organization creatively adapt its resource base to be fit for the future?

B) Pick a product or service you know well and sketch out a value chain analysis for how it is delivered and supported. How could the value chain be modified or reconfigured in order to improve the performance of the organization delivering the product/service or to improve customer value creation?

C) Reflecting on the application of resource base analysis, what are the main limitations you find of using resource base tools as stand-alone methods? How easy is it to understand an organization's resource base and activities as an outsider? How feasible is it to undertake resource base analysis in a meaningful way without complementary market-based analysis?

ONLINE RESOURCES

www.oup.com/he/mackay2e

In addition to the video interviews already highlighted, the book's **online resources** include the following features for this chapter, specifically:

- *links to further reading material* to broaden your knowledge of key issues discussed in this chapter;

- *self-test multiple-choice questions* to test your understanding of the material covered in each section of the chapter; and

- *a flashcard glossary* to help you recall and test your understanding of key terms.

FURTHER READING

'Firm resources and sustained competitive advantage' by Jay Barney

Barney, J. (1991). Firm resources and sustained competitive advantage. *Journal of Management*, **17**(1), 99–120.

This article is required reading for students of the resource-based view topic. It introduces the VRIO framework and has been highly influential in the development of the resource-based perspective in strategy research ever since. The main concepts are covered in this chapter, but students are strongly encouraged to explore the original arguments in this seminal paper.

'Mapping distinctive competencies: A systemic approach' by Colin Eden and Fran Ackermann

Eden, C. and Ackermann, F. (2000). Mapping distinctive competencies: A systemic approach. *Journal of the Operational Research Society*, **51**(1), 12–20.

The approach advocated in this chapter for auditing the resource base, capabilities, and activity outcomes is based on an interpretation of Eden and Ackermann's principles for the use of mapping methods to support strategy work. This article explains how the use of a systematic approach to mapping of the resource base can lead to understanding of distinctiveness and competitive advantage from patterns of resources. Note that Eden and Ackermann's use of competences is synonymous with how capabilities have been defined in this chapter. For a further, detailed example of how to map the resource base, you can see also Chapter 7 *of* Making Strategy *(Ackermann and Eden 2011).*

Dynamic Capabilities: Understanding Strategic Change in Organisations by Constance Helfat et al.

Helfat, C.E., Finklestein, S., Mitchell, W. et al. (2007). *Dynamic Capabilities: Understanding Strategic Change in Organisations*. Oxford: Blackwell.

Dynamic capability remains a hot topic in strategy academia. With the high level of research interest shown in the concept since Teece et al.'s seminal publication in 1997, multiple competing views of dynamic capability emerged in the literature. This book by Helfat and colleagues is an attempt to draw together dynamic capability thinking from leading authors in order to progress understanding and a research agenda for understanding strategic change. Drawing on a range of considerations, it explains dynamic capability in a coherent way and offers valuable insights into resource-based competitive advantage that will benefit students of strategy in general, as well as those interested in knowing more about dynamic capability.

'Innovation, dynamic capabilities, and leadership' by Paul J. H. Schoemaker et al.

Schoemaker, P.J.H., Heaton, S., and Teece, D. (2018). Innovation, dynamic capabilities, and leadership. *California Management Review*, **61**(1):15–42.

In this article, the authors argue that in today's dynamic business environment, those organizations that focus on new product and process developments coupled with business model innovation will leverage their dynamic capabilities. The article brings together dynamic capabilities, business model innovation (see Chapter 11 *for more on business model innovation) and strong strategic and entrepreneurial leadership (see* Chapter 14 *for more on leading strategic change) to help organizations to thrive in an environment that is VUCA (volatile, uncertain, complex, and ambiguous—see* Chapter 11 *for more on this term).*

REFERENCES

Ackermann, F. and Eden, C. (2011). *Making Strategy: Mapping Out Strategic Success*. London: Sage.

Adner, R. and Levinthal, D.A. (2004). What is not a real option: Considering boundaries for the application of real options to business strategy. *Academy of Management Review*, **29**(1), 74–85.

Ashkenas, R. (2011). When the invincible become 'vincible'. *Harvard Business Review* (29 March), https://hbr.org/2011/03/when-the-invincible-become-vin.html (last accessed 10 August 2022).

Augier, M. and Teece, D.J. (2009). Resource, capabilities, and Penrose effects. In: Teece, D.J. (ed.), *Dynamic Capabilities and Strategic Management: Organising for Innovation and Growth*. Oxford: Oxford University Press, pp. 113–35.

Bachmann, J.W. (2002). Competitive strategy: It's OK to be different. *Academy of Management Executive*, **16**(2), 61–5.

Barney, J. (1991). Firm resources and sustained competitive advantage. *Journal of Management*, **17**(1), 99–120.

Barney, J.B. (1995). Looking inside for competitive advantage. *Academy of Management Executive*, **9**(4), 49–61.

Barthelemy, J. and Adsit, D. (2003). The seven deadly sins of outsourcing: Executive commentary. *Academy of Management Executive*, **17**(2), 87–100.

Chang, R. (2019). A Chinese farewell to Six Sigma. *Bloomberg Businessweek European Edition* (11 February), 20–1.

Connor, T. (2002). The resource-based view of strategy and its value to practising managers. *Strategic Change*, **11**(6), 307–16.

Dierickx, I. and Cool, K. (1989). Asset stock accumulation and sustainability of competitive advantage. *Management Science*, **35**(12), 1504–13.

Eden, C. and Ackermann, F. (2000). Mapping distinctive competencies: A systemic approach. *Journal of the Operational Research Society*, **51**(1), 12–20.

The Financial Times (2021). Schools must lay the foundations to bridge Africa's skills gap (12 October), https://www.ft.com/content/d0941cd2-f9bb-4e68-b539-206e32bac955 (last accessed 23 April 2022).

Forbes (2022). Aliko Dangote (10 May), https://www.forbes.com/profile/aliko-dangote (last accessed 23 April 2022).

Frynas, J.G., Mol, M.J., and Mellahi, K. (2018). Management innovation made in China: Haier's Rendanheyi. *California Management Review*, **61**(1), 71–93.

Garbuio, M., Lovallo, D., and Sibony, O. (2015). Evidence doesn't argue for itself: The value of disinterested dialogue in strategic decision-making. *Long Range Planning*, **48**(6), 361–80.

The Guardian (2019). Concrete: The most destructive material on earth, https://www.theguardian.com/cities/2019/feb/25/concrete-the-most-destructive-material-on-earth (last accessed 23 April 2022).

Hamel, G. and Zanini, M. (2018). The end of bureaucracy: How a Chinese appliance maker is reinventing management for the digital age. *Harvard Business Review* Digital *Articles* (November/December), 50–9, https://ournhspeopleprofession.org/bundles/ctclient/uploads/FOW/HBR-Hamel_Zanini%E2%80%93The_end_of_bureaucracy.pdf (last accessed 19 October 2022).

Healey, M.P. and Hodgkinson, G.P. (2017). Making strategy hot. *California Management Review*, **59**(3), 109–34.

Helfat, C.E., Finklestein, S., Mitchell, W. et al. (2007). *Dynamic Capabilities: Understanding Strategic Change in Organisations*. Oxford: Blackwell.

Kaplan, R.S. and Norton, D.P. (2008). Mastering the management system. *Harvard Business Review*, **86**(1), 62–77.

Kornberger, M. (2017). The values of strategy: Valuation practices, rivalry, and strategic agency. *Organization Studies*, **38**(12), 1753–73.

Lampel, J. and Shamsie, J. (2003). Capabilities in motion: New organizational forms and the reshaping of the Hollywood movie industry. *Journal of Management Studies*, **40**(8), 2189–210.

Leonard-Barton, D. (1992). Core capabilities and core rigidities: A paradox in managing new product development. *Strategic Management Journal*, **13**(Special Issue), 111–25.

LVMH (2022). New records for LVMH in 2021 (27 January), https://www.lvmh.com/news-documents/press-releases/new-records-for-lvmh-in-2021 (last accessed 23 April 2022).

Markides, C.C. (2000). *All the Right Moves: A Guide to Crafting Breakthrough Strategy*. Boston, MA: Harvard Business School Press.

MacKenzie, N.G., Perchard, A., Mackay, D., and Burt, G. (2022). Unlocking dynamic capabilities in the Scotch whisky industry, 1945–present. *Business History*, 1–21, https://doi.org/10.1080/00076791.2022.2085251.

Miller, D. (2003). An asymmetry-based view of advantage: Towards an attainable sustainability. *Strategic Management Journal*, **24**(10), 961–76.

Miller, D. and Shamsie, J. (1996). The resource-based view of the firm in two environments: The Hollywood film studios from 1936 to 1965. *Academy of Management Journal*, **39**(3), 519–43.

Penrose, E. (1959). *The Theory of The Growth of The Firm*. Oxford: Basil Blackwell.

Peteraf, M. (1993). The cornerstones of competitive advantage: A resource-based view. *Strategic Management Journal* (1986–98), **14**(3), 179–91.

Peteraf, M.A. and Barney, J.B. (2003). Unraveling the resource-based tangle. *Managerial and Decision Economics*, **24**(4), 309–23.

Petit, N. and Teece, D.J. (2021). Innovating Big Tech firms and competition policy: Favoring dynamic over static competition, *Industrial and Corporate Change*, 30(5), 1168–98, https://doi.org/10.1093/icc/dtab049.

Porter, M.E. (1985). *Competitive Advantage: Creating and Sustaining Superior Performance*. New York: Free Press.

Prahalad, C.K. and Hamel, G. (1990). The core competence of the corporation. *Harvard Business Review*, **68**(3), 79–91.

Schoemaker, P.J.H., Heaton, S., and Teece, D. (2018). Innovation, dynamic capabilities, and leadership. *California Management Review*, **61**(1), 15–42.

Teece, D.J. (2007). Explicating dynamic capabilities: The nature and microfoundations of (sustainable) enterprise performance. *Strategic Management Journal*, **28**(13), 1319–50.

Teece, D.J. (2014). The foundations of enterprise performance: Dynamic and ordinary capabilities in an (economic) theory of firms. *Academy of Management Perspectives*, **28**(4), 328–52.

Teece, D.J., Pisano, G., and Shuen, A. (1997). Dynamic capabilities and strategic management. *Strategic Management Journal*, **18**(7), 509–33.

Teece, D., Peteraf, M., and Leih, S. (2016). Dynamic capabilities and organizational agility: Risk, uncertainty, and strategy in the innovation economy. *California Management Review*, **58**(4), 13–35.

Vergne, J.-P. and Durand, R. (2011). The path of most persistence: An evolutionary perspective on path dependence and dynamic capabilities. *Organization Studies*, **32**(3), 365.

Wernerfelt, B. (1984). A resource-based view of the firm. *Strategic Management Journal*, **5**(2), 171–80.

Wernerfelt, B. (1995). The resource-based view of the firm: Ten years after. *Strategic Management Journal*, **16**(3), 171–4.

Winter, S.G. (2003). Understanding dynamic capabilities. *Strategic Management Journal*, **24**(10), 991–5.

Zeng, J. and Mackay, D. (2019). The influence of managerial attention on the deployment of dynamic capability: A case study of internet platform firms in China. *Industrial and Corporate Change*, **28**(5), 1173–92.

Zollo, M. and Winter, S.G. (2002). Deliberate learning and the evolution of dynamic capabilities. *Organization Science*, **13**(3), 339–51.

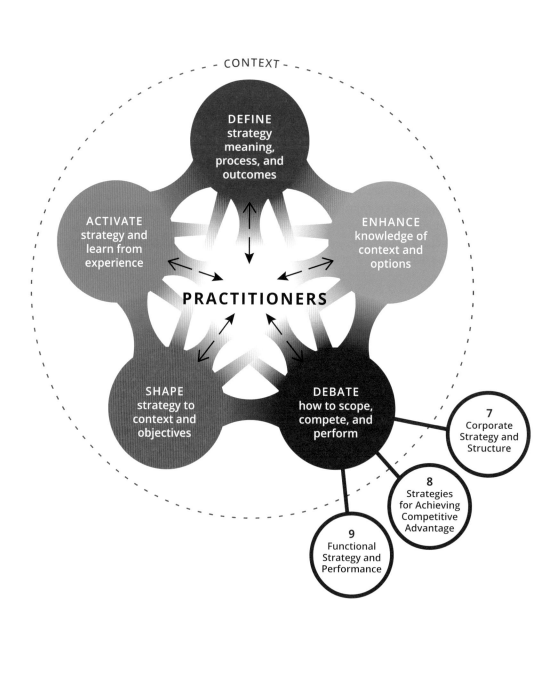

CONTEXT

DEFINE
strategy
meaning,
process, and
outcomes

ACTIVATE
strategy and
learn from
experience

ENHANCE
knowledge of
context and
options

PRACTITIONERS

SHAPE
strategy to
context and
objectives

DEBATE
how to scope,
compete, and
perform

7
Corporate
Strategy and
Structure

8
Strategies
for Achieving
Competitive
Advantage

9
Functional
Strategy and
Performance

PART
THREE

Debate how to scope, compete, and perform

In Part 3 of this book, we explain how strategy might be debated, understood, and scoped within an organization during a strategizing episode. By looking at how questions of competition and strategic performance can be addressed, we will be exploring key recurring topics for practitioners in senior leadership positions in the organization. In Chapter 7, we explore corporate strategy and the relationship between an organization's structure and its strategy. Organizational structure can have a major impact on the dynamics of strategizing and how practitioners are able to act in a coherent manner. We consider the different ways in which activities can be organized in order to help an organization to achieve its goals. In Chapter 8, we address how the important question of competitive advantage might feature in strategizing discussions, building on market- and resource-based thinking introduced in section 8.2. We explore the nature and sources of competitive advantage and how it might be sustained over time through business strategy—how an organization competes. Chapter 9 investigates functional strategy; we discuss how strategy work occurs within organizational units, in alignment with corporate and business strategy demands, and in conjunction with strategic performance management approaches. This chapter broadens our understanding of the full range of 'internal' stakeholders that might influence strategizing from a process–practice perspective.

By the end of Part 3, you should have enhanced abilities to think, talk, and act like a practitioner, debating how to scope, compete, and perform through strategy.

CHAPTER SEVEN

Corporate Strategy and Structure

CONTENTS

By the end of this chapter, you should be able to:

○ Analyse the main organizational structural types—which sit in the simple, complex, and innovation-orientated categories—in terms of their strengths and weaknesses

○ Evaluate the suitability of a range of structural types for organizations against a number of design tests

○ Appreciate the role of systems in supporting the delivery of an organization's strategy

○ Comprehend the relationship between internationalization and organizational structure

TOOLBOX

7

○ **Mintzberg's six ideal structural types**
Henry Mintzberg identifies a number of possible structural configurations adopted by organizations. He suggests that these structural types can result from the strategy an organization adopts and the extent to which it practises that strategy.

○ **Simons' basic control levers**
A framework which can help managers to understand the different ways in which they can exercise control in organizations that require flexibility, creativity, and innovation.

○ **The OLI framework**
OLI stands for ownership, location, and internalization, three potential sources of advantage that may underlie a firm's decision to become a multinational. This framework helps us to explore the reasons why a firm may decide to do so.

○ **The Stopford and Wells matrix**
A model that explores the typical stages of development for companies that are moving towards an international organizational structure. It suggests that the process is driven by both the number of products sold internationally and the importance of international sales to the company.

○ **Porter's configuration/coordination matrix**
A framework proposed by Michael Porter, which gives his view of the relationship between the organization's configuration (i.e. where value chain activities are performed) and coordination, that is, how the organization's value chain is managed.

🎧 Access the online resources to watch a short video clip where Gordon Ramsay shares his top career tips.

OPENING CASE STUDY RESTRUCTURING AT TOYOTA

7

Back in 2009, Toyota, one of the world's largest automobile manufacturers, was caught up in a crisis when the alleged improper installation of a floor mat from a sports utility vehicle (SUV) into a Lexus by a dealer in the United States led to the vehicle's accelerator getting stuck, causing a fatal accident. Since then, we have seen the corporation make a series of far-reaching changes to its organizational structure, with regular announcements of new initiatives intended to respond to its critics and refresh its approach to strategy implementation.

Toyota's reaction to the 2009 tragedy appeared to illustrate some of the concerns that outsiders had expressed about Toyota's organizational structure. The company was accused of moving too slowly in response to external threats (such as mounting customer concerns and complaints), perhaps due to a rigid corporate culture and a very strong hierarchy of seniority. Commentators asked whether, given the company's structure and culture, many managers would be reluctant to pass 'bad news' up the chain of command and pointed out that Toyota had a large, all-male board of directors, all of whom were 'company insiders'. In a traditional Japanese business hierarchy, the most senior managers make the key decisions for the whole organization. Power and decision-making are centralized in the Japanese headquarters of the company, with little delegation of authority—for example to managers in the United States. Most information from its global operations flowed in a single direction—back to Japan, where decisions were made. Individual business units around the world seemed to have very little communication with each other.

It has often been argued that a highly centralized organizational structure is advantageous in promoting efficiency. If a relatively small group of people in the corporate headquarters have good information on what is happening in all of the company's business units around the world, they can seek to ensure that—for example—every factory has exactly what it needs, exactly when it needs it. However, the 2009 crisis highlighted an important disadvantage of a highly centralized organizational structure, such as Toyota's at the time: such a

model can promote secrecy, with only a small number of people at the top of the company having a full picture of events.

By 2013, Toyota was seen to be moving away from its strongly centralized global hierarchy (similar to a spoke-and-wheel structure), and towards a divisional organizational structure. It retained aspects of a global hierarchy, with business unit heads continuing to report to the Japanese headquarters. However, the company increased the decision-making power of its regional heads and business unit heads, making its decision-making processes less centralized. Toyota also introduced *geographic divisions* to its organizational structure—with regional heads representing Japan, North America, Europe, East Asia and Oceania, China, Asia and Middle East, Africa, and Latin America and the Caribbean. This shift was intended to enable the company to improve products and services according to regional market conditions. In addition, *product-based divisions* were also established to support development of brands and product lines such as Lexus.

From 2013 to the present, Toyota has continued to make a range of changes to its organizational structure to speed up decision-making and enable innovation in the business. Its board of directors is now much smaller and includes women and other directors with experience outside the company.

Questions for discussion

1. What do you think will be the main benefits of the restructuring that Toyota is introducing? How does the changing structure support the company's strategy?

2. Can you think of any disadvantages to the organizational changes being introduced? What difficulties or barriers to change is the company likely to face as it makes those changes?

3. Today, Toyota operates in more than 170 countries and regions around the world. Can you think of any ways in which its global profile might help or hinder its plan to change its structure and strategy?

Sources

Gregory, L. (2018). Toyota's organizational structure: An analysis. Panmore Institute (8 September), http://panmore.com/toyota-organizational-structure-analysis (last accessed 18 August 2022).

Liker, J. (2011). Toyota's recall crisis: What have we learned? (11 February), https://hbr.org/2011/02/toyotas-recall-crisis-full-of (last accessed 18 August 2022).

Toyota (2017). Toyota to update its organization structure to boost business innovation (1 March), https://global.toyota/en/detail/15197404 (last accessed 18 August 2022).

Toyota (2020). TMC announces changes to executive structure, senior management responsibilities, and organizational structure (3 March), https://global.toyota/en/newsroom/corporate/31845625.html (last accessed 18 August 2022).

7.1 **Introduction**

Organizations exist to enable us to do things that it would be difficult to do alone. Organizations can form complex networks, and we rely on those networks to satisfy our daily needs. Organizations exist to facilitate joint action, with their structures being determined both by the way in which tasks that need to be completed are divided and by the way that sub-tasks are managed to fulfil overall goals. The way that these tasks are broken down and reintegrated is called structuring; the particular structure adopted by a given organization is known as its **organizational structure**.

An organization's structure enables activities to be carried out in a way that is consistent with its overall purpose. As such, it represents a control mechanism that helps to keep the organization on track. For a large organization in particular, we can consider its structure to operate at several levels—at the top level, the form of the overall organization, then cascading down through sub-units and functions to the level at which products are made or services are delivered.

In this chapter, we consider organizational structure at these different levels. We explore the role of structure in the implementation of strategic change, and we consider how managers can evaluate and choose between alternative structures. From a process–practice perspective, analysis of structure helps us to better understand how decisions are made, how stakeholders interact, and how information and resources flow, all of which impact on how strategizing might occur. We also discuss the concepts of systems and organizational cultures as alternative control mechanisms, and we consider the relationship between internationalization and organizational structure.

7.2 **Relationship between strategy and structure**

We start our discussion of the relationship between an organization's strategy and its structure with the contribution of Alfred Chandler—a US professor of business history and probably one of the most influential strategic thinkers of his time. His book, *Strategy and Structure* (Chandler 1962), describes his research in four large US companies. He argued that they all faced essentially the same internal and external pressures for change. He charted their evolution and demonstrated that they had all developed similar types of **divisionalized** multi-business unit structures (known as **M-form structures**; see section on multidivisional complex structures). A divisionalized organization is typically organized around a number of different products or services, markets, or geographies. This led Chandler to offer two propositions. First, fundamental environmental changes require an adaptive response. Second, the strategies that are put into practice eventually produce a 'fit' between the new types of organization which develop and their competitive environments.

In describing their developmental paths, Chandler showed how each company had taken a different route to reach the new structural form. They had faced different types of difficulties along the way and used different strategy processes to get there, but they had all arrived at the same end point.

Chandler's case studies showed that growth created administrative problems. The companies responded by formalizing techniques for administration and work allocation. He described how they adapted internally by revising their organizational structures and channels of control. The internal strategies they adopted to respond to external environmental change led to the development of new structural forms.

These findings led Chandler to put forward one of the most famous statements in the history of strategic management: 'Structure follows strategy.' It has become self-evident in today's environment that organizations need to adapt to environmental change. The idea that strategy is in part about an organization achieving and maintaining a 'fit' with its environment has also been highly influential.

In this section, we consider the relationship between strategy and structure, the main elements of organizational structure, and Mintzberg's influential theories on organizational structure. We identify the key strengths and weaknesses of the main structural forms that are widely recognizable in contemporary organizations (including simple, complex, and innovation-orientated structures), and we conclude by considering how to choose an effective structure for an organization.

Structure, systems, and culture

Today, we might challenge Chandler's view. Does structure always follow strategy? The Toyota case study that opened this chapter might lead us to reflect on an ongoing tension between an organization's high-level goals and the need, over time, to create an appropriate structure that is likely to help deliver the espoused strategy. The role of structure in operational effectiveness is widely discussed in the existing management literature (e.g. Nadler et al. 1997; Bennet and Bennet 2004). The discussion is typically based on the assumption that an organization relies on its structure in order to coordinate its activities; the right organizational structure may also help to deliver a unique mix of values.

Structural mechanisms include the ways in which people interface and interact while doing their work, the flow of information through the organization, and the coordination and control of essential activities and practices. For example, Google Inc. was restructured in 2015 to become Alphabet Inc., after which Google's search product became a wholly owned subsidiary of a new parent company, Alphabet. Google's other projects and teams were spun out into separate 'Alphabet companies', each with its own CEO (Alphabet Inc. is a holding company with no business operations of its own). Figure 7.1 shows the different 'Alphabet companies', which are now subsidiaries of Alphabet Inc.

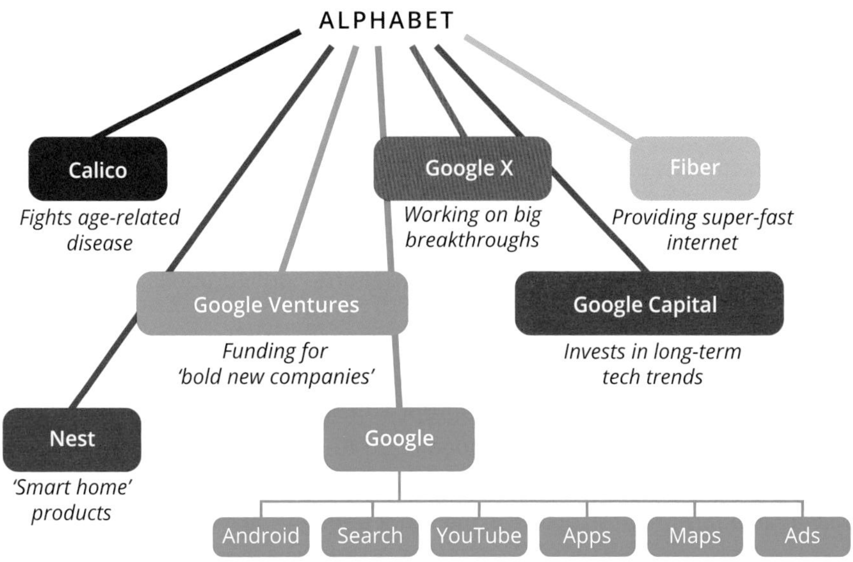

FIGURE 7.1 Different 'Alphabet companies', which are subsidiaries of Alphabet Inc. *Source*: courtesy of Seeking Alpha. Full article: https://seekingalpha.com/article/4213384-alphabet-berkshire-tomorrow-part-1 (last accessed 18 August 2022).

It was reported that the main aim behind this restructuring was to help entrepreneurs build and run companies with the autonomy and speed they need. In other words, the company engaged in a diversification strategy by restructuring to move beyond the search engine business (e.g. Dudovskiy 2017). In 2017, a further step in the reorganization (e.g. Lomas 2017) created a holding company under Alphabet (XXVI Holdings Inc., named for the number of letters in the Latin alphabet, displayed in roman numerals), which legally separates Googles from divisions that were previously technically its subsidiaries, such as Waymo (which focuses on autonomous driving technology) and DeepMind (artificial intelligence).

Such an example may seem to support Chandler's (1962) logic that 'structure follows strategy' and that organizations choose their structures to support their strategic direction. However, the opposing view is that strategy follows structure. This means that an organization's structure and operational practices can dictate future strategy. Put simply, our view of what is desirable, or even possible, in terms of future strategy can be affected if an organization's structure and operational practices become the norm without further question or comment.

In Chandler's view, strategy needs to be developed first; only then do we ask ourselves what structure might be needed to ensure that the strategy can be implemented successfully. For example, a new strategy may create new resource demands in terms of staff, machinery, or infrastructure; these demands could change the way the organization operates, making a new structure necessary.

Main elements of organizational structure

Let us now consider the many configurations that an organization can adopt. A key idea here is that key elements of structure combine to form natural clusters or 'configurations'. The term 'configurations' refers to the natural clusters or groupings that result when the key elements of structure are combined. The idea behind this is that formal structures and processes need to be aligned so that they can more comprehensively influence the informal processes and relationships that occur in all organizations. This is based on the belief that if the formal and informal sides of an organization are closely connected, it becomes easier to undertake more effective strategy work.

A configuration consists of both the broader and the more micro-structures within an organization and includes the processes and relationships through which an organization's strategy is developed.

There are three essential aspects of an organization's configuration: its structural design, processes, and relationships.

- **Structural design**: influences the way in which knowledge and skills are developed within an organization. The wrong (or an inappropriate) structural design can result in essential knowledge and skills not being developed or strategies not being implemented. As such, structural design lies at the heart of the advantage a particular organization may offer. However, an appropriate structure alone is not enough.

- **Processes**: drive and support what people do, both within and around an organization. As such, they strongly influence an organization's likelihood of success (or failure). They help define how strategies are created, and they determine how employees interact when implementing a strategy.

- **Relationships**: connect people within an organization to each other and to those outside the organization who have an impact on its success. In larger organizations, relationships form internally between those in the corporate 'hub' and those located in dispersed organizational units. Externally, relationships are developed through routine interactions with consultants, shareholders, and other stakeholders.

Managers typically describe their organizations in terms of **organization charts**, which are a useful way of depicting formal relationships. Organization charts represent the different 'levels' within larger organizations and typically indicate reporting lines. Redrawn organization charts often lie at the heart of restructuring attempts by signifying the introduction of a new set of skills which may be seen to be crucial to the future success of the organization. For example, a new organization chart which includes a 'director of strategy' role that did not previously appear makes a clear statement that strategy has become more of a concern for the organization and is considered more important to its future success. We will discuss this feature of top management teams further in Chapter 14.

Mintzberg on organizational structure

Henry Mintzberg is a Canadian business and management academic and author and an influential contemporary thinker about strategic management (e.g. Mintzberg 1979, 1989, 1993). Mintzberg does not believe that there is always 'one best way' to design an organization, suggesting that characteristics of organizations appear to fall into natural clusters or configurations. He argues that when structures are designed, organizations need to be viewed as a whole. He suggests (Mintzberg 1979) that the structure of any organization has two essential elements: (a) the *parts* of the structure, and (b) the *mechanisms* that hold them together.

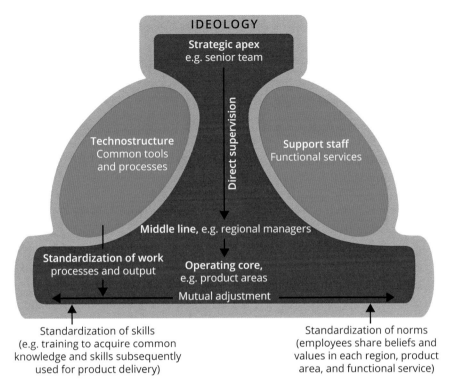

FIGURE 7.2 Mintzberg's six parts of the organization. *Source*: after Mintzberg, H. (1979). *The Structuring of Organisations*. Adapted in Segal-Horn, S. (2004). *The Strategy Reader*. Oxford: Blackwell, 247, Figure 13.1. Reproduced with permission of John Wiley & Sons Limited.

First, he identifies six basic parts, which are illustrated in Figure 7.2:

- the operating core;
- the strategic apex;
- the middle line;
- the technostructure;
- support staff;
- ideology.

He then lists six mechanisms which link the basic parts together:

- direct supervision;
- mutual adjustment;
- standardization of work processes;
- output;
- skills;
- norms.

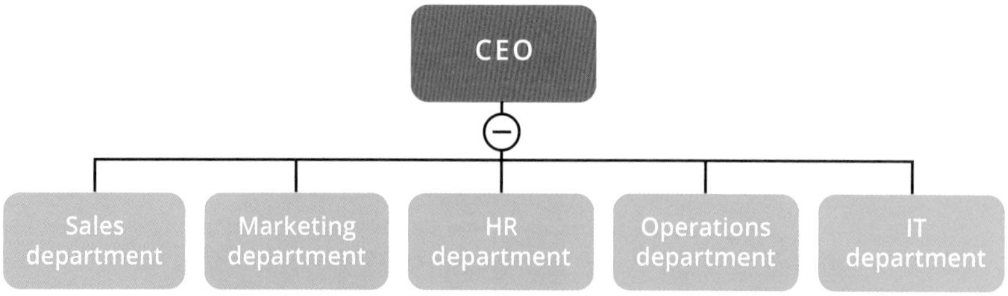

FIGURE 7.3 Example of a simple organizational chart with a functional structure. *Source*: authors.

These mechanisms form the 'glue' that brings together the work of every employee or team in getting the overall work done.

Mintzberg suggests that the combination of these two elements with the centralization or decentralization of power in an organization results in six structural configurations, illustrated in Figure 7.3. 'Centralization' implies that the decision-making power rests at a single point in the organization while 'decentralization' implies that the power is relatively dispersed among many individuals or levels within the organization. So, what are these six structural configurations?

Mintzberg's six ideal structural types

Mintzberg develops six structural configurations (or 'types') by considering the consequences of emphasizing each of the six basic parts listed in turn. This leads us to the six structural configurations described in Table 7.1. The first, 'simple structure', will typically be seen in a small organization or one that is at a relatively early stage in its development, where the 'strategic apex' remains the key part of the organization. As we move across the six structures described in Table 7.1, we see that the size and complexity of the organization can develop in a range of ways, with different parts of the organization seen to be behind the ways in which it develops. We discuss this further as we provide our own summary of organizational forms under the headings 'Simple', 'Complex', and 'Innovation-orientated'. Think about the characteristics of Mintzberg's six types depicted in Table 7.1 as you read the discussion of various organizational structures in the following section.

Simple, complex, and innovation-orientated structures

We now move from Mintzberg's account of organizational structure to our own list of structural forms—forms that are widely reflected in contemporary organizations. We will summarize them under three main categories:

- simple structure (functional);
- complex structure (multidivisional, holding, matrix, network, and transnational);
- innovation-orientated structure (**project-based structure** and adhocracy).

We should stress, however, that many organizations have characteristics of more than one structure and that innovation and strategic change can, of course, take place through more than one category of structure (see the example of Keiretsu, Case Example 7.1). As you read the

TABLE 7.1 Mintzberg's six ideal structural types

	Simple structure	Machine bureaucracy	Professional bureaucracy	Divisionalized form	Adhocracy	Missionary
Key part	Strategic apex	Technostructure	Operating core	Middle line	Support staff	Ideology
Coordinating mechanism	Direct supervision	Standardization of work processes	Standardization of skills	Standardization of outputs	Mutual adjustment	Standardization of norms
Dominant pull to:	Centralize	Standardize	Professionalize	Balkanize	Collaborate	Evangelize
Decentralization	None (centralized)	Limited horizontal	Horizontal	Limited vertical	Selective horizontal and vertical	Full decentralization
Planning and control	Little	Action planning	Little	Much performance control	Limited action planning	Little
Liaison devices	Few	Few	In administration	Few	Many throughout	Few
Situational factors	Age and size, technical system, environment, power					
Examples	Small owner–manager organizations undertaking simple activities, e.g. small shops	Fast-food chains, airlines, telephone banking	Hospitals, colleges, law firms (or other professional service firms or partnerships)	Large conglomerates	Creative advertising agencies, bespoke software boutiques	Evangelical churches, revolutionary movements

Source: authors.

descriptions of each form, try to relate them to any organizations that you are familiar with—including any 'hybrid' structures that seem to incorporate aspects of more than one form. An understanding of different organizational structures is very valuable as you reflect on the different strategies that organizations are pursuing and the barriers that they may encounter as they work on strategy implementation.

Simple structure

An organization is likely to have a **simple structure** during its early stages, with work divided between a number of sections/departments according to their function. This is known as a **functional structure** (Figure 7.3).

The functional structure is perhaps the simplest form of organizational structure and may reflect responsibilities including operations, finance, marketing, and human resources. This type of configuration is usually found in smaller companies or those with narrow (rather than diverse) product ranges. Organizations of this type may evolve into larger, more complex entities that adopt multidivisional structures (discussed later in this section); each of these divisions may retain their functional configuration.

What are the advantages of a functional structure?

- The CEO can keep in touch will all functions and operations relatively easily.
- Control mechanisms are reduced and remain simple.
- Responsibilities and reporting mechanisms are clearly defined and easily understood.
- Specialists are located at senior and middle management levels and are clearly identified within the overall structure.

However, there may be disadvantages.

- Senior managers can become overburdened with routine matters and operational detail as they focus on their functional responsibilities and may fail to monitor the external environment if they become too inward-looking.
- Diversity can become difficult to cope with as functional lines become rigid.
- It may be difficult to coordinate between functions as functional barriers are reinforced.
- It may be difficult for an organization with this configuration to adapt to changes in its size and changes in the external environment.

The advantages and disadvantages listed here both stem from an organization's basic and simple form.

Complex structures

Most organizations become larger and more complex over time, and their structures also tend to evolve as the organization begins to employ more staff, operate in more locations, provide a wider range of products and services and so on. We will look at a number of **complex structures** that reflect these changes in how activities can be organized: **multidivisional structure**, **holding structure**, **matrix structure**, **network structure**, and **transnational structure**. We begin with the multidivisional structure.

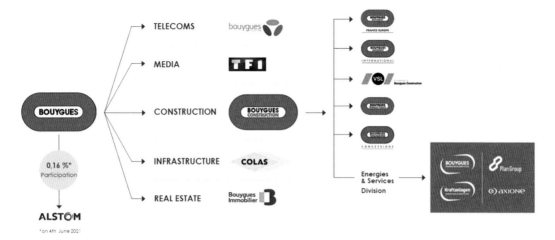

FIGURE 7.4 Example of multidivisional structure. *Source*: courtesy of BOUYGUES Group, https://www.bouygues-es.co.uk/our-group (last accessed 18 August 2022).

The multidivisional structure

As noted earlier in this chapter, organizations often become more complex in structure as they develop. The multidivisional structure, or the M-form, is a configuration built up by multiple divisions defined by products, services, or geographical areas, and a central head office organized by function. For example, Figure 7.4 illustrates the organization chart of the industrial group Bouygues, which shows its interests in construction, roads, property, TV, and telecommunications.

The introduction of divisions often stems from problems that functional structures experience when dealing with diversity or expansion, as noted when we discussed the disadvantages of a simple structure. Divisions are often introduced when domestic organizations expand into other geographical markets. The intention is that each division in a multidivisional structure will be better able to respond to the specific requirements of its product/market strategy using its own set of functional departments.

This type of configuration also exists in many public services, where the organization is structured around service departments such as education, social services, recreation and so forth. For example, in the health sector, it has been argued that the potential benefits of a more decentralized M-form structure, such as flexibility, can outweigh the potential disadvantages, such as a possible increase in costs due to some duplication of effort (Bustamante 2016).

The multidivisional structure has a number of advantages:

- divisions can be added or divested (removed) as appropriate, giving an organization a high degree of operational flexibility;
- each division can be managed by monitoring selected performance indicators, and therefore accountability at the divisional level can be increased;
- divisional managers have greater ownership of their own divisional strategies;
- growth areas can be clearly identified and nurtured;

- conflicts between functional areas can be reduced;
- career progression is promoted: divisional managers can adopt a strategic leadership role within their division that equips them with the skills and experience needed for a move to the corporate centre.

However, the multidivisional structure also has some potential disadvantages:

- central and divisional activity can become duplicated as functions behave more like independent businesses;
- divisional priorities may overshadow those coming from the corporate centre, leading to fragmentation and potential conflict with head office;
- internal competition between divisions can occur as they 'compete' for scarce central resources;
- the sharing of experiences and learning across divisions can become difficult—and may even be discouraged;
- there is a danger of loss of central 'control' over the divisions.

The holding structure

A holding structure groups together a number of diverse businesses under a central head office, as depicted in Figure 7.5. These businesses may have come together through mergers and acquisitions or via joint ventures. An example of a famous holding company is the US multinational conglomerate Berkshire Hathaway Inc. If the name is not immediately familiar to you, many of the brands owned by Berkshire Hathaway are certainly household names in many parts of the world and cover a diverse spread of industries, including Duracell (batteries and smart power systems), Dairy Queen (restaurants), and Fruit of the Loom (textiles and clothing).

In a holding structure, every division operates autonomously as a **strategic business unit (SBU)**, with the head office acting as a central coordinator. Holding structures can be adopted by organizations of differing sizes: smaller organizations may adopt 'holding' structures as part of a strategy of rapid growth predicated upon the exploitation of new opportunities.

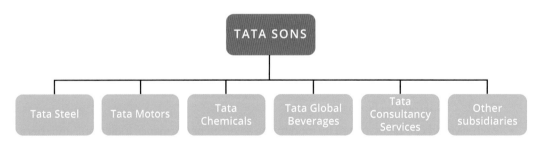

FIGURE 7.5 Example of a holding structure: Tata Group. *Source*: reproduced with permission from *The Economist* (2017). Tata's governance is still faulty (9 February), https://www.economist.com/business/2017/02/09/tatas-governance-is-still-faulty (last accessed 18 August 2022). © The Economist Group Limited, London 2017.

A holding structure has a number of advantages:

- it allows for multiple ownership and hence a greater spread of risk around the companies making up the group;
- the SBUs benefit from being exposed to a wider range of knowledge and expertise through their collaboration;
- the organization has the flexibility to tap into new market opportunities.

Some of the potential disadvantages of a holding structure are:

- minimal control or intervention over strategic issues by the corporate parent;
- the possibility that under-performing SBUs become isolated and difficult to manage;
- the potential for conflicts and competition to emerge between SBUs.

Matrix structure

The matrix structure combines elements of the different structures we have already seen—for example, product divisions and geographical territories or product divisions and functional specialisms (Figure 7.6). As such, it can combine aspects of functional and holding structures to yield a more complex hybrid structure.

Matrix structures are often adopted by multiproduct, multinational, and multifunctional organizations as they make them adept at coordinating resources and capabilities across projects, completing routine production and engineering tasks, and achieving economies of scale (Hobday 2000). Some form of matrix structure has been adopted over the years by a long list of major corporations, including General Electric (GE), Bechtel, Citibank, Dow Chemical, Shell Oil, Texas Instruments, and TRW (Davis and Lawrence 1978).

It can be highly challenging to implement a strategy within an organization that has adopted a matrix structure, not least because of the need to coordinate the needs of different businesses and different countries or regions. However, such a structure brings with it potential benefits; knowledge management can be particularly effective under a matrix structure because it

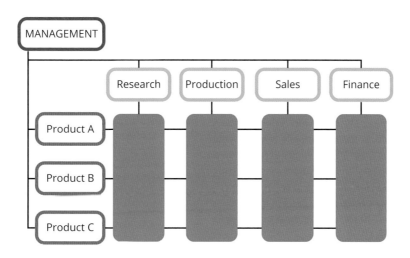

FIGURE 7.6 Example of a matrix structure. *Source*: authors.

allows separate areas of knowledge to be integrated across organizational boundaries. This is reflected in the organizational structure of Starbucks, the US coffee company, which has a matrix structure that has evolved over time to meet the needs of the business, as we discuss in Case Example 7.2.

Case Example 7.2 provides a good illustration of a matrix structure in practice, and as with each different structural type there are associated advantages and disadvantages.

 Access the online resources to watch a short video clip where Gordon Ramsay discusses supply chain management and organizational culture.

CASE EXAMPLE 7.1 **KEIRETSU**

The structure of major companies in Japan, known as **keiretsu**, is steeped in traditional relationships dating back to the seventeenth century. However, the keiretsu model was mainly pursued in the aftermath of the Second World War and soon became the dominant partnership network driving modern Japanese business. The term 'keiretsu' translates as 'lineage' or 'grouping of enterprises' and refers to Japanese business structures comprising networks of different companies including banks, manufacturers, distributors, and supply chain partners.

A **horizontal keiretsu** is an alliance of cross-shareholding companies, led by a Japanese bank, which provides a range of financial services. Mitsubishi is an example of a modern horizontal keiretsu, led by the Bank of Toyko-Mitsubishi. Mitsubishi Motors and Mitsubishi Trust and Banking are part of the core group, followed by Meiji Mutual Life Insurance Company, which provides insurance to all members of the keiretsu. Mitsubishi Shoji is the trading company for the Mitsubishi keiretsu, with its aim of distributing goods around the world on behalf of keiretsu members.

A **vertical keiretsu** is a partnership of manufacturers, suppliers, and distributors that work cooperatively to increase efficiency and reduce costs. A modern example is the automobile giant Toyota (see the Opening Case Study), which depends on a network of suppliers and manufacturers covering parts, production, dealerships, and so on.

Banks typically own a small percentage of their keiretsu members' stock, and members may own a portion of the bank's stock. Member companies may also borrow from the member bank. Interlocking relationships allow the bank to monitor borrowings, strengthen relationships, and help with problems such as supplier networks.

It is argued that keiretsu relationships can increase efficiency (e.g. due to information sharing among customers, suppliers, and employees), leading to speedy investment decisions. The reduction of costs due to dealing with intra-keiretsu firms can also increase efficiency within the supply chain.

Questions for discussion

1. What advantages may be offered to a firm that is a member of a keiretsu or similar grouping?

2. Why is the idea of keiretsu a controversial concept for some commentators?

3. How to you think the idea of keiretsu might continue to evolve in the twenty-first century, for instance, as a result of modern communications and technology?

Sources

Aoki, K. and Lennerfors, T.T. (2013). The new, improved keiretsu (September), https://hbr.org/2013/09/the-new-improved-keiretsu (last accessed 18 August 2022).

Investopedia (2022). Understanding Japanese keiretsu (29 January), https://www.investopedia.com/articles/economics/09/japanese-keiretsu.asp (last accessed 18 August 2022).

CASE EXAMPLE 7.2 **STARBUCKS COFFEE COMPANY'S ORGANIZATIONAL STRUCTURE**

Starbucks is a world-famous coffee house chain, with over 32,000 stores in 80 countries. The organizational structure of Starbucks has been identified as an important part of its success. Its organizational structure has evolved over time to suit changing business needs; it is a matrix structure, which, as we saw earlier in this section, is a hybrid structure combining different structural dimensions.

The main features of Starbucks Coffee's organizational structure are:

- functional hierarchy;
- geographic divisions;
- product-based divisions;
- teams.

Functional hierarchy: indicates how the company's structure is grouped according to function or department, such as human resources, marketing, and finance. Each of these departments is led from the company's headquarters, which means that any decision made in the HR department in the company's headquarters impacts all the Starbucks cafés. This makes the company's functional structure hierarchical and facilitates a top-down management of the whole company, directed by the CEO.

Geographic divisions: Starbucks's organizational structure also involves geographic divisions, which allows it to offer a higher level of flexibility in order to respond to varying geographical needs to support the market conditions. This geographical structure is made up of three regional divisions to support Starbucks's global market: (a) China and Asia–Pacific; (b) the Americas; and (c) Europe, the Middle East, and Africa. Each manager reports to two superiors: the geographic head (e.g. President of US Operations) and the functional head (e.g. Corporate HR Manager).

Product-based divisions: a further way of dividing the company's organizational structure is by product, which allows Starbucks to focus its innovation and product development within specialized areas of the company. For example, apart from coffees and other beverages, Starbucks has other divisions for merchandise and for baked goods.

The organizational structure of Starbucks has been identified as an important part of its success. *Source*: Jiawei Zhao/Unsplash.com.

Teams: day-to-day in each Starbucks branch, teams are organized to deliver the best possible service to customers.

Questions for discussion

1. This case outlines how Starbucks's organizational structure aims to meet the firm's current business needs. Considering the advantages and disadvantages of the range of structures we have discussed so far, comment on how successfully Starbucks's organizational structure appears to help the company to achieve its strategic objectives.

Continued

2. What do you think are the possible advantages and disadvantages of the organizational structure that the firm has adopted—for example, choosing a form of hybrid structure?

3. How do think that the organizational structure of Starbucks might have to evolve in the future? Explain your answer.

Sources

Meyer, P. (2022). Starbucks's organizational structure and its characteristics (16 June), http://panmore.com/starbucks-coffee-company-organizational-structure (last accessed 18 August 2022).

Starbucks company profile, https://www.starbucks.com/about-us/company-information (last accessed 18 August 2022).

The advantages of a matrix structure are that it can:

- encourage overlapping businesses to collaborate to address relevant opportunities (e.g. developing strategies that bring together the range of product lines at Starbucks);

- integrate knowledge and learning across locations (e.g. Starbucks's senior team can take an overview of geographic locations, while local managers can adapt their activities to meet local needs);

- enable the flexibility required to adapt to changing strategic conditions (e.g. creating a renewed focus on customer experience in the case of Starbucks);

- enable two or more individuals to be responsible for strategic decision-making and accountability (e.g. at Starbucks, managers report to both a geographic head and a functional head).

Some of the disadvantages of a matrix structure are that it can:

- be confusing and slow if strategic decision-making involves several participants;

- lead to unclear job and task allocation if there is confusion around roles and responsibilities;

- lead to unclear responsibilities for costs and profits;

- generate tension and potential conflict between individuals in teams if they feel they have divided loyalties.

Some large, international organizations have chosen to adopt different structures in different parts of the world, perhaps driven by changes in their senior team at a particular time. For example, in 2012, GE moved away from a matrix structure in India, while retaining that structure in other parts of the world (Ganguly 2012). For GE, moving away from a matrix structure represented a decentralization of power in India, giving its managers on the ground permission to 'localize the business'. It allowed GE to try something different in a country that represented a very small percentage of its global business at that time.

However, such a decision can also lead to local managers feeling that they have lost the prestige that comes with reporting directly to the company's global headquarters. They may also feel that they have lost some autonomy as their strongest reporting line is now to the head of the local country rather than to an executive on the other side of the world. This illustrates the various complexities and tensions involved in designing an appropriate organizational structure for a very large organization operating in multiple businesses in multiple locations around the world.

Network structure

The network structure is a flexible, non-hierarchical structure in which a series of independent organizations or SBUs are grouped together. As such, it may comprise numerous individuals, project groups, or collaborations who are collectively designing, producing, and marketing a given product or service. All the participating entities are linked by formal or informal relationships (Figure 7.7). The essential feature of a network structure is that the boundaries of the organization are permeable and less distinct so that the organization becomes 'boundaryless' (Arthur and Rousseau 1996).

The majority of the productive activities of an organization with a network structure are outsourced to suppliers and distributors. As a result, its activities may be spread worldwide. Staff may not be employed on a long-term basis; they may instead be hired for specific projects for particular periods of time based on the skills and competencies they offer.

The network structure is common in dynamic and complex environments in which an organization needs to be responsive in terms of its creativity and innovation if it is to be effective and to be able to demonstrate a clear competitive advantage.

The advantages of the network structure are that it gives an organization the flexibility needed to respond to rapid changes and allows it to focus on its areas of particular competence, while drawing on distinct areas of expertise and benefiting from efficiencies exhibited by other firms.

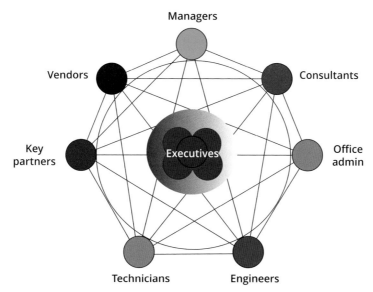

NETWORK ORGANIZATION

FIGURE 7.7 Example of a network structure. *Source*: authors.

What are the possible disadvantages of the network structure?

- Relationships are transitional, unstable, and subject to tensions.

- High levels of trust are required.

- Cultures may diverge as the organizations making up the network evolve over time.

- The coordination required to make the parties operate collaboratively can be time consuming and resource intensive, but such coordination must happen if economies of scale and scope are to be achieved.

- An organization may inhibit its own development and operational optimization by continually outsourcing activities.

The transnational structure

This configuration enables an organization to operate effectively on an international scale and can help to spread knowledge across geographic borders. The transnational structure seeks to maximize the benefits from two extreme international strategies: the multidomestic strategy and the global strategy.

- A **multidomestic strategy** involves a portfolio of separate national companies with a coordinating centre, where the separate national companies have little contact or interaction with each other.

- A **global strategy** involves an organization making the same product available in many different national markets (Segal-Horn and Faulkner 2010). In so doing, the organization attempts to benefit from economies of scale by standardizing its product offer.

A global strategy is supported by global product divisions (e.g. worldwide manufacturing systems), whereas a multidomestic strategy is supported by local subsidiaries, each with a substantial amount of autonomy with respect to the design, manufacture, and marketing of products.

A transnational structure seeks to combine the best of both global and multidomestic approaches. A famous example is HSBC. A long-running advertising campaign, launched in 2002, positioned HSBC as 'The world's local bank'. More recently, its 'We are not an island' campaign was designed to champion the United Kingdom's internationalism (Stewart 2020). HSBC sees itself a bank that has many global connections yet is still flexible enough to care for the needs of local customers (Renteria 2010). The term 'glocalization' has been coined to describe this approach, which essentially aligns high local responsiveness with high global coordination—in other words, the benefits of globally coordinated operation, particularly in terms of scale and scope, are coupled with the merits of being flexible enough to adapt to local market needs.

The transnational configuration has the following characteristics.

- Each national unit operates independently but is a source of ideas and capabilities for the whole corporation. For example, in the oil and gas sector, new technologies developed in one location can then be rolled out around the world. BP points to the deployment of its 'big data' Argus platform for use at 99.5% of its wells, aiming to support critical decisions with state-of-the-art analytical tools (Looney 2017).

- National units achieve greater scale economies through specialization on behalf of the whole corporation, or at least by dividing operations into large regions. Again, BP provides an interesting example of a firm with its roots in a particular location but with key activities around the world. BP is a British multinational oil and gas company headquartered in London, yet nearly one-third of its global business interests are in the United States, and it has important operations in Iraq, Oman, Egypt, Angola, India, the South China Sea, Australia, and Azerbaijan, as well as other locations around the world.

- The corporate centre manages the global network by first establishing the role of each business unit and then sustaining the systems and relationships to make the network of business units operate effectively. In the HSBC example, the intention was to provide a familiar customer experience around the world, despite national variation in the features of products and services.

What are the disadvantages of a transnational structure?

- It requires managers to be willing to focus their work on both local *and* international responsibilities simultaneously, which can be demanding.

- Responsibilities at the local and the global level can be both complex and confusing and potentially even in conflict, placing additional strain on individuals.

- Internal politics may overshadow effective work.

Innovation-orientated structures

The final two configurations described here are the project-based structure and adhocracies. Both structures are associated with a particular intention on the part of an organization to innovate. They share many of the characteristics of network organizations, as described in the section on the network structure, but they go even further in pursuit of dynamic flexibility.

Project-based structure

In this configuration, teams are created, undertake their work (e.g. on a contract basis), usually for a fixed time-span, and then dissolve. Such a structure can be particularly appropriate for organizations that deliver large and expensive goods or services (such as major projects in the fields of civil engineering or information technology) or those delivering time-limited events (such as sporting events, festivals, or large consultancy engagements). The organization structure comprises a constantly changing collection of project teams that are overseen by a small corporate group. Many organizations use such teams on an impromptu basis to complement the 'main' organizational structure. For instance, high-tech companies such as Vodafone, Sharp, Sony, NTT, Mitsubishi Electric, and Matsushita Electric often exhibit project-based structures (Kodama 2007).

What are the advantages of a project-based structure?

- It is highly flexible—projects can be established and dissolved as required. This can be vital in a fast-moving environment, where organizations need to bring together and exploit individual knowledge and competencies quickly and in novel ways.

- It makes accountability and control mechanisms transparent because project teams have defined tasks to achieve with defined timescales.

- Knowledge exchange is effective because project members can be drawn from different departments within an organization.

- Individuals may be more willing to work in different locations around the world because of the relatively short timelines involved, hence making it possible to assemble teams that draw from an organization's global talent pool.

The project-based structure also has potential disadvantages.

- The success of project-based structures can lead to them being used inappropriately, whereby there is an attempt to use them to sort out any and every problem.
- If projects do not have strong programme management, they may drift in focus or activity.
- The constant formation and disbanding of project teams—and associated movement and reassignment of individuals from across an organization—can hinder the development of specialist knowledge and expertise, which may delay organizational learning.

Adhocracies

Mintzberg (1989) suggests that adhocracies are innovation-orientated organizational forms. They have a flexible organic structure with few formal constraints, thereby offering the maximum potential for innovation. They encourage diverse experts to interact and focus on client needs and best practices (Dolan 2010). The emphasis is on an organization's ability to innovate and be creative in an environment in which knowledge is the key strategic asset.

Adhocracies rely on a variety of expertise to win business and are primarily organized around experts or areas of expertise. They may be young firms that rely on one or more charismatic and entrepreneurial founding members to lead the organization. It has been suggested that NASA functioned as an **adhocracy** in its first dozen or so years (Desveaux 2012). It was created in the wake of failures and conflicts between branches of the US military and was given considerable autonomy and a clear problem-solving mandate—to land people safely on the Moon within a decade.

Adhocracies have also been described as 'cellular' (Miles et al. 1997) because they must be highly fluid and adaptive to change while performing complex tasks.

Adhocratic organizations may feature the coordinated operation of multifunctional teams. For example, the UK-based pharmaceutical firm GlaxoSmithKline has broken its drug discovery operation into about 40 units that compete with one another for funding (Birkinshaw and Ridderstale 2015). These configurations are similar to the project-based structure as their focus is driven by the design, development, and delivery of tailor-made projects. The key difference is timescale: project teams tend to be set up for a specific purpose for a fixed period of time, while adhocracies are ongoing configurations.

Adhocracies tend to remove hierarchical layers and 'flatten' the organization wherever possible, with the point of contact with the customer assuming particular importance. For instance, Zappos, the online shoe and clothing retailer, is famous for its ability to deliver an excellent customer experience, based partly on the ability of the customer service staff to understand and deliver what the client wants (Solomon 2018; Frampton 2020). Adhocracies also strive to respond quickly and responsively to customer needs. For example, Zappos offers thousands of product lines and the ability to customize the product to meet the needs of an individual customer. Such an approach requires a departure from the centralized command-and-control mode that we typically see in complex structures.

Access the online resources to watch a short video clip where Gordon Ramsay discusses innovation and implementation.

Organizational structures: The reality

It is important to note that, in reality, few organizations adopt a structure that is exactly like one of the pure structural configurations we have discussed. Similarly, it would be an oversimplification to say that a company adopts one form and has no traces of any of the other types within its structure. In practice, an organization may exhibit many micro-structures within one or more macro-structures. As a consequence, an organization may adopt a blend of different structures that have either been consciously formed or have evolved as the organization has faced and responded to new challenges.

How do strategic leaders choose organizational structure?

We have discussed a range of structural configurations (with the caveat that organizations often use a blend of these types). But how do strategic leaders choose which organizational structure to adopt? Goold and Campbell (2002) offer nine design tests for strategic leaders making a conscious decision to adopt a specific organizational structure. Strategic leaders can evaluate their proposals for possible organizational structures against these nine tests in order to identify a suitable configuration for their organization. This can be a useful way for strategic practitioners to assess whether the formal structure they are working to establish is appropriate and covers the main issues they are seeking to address. The first four tests emphasize the need for a good fit between the proposed structure and the key goals of the organization.

- **The market advantage test**: if we think of Chandler's dictum that 'structure follows strategy', we can see that this test, which represents a test of fit between the firm's structure and its market strategy, is very important. For example, if coordination between two steps in a production process is important to market advantage, then these steps should probably be placed in the same structural unit.

- **The parenting advantage test**: this test holds that there should be a good fit between the organization's structure and the parenting role of the corporate centre. For example, if the corporate centre aims to add value as a manager of synergy, it should design a structure that places important integrative specialisms (such as marketing or research) at the centre. Recall the case study of Toyota that opened this chapter: in the company's traditional structure, decision-making and power were centralized at headquarters, with little delegation of authority or communication between business units around the world. More recently, geographic divisions and product-based divisions were introduced to support a new, less centralized approach to decision-making.

- **The people test**: this maintains that there must be a good fit between the organization's structure and the people available to fill key roles. For example, it is dangerous to switch completely from a functional structure to a multidivisional structure if, as is likely, the organization lacks managers with competence in running decentralized business units.

- **The feasibility test**: this test can be seen as a catch-all category. It reminds us that the structure must fit with a range of constraints that the organization has to address—perhaps including legal constraints or pressures from important stakeholders such as trade unions. Rumelt (2011) gives the example of International Harvester's new strategic plan, which involved structural changes such as cutting costs and strengthening networks. Unfortunately, the plan did not mention important obstacles such as the firm's very poor labour relations or its very inefficient production facilities—and most of the business was sold off a few years later.

These four tests are an important starting point when choosing an appropriate structural design as they highlight a range of important aspects that should not be overlooked. However, Goold and Campbell (2002) go further in identifying five more tests, with the aim of exploring whether the proposed organizational structure appears to be based on good general design principles.

- **The specialized cultures test**: this test is based on the notion that a good organizational design brings together specialist staff. This is important as it allows specialists to develop their expertise in close collaboration with each other. Therefore, a structure will fail this test if it breaks up important specialist cultures.

- **The difficult links test**: this test asks us to consider whether a proposed structure will set up links between parts of the organization where good relationships are important, but such relationships are also likely to be strained. For example, extreme decentralization to profit-accountable business units may strain relationships with a central R&D department. This kind of structure may fail if compensating mechanisms are not put in place.

- **The redundant hierarchy test**: this test reminds us that a proposed structure should be checked in case it has too many layers of management. Redundant levels of hierarchy can cause unnecessary blockages and associated costs for the firm.

- **The accountability test**: this test stresses the importance of clear lines of accountability. The aim is to ensure that managers throughout the organizational structure are totally committed to achieving the organization's goals and are accountable for delivery against the organizational strategy. For example, matrix structures are sometimes accused of lacking clear accountability as managers tend to have dual lines of reporting under such structures.

- **The flexibility test**: another important test is the extent to which an organizational design will allow for change in the future, perhaps in response to changes in a fast-moving external environment; for example, divisional domains should be specified in a sufficiently broad manner to allow divisional managers to follow new opportunities as they emerge.

Kranias (2000) gives a good example of a situation where we can put the nine tests into practice by discussing the case of Japanese multinational companies entering the United Kingdom and the choices that they have made with regard to organizational structure and fit to strategy. Table 7.2 explains why establishing a subsidiary in the United Kingdom (typically following a transnational structure, as discussed in this chapter) represents a fit between strategy and structure for the company.

Goold and Campbell's nine tests provide a useful screening device for forming an effective configuration. However, even if a structural design passes these tests, the structure still needs to match with other aspects of the organization's configuration, processes, and relationships.

TABLE 7.2 **Examples of 'fit' for a Japanese multinational company**

Test	Examples of 'fit' for a Japanese multinational company
The **market advantage test**	• The Japanese firm depends on foreign markets for the supply of raw materials and as export markets for its production • A UK subsidiary may protect the firm against increasing land prices and labour costs in Japan • It may also protect the firm from any increase in protectionism against Japanese products in the world market and against currency fluctuations
The **parenting advantage test**	• The corporate parent controls all operations worldwide and is the source of competitive advantage • Information flows from the centre to the subsidiaries • All subsidiaries are part of the corporate value chain and participate in corporate strategy • Strong centralization is necessary for the coordination of global operations
The **people test**	• Japan is a unique country, relatively isolated from the rest of the world and with a unique culture • The prospect of long-term employment changes both the attitude of the employee towards the company and also the attitude of the company towards the employee, that is, the company considers the employee to be an asset
The **feasibility test**	• Many Japanese firms have seen the United Kingdom not only as a big market but also as a gateway to European markets • The UK economy has been seen as stable • UK legislation and taxes have been seen as favourable • The United Kingdom has also been seen as an attractive location because of the language, and the availability of knowledge-based resources
The **specialized cultures test**	• Japanese firms tend to have non-specialized career paths, which are seen as immersing the employee in the overall philosophy of the organization • Through rotation to different functional areas, the employees encounter and absorb the corporate ideology
The **difficult links test**	• The traditional separation of sales and manufacturing in Japanese multinational companies is one of the reasons why this configuration is appropriate • The separation is motivated by the desire to improve information sharing and achieve better customer service, and there is a general preference for keeping specialized activities separate
The **redundant hierarchy test**	• Japanese expatriate managers tend to assume the top positions in the management hierarchy of the subsidiary company • Expatriates also tend to play a connecting role between the corporate centre in Japan and the subsidiary in the United Kingdom • Expatriates attempt to pass on the corporate philosophy to the subsidiary; their presence in the overseas subsidiary is typically temporary (e.g. not exceeding three years) • Local managers may assume (for example) second and third places in the hierarchy of the UK subsidiary company

Continued

7

TABLE 7.2 *Continued*

Test	Examples of 'fit' for a Japanese multinational company
The **accountability test**	• Although the control exercised by the centre is typically rather flexible, the system of reporting to the centre is detailed • These companies tend to focus on planning procedures, both formal and informal, long-term and short-term • The centre takes a proactive role by setting strategic priorities and actively participating in business-level strategies
The **flexibility test**	• The strategic goal of the company is to increase its flexibility in the face of demands from European markets • The European market is felt to be quite complex, for example, consisting of multiple languages, which, in practice, may mean that a range of different products have to be produced in relatively small volumes • Flexibility can also be translated into a reduction in stock levels. The proximity of customers can reduce lead times and stock levels may be kept as low as possible (e.g. with customers holding just a few days' worth of stock), hence production occurs in small and specific quantities as ordered • The centre tends to reduce its pressure on its overseas operations in the United Kingdom over time. The management tends to become more localized and the subsidiaries more orientated towards meeting the needs of the European market. The centre, and consequently the subsidiaries, tend to realize that their role is to satisfy a different market and not necessarily to attempt to implement the espoused corporate strategy even at the cost of adopting the flexibility required.

Source: authors.

7.3 Impact of systems on strategy

We have looked at the link between strategy and structure and considered the main structural forms in organizations. But within any given organizational structure, how do things get done? All organizations, whatever their broad structural form, will have a number of systems and routines in place. Systems can be thought of as the micro-structures that make organizations work. In Chapter 6, we consider an activity system that could explain competitive advantage from a resource-based view. In this section, we take a broader look at what systems are and why they are so important to the practice of strategy. We explore different types of operational and control systems, and we introduce levers of control (Simons 1995)—a comprehensive approach to the establishment of control systems in organizations that operate in environments where they experience rapid and continuous change. We end the section by discussing 'control via simple rules' as advocated for organizations in turbulent environments where high levels of flexibility and creativity are also required (Eisenhardt and Sull 2001).

What are systems?

In organizational terms, a system can be described as a micro-structure that actually makes an organization work. A system tells people and machines what to do, monitors performance, and provides a means by which to evaluate an organization's overall performance. As such, systems are the building blocks from which capabilities develop; they can make important connections between long-term strategy and short-term actions, supporting communication, planning, feedback, and learning (Kaplan and Norton 1996).

Routines are a particularly important subset of systems in strategic terms because they can be the source of competitive advantage for an organization. At an organizational level, a routine can be considered 'the way we do things around here'; they tend to persist over time and guide people's behaviour. We can think of them as being to the organization what skills are to the individual. A routine increases efficiency and effectiveness by encapsulating the knowledge that is necessary for the standardized performance of a task. Systems provide the link between strategy and operational effectiveness.

Systems perform in two ways.

- **As operational systems**: that is, those mechanisms, including working practices and routines, that underlie the efficient use and deployment of resources and capabilities, for instance, the order fulfilment system in a warehouse, where customer orders that have been placed online are picked and prepared for distribution.

- **As control systems**: that is, those mechanisms that monitor the achievement of strategic goals, for instance, a system that monitors the number of items manufactured per week that meet the required quality standards or the proportion of an airline's flights that arrive at their destination on time. This type of control system relates to the discussion in Chapter 4 of the use of performance indicators as part of deploying systems of goals and objectives; and we can discuss control systems further in relation to Case Example 7.3, AB, InBev.

Why are systems important?

Systems enable, specify, guide, and control behaviours in an organization. They allow the resources and capabilities of an organization to interact in order to create value. They both facilitate activity and control it. As such, they are key to the implementation of strategy. Examples include cost control systems, performance evaluation systems, and reward systems to incentivize staff to focus on certain tasks.

If an organization's strategy and systems don't align, the organization will struggle to implement its planned strategy successfully. For example, a business may be growing so fast that its systems have difficulty keeping up or they develop in directions which are less than ideal; a performance management system may encourage staff to continue to pursue good scores on previously defined performance metrics, even when those metrics are no longer aligned with the organizational strategy. Pongatichat and Johnston (2008) point out that this is an important problem in public-sector organizations as well as private ones:

With three or four tiers of government and elections for each tier every three or four years, new and sometimes distinctly different political agendas may be suddenly forced on the organization. Indeed a change in the political domination in a council (city, borough, county, region or central) may lead to the complete reversal of some policies which will not only affect that level but also all the tiers below it.

Pongatichat and Johnston (2008: 210–11)

In dynamic environments, **operational systems** must include features that allow the organization to change core capabilities over time—for example, in production, technology, or marketing. Without such an ability to change, or dynamic capability, an organization will be unable to learn, innovate, and seize emerging opportunities in products and markets. Operational systems that embody these qualities may be genuine sources of distinctiveness.

We now look at how operational systems can help or hinder an organization to learn and develop.

Operational systems as learning

We know from everyday experience that we learn some things through word of mouth and simply 'having a go', while other learning is more structured: we learn by reading things that are written down (they are 'codified'). The former type of learning encapsulates the acquisition of tacit knowledge, that is, knowledge that is less easily written down.

Organizations face challenges when it comes to the development of systems because the knowledge underlying some skills is largely tacit in nature; it is difficult to articulate and is more easily expressed through performance (Tsoukas 2005). For example, a customer service representative may learn how to deal with difficult customers by experiencing many interactions over time. Through these experiences, the representative can learn how to respond in certain situations. Customer service training can help to a certain extent, but it typically takes experience and practice to learn successful responses. It is difficult to give every example in training, so having an experienced person on hand to mentor new employees can help transfer that knowledge and experience to them.

Tacit systems are ways of doing things that are essentially assumed knowledge: members of an organization take the knowledge needed to do that thing for granted to the point where that knowledge is never written down. Codified systems, on the other hand, are explicitly documented. One could argue that this difference distinguishes routines from systems: routines often embody tacit knowledge, while systems tend to be more explicit.

Implementing strategy requires the integration of many types of knowledge embodied in people and practices across the organization (e.g. Bryson et al. 2009). In a dynamic environment, it can be difficult for organizations to achieve this integration while preserving their operational efficiency. Operational systems can contribute to making the process of integrating knowledge more efficient and also enable the organization to use its knowledge to adapt to its changing circumstances. This is achieved through organizational learning. Routines are key: firms may use routines to help support decisions such as the choice of product designs or the setting of production levels.

The process of learning is likely to be different for every organization. A small organization with a flat hierarchy may be able to achieve close and frequent face-to-face contact between the key people that work there. This means that operational systems need to be flexible to support these interactions. In contrast, in large organizations with complex structures, there is a danger that the operational systems can become sources of inefficiency. In other words, they become such a routine part of day-to-day working that, over time, the organization becomes slow and unresponsive to change as bureaucratic rigidity gradually takes hold. Garvin suggests that this points to a dual challenge: 'a learning organization is an organization skilled at creating, acquiring, and transferring knowledge, and at modifying its behavior to reflect new knowledge and insights' (Garvin 1993: 80). This suggests that the successful management of strategy can require processes of unlearning (Nystrom and Starbuck 1984) and that managers must recognize this. Existing capabilities can become obsolete because of significant environmental shifts; they need to be unlearned in order to adapt new and better ways of doing things.

Montgomery (2008) makes a similar point when she argues that the search for competitive advantage can leave organizations blinkered: they fail to evolve their activities over time. Unless organizations are prepared to evolve, to give up old ways of doing things and adopt new ones, they risk becoming locked into an outmoded view of their own success. For newer recruits, the problem may be less about unlearning and more about ensuring that they really 'get' the organization's strategy—a concept sometimes referred to as 'embeddedness', which is affected by job conditions (such as training opportunities and a clear development path) and also by perceptions of and trust in top management (Galunic and Hermreck 2012).

Control systems

Having considered the different ways in which an organization can be structured, we may find ourselves asking: within a given structure, how does an organization ensure that its employees act in a way that is consistent with its agreed strategy? To answer this question, we explore how control systems help an organization to remain focused on its strategic goals.

Control systems align individuals, locations, and activities with strategic decisions and provide ways to monitor performance against strategic goals. Control systems take different shapes and forms, with some being imposed by outside stakeholders and others being chosen by management. As we see for structural configurations, different organizations require different control systems: it is not a case that 'one size fits all'. We illustrate this by looking at two different types of control systems—financial and dynamic. We finish with an alternative to a control system—control via simple rules.

Financial control systems

In many organizations, the management of performance focuses on the monitoring of finances and budgets, with 'numbers' being used to define budgetary activities and set financial targets. As such, the budgetary process involves setting and monitoring financial estimates—in relation to both income and expenditure—for a fixed period (e.g. a financial year) for the organization as a whole and often for different levels within the organization.

Budgets can be considered to have three purposes: they provide a forecast of future income and expenditure, they represent targets against which required financial performance can be measured, and they represent limits of authority (levels of expenditure up to which spending has been approved).

Budgets are often reviewed and established annually: the previous year's performance is reviewed, and future forecasts are set out (typically over an agreed time period such as three years, for example). The budgetary process may also be a vehicle for analysing the impact of implementing strategic initiatives. While conventional accounting practices and policies exist, organizations vary when it comes to presenting their financial plans. This diversity makes the use of financial plans potentially ambiguous. Generally, the more complex the organization, the more sophisticated and formalized the **financial control systems** are likely to be.

Such financial planning and budgetary control processes also apply to not-for-profit organizations where financial integrity and accountability are of paramount importance. In order to remain fully informed of financial performance, the trustees of most charitable organizations (being accountable to the relevant authority, such as the Charity Commission for England and Wales) will require regular statements covering the financial health of the organization. Examples of such reports include income and expense statements, balance sheets, and cash flow statements.

If financial control is mismanaged in any way, the consequences for an organization can be disastrous. In the **third sector**, which includes charitable organizations, financial control mismanagement is perhaps particularly catastrophic because of the potential loss of trust which can ensue. For example, the reasons behind the closure of Kids Company in the United Kingdom in 2015 received a great deal of analysis in the media. When the charity closed, it said its finances had become stretched because of the number of children needing help. But donors had apparently been withdrawing their support, alarmed by stories of alleged mismanagement (BBC 2016). Earlier that summer, the charity had said that it wanted to restructure and had sought new funds from the UK government and donors. But when it finally closed in August 2015, government ministers said that they wanted to recover a £3 million grant given to the charity a week before. Criticisms included lavish spending and mismanagement, and—in the eyes of the media—the charity's chief executive, formerly seen as an inspirational leader, was labelled a 'disgrace' (Renegade Inc. 2017). The charity was accused of a 'chronic failure of governance' and 'insularity', that is, resisting peer-led scrutiny (Ilott 2016). After a legal case lasting more than three-and-a-half years, the chief executive and other trustees were finally cleared of personal wrongdoing (Casciani 2021; Butler 2021). However, the case illustrates that control must be rigorous and any assessment of strategic performance must be open to the inclusion of issues other than financial criteria alone, such as the ethical behaviour of employees and their achievements.

Dynamic control systems

There is obviously a balance to be struck between the control needed to maintain an organization's activities within agreed strategic parameters and the flexibility needed to foster creativity and innovation, particularly in organizations faced with continuous change. Robert Simons (1995) argues that an effective **dynamic control system** is one that promotes the strategic flexibility and innovative capabilities that the organization needs to adapt to change but in a controlled manner.

Unlike the **financial control systems** discussed in the previous section, Simons' approach to control brings together both feedback and feedforward mechanisms according to broader organizational criteria, such as an organization's culture. Using strong empirical evidence, he describes four 'levers' of control which, when used collectively, can reconcile the conflict between flexibility and control. The interrelationships between these levers are shown in Figure 7.8. We can explore each of these four levers in a little more detail, as follows.

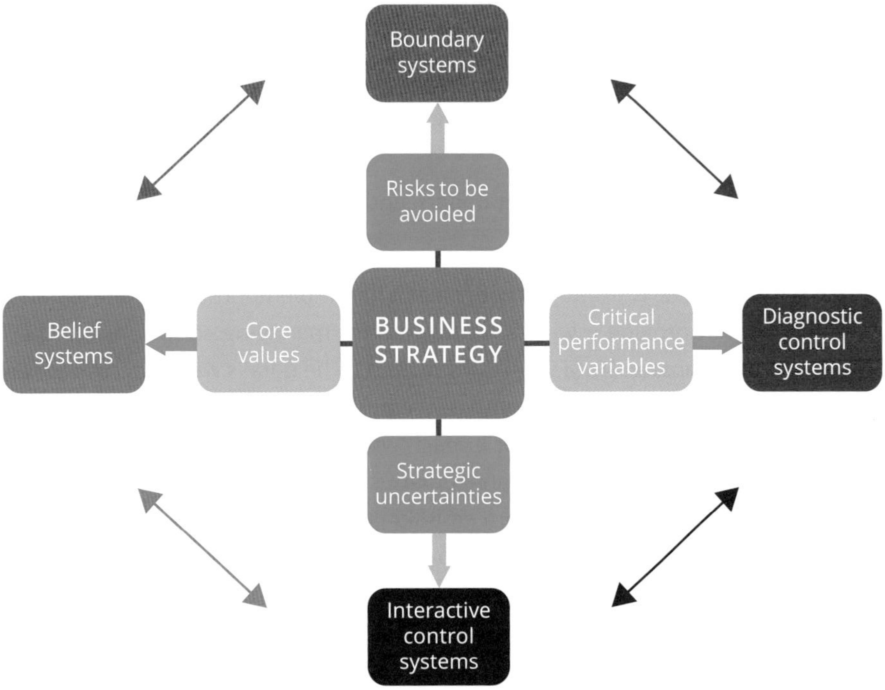

FIGURE 7.8 Levers of control. *Source*: from Simons, R. (1995). *Levers of Control: How Managers Use Innovative Control Systems to Drive Strategic Renewal*. Boston, MA: Harvard Business School Press. By permission of Harvard Business Publishing.

- **Belief systems**: these are the explicit values of the organization, encapsulated in its mission statement and purpose. They inspire and guide the strategy process and provide a framework for implementation decisions. Typically, expressions of belief systems are concise and inspirational. For example, Twitter say that 'our service shows the world what's happening and democratizes access to information' (Twitter 2021). Belief systems promote the commitment of employees to the organization's core values in pursuing its strategic goals.

- **Boundary systems**: these indicate the boundaries of the 'acceptable domain of activity' of an organization and can be closely associated with its belief system. Codes of conduct and ethical principles are examples of 'business conduct boundaries', while planning documents, which define the scope of an organization's activities, are 'strategic boundary systems'. Simons (1995) suggests that these act as an 'organization's brakes' and that every organization needs them to avoid both activities that are off-limits and unacceptable risks. A famous example is Bill Gates's statement of what Microsoft was *not* going to be: they weren't going into hardware (e.g. Brant 2016).

- **Interactive control systems**: these stimulate search and learning, permitting new strategies to develop throughout the organization as individuals respond to perceived opportunities and threats. Here, the focus is on strategic uncertainties and challenging existing assumptions. Typically, an effective interactive control should include four distinct features:

— it keeps strategic information up-to-date for management;

— the information is organized and accessible to managers at all levels in the organization;

— it encourages strategic decision-making in a process of dialogue between superiors, subordinates, and peers;

— it serves as a catalyst for ongoing debate and critical thinking about underlying data, assumptions, and action plans.

For example, Tata Steel is proud to report that it has implemented environmental management systems that provide it with 'a framework for managing compliance and achieving continuous improvement' (Tata Steel Europe 2021). The data is widely accessible and used as a basis for critical debate. The company requires appropriate strategic information in order to minimize its environmental impact 'wherever practicable and cost-effective to do so'. Tata Steel's environmental management systems enable them to monitor its main potential environmental impacts (from emissions to air of particulates, oxides of nitrogen, sulphur dioxide, and carbon dioxide and to water of hydrocarbons and suspended solids), as well as to report annually on its energy usage and waste treatment activities.

- **Diagnostic control systems**: these allow managers to measure outputs and compare them with expected standards of performance over defined time periods. Managers can then adjust and modify inputs and processes in the light of these analyses to ensure that future outputs more closely match organizational targets. Such diagnostic systems help managers to track the progress of individuals and divisions towards the achievement of strategically important goals. An example is the formal review of performance in regular meetings at board, departmental, and team level, commonly referred to as appraisals.

CASE EXAMPLE 7.3 SYSTEMS FOR ESG REPORTING AT AB INBEV

Many organizations publish reports to evidence the environmental, social and governance (ESG) impacts of their activities. ESG reports can be a valuable communication tool in convincing important stakeholders about the value of the organization's activities. However, an organization that wishes to publish such a report must first put in place systems to collect the necessary information; poor data is frequently a major hurdle in ESG reporting.

The world's largest brewer, Anheuser-Busch InBev (known as AB InBev) uses external third parties to verify its ESG reporting. However, when it comes to internal resources, rather than creating a dedicated ESG reporting team, it relies on different business units from procurement to logistics to track the necessary data. The company issued its first ESG report for the year 2020. 'Investors were asking for a lot more information and context to understand the mission, the lessons learned and vision forward', commented Ezgi Barcenas, the company's global head of sustainability.

AB InBev's ESG report for 2020 gives a range of examples that illustrate Simons' levers of control, including:

- **Belief systems**: on renewable energy and land rights, 'We believe our goal to reach 100% purchased renewable electricity is a transformational goal that will also bring additional benefits to local communities.'

FIGURE 7.9 AB InBev ESG report. *Source*: Ab-inbev.com (2020). 2020 Environmental, Social and Governance Report, https://www.ab-inbev.com/news-media/latest-headlines/esg-report (last accessed 18 August 2022).

- **Boundary systems**: the world's largest brewer is keen to establish its place in the global market for no- and low-alcohol (NABLAB) beers, saying, 'we aim to have NABLAB products represent at least 20% of our global beer volume by the end of 2025'.

- **Interactive control systems**: the company points to innovative local sourcing policies and its commitment to produce local beers like Eagle Lager in Zambia or Magnífica in Brazil with alternative starch sources, creating 'new sources of income for crops like cassava and sorghum that have historically been grown as subsistence crops'.

- **Diagnostic control systems**: the company aims to work with retailers and suppliers, understanding their strengths and opportunities for development.

These examples and more are summarized in Figure 7.9, which is taken from the AB InBev ESG report.

Continued

Questions for discussion

1. Give some examples of the ways in which control systems at AB InBev might be used to align individuals, locations, and activities with its strategic goals.

2. Give some examples of the ways in which control systems at AB InBev might be used to monitor performance against strategic goals.

Sources

Ab-inbev.com (2020). 2020 Environmental, Social and Governance Report, https://www.ab-inbev.com/news-media/latest-headlines/esg-report (last accessed 18 August 2022).

Murray, S. (2021) Measuring what matters: The scramble to set standards for sustainable business (14 May), https://www.ft.com/content/92915630-c110-4364-86ee-0f6f018cba90 (last accessed 18 August 2022).

Control via simple rules

Is Simons' model sufficiently flexible to be applied in highly turbulent and relatively creative environments? Eisenhardt and Sull (2001) argue that such environments require an altogether different perspective on control. They give examples of organizations which have done remarkably well in highly chaotic environments, despite few apparent resources, and which have used constantly evolving strategies to make the most of unanticipated one-off opportunities. Sull and Eisenhardt (2012) give the example of ALL (América Latina Logística), which prioritized capital expenditure by asking whether proposals:

- removed obstacles to growing revenues;
- minimized up-front expenditure;
- provided benefits immediately (rather than paying off in the long term);
- reused existing resources.

Examples such as ALL suggest that the organization succeeded by learning to handle strategy as a set of simple rules. Such an approach could work for a wide range of organizations, not least because of the profound impact the new economy has had on all manner of firms whereby they must now capture unanticipated opportunities in order to succeed. Managers of such companies—like Yahoo!, according to Eisenhardt and Sull (2001)—know that the greatest opportunities for competitive advantage lie in market confusion, so they jump into chaotic markets and shift flexibly among opportunities as circumstances dictate. Yahoo! had a clear focus on product innovation, supported by simple rules such as to know the priority rank of each product in development and to ensure that every engineer could work on every project (Eisenhardt and Sull 2001).

Control by simple rules rather than complicated systems is an approach most suited to organizations in the new economy—organizations that have to survive in markets that are both rapidly changing and ambiguous. Sull and Eisenhardt (2012) give the example of Skrill, a provider of online payment services. Skrill decided to woo business from digital service providers like Skype and Facebook. Skrill was faced with hundreds of ideas for payment options it could develop for such customers and had to weigh up complex trade-offs when deciding which opportunities to pursue. Selecting which payment options to adopt became Skrill's critical bottleneck. A cross-functional team was convened; before the meeting, each team member articulated the rules that his or her function would use to evaluate alternatives. The team negotiated all the ideas down to a handful of rules, such as 'The customer can complete payment in fewer than five steps' and 'More than one existing customer requested the payment option.'

It is important to note, then, that simple strategy rules are not broad or vague. Rather, they are specific and flexible, so that managers can approach each opportunity in a controlled and disciplined manner. The simple rules proposed by Eisenhardt and Sull (2001: 114) fall into five broad categories:

- **How-to rules**: these spell out key features of how a process is executed (in the Skrill example, the firm focused on payment options that could be completed in less than five steps).
- **Boundary rules**: these encourage managers to focus on which opportunities can be pursued and which are outside the organization's scope (again, in the Skrill example, they chose options that were requested by more than one existing customer as being within the scope).
- **Priority rules**: these help managers rank the accepted opportunities (see the ALL example).
- **Timing rules**: these help managers synchronize the pace of emerging opportunities with other parts of the organization; this might include prioritizing projects where a strong cross-functional team can be put together and pulling out of projects where key skills may be lacking or key members of staff are leaving the organization.
- **Exit rules**: these help managers to decide when to pull out of yesterday's opportunities; this might include cancelling a project when financial returns do not come in according to previously agreed plans.

To be effective, simple rules must relate to a single process and must be frequently reviewed to keep in step with the rapidly changing contexts they are put in place to operate within. It is also important to minimize the number of rules: Eisenhardt and Sull (2001) recommend between two and seven rules. Their research found that young companies often had too few rules to be effective and more mature companies often had too many.

7.4 **International strategy and structure**

Why do many firms wish to internationalize and what are the perceived economic, operational, and competitive drivers and potential benefits? We will consider these questions, review the different ways in which firms can go about internationalizing, and look at the different conditions under which internationalization may or may not be a robust strategy. We discuss international strategy in greater depth in Chapter 12, when we explore globalization. However, the key themes for this chapter are the international configuration of the international firm and a process approach to internationalization.

Why internationalize?

Until the end of the nineteenth century, international trade was dominated by trading companies or investment houses. Since then, international trade has become increasingly dominated by **multinational corporations (MNCs)**. The difference between the former and the latter is that while the activities of the former were conducted from a base in their domestic markets, the activities of MNCs are based on **foreign direct investment (FDI)**, that is, locating part of the firm's activities—perhaps design, manufacturing, assembly, sales, distribution, or R&D—in other countries (countries that are not the firm's home country). What is more, these investments tend to be actively managed as single operational entities within a unified corporation.

MNCs are complex organizations. They are difficult to manage; they may decline into dysfunctional bureaucracies; they can be inflexible, unresponsive, and slow to change; they sometimes attract negative coverage in the media; and they can be unpopular with the public. So what is the purpose of the MNC in the twenty-first century?

Perhaps the main strategic benefit in being an MNC is that it should provide the organization with flexibility—with a range of strategic options. The firm can choose between a range of ways of pursuing its international strategy. Much domestic market strategy is likely to be defensive, that is, trying to protect existing positions. However, much of the world's trade is across borders. MNCs have a wider range of strategies open to them because they are international and operate across borders. Despite some cross-border global and regional integration, international integration is incomplete, and this allows MNCs to benefit from market imperfections—making international strategy different from national strategy.

Ghemawat (2003) calls this incomplete state of cross-border integration 'semi-globalization'. He makes the point that international strategies take account of such market imperfections in their formulation and implementation. If the world really were one 'global village', global strategies would be irrelevant—they would be the same as domestic strategy.

Governments and MNCs

Governments and supranational organizations can erect regulatory, institutional, and tariff barriers to trade, while MNCs can attempt to configure their international operations to exploit those barriers which favour them and avoid those which do not. Such trade barriers may include:

- high tariffs;
- import quota systems;
- refusal to sanction licences;
- nationalistic purchasing and ownership policies;
- centralized 'command' economies;
- excessively nationalistic domestic demand.

Governments tax immobile assets and nationally based consumption and try to set corporation taxes at levels which will provide them with useful sources of tax revenue without forcing corporations to shift their investments in jobs, buildings, research, or technology to other locations. Governments seek to attract high-quality inward investment by MNCs into their countries by offering capital gains, regional grants (e.g. in employment 'black spots'), tax-free zones, and so on.

MNCs: What, when, and why?

MNCs are companies which have part of their activities located outside their home country and operate in international markets. In MNCs, comparative costs, risks, and regulatory context may influence where a particular activity is carried out. International trade may be carried out in different ways. The four main types of international trade are:

- exporting;
- FDI—the defining characteristic of MNCs;
- licensing;
- joint ventures, strategic alliances, and the like.

The theory of FDI, and of alternative organizational forms to develop business across frontiers, is set out in a simple way via the OLI framework (Collinson et al. 2020). The OLI framework (Figure 7.10) is a decision model which we can use to explore the potential sources of advantage that a domestic firm may have when it considers whether to become a multinational. OLI stands for **o**wnership, **l**ocation, and **i**nternalization, three potential sources of advantage which may underlie a firm's decision to become a multinational. We discuss the three questions that make up the decision model below.

1. Ownership advantages address the question of why some firms but not others go abroad and suggest that a successful MNC has some firm-specific advantages which allow it to overcome the costs of operating in a foreign country. This approach views firms as collections of resources and capabilities (see Chapter 6 for a full discussion) and suggests that if a firm has no such advantages, it might be wise to consider remaining domestic.

2. Location advantages focus on the question of where an MNC chooses to locate. Consider the example of whether a firm should locate its manufacturing facilities in another country, where it hopes to reach customers. The framework suggests that if there is no advantage

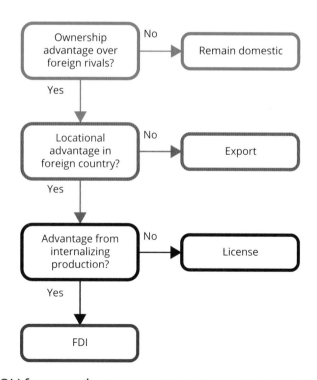

FIGURE 7.10 OLI framework. *Source*: reproduced with permission from Collinson, S. et al. (2020). *International Business* (8th edn). Harlow: Pearson. © Pearson Education Limited, 2012, 2017.

to be gained by going international, such as locating its manufacturing operations near an overseas source of raw materials, it may be better for the firm to remain domestic and export its products to overseas locations rather than manufacturing overseas.

3. Internalization advantages influence how a firm chooses to operate in a foreign country. The firm needs to consider the advantages and disadvantages of keeping its activities internal via an FDI (e.g. setting up a wholly owned subsidiary in an overseas location) compared with other entry modes such as exports, licensing, or a joint venture. For instance, a firm may wish to keep production activities internal because it can keep costs down or maintain control of quality. A joint venture may not be appropriate if the firm has major concerns about avoiding 'leakage' of competitive advantage to rival firms, for example, via proprietary knowledge.

Reasons for internationalization

We live in a world of MNCs—corporate entities selling on a global scale and with activities in many parts of the world. Next, we consider two different approaches which explain why organizations internationalize: the first is internationalization as structural imperative and the second is internationalization as process.

Internationalization as structural imperative

Here, we return to thinking that emerged from Chandler's seminal book *Strategy and Structure* (Chandler 1962). As we know, Chandler argued that 'structure follows strategy'; he described how major companies adopted the M-form or multidivisional organizational structure in order to cope with the need to coordinate their activities around the globe. The economic basis of Chandler's work is the cost advantages that scale and scope provide in technologically advanced, capital intensive industries (Chandler 1990). In sectors where few large firms appeared, it was because neither technological nor organizational innovation substantially increased minimum efficient scale; that is, large plants did not offer significant cost advantages over smaller ones.

Investments in scale, scope, distribution, and management allow large firms to build dominant positions sufficient to influence the basis of competition in their industry in terms of structure, key resources, and capabilities relevant to competing in that industry. Advantages of scale and scope lead to national and international concentration so that competition becomes oligopolistic (i.e. competition is limited to a few, usually large, competitors). Growth becomes a continuous search for improved quality, sourcing, distribution, and marketing and is rooted in continuously enhanced cost structures. Some growth can come from acquisition, but the main emphasis for long-term growth is likely to be twofold:

- **geographic expansion into international markets** in the continuous drive for increments in scale and cost advantages;
- **expansion into related product markets** in the pursuit of enhanced scope economies.

Together, these can create a dynamic spiral of volume, scale, scope, and cost curves, reinforced by organizational capabilities developed to cope with fierce oligopolistic competition. The opportunity to create first-mover investments is short-lived (e.g. Chandler 1990). Therefore, the logic of sustainable international competition is to make long-term scale investments to create organizational capabilities and then to continue to reinvest in them.

In a similar vein, Stopford and Wells (1972) developed a simple model to illustrate the typical stages of development for companies that are moving towards an international organizational structure. They saw this as a process driven by two dimensions (see Figure 7.10):

- foreign product diversity, that is, the number of products sold internationally;
- the importance of international sales to the company, that is, foreign sales as a percentage of total sales.

Stopford and Wells (1972) suggested that international divisions were set up at an early stage of internationalization when the figures for both product diversity and percentage of foreign sales were low. Then, those companies which found that international expansion led to substantial product diversity tended to adopt a worldwide product division structure (Pathway A in Figure 7.11). Or, if companies expanded overseas without increasing product diversity, they tended to adopt a geographical area structure (Pathway B in Figure 7.11). Finally, when both foreign sales and the diversity of products were high, a global matrix emerged. Thus the grid structure of the MNC with a geographic axis and a product group axis emerged.

Internationalization as a process

The internationalization process model (Johanson and Vahlne 1977), also known as the Uppsala model or the 'stages' model, suggests that the process by which a firm increases its international involvement should occur in *stages*. Johanson and Vahlne envisaged a firm gradually internationalizing through increased commitment to and knowledge of foreign markets. Therefore, the firm is most likely to enter markets with successively greater **psychic distance** (e.g. Perlmutter 1969), where psychic distance is a subjective notion of distance based on the *perceived* differences between a 'home' country and 'foreign' country (regardless of time and

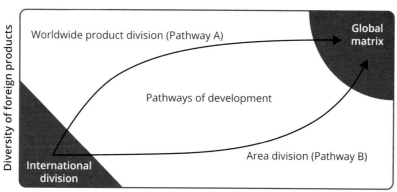

FIGURE 7.11 Stopford and Wells matrix: Pathways for international development. *Source*: Stopford, J.M. and Wells, L.T. (1972). *Managing the Multinational Enterprise: Organization of the Firm and Ownership of the Subsidiary*. New York: Basic Books. Adapted by Segal-Horn, S. and Faulkner, D. (2010). *Understanding Global Strategy*. Andover: Cengage Learning EMEA, Figure 7.2.

spatial factors). At the outset, it sells to countries culturally most similar to its own, before gradually broadening out.

The model depends on the notion that uncertainty, and hence risk, increases with greater psychic distance and unfamiliarity. The problem with this model is that it is very formal; it assumes that a firm is starting out with no existing international organization. However, there are many examples of internationalizing companies which have gone for large rather than familiar markets—and also for many markets at the same time. Consider the expansion of Ikea into China or Carrefour's expansion across countries in Europe, Asia, and South America. The contrast is between a 'water-fall' pattern of global expansion (one country at a time) and a 'sprinkler' pattern (many countries at a time). In current markets, with shortening product life cycles and the strategic importance of rapid time to market, there is often insufficient time to adopt the waterfall approach.

The 'stages' model of the internationalization process is highly sequential and also rather deterministic. Its contribution to theory is to demonstrate how internationalization can cause production to gradually move from the home country. The two approaches described earlier in this chapter are about the process of *becoming* international. However, they can also help us to understand some of the problems that MNCs may face when they are locked into the structures and processes of an earlier stage of internationalization than the stage they have currently reached.

 Access the online resources to watch a short video clip where Gordon Ramsay discusses expansion and globalization.

International configuration

We have discussed how and when MNCs may begin to become international. We can now look at what MNCs can achieve as part of becoming an international organization, and why. Kogut (1985) suggests that MNCs are able to win against most domestic operations because they can both access the comparative advantage of nations in which they carry out FDI and achieve competitive advantage by investing appropriately in their value chains. International location or configuration of the value chain enables the MNC to identify sources of comparative (country/location) advantage and competitive (firm) advantage.

Configuration of the international value chain

An organization that competes internationally must decide how to spread the activities in its value chain among countries (Porter 1986: 23). In our earlier discussion of organizational structure, we used the term 'configuration' to describe the structural design and processes of an organization. In international strategy, 'configuration' refers to where the various value chain activities are performed. It is about *where* we do what we do and *why*. Such decisions result in differing configurations for different organizations and industries. The location of activities in an international value chain is one of the most important concepts in international strategy because it is how MNCs benefit from the geographic dispersion of their activities. It is the means by which large organizations can make the most of the potential advantages identified by Kogut

(1985) mentioned earlier. Organizations typically have a wide choice of possible configurations of their activities; organizations that operate across borders should use their choice of configuration as a source of advantage.

Configuration and coordination

Figure 7.12 shows Porter's (1986) view of the relationship between **configuration** (where value chain activities are performed) and *coordination* of the organization's value chain configuration (how it is managed). To get to the heart of the message, let's start by considering the horizontal axis—where are the organization's key activities configured? Many organizations will begin with a value chain that is geographically concentrated, for example, to achieve economies of scale. However, over time, this concentration may become 'less necessary' (in Porter's language) because modularization of production technologies or variety at low cost means that scale is no longer so important to that organization. On the other hand, a geographic concentration of key activities may become 'less possible', for example, because the organization needs to be closer to its markets and customers (e.g. for R&D or market research). The other arrow in Figure 7.12 makes the same basic point: if you disaggregate your value chain away from being geographically concentrated (top right), you must become very efficient at coordination (i.e. it becomes 'more important') in order to make the disaggregated value chain work. It is also more feasible to do this with modern information and communication technology (ICT); before modern ICT existed, configurations had to be more concentrated.

The high level of coordination required to manage complex global supply chains may result in higher costs. These additional costs must be weighed against the cost savings in other parts of the value chain. Additional potential non-financial costs, such as risk to reputation or brand, can arise from international configuration of value chains.

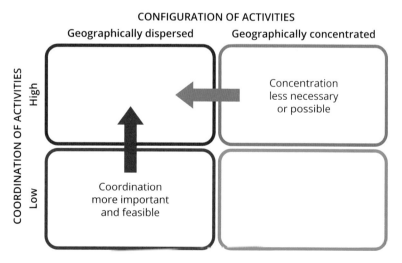

FIGURE 7.12 Porter's configuration–coordination matrix. *Source*: reproduced with permission from Porter, M.E. (1986). *Competition in Global Industries*. Boston, MA: Harvard Business School Press, Figure 1.7. By permission of Harvard Business Publishing.

PRACTITIONER INSIGHT GORDON RAMSAY, PLANT LEADER, P&G

Procter & Gamble (P&G) is a fast-moving consumer goods (FMCG) company headquartered in Cincinnati, Ohio. In 2020, P&G generated net sales of $71 billion through its activities in over 160 countries, supported by operations in more than 80 countries employing 97,000 people. We spoke to Gordon Ramsay, plant leader for their West Virginia operations. He has been involved in the start-up of this multi-category site servicing the Beauty Care and the Fabric and Home Care segments. The plant is the biggest supply chain initiative in P&G's history. Gordon shares his views on corporate strategy and structure within this multinational setting.

Corporate strategy and structure

There are three main components to P&G's corporate structure:

1. A go-to-market structure within a region that presents a single customer-facing organization. This function interacts with our main customers, such as Walmart, Target, Costco etc., to offer them the full P&G product range from one point of contact.

2. In terms of financial flows and reporting lines, we are organized internally in defined segments subdivided into territories (e.g. Fabric and Home Care is a segment, North America is a territory).

3. Business units: within sectors, business units look after categories of products (e.g. Fabric Care is a business unit with multiple brands within the Fabric and Homecare segment).

This isn't a static picture—P&G ebbs and flows in terms of its corporate structure. At present, the corporate strategy is moving away from a highly centralized structure—moving from horizontal functions (e.g. centralized purchasing) to tightly integrated 'verticals' (e.g. more autonomy for sectors). This move will increase the extent to which business unit performance can be enhanced by working in a way that suits the needs of the sector. For me, strategy defines your long-term goals and how you're planning to achieve them. It is our job as a leadership team in the plant to set and implement strategy that steers the site in line with corporate expectations, accommodating the needs of multiple existing and changing structures.

Corporate systems

A vitally important feature in how we manage our organization is IWS—Integrated Work Systems. IWS is our continuous improvement system—the A–Z guide as to how you run a world-class production site. All the tools, processes, and systems to deliver operational excellence are defined in that programme documentation and knowledge. That is our guiding operations strategy for the site. I have a strategy document specifically for my leadership team, on which item number one is 'IWS is the way we do the work.' Having that shared methodology gives us a common way of working, supported by a central corporate team and resources, that allows us to meet the needs of each business unit. For continuing operations, we harmonize around the IWS way to achieve our common corporate key performance indicators.

Being effective in a corporate setting

New employees and graduates coming into a complex and fast-paced business such as ours will succeed if they bring capabilities in collaboration and team-working, tenacity and solutions focus, and problem-solving and analytical thinking. An ability for reflection is important too. I think of it as self-feedback. I am non-stop critiquing what I'm doing, and everything we are doing as a leadership team, in order to check that we are performing as well as we can and achieving our targets. In our leadership team meetings, we discuss our approach, we debate and listen, and we try to reality check our different points of view. I think that people—individual or collective—who have the ability to assess themselves and give themselves feedback will progress, learn, and grow faster.

 Access the online resources to watch a short video clip where Gordon Ramsay talks more about his career.

CHAPTER SUMMARY

In this chapter, we addressed the following learning outcomes:

○ **Analyse the main organizational structural types**—which sit in the simple, complex, and innovation-orientated categories—**in terms of their strengths and weaknesses.** The relationship between strategy and structure was introduced, followed by the main aspects of structure and the coordinating elements that link them. We discussed the 'ideal types' of organizational structure, with examples of simple, complex, and innovation-orientated structures, with an analysis of their main strengths and weaknesses in each case.

○ **Evaluate the suitability of a range of structural types against a number of design tests.** We introduced nine design tests (Goold and Campbell 2002) which can help an organization to select or move towards an appropriate organizational structure. The first four tests fit with the key objectives of the organization—market advantage, parenting advantage, people, and feasibility. The remaining five tests are based on more general principles of good design—specialized cultures, difficult links, redundant hierarchy, accountability, and flexibility.

○ **Appreciate the role of systems in supporting the delivery of an organization's strategy.** We have discussed what we mean by systems in the context of the practice of strategy and why they are such important elements of successful strategy implementation. Different types of operational and control systems were reviewed, alongside Simons' (1995) levers of control as a comprehensive approach to the establishment of control systems in organizations that operate in environments where they experience rapid and continuous change. 'Control via simple rules' was also explored, as advocated for organizations in turbulent environments where high levels of flexibility and creativity are also required.

○ **Comprehend the relationship between internationalization and organizational structure.** Finally, we discussed why firms might wish to internationalize and examined some of the drivers and potential benefits of internationalization. We reviewed the different ways in which firms can go about internationalizing and the different conditions under which internationalization may or may not be a robust strategy. We also explored a process approach to international strategy.

END-OF-CHAPTER QUESTIONS

Recall questions

1. How would you describe the relationship between an organization's strategy and its structure? Do you agree with Chandler that 'structure follows strategy'?

2. Give a brief description of a 'simple' organizational structure and its main advantages and disadvantages.

3. Summarize the key differences between the main types of 'complex' organizational structure—multidivisional, matrix, holding, network, transnational, and innovation-orientated (project-based and adhocracy).

4. Explain why a firm might want to internationalize and what benefits internationalization might bring.

Application questions

A) Ask five people who work in different organizations to describe the structure of their organization (or alternatively, research five different organizations online). Draw a diagram for each organization that summarizes its organizational structure; compare and contrast the diagrams with Mintzberg's six ideal structural types, noting similarities and differences.

B) Choose an organization that you can research online and draw a picture of its organizational structure—at a good level of detail, if possible. Use Goold and Campbell's nine design tests to evaluate whether the organization's configuration is appropriate or not. Reflecting on the organization's context and history, suggest some explanations for any discrepancies that you observe.

C) Imagine that you have been assigned to lead a strategy team within an organization that is currently based in a single country but is considering moving to an international strategy. What are the key issues that you would consider relating to changes in organizational structure and systems? Make brief notes to share with colleagues about the possible benefits and risks and the key actions to take.

ONLINE RESOURCES

www.oup.com/he/mackay2e

In addition to the video interviews already highlighted, the book's online resources include the following features for this chapter, specifically:

- *links to further reading material* to broaden your knowledge of key issues discussed in this chapter;

- *self-test multiple-choice questions* to test your understanding of the material covered in each section of the chapter; and

- *a flashcard glossary* to help you recall and test your understanding of key terms.

FURTHER READING

Structure in Fives: Designing Effective Organizations by Henry Mintzberg

Mintzberg, H. (1993). *Structure in Fives: Designing Effective Organizations*. Englewood Cliffs, NJ: Prentice-Hall.

This book synthesizes messages from research on what it takes to design an effective organization, presented in a form that will be read by managers, staff specialists, and consultants who are concerned with the structuring of organizations.

Building the Innovative Organization: Management Systems That Encourage Innovation by James Christiansen

Christiansen, J.A. (2000). *Building the Innovative Organization: Management Systems That Encourage Innovation*. Basingstoke: Palgrave.

In this book, James Christiansen aims to help managers to learn how to support innovation in their organizations. He explores how everyday systems and practices of management can either encourage or discourage innovation.

'Organisation structure and innovation performance in different environments' by Andy Cosh, Xiaolan Fu, and Alan Hughes

Cosh, A., Fu, X. and Hughes, A. (2012). Organisation structure and innovation performance in different environments. *Small Business Economics*, **39**(2), 301–17.

This study examines the relationship between structure and innovation in small and medium-sized enterprises. The authors find that decentralized decision-making supports the ability to innovate.

REFERENCES

Ab-inbev.com (2020). 2020 Environmental, Social and Governance Report, https://www.ab-inbev.com/news-media/latest-headlines/esg-report (last accessed 18 August 2022).

Aoki, K. and Lennerfors, T.T. (2013). The new, improved keiretsu (September), https://hbr.org/2013/09/the-new-improved-keiretsu (last accessed 18 August 2022).

Arthur, M.B. and Rousseau, D.M. (1996). *The Boundaryless Career: A New Employment Principle for a New Organizational Era*. Oxford: Oxford University Press.

BBC (2016). Kids Company closure: What went wrong? (1 February), https://www.bbc.co.uk/news/uk-33788415 (last accessed 12 July 2021).

Bennet, A. and Bennet, D. (2004). *Organizational Survival in the New World*. London: Routledge.

Birkinshaw, J. and Ridderstale, J. (2015). Adhocracy for an agile age. *McKinsey Quarterly,* **4**, 44–57.

Brant, T. (2016). Ballmer: Bill Gates didn't want Microsoft to make hardware (4 November), https://www.pcmag.com/news/349334/ballmer-bill-gates-didnt-want-microsoft-to-make-hardware (last accessed 18 August 2022).

Bryson, J.M., Crosby, B.C., and Bryson, J.K. (2009). Understanding strategic planning and the formulation and implementation of strategic plans as a way of knowing: The contributions of actor-network theory. *International Public Management Journal*, **12**(2), 172–207, doi:10.1080/10967490902873473.

Bustamante, A.V. (2016). U-form vs M-form: How to understand decision autonomy under healthcare decentralization? Comment on 'Decentralisation of health services in Fiji: A decision space analysis'. *International Journal of Health Policy and Management*, **5**(9), 561–3.

Butler, P. (2021). Mismanagement claims against Kids Company founder thrown out (12 February), https://www.theguardian.com/uk-news/2021/feb/12/mismanagement-claims-kids-company-founder-thrown-out-camila-batmanghelidjh (last accessed 18 August 2022).

Casciani, D. (2021). Kids Company founder and former trustees win disqualification fight (12 February), https://www.bbc.co.uk/news/uk-56044000 (last accessed 18 August 2022).

Chandler, A.D. (1962). Strategy *and Structure: Chapters in the History of American Enterprise* (repr. 1990). Boston, MA: MIT Press.

Chandler, A.D. (1990). The enduring logic of industrial success. *Harvard Business Review,* **68**(2), 130–40.

Collinson, S., Narula, R., Rugman, A.M., and Qamar, A. (2020). *International Business* (8th edn). Harlow: Pearson.

Davis S.M. and Lawrence P.R. (1978). Problems of matrix organisations. *Harvard Business* Review (May), https://hbr.org/1978/05/problems-of-matrix-organizations (last accessed 18 August 2022).

Desveaux, J.A. (2012). Adhocracy, https://www.britannica.com/topic/adhocracy (last accessed 18 August 2022).

Dolan, T.E. (2010). Revisiting adhocracy: From rhetorical revisionism to smart mobs. *Journal of Future Studies*, **15**(2), 33–50.

Dudovskiy, J. (2017). Alphabet Inc. organizational structure: Divisional and flat (20 June), https://research-methodology.net/alphabet-inc-organizational-structure-divisional-and-flat (last accessed 18 August 2022).

The Economist (2017). Tata's governance is still faulty (9 February), https://www.economist.com/business/2017/02/09/tatas-governance-is-still-faulty (last accessed 18 August 2022).

Eisenhardt, K.M. and Sull, D. (2001). Strategy as simple rules. *Harvard Business Review* (January), **79**(1), 106–16.

Frampton, S. (2020). How Zappos customer service WOWs customers to win (13 March), https://chattermill.com/blog/zappos-customer-service (last accessed 18 August 2022).

Galunic, C. and Hermreck, I. (2012). How to help employees 'get' strategy. *Harvard Business Review*, **90**, 24.

Ganguly, D. (2012). Matrix evolutions: How GE underwent a fundamental change in its organisational and matrix structure (17 February), https://economictimes.indiatimes.com/matrix-evolutions-how-ge-underwent-a-fundamental-change-in-its-organisational-and-matrix-structure/articleshow/11921385.cms (last accessed 18 August 2022).

Garvin, D.A. (1993). Building a learning organisation. *Harvard Business Review* (July–August), **71**, 78–91.

Ghemawat, P. (2003). Semiglobalization and international business strategy. *Journal of International Business Studies*, **34**(2), 138–52.

Goold, M. and Campbell, A. (2002). Do you have a well-designed organization? *Harvard Business Review* (March), **80**(3), 117–24.

Gregory, L. (2018). Toyota's organizational structure: An analysis. Panmore Institute (8 September), http://panmore.com/toyota-organizational-structure-analysis (last accessed 18 August 2022).

Hobday, M. (2000). The project-based organisation: An ideal form for managing complex products and systems? *Research Policy,* **29**, 871–93.

Ilott, O. (2016). Kids Company: An anatomy of failure (2 February), https://www.instituteforgovernment.org.uk/blog/kids-company-anatomy-failure (last accessed 12 July 2021).

Investopedia (2022). Understanding Japanese keiretsu (29 January), https://www.investopedia.com/articles/economics/09/japanese-keiretsu.asp (last accessed 18 August 2022).

Johanson, J. and Vahlne, J. (1977). The internationalization process of the firm: A model of knowledge development and increasing foreign market commitments. *Journal of International Business Studies*, **34**(2), 138–52 (1), 23–32.

Kaplan, R.S. and Norton, D.P. (1996). Using the balanced scorecard as a strategic management system. *Harvard Business Review* (January–February), **74**, 75–85.

Kodama, M. (2007). Project-based organization in the knowledge-based society, https://www.researchgate.net/publication/281445331_PROJECT-BASED_ORGANIZATION_IN_THE_KNOWLEDGE-BASED_SOCIETY_Project-based_Organizations_11_Why_Are_Project-based_Organizations_Necessary (last accessed 18 August 2022).

Kogut, B. (1985). Designing global strategies: Profiting from operational flexibility. *Sloan Management Review,* **27**(1), 27–38.

Kranias, D.S. (2000). Cultural control: The case of Japanese multinational companies and their subsidiaries in the UK. *Management Decision*, **38**(9), 638–49.

Liker, J. (2011). Toyota's recall crisis: What have we learned? (11 February), https://hbr.org/2011/02/toyotas-recall-crisis-full-of (last accessed 18 August 2022).

Lomas, N. (2017). Google parent Alphabet forms holding company, XXVI, to complete 2015 corporate reorganization (4 September), https://techcrunch.com/2017/09/04/google-parent-alphabet-forms-holding-company-xxvi-to-complete-2015-corporate-reorganization (last accessed 18 August 2022).

Looney, B. (2017). Digitally enabled, https://www.bp.com/content/dam/bp/business-sites/en/global/corproate/pdfs/investors/bp-strategy-update-2017-bernard-looney-presentation.pdf (last accessed 18 August 2022).

Meyer, P. (2022). Starbucks's organizational structure and its characteristics (16 June), http://panmore.com/starbucks-coffee-company-organizational-structure (last accessed 18 August 2022).

Miles, R.E., Snow, C.C., Mathews, J.A. et al. (1997). Organizing in the knowledge age: Anticipating the cellular form. *Academy of Management Executive*, **11**(4), 7–24.

Mintzberg, H. (1979). The structuring of organisations. Adapted in: Segal-Horn, S. (ed.) (2004). *The Strategy Reader* (2nd edn). Oxford: Blackwell, 246–69.

Mintzberg, H. (1989). *Mintzberg on Management: Inside Our Strange World of Organisations.* New York: Free Press/Collier Macmillan.

Mintzberg, H. (1993). *Structure in Fives: Designing Effective Organizations*. Englewood Cliffs, NJ: Prentice Hall.

Montgomery, C.A. (2008). Putting leadership back into strategy. *Harvard Business Review*, **86**(1), 54–60.

Murray, S. (2021). Measuring what matters: The scramble to set standards for sustainable business (14 May), https://www.ft.com/content/92915630-c110-4364-86ee-0f6f018cba90 (last accessed 18 August 2022).

Nadler, D., Tushman, M., and Nadler, M.B. (1997). *Competing by Design: The Power of Organizational Architecture*. Oxford: Oxford University Press.

Nystrom, P.C. and Starbuck, W.H. (1984). To avoid organizational crises, unlearn. *Organizational Dynamics*, **12**(4), 53–65.

Perlmutter, H.V. (1969). The tortuous evolution of the multinational corporation. *Columbia Journal of World Business*, **4**, 9–18.

Pongatichat, P. and Johnston, R. (2008). Exploring strategy-misaligned performance measurement. *International Journal of Productivity and Performance Management,* **57**(3), 207–22.

Porter, M.E. (1986). *Competition in Global Industries*. Boston, MA: Harvard Business School Press.

Renegade Inc. (2017). Kids Company—what happened?, https://renegadeinc.com/kids-company-what-happened (last accessed 18 August 2022).

Renteria, M. (2010). Executing a global strategy, locally: Lessons from the world's local bank (23 November), https://brandleadership.wordpress.com/2010/11/23/executing-a-global-strategy-locally-lessons-from-the-worlds-local-bank (last accessed 18 August 2022).

Rumelt, R. (2011). The perils of bad strategy. *McKinsey Quarterly* (1 June), https://www.mckinsey.com/business-functions/strategy-and-corporate-finance/our-insights/the-perils-of-bad-strategy (last accessed 18 August 2022).

Seeking Alpha (2018). Alphabet: The Berkshire of tomorrow, part 1 (23 October), https://seekingalpha.com/article/4213384-alphabet-berkshire-tomorrow-part-1 (last accessed 18 August 2022).

Segal-Horn, S. (ed.) (2004). *The Strategy Reader* (2nd edn). Oxford: Blackwell.

Segal-Horn, S. and Faulkner, D. (2010). *Understanding Global Strategy*. Andover: Cengage Learning EMEA.

Simons, R. (1995). *Levers of Control: How Managers Use Innovative Control Systems to Drive Strategic Renewal*. Boston, MA: Harvard Business School Press.

Solomon, M. (2018). How Zappos delivers wow customer service on each and every call. *Forbes* (15 September), https://www.forbes.com/sites/micahsolomon/2018/09/15/the-secret-of-wow-customer-service-is-breathing-space-just-ask-zappos/?sh=4802c0911b2c (last accessed 18 August 2022).

Stewart, R. (2020). HSBC's 'We Are Not An Island' ads return with pro-immigration message (14 January), https://www.thedrum.com/news/2020/01/14/hsbcs-we-are-not-island-ads-return-with-pro-immigration-message (last accessed 18 August 2022).

Stopford, J.M. and Wells, L.T. (1972). *Managing the Multinational Enterprise: Organization of the Firm and Ownership of the Subsidiary*. New York: Basic Books.

Sull, S. and Eisenhardt, K.M. (2012). Simple rules for a complex world. *Harvard Business Review* (September), https://hbr.org/2012/09/simple-rules-for-a-complex-world (last accessed 19 October 2022).

Tata Steel Europe (2021). Respecting and safeguarding the environment is a fundamental principle held by all Tata Group companies, https://www.tatasteeleurope.com/ts/sustainability/environment (last accessed 18 August 2022).

Toyota (2017). Toyota to update its organization structure to boost business innovation (1 March), https://global.toyota/en/detail/15197404 (last accessed 18 August 2022).

Toyota (2020). TMC announces changes to executive structure, senior management responsibilities, and organizational structure (3 March), https://global.toyota/en/newsroom/corporate/31845625.html (last accessed 18 August 2022).

7

Tsoukas, H. (2005). Do we really understand tacit knowledge? In: Little, S. and Ray, T. (eds) (2nd edn), *Managing Knowledge: An Essential Reader.* London: Open University/Sage, 1–18.

Twitter (2021). Civic integrity, https://about.twitter.com/en/our-priorities/civic-integrity (last accessed 18 August 2022).

7

CHAPTER EIGHT

Strategies for Achieving Competitive Advantage

CONTENTS

By the end of this chapter, you should be able to:

- ○ Define the nature and sources of competitive advantage
- ○ Appreciate the link between the organization's business model, its strategic resources, and strategies for achieving competitive advantage
- ○ Recognize the importance of isolating mechanisms, causal ambiguity, and dynamic capabilities in achieving and maintaining competitive advantage
- ○ Explain generic and hybrid strategies that organizations can apply to gain competitive advantage
- ○ Consider the feasibility of maintaining a sustainable competitive advantage in highly competitive and dynamic environments

🔧 TOOLBOX

- ○ **Business model**
  The rationale of how an organization creates, delivers, and captures value in a competitive environment.

- ○ **Isolating mechanisms**
  The impediments to immediate imitation of an organization's resource position by competitors. Isolating mechanisms are to an organization what entry barriers for new entrants are to an industry.

- ○ **Generic strategies**
  An explanation of strategies that describe how a company pursues competitive advantage across its chosen market scope.

- ○ **Strategy clock**
  A model that explores the options for the organization to strategically position its products and services to deliver 'value for money', that is, how an organization can position its product or service offering in the minds of customers to give it a competitive advantage.

8

 Access the online resources to watch a short video clip where Dick Howeson shares his top career tips.

OPENING CASE STUDY **HOW DO YOU BUILD A $100 MILLION BUSINESS FROM SOCKS?**

Swedish friends Mikael Söderlindh and Viktor Tell had a bit of a thing for colourful socks or 'happy socks', as they called them. Spring was late to arrive in 2008 and on a dull Sunday afternoon in Stockholm Mikael and Victor were feeling jaded. It was on that day when Viktor had an idea, Söderlindh recalls. He said: 'What if we'd set up a business making happy socks?'

Söderlindh and Tell registered the name '*Happy Socks*' and co-founded a firm with the same name. By 2016, the firm's retail sales had grown close to $100 million from selling more than 20 million pairs of socks per year in 112 countries through more than 10,000 points of sale, supported by a fast-growing e-commerce channel, extensive social media presence, and an expanding portfolio of retail stores. According to the co-founders, at the time they had the idea for the company, the only bright, printed socks on the market were sold as 'gag gifts', often covered in Bart Simpson's face and hardly appealing to the kind of design-conscious customer they hoped to reach.

From the very start, Happy Socks leveraged their social media presence to target customers globally. With a limited marketing budget and an initial stock of 60,000 pairs of socks manufactured in Turkey, the two co-founders mailed samples and catalogues with a personal letter of introduction to major buyers of leading retailers, market by market, closely imprinting their distinctive personal vision on their products and business culture. They hired wisely by actively recruiting people who would thrive in an open and collaborative culture, although the company had a formal organization structure to ensure that the power of play was harnessed rather than the playfulness and fun becoming a distraction from business.

Happy Socks disrupted the global sock wear market by offering attractively priced, colourfully patterned socks as a fashion accessory, seeking celebrity design and promotion collaborations, and establishing a wide-reaching social media presence. The socks fashion market has attracted new competitors such as *Stance*, a US company best known for its collaboration with US sports leagues; *Bombas*, the buy-one-donate-one start-up; and a wide

Source: © Happy Socks.

variety of smaller labels. Söderlindh argues that the crowded playing field has only improved Happy Socks's game:

> I think competition has grown the business; without the competition, it would not be where it is [. .] you have a lot of brands now that are out on the market, and I think our brand stands for the creativity, the art, the design, and fun. We have a very clear position where we are.

That clarity might come from the **consistency** of the firm's mission and purpose. The firm's first Sustainability Report in 2019 states: 'Happy Socks is a unique company where culture, and diversity is a part of what we do and stand for, our mission is to spread happiness and colour to every corner of the world. This will not change.' In other words, as much as the company may grow or expand its product lines, its ethos will remain the same—produce an accessible, stylish product that makes people smile.

Collaborations have been at the centre of Happy Socks product development strategy. An eclectic array of collaborators has included celebrities, the makers of online social building game *Minecraft*, and a Japanese toymaker *MediCom*, which led to limited edition socks inspired by the firm's iconic *Be@rbrick* figurines accompanied by Happy Sock-wearing collectibles. The company plans on two new collections each year, with best-selling lines always available,

8

and further unique creative collaborations world-wide. The company has extended the Happy Socks brand by stripping David Hasselhoff of his Baywatch swimsuit and dressing him into Happy Socks swim trunks. With the introduction of underwear and a women's sub-label *Hysteria*, there's something to be noted about having a strong brand image, one that universally uplifts people. As a result, the brand that is based on the company's artistic creativity, the ethos of fun, and the mission to deliver happiness is the driving force behind their happy and loyal customers.

Questions for discussion

1. What do you think makes Happy Socks successful?
2. Why do you think Happy Socks focused on global expansion right from the very start?
3. What resources or activities enabled Happy Socks to grow very quickly?

Sources

Fashionista (2017). Happy Socks built a $100 million sock business—and it's coming for women's fashion next (19 July), https://fashionista.com/2017/07/happy-socks-swedish-label (last accessed 8 May 2021).

Fast Company. Happy Socks builds a business and happiness two feet at a time, https://www.fastcompany.com/1679274/happy-socks-builds-a-business-and-happiness-two-feet-at-a-time (last accessed 8 May 2021).

Happy Socks (2019). Sustainability Report 2019, https://a.storyblok.com/f/54304/x/e4d886d315/sustainability-report-2019.pdf (last accessed 8 May 2021).

Quick Books Commerce (2018). How Happy Socks created a $100 million eCommerce business? (11 December), https://www.tradegecko.com/blog/small-business-growth/how-happy-socks-created-100-million-ecommerce-business (last accessed 8 May 2021).

Scan Magazine (2020). Happy Socks: Spreading happiness, one colourful sock at a time. Scan Client Publishing, https://scanmagazine.co.uk/happy-socks (last accessed 8 May 2021).

8.1 **Introduction**

An important task in strategizing is to clarify how the organization competes in a way that creates value for customers for which they are willing to pay more than the cost of creating that value. Therefore, strategy practices that focus on debating how an organization competes—particularly when new information becomes available about shifting context—are a crucial feature of strategizing episodes. In market economies, few organizations have the luxury of having no serious competitors or threats to their market position. More often than not, it is necessary for organizations to change the way they compete in response to evolving competitive conditions and the threat of new competitors. Faced with ever-present competitive pressures, organizations must develop business models that align with strategies that seek to produce a competitive advantage over their rivals. At the same time, they must try to slow down the erosion of this advantage by existing competitors, potential new entrants to the market, or new product innovations and technologies.

Competitive success is achieved through the deployment of the organization's tangible and intangible resources, such as the organization's brand reputation and capabilities to produce a superior customer value proposition that cannot be copied or bettered by the organization's rivals. However, no competitive advantage lasts indefinitely. In highly competitive and dynamic environments, an organization can (at best) hope to achieve a temporary advantage until it is competed away, unless it is able to build barriers against rivals and continually renew its sources of competitive success to stay ahead of the competition to enjoy a sustainable competitive advantage. To do this, an organization must consistently be better or meaningfully different from its rivals.

As you study strategy, it is important to understand possible sources of competitive advantage and how this can be achieved, sustained, or indeed eroded by competitors or shifting external demands, such as a need for establishing sustainability credentials. This is a main concern for strategists. Being able to frame and explain an organization's situation in terms of theories of competitive advantage will increase your ability to lead effective debate and decision-making in strategizing episodes. We begin this chapter by considering what constitutes the nature and the sources of an organization's competitive advantage and how this advantage can be maintained in a competitive marketplace. We then turn to critically evaluate the mechanisms that may protect an organization from competitive imitation and how strategy practitioners can slow down the inevitable competitive erosion in fast-moving competitive environments. In the chapter, we will also consider the most common types of competitive advantage and hybrid strategies that a business can deploy. Building on the concepts introduced in Chapter 6, we emphasize the importance of finding ways for an organization to continually renew its value to customers by creating resources and capabilities to stay ahead of the competition. We conclude the chapter with a critical evaluation of the implications of research (McGrath 2013a, b), which suggests that, in today's intensely competitive environments, organizations cannot maintain a sustainable competitive advantage indefinitely. Instead, organizations can develop a series of temporary advantages that need to be recreated and protected through continual innovation and development. We encourage you to reflect on how the knowledge of new context and options generated by the analytical tools outlined in section 8.3 might provide valuable inputs to debates on how an organization could and should compete.

8.2 Nature of competitive advantage

Companies such as Facebook in social media, Airbnb in owner-managed holiday rentals, Apple in mobile devices and laptops, Amazon in low-cost online retail and entertainment, and Levi's in denim have become names that are recognized throughout the world. The prominence of these firms in their respective competitive spheres is not a result of a clever advertising campaign or a public relations stunt. These businesses have become successful because they have created business models that enable them to offer something unique to their customers that their rivals cannot match. This uniqueness may be based on either these firms' ability to offer products or services to their customers by providing a highly desirable product or service at a premium price or a standard product at a lower price. It is the ability to be different in a meaningful way in the eyes of their customers which sets these firms apart from their closest rivals.

Business model

Competitive strategy is about winning business with a product or service that customers perceive to be superior in terms of 'value for money' than alterative offerings available in the market. How customers perceive 'value for money' is the difference between what the customer would be willing to pay for the product less the price charged by the organization. This difference is what economists call **consumer surplus**. A superior offer can be achieved in two ways:

1. The value, or utility, of the organization's product as perceived by the customer is superior to competitors.

2. The value, or utility, of the organization's product as perceived by the customer is equivalent to competing offers but the price charged by the organization is lower (Bowman and Schoenberg 2008).

Every successful organization will need to bring its value-creating resources and activities together in a way that delivers a product or a service of superior 'value for money' to the customer. These interlocking elements of value-creating activities constitute the organization's **business model**. Think about Happy Socks in our opening case—how the firm developed a successful business model to attract customers to its colourful and stylish socks through artistic design, manufacturing located in Turkey, strong social media and e-commerce presence, collaborations, and physical distribution outlets in over 100 countries.

By identifying the constituent parts of the business model, strategists can understand how the organization fulfils its value proposition in a profitable way through the application of value-creating resources and activities. Johnson, Christensen, and Kagermann (2008) identify three components that make up the business model: customer value proposition, profit formula, and key resources and processes. The three components of the business model are depicted in Figure 8.1.

Customer value proposition is the way an organization satisfies customer needs. It is often said that customers don't buy features but benefits. This means that a customer's perceived value of a product is dependent how well the product matches the needs that may be complex and context specific. To understand their customers better, organizations should think what the customers' 'jobs to be done' are that a product or service should satisfy. Jobs to be done is shorthand for what the customer seeks to accomplish with the product in any given circumstances that may have either a material or psychological dimension to them, or both. Understanding

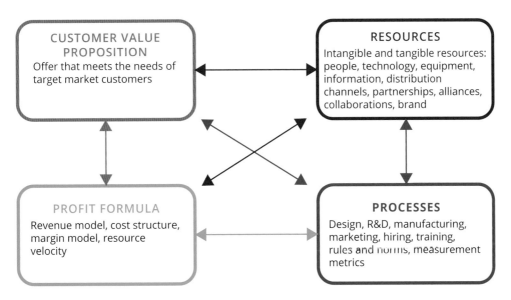

FIGURE 8.1 Business model. *Source*: adapted from figure/textual content in Johnson, M.W., Christensen, C.M., and Kagermann, H. (2008). Reinventing your business model. *Harvard Business Review* (December).

these circumstances is more important than customer characteristics, product attributes, new technologies, or trends (Christensen et al. 2016).

Profit formula is a quantifiable analysis that reveals how a company creates value (profit) for itself while providing value to customers. The profit formula consists of the following:

1. *Revenue model*: price x sales volume = total revenue.

2. *Cost structure*: the cost of resources required by the business that includes direct and indirect costs and production economies of scale.

3. *Margin model*: the financial contribution needed from each transaction to achieve desired profits, given the expected sales volume and total costs.

4. *Resource velocity*: how fast the organization turns over inventory and other assets, for example, how well the organization utilizes its resources to support the expected sales volume and achieve anticipated profits.

Key resources include all value-creating tangible and intangible resources to deliver the organization's value proposition and generate profit for the company and how these elements interact with each other (see Chapter 6 for a discussion of resource bundles and complementary effects). These resources include both key value-creating strategic resources and generic 'threshold' resources that do not, on their own, give the organization a competitive advantage. Generic threshold resources are required at a minimum level for a company be a participant in its industry.

Key processes are operational and managerial activities and processes that enable the organization to deliver value to its customers in a unique way. These processes also include recurrent day-to-day activities as well as rules, norms, control systems, and performance measurement metrics as examined in Chapter 7.

These four elements are the building blocks of any organization. Although the framework may seem simple, it is a powerful tool in understanding the interdependences of the parts of the business model. Major changes in any of the individual components will have an impact on the other elements as well as the whole of the business model. It is therefore important that those leading an organization are able to develop a more or less stable system in which the four elements of the business model align with each other in consistent and complementary ways (Johnson et al. 2008).

Competitive advantage

An organization is said to have a competitive advantage when it is able to create or has the potential to create more economic value than its competitors. An organization's competitive advantage can be temporary or sustainable. A temporary advantage lasts for a finite period of time until it is competed away. A sustainable advantage, in contrast, may last much longer. A critique of the feasibility of organizations to create and maintain sustainable competitive advantage is discussed in more detail in section 8.5. In mature and stable sectors, organizations able to defend and deploy their distinctive resource in line with external success factors may be able to maintain an advantage over their competitors for an extended period. For example, Levi Strauss began manufacturing denim overalls in the 1870s and the company created their first pair of Levi's 501 Jeans in the 1890s. Although the company's fortunes have been buffeted by the winds of fashion over the years, denim is an everyday staple for many people and the company still possesses an enduring appeal. Its products have been worn by people from all walks of life from cowboys, to miners, even to Nobel prize winners, including Albert Einstein, whose Levi's leather jacket was sold at auction for over £90,000 in 2016 (https://www.levistrauss. com/2016/07/29/sold-the-story-behind-the-albert-einstein-auction/).

We define a sustainable competitive advantage as a set of distinctive tangible and intangible resources and capabilities that allow an organization to consistently outperform their rivals' competitive efforts. The emphasis in our definition is the idea of consistency in outperforming rivals. This does not mean that the organization merely matches the performance of its competitors, but the organization should consistently be performing better than the break-even competitors in its sector. Most organizations are able to have a good year or two when they outperform the competition, but few organizations are able to consistently produce performance above sector average year after year. Hence, for profit-seeking organizations, it is important to analyse market position in terms of relative profitability over an extended period of time. An organization's market position may vary from one year to another, and profitability may even dip below the performance of its closest competitors for a short period of time. However, this does not necessarily mean that the firm has lost its competitive advantage as a decision may be taken to forgo today's profitability by investing in the acquisition of market share, new technology development, or hiring and compensating talented people, with the expectation that these investments will result in superior future performance (Rumelt 2003). For not-for-profit organizations, such as charities or government departments, similar analysis can be completed based on funding profiles achieved over a multi-year period. Not-for-profit organizations that are sustaining or growing funding levels despite alternative options for deployment of funder financial resources can be said to be sustaining competitive advantage.

 Access the online resources to watch a short video clip where Dick Howeson discusses competitors and strategic thinking.

8.3 Sources of competitive advantage

Having defined competitive advantage, what are the potential sources of competitive advantage? Building on the market-based view (MBV) and the resource-based view (RBV) concepts introduced in Chapters 5 and 6, we will discuss three different sources of competitive advantage:

1. the organization's position in the industry (MBV);
2. its internal resources and capabilities (RBV);
3. the impact of external and internal changes on competitive advantage.

The first view (MBV) is based on the assumption that the organization's competitive advantage is derived from securing a defensible position in the most attractive segments of a given industry (Porter 1980). Hence, the organization's competitiveness is greatly influenced by external industry and competitive factors. Porter's industry forces analysis is discussed in more detail in Chapter 5.

The second view, RBV (Wernerfelt 1984; Barney 1991), in contrast with the industry forces perspective, considers competitive advantage to result from distinctive and socially complex combinations of the organization's internal resources and capabilities. As explained in Chapter 6, these distinctive resources and capabilities are 'sticky', proving hard to transfer outside the organization or for competitors to imitate, which, in turn, creates value as they will not be available to competing organizations. It is this resource specificity that may provide the organization with a competitive advantage until its resource combinations either become obsolete or are competed away through rival innovation should the organization be unable to continually renew its resource base to keep ahead of the competition (Dierickx and Cool 1989).

The third view is a more holistic way of thinking about the emergence of competitive advantage by considering the impact of both external and internal changes as a source of competitive advantage. External changes have a varying impact on organizations in the same industry as no organization, not even very close competitors, possesses identical resources and capabilities. This is frequently referred to as **resource heterogeneity**, meaning that organizations in the same industry possess and compete with different resource and capability mixes. For example, although both British Airways and Virgin Atlantic have similar tangible resources, such as airplanes, landing slots at airports, lounges, pilots and crew, catering services, jet fuel and so on, the way these similar resources are combined together produces flying experiences that are perceived to be different by travellers. The way that these resources are combined are a result of how the organization has produced the service in the past but also a reflection of how the organization's strategists perceive the present and future state of air travel and what aspects of flying their customers value the most.

A seminal example of how resource heterogeneity influences competitive advantage of different organizations in the same industry is the effect that the creation of the Organization of the Petroleum Exporting Countries (OPEC) in the early 1970s had on the automotive industry. The formation of the oil cartel resulted in a fourfold increase in the price of oil and gasoline within a year between 1973 and 1974. High gasoline prices almost brought the US automotive industry to its knees as the US carmakers produced almost exclusively large, 'gas-guzzling' cars which consumers began to shun because of the skyrocketing gasoline prices at the pumps and the subsequent high running costs of the vehicles. In contrast, the high gasoline price was great news for the Japanese and European car manufactures, who were able to take advantage of this external change to enter the US market with small automobiles with frugal engines. The oil shock enabled the Japanese and European car manufactures to gain a foothold in the US market and use that as a base to build their reputation as manufacturers of high-quality, energy-efficient vehicles. Some argue that the US automotive manufacturers never fully recovered from the oil shock and were not able to catch up with the foreign manufacturers in terms of efficiency and quality. It is worth noting that not all external changes have the same magnitude as the 1973 oil crisis, but it is true that the greater the external change, the greater the entrepreneurial opportunities that become available for exploitation by organizations that are positioned to take advantage of them.

Opportunities presented by external changes must be accompanied by the organization's ability to take an advantage of these changes. Apple's late CEO, Steve Jobs, perceived that consumers would be willing to pay a dollar for a music download rather than 'stealing' tracks that had been made available by pirate sites.

> *We believe that 80% of the people stealing stuff don't want to be, there's just no legal alternative. Therefore, we said: Let's create a legal alternative to this. Everybody wins. Music companies win. The artists win. Apple wins. And the user wins, because they get a better service and don't have to be a thief.*

> (Jobs 2003)

Mr Jobs had spotted an emerging change in consumer attitudes, and he was able to harness Apple's technological knowhow and innovative capability to create the iTunes music store to take an advantage of the change in consumer attitudes towards music piracy. There may have been other businesses who had also identified this new emerging consumer trend before Steve Jobs, but Apple was the first business to be able to mobilize its resources to take advantage of it.

In addition, Apple had introduced its first iPod in 2001 and the iTunes music download service provided added benefit and functionality to the customers who had purchased the firm's iPods. The additional music download service tied Apple's iPod customers even closer to the firm's product and service offer through the iTunes platform. This seamless hardware and software integration became a powerful protective mechanism for maintaining Apple's competitive advantage. Even today, rivals still have difficulty challenging Apple's dominance in music downloads with superior product/service features or quality. However, Apple's story did not end with iPods and iTunes. Having successfully launched the iPod, the company began actively thinking how else the firm could leverage the technological knowhow it had acquired by developing iPod and the music platform. Six years later, in 2007, Apple launched the world's first smart phone, the iPhone, which revolutionized the mobile telephone industry, and, in 2010, the firm launched the iPad, which redefined how we browse the web, watch movies and photos, and send and read emails. It should not come as a surprise that the iPad, the iPhone, and the original iPod look uncannily similar, although with much improved and different functionality, as they all share the technological and design competencies of the firm. Apple is a classic example of a firm that has managed to maintain its competitive advantage in a fast-moving competitive environment by marrying evolving external opportunities with continual development of its core competencies in technology and design (Schoemaker et al. 2018).

Figure 8.2 depicts the relationship between external and internal factors and competitive advantage.

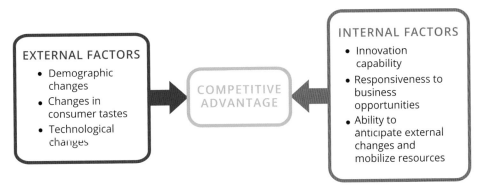

FIGURE 8.2 Sources of competitive advantage. *Source*: authors.

Sustaining competitive advantage

From a process–practice perspective, the creation and maintenance of competitive advantage is a continuous cycle that is subject to erosion by competitor moves and changes in the external environment, as illustrated in Figure 8.3. Competitive erosion refers to a gradual destruction (or chipping away) of an organization's competitive advantage. In a competitive environment, the organization has two main priorities:

1. The protection of the existing sources of competitive advantage from competitive erosion: this can be achieved by building barriers to imitation or avoiding resource mobility (preventing valuable resources from leaving the organization and ending up with rivals).

2. The process of resource renewal: this can be achieved by investing in new strategic resources and capabilities.

An organization's strategic resources and capabilities enable attainment of a favourable market position that underpins its competitive advantage. The benefits of competitive advantage may result in higher customer satisfaction and loyalty and increased market share as well as a higher profitability levels or achievement of organizational purpose. The improved financial performance should then enable the organization to invest in the continuous development of new strategic resources and capabilities in order to maintain its advantage. As discussed in Case Example 8.1,

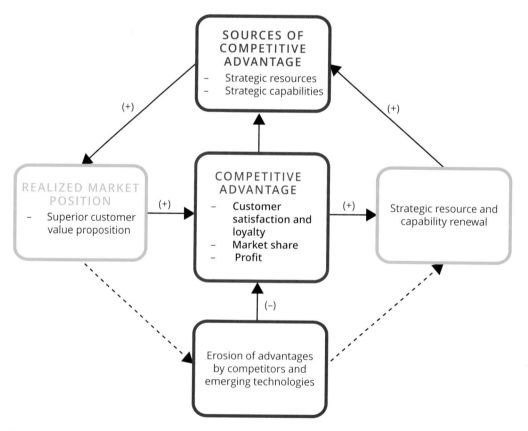

FIGURE 8.3 Cycle of competitive advantage. *Source*: reproduced with permission from Day, G., Reibstein, D., and Gunther, R. (eds) (1997). *Wharton on Dynamic Competitive Strategy*. New York: John Wiley. Copyright © 1997, John Wiley & Sons.

CASE EXAMPLE 8.1 **AMAZON: THE EVERYTHING STORE**

Founded by entrepreneur Jeff Bezos in Seattle in 1994 as one of the first dotcom firms, Amazon's business model is built entirely around emerging digital technology. It has grown to become a $386 billion turnover e-commerce mega-retailer and cloud computing business, the second largest US retailer behind Walmart (*Forbes* 2021).

As it started life as a small bookseller, at the heart of Amazon's success is the firm's ability to sell books at a significantly reduced price compared with more traditional book retailers by leveraging its e-commerce platform as a value-creating strategic resource. The more Amazon achieved increasing economies of scale, the more significant the cost savings it could make to its books, which allowed Amazon to sell its product at an unmatchable price compared with its competitors.

Additionally, Amazon was at helm of an emerging new technology, developing the Kindle, which gave booklovers the convenience of hundreds of book titles on a single device. Amazon sold Kindles at a break-even price, but the additional book downloads from Amazon's cloud server drove the firm's marginal costs down even further and compensated for the lack of profits generated from Kindle sales. Amazon's ability to invest in emerging technologies put enormous pressure on other booksellers, who were struggling to compete. Had Waterstones, one of the largest 'bricks-and-mortar' book retailers in the United Kingdom, not been able to reconfigure its activities to provide incentives for people to visit their stores rather than buy their books from Amazon, the company would have followed other well-known book retailers, such as Borders in the United States, into administration. Amazon remains a constant threat to many iconic independent bookshops today, despite a rise in the number of independent bookshops in the United Kingdom and the United States in more recent years. This revival has been driven more by a backlash against Amazon's retail power and the willingness of book lovers to support local businesses even if this would entail paying more for their book purchases from a physical store.

Amazon has also expanded into new markets. It continues to react to changing external environments, such as technological change and innovation, as well as changes in consumer tastes, which has led them to expand into fashion retailing (Prime Wardrobe), movie entertainment production (Amazon Studios), everyday electronics (AmazonBasics), voice recognition technology (Echo- and Alexa-enabled smart speakers), and even book publishing by exploiting the opportunities to sell more physical and digital products to a loyal customer base.

Amazon has also increased the rate of its acquisitions since 2015, with its most significant acquisition being Whole Foods, a premium grocery retailer, in 2017. This acquisition gives Amazon access to premium retail sites and may allow Amazon to use Whole Foods to expand its own food offer and use the physical space for customers to pick up their Amazon orders and to sell items that may be less suitable for online retailing. In September 2020, Amazon opened its first supermarket, Amazon Fresh, in Los Angeles, California. Shoppers are assisted by an array of technology: trolleys with fitted computer vision to monitor the items they pick, while Alexa voice assistants are available to answer questions on every isle. Since the opening of the first Amazon Fresh store, at least a dozen more have been opened across the United States, with several more under construction. This store-opening programme signals an acknowledgment that the firm won't be able to establish itself as a serous player in the United States' $1.3 trillion grocery market without traditional physical retailing.

Although Amazon continues to beat its competitors' customer order fulfilment times, its customers' shopping beyond buying groceries has been limited to simply browsing a webpage. Some of Amazon's competitors have seen this as a potential source for competitive advantage and have responded by enhancing their own customer experience by creating 'living spaces' beyond a traditional shopping experience, such as the cosy cafés in Waterstones and other bricks-and-mortar booksellers. However, Amazon has responded by disruptively opening bricks-and-mortar stores, including book shops in several US cities. These stores are designed to meet

Continued

the supercharged expectations of the modern-day consumer by rotating inventory out on a weekly basis as items become more or less popular on their website, and tagging items with exclusive prices for Prime customers, and presenting customer ratings and reviews. Through this new move, Amazon seeks not just to replicate other retailers' in-store experience but also to identify new ways to engage customers through physical retail outlets.

The company has truly become an 'everything store'. As Jeff Bezos is fond of saying, 'Amazon wants to continually give more to their customers without charging more.'

Questions for discussion

1. What do you consider is/are Amazon's strategic resource(s)?

2. How does Amazon use these resources to create and sustain competitive advantage?

3. Do you consider Amazon's venture in physical retailing logical, given the firm's source(s) of competitive advantage? If so, why, and, if no, why not?

Sources

BloombergUK (2019). Amazon plans to launch thousands of satellites to provide broadband (4 April), https://www.bloomberg.com/news/articles/2019-04-04/amazon-plans-to-launch-thousands-of-satellites-for-broadband (last accessed 18 August 2022).

CBInsights (2019). Infographic: Amazon's biggest acquisitions (19 June), https://www.cbinsights.com/research/amazon-biggest-acquisitions-infographic (last accessed 18 August 2022).

CNBC (2018). Amazon just opened a new store that sells popular items from its website. Here's what it looks like inside (27 September), https://www.cnbc.com/2018/09/27/amazon-just-opened-its-4-star-store-in-new-york-heres-a-look.html (last accessed 18 August 2022).

The Economist (2017). Amazon, the world's most remarkable firm, is just getting started (25 May), https://www.economist.com/leaders/2017/03/25/amazon-the-worlds-most-remarkable-firm-is-just-getting-started (last accessed 18 August 2022).

The Financial Times (2021). Walmart vs Amazon: The battle to dominate grocery (11 May), https://www.ft.com/content/9ab41b9e-a294-430f-951d-49cfc3415460 (last accessed 18 August 2022).

Forbes (2018). Five reasons why Amazon is driving into bricks-and-mortar retail (19 December), https://www.forbes.com/sites/annaschaverien/2018/12/29/amazon-online-offline-store-retail/#76bf35f51287 (last accessed 18 August 2022).

Forbes (2021). Amazon's net profit soars 84% with sales hitting $386 billion (2 February), https://www.forbes.com/sites/shelleykohan/2021/02/02/amazons-net-profit-soars-84-with-sales-hitting-386-billion/?sh=7b-9be73a1334 (last accessed 18 August 2022).

The Guardian (2019a). Amazon blamed as 'iconic' bookshops announce closure (30 May), https://www.theguardian.com/books/2019/may/30/amazon-blamed-as-iconic-bookshops-announce-closure (last accessed 18 August 2022).

The Guardian (2019b). Unputdownable! The bookshops Amazon couldn't kill (6 June), https://www.theguardian.com/books/2019/jun/06/amazon-booksellers-beating-odds-book-shops (last accessed 18 August 2022).

The Verge (2019). Here's Amazon's new transforming Prime Air delivery drone (5 June), https://www.theverge.com/2019/6/5/18654044/amazon-prime-air-delivery-drone-new-design-safety-transforming-flight-video (last accessed 18 August 2022).

Amazon used its experience and success in online retailing to branch into new digital content provision and even physical retailing, which combines traditional stores with the firm's e-commerce technology. Similarly, Apple used its technology knowhow to launch successive products from iPod to iPad, and it is in the process of expanding its successful iTunes and App store to a games arcade subscription service (https://www.ft.com/content/44236e86-5ba3-11e9-9dde-7aedca0a081a).

Continual investment in developing resources and capabilities is vital as any organization with a superior competitive position will be subject to competitive imitation, and unless it is able to stave off competition, its advantage will be lost or 'eroded'.

How fast is an organization's competitive advantage eroded by its competitors? This depends on how easy it is for the competition to imitate the leading company's strategic resources and capabilities as imitation is the most direct form of competition. Imitation is particularly easy where the leading organization possesses no significant proprietary resources, technologies, or other barriers for competitive imitation, such as brand equity.

As will be discussed further in Chapter 11, rivals may also seek to divert resources and attention towards **innovation**, which may change the competitive landscape through new products, technologies, platforms, or ways of working. For example, as addressed in Chapter 6, a generation ago, most people associated a 'Kodak moment' with happy events that were saved for posterity on film using an Eastman Kodak Instamatic camera. Today, the name Kodak serves as an example of a corporate blunder and a missed opportunity that warns strategists of the need to stand up and respond when disruptive developments encroach on their market (Anthony 2016). As Kodak's core business was selling film, it is not hard to see why the past few decades proved challenging for the firm. Cameras went digital and then disappeared into smartphones. People went from printing pictures to sharing them online. Of course, some people do still print photo books and holiday cards, but that volume pales in comparison with Kodak's heyday. The company filed for bankruptcy protection in 2012, exited legacy businesses, and sold off its patents before re-emerging as a much smaller company in 2013. Once one of the most powerful companies in the world, the firm's market capitalization had plunged to $109 million in April 2019 (New York Stock Exchange: Kodiak Copper Corp.).

However, innovation can be costly and, at a minimum, requires slack resources and involves a degree of risk, which is why imitation remains a more common mode of direct competition. This means that if an organization is to maintain a sustainable competitive advantage, it must have or develop effective barriers to imitation, which are referred to as **isolating mechanisms** (Rumelt 1984). The more effective these isolating mechanisms are, the longer the organization can expect to enjoy a competitive advantage.

Isolating mechanisms

Isolating mechanisms can take different forms. Some isolating mechanisms are a mixture of resource characteristics whereas others involve managerial practice, and each type offers varying success in protecting and sustaining competitive advantage and combating competitive imitation. In this section, we examine the following examples of the most common isolating mechanisms and their effectiveness in protecting and sustaining competitive advantage:

- unique historical conditions;
- path dependency;
- patents;
- social complexity;
- causal ambiguity.

Unique historical conditions

As explained in the concept of path dependence (see Chapters 4 and 6), unique historical conditions may have been present at a time when an organization was able to acquire or develop a particular resource or a resource mix upon which its competitive advantage is based. This is often referred to as **time compression diseconomies** as some resources are almost impossible to imitate because they have arisen from unique historical conditions (Dierickx and Cool 1989). For a competitor to imitate such a resource, it would require those same historical conditions. In other words, history would need to repeat itself. An example of time compression diseconomies is Caterpillar's global service and supply network, which was created through US Federal Aid. When the United States entered the Second World War, the country needed a primary supplier of construction equipment to build and maintain military bases throughout the world. For a competitor to build and replicate a competing network of such a global reach and magnitude could potentially be prohibitively expensive and difficult, so Caterpillar sought to secure a competitive advantage with these unique historical resources. The global service network was Caterpillar's strategic resource and the business managed to enjoy a leading position globally in earth-moving equipment.

This advantage lasted until Komatsu, a Japanese upstart, decided to challenge Caterpillar. It would have been financially impossible for Komatsu to replicate Caterpillar's service network. Instead, Komatsu adopted a long-term strategy by beginning to design and produce machinery that did not break down, or at least did not require as much servicing as Caterpillar's heavy-duty earth-moving equipment. By producing more reliable machinery, Komatsu effectively devalued Caterpillar's service network as a strategic resource and a source of competitive advantage.

Path-dependent competitive advantage

In Chapters 4 and 6, we explained that what an organization can do today depends on what it has done in the past—a concept known as path dependency. Path-dependent evolution of competitive advantage occurs when an organization gains a competitive advantage today, based on the acquisition or development of a resource or processes in the past. Returning to Case Example 8.1, when Jeff Bezos of Amazon first developed the company's online platform for selling books, he may not have been fully aware of the future value potential of leveraging the resource across different product categories. Once the value of Amazon's e-commerce platform became more widely known, Amazon had already moved along the learning curve and the cost of replicating the resource by potential imitators placed these rivals in a cost disadvantage. Path dependency is linked to the concept of **first-mover advantage**, which refers to circumstances when the first organization to offer a product, process, technology, business model, or platform can gain such a solid foothold in the market by earning customer loyalty, economies of scale, or learning benefits that subsequent entrants are unable to successfully challenge the first mover's dominant position. This is a key question for practitioners involved in strategizing episodes considering innovation: 'Should we seek to capture first-mover advantage? Or should we let others go first, let them make the main mistakes, and then imitate the successful path?'

Isolating mechanisms are examples of strategic resources, practices, and processes that have evolved over a long time and therefore might make up much of the 'taken for granted' characteristics of the organization, its culture, how business is conducted, and how strategizing tends to happen. They are also a part of the day-to-day experience of practitioners. If these resources, practices, and processes are valuable and inimitable by an organization's competitors, they can form the basis of the organization's sustainable competitive advantage. However, a downside to these mechanisms is that they can become value-destroying 'core rigidities' (Leonard-Barton 1992), as explained in Chapter 6. In other words, they can deteriorate in value in competitive environments characterized by a significant degree of new product or process innovation and become a source of competitive disadvantage (as gauged by financial losses or loss of funding). For example, Caterpillar lost its leading industry position in earth-moving machinery when competitors brought more reliable and less service-intensive products to the market. This eroded the value of Caterpillar's superior global service network. Similarly, Nokia lost its position in the market to smartphones when consumers began to attribute less value to the durability of Nokia phones than to the functionality offered by Apple's iPhone.

Patents

Another example of an isolating mechanism is the **patent**. Patents can act as powerful isolating mechanisms as they can be used to exclude others from a product market for the duration of patent protection. Patents raise the cost of competitive imitation and protect an organization's revenue streams. The only way that potential competitors can challenge patent protection is by creating a substitute product or a new, more innovative product that does not infringe the existing patent protection of the leading organization.

However, some scholars argue that, instead of cementing an organization's sustainable competitive advantage, patents may have the opposite effect (Barney 1986). Patents may, in effect, reduce the costs of imitation, especially for patents that seek to protect specific products from competitive imitation. When a patent application is submitted to the Patent Office, the organization must reveal significant details about the product, and this important information is then available to competitors. This information can effectively provide a blueprint for product imitation that is only temporarily protected by the patent. Moreover, patent infringements are very expensive to defend. In most cases, small-to-medium-sized organizations lack the financial resources to defend against such infringements. Hence, some scholars (Rumelt 1984; Thurm 1998) question the wisdom of patent protection for new innovative products by small entrepreneurial organizations.

Patent disputes and theft are by no means a new phenomenon. Individual inventors and entrepreneurs have always been at the risk of theft of their inventions. A famous case that underpins our digital world as we know it today involved Nikola Tesla and Guglielmo Marconi. In the 1890s, Tesla discovered that he could use electrically charged 'Tesla coils' to transmit messages over long distances by setting them to resonate at the same frequency. Tesla's patent for this design was accepted in 1900. At the same time, Marconi was working on his own device for transmitting signals over long distances. However, Marconi's patents were repeatedly turned down due to the priority of previous inventors. Undeterred, Marconi experimented with technologies like the Tesla oscillator to transmit messages over long distances. Tesla initially tolerated Marconi using his work. He is quoted as having said, 'Marconi is a good fellow. Let him continue. He is using seventeen of my patents.' Yet, this changed in 1904, when the US Patent Office decided to award credit for the invention to Marconi. A furious Tesla attempted to sue Marconi, but he didn't have sufficient financial resources to prosecute successfully. The patent was not restored to Tesla until after the inventor's death in 1943 (http://www.businesscareersguide.com/10 great business ideas that were-actually-stolen/).

Social complexity

An organization's resources may be difficult to imitate due to their **social complexity**. As the Case Example 8.2 illustrates, social complexity can provide a firm with competitive advantage. Social complexity arises because the composition and configuration of the organization's

CASE EXAMPLE 8.2 COMPETITIVE ADVANTAGE FROM COMPLEX INTERACTIONS

Companies are increasingly aware that sustainable competitive advantage can no longer be based on tangible products and services that can be copied or substituted with relative ease by rivals. Organizations are looking for intangible, socially complex resources within the organization to find ways to improve the effectiveness of solving their strategic business problems.

Tacit interactions between employees are becoming a focus of daily strategic activity and are increasingly a fundamental part of organizations' way of working within particularly competitive markets. 'Tacit' activities involve the exchange of information, making judgements, and drawing on multifaceted forms of knowledge between co-workers, customers, and suppliers.

For example, at Toyota Motor Company, employees from different function groups, such as production workers, engineers, and managers, work together to establish cost-cutting strategies without risking product quality. Managers are an example of those employees within an organization who are primarily responsible for these types of collaborative activities. At Toyota, they make up 25–50% of the workforce and typically have the highest salaries to reflect their involvement in shaping competitive strategies within a volatile external environment.

Not only do companies that make these activities central to their strategy raise their top and bottom lines, but also this type of activity enables organizations to establish a competitive advantage against its rivals through the collective talent of their workforce. Establishing competitive advantage is challenging, but in order to build on this competitive advantage, companies must channel this talent to evolve their strategy, design organizations, and maximize use of technology—this is no mean feat. The best way for executives to begin to think strategically about these socially complex resources and capabilities is to understand the nature of tacit interaction: the searching, coordinating, and monitoring activities required to exchange goods, services, and information.

The faster pace of specialization, globalization, and technical change that we see today has also significantly improved the way in which companies, their customers, and their supply chains interact. The result has been a dramatic increase in the volume and value of interactions. In most advanced economies, four out of five non-agricultural jobs involve interactions such as these, but only one in five of these roles in today's economy involves actually extracting raw materials or working on a production line, whereas during the pre-globalization era this may have been more proportionate. What this tells us is that the number of jobs which require the more 'tacit' interactions between different highly paid function groups is growing faster than any other type of role within a supply chain. Examples of today's more 'tacit' roles include managing supply chains, managing the way customers buy and experience products and services, rebranding, and negotiating acquisitions.

Questions for discussion

1. If organizations' competitive advantage is increasingly derived from intangible resources, such as employees and their social interactions, what managerial challenges do you consider such intangible resources present and why?

2. How do you think you could identify the link between the most valuable resources and business performance if they are intangible?

Source

Beardsley, S.C. et al. (2006) Competitive advantage from better interactions. *McKinsey Quarterly* (May), http://www.mckinsey.com/business-functions/organization/our-insights/competitive-advantage-from-better-interactions (last accessed 18 August 2022).

resources are a mix of socially complex phenomena such as interpersonal relationships among managers and employees (including tacit interactions between them), cultural norms, and the organization's reputation among customers and suppliers (Strebel 1996). It can be argued that socially complex resources such as an organization's culture can be a source of sustainable competitive advantage. Organization culture (see Chapter 4) has been cited, at least partially, as the source of the sustained superior performance of companies such as IBM, Hewlett-Packard, McDonald's, and Proctor & Gamble (Peters and Waterman 1982). Successful cultures are very difficult to imitate. Rivals who try to change their cultures to emulate a leading organization will rarely achieve sustainable advantage. Although the rivals may successfully incorporate valuable new attributes to their organizational cultures, such activities rarely result in sustained superior performance (Barney 1986).

Causal ambiguity

We have already seen that if an organization is to imitate the competitive advantage of a rival, it must understand the basis of the rival's success. If the organization's sources of success are transparent and there are no isolating mechanisms present, competitive imitation should be a relatively easy process. In such circumstances, sustainable competitive advantage is not possible. An increasing amount of research has focused on the implications that resource inimitability has on the sustainability of competitive advantage from the perspective of both the imitating and the imitated organizations (Ambrosini and Bowman 2008).

Causal ambiguity (King 2007; McIver and Lengnick-Hall 2018) is a concept that describes the degree to which would-be imitators, as well as the managers of the organization that is being imitated, understand the relationships between resources and business results. Causal ambiguity exists when the value of the resource itself, the characteristic of the resource, or the linkage between the resource and business performance is not fully understood. If the link between the organization's resources and competitive advantage is opaque, it is difficult for competing organizations to duplicate the resources through imitation as they do not know which resources to imitate. The framework of causal ambiguity is depicted in Figure 8.4.

In quadrant A, the nature of the resource and its link to business performance is known to the organization's managers and so both characteristic and linkage ambiguity are low. The resource can be imitated relatively easily by hiring away the organization's managers, who understand the nature and linkage between resources and business performance, or by engaging in systematic intelligence gathering and analysis of the organization's competitive success. Once the resource becomes disseminated across the organizations in a sector, it will only be able to provide competitive parity (the resource won't provide a competitive advantage for any of the organizations). The managerial challenge for the organization is to develop the existing resource or replace it with a new resource that possesses at least some inimitable characteristics in order to protect the organization's competitive position.

In quadrant D, sustained competitive advantage is possible as both the organization and its competitors face perfect characteristic and linkage ambiguity. In other words, the nature of the resource and the link between the resource and the organization's performance are not known (to either the organization or its competitors). Since imitation is not possible, sustained competitive advantage can only be destroyed through resource substitution where the competitor develops a competing product by using a different set of resources from that of the leading organization.

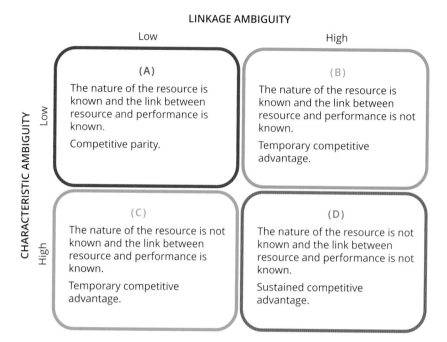

FIGURE 8.4 Characteristic and linkage ambiguity: The framework of causal ambiguity. *Source*: authors.

However, as the organization that possesses the valuable resource also faces perfect causal ambiguity, it does not have the means to develop the resource further. At worst, the organization may inadvertently destroy the resource because it does not understand its value and its link to performance (Barthelemy and Adsit 2003). This can happen when organizations divest or outsource activities that may mistakenly be considered of secondary importance. For example, many banks rushed to cut their operating costs by offshoring their call centres. However, it was only once their customers had difficulties in communicating with the offshore call centre staff (due to language and cultural barriers) that the banks realized that domestic call centres were, in fact, the key differentiating service that customers valued the most.

The strategic challenge for the organization that faces perfect ambiguity is to reduce both characteristic and linkage ambiguity but preserve or develop alternative barriers to competitive imitation as the degree of causal ambiguity is reduced.

(We should note that causal ambiguity presents a critique of the resource-based view, which posits that competitive advantage is derived from an organization's distinctive resources and capabilities. However, causal ambiguity makes it difficult for practitioners to identify and manage the organization's internal sources of success. And, as quadrant D shows, at least in theory, sustainable competitive advantage is possible only if the sources of success are perfectly ambiguous to both the organization's practitioners and would-be imitators.)

Quadrants B and C have differing types of causal ambiguity, either linkage or characteristic ambiguity. A resource that only has one type of ambiguity can be considered to provide the organization with a temporary competitive advantage. Depending on the type of ambiguity of the resource, the organization has some managerial visibility and influence over the resource. However, the strategic challenge is to reduce ambiguity in terms of either linkage or characteristic ambiguity, while simultaneously either preserving or developing barriers to competitive imitation as the degree of causal ambiguity is reduced.

The causal ambiguity framework introduces a dynamic aspect in terms of managerial processes to reduce the degree of characteristic and linkage ambiguity while, at the same time, preserving and/or developing barriers against the threat of competitive imitation. As you study strategy, it is important to understand that strategy practitioners should develop techniques that allow various types of factors to be brought to light, including those that are causally ambiguous. Some of these tools were covered in Chapter 3, where we considered the challenges of strategic decision-making in organizations. The surfacing of causally ambiguous success factors may provide a trigger for organizational learning. The debate and the unpacking of what the causes of success are can facilitate the reframing of the basic assumptions underlying managers' beliefs about sources of success. This could ultimately lead to a reframing of managers' strategic choices as they begin to understand the sources of the organization's success in more depth.

To illustrate the concept of causal ambiguity, consider Richard Branson's Virgin Group of companies. Having created more than 400 Virgin companies, Branson shared his secrets of success in a blog post (https://www.virgin.com/entrepreneur/richard-bransons-secrets-success?amp) and how others might replicate it. 'One of the tried-and-true methods of building a business is by offering such useful products and terrific service that you disrupt the local market, winning customers away from your competitors', he says. 'We at Virgin have done this with a particular focus on disruptive change.'

Virgin won't venture into a new business unless it believes it can offer something that is distinct from what already exists. 'From our first ventures, like our music stores and record label, to some of our flagship businesses today, including our airlines and space tourism companies, we have approached business development proactively and opportunistically, looking for openings where we can surprise and delight customers by offering something truly different.'

'Success in one area tended to lead to success in other fields, and so it has been sustained', he says. 'We built up an extensive network of relationships, and now entrepreneurs and companies often approach us with ideas for partnerships that will help them to start a new business, or to attract new customers.'

'There is a lot of cross-over between sectors in everything from technology and design to trends in customer preferences', he explains. 'The lessons we learn from one business can often be applied to another.' Companies across the Virgin Group often work together to achieve common goals, meeting at forums based around either a sector, such as mobile technology, or a department, such as communications.

But what is the real secret of Virgin's success? Branson says: 'Consider the importance of what seems to be the final magic ingredient: since we started Virgin over 40 years ago with such strong personal relationships, we have always also had close ties with our customers.'

Virgin, under Richard Branson's leadership, seems to have a clear strategy and, although there have been failures along the way, on aggregate It has succeeded. Eight businesses that have been created in eight completely different sectors have an enterprise value of more than $1 billion. However, the question remains as to whether, due to causal ambiguity, any would-be imitator, or even Branson himself, could replicate Virgin's success based on the insight provided.

Dynamic capabilities and competitive advantage

The ability of organizations such as Apple and Amazon to adopt and take advantage of changes in the competitive environment while other organizations stagnate implies differences in the capabilities of these organizations. As introduced in Chapter 6, this capacity to continually renew the organization's resource base and capabilities is referred to as organizational dynamic capability (Teece et al. 1997). In relation to competitive advantage, we can think of dynamic capability as arising from:

> [...] the firm's processes that use resources, specifically the processes to integrate, reconfigure, gain and release resources, to match or even create market change. Dynamic capabilities are the organisational and strategic routines by which firms achieve new resource configurations as markets emerge, collide, split, evolve, and die.

> (Eisenhardt and Martin 2000: 1,107)

Dynamic capability arises from organizational resources, routines, and processes that can be used for sustaining existing competitive advantage or creating **disruptive change** and new sources of advantage. Dynamic capabilities refer to specific routines, processes, or capabilities that might be deployed through organizational activity (e.g. dynamic marketing capabilities as described by Bruni and Verona 2009). Having dynamic capabilities doesn't directly result in competitive advantage, but, instead, the use of dynamic capabilities might create valuable new resource-based configurations through which competitive advantage is gained (Wang and Ahmed 2007). In other words, the customer may be willing to pay an organization for the resource-based outcomes of deploying dynamic capabilities (e.g. new products from improved quality processes) but not the dynamic capabilities themselves (e.g. in-house R&D and technology development capabilities).

Examples of dynamic capabilities include processes for:

- **Reconfiguration**: the transformation and recombination of resources (e.g. the consolidation of central support functions). Such consolidations often occur as a result of mergers and acquisitions or a reorganization of operations in large multinational corporations. Large-scale bank mergers such as that of J.P. Morgan and Chase Manhattan Bank achieved significant economies of scale from the amalgamation and reconfiguration of their banking operations activities.

- **Leveraging**: replication of a system or a process from one business unit to another or extending a resource by deploying it into a new domain (e.g. by applying an existing brand to a new set of products). The Virgin Group of companies has successfully leveraged its brand from an airline, to an internet and entertainment service provider, to a high street bank.

- **Learning**: allows tasks to be performed more effectively and efficiently as an outcome of experimentation, reflecting on both failures and successes. Amazon's Jeff Bezos has stated that the firm explores all avenues, although some of them may lead into blind alleys. Prime Air is a future delivery system from Amazon designed to get packages safely to customers in 30 minutes or less using drones.

- **Creative integration**: relates to the ability of an organization to integrate its resources in a novel way that may result in new resource configurations. As we have already seen, Apple has used its technical and product design capabilities from iPod to launch iPad, a product that revolutionized the way people use the internet, view photos, send email, etc.

8

Dynamic capabilities also link with causal ambiguity and path dependence in explaining sustainable competitive advantage. As we already know, sustainable advantage can only be maintained if the organization's advantage is based on strategic resources, including routines and capabilities that are difficult to imitate. The transfer of capabilities from one setting to another can be accomplished only if the capability that is being transferred is fully understood by the organization's managers. This could make it imitable, but in managerial practice this is not often the case. Not only does the tacitness of organizational routines hinder imitation, but also a change in an organizational routine in one part of the organization impacts a routine in another part of the organization, making competitive imitation even more difficult.

Zollo and Winter (2002) relate high causal ambiguity to 'learning investments' or learning by doing, which produce routines that govern organizational activity. These routines emerge over time and hence will be path-dependent and shrouded in ambiguity. The higher the degree of causal ambiguity between the emerging routines and business performance, the higher the likelihood that explicit articulation of such routines, if possible, will provide a better effectiveness in developing dynamic capabilities. In order to achieve this, in your future career as a strategy practitioner you must try to make explicit the link between routines and performance outcomes. This is a very difficult thing to do, but organizations that are able to reduce causal ambiguity to gain an insight into the relationship between their resources, routines, and performance outcomes are better able to leverage these capabilities to gain and sustain a competitive advantage.

8.4 Types of competitive advantage

So far in this chapter, we have considered the sources of competitive advantage. How, then, can organizations compete effectively, given the nature of their strategic resources?

It is unlikely that any two organizations will employ competitive strategies that are exactly alike in every sense. Even close competitors in the same industry possess slightly different resources and resource mixes that are used to produce a product or a service. Moreover, managers in different organizations have different perceptions of industry driving forces, the nature of future threats and opportunities, and how best to deal with competitive pressures. Organizations try to avoid competing head-on with rivals as this ultimately results in dynamics that are destructive to all industry participants. Even in the most competitive industries, organizations try to find different customer segments and adjust their strategies in order to find ways to protect their organization from the problematic effects of cut-throat competition.

Porter's generic strategies and competitive scope

It is possible to classify organizations by general strategic orientation. Porter (1985) identified two basic dimensions on which organizations base their competitive strategies. The first dimension involves the organization's competitive scope: whether the organization's target market segment is broad or narrow. The second dimension is whether the organization pursues low-cost or product/service differentiation strategy. These strategy frameworks are referred to as Porter's generic strategies.

Four generic competitive strategy frameworks

Porter's two strategy dimensions give rise to four **generic strategy** options for establishing a market position to deliver value to customers. The four generic strategy options are broad low-cost strategy, broad differentiation strategy, low-cost focus strategy, and differentiation focus strategy. We will start by briefly explaining each strategy before looking at the key considerations of low-cost and differentiation strategies in more detail. We will conclude by considering the possibility of hybrid strategies.

Broad low-cost strategy

Broad low-cost strategy aims to achieve the lowest overall costs in the industry by offering similar products to rivals at better value for money for a broad range of buyers. An example of broad low-cost strategy is Timex. Timex is the original dollar watch company, which means that it is a high-volume provider of inexpensive but stylishly branded watches. The company constantly tries to drive down costs by exploiting low-cost manufacturing resources and using extensive advertising to drive up volumes to increase economies of scale. The organization produces hundreds of watch variations of its no-nonsense timekeepers so that customers can always have a fashionable Timex to match their outfits or activities from camping to Ironman competitions. This strategy has helped Timex to become one of the best-known watch brands in the world.

Broad differentiation strategy

Broad differentiation strategy seeks to differentiate the organization's product/service offer from that of rivals so that it will appeal to a broad range of buyers who are willing to pay a premium price for the offering. An example of broad differentiation strategy is Starbucks (see Case Example 7.2 for more information about Starbucks). Starbucks's baristas are happy to prepare orders to meet their customers' wishes, no matter how detailed. The company is also well known for quality products, with strict guidelines on coffee roasting and brewing—a cup of espresso must be served within 23 seconds of brewing. Food offering and preparation is strictly controlled so as not to overpower the smell of coffee in its shops, which the company likes to call a 'third place'—a place alongside one's home and office. The quality of coffee, personal attention, and the network of 24,000 stores has made Starbucks the coffee lovers' choice in 70 countries.

Low-cost focus strategy

Low-cost focus strategy concentrates on a narrowly defined target market segment by out-competing rivals on costs by being able to offer a low-priced product to a customer segment whose needs may be slightly below average. Therefore, the organization may use demographic profiling as a basis for identifying its target market. Papa Murphy's is a take-and-bake pizza company. It was formed in 1995 as the merger of two local take-and-bake pizza companies, Papa Aldo's Pizza and Murphy's Pizza. The company and its franchisees operate more than 1,300 outlets in the United States and Canada. Papa Murphy's is authorized to accept food stamps as payment. This allows Papa Murphy's to attract customers who might not otherwise be able to afford a prepared pizza.

Differentiation focus strategy

Differentiation focus strategy concentrates on a narrowly defined target market segment who are willing to pay a premium for a product/service that meets their specific needs better than the rival product/service offerings. An example of differentiation focus strategy is Bang & Olufsen, a Danish high-fidelity audio-visual products firm. Bang & Olufsen products are marketed as 'lifestyle' products, and they are carefully targeted at wealthy customers with particular tastes that reflect individualism, and self-expression, and motivation. Bang & Olufsen often refers to Mercedes Benz as its primary competitor and perceives that it is competing for upper-middle-class discretionary spending rather than directly with other audio-visual companies. The company's designs attract both men and women with their combination of high technology, spectacular and often audacious Danish modern styling, excellent performance, and extremely functional integration into the typical upper-middle-class home.

Generic strategies and organizational resources

Porter's generic strategies are directly linked to an organization's business model as the strategy adopted must be aligned with the organization's overall operating system through which value creation occurs. This requires the organization's resources to be harnessed to deliver a satisfactory customer value proposition (refer to our discussion of the business model in section 8.2). The nature of the organization's resources and isolating mechanisms largely determine which generic strategy is a feasible option for the organization. There would be little sense in identifying the product/service attributes that are valued by customers if the business was not able to supply those attributes. Similarly, there is little purpose in developing resources to deliver product/services with attributes that are not valued by customers. For example, the organization that pursues a low-cost strategy must possess resources and capabilities that are focused on delivering a product at an acceptable price which customers value for its value/quality at a lower cost than the organization's rivals. For example, the whole business model of Ryanair, the leading European low-cost airline, is based on a resource configuration that is focused on delivering an acceptable service at the lowest possible cost and price to the customer.

Low-cost strategy should not be equated with selling products and services that are perceived as 'cheap and nasty' or of inferior quality by customers. Organizations that pursue low-cost strategies must be able to offer products and services that are of acceptable quality and comparable to industry standards but be able to do so at a lower overall cost than that of rival organizations. It is unlikely that any organization can survive very long by offering a poor-quality product or service, however low the price.

Similarly, companies that pursue differentiation strategies must ensure that the organization's resources and any materials used in the production process are consistent with supplying a highly differentiated product/service for which customers would be willing to pay a premium price compared with rival offers. Organizations, such as the opening case of LVMH in Chapter 6, that offer highly differentiated premium-priced products or services must use high-quality materials in their production processes and have highly sophisticated market research, advertising, and promotion capabilities to provide customers with an appropriate justification to make a decision to pay a premium price for what is offered to them.

Low-cost strategies

Organizations with costs that are lower than those of their rivals are likely to enjoy a competitive advantage in the marketplace because they can offer their customers lower prices and hence gain increases in sales and market share. Competitive advantage can be sustained as long as the organization is able to maintain its cost advantage over its competitors and as long as its customers will consider the organization's offer as value for money.

Organizations that pursue a low-cost strategy on a broad market basis will be able to exploit economies of scale and learning effects that will drive the organizations' costs even lower as the volume of production or service increases. In contrast with broad market-based low-cost strategy, an organization that follows the low-cost focus, or niche cost focus, strategy is not able to earn significant economies of scale or learning effects as its production volumes and market share are low as a result of the organization's focus on a narrow market segment. An organization in the low-cost niche tends to produce a basic product or service resembling the average market-leading product to the extent that it is acceptable to enough customers for the organization to make a profit. An example of a niche cost focus company could be a local supermarket stocking budget food and other household items.

Achieving a low-cost position affords an organization with greater pricing flexibility than its rivals, which can be used as a tool for sustaining competitive advantage. It is important to note that cost and price are not used interchangeably here. An organization that achieves a low-cost position can maintain flexibility in its pricing strategy. In a less competitive market, the organization may choose to maintain the price at the same level as its competitors, thus earning a higher level of profit due to its low-cost base. In a fiercely competitive market, the organization may wish to set the price below its rivals' price to maintain market share, given that competitors with a higher cost base would find it difficult to match the lower price without incurring losses.

Low-cost strategy is usually most effective in industries in which the material characteristics or the reputation of the product/service is less important than the price. This is especially true in commodity markets where competing offerings are virtually indistinguishable from each other. The airline industry has suffered from commoditization for a long time. Although airlines have tried to differentiate their services in the eyes of the travelling public, customers don't seem to value the airlines' differentiation efforts to build customer loyalty. Travellers usually make their buying decisions based on price and choose an airline that best fits their travel schedule.

On the other hand, a low-cost strategy is less likely to be successful in industries or markets that are characterized by expectations of differentiation. This is particularly true for services such as legal advice, consulting advice, and medical care. Customers are more concerned about the reputation and quality of advice and care than the price of the service. Most customers would probably be wary of a lawyer or financial advisor who emphasized low fees.

To achieve an overall low-cost position, the focus of the organization's operating activities is a relentless focus on improving efficiency and lowering the overall costs. Successful low-cost strategies are often characterized by:

- low labour costs achieved through capital-intensive production processes;
- product design that can be manufactured easily with shared components;
- sophisticated inventory and supply chain management systems;
- low-cost distribution networks.

Efficiency-focused value-creation processes must be accompanied by a culture and managerial attitude that emphasizes close supervision of labour, cost control in all activities across the organization, and incentives that are based on achieving cost and efficiency targets.

Differentiation strategies

Differentiation strategies aim to give an organization a competitive advantage by offering customers products that are perceived as unique on either a broad or narrow market basis. Differentiation strategy works best in industries and markets where the characteristics of products and services themselves offer opportunities for differentiation. Automotive, fashion, and consumer product industries are prime examples of industries where differentiation strategies work best. However, innovative differentiation strategies can be found in even the most basic commodity industries. An example is Morton Salt, an old US brand and a very basic commodity. Morton Salt is packaged in a container with a distinctive blue label with a yellow illustration of a girl holding an umbrella (Figure 8.5).

The company's strapline 'When it rains it pours' implies that even in humid conditions Morton's salt pours without getting clogged up. Morton has recently launched its first major brand campaign in the firm's 168-year history, which sponsored the music video of OK Go's *The One Moment*. It was one of the breakout videos of 2016 and by 2019 it had attracted over 25 million YouTube and 24 million Facebook views. The video was just one small part of the brand's effort to recreate itself as a much more 'on trend' company that speaks directly to millennials who

FIGURE 8.5 Evolution of the Morton Salt girl. *Source*: Copyright © 1995–2019 Morton Salt, Inc. All rights reserved.

reputably value quality ingredients and foods. The strategy seems to work as Morton Salt products usually retail at a premium of over 30% compared with competing salt products.

Differentiation necessitates differences between competing products or services, but it is the customer's perception of the experience that the product or service offers which is critical to the long-term success of a differentiation strategy. Organizations that can create an emotional bond with their customers are more likely to benefit from long-lasting customer loyalty towards their offering. This is especially important in markets that are characterized by fickle trends or fads.

Morton Salt attempts to cement this type of emotional bond by creating an image of Morton Salt beyond the salt itself and making it what the firm calls an 'emotional lifestyle choice'. It is increasingly imperative for the Morton brand to connect on a more emotional level. This comes even as competition grows from other products like kosher salt or Himalayan pink salt and as Morton tries to tell customers that its product is key to their everyday lives beyond food—for example, it is used in health care and farming.

The ability to innovate, in addition to strong marketing skills, is an important organizational capability for organizations that pursue differentiation strategies. They must continuously be able to develop new products or product extensions that are perceived as unique by customers. Gillette has been the dominant firm in the wet-shaving market and it has maintained its lead by continuously launching new product iterations and extensions. Although online sellers like Dollar Shave Club have eaten into its market share in the United States, Gillette still controls 65% of the global blades and razors market with the slogan 'The best a man can get'. However, the main risk of differentiation strategies is that, in their attempts to constantly increase the functionality of their products in order to maintain or even increase premium pricing, companies may add features that are no longer considered of added value and price by customers. For example, in 2016, Philips launched a 'OneBlade' razor in the United Kingdom that mocks Gillette's strategy of introducing an ever-increasing number of blades into their shaver cartridges.

To sustain a differentiation advantage, organizations must possess or be able to enhance their:

- innovation and research capabilities to improve the perceived value of their products and services by customers;
- ability to coordinate R&D, manufacturing, and marketing to ensure a high-quality product or service;
- ability to attract highly skilled scientists, designers, marketers, and creative people.

The organizational culture and management focus of successful differentiators is to ensure that the organization produces offerings of the highest possible quality and undertakes support activities in communicating with and distributing to customers that ensure superior customer satisfaction.

Hybrid strategies

Porter (1985) argues that successful organizations must select and concentrate on effectively implementing one of the generic strategies. According to Porter, an organization that attempts to pursue low-cost and differentiation strategies simultaneously ends up 'stuck in the middle' without clear strategic focus, which will ultimately lead into failure.

New strategy playbook

The end of (sustainable) competitive advantage means that prior assumptions about effective strategies for sustaining organizations are no longer relevant. A new playbook is required that prompts organizations to explore how they can build their capabilities to move from one competitive arena to another rather than attempting to defend existing or ageing sources of competitive advantage. Organizations that can do this are likely to show a notable continuing degree of dynamism. Moving from one advantage to another advantage will become perceived as quite normal, not exceptional. Clinging to older advantages is seen as potentially dangerous. Disengagement from old advantages is seen as intelligent and failures as potential harbingers of useful insight. Most importantly, organizations develop a rhythm for moving from one arena to another, and rather than the wrenching downsizings and restructurings that are so common in organizational life today, disengagements will occur in a steady rhythm, rather than as a result of radical change (McGrath 2013b).

Finally, as the pace of competition becomes faster, decisions that are made quickly, that are roughly right, and that are satisfactory are likely to beat a decision-making process that is more precise but slower. Prediction and being right will be less important than reacting quickly and taking corrective action (see Chapter 3).

PRACTITIONER INSIGHT **DICK HOWESON, CEO, UTALK**

We were not too concerned about competition as Andrew and I knew that we were going to be different—we have always been different.

(Richard Howeson, CEO)

How would you like to learn 134 languages including Kinyarwanda, Greenlandic, Oromo, Cockney, or even Star Trek Klingon? This is what uTalk, a London-based educational publisher known primarily for its interactive language learning, is able to offer its globe- and galaxy-trotting customers.

The company was established in 1999 by Richard (Dick) Howeson and Andrew Ashe. uTalk is distinctive among language self-study programmes in teaching most of the target languages with a choice of over 130 base languages, so the programmes can be used all over the world. The company's products are sold worldwide through their website and a network of distributors; 70% of the firm's

revenue comes from outside the United Kingdom. uTalk content is also sold under the Instant Immersion brand in the United States. As a differentiating feature, uTalk's customers have access to language-learningprogrammesfrom uTalk's websites that have been localized for global audiences and through Apple's App Store.

Competition in the language-learning market is fierce and most self-study programme businesses aim to provide their customers fluency, but 'We don't do that', says Dick Howeson, uTalk's CEO. Instead, the company focuses on providing solutions for a 'job to be done'—helping people to get by in a foreign country. 'If you ask anyone on the street if they would like to learn a foreign language most will

Continued

say "Yes", but if you ask them how much time they have, the answer is "Not much", but most would like to learn enough to get by. That's what we do and we make learning a language fun and simple.'

Dick tells a story of landing at the airport in Hungary and needing to visit the restroom but not being able to figure out which door was for men and which for women as the doors did not have pictures on them. This was his Eureka moment as he realized that most travellers would love to learn the basics, if only just being able to understand the restroom signage. People should be able to open up their laptop on the plane to their destination and learn the rudimentary basics by the time they land. The focus should be on the spoken word, not writing or grammar. 'Many people have been telling us that we should add grammar courses, but we don't do that [...] you can go and buy a grammar book if you are interested.' The company does not use focus groups, but it has begun running pop-up learning sessions in Costa Coffee shops in London. Participants get the app, which normally costs £49, free of charge. Although uTalk does not make a profit from the classes, they do help to build brand awareness, and the workshops give a chance to get feedback on the firm's language-teaching techniques.

Dick's airport Eureka moment occurred at the time when digital technologies and laptops with CD-ROM readers were becoming available to consumers at a reasonable price. Andrew trained himself as a multimedia designer and Dick visited a library to read everything he could find on learning a foreign language. He came across six different theories which all contradicted each other. Dick concluded that, as there was no conclusive evidence of a best way to learn a language, then uTalk would come up with its own language-learning theory. Armed with Dick's insight and Andrew's programming skills, the pair set out to develop their own CD-ROM-based interactive language-learning programme. 'As Englishmen, we naturally began by designing a French course with English as a base language.' The course sold well, but soon uTalk began receiving inquiries from distributors and agents for an English language course with French as a base language and a French language course with German as a base language. 'We realised very early on that whenever we developed a new language learning course we

also needed to make sure that this language could be used as a base language platform for another language program.'

Another differentiator for the firm is that thinking about languages both as a target and as a base language gave uTalk an unprecedented number of theoretical language programme combinations. With 134 languages and 130 base languages, the firm is able to offer 17,430 language combinations. To reach the maximum target audience for the most popular language combinations, uTalk hired website designers and coders to create websites in base languages that could be accessed by anyone with internet access, anywhere in the world, in local language.

uTalk had always used Apple Mac-based technology and when Steve Jobs launched iPad in 2010, Andrew, uTalk's chief technologist, called it a truly revolutionary product that would permanently change how people learn things. The firm's CD-ROM-based product was still selling strongly alongside internet downloads, but the company saw apps as the way forward. By this time, the company had a built an in-house technology development capability, and today most of uTalk's most popular languages are available in the Apple and Google App stores.

'Andrew and I have always been a bit different', says Dick. 'We have lunch out together every week and we think about the world, not only business, and come up with ideas to make the world a better place. When people say that something can't be done, we try to go and do it to prove people wrong.' Learning a language can be a step in making the world better. uTalk has developed Chatterbox, a classroom teaching tool for primary-aged children, which can be used the world over, and the firm supports the charity onebillion.org to educate one billion children in maths and languages with the help of apps wherever they are in the world. 'The key to our success is to build a product that we are passionate about and that we know works.'

Dick's guide to uTalk apps can be found at https://youtu.be/fhxnNKNwd58.

 Access the online resources to watch a short video clip where Dick Howeson talks more about his career.

CHAPTER SUMMARY

In this chapter, we addressed the following learning outcomes:

○ Define the nature and sources of competitive advantage.

We defined competitive advantage as the difference between the economic value that the organization creates from its business model and the economic value created by its rivals. Two prominent views on competitive advantage show that advantage can arise from the organization's position in the industry and/or its internal resources and capabilities.

○ Appreciate the link between the organization's business model, its value-creating strategic resources, and strategies for achieving competitive advantage.

The resource-based perspective of the organization states that the organization's competitive advantage arises from the exploitation of its strategic resources to produce a product or service that is different from a competitive offer. Such an offer has to be better in terms of either providing better value for money or by being significantly different so that customers are willing to pay a premium price for it. The organization's configuration of strategic resources will influence the organization's orientation to pursue either low-cost or differentiation strategies.

○ Recognize the importance of isolating mechanisms, causal ambiguity, and dynamic capabilities in achieving and maintaining competitive advantage.

Imitation is the most direct form of competition. Isolating mechanisms (unique historical conditions, path dependency, patents, social complexity) and causal ambiguity can act as deterrents to such competitive erosion. Another threat to the organization's competitive advantage is competitive and technological innovation. Therefore it is imperative that the organization is continually able to renew its strategic resources and capabilities.

○ Understand generic strategies that organizations can apply to gain competitive advantage.

We presented two main frameworks for an organization's strategic orientation: Porter's generic strategies of cost leadership, differentiation, and focus and Bowman's strategy clock, also often referred to as the customer matrix. We also considered the feasibility of hybrid strategy. An organization's strategic orientation is greatly influenced by its business model and the configuration of its strategic resources and capabilities.

○ Consider the feasibility of maintaining a sustainable competitive advantage in highly competitive and dynamic environments

We demonstrated that in highly dynamic and competitive markets it may not be possible for organizations to enjoy a sustainable competitive advantage for an extended period of time. Instead, organizations should focus on earning successive temporary advantages, which requires them to continually reconfigure their business operations and even disengage from activities that no longer create value and a competitive advantage.

? END-OF-CHAPTER QUESTIONS

Recall questions

1. What is a business value proposition?
2. Define competitive advantage.
3. What is an isolating mechanism?

Application questions

A) What impact does resource heterogeneity have on how organizations in the same industry compete?
B) What are the differences between characteristic and linkage ambiguity and what impact do they have on competitive imitation?
C) Compare and contrast the similarities and differences between Porter's generic strategies, the strategy clock, and hybrid strategies.

8

; ONLINE RESOURCES

www.oup.com/he/mackay2e

In addition to the video interviews already highlighted, the book's **online resources** include the following features for this chapter, specifically:

- *links to further reading material* to broaden your knowledge of key issues discussed in this chapter;
- *self-test multiple-choice questions* to test your understanding of the material covered in each section of the chapter; and
- *a flashcard glossary* to help you recall and test your understanding of key terms.

FURTHER READING

'Firm resources and sustained competitive advantage' by Jay Barney

Barney, J. (1991). Firm resources and sustained competitive advantage. *Journal of Management*, **17**(1), 99–120.

Understanding sources of sustained competitive advantage has become a major area of research in strategic management. Building on the assumptions that strategic resources are heterogeneously distributed across firms and that these differences are stable over time, this article examines the link between firm resources and sustained competitive advantage.

'Dynamic capabilities: What are they?' by Kathleen M. Eisenhardt and Jeffrey A. Martin

Eisenhardt, K.M. and Martin, J.A. (2000). Dynamic capabilities: What are they? *Strategic Management Journal*, **21**(10–11), 1105–21.

This seminal article focuses on dynamic capabilities and, more generally, on the resource-based perspective of the firm. The authors argue that dynamic capabilities are a set of specific and identifiable processes such as product development, strategic decision-making, and alliancing. They are detailed, analytic, stable processes with predictable outcomes.

The End of Competitive Advantage: How to Keep Your Strategy Moving as Fast as Your Business by Rita Gunther McGrath

McGrath, R.G (2013). *The End of Competitive Advantage: How to Keep Your Strategy Moving as Fast as Your Business*. Boston, MA: Harvard Business School Publishing.

This book argues that it's time to go beyond the very concept of sustainable competitive advantage. Instead, organizations need to forge a new path to winning: capturing opportunities fast, exploiting them decisively, and moving on even before they are exhausted. McGrath shows how to do this with a new set of practices based on the notion of transient competitive advantage.

'The causal ambiguity paradox: Deliberate actions under causal ambiguity' by Derrick McIver and Cynthia Lengnick-Hall

McIver, D. and Lengnick-Hall, C. (2018). The causal ambiguity paradox: Deliberate actions under causal ambiguity. *Strategic Organization*, **16**(3), 304–22.

Causal ambiguity describes a lack of understanding of cause-and-effect interactions between resources and competitive advantage. As a central construct in strategic management, causal ambiguity constrains an organization's ability to replicate valuable capabilities internally, yet simultaneously offers a means of protecting those capabilities from imitation by external agents. This shifts the attention from looking at casual ambiguity as a given characteristic within organizations and examines the causal ambiguity paradox by looking at how organizations can strategically act on causal ambiguity as a mechanism for extending advantages.

'From customer understanding to strategy innovation: Practical tools to establish competitive positioning' by Cliff Bowman and Richard Schoenberg

Bowman, C. and Schoenberg, R. (2008). From customer understanding to strategy innovation: Practical tools to establish competitive positioning. In Galvan, R., Murray, J., and Markides, C. (eds), *Strategy, Innovation, and Change.* Oxford: Oxford University Press.

This chapter is a full discussion of the customer matrix that is derived from the perceptions that customers have of the products or services offered to them and the prices charged by firms. Perceived use value and price represent the two elements of 'value for money'. The customer matrix separates perceived use value and price from each other to assist strategists in analysing competitive strategy.

REFERENCES

Ambrosini, V. and Bowman, C. (2008). Surfacing tacit sources of success. *International Small Business Journal*, **26**(4), 403–32.

Anthony, S. (2016). Kodak's downfall wasn't about technology. *Harvard Business Review* (July) (reprint H02ZWT).

Barney, J.B. (1986). Organizational culture: Can it be a source of sustained competitive advantage? *Academy of Management Review* **11**(3), 656–65.

Barney, J. (1991). Firm resources and sustained competitive advantage. *Journal of Management*, **17**(1), 99–120.

Barthelemy, J. and Adsit, D. (2003). The seven deadly sins of outsourcing. *Academy of Management Executive*, **17**(2), 87–100.

Beardsley, S.C. et al. (2006). Competitive advantage from better interactions. *McKinsey Quarterly* (May), http://www.mckinsey.com/business-functions/organization/our-insights/competitive-advantage-from-better-interactions (last accessed 18 August 2022).

BloombergUK (2019). Amazon plans to launch thousands of satellites to provide broadband (4 April), https://www.bloomberg.com/news/articles/2019-04-04/amazon-plans-to-launch-thousands-of-satellites-for-broadband (last accessed 18 August 2022).

Bowman, C. (1988). *Strategy in Practice*. Harlow: Prentice Hall.

Bowman, C. and Faulkner, D. (1997). *Competitive and Corporate Strategy*. London: Irwin.

Bowman, C. and Schoenberg, R. (2008). From customer understanding to strategy innovation: Practical tools to establish competitive positioning. In Galvan, R., Murray., J. and Markides, C. (eds), *Strategy, Innovation, and Change.* Oxford: Oxford University Press.

Bruni, D.S. and Verona, G. (2009). Dynamic marketing capabilities in science-based firms: An exploratory investigation of the pharmaceutical industry. *British Journal of Management*, **20**(Special Issue—March), S101–S117.

CBInsights (2019). Infographic: Amazon's biggest acquisitions (19 June), https://www.cbinsights.com/research/amazon-biggest-acquisitions-infographic (last accessed 18 August 2022).

Christensen, C.M., Hall, T. Dillon, K., and Duncan, D.S. (2016). Know your customers' 'jobs to be done'. *Harvard Business Review* (September), 54–62.

CNBC (2018). Amazon just opened a new store that sells popular items from its website. Here's what it looks like inside (27 September), https://www.cnbc.com/2018/09/27/amazon-just-opened-its-4-star-store-in-new-york-heres-a-look.html (last accessed 18 August 2022).

Day, G., Reibstein, D., and Gunther, R. (eds) (1997). Wharton on Dynamic Competitive Strategy. New York: John Wiley.

Denning, S. (2013). It's official! The end of competitive advantage, *Forbes* (2 June), https://www.forbes.com/sites/stevedenning/2013/06/02/its-official-the-end-of-competitive-advantage/#3fbb9c831565 (last accessed 18 August 2022).

Dierickx, I. and Cool, K. (1989). Asset stock accumulation and the sustainability of competitive advantage. *Management Science*, **35**(12), 1504–11.

The Economist (2017). Amazon, the world's most remarkable firm, is just getting started (25 May), https://www.economist.com/leaders/2017/03/25/amazon-the-worlds-most-remarkable-firm-is-just-getting-started (last accessed 18 August 2022).

Eisenhardt, K.M. and Martin, J.A. (2000). Dynamic capabilities: What are they? *Strategic Management Journal*, **21**(10–11), 1105–21.

Fashionista (2017). Happy Socks built a $100 million sock business—and it's coming for women's fashion next (19 July), https://fashionista.com/2017/07/happy-socks-swedish-label (last accessed 8 May 2021).

Fast Company (2011). Happy Socks builds a business and happiness two feet at a time (16 December), https://www.fastcompany.com/1679274/happy-socks-builds-a-business-and-happiness-two-feet-at-a-time (last accessed 8 May 2021).

The Financial Times (2021). Walmart vs Amazon: The battle to dominate grocery (11 May), https://www.ft.com/content/9ab41b9e-a294-430f-951d-49cfc3415460 (last accessed 18 August 2022).

Forbes (2018). Five reasons why Amazon is driving into bricks-and-mortar retail (19 December), https://www.forbes.com/sites/annaschaverien/2018/12/29/amazon-online-offline-store-retail/#76bf35f51287 (last accessed 18 August 2022).

Forbes (2021). Amazon's net profit soars 84% with sales hitting $386 billion (2 February), https://www.forbes.com/sites/shelleykohan/2021/02/02/amazons-net-profit-soars-84-with-sales-hitting-386-billion/?sh=7b9be73a1334 (last accessed 18 August 2022).

The Guardian (2019a). Amazon blamed as 'iconic' bookshops announce closure (30 May), https://www.theguardian.com/books/2019/may/30/amazon-blamed-as-iconic-bookshops-announce-closure (last accessed 18 August 2022).

The Guardian (2019b). Unputdownable! The bookshops Amazon couldn't kill (6 June), https://www.theguardian.com/books/2019/jun/06/amazon-booksellers-beating-odds-book-shops (last accessed 18 August 2022).

The Guardian (2022). John Lewis drops 'never knowingly unsold' pledge (25 February), https://www.theguardian.com/business/2022/feb/25/john-lewis-drops-never-knowingly-undersold-pledge (last accessed 15 July 2022).

Happy Socks (2019). Sustainability Report 2019, https://a.storyblok.com/f/54304/x/e4d886d315/sustainability-report-2019.pdf (last accessed 8 May 2021).

Hendry, J. (1990). The problem with Porter's generic strategies. *European Management Review*, 8(4), 443–50.

Jobs, S. (2003). Steve Jobs rare interview. 60-minutes, https://www.youtube.com/watch?v=ZUfzXz23ndo (last accessed 18 August 2022).

Johnson, M.W., Christensen, C.M. and Kagermann, H. (2008). Reinventing your business model. *Harvard Business Review* (December) (reprint).

King, A.W. (2007). Disentangling interfirm and intrafirm causal ambiguity: A conceptual model of causal ambiguity and sustainable competitive advantage. *Academy of Management Review*, **32**(1), 156–78.

Leonard-Barton, D. (1992). Core capabilities and core rigidities: A paradox in managing new product development. *Strategic Management Journal*, **13**(S1), 111–25.

McGrath, R.G. (2013a). *The End of Competitive Advantage: How to Keep Your Strategy Moving as Fast as Your Business*. Boston, MA: Harvard Business School Publishing.

McGrath, R. (2013b). The end of competitive advantage. European *Business Review* (7 November), https://www.europeanbusinessreview.com/the-end-of-competitive-advantage (last accessed 18 August 2022).

McIver, D. and Lengnick-Hall, C. (2018). The causal ambiguity paradox: Deliberate actions under causal ambiguity. *Strategic Organization*, **16**(3), 304–22.

McMaken, M. (2012). E-books vs print books (7 April), http://www.investopedia.com/financial-edge/0812/e-books-vs.-print-books.aspx (last accessed 18 August 2022).

Peters, T.J. and Waterman, R.H. (1982). *In Search of Excellence.* New York: Harper & Row.

Porter, M.E. (1980). *Competitive Strategy: Techniques for Analyzing Industries and Competitors*. New York: Free Press.

Porter, M.E. (1985). *Competitive Advantage: Creating and Sustaining Superior Performance*. New York: Free Press.

Quick Books Commerce (2018). How Happy Socks created a $100 million eCommerce business? (11 December), https://www.tradegecko.com/blog/small-business-growth/how-happy-socks-created-100-million-ecommerce-business (last accessed 8 May 2021).

Rumelt, R.P. (1984). Toward a strategic theory of the firm. In: Lamb R. (ed.), *Competitive Strategic Management*. Upper Saddle River, NJ: Prentice Hall, pp. 556–70.

Rumelt, R.P. (2003). What in the world is competitive advantage? Working paper, Anderson School, University of California, Los Angeles.

Scan Magazine (2020). Happy Socks: Spreading happiness, one colourful sock at a time. Scan Client Publishing, https://scanmagazine.co.uk/happy-socks (last accessed 8 May 2021).

Schoemaker, P.J.H., Heaton, S., and Teece, D. (2018). Innovation, dynamic capabilities, and leadership. *California Management Review*, **61**(1), 15–42.

Strebel, P. (1996). Why do employees resist change? *Harvard Business Review*, **74**(3), 86–92.

Teece, D.J., Pisano, G., and Shuen, A. (1997). Dynamic capabilities and strategic management. *Strategic Management Journal*, **18**(7), 509–33.

Thurm, S. (1998). Copy this typeface? Court ruling counsels caution. *Wall Street Journal*, 15 July.

The Verge (2019). Here's Amazon's new transforming Prime Air delivery drone (5 June), https://www.theverge.com/2019/6/5/18654044/amazon-prime-air-delivery-drone-new-design-safety-transforming-flight-video (last accessed 18 August 2022).

Wang, C.L. and Ahmed, P.K. (2007). Dynamic capabilities: A review and research agenda. *International Journal of Management Reviews*, **9**(1), 31–51.

Wernerfelt, B. (1984). A resource-based view of the firm. *Strategic Management Journal*, **5**, 171–80.

Zollo, M. and Winter, S.G. (2002). Deliberate learning and the evolution of dynamic capabilities. *Organization Science*, **13**(3), 339–51.

8

CHAPTER NINE

Functional Strategy and Performance

CONTENTS

By the end of this chapter, you should be able to:

○ Describe the role of functional strategy in supporting organizational strategy

○ Outline the main types of functional strategy: financial strategy, HRM strategy, marketing strategy, operations strategy, IT strategy

○ Discuss the potential advantages and disadvantages of functional strategy

○ Explain the role of strategic performance management tools (e.g. balanced scorecard) in connecting functional strategy with the effective implementation of organizational strategy

TOOLBOX

○ **Functional strategies: financial, HRM, marketing, operations, IT**
Functional strategies are the strategies adopted by each functional area of the organization such as finance, human resource management, marketing, operations, and IT. Functional strategies need to be in line with the overall business/corporate strategy to help the organization to achieve its overall objectives.

○ **McFarlan's strategic grid**
This model can help an organization to assess the relationship between IT projects, business operations, and business functions. One axis of the grid focuses on IT's relationship with business strategy, the other focuses on its relationship with business operations. IT projects and initiatives, both current and proposed, are placed on the grid based on their expected impact.

○ **Balanced scorecard (Kaplan and Norton)**
This is a strategic performance measurement model that can help managers to translate an organization's mission and vision into functional plans and activities. It can provide information on the organization's performance against its chosen strategy, aiding feedback and learning.

○ **Strategy map (Kaplan and Norton)**
This is a diagram that represents the organization's strategy on a single page and is a useful tool for making clear connections between the performance of each function and the performance of the organization as a whole.

9

OPENING CASE STUDY **VAIL RESORTS**

Founded in the early 1960s in the Vail Valley, Colorado, Vail Resorts Inc. is the parent company for three 'highly integrated and interdependent business segments'—Mountain, Hospitality, and Development. The Mountain segment operates 37 ski resorts in the United States, Canada, and Australia and includes lift ticket, ski and snowboard school, dining, and retail and rental businesses. The Hospitality segment includes a portfolio of hotels and properties near mountain resorts. The Development segment holds, develops, buys, and sells real estate in and around Vail's resort communities.

As reported by Bloomberg, an important innovation for Vail was:

the introduction of the Epic Pass in 2008 for unlimited lift rides at all of its (then five) resorts for $579, roughly one-third the cost of other existing passes. It has an important catch: pass sales were offered only before the season hit its stride, closing right before Thanksgiving. By getting skiers to buy early, the company locked in a mass of customers and raked in a pile of revenue during its slowest months.

The company achieved a 22% increase in revenue in the first year, and over the subsequent decade invested in adding resorts across North America as a hedge against weather.

Building on the lock-in achieved by the 'pass' model, CEO Rob Katz reportedly realized that the key to making money in the ski industry isn't necessarily finding more skiers—it's getting more money from the ones you already have. In 2018, for every daily visit to a resort by a skier, it collected $168 and paid only $135, a 20% profit margin. Half the revenue came from lift passes and the rest from ancillary products and services.

Vail uses technology extensively throughout its operations. According to Bloomberg:

Every Vail pass or ticket is embedded with a radio frequency identification chip, which is automatically scanned at every ski lift. Vail knows how much, where, and with whom each guest skis. The data are used to predict how likely the person is

to return to a Vail resort. It's a Big Data play in an historically analogue industry.

Cross-functional work helps deliver gains for Vail. IT and marketing teams work together to brainstorm and realize new customer apps, express day tickets (digital downloads), lift wait-time transparency, and an on-mountain digital assistant to keep visitors informed and happy. The IT function makes sure that the digital support structure exists to make marketing's understanding of what matters most to customers a reality.

Vail employs around 55,000 full-time or seasonal staff. The company prescribes a set of foundational values to be lived out 'every day in everything we do—Serve Others, Do Right, Be Inclusive, Drive Value, Do Good, Be Safe, Have Fun'. To help manage growth and consistency of experience across locations, Vail has agreements with a number of corporate partners—for example, Pepsi for drinks, Helly Hansen for clothing, and a zero-waste partner, Eco-Products.

Vail Resorts was awarded the 2019 Golden Eagle Award for Environmental Excellence by the National Ski Areas Association; it was also recognized by *Forbes* as one of 'America's Best Large Employers' in 2021 and a 'Best Employer for Diversity' for efforts to advance women in a traditionally male-dominated industry.

Questions for discussion

1. How would you summarize Vail Resorts' IT strategy? How core is its competence in technology to its business strategy?

2. How would you summarize Vail Resorts' financial strategy? How does it manage the flow of funds to support its business strategy?

3. How would you summarize Vail Resorts' HR strategy? How important is the right corporate culture to its business strategy?

Sources

BloombergUK (2019). The battle for the best ski pass (1 March), https://www.bloomberg.com/news/features/2019-03-01/epic-vs-ikon-battle-for-the-best-ski-pass (last accessed 18 August 2022).

9

Cision PR Newswire (2019). Vail Resorts named one of 'America's best employers' by *Forbes* (19 April), https://www.prnewswire.com/news-releases/vail-resorts-named-one-of-americas-best-employers-by-forbes-300835166.html (last accessed 18 August 2022).

Cision PR Newswire (2021). Vail Resorts named one of 'America's Best Largest Employers 2021' by Forbes (11 February), https://www.prnewswire.com/news-releases/vail-resorts-named-one-of-americas-best-large-employers-2021-by-forbes-301227357.html (last accessed 18 August 2022).

Magzter (2019). The Great M&A Ski War (4 March), https://www.magzter.com/stories/Business/Bloomberg-Businessweek/The-Great-MA-Ski-War (last accessed 18 August 2022).

Mountain Times (2021). Major reset in Epic Pass prices a game changer (31 March), https://mountaintimes.info/major-reset-in-epic-pass-prices-a-game-changer (last accessed 18 August 2022).

SkitheWorld.com (2019). One pass to ski them all (3 March), https://skitheworld.com/2019/03/one-pass-to-ski-them-all (last accessed 18 August 2022).

The Storm Skiing Journal and Podcast (2021). Vail slashes epic pass prices by 20 percent, further de-mystifying the season pass (24 March), https://www.stormskiing.com/p/vail-slashes-epic-pass-prices-by (last accessed 18 August 2022).

Vail Resorts, http://www.vailresorts.com/Corp/info/values.aspx (last accessed 18 August 2022).

Vail Resorts. Partners, https://www.vail.com/footer/strategic-alliance-partners.aspx (last accessed 18 August 2022).

Vail Resorts (2019). Vail Resorts receives NSAA Gold Eagle Award for Environmental Excellence (6 May), http://news.vailresorts.com/corporate/vailresorts/vail-resorts-wins-golden-eagle-award-environmental-excellence.htm (last accessed 18 August 2022).

9.1 **Introduction**

A discussion of strategic management often focuses at the level of the corporate or the whole organization (see Chapter 1). However, strategizing can occur within elements of an organization in which the aims and activities of the rest of the organization form part of the context influencing what people do in relation to strategy. The same dynamic frameworks of strategy identified in Chapter 2 still apply but the practitioners involved in making and realizing decisions are focused on specific functional concerns. In this chapter, we consider the functional strategies which, particularly in medium and large organizations, support the organizational strategy and ensure that it is delivered as intended. We can think of functional strategy as the organizational strategies and plans prepared for various functional areas of the organization such as financial strategy, human resources management (HRM) strategy, marketing strategy, operations strategy, and information technology (IT) strategy. Functional strategies can be both part of the organization's overall strategy and a key element of 'cascading' or implementing the organizational strategy within each functional area. In this chapter, we explore each of the main areas of functional strategy, summarizing what each type of strategy involves and highlighting some of the key factors to be considered when developing a successful strategy in each area. In our final section on managing strategic performance, we look at tools, such as the balanced scorecard, which can help us to understand the relationship between the organization's overall strategy and the operation of its key functions; we also explore how the firm can use functional strategies in order to manage the implementation of organizational strategy.

9.2 **Types of functional strategy**

As discussed in Chapter 1, organizational strategy formation is made up of three main types of strategy (see Figure 9.1):

- **Corporate strategy**: relating to the entire organization, asking the question, 'Where should we operate and compete?'
- **Business strategy**: strategies for individual business units or sectors of industry, asking, 'How should we compete?'
- **Functional strategy**: strategies for each function, such as finance, marketing, and operations, asking the question, 'How should we operate?'

We can break this functional strategy down into common areas (see Figure 9.2) in order to provide an understanding of how organizations can operate successfully. These common areas are:

- **Financial strategy**: includes selecting the main source(s) of funding, the development of the organization's own funds, and so on.
- **HRM strategy**: includes decisions about how staff are recruited and organized such as the type of organizational structure, compensation system, etc.
- **Marketing strategy**: includes decisions around the pricing of products and services, their promotion and distribution, the image and public relations of the organization and so on.
- **Operations strategy**: may include the crucial 'make or buy' decisions that define what the company produces itself and what it purchases from suppliers or partners.
- **IT strategy**: outlines how information technology should be used to help achieve the organization's goals, including an outline of current and future IT projects and initiatives.

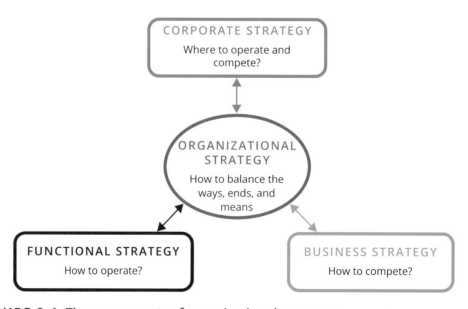

FIGURE 9.1 The components of organizational strategy. *Source*: authors.

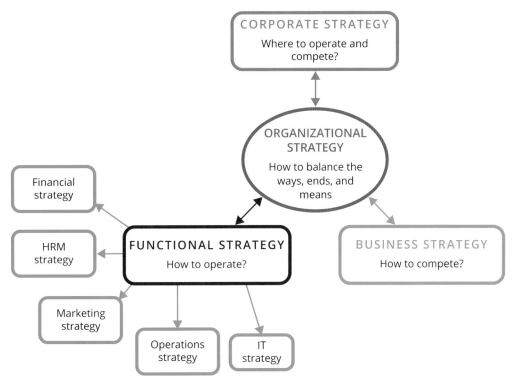

FIGURE 9.2 The components of functional strategy. *Source*: authors.

Advantages and disadvantages of functional strategy

A strong functional strategy is a valuable tool for helping leaders and individuals within each function to understand the overarching strategy of the organization and align with that strategy and help deliver it. When many people encounter the notion of 'strategy' for the first time, they assume that strategic thinking and strategy implementation are only for the senior executives of the organization. However, we argue that 'strategy is everyone's job'; that is, strategic thinkers are needed within every function of the organization—starting from entry level. If a company can establish a difference at each level, or in each activity of the business, it is in a strong position to outperform its competitors. This highlights that functional and departmental leaders play a very demanding role in that they must be in tune with the organization's senior management and strategy and the needs and wants of customers, as well as the business environment, market, competitors and so on.

Therefore, functional strategy can provide many advantages to the organization, such as:

- **Coherence**: bringing together a complex set of operational level plans into a coherent strategic statement that clarifies the contribution of each function to the overall strategy.

- **Purpose**: highlighting the purpose and contribution of each function to the achievement of the organization's goals for the benefit of all parties (both within the function and in the rest of the organization).

- **Delegating roles and responsibilities**: assisting with the efficient allocation of employees and resources to the tasks where they have most knowledge and experience.

- **Motivation**: ensuring that employees feel that their abilities are being used effectively towards the attainment of both the function's and the organization's goals.
- **Leading to action**: helping each functional team to turn high-level strategic statements into actionable plans.

However, functional strategy can also have its disadvantages, such as:

- **Being ineffective in smaller organizations**: seen as a drain on resources and staff time.
- **Leading to potential conflicts**: causing conflict between the organization's overall strategy and one or more specific functional strategies, which must then be resolved.
- **Overstretching managers**: leaving functional managers feeling that they are facing too many conflicting requests and that they are 'stretched too thinly' across a range of priorities.
- **Distracting functional managers**: causing too much distraction to the point where functional managers can lose sight of the main objectives of the organization.

To seek to maximize the advantages of functional strategy while avoiding the downsides, organizations can focus on developing actionable programmes in each functional area. These actionable programmes should be closely aligned with the higher-level strategic statements of their business unit and/or organization and help to bring such statements to life for staff in each function. For example, consider the Opening Case Study on Vail Resorts. Its financial strategy includes investing in and managing a portfolio of real estate, hotels, and other accommodation and a sharp focus on revenue management with an innovative customer proposition. Its HR strategy includes a clear focus on a set of foundational values to be lived out by all employees, and these values are seen as key to supporting the organization's mission. Its IT strategy includes gathering and analysing rich customer data; the insights from this data are used to inform future marketing to customers and enhance the customer experience; and so on for each function. Each functional area has a clear sense of purpose and of what that function needs to do to support the overall organizational strategy. These functional strategies and action plans are not felt to be a distraction, a source of conflict, or a drain on resources; they are at the heart of what each function is about.

In the next five sections, we discuss each of the main areas of functional strategy in turn—financial, HRM, marketing, operations and IT.

9.3 Financial strategy

Financial strategy is core to the start-up and ongoing operation of any successful organization. What is meant by financial strategy? And how does it add value to an organization's strategy? It is important for strategists to consider how organizations that are seeking to implement their strategies and track their progress need clear financial goals and metrics. Managers make important decisions on a daily basis, and those decisions have financial implications. Such decisions might include recruiting staff, planning a marketing campaign, scheduling the organization's operations, or approving investment in an IT project. In other words, they connect with all of the other aspects of functional strategy that we discuss in this chapter. All of these decisions have important financial implications for the organization. We will consider what is meant by financial strategy in different kinds of organizations and how it can add value by supporting strategic planning and decision-making.

What is financial strategy?

Financial strategy has two components (Bender 2014):

- raising the funds needed by the organization in the most appropriate manner;
- managing the employment of those funds within the organization, including whether to reinvest or distribute any profits and how to do so in a way that is appropriate to the goals of the organization.

Imagine you are a manager in an organization, charged with making strategic decisions. In particular, your decisions are likely to impact upon the second component of Bender's definition of financial strategy, which concerns the appropriate use of funds within the organization. However, for a publicly listed company, we also need to remember the first component (raising funds), which leads us to consider the linkages between strategic decisions and the interests of shareholders, and hence the firm's relationship with capital markets. For any organization, a good financial strategy must reflect the interests of all internal and external stakeholders—as, indeed, should the overall strategy.

In Bender's definition of financial strategy, she uses the term 'appropriate to the goals of the organization'—highlighting that the aim of the financial strategy is to add value for the organization. She discusses the definitions of value in relation to a two-stage investment process for private firms as follows:

1. The **first step** is for shareholders and others to decide to invest in a company. This leads to a definition of **investor value** (Bender 2014), which reflects the required returns of the capital markets and is mirrored in the financial value placed on the company's securities by the markets.

2. The **second step** is the set of decisions by the organization with regard to how it invests in a portfolio of projects. This links to a definition of **corporate value** (Bender 2014), which is the present value of the expected returns from a combination of the current business strategies and future investment programmes.

To put this another way, elaborating on the first step in Bender's process: imagine that you are a venture capitalist—an investor who is interested in providing capital to a firm that is exhibiting high growth potential in return for an equity stake in the firm, as in *Dragon's Den* in the United Kingdom, or similar to *Shark Tank* in the United States. You might be interested in funding a start-up venture or a small firm with an exciting business idea that wants to expand.

What criteria will you be seeking to evaluate when you make your choice to invest in a particular firm? First, you will probably be looking for significant potential for earnings growth. However, venture capitalists have a range of questions in mind when choosing firms to invest in (Fried and Hisrich 1994; Mason and Stark 2004). Can the business idea be brought to market within a reasonable timescale (perhaps two or three years)? Can the business gain competitive advantage (see Chapter 8 for a longer discussion of competitive advantage)? And what is your opinion of the management of the firm? Do they have a good 'track record' in business? Do they exhibit leadership and demonstrate an ability to identify risks?

Putting ourselves in the shoes of a venture capitalist can help to make the connection between the two stages in Bender's investment process. Most managers will tend to focus on the second step of improving the organization's (internal) investments in its project portfolio to make it a 'better business'. However, the aims of corporate financial strategy remind us to focus on the first step as well. In profit-seeking organizations, this means creating (external) shareholder value and making the organization a better investment for shareholders or other potential investors. In the case of General Electric (Case Example 9.1), we can see the extreme pressure put on CEOs who are not seen to be delivering in this way. In not-for-profit organizations, the first step means creating stakeholder value through the delivery of an organizational purpose or mandate better than any alternative organizations.

Drivers of value

Bender (2014) suggests that there are seven drivers (based on Rappaport 1998) which can be utilized to create value. This model is widely adopted to underpin most corporate valuations and applied to explore sensitivity analysis and to evaluate synergies in mergers and acquisitions. The seven drivers are:

1. **Increase sales growth**: for example, launching new products or finding new markets for existing products (see Ansoff's matrix in Chapter 10).

2. **Increase the operating profit margin** (the relationship between money flowing in and expenses): for example, cutting costs or achieving economies of scale (discussed in Chapter 10), perhaps at the same time as boosting revenue.

3. **Reduce incremental investment in capital expenditure**: meaning the funds used to acquire and upgrade physical assets such as buildings and equipment.

4. **Reduce investment in working capital**: meaning the amount of money you need to expand your business and meet short-term responsibilities and expenses.

5. **Reduce the cost of capital**: that is, the cost of the firm's funds.

6. **Increase the time period of competitive advantage**: such as the time period over which the business is expected to generate returns on incremental investment which exceeds its cost of capital.

7. **Reduce the cash tax rate**: that is, tax payments over a particular time period.

If we look across different businesses, different drivers will be more or less important. In the hotel business, we may find that sales (i.e. the hotel occupancy rate) is the most important driver because of high fixed costs of property ownership in that sector. However, for a bank lending to corporate clients, profits are derived from a slim margin between the rate at which the bank borrows money and the rate at which it lends money to its customers. Therefore, the bank may create more value by seeking to improve interest margins and reducing its operating costs than by seeking to increase the volume of sales (lending).

So, how do we identify the key drivers of value in a particular organization? Researchers offer advice on this (e.g. Marr et al. 2004), with most approaches to identifying value drivers starting from the resource-based view (RBV) of the firm, given the importance of understanding an organization's resources and capabilities (see Chapter 6 for more on RBV) when considering how it adds value. The work of Amit and Zott (2001) is particularly important to today's organizations in that it explores new business models in the digital economy and argues that managers should focus on four interdependent dimensions of value creation:

- **Efficiency**: the greater the transaction efficiency gains that are enabled by a particular e-business, the lower the costs and hence the more valuable it will be.

- **Complementarities**: e-businesses can leverage the potential for value creation by offering bundles of complementary products and services to their customers.

- **Lock-in**: the greater the switching costs (i.e. the costs of switching to a rival firm), the lower the likelihood of customers and strategic partners migrating to competitors.

- **Novelty**: e-businesses innovate in the ways in which they do business, that is, in the structuring of transactions.

Consider Vail Resorts (our Opening Case Study): one of their value drivers is clearly 'novelty' (i.e. the introduction of the 'Epic Pass') and bringing valuable revenue before the height of the season by requiring skiers to buy early. Yet, half of Vail's revenue comes from ancillary products and services, suggesting that they have also given careful thought to 'complementarities'. Their use of IT is likely to allow developments in the 'efficiency' category, and their focus on understanding and delighting their customers is intended to encourage loyalty and repeat purchase.

A more recent study has both confirmed Amit and Zott's (2001) dimensions of value creation and found evidence of how they may interplay and reinforce one another. Caterpillar, a leading manufacturer of construction and mining equipment, engines, etc., collects valuable data on the performance of its equipment, such as engines (Visnjic et al. 2017); this can support powerful data analytics and give insight into the performance of a machine—a 'novelty' value driver. However, it can also represent an 'efficiency' value driver by supporting better cost management of expensive equipment over its lifetime, alongside other benefits such as better predictions of the future maintenance requirements of the machinery. Marr (2005) advocates using strategy maps (Kaplan and Norton 2004a, b) to identify key resources (we return to this in section 9.8 on managing strategic performance).

Financial strategy in different types of organization

Much of what we discuss in this section is applicable to all sorts of organizations. However, some of it only applies to publicly listed firms. In such a firm, the shareholders own the company and it is run by the directors. This raises a number of issues. First, there is a potential conflict of agency between the directors and the shareholders; directors' actions may not always be in line with shareholders' goals. Second, most publicly listed companies have thousands of shareholders; it is not possible for the directors to determine and act upon the goals of so many individuals. Therefore, we make assumptions about a generic 'shareholder value' as the company's target for performance—noting that if a listed company's share price does not perform as well as expected, it may become a target for a takeover bid. For example, in 2018, Melrose Industries, a company specializing in buying underperforming businesses, acquired GKN, a multinational automotive and aerospace components company, for around £8 billion. The deal hit the headlines again in 2019 when Melrose announced plans to close a GKN factory, leading to accusations of 'asset stripping' (*The Guardian* 2019). Critics were clearly questioning whether, if we look beyond a narrow definition of shareholder value, the steps taken by Melrose were in the interests of a wider set of stakeholders such as the employees of the GKN factory in question (see Chapter 14 for more discussion on the strategizing impact of the roles and activities of practitioners at the top of the organization).

As an alternative to publicly listed firms, consider the (rather different) situation in a private company. The company is often owned by its directors. Where this is not the case, there is still likely to be a strong link between the owners and the directors, so the directors can still communicate with the key stakeholders to discuss their goals. The main objectives may be financial security for family shareholders, for example, and/or the creation and maintenance of a business that will be passed on to future generations of the family. Such companies may be reluctant to take on debt; and they may be in a strong position to respond to the threat of a hostile takeover bid. For example, for a number of years, LVMH (or Louis Vuitton, the luxury goods conglomerate) pursued Hermès, the French high fashion manufacturer that has been led by the same family since it was founded in 1837. LVMH slowly acquired shares in Hermès in what was seen as the start of a hostile takeover. Hermès responded by, amongst other things, 'locking up' just over 50% of its shares in a holding company and challenging LVMH's actions in the French courts (Adams 2014). These tactics have been successful in supporting Hermès in its desire to remain as an independent family-led firm—but such challenges to private companies are not unusual and illustrate the need to align financial strategy with the overall organizational strategy in different ways in different types of organizations.

Linking financial strategy with business/corporate strategy

In this section, we have identified some of the important connections between financial strategy and the overall business strategy, including the impact of investment decisions in key strategic projects and the implications of those decisions for the organization's performance. We have explored the creation of value from a financial perspective (discussing the seven drivers), and we have touched on the different views of financial strategy that may emerge in different types of organization such as publicly listed and private firms. Case Example 9.1 gives us the opportunity to consider the financial strategy of General Electric, which includes a sharp focus on managing the firm's assets. But General Electric also needs to consider changing other important elements of its business such as the skills and capabilities of its senior executives. This illustrates that financial strategy is pursued alongside other elements of functional strategy such as human resource management—and we turn to this next.

CASE EXAMPLE 9.1 GENERAL ELECTRIC (GE) BREAKS UP

General Electric (GE) is a multinational conglomerate that has historically operated across a huge range of industries including aviation, health care, power, digital technologies, renewable energy, transportation, and capital. In 2001, GE's market value was over $400 billion; during the tenure of CEO Jack Welch, the company's value had risen by 4,000%. Yet, in late 2021, its current CEO, Laurence Culp, announced that GE would split its remaining operations into three remaining companies covering jet engines, power, and health care. As *The Economist* comments, this represents a modest reach compared to its past sprawl; what has driven the break-up of GE?

Following Welch's departure in 2001, Jeffrey Immelt became CEO, four days before the attacks on the World Trade Center in New York. This, combined with the global financial crisis some years later, had serious impacts on the aviation and financial services arms of GE. By 2018, the company hit a low point, valued at only $60 billion. Where Welch preferred organic growth, Immelt focused on acquisitions. In August 2017, Immelt was succeeded by John Flannery, and, in October 2017, the company revealed terrible third-quarter results. Flannery announced the need for urgent change. He sold GE's health-care unit for $1 billion; by disposing of other units, Flannery sold assets worth $20 billion. However, as GE had assets worth over $300 billion, this was a drop in the ocean. GE's shares fell by 12% as analysts were underwhelmed by the divestments.

Flannery's tenure was short; in October 2018, he was replaced by Laurence Culp. Culp was brought in from outside GE—a step last taken in the nineteenth century. *The Economist* notes that Culp speaks of the 'illusory benefits of synergy', arguing that 'a sharper purpose attracts and motivates people'. Commentators will be watching GE closely: is this the story of a demise of a famous conglomerate or will Culp's sharper purpose mark the beginning of a new era for the company?

Questions for discussion

1. How would you summarize GE's shifting financial strategy under CEOs Welch, Immelt, Flannery, and Culp?

2. How would you summarize the fit between GE's new business strategy and its financial strategy under the current CEO, Laurence Culp? Are there any aspects of the strategy that seem to be missing? What else would you like to know, before commenting on Culp's approach?

Sources

The Economist (2017). Flannery unveils his strategy to revive GE (16 November), https://www.economist.com/business/2017/11/16/flannery-unveils-his-strategy-to-revive-ge (last accessed 18 August 2022).

The Economist (2021a). General Electric breaks up (13 November), https://www.economist.com/business/2021/11/13/general-electric-breaks-up (last accessed 18 August 2022).

9.4 Human resource management strategy

In this section, we consider another key area of functional strategy: human resource management (HRM) strategy. This is generally considered to include an organization's plans for managing people, their performance, their training, and their development. It also covers the organization's culture and its approach to determining how people and culture fit into the organization's future growth strategies and plans. We will explore what HRM strategy involves, how it can be framed around five key questions, and how it links to the organization's overall business strategy.

What is HRM strategy?

Human resource management is the process through which management builds the workforce and creates the human performance that the organization needs (Boxall and Purcell 2016). This definition raises questions about the fit between the activities of the HR function and the organization's overall strategy. Strategic analysis in HRM can be framed around five questions (Boxall and Purcell 2016):

- **Talent**: can the firm recruit and retain the people it needs?
- **Performance**: is the model of HRM helping to deliver the kind of performance that the organization needs?
- **Strategic fit**: does the organization have a set of HRM models that fits its environment, its goals, and its configuration of activities?
- **Dynamism**: what economic and socio-political changes are likely to affect the firm's HR strategy and how should it prepare for them?
- **HR function**: how can HR departments contribute more strategically?

Managing HRM strategy

Next, we consider each of these five questions in turn to explore how HRM strategy can be managed.

Managing 'talent' via HRM strategy

In Chapter 1, we introduced the idea that when considering how to build competitive advantage, an organization can use the RBV (discussed in Chapter 6) to consider the ways in which valuable resources can be built and barriers to imitation can be created. HRM issues are, of course, a very important element of the RBV perspective. Therefore, we begin with the first of the five questions, which is sometimes summarized as 'talent management'.

When we think about identifying and building the distinctive capabilities of the organization, the role of the firm's workers and their skills must be central to our thinking. The HR strategy of the organization should help it to survive, thrive, and 'add value'. This leads to key questions (Boxall and Purcell 2016) such as how to enhance the motivation and development of those individuals whose human capital is core to the firm's mission and renewal. And, how to build the kinds of organizational processes and/or social capital that enable individuals to function effectively. Therefore, a first key aspect of HR strategy must be to build and maintain a workforce of appropriate quantity and quality. Such 'talent management' must be a critical concern of strategic HRM, even when the labour market may contain a surplus of jobseekers (Collings and Mellahi 2009; Lanvin and Evans 2017).

Managing 'performance' via HRM strategy

If an appropriate workforce can be built, attention turns to the achievements of the workforce, including operating and financial outcomes such as the levels of productivity and quality that the organization can reach. In attempts to explain how HRM affects performance, the AMO model is a popular starting point (Boxall and Purcell 2016; Vroom 1964); it argues that performance depends on the individual's *ability*, *motivation*, and *opportunity* to perform (Blumberg and Pringle 1982; Guest 1997). Hence, the role of any HRM process is to put in place the policies and practices that will enhance employee ability, motivation, and opportunity to perform (Boselie et al. 2005; Jiang et al. 2012). For example, a lot of attention has been paid to Google's policies of offering employees free meals, free shuttles to work, and other 'perks' (Quora 2018), which may result in staff feeling more highly valued, spending more time at work, and socializing with colleagues—perhaps leading to higher levels of productivity which benefit their employer. And in 2018, London transport organization TfL came top of a survey to find the best employers in the United Kingdom for work–life balance (McCulloch 2018), having introduced policies on flexible working hours and generous holidays for staff.

Managing 'strategic fit' via HRM strategy

HR strategy must also reflect the context in which it is implemented such as the type of organization in question. Let's consider some examples—manufacturing, services, and **public sector**—in order to understand the variety of issues that HR strategy may need to address.

First, we might look at the context of manufacturing. HR strategy in manufacturing has had to address many challenges in recent decades, such as the development of lean manufacturing (Ohno 1988), a philosophy that combines high utilization of manufacturing capacity with low inventory, eliminating the buffers built into traditional approaches to mass production (Womack et al. 1990). In other words, where a traditional manufacturing process might have a stock of items waiting to be worked on at each stage in the process, a lean approach demands the elimination of any 'waste' so that the organization can focus only on activities that are directly 'adding value'. Lean production calls for the application of skills that are less important in traditional mass production, such as technical skills in the diagnosis of waste and quality problems and team-working skills (Sterling and Boxall 2013).

Following on from lean manufacturing, the idea of agile manufacturing has also gained traction in many businesses. Agile manufacturing focuses on thriving in an unpredictable environment, reflecting the fact that most organizations now operate in dynamic markets with fast-changing customer requirements. Staff must be responsive to the market and able to integrate operational information and processes (e.g. across different partners such as suppliers) to create systems that are reliable, flexible, and capable of rapid change (Krishnamurthy and Yauch 2007; Soltan and Mostafa 2015). HRM strategy has an important role to play in building and mobilizing such core competencies. An exciting example is that of Wikspeed, a registered car manufacturing company that developed a functioning prototype within just three months (much faster than a 'traditional' approach to designing a new car) using an agile approach based on self-organizing teams and effective horizontal communications (Denning 2012).

Turning to the context of service industries, we can identify a number of differences between services and other industry sectors, leading to a different set of challenges for HRM strategy and the management of performance (Boxall and Purcell 2016). First, service firms are typically much more labour intensive than manufacturing firms (Frenkel 2000). Second, services differ from manufacturing in terms of the balance between tangibility and intangibility in the offering to the customer (Bowen and Ford 2002). Third, services are typically produced and consumed as and when consumers demand them, and, fourth, consumers are involved in co-producing a range of services (Lovelock et al. 2010). Consider the example of Vail Resorts, our Opening Case Study. With a large workforce of full-time and seasonal staff, the challenges of managing performance are considerable. One approach that they adopt is the clear prescription of a set of values to be lived out 'every day in everything we do—Serve Others, Do Right, Be Inclusive, Drive Value, Do Good, Be Safe, Have Fun'. These values focus employees on key issues, from corporate value, safety, and customer service to the needs of a wider range of stakeholders such as the environment.

When considering service industries, we should not overlook the importance of HR strategy in the public sector. Under the 'New Public Management' (Greener 2013), HRM is regarded as 'one of the key ways that an organization can achieve a competitive edge over its rivals' (Greener 2013: 197). This comprises aspects such as the determination of performance standards, measurement to ensure compliance, and intervention when performance falls below the expected standards; proactive recruitment of key individuals, sometimes from a global labour market; training and development, with a focus on new ways of working and the constant updating of skills and knowledge; and even the adoption of performance-related pay as an element of individual appraisal (Boxall and Purcell 2016).

Managing in a dynamic environment via HRM strategy

Many organizations seek to anticipate important changes in the external environment—social, political, economic, etc.—and plan initiatives to help the organization to prepare for such changes. However, it is widely argued that many change initiatives are unsuccessful. Ulrich (1997) suggests that the HR function has an important role as an agent of change, helping to identify and implement processes for change. This role is highly strategic: 'the actions of change agents include identifying and framing problems, building relationships of trust, solving problems, and creating—and fulfilling—action plans' (Ulrich 1997: 31).

According to Ulrich, HR professionals must help their organization to meet new objectives and do so quickly. They must enhance the ability of the organization to improve the design and implementation of its initiatives and to reduce cycle time in all organizational activities. A key step in the process of change is to identify key success factors for building the capacity to change. This requires HR professionals to assist with aligning the internal culture to the desired market identity, understanding the process for creating a shared mindset, having a model of change that is used throughout the business, and keeping the pressure on the business to respond to change, even in the midst of creating new strategies (Ulrich 1997). Consider the example of GE (Case Example 9.1): we followed a series of CEOs as they sought to introduce strategic shifts—yet at times, the firm's poor performance suggests that the senior team was struggling to change the organization to meet its new goals and strategies in a challenging and dynamic environment.

How HRM can contribute strategically

Ulrich (1997) argues that HR will play a 'strategic partner' role when it has the ability to translate business strategy into action. To achieve this role, Ulrich advocates the design of an organizational 'architecture' and the assessment or audit of the organization against this architecture to identify areas of strength and weakness. Moreover, HR should be playing a role in leading improvement practices and setting priorities (Ulrich 1997). In this world view, HR managers collaborate with line managers to turn strategies into action.

Such advice can perhaps be expanded by considering the strategic role of HR in particularly challenging contexts. Consider a multidivisional company, where HR strategy may face a particular set of issues. For example, HR strategies may have to deal with the restructuring and downsizing associated with strategic projects (discussed further in Chapter 10) such as acquisitions and divestments (Boxall and Purcell 2016). In a multinational firm, HR strategy must address the tensions between global integration and local adaptation or decentralization (Dowling et al. 2013). Ulrich's (1997) notions of designing an organizational architecture and assessing the organization against the desired framework may be particularly pertinent in such a demanding setting where organizational strategy is facing many pressures and forces for change.

Linking HRM strategy with business/corporate strategy

To conclude, we return to the key issue of people as a critical (human) resource in any organization and how resources are combined into capabilities to support the organization's strategy. Ulrich and Smallwood (2004) shed some light on the importance of organizational capabilities in a strategic HR context and how leaders can evaluate the organization's capabilities and build the ones needed to create value for the business. They advocate the use of a 'capabilities audit' to build a high-level picture of an organization's strengths and areas for improvement (see Table 9.1). They suggest that such an audit is a powerful way to evaluate **intangible assets** and render them concrete and measurable.

Ulrich and Smallwood suggest that the first step is to select the focus for your study—it might be the whole organization or just a business unit, division, region, etc. The second step is to assess the organization's performance against each of the 11 organizational capabilities proposed

TABLE 9.1 **How to perform a capabilities audit**

Organizational capabilities	Questions	Assessments	Ranking
Talent	Do our employees have the competencies and the commitment required to deliver the business strategy in question?		
Speed	Can we move quickly to make important things happen fast?		
Shared mindset and coherent brand identity	Do we have a culture or identity that reflects what we stand for and how we work? Is it shared by both customers and employees?		
Accountability	Does high performance matter to the extent that we can ensure execution of strategy?		
Collaboration	How well do we collaborate to gain both efficiency and leverage?		
Learning	Are we good at generating new ideas with impact and generalizing those ideas across boundaries?		
Leadership	Do we have a leadership brand that directs managers on which results to deliver and how to deliver them?		

TABLE 9.1 *Continued*

Organizational capabilities	Questions	Assessments	Ranking
Customer connectivity	Do we form enduring relationships of trust with targeted customers?		
Strategic unity	Do our employees share an intellectual, behavioural, and procedural agenda for our strategy?		
Innovation	How well do we innovate in product, strategy, channel, service, and administration?		
Efficiency	Do we reduce costs by closely managing processes, people, and projects?		

Source: from Ulrich, D. and Smallwood, N. (2004). Capitalizing on capabilities. *Harvard Business Review*, June, 119–27. By permission of Harvard Business Publishing.

in Table 9.1. However, they note that the questions posed can be flexed to reflect the overall strategy of the organization. The assessment, via a survey, can be done by a small team or a large number of staff, depending on the organization's particular needs. Respondents can make their assessments on a scale from 0 (worst) to 10 (best); they can also rank the capabilities in terms of improvement needed, where 1 represents the highest priority, 2 represents the next highest, and so on.

To illustrate this suggested approach, Ulrich and Smallwood give the example of InterContinental Hotels Group (IHG). A capabilities audit was undertaken by their executive team (see Figure 9.3). Respondents were asked about the firm's 'actual state' and 'desired state' with regard

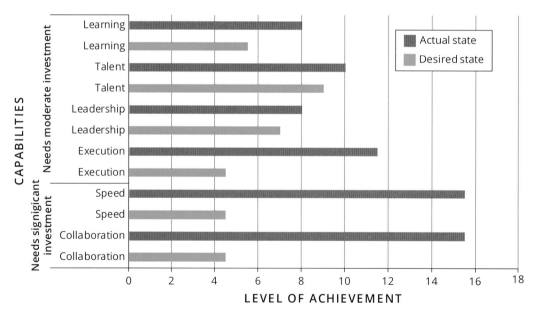

FIGURE 9.3 Snapshot of IHG's capabilities audit results. *Source*: from Ulrich, D. and Smallwood, N. (2004). Capitalizing on capabilities. *Harvard Business Review*, June, 119–27. By permission of Harvard Business Publishing.

to a set of key capabilities for IHG (similar to the 11 capabilities listed in Table 9.1, but adapted to meet the particular needs of IHG). The audit enabled the firm to identify areas where the respondents recognized a large gap between the current and desired future performance of the firm. The data indicated no difference between the scores for actual and desired capabilities categorized as 'shared mindset', and 'accountability', in which case, efforts can focus elsewhere. The audit highlighted two priority areas (Figure 9.3) where current performance fell short and most investment was needed: 'collaboration' and 'speed'. Another four areas were identified where moderate investment was needed: 'execution', 'leadership', 'talent', and 'learning'. The results of such an audit can be used to summarize an organization's actual and desired position and prioritize future attention and investment in relation to any of the key areas discussed in this section and highlighted by an organization's business strategy—managing talent, performance, strategic fit, and HR's contribution to strategy in a dynamic environment.

9.5 Marketing strategy

We now turn to a third important area of functional strategy—marketing. A marketing strategy for a firm aiming to make a profit sets out the firm's overall approach to reaching people and turning them into customers of its product or service, as well as its approach to retaining existing customers. A sound marketing strategy will be based on market research and a good knowledge of the firm's existing and target customers. When the managers of a company develop its marketing strategy, they have to think about the product or service that they are promising to deliver to customers and how they plan to do so. This is typically followed by the development of a more detailed marketing plan, covering types and timing of marketing activities, key marketing messages, and so on.

What is marketing strategy?

A marketing strategy can be defined as 'a plan designed to influence exchanges to achieve organizational objectives', and 'typically [...] intended to increase the probability or frequency of consumer behaviours, such as frequenting particular stores or purchasing particular products' (Peter et al. 1999: 10). The marketing plan is often accomplished by developing and presenting marketing 'mixes' directed at selected target markets. A marketing mix consists of elements such as product, promotion, pricing, and placing/distribution (Borden 1964), known as the 4Ps framework. Therefore, Kotler and Armstrong (2017) argue that a marketing strategy needs to be based on a good understanding of a range of consumer issues, such as:

- **Product**
  - What products do consumers use now?
  - What benefits do consumers want from these products?
- **Promotion**
  - What promotion appeal would influence consumers to purchase and use our product?
  - What advertising claims would be most effective for our product?

- **Pricing**
  - How important is price to consumers in various target markets?
  - What effects will a price change have on purchase behaviour?
- **Placing/distribution**
  - Where do consumers buy our product?
  - Would a different distribution system change consumers' purchasing behaviour?

In the 1980s, the 4Ps framework was challenged for not paying sufficient attention to customer service. The result was that the mix was extended to 7Ps, including three elements (the service mix) that better reflect service delivery: people, process, and physical evidence (Booms and Bitner 1981). The additional Ps can be illustrated as:

- **People**
  - What is the role of our staff in delivering our services to our customers?
  - What training and skills do they require? What recruitment policies should we adopt?
- **Process**
  - How should we design the process of delivering our services to our customers?
  - What role does IT play in the process of service delivery?
- **Physical evidence**
  - How do our customers experience our brand?
  - How is this experience embodied and delivered, for example, through our staff, our product packaging, or our website?

Chaffey and Ellis-Chadwick (2019) summarize the 7Ps in an era of digital marketing (Figure 9.4). For example, they suggest that, under 'product', if a firm provides its services via the internet,

USING THE INTERNET TO VARY THE MARKETING MIX

PRODUCT	PROMOTION	PRICE	PLACE	PEOPLE	PROCESS	PHYSICAL EVIDENCE
• Quality • Image • Branding • Features • Variants • Mix • Support • Customer service • Use occasion • Availability • Warranties	• Marketing communications • Personal promotion • Sales promotion • PR • Branding • Direct marketing	• Positioning • List • Discounts • Credit • Payment methods • Free or value-added elements	• Trade channels • Sales support • Channel number • Segmented channels	• Individuals on marketing activities • Individuals on customer contact • Recruitment • Culture/ image • Training and skills • Remuneration	• Customer focus • Business-led • IT-supported • Design features • Research and development	• Sales/staff contact experience of brand • Product packaging • Online experience

FIGURE 9.4 Using the internet to vary the marketing mix. *Source*: reproduced with permission from Chaffey, D. and Ellis-Chadwick, F. (2019). *Digital Marketing: Strategy, Implementation and Practice* (7th edn). London: Pearson Education. © Pearson Education Limited 2012, 2016, 2019.

its staff should understand customer behaviour such as when the customer uses the online service. The firm then needs to consider factors such as the availability of the service and the provision of customer service and online support.

The elements of the marketing mix, summarized in Figure 9.4, can give us an insight into the key needs and wants of existing and potential customers. However, many markets are large, with diverse customer requirements. Next, we discuss how marketers can divide a broad market into subgroups based on the shared characteristics of some customers. The elements of the marketing mix can then be varied to meet the distinct needs of different subgroups or segments, enabling the organization to build a more targeted approach to marketing to its chosen customers.

Market segmentation

The buyers in a market typically differ in terms of their needs and wants. Organizations use a process known as **market segmentation** to divide large heterogeneous markets into smaller segments—an integral part of marketing strategy (Baines et al. 2022). Market segmentation can allow an organization to reach different segments of customers more efficiently and effectively with products and services that meet their varying needs. Table 9.2 outlines some of the criteria that can be used to segment customer markets.

In Case Example 9.2, we explore a highly successful advertising campaign to promote Marmite, a savoury food spread made from yeast extract. The campaign was designed to strike a chord with young adults who had become cynical about traditional marketing strategies. As an example of a segmented **digital** marketing campaign, consider the targeting of young business professionals in the United Kingdom by the *Financial Times* (*The Financial Times* 2014). In terms of the dimensions of the **marketing mix**, their mix of 'product', 'place', and 'promotion' was all carefully chosen. The goal was to tempt readers (typically aged 24–34) who were unlikely to buy the print version of the newspaper, likely to be time poor, digital savvy, and tend to access news on the go, to use FT.com on their mobile phones, under the tagline 'Find your personalised Financial Times at FT.com'. The campaign ran at digital poster sites at London commuter stations alongside a digital media acquisition campaign across Facebook and Twitter, and it stressed a business-focused offering drawing

TABLE 9.2 **Criteria that can be used to segment customer markets**

Segmentation criteria	Example
Demographic	Age, sex/gender or gender identity, life-cycle stage, income, occupation, education, religion, ethnicity, social class
Geographic	Nations, regions, states, counties, cities, neighbourhoods, population density (urban, suburban, rural), climate, customs and traditions
Life stage	Childhood, adulthood, young couples, retired people
Psychographic (lifestyles)	Social demographic or culture, activities, interests, personality
Behavioural	Occasions, benefits, user status, usage (frequency, time of usage, or situations), loyalty status, media channels used

Source: based on Baines, P., Fill, C., Rosengren, S., and Antonetti, P. (2022). *Marketing* (6th edn). Oxford: Oxford University Press.

on technology and exciting creative formats. This segmentation exercise sits at the intersection of a number of segmentation variables—geographic (focused on London commuters in the United Kingdom), demographic (many variables, including age and level of education), psychographic (likely to appeal to young professionals with career aspirations), and behavioural (given patterns of accessing the news and likely benefits sought, etc.).

Having identified some potentially attractive market segments to target, marketers need to understand how the customers in that segment make decisions about which products or services to try, and we turn to this issue next.

Understanding the decision-making behaviour of customers

To develop effective marketing strategies, and to reach a particular segment of customers that they wish to target, marketers also need to know the type of problem-solving process their customers use to make purchase decisions. Marketers who want to target several customer segments with different problem-solving processes may have to develop multiple strategies to influence the different decision outcomes. A brief overview of three widely cited choice behaviours is given below (see, e.g. Betsch et al. (2002) and Sirakaya and Woodside (2005) for a discussion of the decision-making behaviour of travellers/tourists).

- **Routinized choice behaviour**: occurs when consumers think they know all they need to know about a product category and are not motivated to search for more information. Their choice behaviour is based on a learned decision plan stored in their memory. Marketers of established brands may want consumers to continue to follow a routine choice approach as they are already well positioned in the consumers' minds. Marketers of new brands, or brands with low market share, may be seeking to interrupt the consumers' automatic problem-solving process.

- **Limited decision-making**: occurs when consumers already have a lot of information about the product. The basic marketing strategy will likely be to make additional pieces of information readily available to consumers when and where they may need them.

- **Extensive decision-making**: occurs when consumers' level of knowledge is low and a wide range of information is being sought. Marketers will typically seek to make the necessary information available in a format and at a level that consumers can understand and use in the problem-solving process.

In Case Example 9.3, we will explore Primark's approach to opening new outlets in the United States, away from its base in Europe. Unlike its rivals, Primark has avoided online shopping, preferring a more traditional 'pile-it-high-sell-it-cheap' approach to retailing. This example indicates the importance of understanding the decision-making behaviour of consumers, as well as creating the right physical and social environment for the consumer with a purchase decision to make, and we turn to this issue—the consumer's environment—next.

Understanding the social and physical environment

As well as understanding the consumer's problem-solving process, marketers need to understand the social and physical environment in which consumers operate. Marketing strategies can then seek to alter aspects of the environment with the intention of influencing consumers

TABLE 9.3 **Examples of possible environmental changes to influence consumer behaviour**

Type of strategy	Example(s) of changes
Product strategies	New product design or new packaging
Pricing strategies	Notification of a 'sale' in the window of a high-street store or online or price labelling on physical products
Promotion strategies	Advertisements in magazines or on electronic displays in major railway stations
Place/distribution strategies	Design of websites or the location or layout of a retail store

Source: authors.

and their behaviour. Table 9.3 provides examples of how aspects of the physical environment can be changed.

Other marketing strategies can seek to alter aspects of the social environment. For example, consumers are influenced by the behaviour of sales and service staff—whether their attitude is friendly, aggressive, or pushy, etc. A study of 48 branches of a major UK bank (Wilson 1997) showed that distinct subcultures existed across the different locations; this highlights the difficulties and complexities of designing and controlling a single style of 'corporate behaviour'. Going beyond the interactions between staff and customers, another increasingly important aspect of the social environment is the interaction between customers themselves. Studies suggest that we are much more likely to believe word-of-mouth recommendations from our own friends and family than from other sources (Nielsen 2012). For example, the firm Three (a telecommunications and internet provider) encourages its customers to 'refer a friend' and share financial rewards (Three.co.uk 2022).

Linking marketing strategy with business/corporate strategy

In Chapter 8, we discussed how corporate strategy is summarized in an organization's business model (also discussed further in Chapter 11). In Table 9.4, we explore the fit between a business model and marketing strategy, including some key questions that management should pose. This summary clearly indicates that an effective marketing strategy is a strong complement to—and not a substitute for—a robust business model and organizational strategy. Marketing strategy can be seen as taking a desired organizational strategy and elaborating on the organization's interactions with its customers, and with its use of resources and capabilities, to achieve a desired position in the market.

TABLE 9.4 **Fit between an organization's marketing strategy and its business model**

	Business model	Marketing strategy
Definition	A business model can provide a template of how an organization interacts with other parties	Marketing strategy summarizes a pattern of managerial actions that are deployed to achieve competitive advantage through market positioning

TABLE 9.4 *Continued*

	Business model	Marketing strategy
Some key questions addressed	Which parties to bring together and how to interact with them? What goods or information to exchange? What resources and capabilities to deploy?	What products/services to provide? Which customers to serve? What positioning to adopt against rivals? When to enter certain markets? Etc.
Unit of analysis	The organization and its partners	Primarily focused on the organization itself
Focus	Externally orientated: the exchanges between the organization and other parties	Internally orientated: how should the organization act in the light of competition?

Source: based on Zott and Amit (2008: 5).

CASE EXAMPLE 9.2 MARKETING MARMITE

When it comes to Marmite, 'you either love it or hate it'. Marmite has become a byword for something or someone polarizing. Yet, this idea was planted in the 1990s by an advertising agency.

In 1902, the Marmite Food Extract Company was formed in Burton-upon-Trent, capital of the United Kingdom's brewing industry. Marmite was packed full of Vitamin B, and *The Lancet* recommended it as a cure for anaemia. It was sent to nourish troops in the First World War and to prisoner-of-war camps in the Second. Marmite's fortunes declined in the 1970s due to worries about salt consumption and the rise of breakfast cereals. By the mid-1990s, the brand was failing. It fell to the advertising agency BMP DDB to make Marmite 'cool'. Andy McLeod and Richard Flintham had a tough job: their research indicated that Marmite smelt 'disgusting' and looked 'like a brown stain on toast'.

McLeod recalls the moment they cracked the problem. 'I remember [...] saying to Richard, "I f***ing hate Marmite." And he said "Oh, I love it." And we both just looked at each other.'

The 'Hate/Mate' campaign launched in 1996 with two adverts. The first featured people salivating over and bathing in the product, to the refrain 'My Mate, Marmite'. The second showed people spitting it out, sticking pins in jars, etc., to the lyrics 'I Hate Marmite'. The campaign's irony and self-awareness appealed to Generation X. Sales to

Source: © Brett Ryder/heartagency.com

'pre-family households' increased by 50% between 1995 and 2001. More than 25 years later, this advertising campaign remains central to Marmite's lasting success. The 'Hate/Mate' campaign presaged the absolutism of social-media debates, where you're either on one side or the other. Each new Marmite product (popcorn, peanut butter, sausages) is greeted by a Twitterstorm that does more for brand awareness than any paid marketing.

Questions for discussion

1. Use the marketing mix (4Ps; 7Ps; and internet/ digital marketing (Figure 9.4)) to analyse the marketing strategy for Marmite. What insights

does it offer into the needs and wants of existing and potential customers?

2. Apply market segmentation thinking, such as the segmentation criteria listed in Table 9.2, to analyse Marmite's market. What does this approach suggest about the identification of potentially attractive market segments with different needs and wants?

Sources

The Economist (2021c). Marketing Marmite: How an advertising agency started a culture war (17 June), https://www.economist.com/1843/2021/06/17/marketing-marmite-how-an-advertising-agency-started-a-culture-war (last accessed 18 August 2022).

9.6 Operations strategy

Next, we turn to the crucial area of operations strategy, the driver behind an organization's operations which produces and distributes its goods and services. It addresses important issues, including the allocation of resources to ensure that the organization's infrastructure and activities, such as production or distribution, are properly supported in a manner that is both effective and efficient.

What is operations strategy?

It has been noted that the term 'operations strategy' can at first sound like a contradiction. Slack and Lewis (2017) ask, 'How can the term "operations", which is generally concerned with the day-to-day delivery of goods and services, be strategic?' However, it can be argued that the effective management of an organization's operational resources (including workers, facilities, machines, and tools, etc.) is key to its long-term success. Operations strategy can be defined as the total pattern of decisions which shape the long-term capabilities of an operation and their contribution to overall strategy. Operations strategy should certainly 'prevent strategic decisions being frustrated by poor operational implementation' (Slack and Lewis 2017: 1); it should also be able to ensure that the management of operations resources can itself provide competitive advantage. This emphasizes the role of operations strategy in both facilitating planned strategic activity (e.g. supporting the delivery of a marketing plan) and potentially contributing to the ability of the organization to survive and thrive in the future via sustainable competitive advantage.

Operations strategy in different contexts

In order to understand operations strategy, it is important to consider distinctions between operations strategy in different contexts. Two key contexts to compare are manufacturing and service industries.

Manufacturing industries

In a manufacturing context, Hill (2000) highlights the need to embed manufacturing strategy within a wider process of both corporate strategy development and marketing strategy and advocates a five-step process for doing so. Having (a) defined corporate objectives and (b) determined marketing strategies to meet these objectives, manufacturing strategy should be developed by (c) assessing how different products qualify in their respective markets and win orders against competitors, (d) establishing the appropriate process to manufacture these products (i.e. process choice), and (e) providing the manufacturing infrastructure to support production.

Consider the automotive industry, under pressure to customize its products for customers and worth an estimated trillion dollars worldwide (Nathan 2019). This industry can provide a context for critical decisions about establishing appropriate manufacturing processes and providing infrastructure to support production. A key driver is the Industrial IoT, or Internet of Things (e.g. Boyes et al. 2018), a term which is widely applied to connected devices in consumer, domestic, business, and industrial settings. The Industrial IoT allows managers to gather machine data and analyse it against various key performance indicators such as productivity, quality, and maintenance (see Table 9.5 for further examples). This type of initiative would align to organizational strategy interests in digitalization, discussed further in Chapter 11.

Service industries

In the context of service industries, the notion of customer experience is often stressed. Pullman and Gross (2004: 553) define an experience as occurring when:

> a customer has any sensation or knowledge acquisition resulting from some level of interaction with different elements of a context created by a service provider. Successful experiences are those that the customer finds unique, memorable and sustainable over time, would want to repeat and build upon, and enthusiastically promotes via word of mouth.

Voss et al. (2008) propose a construct that they label 'experience capability', defined in terms of the firm's ability to choreograph customer experiences. Therefore, their view of service operations strategy comprises three main classes of deliberate design choices, which are termed 'stageware' (physical environment), 'orgware' (management organization focused on customer

9

TABLE 9.5 **Industrial Internet of Things in automotive manufacturing**

Potential area of benefit	Example
Productivity	Improved throughput, reduced cycle time, better understanding of bottlenecks in the manufacturing process
Predictive maintenance	Reduction in lost time due to equipment malfunctions
Predictive quality	Migration from statistical or sample-based control to online measurement of every part in a car, with alerts to management if the quality falls outside specified ranges
Energy monitoring and conservation	Sensors can monitor every stage in the manufacturing process to identify where energy is being wasted
Health-and-safety monitoring	The use of connected sensors and monitors can make compliance automatic and/or influence worker behaviour
Process traceability	In the case of failure of a part, manufacturers can trace the part to where it was manufactured and determine if it is a machine-level problem, a part-level problem, or a component-level problem, potentially limiting the scope of the recall

Source: authors.

experience), and 'customerware' (the key role of customer contact employees). We can consider the example of Primark (Case Example 9.3) in choosing to open enormous outlets beyond the United Kingdom—on average, nearly six times the size of those run by its rival Inditex (owner of Zara) and often in out-of-town malls where rents are cheap. The atmosphere created in its

CASE EXAMPLE 9.3 WHAT IS PRIMARK DOING DIFFERENTLY?

Primark, the discount clothing retailer, is well-known for its low prices and is currently expanding aggressively in the United States from its base in Europe. Although it appears to be in the same business as its budget rivals, its approach is different. Primark has stuck to a stack-it-high-sell-it-cheap approach to retailing. Other giants of fast fashion have grown by embracing speed. Back in the 2000s, Inditex, which owns Zara, began manufacturing some of its products in Europe, enabling it to get designs into shops within a few weeks. Previously, shoppers had to wait entire seasons for high-street brands to imitate the latest catwalk styles. It took at least that long to get clothes made and shipped from Asian factories with long lead times. Zara's business model was soon copied across the industry.

Primark has stayed in the slower lane, betting that shoppers will accept being less cutting-edge in return for big savings. Designs are simple to keep stitching costs down. This strategy allows it to concentrate manufacturing in lower-cost countries such as Bangladesh, where monthly wages start at around $100. Its orders can be fulfilled in off-peak periods; factories produce Primark clothing during quiet weeks, while slotting in more lucrative short-turnaround work for more demanding brands.

Primark stands out amongst rivals for refusing to sell anything online, which it sees as impossible at its price points. It lost up to 100% of sales as the COVID-19 pandemic shut shops around the world. Extended closures, especially in the United Kingdom, home to about half of its 380 outlets, cost it £3bn in sales and perhaps £1bn in profit.

Critics of the company continue to raise serious concerns about whether the real price of budget clothing is being paid by workers, the environment, and animals. The company has responded to such challenges with commitments to make its clothes more sustainable by 2030.

Questions for discussion

1. How would you summarize Primark's business strategy and business model? What are the key resources and capabilities supporting that strategy and business model?

2. How would you summarize Primark's operations strategy? What challenges does it face regarding the sustainability and ethics of its business model?

3. How would you summarize Primark's marketing strategy and IT strategy? Describe the customer's choices and 'experience' when shopping at Primark.

Sources

The Economist (2021b). How Primark makes money selling $3.50 t-shirts (21 August), https://www.economist.com/business/2021/08/21/how-primark-makes-money-selling-350-t-shirts (last accessed 18 August 2022).

The Guardian (2021). Primark pledges to make all its clothes more sustainable by 2030 (15 September), https://www.theguardian.com/business/2021/sep/15/primark-clothes-sustainable-retailer-carbon-emissions-plastics (last accessed 18 August 2022).

Primark, https://www.ethicalconsumer.org/company-profile/primark (last accessed 18 August 2022).

Robertson, L. (2021). How ethical is Primark? *Good on You* (21 August), https://goodonyou.eco/how-ethical-is-primark (last accessed 18 August 2022).

stores has been described as 'jumble-emporium'—and it appears to work as Primark sells about ten times as many items as its rival H&M per square metre (*The Economist* 2021b).

These design choices (stageware, orgware, and customerware) emphasize the unique challenges faced by managers who are developing operations strategy in a service industry context. It has been argued (Roth and Menor 2003) that an operations strategy perspective is needed to determine the theoretical and practical insights which will enable firms to effectively deploy their operations in order to provide the right offerings to the right customers at the right times. Organizations should consider the strategic alignment of three elements:

- their targeted market and customer segments;
- the notion of the service concept as a complex bundle of offerings;
- their choice of service delivery system design.

Each element combines with the others to influence the customer encounter and, in turn, the evoked customer response to the service delivery system (Roth and Menor 2003; Voss et al. 2008). As an example of outstanding customer experience, consider Zappos, the online shoe store frequently praised for its customer service (Solomon 2018). The excellent customer experience at Zappos is achieved via a mix of important elements (Glassman 2013), illustrated in Table 9.6.

Key dimensions of operations strategy

Having looked at operations strategy in two distinct contexts (manufacturing and service industries), we now consider two key dimensions of operations strategy: servitization and outsourcing.

TABLE 9.6 Design choices at Zappos to deliver outstanding customer experience

Category of design choice	Example	Result
Customerware: the key role of customer contact employees	Employees create an emotional connection with customers (e.g. over the problems of finding a comfortable shoe for narrow feet), leading to variable call length	Future customer loyalty and word-of-mouth recommendations; for example, customer delighted by a free delivery upgrade to ensure shoes arrive in time for a special event
Orgware: management organization focused on the customer experience	Low agent occupancy targets; that is, the proportion of time spent on calls is typically 60–70% compared with 80% or more in many other businesses	The communication style and actions of agents appear to be highly sympathetic to customers and offer a customized service for each individual
Stageware: physical environment	Zappos observe and track behaviour to understand exactly what customers want—enormous selection and convenience, with an easy-to-use interface/delivery package	Appropriate mix of technology and excellent human interface; customers find it easy to make purchases and to return any that they are not entirely happy with

Source: authors.

Servitization

The concept of servitization takes us beyond an overly simple view of operations strategy as being concerned with either products or services (but never both). Servitization is now widely recognized as the innovation of a manufacturer's capabilities and processes to move from selling products to selling integrated product–service offerings that deliver value in use (Baines et al. 2008; Vandermerwe and Rada 1988). In many organizations, operations strategy still suffers from a decoupling between product manufacture and service delivery (Baines et al. 2008). A decoupled approach to operations strategy is unsatisfactory as it creates many challenges emerging from a traditional approach to product manufacture. Such an approach means that it is problematic for the firm to deliver its offering to the marketplace in an effective manner. An operations strategy that integrates a range of features is desirable, covering typical structural aspects of operations (such as process, capacity, facilities, and supply chains) as well as a range of infrastructure issues (such as human resources, customer relations, and supplier relations).

An innovative example of servitization is the relationship between Philips, the Dutch multinational technology company, and Amsterdam Airport Schiphol (Wright 2015). Philips provides lighting for the terminal buildings inside Schiphol and owns the fixtures and installations inside the airport, which were specifically designed for the purpose and are planned to last 75% longer than conventional fixtures. LED lighting is very efficient but has high up-front purchase costs. Under this model of lighting as a service, Schiphol pays for the energy it uses, benefiting from low electricity usage while avoiding the cost of buying the lamps initially, and aims to be one of the most sustainable airports in the world. Philips and its partners will be responsible for the performance, durability, and re-use of the LED lamps that will be installed in the airport, with a predicted saving of 50% in electricity consumption.

Outsourcing

A key element of operations strategy for many organizations will be a consideration of its decisions around outsourcing. Outsourcing has been defined as the act of obtaining finished or semi-finished products or services from an outside company if these activities were traditionally performed internally (Dolgui and Proth 2013). Outsourcing first came to prominence in the early 1990s and was soon described as one of the most important new management ideas and practices of the twentieth century (Sibbert 1997). According to Corbett (2004), for outsourcing to be fully effective, it needs to be integrated into the organization's overall business strategy.

> This means shifting from a view of outsourcing as a reactive tool—where opportunities are sought only in response to external pressures for change or a consultant's report on the latest opportunity—to one of weaving outsourcing into the very fabric of the business's decision-making and operations.

> (Corbett 2004: 77)

A top-down approach to identifying outsourcing opportunities involves making sourcing decisions an integral part of the organization's strategic decision-making. A more bottom-up approach suggests that the identification of external sourcing opportunities begins with those areas of the organization than can offer little opportunity for competitive advantage. For Corbett (2004), the most important factor is to elevate sourcing to the level of an important

9

FIGURE 9.5 Four perspectives on operations strategy: Top down, bottom up, market requirements, and operations resources. *Source*: reproduced with permission from Slack, N. and Lewis, M. (2019). *Operations Strategy* (6th edn). Harlow: Financial Times/Prentice Hall. © Pearson Education Limited 2011, 2015, 2017, 2019.

management decision. New sources of competitive advantage can be sought via the unique ways that a firm aims to blend its internal and external sources.

However, outsourcing is a controversial topic, particularly in the public sector. Its supporters point to money saved and innovations successfully introduced. The Forth Valley Royal Hospital, run by Serco, was the first in the United Kingdom to use automated guided vehicles to move laundry and waste around in the basement, saving money by cutting about 40 jobs (*The Economist* 2018). A survey of evidence from around the world (Hodge 2000) found that outsourcing had resulted in an overall saving in government expenditure of between 6 and 12%. But critics argue that the average cost savings have fallen dramatically over time as private contractors trim any 'slack' from the services that they now operate and public providers have become more efficient.

Moreover, evaluating whether outsourcing has delivered improved services is a complex issue—particularly when we look beyond relatively simple services, such as refuse collection, and consider more complex activities such as the running of a prison. In the United Kingdom, some have pointed to a crisis in outsourcing projects. For example, Carillion, the giant construction firm, collapsed in January 2018, leading to, amongst other problems, delays in building new hospitals for the United Kingdom's National Health Service (*The Guardian* 2020). Capita, the largest business process outsourcing and professional services company in the United Kingdom, has been criticized for its financial performance, along with its failure to deliver targets for army recruitment and a website that 'cost three times its budget and was 52 months late' (BBC 2018).

Linking operations strategy with business/corporate strategy

As with marketing strategy, it is important to understand how operations strategy links to business strategy. Slack and Lewis (2017) propose four perspectives on operations strategy, which can help to draw out some of its key dimensions. First, operations strategy must reflect the aims and objectives of the whole organization and what it is seeking to achieve, that is, a top-down perspective. Second, operations strategy must also adopt a bottom-up perspective; in this view, operational activities and improvements cumulatively help to build the organization's strategy. Third, operations strategy should help to translate market requirements into operations decisions. Finally, operations strategy involves exploiting the capabilities of operations resources in chosen markets. This is highlighted in Figure 9.5.

9.7 IT strategy

We have now discussed four of the five key functional strategies: financial, HRM, marketing, and operations. In this section, we consider the final functional strategy: IT (information technology). What is IT strategy and how does it align with business strategy? A number of frameworks have been developed to help managers analyse their organization's portfolio of IT projects, think through the problem of alignment with business strategy, and identify appropriate actions. In this section, we will focus on one such key framework.

What is IT strategy?

We can think of IT strategy as the total pattern of decisions relating to the use of technology within an organization. An organization's IT strategy sets out how IT will be used to help the organization to meet its goals. IT strategy is often implemented via IT projects, where a project is a set of interrelated activities that are time limited and use a defined set of resources to achieve a particular objective (PMI 2019). To manage its IT strategy, an organization must typically monitor and control a set of projects and ensure that the IT strategy is fully supporting the organization's overall strategy. Next, we introduce a model designed to address these questions around how to manage a portfolio of IT projects and ensure that business strategy and IT strategy are aligned.

McFarlan's strategic grid

McFarlan's strategic grid (1984) was developed to assist managers with analysing the portfolio of IT projects that their organization is pursuing. According to Burgelman et al. (2009. 989), in a technology-intensive environment, 'projects are where the action is. They're where the "rubber

9

meets the road".' This is because development projects can lead to a host of benefits, from success in a new market to barriers to entry for competitors due to a new delivery system. The portfolio of IT projects can be an important indicator of an organization's priorities and strategic intent—and the changes that it is seeking to introduce. If important resources (such as money, people, time, and management attention) are being allocated to support current projects, the make-up of the project portfolio may shed light on changes in performance, productivity, re-turns, and innovation across the organization.

The strategic grid helps managers to analyse the portfolio of IT initiatives along two dimensions—the impact on business operations (focusing on the organization's current activi-ties) and the impact on strategy (with a focus on future plans). The aim is to help managers to assess the alignment of IT with the organization's strategic goals and also to ensure that the approaches for organizing and managing IT are appropriate, given the position of the projects on the grid (Figure 9.6). Next, we review the four quadrants in Figure 9.6 to consider how the framework can be used to analyse different types of IT project.

- **Support (low impact on business operations/low impact on strategy)**: these proj-ects have little impact on an organization's core strategy or operations. They may aim to achieve local improvements or incremental cost savings and are typically carried out by IT specialists in partnership with local end-users.

- **Factory (high impact on business operations/low impact on strategy)**: these projects are typically designed to improve the performance or reduce the costs of the core opera-tions of an organization. Business unit managers and IT managers will work in partnership on such projects, given their high operating impact/risk.

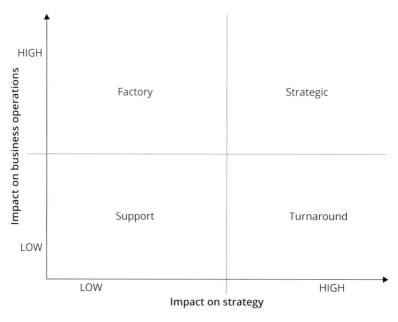

FIGURE 9.6 Strategic grid. *Source*: reproduced with permission from Applegate, L., Austin, R., and McFarlan, F. (2007). *Corporate Information Strategy and Management: Text and Cases* (7th edn). Boston, MA: McGraw-Hill.

- **Turnaround (low impact on business operations/high impact on strategy)**: these projects are designed to exploit emerging strategic opportunities. They require input from business managers (e.g. those involved with business development), IT managers, and those with expertise in emerging technologies.

- **Strategy (high impact on business operations/high impact on strategy)**: finally, firms which have important IT projects in this quadrant are making a commitment to use IT to enable both core operations and core strategy. Such projects are typically defined, implemented, and managed with key input from the most senior levels of the organization.

This framework can help managers to describe their current portfolio of IT projects, to understand whether the allocation of resources is appropriate given the organization's overall goals, and to identify whether they wish to make changes to their stance on IT from a more defensive to a more offensive approach. In a later study, Nolan and McFarlan (2005) place 'need for reliable IT' (rather than 'current operational impact') on the vertical axis and 'need for new IT' (rather than 'strategic/future impact') on the horizontal axis. Their point is that companies focusing on the left-hand side of the grid ('factory' and 'support' quadrants) are typically adopting a defensive stance with their IT, while companies on the right ('turnaround' and 'strategic' quadrants) are using IT in a more offensive manner to support and move their business strategy forward.

Some of the world's most innovative companies are using IT in this 'strategic' manner. The CEO of Alphabet/Google has described it as an 'AI first' company. AI (artificial intelligence) can be described as the simulation of human intelligence processes by machines, especially computer systems. For instance, Gmail suggests to its users how to finish their sentences when composing emails (Ringel et al. 2019). This Smart Compose feature relies on Google's expertise in AI; for Google, such AI-driven initiatives are likely to represent projects on the right-hand side of McFarlan's grid, where impact on strategy is high.

In order to assess the strategic impact of IT, McFarlan poses five questions about IT applications in relation to the competitive forces (Porter's Five Forces, introduced in Chapter 5):

Can IT applications:

- build barriers to the entry of new competitors into the industry;
- build switching costs for existing customers;
- change the basis of competition;
- change the balance of power in supplier relationships;
- create new products?

Consider companies which can be viewed as pioneers in voice recognition technology and virtual assistants, such as Amazon (with Alexa) and Apple (with Siri). These innovations have created new products and services and potentially built barriers to entry for competitors while changing the basis of competition for these innovative companies. Customers who enjoy these innovations may also become more loyal to the firm. The five questions appear to focus our thinking on the right-hand side of the grid, that is, the scope for the organization to use IT offensively as part of its strategic positioning.

Having discussed a key framework for exploring IT strategy, we next consider how IT can drive strategic opportunities for an organization.

Strategic opportunities

IT can be an important part of an organization's search for new strategic opportunities (Applegate et al. 2007; Tidd and Bessant 2018).

- **IT can change the basis of competition**: consider the automotive industry. Many customers focus on the features, function, and appearance of a car when making a buying decision. However, more recently, some customers have become more focused on both their experience at the dealership when making their purchase and the quality of service after the purchase. This shift offers a potential advantage to companies who can use IT to support the customer experience, both during and after the sale.

- **IT can change the nature of relationships** and balance of power among buyers and suppliers. Today, many organizations are allowing data, and knowledge of their operations, to flow through their supply chain as they collaborate more closely with suppliers. Data flows and collaborations are supported and facilitated by new technology, for example, manufacturers who can easily share information such as stock levels and specifications for particular parts with other firms in the supply chain. In addition, online communities are growing, allowing organizations to discover and collaborate more easily with new partners.

- **IT can build or reduce barriers to entry**: Amazon initially took advantage of the fact that the internet had reduced barriers to entry in certain sectors such as selling books; anyone who wanted to become a bookseller could do so via a website (no longer needing a shop on the high street). However, Amazon's business model required the company to take ownership of physical inventory (i.e. stocks of books and other products, waiting for customer orders), and this required significant investment in infrastructure such as stock warehouses.

- **IT can increase or decrease switching costs**: for example, the costs incurred when opening or closing an account with a financial services provider can be reduced by using new IT systems. NatWest attracted attention when it launched a 'paperless mortgage', allowing customers and staff to share and verify documents online (Finextra 2019), potentially cutting costs in terms of paper processing and staff time as well as improving customer service.

- **IT can add value to existing products or services or create new ones**: for example, the digitization of books, magazines, music, video games, etc. A total of 191 million e-books were sold in the United States in 2020 (Statista.com 2021). The global number of readers of e-books is predicted to reach 1.18 billion by 2026 (Statista.com n.d.).

Linking IT strategy with business/corporate strategy: Digital strategy

In an increasingly digital world, for many managers, the term 'IT strategy' has become inextricably linked with 'digital strategy'. We will discuss digital strategy in greater depth in Chapter 11 when we explore innovation and disruption. However, for Dave Aron, an analyst at Gartner, the distinction between IT strategy and digital strategy can be explained as follows:

- *IT Strategy is a technical answer to a business question: 'How will IT help the business win?' It assumes the business strategy is set, then considers how to use IT to make that strategy successful. IT Strategy is usually conducted after business strategy.*

- *Digital Business Strategy is a business answer to a digital question: 'How should our business evolve to survive and thrive in an increasingly digital world?' It is not a separate strategy, but instead a lens on business strategy. All aspects of the business strategy should be informed by digital considerations.*

(Aron 2013)

For example, Kaiser Permanente, a provider of health care and not-for-profit health plans (Ross et al. 2017), has a digital strategy that can be summarized using some of the elements of functional strategy we have discussed in this chapter:

- **Marketing**: Kaiser's approach begins with its customer engagement strategies. Data analytics are applied to achieve personalized medical outreach, and digital channels provide access to personal health records, secure messaging between patients and providers, and remote care.

- **HR**: Kaiser approaches its business as a collaboration between care providers and patients/members of the organization.

- **Operations**: Kaiser's operational 'backbone' starts with its electronic health records system, which facilitates meaningful patient interactions and enables new digital initiatives that require accurate, accessible patient data.

We will explore further details of Kaiser Permanente's approach to digitalization in Chapter 11. Bharadwaj et al. (2013) suggest that there are four key themes that should guide our thinking on digital business strategy and may help to provide insights for the future. These themes are:

1. Scope of digital business strategy
2. Scale of digital business strategy
3. Speed of decision-making
4. Sources of value creation and capture.

As shown in Figure 9.7, there are a number of drivers of these four themes, including external digital trends and internal organizational 'shifts'. Examples include:

- **Scope of digital business strategy**: Netflix moves beyond being a subscription service to a wide range of content development.

- **Scale of digital business strategy**: airline alliances such as Star Alliance and Oneworld can choose to share aspects of their business operations, including reservation systems, loyalty programmes, and online cross-selling.

- **Speed of decision-making**: organizations can respond to customer service requests in real time through Twitter, Facebook, and other social media platforms.

- **Sources of value creation and capture**: Google's entry into the smartphone business based on giving away the software (Android) free and monetizing it through its ability to influence and control advertising.

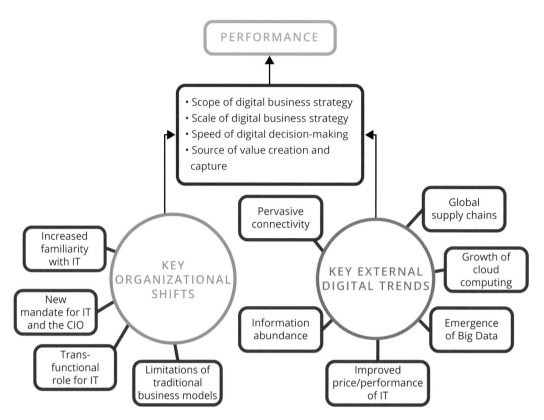

FIGURE 9.7 Four key themes of digital business strategy and their drivers. *Source*: reproduced with permission from Bharadwaj, A., El Sawy, O.A., Pavlou, P.A., and Venkatraman, N. (2013). Digital business strategy: Toward a net generation of insights. *MIS Quarterly*, **37**(2), 471–82, Figure 1.

Bharadwaj et al. (2013) also suggest a series of key questions for understanding digital business strategy (see Table 9.7) under the four key themes. These questions emphasize the important relationship between digital business strategy and the functional strategies we have discussed in this chapter, for example, by asking whether the organization's digital business strategy transcends the traditional functional 'silos' (i.e. helping to break down barriers between business functions and departments), whether digital business strategy can speed up operational decision-making and supply chain orchestration, and whether digital business strategy is effective in creating and capturing value.

9.8 Managing strategic performance

At the beginning of the chapter, we explored how functional strategies can contribute to and deliver an organization's overall strategy (see Figure 9.2). In sections 9.3–9.7 we discussed how different types of functional strategies can play this key role.

But how can the firm use these functional strategies in order to manage the implementation of its organizational strategy? In this final section, we introduce tools to support the organization as it seeks to manage the implementation of its strategy through the activities of its various functions.

Link between organizational strategy and functional strategies

In order to understand how an organization can use functional strategies to manage the implementation of organizational strategy, we first need to understand the relationship between the organization's strategy, on the one hand, and the operation of its key functions, on the other. Kaplan and Norton argue that:

> A visionary strategy that is not linked to excellent operational and governance processes cannot be implemented. Conversely, operational excellence may lower costs, improve quality, and reduce process and lead times; but without a strategy's vision and guidance, a company is not likely to enjoy sustainable success from its operational improvements alone.

(Kaplan and Norton 2008: 1)

Kaplan and Norton's proposition is that an organization is likely to fail at implementing a strategy or managing operations if they lack an overarching management system to integrate and align these two vital processes (the organization's strategy and the operation of its functions). They argue for a number of strategy execution processes that organizations need to put in place:

- translate the strategy, that is, create a clear articulation of the organization's strategy and its accompanying measures;
- manage (a limited number of) strategic initiatives;
- align the organization's units (business units and support units) to deliver the strategy;
- communicate the strategy;
- review the strategy, that is, conduct regular meetings to report on and manage the strategy;
- update the strategy regularly to account for changing conditions.

Kaplan and Norton also stress the role of the functional strategies in working towards overall organizational goals. For example, the financial strategy should link the strategic initiatives to the budget; the IT strategy may include the development of key service level agreements; the HR strategy is likely to address organizational development and so on.

Next, we discuss two tools that an organization can use to manage the implementation of its strategy through the activities of its various functions.

Balanced scorecard

Kaplan and Norton (1992) introduced the notion of the **balanced scorecard** as a set of measures that give senior managers a fast but fairly comprehensive view of key aspects of the organization. The tool allows managers to look at the organization from four important perspectives (see Figure 9.8):

- **Financial perspective**: How do we look to shareholders?
- **Customer perspective**: How do customers see us?
- **Internal business perspective**: What must we excel at?
- **Innovation and learning perspective**: Can we continue to improve and create value?

TABLE 9.7 **Key questions on digital business strategy**

Key theme	Key questions	Examples of impact on functional strategies
Scope of digital business strategy	What is the extent of fusion/integration between IT strategy and business strategy?	Can be addressed with IT strategy models (section 9.7)
	How encompassing is digital business strategy? How effectively does it transcend traditional functional and process silos?	Can be addressed by integrated working between IT and all of the functional areas—finance, HRM, marketing, and operations
	How well does digital business strategy exploit the digitization of products and services and the information around them?	Can be addressed by integrated working between IT and marketing Example: Vail Resorts embedding chips in ski passes
	How well does digital business strategy exploit the extended business community?	Can be addressed by partnerships/alliances (see Chapter 10 for more on strategic alliances); opportunities may arise in any functional area
Scale of digital business strategy	How rapidly and cost effectively can the IT infrastructure scale up/down to enable a firm's digital business strategy to bolster a strategic dynamic capability?	Can be addressed by integrated working between IT and operations
	How effective is digital business strategy in scaling volume through alliances/partnerships?	Can be addressed by alliances/partnerships (see Chapter 10 for more on strategic alliances); opportunities may arise in functional areas such as operations (e.g. outsourcing, section 9.6)
	How well does digital business strategy take advantage of data/information/knowledge abundance?	Can be addressed by building new capabilities as IT maturity develops

Speed of digital business strategy	How effective is digital business strategy in accelerating new product launches?	Can be addressed by integrated working between IT and marketing Example: Vail Resorts launch of Epic Pass
	How effective is digital business strategy in speeding up learning for improving strategic and operational decision-making?	Can be addressed by integrated working between IT and other functions Example: Vail Resorts analysis of customer data to gain new insights
	How quickly does digital business strategy bolster the speed of dynamic supply chain orchestration?	Can be addressed by integrated working between IT and operations
	How quickly does digital business strategy enable the formation of new business networks that provide complementary capabilities?	Can be addressed by alliances/partnerships (see Chapter 10 for more on strategic alliances); opportunities may arise in functional areas such as operations (e.g. outsourcing, section 9.7)
Sources of value creation and capture	How effective is digital business strategy in leveraging value from information?	Can be addressed by integrated working between IT and other functions Example: Vail Resorts analysis of customer data to gain new insights
	How effective is digital business strategy in capturing value through coordinated business models in networks?	Can be addressed by new approaches to business models (Chapters 8 and 11), alliances/partnerships (Chapter 10)
	How effective is digital business strategy in appropriating value through the control of the firm's digital architecture?	Can be addressed by Aron's approach to IT strategy and digital strategy (section 9.7), that is, all aspects of business strategy informed by digital considerations

Source: adapted from Bharadwaj, A., El Sawy, O.A., Pavlou, P.A., and Venkatraman, N. (2013). Digital business strategy: Toward a net generation of insights. *MIS Quarterly*, **37**(2), 471–82, p. 479, https://misq.umn.edu/misq/downloads/download/editorial/581 (last accessed 2 October 2022).

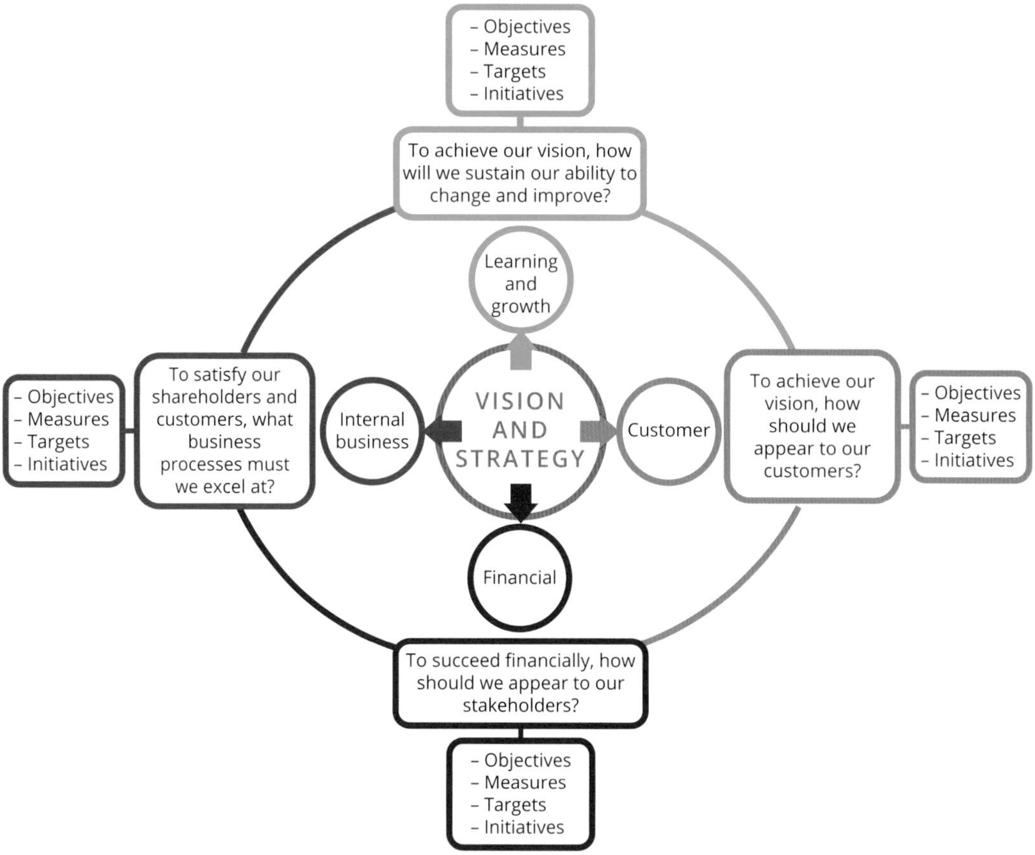

FIGURE 9.8 Balanced scorecard provides a framework to translate a strategy into operational terms. *Source*: adapted from Kaplan, R.S. and Norton, D.P. (1996b). *The Balanced Scorecard: Translating Strategy into Action*. Boston, MA: Harvard Business School Press. By permission of Harvard Business Publishing.

These four perspectives can be linked to the areas of functional strategy that we have been discussing in this chapter. The first, the **financial perspective**, addresses the organization's financial strategy in a direct manner. The second, the **customer perspective**, is probably easiest to connect with marketing strategy in the first instance. The third, **internal business**, encompasses all of the functions that support the organization in the implementation of its strategy—HRM, operations, and IT. The fourth perspective, the **innovation and learning perspective**, emphasizes the importance of considering how the organization will continue to improve in all these areas and create value in future.

The framework also stresses the connections between the different perspectives. For example, if customers are satisfied (**customer perspective**), they are more likely to choose to spend more money with the firm, leading to increased revenue (**financial perspective**). And customers are more likely to be satisfied (customer perspective) if the firm's staff are well motivated and providing excellent service via smoothly running internal processes (**internal business perspective**).

Kaplan and Norton argue that the financial and non-financial measures on a balanced scorecard should be derived from the company's unique strategy (Kaplan and Norton 1996a, b).

The scorecard is viewed by many as a 'classic' model that has been widely applied in organizations in all sectors from banks (Balkovskaya and Filneva 2016) to local government (Sharma and Gadenne 2011). Kaplan and Norton (1996a: 55) write that 'the Balanced Scorecard provides executives with a comprehensive framework that can translate a company's vision and strategy into a coherent and linked set of performance measures'. They suggest that the measures should include both outcome measures and the performance drivers of those outcomes. By articulating the outcomes desired by the firm, as well as the drivers of those outcomes, managers can channel the knowledge and energies of people throughout the organization towards achieving the business's long-term goals.

Kaplan and Norton reject the traditional view of measurement as a tool to control behaviour and evaluate past performance. While many systems of control and performance measurement attempt to keep individuals and organizational units in compliance with a pre-established plan, Kaplan and Norton argue that the measures on a balanced scorecard can be used by executives in a different way:

> [...] to articulate the strategy of the business, to communicate the strategy of the business, and to help align individual, organizational, and cross-departmental initiatives to achieve a common goal. These executives are using the scorecard as a communication, information, and learning system, not as a traditional control system. For the Balanced Scorecard to be used in this way, however, the measures must provide a clear representation of the organization's long-term strategy for competitive success.
>
> (Kaplan and Norton (1996a: 56)

Strategy maps

In their later work, Kaplan and Norton (e.g. 2004a) propose strategy maps as a way to describe an organization's strategy, so that objectives and measures can be established and managed. Consider Figure 9.9: on the left-hand side of the strategy map, we see the four perspectives of the balanced scorecard; each perspective has a 'row' of the model that contributes to the overall strategy of the organization. As we drill down into the detail of the four perspectives of the balanced scorecard, each organization will have its own unique strategy map, reflecting the aspects that are most important to its own unique strategy. For example, in Figure 9.9:

- the financial perspective contains elements concerning productivity (improving the cost structure and utilization of assets) and growth (expanding revenue and enhancing customer value);
- the financial perspective is supported by a customer perspective showing the key elements of the customer value proposition—price, quality, etc.;
- the customer perspective is supported by an internal perspective, which highlights the importance of sound processes for managing operations, customers, innovation and so on;
- all of the above is supported by a focus on learning and growth, which reflects the importance of human capital, information capital, etc.

The strategy map is 'the missing link between strategy formulation and strategy execution' (Kaplan and Norton 2004a: 10). Based on the balanced scorecard with its four perspectives,

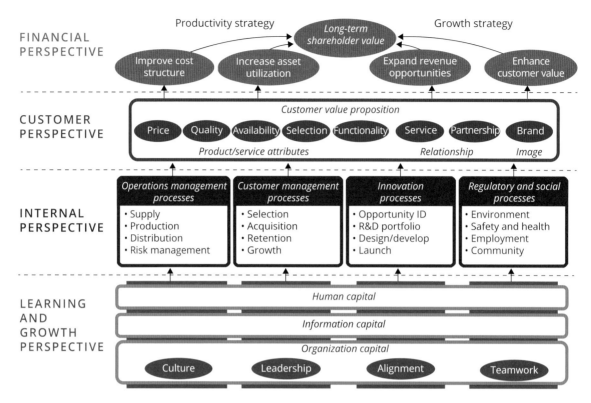

FIGURE 9.9 Strategy map represents how an organization creates value. *Source*: adapted with permission from Kaplan, R.S. and Norton, D.P. (2004b). The strategy map: Guide to aligning intangible assets. *Strategy & Leadership*, **32**(5), 10–17, https://doi.org/10.1108/10878570410699825. Copyright © 2004, Emerald Publishing Limited.

it adds an additional layer of detail that illustrates the time-based dynamics of strategy. The intention is to add granularity, clarity, and focus and to provide a framework that illustrates how strategy links intangible assets to value-creating processes:

> *A strategy map for a Balanced Scorecard makes explicit the strategy's hypotheses. Each measure of a Balanced Scorecard becomes embedded in a chain of cause-and-effect logic that connects the desired outcomes from the strategy with the drivers that will lead to the strategic outcomes. The strategy map describes the process for transforming intangible assets into tangible customer and financial outcomes. It provides executives with a framework for describing and managing strategy in a knowledge economy.*

(Kaplan and Norton 2001: 69)

To illustrate the use of a strategy map, Figure 9.10 provides an example for Crown Castle, a large technology firm:

- **Financial strategy**: the strategy map illustrates the relationship between the customer perspective (with dimensions such as price and speed to market) and the financial perspective which emphasizes revenue, operating costs, etc.

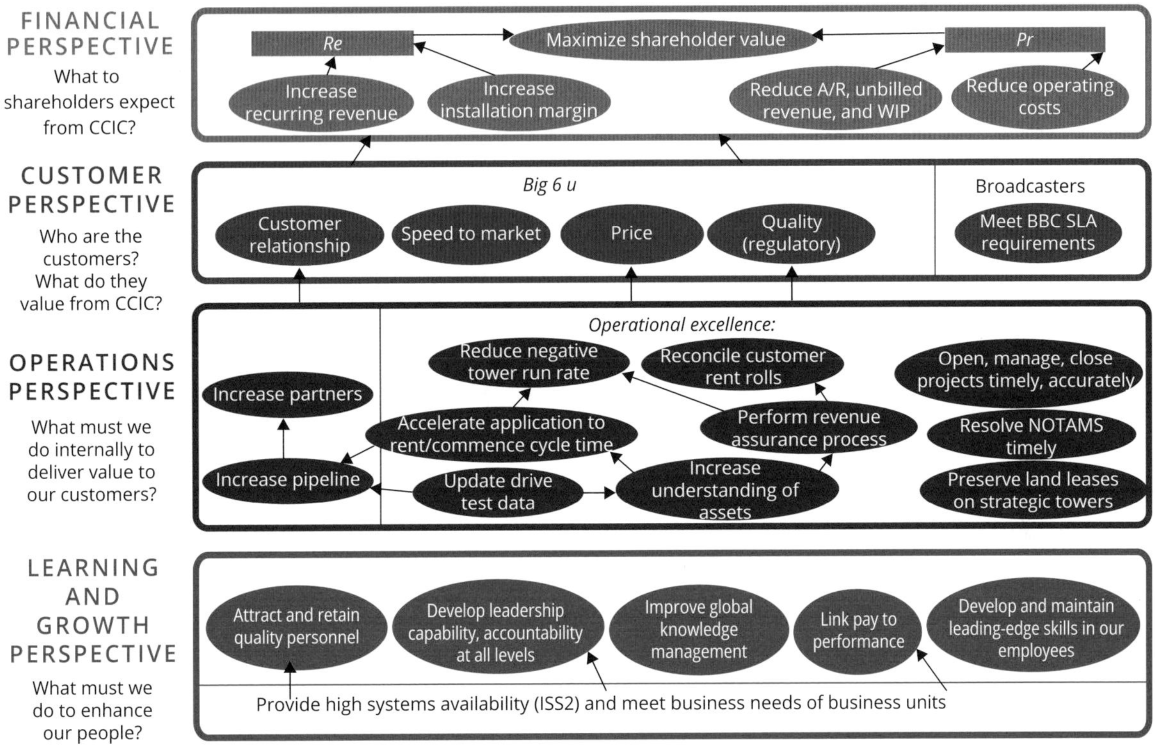

FIGURE 9.10 Kaplan and Norton's strategy map applied to Crown Castle. *Source*: adapted with permission from Kaplan, R.S. and Norton, D.P. (2004b). The strategy map: Guide to aligning intangible assets. *Strategy & Leadership*, **32**(5), 10–17, https://doi.org/10.1108/10878570410699825. Copyright © 2004, Emerald Publishing Limited.

- **HRM strategy**: the strategy map illustrates the importance of HR in the learning and growth of the organization by highlighting aspects such as attracting and retaining personnel, developing leadership capabilities, linking pay and performance, etc.

- **Marketing strategy**: the customer perspective of the strategy map stresses the importance of building customer relationships in supporting future financial success. It also identifies key dimensions of achieving customer satisfaction such as quality and speed to market.

- **Operations strategy**: the strategy map places key operational issues at the heart of the organization's strategic performance, highlighting dimensions from successful project management to appropriate partnerships.

- **IT strategy**: Kaplan and Norton (2004b) stress that Crown Castle's operating environment is highly dynamic, competitive, and fluid. The strategy map must be updated regularly, for example, to reflect shifting pressures in the external business environment as well as to respond to any changes required in the firm's portfolio of IT projects as suggested by **McFarlan's strategic grid** (section 9.7).

PRACTITIONER INSIGHT **KYLIE JAMIESON, SENIOR MANAGER, BEACONFIELD PARTNERS**

Kylie Jamieson is a Senior Manager with Beaconfield Partners in Australia—a specialist technology and commercial advisory, strategy, transformation and sourcing-as-a-service firm focused on the Asia-Pacific region. Kylie has an extensive track record of leading strategy implementation, digital transformation, and organizational change projects for a range of clients, locally and internationally.

'Can you tell us about your career to date and your current role?'

I have spent the majority of my career leading functional strategy implementation, transformative initiatives, and organizational change projects. I work with executives, senior leaders, and their teams to implement strategy using project and change management disciplines. I have experience in a range of settings, including large organizations spread across Australia and multinational organizations with teams spread across geographies, time zones, and diverse cultural environments.

At Beaconfield Partners, we define, source, negotiate and run next-generation technology services for clients. These capabilities are so crucial for organizations in a disrupted world—digitalization and digital change is here to stay, and we support clients adapt and thrive in this setting. I'm a Senior Manager leading the implementation of projects and providing programme management for clients' complex strategic technology initiatives.

'What tools do you use to manage strategy implementation?'

As a project manager, my profession has a tried and trusted kitbag of tools that I use. Projects involve change and I leverage methods of strategic change management as part of the key tools in my kitbag. I use visual representation and diagrams extensively in communicating with stakeholders. I find roadmaps to be particularly helpful in describing the activities and steps required to achieve the vision and objectives of any initiative. Roadmaps can help stakeholders to visually connect with your implementation plan. Project plans are really important too in communicating and managing how to handle the actual doing and timescales of

strategy execution. There are many tools that are used in project management so I won't name them all, but a risk and issue log is also key to successful implementation.

Successful transformation requires strong collaboration across functions, people, and customers. A key intervention would include understanding the business processes to determine where the introduction of new technology will impact existing business processes and roles performed within the business.

Kylie shares her views on strategy implementation and initiative delivery

Whether working internationally or locally, I tend to use the same tools and interventions. However, it is important to adjust your communication to suit the style of the audience, particularly across levels of an organization. How you discuss strategy execution with an operational colleague versus a member of the executive should be respectfully adjusted so that messages are relevant and accessible to whomever you are dealing with. I build rapport with my teams and key stakeholders and discuss and agree ways to engage. In cross-geographical teams, it is vital you are aware of cultural differences to get the best out of people whilst optimizing their experience. Using language and focusing on aspects of implementation that address the diverse needs of a mixed group of stakeholders helps keep them engaged whilst demonstrating that you understand their needs. The use of stakeholder matrices are helpful when working with a large number of stakeholders.

In managing implementation progress, risk and issue identification are key. To mitigate risks and handle issues effectively it is really important to stay close to the project team and stakeholders—open communication is key to achieving successful outcomes. I like to keep my key stakeholders informed along the way, engaging with them continually. When you uncover new risks, you should not be afraid to call them out and facilitate honest conversations.

In any long-standing implementation project, you will likely have to adjust your approach and activity plans to hit objectives. This is where the concept of 'agile' can be really important. An agile approach is iterative, allowing for changing needs and realizing benefits throughout the process. With origins in IT projects, an agile mentality has permeated general project approaches now too. An iterative approach is key to delivering objectives and key measures of success on time and on budget in a dynamic world.

'Could you share your views on how best to undertake strategic transformation/implementation work in organizations?'

Project management involves a feasibility assessment of a proposed project. As a project manager, it is my role to assess the proposed project by way of a written document and/or presentation to inform the best way forward. A project feasibility assessment includes:

Suitability—does the proposed strategy address the strategic problem?

Feasibility—can the strategy be resourced? Will the strategy deliver the required level of operational performance? What are the social impacts and environmental outcomes of implementation alongside financial objectives?

Acceptability—what is the cost of delivering the project? What are the risks and can they be mitigated? How will the project impact internal systems, procedures, and people?

The feasibility assessment translates into a decision to continue to fund a project or not. If the project is agreed, key measures of success can be defined with the sponsor—that is, a set of indicators and targets that will determine whether the delivered initiative has been successful. Once the initiative is underway, key milestones are reported against to meet the interests of the main project stakeholders. One of the key control activities is leading working group meetings with the team, getting close to what is actually happening, and building an understanding of the activity progress and roadblocks.

It is also valuable to collaborate with subject matter experts from functional business areas, such as finance, human resources, and marketing, to map out existing processes before implementation starts. I find operations colleagues in particular can help you to develop a deep understanding of how to balance implementation change demands with ongoing performance targets. Collaborating with subject matter experts will help you plan effectively.

There are many practicalities to implementing strategic initiatives internationally. There are cultural differences not only internally to the organization but also externally in the consumer environment. For example, customers in some markets will only deal with a local representative. Relationships are important and those who are operating in another country bring the strength of well-established relationships with them. There are also legal, human resource management, and finance differences that need to be well understood and considered. The more you engage across geographies, the better you'll be able to understand these differences and harness diversity for implementation success. Taking this back to the feasibility assessment, all of these considerations would be thought through and discussed with key stakeholders, including the project sponsor, as part of project feasibility.

'Generally, what would you advise strategic leaders to prioritize in the current climate?'

Prioritize people! People are your greatest asset and will thrive if you can create an inclusive culture, community, and environment. This is super-important in geographically distributed teams. You can't assume that ways of working will transfer well between locations. As an implementation leader, adapting your approach to ensure stakeholders understand, engage, and feed into planning will make you more effective in delivering change.

I would also highlight the importance of strategic leaders enabling colleagues to skill up in data and digitalization as central features of the future of work and strategy. Digital and data analysis skills are now crucial to implementation work. More broadly, building data and digital literacy can have a demystifying effect that unlocks new capabilities for colleagues. For example, through business intelligence tools, leaders can drill into data to help drive strategic improvements. There is no doubt that digitalization is making strategy implementation more complex and adding new considerations and possibilities to projects. But it is vital to embrace this technology—as individual leaders and as organizations collectively, as business processes—including strategy—will increasingly need to adapt to keep pace with technological change.

CHAPTER SUMMARY

In this chapter, we addressed the following learning outcomes:

○ **Describe the role of functional strategy in supporting organizational strategy.**
Functional strategy can help managers within each functional area of the organization to align their own activities with the organization's overall strategy—and hence ensure that the strategy is delivered. The functional strategy can bring the organization's operational plans together into a coherent strategic statement that clarifies the contribution of each function to the overall organizational strategy. It can highlight the contribution of each function to the achievement of the organization's goals and assist with the efficient allocation of resources to the tasks where they can be most effective. A good functional strategy will help each functional team to turn high-level strategic statements into actionable plans and ensure that employees feel that their abilities are being used effectively towards the attainment of both the function's and the organization's goals.

○ **Identify and outline the different types of functional strategy.**
We have discussed functional strategy for five key areas of the organization—finance, HRM, marketing, operations, and IT—in relation to a number of case examples. For example, we saw that Primark is constantly refreshing its operations strategy in response to external factors, such as shifting patterns of retail behaviour; we reflected on Marmite's innovative marketing strategy as it sought to revive a struggling brand; and we saw GE renew its approach to **financial strategy** under the organization's changing leadership. In our Opening Case Study of Vail Resorts, we see many of these elements come together as they adopt innovative approaches to generating income from their target markets and their use of technology, as well as focusing on the values espoused by staff. We have noted the complex interactions between these dimensions and their contribution to the overall strategy of the organization.

○ **Discuss the potential advantages and disadvantages of functional strategy.**
We have discussed the potential value of functional strategy, for example, in aligning functional areas with the organization's overall strategy, articulating and highlighting the contributions of the functional areas, assisting in planning and resource allocation, and ensuring that the overall strategy is delivered. However, attention must also be paid to the context of the strategy, such as the type of the organization in question and its unique needs. For example, functional strategy may be seen as ineffective in smaller organizations; managers may argue that functional strategy is an unnecessary drain on resources and staff time. In particular cases, it may lead to (real or perceived) conflicts between the organization's overall strategy and one or more specific functional strategies, which must then be resolved. Moreover, functional strategies may leave functional managers feeling that they are facing too many conflicting requests and that they are 'stretched too thinly' across a range of priorities; they may even distract functional managers to the point where they can lose sight of the main objectives of the organization.

9

○ Explain the role of strategic performance management tools, such as the balanced scorecard, in connecting functional strategy with the effective implementation of organizational strategy.

We have introduced tools such as the balanced scorecard and strategy maps to help to elaborate the relationship between the organization's strategy, on the one hand, and the operation of its key functions, on the other. This is an important step as organizations often fail to implement their strategy because they lack an overarching management system to integrate and align these two processes. These tools illustrate the role of functional strategy in working towards the overall organizational goals. The balanced scorecard gives senior managers an overview of key aspects of the organization, while a strategy map can show how strategy links intangible assets to value-creating processes within the organization.

END-OF-CHAPTER QUESTIONS

Recall questions

1. What is functional strategy, and how might it be of value to an organization?

2. Describe the relationship between functional strategy, business unit strategy, and organizational/corporate strategy. Explain how the different levels of strategy may interact.

3. Draw Kaplan and Norton's balanced scorecard, labelling the four perspectives and giving examples of performance measures in each of the four quadrants.

4. Define the concept of market segmentation and how the marketing mix can build customer insight and support marketing planning in an organization.

5. Describe the relationship between digital strategy, IT strategy, and business strategy.

Application questions

A) Describe some of the advantages and disadvantages of functional strategy, relating your comments to an organization that you know well.

B) Choose an organizational function that you are familiar with—finance, human resources, marketing, operations, or IT. Make notes on the strategy of that function within an organization that you know well or can research online. Highlight the key topics and issues that the functional strategy covers and any that it might be missing. How does the functional strategy influence and how is it influenced by the organization's overall strategy?

C) Develop a strategy map for an organization that you know well or can research online. Make notes on the connections that the map highlights between the strategies of the functions within the organization and the organization's strategy as a whole. What does your work tell you about how functional strategy should be developed and managed in organizations?

ONLINE RESOURCES

www.oup.com/he/mackay2e

In addition to the video interviews already highlighted, the book's **online resources** include the following features for this chapter, specifically:

- *links to further reading material* to broaden your knowledge of key issues discussed in this chapter;
- *self-test multiple-choice questions* to test your understanding of the material covered in each section of the chapter; and
- *a flashcard glossary* to help you recall and test your understanding of key terms.

FURTHER READING

'Big Data consumer analytics and the transformation of marketing' by Sunil Erevelles, Nobuyuki Fukawa, and Linda Swayne

Erevelles, S., Fukawa, N., and Swayne, L. (2016). Big Data consumer analytics and the transformation of marketing. *Journal of Business Research*, **69**(2), 897–904.

This article seeks to understand the impact of big data on various marketing activities. The authors argue that three resources—physical, human, and organizational capital—impact on the process of collecting and storing evidence of consumer activity as big data, the process of extracting consumer insight from big data, and the process of utilizing consumer insight to enhance dynamic/adaptive capabilities.

'Global talent management and global talent challenges: Strategic opportunities for IHRM' by Randall S. Schuler, Susan E. Jackson, and Ibraiz Tarique

Schuler, R.S., Jackson, S.E., and Tarique, I. (2011). Global talent management and global talent challenges: Strategic opportunities for IHRM. *Journal of World Business*, **46**(4), 506–16.

The authors discuss the vital role of international human resource management for international organizations. The management of talent, in a global setting, can entail dealing with talent shortages, talent surpluses, locating and relocating talent, and compensation levels of talent. They label these issues as 'global talent challenges' and discuss their implications for organizations.

'Internet marketing capabilities and international market growth' by Shane Mathews et al.

Mathews, S., Bianchi, C., Perks, K.J. et al. (2016). Internet marketing capabilities and international market growth. *International Business Review*, **25**(4), 820–30.

This study explores how the internet, combined with marketing capabilities, can drive international market growth. It suggests that internet marketing capabilities indirectly lead to international market growth when the firm has a high level of international strategic orientation and international network capabilities. Overall, internet marketing capabilities enhance the firm's ability to generate other internal capabilities within the firm.

9

REFERENCES

Adams, S. (2014). Hermès and LVMH make peace. *Forbes* (11 September), https://www.forbes.com/sites/susanadams/2014/09/11/hermes-and-lvmh-make-peace/#3c844d0d6288 (last accessed 25 February 2022).

Amit, R. and Zott, C. (2001). Value creation in e-business. *Strategic Management Journal*, **22**, 493–520.

Applegate, L.M., Austin, R.D., and McFarlan, F.W. (2007). *Corporate Information Strategy and Management* (7th edn). New York: McGraw-Hill.

Aron, D. (2013). The difference between IT strategy and digital strategy. *Gartner* (12 November), https://blogs.gartner.com/dave-aron/2013/11/12/the-difference-between-it-strategy-and-digital-strategy (last accessed 25 February 2022).

Baines, P., Fill, C., Rosengren, S., and Antonetti, P. (2022). *Marketing* (6th edn). Oxford: Oxford University Press.

Baines, T., Lightfoot, H., Peppard, J. et al. (2008). Towards an operations strategy for product-centric servitization. *International Journal of Operations & Production Management*, **29**(5), 494–519.

Balkovskaya, D. and Filneva, L. (2016). The use of the Balanced Scorecard in bank strategic management. *International Journal of Business Excellence*, **9**(1), 48–67.

BBC (2018). Army's £113m recruitment website 'was 52 months late' (14 December), https://www.bbc.co.uk/news/uk-46561779 (last accessed 25 February 2022).

Bender, R. (2014). *Corporate Financial Strategy* (4th edn) London: Routledge.

Betsch, T., Haberstroh, S., and Hohle, C. (2002). Explaining routinized decision making: A review of theories and models. *Theory & Psychology*, **12**(4), 453–88.

Bharadwaj, A., El Sawy, O.A., Pavlou, P.A., and Venkatraman, N. (2013). Digital business strategy: Toward a net generation of insights. *MIS Quarterly*, **37**(2), 471–82.

BloombergUK (2019). The battle for the best ski pass (1 March), https://www.bloomberg.com/news/features/2019-03-01/epic-vs-ikon-battle-for-the-best-ski-pass (last accessed 18 August 2022).

Blumberg, M. and Pringle, C. (1982). The missing opportunity in organizational research: Some implications for a theory of work performance. *Academy of Management Review*, **7**(4), 560–9.

Booms, B.H. and Bitner, M.J. (1981). Marketing strategies and organization structures for service firms. In: Donnelly, J.H. and George, W.R. (eds), *Marketing of Services*. Chicago, IL: American Marketing Association, pp. 47–51.

Borden, N.H. (1964). The concept of the marketing mix. *Journal of Advertising Research*, **2**, 7–12.

Boselie, P., Dietz, G., and Boon, C. (2005). Commonalities and contradictions in HRM and performance research. *Human Resource Management Journal*, **15**(3), 67–94.

Bowen, J. and Ford, R. (2002). Managing service organizations: Does having a 'thing' make a difference? *Journal of Management*, **28**(3), 447–69.

Boxall, P. and Purcell, J. (2016). *Strategy and Human Resource Management* (4th edn). London: Palgrave Macmillan Education.

Boyes, H., Hallaq, B., Cunningham, J., and Watson, T. (2018). The Industrial Internet of Things (IIoT): An analysis framework. *Computers in Industry*, **101**, 1–12.

Burgelman, R., Christensen, C., and Wheelwright, S. (2009). *Strategic Management of Technology and Innovation*. New York: McGraw-Hill.

Chaffey, D. and Ellis-Chadwick, F. (2019). *Digital Marketing: Strategy, Implementation and Practice* (7th edn). Harlow: Pearson.

Cision PR Newswire (2019). Vail Resorts named one of 'America's best employers' by Forbes (19 April), https://www.prnewswire.com/news-releases/vail-resorts-named-one-of-americas-best-employers-by-forbes-300835166.html (last accessed 18 August 2022).

Cision PR Newswire (2021). Vail Resorts named one of 'America's Best Largest Employers 2021' by Forbes (11 February), https://www.prnewswire.com/news-releases/vail-resorts-named-one-of-americas-best-large-employers-2021-by-forbes-301227357.html (last accessed 18 August 2022).

Collings, D. and Mellahi, K. (2009). Strategic talent management: A review and research agenda. *Human Resource Management Review*, **19**(4), 304–13.

Corbett, M.F. (2004). *The Outsourcing Revolution: Why It Makes Sense and How to Do It Right*. New York: Kaplan Publishing.

Denning, S. (2012). Wikispeed: How a 100 mpg car was developed in 3 months. *Forbes*, https://www.forbes.com/sites/stevedenning/2012/05/10/wikispeed-how-a-100-mpg-car-was-developed-in-3-months/?sh=4ba53b28bf (last accessed 22 October 2022).

Dolgui, A. and Proth, J. (2013). Outsourcing: Definitions and analysis. *International Journal of Production Research*, **51**(23–24), 6769–77.

Dowling, P.J., Festing, M., and Eagle, A. (2013). *International Human Resource Management* (6th edn). Andover: Cengage Learning EMEA.

The Economist (2017). Flannery unveils his strategy to revive GE (16 November), https://www.economist.com/business/2017/11/16/flannery-unveils-his-strategy-to-revive-ge (last accessed 18 August 2022).

The Economist (2018). Britain's outsourcing model, copied around the world, is in trouble (28 June), https://www.economist.com/britain/2018/06/28/britains-outsourcing-model-copied-around-the-world-is-in-trouble (last accessed 25 February 2022).

The Economist (2021a). General Electric breaks up (13 November), https://www.economist.com/business/2021/11/13/general-electric-breaks-up (last accessed 18 August 2022).

The Economist (2021b). How Primark Makes Money Selling $3.50 T-Shirts (21 August), https://www.economist.com/business/2021/08/21/how-primark-makes-money-selling-350-t-shirts (last accessed 25 February 2022).

The Economist (2021c). Marketing Marmite: How an advertising agency started a culture war (17 June), https://www.economist.com/1843/2021/06/17/marketing-marmite-how-an-advertising-agency-started-a-culture-war (last accessed 18 August 2022).

The Financial Times (2014). *Financial Times* targets younger readers with new digital advertising campaign (23 April), https://aboutus.ft.com/en-gb/announcements/financial-times-targets-younger-readers-with-new-digital-advertising-campaign (last accessed 25 February 2022).

Finextra (2019). NatWest paperless mortgage process picks up 100,000 customers (16 May), https://www.finextra.com/pressarticle/78431/natwest-paperless-mortgage-process-picks-up-100000-customers?utm_medium=rssfinextra&utm_source=finextrafeed (last accessed 25 February 2022).

Frenkel, S. (2000). Introduction: Service work and its implications for HRM. *International Journal of Human Resource Management*, **11**(3), 469–76.

Fried, V.H. and Hisrich, R.D. (1994). Toward a model of venture capital investment decision making. *Financial Management*, **23**(3), 28–37.

Glassman, B. (2013). What Zappos taught us about creating the ultimate client experience. *Forbes* (13 May), https://www.forbes.com/sites/advisor/2013/05/13/what-zappos-taught-us-about-creating-the-ultimate-client-experience/#165626220fbd (last accessed 25 February 2022).

Greener, I. (2013). *Public Management* (2nd edn). London: Red Globe Press.

Guest, D. (1997). Human resource management and performance: A review and research agenda. *International Journal of Human Resource Management*, **8**(3), 263–76.

The Guardian (2019). Melrose plan to shut GKN Aerospace factory is 'breach of faith' (5 April), https://www.theguardian.com/business/2019/apr/05/melrose-plan-to-shut-gkn-aerospace-factory-is-breach-of-faith (last accessed 25 February 2022).

The Guardian (2020). Two hospitals held up by Carillion collapse are delayed further (17 January), https://www.theguardian.com/society/2020/jan/17/two-hospitals-held-up-by-carillion-collapse (last accessed 25 February 2022).

9

The Guardian (2021). Primark pledges to make all its clothes more sustainable by 2030 (15 September), https://www.theguardian.com/business/2021/sep/15/primark-clothes-sustainable-retailer-carbon-emissions-plastics (last accessed 18 August 2022).

Hill, T. (2000). *Manufacturing Strategy: Text and Cases* (2nd edn). Basingstoke: Palgrave.

Hodge, G.A. (2000). *Privatization: An International Review of Performance.* Boulder, CO: Westview Press.

Jiang, K., Lepak, D., Hu, J., and Beer, J. (2012). How does human resource management influence organizational outcomes? A meta-analytic investigation of mediating mechanisms. *Academy of Management Journal*, **55**(6), 1264–94.

Kaplan, R.S. and Norton, D.P. (1996a). Linking the Balanced Scorecard to strategy. *California Management Review*, **39**(1), 53–79.

Kaplan, R.S. and Norton, D.P. (1996b). *The Balanced Scorecard: Translating Strategy into Action*. Boston, MA: Harvard Business School Press.

Kaplan, R.S. and Norton, D.P. (2001). *The Strategy-Focused Organization: How Balanced Scorecard Companies Thrive in the New Business Environment*. Boston, MA: Harvard Business School Press.

Kaplan, R.S. and Norton, D.P. (2004a). *Strategy Maps: Converting Intangible Assets into Tangible Outcomes*. Boston, MA: Harvard Business School Press.

Kaplan, R.S. and Norton, D.P. (2004b). The strategy map: Guide to aligning intangible assets. *Strategy & Leadership*, **32**(5), 10–17.

Kaplan, R.S. and Norton, D.P. (2008). *The Execution Premium: Linking Strategy to Operations for Competitive Advantage*. Boston, MA: Harvard Business School Press.

Kotler, P. and Armstrong, G. (2017). *Principles of Marketing* (17th edn). Harlow: Pearson.

Krishnamurthy, R. and Yauch, C.A. (2007). Leagile manufacturing: A proposed corporate infrastructure. *International Journal of Operations & Production Management*, **27**(6), 588–604.

Lanvin, B. and Evans, P. (2017). The Global Talent Competitiveness Index, https://www.insead.edu/sites/default/files/assets/dept/globalindices/docs/GTCI-2018-report.pdf (last accessed 25 February 2022).

Lovelock, C., Patterson, P., and Wirtz, J. (2010). *Services Marketing: An Asia–Pacific and Australian Perspective* (5th edn). Sydney: Pearson Australia.

Magzter (2019). The Great M&A Ski War (4 March), https://www.magzter.com/stories/Business/Bloomberg-Businessweek/The-Great-MA-Ski-War (last accessed 18 August 2022).

Marr, B. (2005). Strategic management of intangible value drivers. *Handbook of Business Strategy*, **6**(1), 147–54.

Marr, B., Schiuma, G., and Neely, A. (2004). The dynamics of value creation: Mapping your intellectual performance drivers. *Journal of Intellectual Capital*, **5**(2), 312–25.

Mason, C. and Stark, M. (2004). What do investors look for in a business plan? A comparison of the investment criteria of bankers, venture capitalists, and business angels. *International Small Business Journal*, **22**(3), 227–48.

McCulloch, A. (2018). TfL tops league table of best organisations in UK for work–life balance, *Personnel Today* (8 June), https://www.personneltoday.com/hr/tfl-tops-league-table-of-best-organisations-in-uk-for-work-life-balance (last accessed 25 February 2022).

McFarlan, F.W. (1984). Information technology changes the way you compete. *Harvard Business Review*, **62**(3), 98–103.

Mountain Times (2021). Major reset in Epic Pass prices a game changer (31 March), https://mountaintimes.info/major-reset-in-epic-pass-prices-a-game-changer (last accessed 18 August 2022).

Nathan, V. (2019). Auto makers are improving operations with help from Industrial IoT. *Forbes*, https://www.forbes.com/sites/vinaynathan/2019/03/29/the-iiot-is-driving-results-for-the-automotive-industry/?sh=75b94d8934ad (last accessed 22 October 2022).

Nielsen (2012). Global trust in advertising and brand messages, https://www.nielsen.com/us/en/insights/reports/2012/global-trust-in-advertising-and-brand-messages.html (last accessed 25 February 2022).

9

Nolan, R. and McFarlan, F.W. (2005). Information technology and the board of directors. *Harvard Business Review*. **83**(10), 96–106.

Ohno, T. (1988). *Just-in-Time: For Today and Tomorrow*. Cambridge, MA: Productivity Press.

Peter, J.P., Olson, J.C., and Grunert, K.G. (1999). *Consumer Behaviour and Marketing Strategy*. London: McGraw-Hill.

PMI (Project Management Institute) (2019). What is project management?, https://www.pmi.org/about/learn-about-pmi/what-is-project-management (last accessed 25 February 2022).

Pullman, M.E. and Gross, M.A. (2004). Ability of experience design elements to elicit emotions and loyalty behaviors. *Decision Science*, **35**(3), 531–76.

Quora (2018), Are Google employees more productive because of company perks? *Forbes*, https://www.forbes.com/sites/quora/2018/07/09/are-google-employees-more-productive-because-of-company-perks/?sh=38fceb474b4d (last accessed 22 October 2022).

Rappaport, A. (1998). *Creating Shareholder Value*. New York: Free Press.

Ringel, M., Grassi, F., Baeza, R. et al. (2019). Innovation in 2019: The most innovative companies 2019 (21 March), https://www.bcg.com/en-gb/publications/2019/most-innovative-companies-innovation.aspx (last accessed 25 February 2022).

Robertson, L. (2021). How ethical is Primark? Good on You (21 August), https://goodonyou.eco/how-ethical-is-primark (last accessed 18 August 2022).

Ross, J.W., Sebastian, I.M., and Beath, C.M. (2017). How to develop a great digital strategy. *Sloan Management Review*, **58**(2), 6–9.

Roth, A.V. and Menor, L.J. (2003). Insights into service operations management: A research agenda. *Production Operations Management*, **12**(2), 145–64.

Sharma, B. and Gadenne, D. (2011). Balanced Scorecard implementation in a local government authority: Issues and challenges. *Australian Journal of Public Administration*, **70**(2), 167–84.

Sibbert, D. (1997). 75 years of management ideas and practice 1922–1997. *Harvard Business Review*, **75**, 2–12.

Sirakaya, E. and Woodside, A.G. (2005). Building and testing theories of decision making by travellers. *Tourism Management*, **26**, 815–32.

SkitheWorld.com (2019). One pass to ski them all (3 March), https://skitheworld.com/2019/03/one-pass-to-ski-them-all (last accessed 18 August 2022).

Slack, N. and Lewis, M (2017). *Operations Strategy* (5th edn). Harlow: Financial Times—Prentice Hall.

Slack, N. and Lewis, M. (2019). Operations Strategy (6th edn). Harlow: Financial Times/Prentice Hall.

Solomon, M. (2018). How Zappos delivers wow customer service on each and every call. *Forbes* (15 September), https://www.forbes.com/sites/micahsolomon/2018/09/15/the-secret-of-wow-customer-service-is-breathing-space-just-ask-zappos/#7b527d521b2c (last accessed 25 February 2022).

Soltan, H. and Mostafa, S. (2015). Lean and agile performance framework for manufacturing enterprises. *Procedia Manufacturing*, **2**, 476–84.

Statista.com (n.d.). eBooks worldwide, https://www.statista.com/outlook/dmo/digital-media/epublishing/ebooks/worldwide (last accessed 25 February 2022).

Statista.com (2021) Unit sales of ebooks in the United States (18 May), https://www.statista.com/statistics/191992/sales-of-e-books-in-the-us-since-2006/#:~:text=A%20total%20of%20191%20million,the%20most%20recently%20available%20data (last accessed 25 February 2022).

Sterling, A. and Boxall, P. (2013). Lean production, employee learning, and workplace outcomes: A case analysis through the ability–motivation–opportunity framework. *Human Resource Management Journal*, **23**(3), 227–40.

The Storm Skiing Journal and Podcast (2021). Vail slashes epic pass prices by 20 percent, further demystifying the season pass (24 March), https://www.stormskiing.com/p/vail-slashes-epic-pass-prices-by (last accessed 18 August 2022).

Three.co.uk (2022) Refer a friend, https://www.three.co.uk/refer-a-friend (last accessed 21 October 2022).

Tidd, J. and Bessant, J.R. (2018). *Managing Innovation: Integrating Technological, Market, and Organizational Change* (6th edn). Chichester: John Wiley.

Ulrich, D. (1997). *Human Resource Champions: The Next Agenda for Adding Value and Delivering Results*. Boston, MA: Harvard Business School Press.

Ulrich, D. and Smallwood, N. (2004). Capitalizing on capabilities. *Harvard Business Review*, **82**(6), 119–27.

Vail Resorts (2019). Vail Resorts receives NSAA Gold Eagle Award for Environmental Excellence (6 May), http://news.vailresorts.com/corporate/vailresorts/vail-resorts-wins-golden-eagle-award-environmental-excellence.htm (last accessed 18 August 2022).

Vandermerwe, S. and Rada, J. (1988). Servitization of business: Adding value by adding services. *European Management Journal*, **6**(4), 314–24.

Visnjic, I., Jovanovic, M., Neely, A., and Engwall, M. (2017). What brings the value to outcome-based contract providers? Value drivers in outcome business models. *International Journal of Production Economics*, **192**, 169–81.

Voss, C., Roth, A.V., and Chase, R.B. (2008). Experience, service operations strategy, and services as destinations: Foundations and exploratory investigation. *Production and Operations Management*, **17**(3), 247–66.

Vroom, V. (1964). *Work and Motivation*, New York: John Wiley.

Wilson, A. (1997). The culture of the branch team and its impact on service delivery and corporate identity. *International Journal of Bank Marketing*, **15**(5), 163–8.

Womack, J., Jones, D., and Roos, D. (1990). *The Machine that Changed the World: The Triumph of Lean Production*. New York: Rawson Macmillan.

Wright, M. (2015) Philips Lighting supplies LED lighting as a service to Amsterdam airport (16 April), https://www.ledsmagazine.com/smart-lighting-iot/smart-cities/article/16696783/philips-lighting-supplies-led-lighting-as-a-service-to-amsterdam-airport (last accessed 25 February 2022).

Zott, C. and Amit, R. (2008). The fit between product market strategy and business model: Implications for firm performance. *Strategic Management Journal*, **29**, 1–26.

9

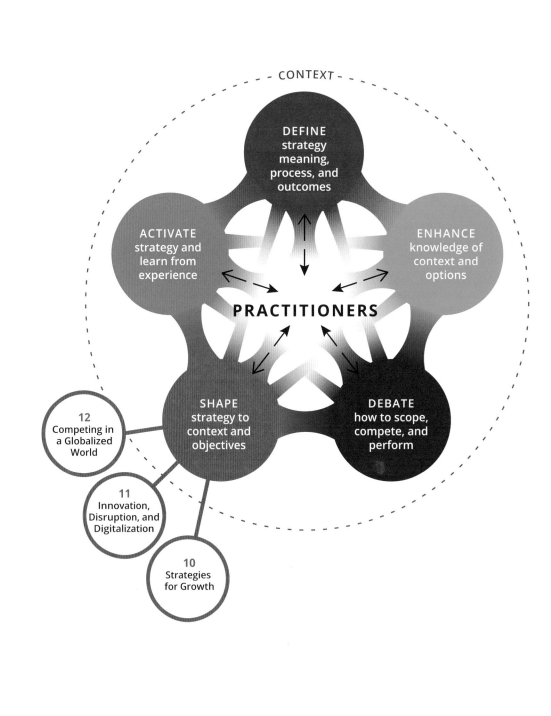

PART
FOUR

Shape strategy to context and objectives

In this part, we address contemporary concerns of wide relevance to organizations during strategy development to meet specific situational needs. Chapter 10 extends corporate strategy thinking by examining how organizations—as multi-business enterprises— might strategize about growth in ways that include both related and unrelated diversification strategies. In Chapter 11, we examine how incorporating innovation and digitalization into strategizing might sustain organizational relevance, improve efficiency, or create new sources of value creation with disruptive market potential.

Finally, strategic options for internationalization of the organization's operations, including a consideration of various business models to manage global expansion and the emerging strategy of 'born global' organizations, are discussed in Chapter 12. By the end of this part, you should have enhanced abilities to think, talk, and act like a practitioner, shaping strategy in response to organization-specific influences and opportunities.

CHAPTER TEN

Strategies for Growth

CONTENTS

By the end of this chapter, you should be able to:

○ Analyse the role of 'corporate parenting' in supporting strategy

○ Define the concepts of economies of scale and scope

○ Explain how you would use the Ansoff matrix to generate and evaluate the various growth options that an organization might consider

○ Appreciate the role of relatedness and synergy in the development of strategy

○ Recognize, develop, and evaluate strategic options based on related and unrelated diversification, vertical and horizontal integration, mergers and acquisitions, joint ventures, and other forms of alliance

○ Assess the risks and rewards associated with a range of approaches to diversification

○ Apply a range of tests of suitability to potential strategic options

TOOLBOX

○ **Economies of scale and scope**
Economies of scale and economies of scope are two concepts that can help an organization to assess the possible benefits of a growth strategy such as reducing its costs. Economies of scale focus on the cost advantages that can arise when the organization increases the level of production of a particular product or service. Economies of scope focus on the cost advantages that can occur when the organization's costs are shared across a variety of goods or activities.

○ **The Ansoff matrix, also known as Ansoff's growth vectors**
The Ansoff matrix is a tool which can help an organization identify and plan its product and market growth strategies. We can think of the organization's products as new or existing and its target markets as new or existing. As part of our strategic planning, the Ansoff matrix helps us to see the possible growth strategies, or growth vectors, for an organization—market penetration, market development, product development, and diversification.

○ **Diversification: related and unrelated**
A diversification strategy involves expanding or adding to the organization's current range of products and markets. A related diversification is one in which the organization expands its activities into products and/or services that are similar to those it currently offers. Unrelated diversification involves entering a new line of business that lacks any important commonalities with the organization's existing industry or industries.

10

Synergy

Synergies occur when the whole is greater than the sum of its parts. It refers to the situation where two or more business units or organizations combine their efforts and find that they can accomplish more together than they can separately. Achieving synergy is often an important goal within a growth strategy, for example, when two companies are planning a merger or alliance of some kind.

Vertical and horizontal integration

When an organization engages in a growth strategy of horizontal integration, it acquires a similar organization in the same industry to increase its size and perhaps achieve economies of scale. An organization adopting a growth strategy of vertical integration acquires an organization that operates in the production process of the same industry, either before or after it in the supply chain process, perhaps to strengthen its supply chain or capture upstream or downstream profits.

Different approaches to diversification

An organization seeking a suitable growth strategy might consider a merger, where two organizations combine into a single legal entity, or an acquisition, where one organization purchases a portion or all of another. A range of cooperative strategies can also be considered, including a joint venture, where two or more organizations create a new entity, and a strategic alliance, which is a less formal agreement between two or more organizations to cooperate.

Testing and evaluating strategic options

Having generated a set of possible growth strategies for the organization, the strategist can apply a set of tests to evaluate how the organization should proceed. For example, does a particular strategic option seem to be consistent with any prior strategic analysis of the organization's external environment and internal resources? Is the strategy likely to work well in practice, and how difficult will it be to achieve? And how acceptable is any new strategic option to the organization's range of stakeholders?

 Access the online resources to watch a short video clip where Kieran Phelan shares his top career tips.

OPENING CASE STUDY AUDI AND FAW ESTABLISH A JOINT VENTURE TO PRODUCE ELECTRIC VEHICLES IN CHINA

An electric car joint venture between Audi and FAW ('First Automobile Works') in China was first officially announced in October 2020. The new company is 60% owned by Audi AG and Volkswagen Group China and 40% by FAW. According to Audi CEO Markus Duesmann, 'this decision emphasizes the strategic importance of the Chinese market'.

The Volkswagen Group is a multinational automotive manufacturing corporation headquartered in Germany. It sells passenger cars under popular marques, including Audi, Bentley, Bugatti, Lamborghini, Porsche, SEAT, and Skoda. FAW is a Chinese state-owned automotive manufacturing company headquartered in Changchun, China. Its main products are automobiles, buses, trucks, and auto parts.

The new joint venture builds on an existing one between FAW and Volkswagen, established in 1991 to manufacture Audi and Volkswagen marque cars for sale in China. However, the new joint venture between Audi and FAW will concentrate on the local production of purely electric Audi models. For Audi, this is the first joint venture with a majority shareholding in China.

Audi's CEO commented:

With the new Audi-FAW company in Changchun, we are further expanding our presence on the Chinese market and strengthening our position as a manufacturer of fully electric premium vehicles through local production [. . .] In doing so, we are continuing the Audi success story in China and actively helping to shape the transformation of the Chinese automotive industry as it moves toward sustainable mobility.

Local production of the first vehicles built jointly with FAW is scheduled to start by 2024.

In making this strategic decision, Audi is further strengthening its presence in China, its biggest foreign market. The company plans to offer or localize further fully electric models from the e-tron family (the e-tron was Audi's first electric mass-production car) in China in the coming years. By 2025, Audi aims to achieve around one-third of its sales in China with electrified cars.

The new joint venture with FAW has allowed Audi to increase the number of locally produced models to 12 by the end of 2021. The models produced by a second partner, SAIC Volkswagen, are set to be introduced in 2022. Audi has so far delivered almost 7 million vehicles on the Chinese market. In 2020 alone, Audi sold 727,358 vehicles in China, the brand's best ever result in over 30 years of business on the Chinese market.

According to Audi's CEO Markus Duesmann, the company is taking 'a further step in the electrification strategy in China', and added that the team was 'extremely well-prepared'. However, it will face tough competition. Domestic EV makers such as China's Nio and Xpeng, as well as companies such as Tesla, are expanding manufacturing capacity in China, where the government promotes greener vehicles to reduce air pollution.

Questions for discussion

1. What do you think motivated Audi to consider a joint venture with FAW—and similarly, what is the motivation for FAW? What do you think

Representatives from the Volkswagen Group, the FAW Group Co., and Chinese government officials celebrate the signing of the memorandum of understanding (MoU) for the joint production of electric vehicles during the Germany-China Automobile Conference *Source*: https://www. audi-mediacenter.com/en/press-releases/audi-and-faw-establish-new-company-to-produce-electric-vehicles-in-china-13266 (last accessed 10 August 2022).

both parties hope to achieve by working together in this way?

2. Can you identify other strategic options that Audi or FAW could have pursued, apart from a joint venture? Do you think that those options would have achieved the same objectives?

3. What are the potential downside risks associated with the joint venture from the perspective of both Audi and FAW?

Sources

Audi MediaCenter (2020). Audi and FAW establish new company to produce electric vehicles in China (13 October), https://www.audi-mediacenter.com/en/press-releases/audi-and-faw-establish-new-company-to-produce-electric-vehicles-in-china-13266 (last accessed 10 August 2022).

Automotive News Europe (2020). Audi, FAW sign deal on a new EV joint venture in China (13 October), https://europe.autonews.com/automakers/audi-faw-sign-deal-new-ev-joint-venture-china (last accessed 10 August 2022).

Electrive.com (2020). Audi reveals more on EV joint venture with FAW (18 January), https://www.electrive.com/2021/01/18/audi-reveals-new-details-about-ev-joint-venture-with-faw/#: :text=The%20electric%20car%20joint%20venture,Changchun%20in%20north%2Deastern%20China (last accessed 10 August 2022).

10

10.1 **Introduction**

To begin our discussion of strategies for growth, it is helpful to restate the distinction between *corporate strategy* and *competitive strategy* (also known as business strategy) introduced in chapter 1. Bourgeois (1980) offers the following definitions:

- corporate strategy discusses *where* a company seeks to compete, a decision sometimes known as 'domain selection';

- competitive strategy discusses *how* a company seeks to compete, a decision sometimes known as 'domain navigation'.

Therefore, corporate strategy occurs at a higher level than business or competitive strategy. It involves choices such as which industries, markets, or segments an organization should compete in and whether and how an organization should collaborate with another organization. Competitive strategy follows these decisions. Having decided where to compete, competitive strategy focuses on how this can be done. For example, a firm may intend to compete in a particular market, but what will be the basis of its competitive advantage (the important idea of competitive advantage is discussed in Chapter 8)? Will it be differentiation, for example? Or perhaps price? Before we can analyse and engage in strategic decisions about which growth strategies to pursue, we need to consider both of these 'levels' of strategy. We also need to reflect for a moment on what we mean by 'growth' in this context. Many organizations will reach a point in their development or life cycle when they want to consider whether and how to expand. This may be about a desire to increase profits or to serve more clients. It might be driven by new opportunities present in the external environment or the financial ambitions of the owner of a firm triggering a strategizing episode. In any case, in this chapter we will be exploring questions of *where* to compete and *how* to compete from the perspective of an organization that is interested in increasing the scale of its current activities.

In this chapter, we will focus on some classic questions of corporate strategy as we discuss how to shape strategy to context and objectives (Part Four of the process–practice framework, Figure 2.4). We begin by exploring the role of the 'corporate parent' in supporting strategy. This is often an important corporate strategy issue as the 'headquarters' of a large organization is typically responsible for high-level decisions around what business the organization participates in. We introduce some important ideas that the strategy practitioner should consider when planning growth strategies as they help us to understand the pros and cons of a range of strategic options. The first is economies of scale and scope; this addresses the potential benefits of either increasing business volumes to reduce unit costs or sharing costs across multiple lines of business. The second is **synergy**—when two business units find that they can achieve more working together than they can independently. We also discuss strategies of diversification (when the organization moves into products and markets that are new to it), and we explore diversification strategies that are both related and unrelated, depending on the degree of similarity between the existing and new lines of business. We explore a range of approaches to growth, including mergers and acquisitions, joint ventures, and other forms of alliance. Finally, we will consider tests for evaluating whether such options are suitable and explore some of the issues around their implementation.

10.2 **Role of corporate parenting**

We begin our discussion of corporate strategy by considering the role of **corporate parenting**. As mentioned briefly in section 10.1, a corporate 'parent' is the head office of a business and its senior managers. In a multi-business organization, this is often a separate entity from the business units themselves. In a small or medium-sized company (SME), it may simply be one person. In any case, 'parenting' is about the influence of the corporate centre on its business units and the type of relationship it has with them, both in strategy formulation and in controlling or enhancing the sources of competitive advantage of the business units within the organization's portfolio. Before understanding the different types of growth strategy, it is important for the strategy practitioner to understand the impact of the corporate parent on corporate strategy. In this section, we will focus on two key aspects of the 'corporate parenting' role (Furrer 2016):

- the responsibility of the corporate parent for value creation;
- the corporate parent's role as a bridge between the corporate- and business-level strategies.

Parenting in single- or multi-business organizations

First, it is helpful to distinguish between single- and multi-business organizations. A single-business organization focuses upon a single industry or product market. The organization may be based around the exploitation of a single technology or product or even an individual owner-manager. This type of organization is common amongst new start-ups, such as a local hairdresser or beauty salon, and across the small and micro-organizational sectors, such as a local restaurant or coffee roaster that has ambitions to grow the scale of its business. It is also possible to identify medium or large single-business organizations, such as a retailer, IT firm, or law firm that confines itself to a core set of products or services, perhaps in a well-defined geographic market.

In contrast, a multi-business organization operates in multiple markets through several distinct units (Paroutis and Pettigrew 2007). It may be organized around different geographical markets, such as Unilever, which operates in 190 countries around the world with key units in Europe, the United States, and Asia; different product markets, such as Samsung Electronics, with its presence in consumer electronics, mobile communications, etc.; or different vertical stages, such as ExxonMobil's structure, which includes 'upstream' businesses that cover searching and drilling for oil and gas, through to 'downstream' businesses that involve refining, distributing, and selling fuel. Therefore a multi-business organization is an organization which has chosen to diversify away from its original product, market, or industry focus and engages in a number of subsidiary activities. These activities could take place in different markets or possibly with different modes of operation.

Role of the corporate parent

The role of the corporate parent in a single-business organization, such as an SME, is relatively clear. The single-business organization is its own corporate parent and there will be no separation in practice between business and corporate levels of strategy, although they remain

10

conceptually distinct. In a single-business organization, the parent is present at all stages of the strategy process and can influence the operation of the organization at first hand. Inevitably, as organizations grow, their processes tend to become more complex. And as complexity grows, the role of the corporate parent changes.

In multi-business organizations, the focus is not upon controlling day-to-day activities across the managerial hierarchy but on making a significant contribution to the overall performance of the organization. The key strategic issue for the organization becomes the evaluation of how the corporate centre adds value. In a 'typical' multi-business organization, the parent is likely to be located in a corporate headquarters (HQ). This HQ will provide a hub around which a variety of subsidiary activities in separate business units will revolve. What is the relationship between the HQ and the business units? Traditionally, the corporate parent has performed a largely functional role aimed at assisting its business units. Based on Porter (1987), Henry (2018) identifies four such areas:

1. **Standalone influence**: this concerns the parent company's impact upon the strategies and performance of each business the parent owns. Standalone influence includes such things as the parent company setting performance targets and approving major capital expenditure for the business. There is an opportunity here for the parent to create substantial value. However, where the parent imposes inappropriate targets or fails to recognize the needs of the business for funds, it will destroy value.

2. **Linkage influence**: this occurs when the parent seeks to create value by enhancing the linkages that may be present between different businesses. For example, this might include transferring knowledge and capabilities across business units. The aim is to increase value through synergy.

3. **Functional and services influence**: the parent can provide functional leadership and cost-effective services for the businesses. The parent company creates value to the extent that it provides services which are more cost effective than the businesses can undertake themselves or purchase from external suppliers.

4. **Corporate development activities**: this involves the parent creating value by changing the composition of its portfolio of businesses. The parent actively seeks to add value through its activities in acquisitions and alliances. In reality, the parent company often destroys value through its acquisitions by paying a premium which it fails to recover.

However, the parent can do more than perform these functional tasks in order to add value to the organization. It can also manage the relationships between the business units more actively. Authors such as Furrer (2016) and Goold et al. (1998) discuss the question of how corporate parents can identify synergy (see section 10.6) and the circumstances in which they might encourage value creation. As an example, consider economies of scope. A brief definition of economies of scope (we will return to this in section 10.3) is the cost savings that the firm creates by successfully transferring some of its capabilities and competencies that were developed in one of its businesses to another of its businesses. Therefore, economies of scope are made possible when an organization moves from being a single- to a multi-business organization. This is particularly relevant when an organization engages in related diversification (see section 10.7 for a fuller discussion). A related diversification is one that occurs within the same product, market, or industry area; it should offer opportunities for activities to be shared or for core competencies and skills to be transferred across businesses (as in the Opening Case Study of Audi and FAW).

If an organization is pursuing a strategy based on diversification (we define diversification in section 10.4 and discuss it further in section 10.7), it will be part of the role of the corporate parent to ensure that value is added by the effective implementation of any possible economies of scope offered by the diversification. This is what is meant by potential 'synergies' which may be attainable as a result of a diversification, that is, any potential economies of scope that can be achieved across two businesses. The parent can assume a coordinating role, aiming to explore and exploit interrelationships amongst business units.

Considering all this, how might the HQ add value, rather than just using up the time and resources of the managers of the business units? One way they could add value is through their responsibility to encourage strategic decisions to be taken as close as possible to its markets. In the public sector, this has been illustrated by trends towards deregulation and privatization of local government services or public utilities. The aim of this kind of deregulation is to shift responsibility for the development of capabilities and competitive strengths down to the business unit level and away from the corporate parent, in this case, the government. However, this is a controversial topic. For example, studies of the deregulation of public transport in the United Kingdom report a mixed picture of success, with bus travellers outside the capital city London facing rising prices and a falling number of journeys (*The Guardian* 2014), leading critics to question whether all the intended benefits of the deregulation have been achieved in this case.

10.3 Understanding economies of scale and scope

When an organization pursues a strategy of growth, there are several potential advantages of growth that it may be pursuing. In this section, we discuss two such benefits—economies of scale and scope. These are important ideas which can help us to understand why some organizations seek to implement growth strategies—and why it can be difficult to achieve all the potential benefits of such strategies in practice.

Economies of scale

Economies of scale are the cost advantages that an organization can achieve when it increases the scale of its operations. Put simply, economies of scale occur when the cost per unit of output decreases as output increases. For example, this may occur when a manufacturing business makes improvements to its production process, allowing faster production of goods at lower unit costs. Economies of scale apply to a variety of situations and at various levels, such as a business or manufacturing unit, a plant, or an entire enterprise. When average costs start falling as output increases, economies of scale are occurring.

One possible source of economies of scale is that the firm may be able to purchase inputs at a lower cost per unit when they are purchased in large quantities. Examples include a large supermarket that has the buying power to negotiate a significant 'bulk discount' when purchasing from farmers and other suppliers or an energy firm negotiating its supply contracts for large quantities of coal and gas.

It's important to remember that economies of scale often have limits. An example might be when the firm's demand for a particular raw material exceeds nearby supply. For example, 'rare earths' are a group of 17 similar chemical elements (BBC 2012), crucial to the manufacture of many high-tech products. Ninety-five per cent of global production of rare earths takes place in China, a fact that occasionally leads to expressions of concern in other parts of the world (Blau 2010). Similarly, a firm may reach a point when its local markets are saturated and therefore transport costs rise because of having to transport its products over greater distances to reach its customers. Another example might arise when its defect rate increases; in other words, a higher proportion of goods produced are faulty. For example, changes to a production process—intended to allow higher volumes and lower unit costs—may result in an increase in the percentage of output that fails to meet the desired quality target, such as the precise specifications for the dimensions of a car axle in the automotive industry.

Economies of scope

Economies of scope operate in a similar way to economies of scale except that where economies of scale result from increasing the volume of production of a single product, economies of scope can be seen as the cost benefits resulting from using the same resource across a range of outputs. They are the result of a more intensive use of a shared resource across business units rather than within a **single business unit**.

Farsi et al. (2007) discuss economies of scope in the case of local public transport in the Swiss marketplace, where a single operator may offer trolley bus, motor bus, and tramway systems. Shareable inputs are labour, capital, and energy. 'Local public transport companies that combine several transport modes use similar equipment such as wires, overhead lines, and similar skills such as driving, management, and network maintenance. Such synergies also apply to activities such as advertising, scheduling, and ticketing' (Farsi et al. 2007: 347).

Achieving economies of scope can clearly have an impact upon cost if, for instance, they permit the sharing of primary activities, such as marketing or operations, or support activities, such as human resources or IT functions. As an example, it is easier for large firms to carry the overheads of sophisticated research and development (R&D). R&D is crucial in the pharmaceuticals industry. Yet, the cost of discovering the next blockbuster drug is enormous and increasing. Several of the mergers between pharmaceuticals companies in recent years have been driven by the desire of companies to spread their R&D expenditure across a greater volume of sales (*The Economist* 2008).

10.4 Corporate strategy: Ansoff's growth vectors

Having explored the key ideas of economies of scale and scope as potential benefits of the implementation of growth strategies, what are the growth options that are available to an organization? In this section, we will introduce a classic strategy framework, the **Ansoff matrix**

(Ansoff growth vectors), which allows the strategist to begin to generate and evaluate the various growth options that an organization might consider.

In section 10.1, we noted Bourgeois' definition of corporate strategy as being concerned with domain selection. In other words, corporate strategy is about where (not how) an organization chooses to compete. So, as we discuss corporate strategy, we are interested in the options available to an organization when they come to choose the industry or market segments that they will compete in. At the simplest level, this may mean that an organization chooses to stay within its original market or product area. However, in a complex global environment, an organization may feel that it is faced with a very wide range of options for extending its activities into new markets or product sectors.

 Access the online resources to watch a short video clip where Kieran Phelan discusses supply chain management and corporate strategy.

Ansoff matrix

Ansoff (1965, 1987) identified that there are a number of broad alternative approaches to growth that an organization can consider. He establishes the idea of the 'strategic portfolio strategy' to assist an organization in mapping out the 'business we are in'. We can think of any organization as an 'assembly of distinctive strategic business areas (SBAs), each of which offers different future growth/profitability opportunities and/or will require different competitive approaches' (Ansoff 1987: 108). Ansoff seems to assume that the organization we are considering is relatively complex; his notion of the organization as an assembly of SBAs is probably less appropriate for a relatively simple, single-business firm and more useful when we are thinking about larger multi-business organizations. However, more recent research has also emphasized that analysis based on the ideas behind the Ansoff matrix, such as the four growth vectors, can also be insightful for small organizations (Byrom et al. 2003)—by exploring an appropriate growth strategy for an SME, for example.

Ansoff's work encourages us to be clear about where each SBA is located and how SBAs can be distinguished from each other. This is explored by introducing the idea of a growth vector. A growth vector is defined as 'the direction in which growth can occur'. It is argued that growth vectors arise when we consider two important criteria:

- **The geographical scope of the firm**, meaning either the organization's existing 'present market', or an alternative 'new market', or both at the same time in complex organizations.

- **The scope of the firm's mission**, meaning the dominant product sector it is seeking to serve. This can be focused on either its existing product market, or an alternative different product market ('diversification'), or both its existing market and a number of different markets for more complex organizations.

Here, we use Ansoff's matrix to highlight the possible strategic options that a firm may wish to pursue in the future. However, it is important to remember that Ansoff himself describes his ideas as addressing growth (i.e. as focusing upon the opportunities for an organization to consider where it should be located in the future), based on the assumption that every organization is always keen to pursue growth. Of course, this may not always be true. For instance, some firms may be focused on survival rather than growth, and some very small organizations may

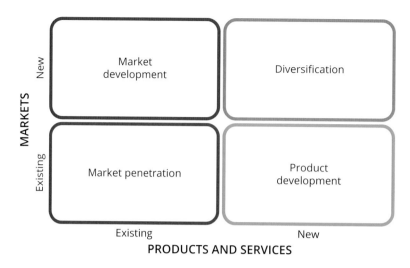

FIGURE 10.1 Ansoff matrix. *Source*: authors.

not be actively pursuing opportunities for growth at all. But what we can assume is that most organizations, once established, are interested in pursuing growth opportunities, and, with that, we can use Ansoff's matrix to explore their strategic options.

Ansoff suggests that there are four broad approaches to growth, or growth vectors, based on whether or not the organization is going to extend beyond its existing market and whether or not it is going to extend its product range. These are depicted in Figure 10.1 and explained in Table 10.1. A market penetration strategy is focused on increasing market share for its present products in its present markets. A strategy of **market development** seeks new markets (for existing products), and a strategy of product development introduces new products (in existing markets). Finally, a strategy of diversification focuses on both new products and new markets.

Having identified these categories of corporate strategic options, it is useful to develop an understanding of how an organization might pursue some or all of these options. This allows us to analyse the strategies that we observe in organizations around the world and to begin to evaluate the range of strategic options that an organization might or should be considering.

Market penetration

This strategic option emphasizes stability in terms of the products or services provided and the market where the organization operates. However, it also stresses that the organization is seeking to increase the amount or value (or both) of the products or services that it sells as a means of achieving growth. For example, if we look at a list of firms spending the most on advertising in the United Kingdom during 2019–20, supermarkets such as Tesco (the United Kingdom's largest supermarket by market share) and Aldi (a German discounter) are amongst the biggest spenders. These firms are battling to protect their current positions, to sell more to their current customers, and to take market share from each other. In 2018, as an important tactic in this competitive battle, Tesco launched Jack's (Barrie 2018), a discount chain which is seeking to compete more directly with the rapidly expanding discounters Aldi and Lidl, both of which are eating into the market share of the traditional supermarkets.

TABLE 10.1 **Ansoff's growth vectors**

Growth vector	Aim	Target market	Strategic action
Market penetration	Identifies a direction for growth based upon an organization increasing the market share for its present product market	Its existing market with existing products	Selling more of its existing products and services to its existing customers
Market development	Identifies new missions for the firm's products	A new market with its existing products	Selling its existing products or services to new customers
Product development	Creates new products to replace or add to current ones	Its existing market with new products	Anticipating changes in existing customer needs and developing the appropriate products to meet those needs
Diversification	Both products and missions are new to the firm	A new market with a new product	Moving into a completely new market or product area to that in which it is used to competing

Source: authors.

The potential of a **market penetration** strategy may be determined by a number of factors, including the prospects for growth in the sector, the organization's capabilities in delivering more of its products or services to meet increased demand, its ability to resist the challenges it faces with regard to existing or new entrants who may be attracted by the prospects for growth or evidence of growing demand and so on. It is also important to remember that selling to existing customers has often been shown to be considerably cheaper than attracting new customers (Gallo 2014).

A growing market is likely to attract a market penetration strategy on the part of existing participants. However, market penetration may also be viable in mature or stable markets, where competition is likely to be well established and the focus is on obtaining market share at the expense of competitors. Market penetration may even be possible in declining markets, where existing firms aim to 'harvest' the remaining opportunities in the sector as other firms decide it is no longer economically viable to compete there. For example, although the car industry in the United States struggled during 2020, major players such as General Motors continued to spend heavily on advertising to promote their brands and shore up their positions.

The concept of market penetration is also applicable in a not-for-profit (NFP) context, even if describing the strategy as 'market penetration' seems inappropriate, as many NFP organizations do not see themselves as 'serving markets' as such. However, voluntary organizations might aim to provide a more complete service to the same group of beneficiaries that they currently serve. For example, under its 'Change Please' programme, the *Big Issue* (perhaps best known for its magazine sold by homeless or marginalized people) is backing a scheme to offer homeless people the opportunity to work as baristas at coffee carts across London (Burns 2017). This initiative enables the organization to help more homeless people and get them into work faster.

 Access the online resources to watch a short video clip where Kieran Phelan discusses organizational structure and growth.

Market development

In a market development strategy, the organization takes its existing products and services into new markets. These may be new geographic markets or new segments of existing markets where the firm has identified customer needs that are currently unmet.

Motivations for pursuing a market development strategy vary by firm. For instance, it may be an appropriate way to secure a foothold in a sector that is currently small or where the extent of demand is as yet unknown. Alternatively, the firm may undertake a major launch of an established brand in a new area. Well-known firms may seek to establish a presence in mature but profitable markets where they have no presence to date. For instance, outside the United States, Amazon's second biggest market is Germany, followed by the United Kingdom and Japan (we discuss Amazon's international goals further in Case Example 10.1). In 2017, Amazon spent $580 million to acquire the e-commerce platform souq.com in order to establish a strong presence in the Middle East market, which it believes is poised for strong growth. In May 2019, as it announced that souq.com would be rebranded amazon.ae in the United Arab Emirates (UAE), the company said that it was proud that its team in the region had grown to more than 3,600 employees since 2017 and that its customers would now have access to a wider range of products and be able to opt to shop online using the Arabic language for the first time (Maceda 2019).

For some companies, market development can be a key feature of a corporate strategy based upon a competitive approach to building global brands as a vital source of product differentiation for what are essentially commodity products. Consider the international strategies of leading footwear firms like Adidas, Nike, and Reebok. These companies have entered international markets for the purposes of expansion. For example, Adidas has identified a 'Key Cities portfolio' comprising London, Los Angeles, New York, Paris, Shanghai, and Tokyo, more recently supplemented by Mexico City, Berlin, Moscow, Dubai, Beijing, and Seoul. The company argues that 'these cities represent the beating heart of our global consumer experience and exert influence on the rest of the world, while at the same time offering commercial opportunities as urbanization continues' (Adidas 2021). This approach can also be viewed as a differentiation strategy Adidas seeks to build and maintain a strong global brand.

In terms of understanding the risks associated with this option, it is worth noting that market development is usually viewed as second only to market penetration in terms of cost advantage and risk avoidance. This is because the emphasis is typically upon marketing existing products (possibly in a marginally modified form) to customers in related market areas, primarily through adding new channels of distribution. For example, consider a manufacturer of electric vehicles that is currently based in Europe and wants to sell its existing products in Asia (e.g. Opening Case Study, Audi and FAW).

Once again, the concept of market development is also applicable in an NFP context, albeit with some modification. Market development for a voluntary organization may involve extending the range of coverage of its activities. For instance, Depaul (a charity that focuses on helping homeless, vulnerable, and disadvantaged people) began in the United Kingdom but has expanded its operations internationally to include Slovakia, Ukraine, the United States, and France, allowing it to help more people beyond the United Kingdom (Depaul 2019).

Product development

In contrast with market development, where an existing product enters a new market, product development (or service development) offers a strategic route to growth in areas where existing product ranges do not fully exploit all the available existing opportunities, where there are advantages to offering a full range of products, or where the demand for a product or service is evolving. For example, Blizzard Tecnica, which produces ski gear, has received a great deal of positive coverage for redesigning items of ski equipment (such as boots and skis, which are traditionally designed with men in mind) to offer a product range that is better suited to female customers, who now make up a large part of the market for such goods (Terwilliger 2017). In 2019, it was reported that, thanks to the Blizzard Black Pearl, the best-selling ski in the United States was, for the first time, one aimed at women (Kestenbaum 2019).

NFP organizations may alter the nature of the service they offer as needs and circumstances change. For example, Marie Curie is a UK-based charity best known for giving care and support to the terminally ill via hospices and nursing staff. However, its strategic plan describes a broadening in the range of services it offers to include information, helpers, and support for the bereaved. It launched information and support services in 2015; in the year 2019–20, the information and support pages on its website were viewed more than 2.3 million times (a 23% increase on the previous year) and more than 15,000 enquiries were answered by phone or live web chat (Marie Curie 2020).

CASE EXAMPLE 10.1 **AMAZON VS ALIBABA**

Amazon, the world's largest e-commerce company based in the United States, competes for dominance in foreign markets with Alibaba, a Chinese multinational also specializing in e-commerce. The two firms—discussed separately in Chapters 8 and 1, respectively—often choose to adopt different approaches around the world.

In some cases, Alibaba's moves towards international expansion have begun with digital payments. Alibaba has a broader reach than Amazon, particularly with its affiliate Ant Group, owner of the giant payments business Alipay. In other cases, Alibaba has invested in e-commerce sites, as with Lazada in South-East Asia. Alibaba aims to build a broad range of services within each market, including payments, e-commerce, and travel services, and then link local platforms with Alibaba's platforms in China. Alibaba helps Chinese companies sell in places such as Brazil and Russia and assists foreign firms with marketing, logistics, and customs in China.

Amazon, on the other hand, earns more than one-third of its revenue from e-commerce outside North America. Its second-largest market is Germany, followed by the United Kingdom and Japan. In 2017, it bought Souq.com, an e-commerce firm in the Middle East. Its criteria for expansion elsewhere include the size of the population and the economy and the density of internet use. It typically owns inventory and warehouses, while Alibaba tends not to do so directly. Amazon also wants to help suppliers in any country to sell their products abroad.

Amazon and Alibaba may need to adapt their business models in new markets, and their models may start to look more similar. They remain each other's fiercest international rivals. Success in e-commerce requires scale, which needs lots of capital. Big firms also have a natural advantage as they expand because technologies developed for one market can be introduced across many.

Questions for discussion

1. Analyse the growth strategies of Amazon and Alibaba using Ansoff's matrix (Figure 10.1).

Continued

Identify and describe any elements of the four growth vectors—market penetration, product development, market development, and diversification—that you think are informing their plans.

2. Do you think that economies of scale and/or scope currently play an important part in the strategies of either business? Explain your answer.

3. In each case, what role do you think the corporate parent could or should be playing in the strategic development of the business?

Sources

Businesswire (2019). Alibaba unveils five-year goals for China consumer business (24 September), https://www.businesswire.com/news/home/20190924005631/en/Alibaba-Unveils-Five-Year-Goals-for-China-Consumer-Business (last accessed 18 August 2022).

The Economist (2021). Forget winning, can Amazon survive in India (25 January), https://techcrunch.com/2021/01/25/india-plays-hardball-with-amazon (last accessed 18 August 2022).

The Financial Times. Alibaba steps up competition with Amazon in global commerce market (8 May), https://www.ft.com/content/3d25007c-713d-11e9-bbfb-5c68069fbd15 (last accessed 21 October 2022).

Statistica (2022). Annual net sales of Amazon in selected leading markets from 2014 to 2021 (14 February), https://www.statista.com/statistics/672782/net-sales-of-amazon-leading-markets (last accessed 18 August 2022).

Diversification

The first three of Ansoff's growth vectors (see Figure 10.1) represent strategic decisions linked to familiar products, services, or missions (markets). The final vector, diversification, suggests diversifying slightly from the familiar. So, what does 'diversification' actually mean, and what is the variety of strategic options available to an organization through diversification? Ansoff (1987) defines diversification as a situation where both products and missions are new to the firm such that the firm moves into a completely new market and product area than that in which it is used to competing. Given our discussion of resources and capabilities, you may be asking why, if there is a close link between an organization's existing capabilities and competitive advantage, a firm would opt to explore opportunities in areas where it has no prior experience and where its resources and capabilities may not be well suited or might not offer any potential to create value for the firm. This is a very important question, and leads us to a discussion of two key concepts, relatedness and synergy (see sections 10.5 and 10.6, respectively), before we go on to a fuller discussion of different strategic options that may represent diversification strategies (section 10.7). In order to explore the potential reasons for and drivers of growth strategies such as diversification, we first explore the idea of related and unrelated diversification in multi-business organizations (Rumelt 1974; Palepu 1985).

10.5 Understanding related and unrelated diversification

Having introduced Ansoff's four growth vectors, we next develop our understanding of the final vector—diversification.

A diversification strategy generally emphasizes both a move away from a single industry approach and some interrelationship with one or more other organizations. There are also different degrees of diversification that an organization can pursue. For example, if 95% of its revenue were generated by a single business, it would be undertaking a low level of diversification. This contrasts with highly diversified multi-business organizations where no single business unit is responsible for the majority of revenues. For example, Johnson & Johnson produces a wide range of prescription and over-the-counter drugs. IT also makes medical devices and runs a sports performance research institute for athletes. This example demonstrates how there can also be different degrees of relatedness within diversified organizations. But what types of relatedness can an organization pursue, and how does this relate to the strategy's ability to create value? In this section, we will consider two main areas of relatedness, corporate and operational relatedness, before considering the question of synergy in section 10.6.

Corporate and operational relatedness

The opportunity to create value through diversification is usually achieved by identifying economies of scope (see section 10.3). Economies of scope exist where a saving is made by producing two or more distinct goods together, when the cost of doing so is less than that of producing each good separately (Teece 1980). If economies of scope can be realized, potential synergies can also be achieved.

In order to understand how an organization can realize economies of scope, it is useful to think about exactly where in the organization the costs savings can be made or synergies achieved. Hitt et al. (2007) point out that we should consider whether two organizations are related at the corporate level or the operational/business unit level. Figure 10.2 illustrates the types of value-creating opportunities that are offered by different types of diversification.

Figure 10.2 has two axes. The first (vertical axis, labelled 'sharing') considers the potential offered by the diversification to share assets. This emphasizes the **operational relatedness** between the two organizations. The second (the horizontal axis, labelled '**corporate relatedness**')

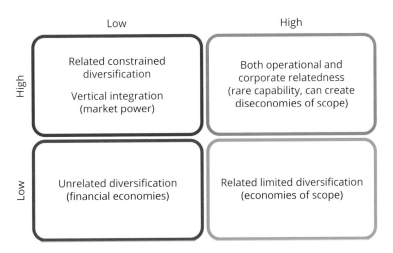

FIGURE 10.2 Hitt et al.'s 2 × 2 matrix on 'value-creating strategies of diversification'. *Source*: adapted from MacMillan, I. (1988). Controlling competitive dynamics by taking strategic initiative. *Academy of Management Perspectives*, **2**(2), 111–18, https://doi.org/10.5465/ame.1988.4275518. © Academy of Management Perspectives.

considers the potential offered by the diversification to combine capabilities and pursue asset creation or improvement. We will now briefly review each of the four quadrants of Figure 10.2 to consider how they offer the opportunity to add value.

Low opportunity for sharing assets/low corporate relatedness

With no **relatedness** of either kind, diversification in this quadrant is known as 'unrelated diversification'. The only opportunities for value creation are likely to lie in the area of financial economies, that is, cost savings realized through the improved allocation of financial resources. These can be based on investments inside or outside the firm. The motivation may be to build a portfolio of businesses, each of which possesses a different profile of risk and reward, with the aim of reducing the total business risk to the organization as a whole. This type of thinking, leading to a portfolio approach, was particularly popular among large, diversified conglomerates during the 1970s. While it can be argued that the popularity of the concept of synergy (Goold and Campbell 1998) has undermined this approach, conglomerates continue to exist. Consider the success of the Virgin Group, which began in the 1970s as a record mail order and record store business and has since engaged in unrelated diversification into the airline industry (Virgin Atlantic), the travel sector (Virgin Trains), the financial services sector (Virgin Money), and so on. However, not every initiative has been a success. For example, in the mid-1990s, the Virgin Group launched Virgin Cola and achieved a very low level of market share and rapidly exited the market. The reason for this unsuccessful example of diversification is that existing powerful players in the soft drinks market were able to make distribution difficult for Virgin and engage in expensive advertising campaigns.

High opportunity for sharing assets/low corporate relatedness

For an example of a firm adopting strategies of diversification where corporate relatedness is low yet there are good opportunities for asset sharing, consider Procter & Gamble, the US multinational consumer goods corporation. With around 65 brands across 10 product categories (dishwashing, laundry detergents, haircare, skincare and so on), this company has the potential to take advantage of considerable **economies of scope**. The cost of undertaking many of its activities (around manufacturing, distribution, etc.) can be shared across a number of business units; hence, the average cost is lower than if each business unit operated in isolation (see Gordon Ramsey's practitioner interview for further insights about P&G's operation in Chapter 6). In this quadrant, we also find firms that are seeking to achieve market power through **vertical integration**. An example is the US retailer Target, which has a wide range of 'own brand' products—hence controlling manufacturing and distribution.

Low opportunity for sharing assets/high corporate relatedness

A similar position occurs in this quadrant, but the opportunities for economies of scope emerge from relatedness at the corporate level. These opportunities are based on the ability to transfer skills across a range of businesses through the activities of the corporate parent. An example is provided by the transformation that is taking place at General Electric (GE)—from a 'classic conglomerate', with a portfolio that had been described as opaque and too broad, to a 'digital industrial company', according to its CEO (Imelt 2017). GE sees itself as a global technology company, has doubled its R&D investment, and has divested slower-growth, lower-tech, non-industrial

10

businesses in favour of higher growth, manufacturing-based products and services (see Case Example 9.1 for further information about changes at GE).

High opportunity for sharing assets/high corporate relatedness

Finally, we consider the situation where significant opportunities exist for both operational and corporate relatedness; this situation may offer the greatest potential for value creation. For example, the Honda Motor Company began in the motorcycle business before moving into cars and trucks, arguably drawing on both operational relatedness and corporate relatedness across the different lines of business.

In summary, Hitt et al.'s matrix helps us to think through the different types of relatedness that might exist between two organizations and the different types of diversified strategies that might be open to an organization when pursuing growth strategies. We can discuss the matrix further in relation to Case Example 10.3 'South Korea's Chaebol'.

10.6 Understanding synergy

In section 10.5, we set out different types of diversification strategies an organization might pursue based on how related they are to another organization at corporate and/or operational level. Each of the quadrants offers different opportunities to add value. But why might achieving the added value be very challenging? To understand this, we explore the concept of synergy, which underpins the strategies of diversification discussed in the previous section.

Synergy 'exists when the value created by business units working together exceeds the value those units create working independently' (Hitt et al. 2007: 211). It is the concept of the whole being greater than the sum of the parts, and it is sometimes the key driver behind mergers and acquisitions or other collaborative arrangements between organizations. For example, a company that is excellent at manufacturing—having the latest manufacturing technology and able to make one of the best products on the market—may be quite poor at logistics, with inefficiencies in its systems for getting products to customers. Therefore, it might choose to merge with another firm that is excellent at logistics but has a rather outdated manufacturing operation. Thus, synergy can be an explanation for and/or a driver of diversification strategies.

Synergy sounds like a relatively simple concept, although it can be difficult to realize and sustain in reality. If it is successful, it creates greater value, as the definition suggests. On the other hand, it also creates interdependence between separate business units, which may, in turn, limit their flexibility and make them less effective as a source of competitive advantage. For example, a decision to pursue synergy may lead an organization to limit itself to the use of certain technologies in order to achieve the synergistic benefits associated with activity sharing. The organization may become more risk averse and less willing to experiment or innovate, and this may be unwise in a dynamic competitive environment. In the discussion of dynamic capabilities in Chapter 9, it was clear that it was the relationship between such capabilities and strategic flexibility that delivered potential competitive advantage. Any search for synergy could result in this kind of flexibility being undermined.

To overcome this contradiction between flexibility and synergy, the concept of co-evolution (Eisenhardt and Galunic 2000) suggests ways of reconnecting flexibility and synergy. They argue that successful firms adopt a flexible approach to building synergy. For example, relationships between two organizations should be allowed to emerge at business unit level rather than be dictated from the top of the organization; and the links between two organizations should be allowed to evolve over time, with new links emerging and old ones ceasing to exist. The ability to manage synergies in this flexible way is likely to represent a type of capability that is probably rare, difficult to imitate, and therefore valuable.

10.7 Understanding different approaches to diversification

We have discussed *why* organizations might choose to diversify—for example, to obtain synergies or economies of scope or to improve the long-term value of their strategic assets, resources, and capabilities. But *how* might an organization pursue a strategy of diversification? This is what we turn to in this section.

We have already introduced Ansoff's (1987) definition of diversification (see Table 10.1), involving a situation where an organization pursues new opportunities where both products and missions are new to the firm. In other words, it enters a completely new market and product area from the area in which it usually competes. But what does this mean in practice? One option is that the organization could create a presence in the new market itself or begin to produce a new product in order to enter a new market. This would be a more organic approach and would usually result in a conglomerate or a corporation made up of a number of seemingly unrelated businesses formed over time. Alternatively, the organization could recognize that it does not have all the required resources or capabilities to undertake all aspects of diversification by itself. This means that it might opt to take a more collaborative approach, that is, work with another organization.

Collaborative approaches to diversification

In this section, we focus on approaches which permit an organization to overcome resource deficiencies, mitigate risk, or take advantage of opportunities by diversification through a number of collaborative approaches. The main options are introduced in Table 10.2. We can think about the decision whether to engage in diversification or not (and if so, which approach to adopt) as being based upon a number of criteria:

- **risk**: the risk of deciding to pursue diversification or the risk to the organization of doing nothing;
- **cost**: the cost of the decision to diversify or not to diversify;
- **reward**: the potential benefits of a decision to diversify;
- **control**: the degree to which the organization is prepared to share control over the diversification approach.

In this section, we explore strategies that affect the interrelationships between business units, either within the corporate portfolio or among business units across different organizations. The strategies we describe here look at opportunities for an organization to seek potential competitive advantage from shared activities with other organizations. We include vertical and horizontal integration, mergers and acquisitions (M&A), joint ventures, and strategic alliances. These strategic options differ on the basis of the levels of risk and control that they involve; they also reflect requirements in terms of the organization's resources, such as resource gaps or deficiencies, or an ability to overcome barriers to entry. These ideas are summarized in Table 10.2.

We now discuss each of the approaches mentioned in Table 10.2 in more depth.

Vertical and horizontal integration

Consider the situation where a manufacturer decides to set up a chain of retail outlets to sell its products. This could be regarded as related diversification into retailing. We might also refer to it as 'forward vertical integration' as the firm has acquired control of a business activity that lies nearer to the end-user market than its core activity as a manufacturer. In contrast, a firm may choose to 'integrate backwards' towards the raw material or other supply inputs that go into making its own products. This issue, sometimes called the 'make-or-buy' decision, leads managers to consider, for example, the costs of a transaction. Is it cheaper for an organization to perform an activity, such as distributing its products, itself or to pay another organization to do it? These questions will also lead managers to consider the boundaries of the firm.

In contrast with vertical integration, a firm which acquires a provider of complementary products or services is said to be engaging in 'horizontal integration'. For example, in 2012, Facebook acquired Instagram. The two companies operate in the same sector (social media), but Instagram was seen as a social networking app with particular strengths in the area of sharing photos and videos from a smartphone, so its resources and capabilities could be seen as complementary to those of its acquirer. Facebook's aims in acquiring Instagram included growing its market share and reducing competition.

Figure 10.3 provides an illustration of vertical and horizontal integration in the car industry. If one manufacturer buys another, this is an example of horizontal integration. If a car manufacturer buys one of its suppliers, this is (backward) vertical integration. If a car manufacturer buys a chain of outlets that sell vehicles directly to customers, this is (forward) vertical integration. These strategic options can provide the organization with a range of benefits, including increased market share, greater control over its own operations, and increased opportunities for economies of scale and scope. On the downside, vertical or horizontal integration may make the organization less flexible. It may also lose out on the benefits of outsourcing to third parties (such as higher quality or lower costs) as it has effectively brought some activities 'in house'.

Both vertical and horizontal integration can be achieved by another type of diversification strategy, that is, mergers and acquisitions—and we turn to this strategy now.

Mergers and acquisitions

Before looking at mergers and acquisitions (M&A) as strategic options, we should first clarify the differences between the two. A merger involves a decision taken by two organizations to integrate their operations on a relatively equal basis. An acquisition, on the other hand, involves

TABLE 10.2 **Different approaches to diversification**

Approach to diversification	Features	Possible rewards	Possible risks
Vertical or horizontal integration	*Vertical integration*: an organization extends its operations closer to its customers (forward vertical integration) or its suppliers (backward vertical integration) Example: Netflix has moved from distributing content to owning and producing its own content *Horizontal integration*: an organization takes over one of its main competitors Example: Disney's acquisition of Pixar in 2006	• Increased control over its own operations • Greater potential for economies of scale and scope • Greater effectiveness of value-chain operations • Improved value appropriation • Increased market share in a growing industry or increased ability to 'harvest' in a declining industry	• Reduction in organizational flexibility • The potential benefits of outsourcing to third parties, such as access to higher quality or cost reduction, may not be realized
Mergers and acquisitions (M&A)	A **merger** is a decision between two companies to integrate their operations on a relatively equal basis Example: AOL and Time Warner in 2000 An **acquisition** involves one organization taking over another Example: Walmart bought the e-commerce company Flipkart in 2018 as an entry into the Indian market	• Increased market power • Overcoming entry barriers • Reduced cost of new product development • Increasing speed to market • Increased diversification • Avoidance of excessive competition • Organizational learning and development of new capabilities	• Integration difficulties • Inadequate evaluation of the target firm • Large or extraordinary debt • Inability to achieve synergy • Too much diversification • Managers becoming too focused upon the M&A deal itself • Organization becoming too large (e.g. Hitt et al. 2007)

10

Cooperative strategies: joint ventures (JVs)	A JV is a new corporate entity created by two separate organizations; it may be created to serve a specific purpose, enter a new market, or exploit new or complementary capabilities Examples: Vistara, an Indian full service airline, is a JV between Tata Sons and Singapore Airlines, utilizing the capabilities of both firms.	• Combination of expertise, to the benefit of both 'parent' organizations • If a home government is unwilling to allow foreign organizations unlimited access to its markets, a JV may be the only way for a foreign firm to access particular industries • The JV shares the risks associated with a new venture between the partners	• The JV shares the control between the partners as well as the ability to appropriate value; this lack of control may be a cause for concern (e.g. control of proprietary information)
Cooperative strategies: strategic alliances (SAs)	A strategic alliance is a decision by two or more organizations to cooperate in the development, manufacture, or sale of products or services; there are a range of types of alliance Examples: In 2014, Google and Samsung signed a broad agreement to cross-license a range of each other's patents Disney use Hewlett Packard's technology platforms in ride creation, animation, etc.	• A strategic alliance is less formal than a JV, so there is typically less risk associated with a strategic alliance • Access to new technology and/or intellectual property rights • Improved agility • Reduced costs (administration or R&D)	• Sharing of resources and profits, possibly also skills and know-how • Focusing and committing to an SA may lead the firm to overlook other opportunities • In an uneven alliance, the weaker partner may be forced to act according to the will of the stronger partner • Difficulties and costs associated with coordination and resolving disputes

Source: authors.

10

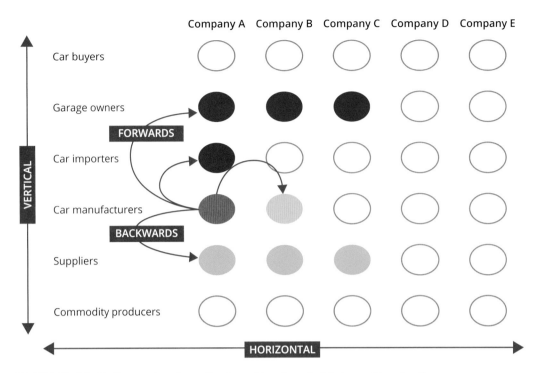

FIGURE 10.3 Example of vertical and horizontal integration in the car industry. *Source:* authors.

one organization buying a controlling interest in another organization. The acquisition often becomes a subsidiary of the acquiring organization, operating within its portfolio of other business units. If the acquisition was not agreed with the managers and owners of the acquired organization, this is known as a (hostile) takeover. For example, during 2018, GKN (a maker of car and plane parts) was the target of a hostile takeover bid from a buy-out firm called Melrose (*The Economist* 2018). Melrose found itself facing a campaign led by customers, politicians, and industry groups, but the deal was completed, and Melrose is now predicted to break up GKN in order to sell off some business units (*The Guardian* 2021).

The popularity of M&A as a corporate strategy is cyclical in nature. M&A activity tends to come in waves. In fact, seven waves of M&A activity have been identified since the late nineteenth century. The most recent wave (since 2007) led to a peak year in 2017, with more than 50,000 M&A transactions worldwide (Boyden 2019). Following a slight decline, the value of global M&A deals in 2020 still amounted to $2.8 trillion, down from $3.4 trillion in the previous year (Statista 2021).

An M&A deal can provide growth opportunities, increasing an organization's market power through horizontal integration. It may achieve entry into a new market because either an organization possesses excess resources it cannot profitably use in its own market or its existing market is declining and revenue growth is slowing. It may spread an organization's exposure to risk across a variety of industries. It may secure resources not currently possessed by the acquiring firm. M&A, in theory at least, should achieve two key objectives: improve competitiveness and deliver superior shareholder value.

However, considerable evidence exists that pursuing an M&A strategy is both risky and uncertain to satisfy the desired objectives. The business world is full of examples of large-scale mergers that have failed to deliver the intended outcomes. Perhaps the biggest disaster of all was the purchase of AOL by Time Warner in 2000 for $165 billion. Time Warner was attracted by AOL's online presence and subscriber base. Shortly after the deal, the 'dot com bubble' burst (the price of leading technology shares reached their peak and then fell very sharply (Madslien 2010)), and the economy went into recession. Over the next few years, the losses resulting from the deal were huge, and the two companies went their separate ways in 2009. In the next section, we review why many firms engaging in M&A experience such poor performance when such deals seem to offer the strategist a constructive route to achieving organizational goals.

Problems with making M&A work

Not all organizations engaging in M&A have an entirely successful experience; for instance, while the shareholders of acquired firms tend to earn above average returns, shareholders of acquiring firms are less likely to do so and often receive zero returns (Fuller et al. 2002; Shah and Arora 2014). Indeed, the value of shares in an acquiring firm often fall when the intention to acquire is announced (Roll 1986), a sign that stock markets view the potential of the M&A to achieve any genuine added value to be low. We might ask why this should be the case. Why is it often so hard for the acquiring organization in particular to realize all the potential benefits of an M&A deal?

There is a wide variety of potential difficulties that an acquiring organization may face; and we can discuss these further in relation to Case Example 10.2 'Univision and Televisa Merger Creates a Spanish-Language TV Giant'. The first of these is difficulty in integrating the two organizations. Integration is a complex and time-consuming task, made even more complex if the merging organizations are long-established entities with entrenched organizational cultures, practices, and processes. However, achieving an effective post-merger integration is crucial. A high level of organizational resource needs to be allocated to the M&A activity. Acquisition targets need to be carefully chosen, and considerable effort needs to be focused upon integrating technical, financial, and human resources into the acquiring organization. Some organizations appear to build, over time, a valuable capability in post-merger integration management. For example, Danaher Corporation is a global conglomerate that has grown via hundreds of acquisitions since its formation in 1984—an example of a successful 'serial acquirer'. However, in other successful organizations, an M&A can act as a distraction, undermining the recipe that has brought them success in the first place. Similarly, managers who are primarily focused on assimilating new acquisitions into the organization may lose sight of the core business, leading to an overall deterioration in performance. There is also a risk that acquisitions may simply produce an organization that is too large for its control systems or for a consistent culture to emerge.

Poor choice of takeover target is a common problem, reflecting a failure in due diligence. For example, Sprint acquired a majority stake in Nextel Communications in 2005, creating the world's third largest telecommunications provider. However, the two networks had very different technologies, very different customers, and very different brand positioning. Compromises were made, staff left citing cultural differences and incompatibility, and the merger generally came to be viewed as a disappointing failure (*Forbes* 2012).

Other acquisitions have been undermined by taking on too much debt to pay for the deal; for example, the acquisition by Cnooc, the Chinese state-owned oil company, of Nexen, a Canadian oil producer, for US$15 billion, which hit trouble when global oil prices slumped. This is especially serious if the revenue-generating effect of the acquisition has been overestimated and sufficient income does not exist to service the debt.

A failure to deliver any expected synergies could also undermine the M&A and ultimately lead to **divestment**, that is, the sale or disposal of one or more of an organization's activities. For example, in the financial services sector, two merging banks often plan to achieve cost savings by consolidating their branch networks. However, in practice, estimated cost savings may be difficult to achieve in full, and calculations should also be made about the likely loss of revenue, such as if customers choose to leave the target bank.

So, what are the other growth strategies that two organizations that want to collaborate without making the major and potentially risky step of a merger or acquisition can explore? Next, we consider some cooperative strategies, where two or more organizations choose to work together while remaining separate entities.

CASE EXAMPLE 10.2 UNIVISION AND TELEVISA MERGER CREATES A SPANISH-LANGUAGE TV GIANT

In April 2021, a merger was announced between Grupo Televisa, a Mexican mass media company, and US broadcaster Univision to create a new Spanish-language media company with plans to launch a global streaming platform.

The new company, Televisa-Univision, plans to feature content and media assets from both broadcasters, including series, movies, sports and soap operas. Televisa pointed out that it will be the 'largest Spanish-language media company in the world'.

Televisa plans to contribute its content assets, as well as its four free-to-air channels, 27 pay-TV networks channels and stations, its Videocine movie studio, and Blim TV subscription video on demand (SVOD) service. Those assets will merge with Univision's, which include Univision and UniMás broadcast networks, 9 Spanish-language cable networks, 61 television stations, and 58 radio stations in major US Hispanic markets and Puerto Rico, and digital properties, including PrendeTV, its advertising video on demand (AVOD) streaming service.

'This strategic combination generates significant value for shareholders of both companies and will allow us to more efficiently reach all Spanish language audiences with more of our programming', said Televisa's executive chairman. Meanwhile, Univision's CEO commented that 'Televisa-Univision will emerge as the leading global Spanish-language multi-media company, uniquely positioned

Source: Schneider/Shutterstock.com.

to capture the significant market opportunity for Spanish speakers worldwide.' The new company should hold one of the largest libraries of content in the world, a considerable portfolio of intellectual property and global sports rights, and a rich Spanish-language production infrastructure.

Televisa-Univision plans to launch a global streaming platform for the 'significantly underserved Spanish-language market' in early 2022, competing with other major companies such as Netflix. A Televisa spokeswoman commented that 'the objective of this transaction is to create a player that competes globally in the streaming market'.

Questions for discussion

1. Before deciding to pursue a merger, what alternative options (other than an M&A deal)

would you recommend that Univision or Televisa should consider?

2. What benefits are the two parties seeking to achieve via a merger deal? For example, what synergies might be possible?

3. What do you see as the key challenges that the two companies may face if the deal proceeds? What risks and challenges should they plan for?

Sources

Forbes (2021). Televisa and Univsion to merge in $4.3 billion transaction (13 April), https://www.forbes.com/sites/veronicavillafane/2021/04/13/televisa-and-univision-to-merge-in-48-billion-transaction/?sh=17df6ea074d6 (last accessed 18 August 2022).

Reuters (2021). Mexico's Televisa says to merge content with Univision in new media company (14 April), https://www.reuters.com/business/media-telecom/mexicos-televisa-says-merge-content-with-univision-new-media-company-2021-04-13 (last accessed 18 August 2022).

Variety (2021). Univision and Televisa set merger deal to create Spanish-language content powerhouse (13 April), https://variety.com/2021/tv/news/univision-televisa-merger-spanish-deal-1234950743 (last accessed 18 August 2022).

Cooperative strategies

Both strategic alliances and joint ventures involve the formation of some sort of partnership with another organization, and this involves losing some degree of control over the organization's operations on the part of senior managers. First, we examine joint ventures.

Joint ventures

A joint venture (JV) can be seen as the child of two organizational parents. The JV may be created to deliver a specific project, to pursue a particular market opportunity, or to capitalize on complimentary resources which would otherwise not be utilized effectively. For example, in 2012, Jaguar Land Rover (JLR), a British automotive company and subsidiary of the Indian firm Tata Motors, and Chery, a Chinese automobile manufacturer, began to put in place a joint venture to build a new plant in China which would bring together strengths in manufacturing, production, and logistics with local R&D and an iconic British brand. In 2018, it was announced that the JV will invest 7 billion yuan (over 900 million euros) in the development and production of electric cars—as well as producing more than 200,000 conventional cars per year at its local facility—suggesting that the two partners are continuing to see the benefits of their collaborative activities (Manthey 2018).

At the time of its JV with Chery, JLR saw China as a fast-growing market where it was aiming to achieve better access. In some instances, JVs may be the only way for an organization to access a new market. Governments of some countries can insist upon local JV partners before allowing market entry to foreign companies to minimize the threat of foreign domination and to enhance the development of skills, employment opportunities, and revenue generation within the host economy of the JV. One such example is the Chinese government's approach to protecting key industries such as its financial services sector. Late in 2018, American Express (AmEx) became the only foreign payment provider allowed to work in China through a 50–50 partnership with a domestic company LianLian Group. Visa and Mastercard, the world's two leading credit card brands, were kept waiting for the go-ahead to process yuan payments (Pham 2018). Finally, in February 2020, Mastercard won approval to begin formal preparation to set up a bank card clearing institution in China, thanks to a joint venture with NetsUnion

10

Clearing Corp, a clearing house for online payments whose stakeholders include the Chinese central bank (Perez 2020).

In JVs, both risk and control are shared. They are consequently viewed with some caution by many managers, who value the opportunities that they can provide and appreciate the ability to share risk but dislike having to giving up a degree of control over the new venture. Public–private partnerships (PPPs) have been used widely to deliver public-sector services in the United Kingdom and elsewhere. Such partnerships can involve complex JVs between public- and private-sector organizations. Researchers have argued that one such project, Building Schools for the Future, entailed 'limited and aggregated financial reporting and patchy oversight and scrutiny, leading to a loss of control over public expenditure' (Shaoul et al. 2013), as well as a loss of accountability. This illustrates the need to design and implement appropriate structures for managing risks and rewards in JV projects.

Strategic alliances

One key difference between joint ventures and strategic alliances (SAs) is that while JVs involve joint ownership, SAs do not. Strategic alliances are voluntary, cooperative, inter-firm agreements aimed at achieving competitive advantage for the partners (Das and Teng 2000a). In practice, this typically means that two or more independent organizations have decided to cooperate in the development, manufacturing, or sale of products and services: 'The proliferation of strategic alliances in recent years marks a shift in the conception of the intrinsic nature of competition, which is increasingly characterized by constant technological innovations and speedy entry into new markets' (Das and Teng 2000a: 34).

An SA is less formal than a JV, so there is typically less risk associated with an SA; it is easier for an organization to end the partnership if it wishes to do so. The alliance may provide an organization with access to new technology or intellectual property rights (see the Google–Samsung and Disney–Hewlett Packard examples in Table 10.2). It may make the organization more agile in its capacity to move into new product lines or markets and it may reduce costs in certain areas (e.g. in R&D) if that activity is now being shared. However, alliances inevitably involve additional costs such as the cost of searching for and selecting a suitable partner.

An SA can also bring some inherent disadvantages. For instance, the need to focus on and commit to a strategic alliance may lead an organization to overlook other opportunities. Organizations may feel that they can no longer act solely in their own interests as they must consider the interests of the alliance, and a 'stronger' partner may be able to force a 'weaker' partner to do its bidding. The frustrations of working in partnership can be considerable. They may include the need for trade-offs and compromise and the need to take account of partners' different cultures, practices, and processes. For instance, a four-year dispute between VW and Suzuki was settled in court in 2015. The two automotive firms established an SA in 2009, working together on fuel-efficient cars, but 'cultural differences' were cited as one of the reasons for the termination of the alliance, after Suzuki accused VW of withholding information it had promised to share, and VW objected to a Suzuki deal to buy diesel engines from Fiat (BBC 2015). There may be difficulties and costs associated with coordination or dispute resolution between two organizations in an SA. Of course, profits and other resources must be shared, perhaps even skills and know-how, and organizations may feel that they are at risk of having to disclose proprietary knowledge relating to their own activities, which may weaken their own ability to capture value in the future.

Management issues affecting strategic alliances

Particular demands are placed upon the managers in an SA. The success of an alliance may lie more in its management than in the circumstances of its initial creation (Elmuti and Kathawala 2001). Managers from partner companies often come from different national and corporate cultures and have difficulty in understanding or approving of their new allies' practices and ways of operation. They may have been trained to operate in hierarchically organized firms and are somewhat disadvantaged when faced with the need to cooperate and act through consensus. SAs are often referred to as 'cooperative strategies' rather than competitive ones; this often implies a need to focus upon operational issues rather than strategic ones. According to Das and Teng (2000b), alliances become unstable due to three kinds of internal tension: cooperation versus competition, rigidity versus flexibility, and short-term versus long-term orientation.

It has been estimated that large firms (e.g. the Fortune 500 list in the United States) have an average of 50–70 strategic alliances each (*The Economist* 2009). This suggests that there is scope for organizations to learn from their own experiences of strategic alliances over time and to improve their capabilities at managing such relationships. Kale et al. (2002: 747) argue that 'firms with greater alliance experience and, more importantly, those that create a dedicated alliance function (with the intent of strategically coordinating alliance activity and capturing/ disseminating alliance–related knowledge) realize greater success with alliances'.

Making international alliances work

There are difficulties involved not just in setting up international strategic alliances but also in maintaining positive cooperative attitudes as the alliance progresses. The actions that must be taken to ensure that the gap between organizations in an alliance is bridged are known as 'boundary-spanning'. Enhanced capabilities in boundary-spanning can mean that an alliance is more likely to work both formally and informally and more likely to achieve its objectives (Albers et al. 2013).

An example of a boundary-spanning action is a 'gateway' system (Badaracco 1991; Killing 1992). This is a system in which, at least in the early months of the alliance, all communications must pass through the office of only one 'gatekeeper' in each partner company in order to avoid the risk of misunderstandings. The gatekeeper is normally the sole interface between the companies and is kept informed of all contacts and therefore, by implication, any areas of potential dispute. By careful selection of appropriate boundary-spanners, and by gradually increasing areas of involvement as the partners get to know each other, the effects of organizational incompatibilities may be reduced. This is a strategic role, and the human resource function is likely to play an important part in it. For instance, Søderberg and Romani (2017) discuss the complexity of global IT development projects where Western firms outsource to Indian service companies. In such situations, key boundary-spanners play an important role in developing trustful and sustainable client relationships and coordinating highly complex projects.

10

A common example of an alliance objective is to encourage the absorption of know-how, embedded knowledge, tacit routines, and organizational practices from the partner (e.g. the alliance between Hewlett Packard and Disney mentioned in Table 10.2). Many alliances are set up for short-term gains in order to deal with temporary situations such as resource deficiencies or lack of market knowledge. Specific short-term objectives may be perfectly satisfactory. Alliances are, of course, not confined to the private sector. CRUK, a cancer research and awareness charity based in the United Kingdom, works with a wide range of strategic partners, including pharmaceutical companies, technology companies, and bodies from the public and charity/not-for-profit sectors, both in the United Kingdom and internationally. The aims of such partnerships include co-funding of research, sharing expertise, and investing in people and training (Cancer Research UK 2014). Many of these aims, such as pooling of certain training and expertise, or conducting a specific research project, can potentially be met over a relatively short timescale, such as between one and three years, with a plan to dissolve the alliance at that point.

Whilst a strategic alliance can bring many benefits to organizations, ending a strategic alliance can be a painful and lengthy process. As noted earlier, VW and Suzuki established a strategic alliance in 2009, but, in 2015, a court ruling was required to settle a four-year dispute between the two firms (BBC 2015). In order to avoid this sort of dispute, many successful alliances form an agreement at formation, in anticipation of their eventual dissolution—a sort of 'divorce' procedure. This can help to reduce anxiety about the costs of potential failure.

Ultimately, it is helpful for a strategist to understand the degree to which the management of an alliance involves constant negotiation to find overlaps between goals rather than to clarify totally congruent goals. As Walter et al. (2012: 1582) note, 'alliance-related decision processes have to balance each partner's self-interest on one hand and collective actions on the other hand, with both partners being dependent on each other's collaboration'. A substantial contribution to success must depend upon the management of internal tensions (Das and Teng 2000b). Both partners must remember that they are partners and not seek to achieve advantages which benefit one at the expense of the other.

A less contentious form of strategic alliance involves **licensing** agreements. Under a licensing agreement, the rights to use a brand, product, process, or other trademarked or patented resource is passed to an alliance partner for the payment of a fee or a share in revenues. Licensing agreements are frequently used to allow major brands to migrate across borders as a rapid and cheap way to establish themselves as global brands. For instance, the Coca-Cola Corporation licenses regional bottling companies to manufacture and distribute soft drinks under the Coca-Cola and other brand names. Strategic alliances can permit organizations to establish manufacturing plants in new territories and to outsource some activities for a variety of reasons; operating in partnership can allow an organization to tap into local knowledge in a new market, managing its risks and lowering its expenditure on fixed costs such as manufacturing plant without losing focus on its core business.

To sum up, a strategist who is considering pursuing a cooperative strategy should be aware of the range of options available, including JVs and SAs. Their relative advantages and disadvantages are associated with a spectrum of flexibility and formality.

CASE EXAMPLE 10.3 **SOUTH KOREA'S CHAEBOL**

South Korea is one of Asia's most affluent countries; its economy is the fourth largest in Asia (after China, Japan, and India) and the twelfth largest in the world. Its economy is dominated by family-run conglomerates known as '**chaebol**'; there are several dozen chaebol, including organizations such as Samsung, LG, Hyundai, SK, and Lotte. The top ten chaebol own more than 27% of all business assets in South Korea. In recent years, the chaebol have been scrutinized following a corruption scandal so significant it led to the impeachment and arrest of the then president, Park Geun-hye.

In January 2017, Jay Y. Lee, the vice-chairman of Samsung, was accused of bribery, embezzlement, and perjury by special prosecutors. He was arrested for handing bribes to Park Geun-hye and her associate Choi-Soon-sil, reportedly worth almost £30 million. Mr Lee handed over the bribe to try to win government support for a smooth leadership transition in his bid to achieve greater control of the company. He was sentenced to five years imprisonment, but the high court reduced that sentence and he served less than a year.

The public was angry about his release; this was not the first time a business leader had been convicted for corruption only to be let off. According to Bloomberg, public discontent with chaebol has long been brewing; in December 2017, the 95-year-old founder of the Lotte retail group was sentenced to 4 years in jail for embezzlement and breach of fiduciary duty. In February 2018, Lotte's chairman was convicted in a separate corruption trial. At a hearing in 2016, nine chaebol leaders faced a barrage of questions from lawmakers, and anger from hundreds of thousands of protesters. Sixteen months later, former president Park was sentenced to 24 years in prison after being found guilty of crimes ranging from bribery to coercion, abuse of power, and the leaking of state secrets. In November 2018, more than 150,000 workers walked out of work in protest at the lack of progress in reforming the chaebol. The cross-shareholdings and intragroup deals within chaebol has led to a perception of cronyism by investors across the world—and critical voices continue to call for reform for the benefit of the future of South Korea.

Questions for discussion

1. List some of the possible ways that being a member of a chaebol might help a firm to survive and thrive in a competitive economy. Can you think of any disadvantages of being a member of a chaebol?

2. What other strategic options might be open to such firms other than being a member of a chaebol? What might be some of the advantages and disadvantages of those alternative options?

3. Consider our discussion of related and unrelated diversification and asset sharing (refer to the axes of the 2 × 2 matrix on value-creating strategies of diversification shown in Figure 10.2). How do these ideas help us to understand the mix of firms that are members of a particular chaebol?

Sources

Bloomberg.com(2019). South Korea's chaebol (29 May 2014, updated 29 August 2019), https://www.bloomberg.com/quicktake/republic-samsung (last accessed 18 August 2022).

EastAsiaForum (2021). Chaebol reforms are crucial for South Korea's future (24 March), https://www.eastasiaforum.org/2021/03/24/chaebol-reforms-are-crucial-for-south-koreas-future (last accessed 18 August 2022).

The Economist (2017). Lee Jae-yong dodges arrest over charges of bribery (21 January), https://www.economist.com/business/2017/01/21/lee-jae-yong-dodges-arrest-on-charges-of-bribery (last accessed 18 August 2022).

The Financial Times. South Korea hit by strikes over lack of chaebol reform (21 November), https://www.ft.com/content/b55b2d6a-ed43-11e8-89c8-d36339d835c0 (last accessed 21 October 2022).

Investopedia (2022). The top 25 economies of the world (1 September), https://www.investopedia.com/insights/worlds-top-economies (last accessed 18 August 2022).

The Telegraph (2017). Samsung heir Lee Jae-yong arrested amid bribery allegations (17 February), https://www.telegraph.co.uk/business/2017/02/16/south-korean-court-issues-warrant-arrest-samsung-heir (last accessed 18 August 2022).

The Wall Street Journal (2016). A presidential scandal transfixes South Korea (27 November), https://www.wsj.com/articles/a-presidential-scandal-transfixes-south-korea-1480112351?mod=article_inline (last accessed 18 August 2022).

10.8 **Testing and evaluating strategic options**

Recall that we are currently in Part Four of the process–practice framework (Figure 2.4), learning how to shape strategy to context and objectives. So, having discussed a range of possible strategies that present opportunities for growth of the organization, how can strategists evaluate the set of strategic options that are open to them? In what ways might they assess how successful the strategies might be in serving the purposes of the organization? In this section, we consider a range of tests that strategists might use to evaluate strategic options.

Tests of consistency, consonance, advantage, and feasibility

Rumelt (1995) suggests four tests of consistency, consonance, advantage, and feasibility that provide a set of screening tools for possible strategic options. Respectively, these mean the extent to which options are *consistent* with what an organization hopes to achieve; *consonance* is the compatibility of an option with the long-term future of the organization in the environment in which it is embedded; *advantage* relates to how much of the value an option creates can be captured by the organization, and *feasibility* refers to the extent to which an option is achievable within current operating realities. Rumelt acknowledges that it may be impossible to demonstrate conclusively that a particular strategy can or will work, let alone that it is an 'optimal' strategy. However, he points out that all strategies could be tested for these four types of problem.

Consistency

First, the proposed strategy must not present goals and policies that lack consistency. You may feel that failing this test is unlikely, but it may be a particularly necessary test for strategies that have emerged over time, rather than being explicitly formulated. Even deliberate strategies may contain compromises between different power groups within the organization, for example.

Inconsistency in strategy is not simply a flaw in logic. A key function of strategy is to provide a coherent framework for organizational activity and a clear sense of vision, direction, and purpose for the organization. Sears Holdings, the parent of US retailer Kmart, finally filed for bankruptcy in October 2018. For some years, Kmart had been widely criticized for a lack of focus in comparison with key competitors such as Walmart ('always lowest prices') and Target ('cheapchic clothing styles'). It can be argued that Kmart's strategy was unsuccessful because it lacked the clear sense of vision and purpose that Rumelt refers to, at least in comparison with the coherent and consistent approach to the market adopted by its competitors.

Rumelt goes on to argue that an organization relates to its environment in two main aspects, which we will consider next. First, its products or services must create more value than they cost (leading us to consider a criterion around consonance). Second, it must compete with other organizations that are also trying to adapt and prosper (hence, a concern for advantage, discussed after consonance).

Consonance

This test is focused on the creation of social value. For Rumelt, the test seeks to evaluate the economic relationships that are the key characteristics of the business. The aim of the test is to explore whether sufficient value is being created to sustain the demand for the firm's strategy over the longer term. An evaluation of consonance is a difficult task, not least because many of the critical threats from the external environment will also threaten the firm's entire industry. The firm's senior team may be so intent on doing battle with existing rival firms that a serious threat to the whole industry is only recognized at a relatively late stage. According to Rumelt, many forecasting techniques do not help managers to identify potentially critical changes that arise from interactions between combinations of trends. In order to apply this test effectively, we have to ask ourselves why the organization exists and question the basic economic foundations that support and define it. We can then explore the consequences of significant changes in the firm's external environment. As a classic example, consider Blockbuster, the former movie rental chain. In 2004, its revenue was around $6 billion, but just six years later it was bankrupt, having failed to respond to a changing business landscape and adapt its operating model.

Advantage

Rumelt's third test is about competitive advantage or whether the organization can capture enough of the value it creates. Competitive strategy can be viewed as the art of creating and exploiting those advantages that are most enduring and most difficult to duplicate. The strategy must provide for the creation and/or maintenance of a competitive advantage from one or more of three sources: superior skills, superior resources, or superior position.

Feasibility

Feasibility refers to how well the strategy might work in practice and how difficult it might be to achieve. Once again, we might ask whether the strategy can be resourced, whether the organization can actually achieve the required level of performance, such as quality, and how competitors might react.

Is it real? Can we win it? Is it worth doing?

As an alternative to Rumelt's evaluative concepts (1995), we can adopt a framework proposed by Day (2007) as a screening test for strategic options for growth. Day advocates evaluating growth options based on three criteria—'Is it real?', 'Can we win it?' and 'Is it worth doing?' A matrix can be used to summarize the results of the strategist's assessment of each strategic option that's open to the organization against each of the three questions (see Figure 10.4, based on a scale of 1 to 5). For example, an organization might be considering three options for strategic growth into a new international market:

	Option A	Option B	Option C
Is it real?	1	3	5
Can we win it?	2	3	4
Is it worth doing?	4	4	3
Total	7	10	12

FIGURE 10.4 Example of a summary matrix for the application of Day's (2007) framework. *Source*: authors.

Option A: acquisition of an established player in the new market;

Option B: joint venture with another organization also wanting to expand into the new market;

Option C: strategic alliance with another organization also wanting to expand into the new market.

We will now examine each of the tests and the steps involved.

Is it real?

This first criterion addresses the extent to which an option might be considered 'real', given how stakeholders feel about the expected outcomes of the option—typically in terms of risk, profitability, reward, ethics, and the effect on relationships. Meeting reasonable stakeholder expectations would appear to be a crucial test for whether any option will be accepted by enough stakeholders as 'real' enough to pursue. The steps involved in establishing if an option is 'real' or not are:

1. What will be the financial or cost–benefit performance? Is there an unacceptable risk of endangering overall liquidity or affecting capital structure?

2. Is there a risk that the organization's relationships with its stakeholders could be unacceptably affected? The proposed option may be unpopular with employees, institutional shareholders, existing customers/clients, or governmental organizations.

3. What is the effect of the proposed option on the internal systems and procedures? Even if winnable, will there be an unacceptable level of additional pressure upon staff?

Having considered each of these questions, the strategist can arrive at an assessment of the extent to which an option will be considered a 'real' opportunity and record the results in the first row of the evaluation matrix (see Figure 10.4), perhaps using a scale of 1 to 5, where 5 indicates that the option is highly acceptable to stakeholders and 1 indicates that it is not acceptable at all. For instance, in the example cited earlier, the firm may feel that an SA would be the most acceptable to key stakeholders and an acquisition the least acceptable.

Next, we consider the second test, which concerns whether an option is winnable for an organization.

Can we win it?

A second test of 'Can we win it?' applied by the strategist evaluates the potential for success in pursuing an option. This test of a proposed option considers how well the strategy will work in practice and how difficult it might be to achieve. The steps for this test are:

1. Can the option be resourced? Even the most brilliant strategy cannot be implemented if, for example, the organization's financial position is too weak to raise the necessary capital.

2. Can the organization actually achieve the required level of operational performance, say, in quality and service levels? For example, an option aimed at cutting costs in a manufacturing environment may run into problems associated with inadequate managerial resources, insufficient numbers of trained staff, insufficient plant, or inadequate process and product technologies.

3. How will the competition react, and how will the organization cope with that reaction? For example, an option to increase market share by reducing prices may lead to a fierce response from competitors.

Having considered each of these questions, the strategist can arrive at an assessment of the likelihood of success for each strategic option that the organization is considering—and record the results in the second row of the evaluation matrix (see Figure 10.4), perhaps using a scale of 1 to 5, where 5 indicates that the option is highly feasible and 1 indicates that it is not feasible at all. In the example cited earlier, the organization may feel that an acquisition would be the most difficult to achieve and an SA would be the least difficult.

Is it worth doing?

Whether a proposed option 'is worth doing' can be assessed by the extent to which it matches the needs identified from a strategic analysis. Such a test of worth, or value, can be regarded as a test of consistency with the environmental and resources analyses and the options potential to contribute to attainment of organizational objectives. In order to assess the value of a possible strategic option, the strategist can consider the following set of four questions:

1. Is the proposed option consistent with and does it fulfil the market key success factors (KSFs) (see the discussion of competitive advantage in Chapter 5). The KSFs apply to the industry within which the organization operates and represent the minimum entry requirements of that market.

2. Does the proposed option address the strategic problem or opportunity identified in the strategic analysis? Does it overcome an identified resource weakness or environmental threat?

3. Does the proposed option capitalize on the organization's identified resources and capabilities and the ways in which they relate to the external opportunities?

4. Does the option fit the organization's objectives, such as required rates of return on capital, profitability measures, and other non-financial performance indicators? These may involve considerations of the organization's role in a wider context, including an acknowledgment of social responsibility.

Having considered each of these questions, the strategist can arrive at an assessment of the extent to which each strategic option is worth pursuing—and record the results in the third row of the evaluation matrix (see Figure 10.4), perhaps using a scale of 1 to 5, where 5 indicates that the option is highly suitable and 1 indicates that it is not suitable at all. For instance, in the example cited earlier, the firm may feel that an acquisition or a JV would be more valuable than an SA as these options may give more controlled access to new resources and capabilities.

A total score can then be calculated for each option, giving the strategist an indication of which strategies perform well on the three tests and which do not. Of course, in practice, it may not be as simple as then choosing the option with the highest score. For instance, a particular strategic option may score well as a real and winnable opportunity, but managers may judge that it should not be pursued because it doesn't deliver sufficient returns to make it worthwhile. Or this exercise may lead managers to debate how they can take that real, winnable option and adapt it so that it becomes more valuable.

10

These three tests of 'Is it real?', 'Can we win it?', and 'Is it worth it?' provide a set of screening tools for possible strategic options. They prompt managers to be explicit about the rationale that underpins potential options and to assess the associated risks and uncertainties. The criteria can also guide the softer process of assessing how acceptable the proposed strategies might be to stakeholders. However, it is usually helpful to test proposed strategies from a number of perspectives, such as those highlighted by Rumelt (1995).

Not-for-profit and public organizations: Testing for efficiency, effectiveness, economy, and equity

Public and private not-for-profit organizations may question whether all these tests apply to them. For example, a test of 'advantage' may not seem appropriate to managers who feel that they are not in a competitive situation. It has been suggested that such organizations may choose to test proposed strategies against objectives that are founded on the **'four Es'**: efficiency, effectiveness, economy, and equity (Norman-Major 2011). We should note that there can be conflicting objectives if, for example, both efficiency and effectiveness are to be served. Take the example of something as simple and uncontroversial as filling potholes in the road: using a cheaper mix to fill the holes may be economical in the short term; however, it may not be effective, efficient, or even economical in the long term if the potholes need constant refilling (Norman-Major 2012).

In this section, we have explored a range of tests that strategists can use to evaluate possible strategic options for growth. As you study strategy, it is important to understand how strategists can use tests to ensure that they select the most suitable option. These tests can be seen as complementing each other, and a skilled strategist will use a variety of tests when considering their strategic options.

10

PRACTITIONER INSIGHT **KIERAN PHELAN, GLOBAL SUSTAINABILITY AND COMPLIANCE DIRECTOR, WILLIAM GRANT & SONS**

Kieran is Global Sustainability and Compliance Director with William Grant & Sons (WG&S). He previously worked for several multinationals in operational improvement, environmental affairs, and international health and safety. He is part of the leadership team that contributes to the strategy process in WG&S.

The company started in 1887 in Speyside, when the founder, William Grant, wished to make 'the best dram in the valley' (a dram is a measure of whisky). From an initial malt whisky distillery has grown the diverse organization of today. Alongside malt whisky and grain whisky, WG&S now produces premium vodka, gins, tequila, rums, and liqueurs. WG&S has distilleries throughout Scotland and bottling facilities in the United Kingdom, Ireland, the United States, and Mexico, as well as a large network of third-party bottling support across the globe. Still family-owned, WG&S has

grown rapidly in recent decades to be one of Scotland's largest family-owned businesses, with revenues of more than £1 billion.

Kieran shares his views on strategy and growth in WG&S.

Growth strategy

Our strategy is to be the market leader in the whisky sector and challenge the premium spirit categories in which we compete. As a growing organization, we're always looking at the brand portfolio to ensure that it fits with our aspirations as a business. We have a continual debate about brands that may need to be refreshed, extended, or retired. We focus on the premium end of the spirits market. Some of the pressures that apply at the other end of the sector don't affect us. We aren't in a race for high-volume, low-price output. We're about exclusivity, quality, and premiumization—a commitment to these product traits drives our growth.

The company has diversified in part through acquisitions to address what we consider gaps in our portfolio. For instance, in 2014, we acquired Drambuie, which is a great fit for the business as a premium liqueur. We also bought Tullamore D.E.W., an Irish whiskey, in 2010.

Trends affecting the organization

There are many parts of the world (e.g. China and India) that are opening up to the increasing tastes of Western premium products through burgeoning middle classes with disposable incomes. These are exciting markets for us and we find ourselves responding to rising demand.

Like many businesses, we also have to respond to cyclical availability of raw materials, such as agave. We use this to produce tequila and it grows on a seven- or eight-year cycle where availability affects price. We try to mitigate those cycles by having a diverse portfolio of products.

Another factor is an increasing focus on the effects of alcohol on health. We manufacture products for special occasions and don't subscribe to the 'pile it high, sell it cheap' philosophy. Low- and no-alcohol drinks, experiencing high uptake from the younger generation, is another trend that's looming on the innovation horizon for our business and the whole industry.

Adapting to diverse customer needs

We sell to more than 180 countries worldwide directly or through distributors, and demand often outstrips supply. We are a branded business that aims to appeal to specific consumer needs in different parts of the world. For example, in China, the number 8 is of high significance, and therefore we will develop 18- or 28-Year-Old spirits to meet those consumer needs.

We are fortunate to have stocks of liquids that have been sourced very carefully and laid down over the years, a position to which larger organizations may not have paid enough attention. This is a real benefit of being a family business and means that we can make the best decisions for the long term, not just to hit quarterly results. That long-term perspective is vital in an industry where the age of the product has been an authenticator of quality.

Alliancing and collaborations

An important alliance for us is the Scotch Whisky Association (SWA), which is the umbrella organization that ensures that industry standards and legal definitions are maintained for Scotch whisky.

The SWA will resist calls from other nations seeking to open up the legal definition to retain geographical exclusivity to Scotland, much in the same way that champagne has a protected heritage and definition. Although, having said that, as globalization continues, an evolution of industry boundaries is inevitable over time and the SWA can help to minimize the possibility of major disruption.

In operations, we deal with many partners and stakeholders. Akin to the SWA, we work with the Tequila Board in Mexico and the Irish Whiskey Association in Ireland. We have a number of partners with whom we co-pack and bottle our products, and several third-party supply chain organizations that service our significant distribution needs around the world. These partners give us global production capacity and flexibility which support our growth needs. In an ever more complex world, the necessity to have strong relationships with all stakeholders is a critical factor for the continued success of our business.

Access the online resources to watch a short video clip where Kieran Phelan talks more about his career.

CHAPTER SUMMARY

In this chapter, we addressed the following learning outcomes:

○ Analyse the role of 'corporate parenting' in supporting strategy for single- and multi-business organizations.

We have looked at the role of the 'corporate parent' for a small organization, where that role might be played by a single person or a large organization, where the corporate parenting role is complex and multifaceted. We have discussed the responsibility of the corporate parent for value creation and examined its role as a bridge between the corporate- and business-level strategies.

○ Comprehend the concepts of economies of scale and scope.

We have introduced the idea that economies of scale are the cost advantages that an organization can achieve when it increases the scale of its operations. We also noted that economies of scope are the cost benefits that can result from using the same resource across a range of outputs.

○ Appreciate the role of relatedness and synergy in the development of corporate strategy.

The idea of relatedness was explored, both at the corporate and operational level. The notion of related and unrelated diversification was also set out in the context of the framework proposed by Hitt et al. (2007) showing value-creating strategies of diversification. We have introduced the concept of synergy, which may help the organization to decide whether to pursue a particular strategic option. We noted that synergy exists when the value created by business units working together exceeds the value that those units create working independently. If a firm is successful in pursuing synergy, it may create greater value.

○ Recognize, develop, and evaluate strategic options based on related and unrelated diversification, vertical and horizontal integration, mergers and acquisitions, joint ventures, and other forms of alliance.

We have explored a range of strategic options that may be open to an organization that is seeking to survive and thrive in a challenging external environment. We introduced the Ansoff matrix as a tool for mapping the various growth options that an organization might choose to pursue—under the headings of market penetration, market or product development, and diversification.

○ Assess the risks and rewards associated with a range of approaches to diversification.

We have looked at a range of strategies for growth under the headings of related and unrelated diversification, including vertical and horizontal integration, mergers and acquisitions, and collaborative initiatives such as joint ventures and strategic alliances. We have explored the risks and rewards that these options may entail for the organization.

○ Apply a range of tests of suitability to potential strategic options.

Finally, we looked at a range of tests of suitability that a management team might apply when deciding which strategies to pursue. These tests address consistency, consonance, advantage, and feasibility (Rumelt 1995), as well as appraisal of the extent to which options are real, winnable, and worth it (Day, 2007).

END-OF-CHAPTER QUESTIONS

Recall questions

1. Give definitions of both 'corporate strategy' and 'competitive strategy', highlighting the main differences between the two. Give examples of both levels of strategy from an organization that you know well.

2. Explain what is meant by the term 'corporate parent'. Outline some of the functions that an effective corporate parent can perform.

3. Give definitions of 'economies of scale' and 'economies of scope', with an example in each case. What is the key difference between the two concepts?

4. Explain what is meant by the term 'synergy'. Give some examples of possible synergies in a range of organizations and outline why synergies are sometimes difficult to achieve.

5. Give definitions of the terms 'related diversification' and 'unrelated diversification', with an example in each case. List some of the strategic options for diversification (related or unrelated) that a firm might pursue.

Application questions

A) Select an organization that you can research online. Imagine you have been assigned to lead a strategy team within that organization. Your task is to apply Ansoff's matrix (Figure 10.1) to identify opportunities for growth. Generate ideas for possible new strategies in each of the four quadrants of the matrix. Make brief notes to share with other students on your course about the likely benefits and risks associated with the possible new strategies in each quadrant.

B) Research five different large organizations online and describe the activities of the corporate parent in each of them. Identify some of the ways in which corporate parenting might be improved in the organizations in question in order to increase the benefits for the business units concerned and the organization as a whole.

C) Choose an organization that you know well (or one you can research online) and identify a strategic option that is or could be under consideration in that organization at present. Use the tests covered in this chapter (consistency, consonance, advantage, and feasibility, etc.) to evaluate whether or not the strategic option is appropriate.

ONLINE RESOURCES

www.oup.com/he/mackay2e

In addition to the video interviews already highlighted, the book's online resources include the following features for this chapter, specifically:

- *links to further reading material* to broaden your knowledge of key issues discussed in this chapter;

- *self-test multiple-choice questions* to test your understanding of the material covered in each section of the chapter; and

- *a flashcard glossary* to help you recall and test your understanding of key terms.

FURTHER READING

'The role of social identity and communities of practice in mergers and acquisitions' by Jennifer Spoor and Mei-Tai Chu

Spoor, J.R. and Chu, M.-T. (2018). The role of social identity and communities of practice in mergers and acquisitions. *Group & Organization Management*, **43**(4), 623–47.

Spoor and Chu recommend the use of communities of practice (CoPs) in post-merger organizations to share knowledge and ease identity concerns.

'The characteristics of partnership success' by Jakki Mohr and Robert Spekman

Mohr, J. and Spekman, R. (1994). The characteristics of partnership success. *Strategic Management Journal*, **15**, 135–52.

This study explores vertical partnerships between manufacturers and dealers and finds that important characteristics of partnership success include partnership attributes of commitment, coordination, and trust, communication quality and participation, and the conflict resolution technique of joint problem solving. It offers insights into how to manage partnerships more effectively to increase the chances of success.

'To diversify or not to diversify' by Constaninos C. Markides

Markides, C. (1997). To diversify or not to diversify. *Harvard Business Review*, **75**, 93–9.

Constantinos Markides, professor at London Business School, argues that before diversifying, managers must think not about what their company does but what it does better than its competitors and whether their strategic assets are transportable to the industry that they want to target.

REFERENCES

Adidas (2021). Company strategy, https://www.adidas-group.com/en/group/strategy-overview (last accessed 18 August 2022).

Albers, S., Wohlgezogen, F., and Zajac, E.J. (2013). Strategic alliance structures: An organization design perspective. *Journal of Management,* **42**(30), 582–614.

Ansoff, H.I. (1965). *Corporate Strategy*. New York: McGraw-Hill.

Ansoff, H.I. (1987). *Corporate Strategy* (rev. edn). London: Penguin.

Audio MediaCenter (2020). Audi and FAW establish new company to produce electric vehicles in China (13 October), https://www.audi-mediacenter.com/en/press-releases/audi-and-faw-establish-new-company-to-produce-electric-vehicles-in-china-13266 (last accessed 10 August 2022).

Automotive News Europe (2020). Audi, FAW sign deal on a new EV joint venture in China (13 October), https://europe.autonews.com/automakers/audi-faw-sign-deal-new-ev-joint-venture-china (last accessed 10 August 2022).

Badaracco, J.L. (1991). Alliances speed knowledge transfer. *Planning Review*, **19**(2), 10–16.

Barrie, J. (2018). Tesco launching Jack's, a new discount chain to compete with Aldi and Lidl (19 September), https://inews.co.uk/news/consumer/jacks-tesco-new-discount-store-when-open-lidl-aldi (last accessed 18 August 2022).

BBC (2012). What are 'rare earths' used for? (13 March), https://www.bbc.co.uk/news/world-17357863 (last accessed 18 August 2022).

BBC (2015). VW and Suzuki settle four-year dispute (30 August), https://www.bbc.co.uk/news/business-34103944 (last accessed 18 August 2022).

Blau, J. (2010). Europe worries over raw materials (25 June), https://www.dw.com/en/europe-worries-over-raw-materials/a-5731662 (last accessed 18 August 2022).

Bloomberg.com (2019). South Korea's chaebol (29 May 2014, updated 29 August 2019), https://www.bloomberg.com/quicktake/republic-samsung (last accessed 18 August 2022).

Bourgeois, L.J. (1980). Strategy and environment: A conceptual integration. *Academy of Management Review*, **5**(1), 25–39.

Boyden (2019). Industry insights: A supersized year for M&A, https://www.boyden.com/media/a-supersized-year-for-ma-3770192/index.html (last accessed 18 August 2022).

Burns, A. (2017). Big Issue-backed Change Please coffee now available nationwide (13 September), https://www.bigissue.com/latest/big-issue-backed-change-please-coffee-now-available-nationwide (last accessed 18 August 2022).

Businesswire (2019). Alibaba unveils five-year goals for China consumer business (24 September), https://www.businesswire.com/news/home/20190924005631/en/Alibaba-Unveils-Five-Year-Goals-for-China-Consumer-Business (last accessed 18 August 2022).

Byrom, J., Medway, D., and Warnaby, G. (2003). Strategic alternatives for small retail businesses in rural areas. *Management Research News*, **26**(7), 33–49.

Cancer Research UK (2014). Strategic partnerships, https://www.cancerresearchuk.org/sites/default/files/cruk_strategic_partnerships_brochure.pdf (last accessed 18 August 2022).

Das, T.K. and Teng, B. (2000a). A resource-based theory of strategic alliances. *Journal of Management*, **26**(1), 31–61.

Das, T.K. and Teng, B. (2000b). Instabilities of strategic alliances: An internal tensions perspective. *Organization Science*, **11**(1), 1–117.

Day, G.S. (2007). Is it real? Can we win? Is it worth doing? *Harvard Business Review*, **85**(12), 110–20.

Depaul (2019). About us, https://uk.depaulcharity.org/about-us (last accessed 18 August 2022).

EastAsiaForum (2021). Chaebol reforms are crucial for South Korea's future (24 March), https://www.eastasiaforum.org/2021/03/24/chaebol-reforms-are-crucial-for-south-koreas-future (last accessed 18 August 2022).

The Economist (2008). Idea: Economies of scale and scope (20 October), https://www.economist.com/news/2008/10/20/economies-of-scale-and-scope (last accessed 18 August 2022).

The Economist (2009). Idea: Strategic alliance (10 November), https://www.economist.com/news/2009/11/10/strategic-alliance (last accessed 18 August 2022).

The Economist (2017). Lee Jae-yong dodges arrest over charges of bribery (21 January), https://www.economist.com/business/2017/01/21/lee-jae-yong-dodges-arrest-on-charges-of-bribery (last accessed 18 August 2022).

The Economist (2018). Dogfight: Melrose's bid for GKN raises questions about Britain's defence industry (25 January), https://www.economist.com/britain/2018/01/25/melroses-bid-for-gkn-raises-questions-about-britains-defence-industry (last accessed 18 August 2022).

The Economist (2021). Forget winning, can Amazon survive in India (25 January), https://techcrunch.com/2021/01/25/india-plays-hardball-with-amazon (last accessed 18 August 2022).

Eisenhardt, K.M. and Galunic, D.C. (2000). Coevolving: At last, a way to make synergies work. *Harvard Business Review*, **78**(1), 91–101.

Electrive.com (2020). Audi reveals more on EV joint venture with FAW (18 January), https://www.electrive.com/2021/01/18/audi-reveals-new-details-about-ev-joint-venture-with-faw/#:~:text=The%20electric%20car%20joint%20venture,Changchun%20in%20north%2Deastern%20China (last accessed 10 August 2022).

Elmutl, D. and Kathawala, Y. (2001). An overview of strategic alliances. *Management Decision*, **39**(3), 205–18.

Farsi, M., Feltz, D., and Filippino, M. (2007). Economies of scale and scope in local public transportation. *Journal of Transport Economics and Policy*, **41**(3), 345–61.

The Financial Times. Alibaba steps up competition with Amazon in global commerce market (8 May), https://www.ft.com/content/3d25007c-713d-11e9-bbfb-5c68069fbd15 (last accessed 22 October 2022).

The Financial Times. South Korea hit by strikes over lack of chaebol reform (21 November), https://www.ft.com/content/b55b2d6a-ed43-11e8-89c8-d36339d835c0 (last accessed 22 October 2022).

10

Forbes (2012). Was Sprint buying Nextel one of the worst acquisitions ever at $35b? (29 November), https://www.forbes.com/sites/quora/2012/11/29/was-sprint-buying-nextel-one-of-the-worst-acquisitions-ever-at-35b/#317d267448e3 (last accessed 18 August 2022).

Forbes (2021). Televisa and Univsion to merge in $4.3 billion transaction (13 April), https://www.forbes.com/sites/veronicavillafane/2021/04/13/televisa-and-univision-to-merge-in-48-billion-transaction/?sh=17df6ea074d6 (last accessed 18 August 2022).

Fuller, K., Netter, J., and Stegemoller, M. (2002). What do returns to acquiring firms tell us? Evidence from firms that make many acquisitions. *Journal of Finance*, **57**(4), 1763–93.

Furrer, O. (2016). *Corporate Level Strategy: Theory and Applications.* Abingdon: Routledge.

Gallo, A. (2014). The value of keeping the right customers. *Harvard Business Review* (29 October), https://hbr.org/2014/10/the-value-of-keeping-the-right-customers (last accessed 18 August 2022).

Goold, M. and Campbell, A. (1998). Desperately seeking synergy. *Harvard Business Review* (September/October), 131–43, https://hbr.org/1998/09/desperately-seeking-synergy (last accessed 21 October 2022).

Goold, M., Campbell, A., and Alexander, M. (1998). Corporate strategy and parenting theory. *Long Range Planning*, **31**(2), 308–14.

The Guardian (2014). Bus deregulation outside London has been a failure—thinktank report (26 August), https://www.theguardian.com/uk-news/2014/aug/26/bus-deregulation-outside-london-failure-thinktank (last accessed 18 August 2022).

The Guardian (2021). Melrose under fire over plans to close GKN factory in Birmingham (25 February), https://www.theguardian.com/business/2021/feb/25/melrose-plans-close-gkn-factory-birmingham (last accessed 18 August 2022).

Henry, A.E. (2018). *Understanding Strategic Management* (3rd edn). Oxford: Oxford University Press.

Hitt, M.A., Ireland, R.D., and Hoskisson, R.E. (2007). *Strategic Management: Competitiveness and Globalisation: Concepts* (7th edn). Mason, OH: Thomson/South-Western.

Imelt, J.R. (2017). How I remade GE and what I learned along the way. *Harvard Business Review* (September/October), 42–51, https://hbr.org/2017/09/how-i-remade-ge (last accessed 21 October 2022).

Investopedia (2022). The top 25 economies of the world (1 September), https://www.investopedia.com/insights/worlds-top-economies (last accessed 18 August 2022).

Kale, P., Dyer, J.H., and Singh, H. (2002). Alliance capability, stock market response, and long–term alliance success: The role of the alliance function. *Strategic Management Journal*, **23**(8), 747–67.

Kestenbaum, R. (2019). Active outdoor sports may have a new group of customers: Women. *Forbes* (24 February), https://www.forbes.com/sites/richardkestenbaum/2019/02/24/women-in-action-outdoor-sports-ski-snowboard-climbing-hiking-camping-fishing-rei-camber-outdoor/#1e13047c4c80 (last accessed 18 August 2022).

Killing, P.J. (1982). How to make a global joint venture work. *Harvard Business Review* (May/June), 120–7, https://hbr.org/1982/05/how-to-make-a-global-joint-venture-work (last accessed 22 October 2022).

Maceda, C. (2019). Amazon officially launches in UAE, replaces Souq.com (1 May), https://gulfnews.com/business/retail/amazon-officially-launches-in-uae-replaces-souqcom-1.1556686706424 (last accessed 18 August 2022).

MacMillan, I. (1988). Controlling competitive dynamics by taking strategic initiative. *Academy of Management Perspectives*, **2**(2), 111–18, https://doi.org/10.5465/ame.1988.4275518.

Madslien, J. (2010). Dotcom bubble burst: 10 years on (9 March), http://news.bbc.co.uk/1/hi/business/8558257.stm (last accessed 18 August 2022).

Manthey, N. (2018). JLR & Chery turn China factory into EV centre (27 November), https://www.electrive.com/2018/11/27/jlr-chery-to-turn-china-factory-into-e-mobility-centre (last accessed 18 August 2022).

Marie Curie (2020). Annual Report and Accounts 2019–20, https://www.mariecurie.org.uk/who/plans-reports-policies/vision-strategic-plan (last accessed 18 August 2022).

Norman-Major, K. (2011). Balancing the Four Es: Or can we achieve equity for social equity in public administration? *Journal of Public Affairs Education*, **17**(2), 233–252.

Norman-Major, K. (2012). The Four Es of great governance. *Minnesota Cities* (May/June), 13.

10

Palepu, K. (1985). Diversification strategy, profit performance and the entropy measure. *Strategic Management Journal*, **6**(3), 239–55.

Paroutis, S. and Pettigrew, A. (2007). Strategizing in the multi-business firm: Strategy teams at multiple levels and over time. *Human Relations*, **60**(1), 99–135.

Perez, S. (2020). Mastercard given approval to prepare for entry into China's payments markets (11 February), https://techcrunch.com/2020/02/11/mastercard-given-approval-to-prepare-for-entry-into-chinas-payments-market/?guccounter=1&guce_referrer=aHR0cHM6Ly93d3cuZ29vZ2xlLmNvbS8&guce_referrer_sig=AQAAACT3iIuUx9MJoRZc2PpBywNakURZJ2d5vRRjP7g9a6AX78m_bXPD1O34Fu8Ymdj-DQD6cZ_tkGHDL_Lf0QCPRbcCn-kh7_DsRxlRvY96ovnMp-LRSfKLFvatTlJAGtkRg6oq7CitNUfyRZSsLoqUoHACLGQ9sI2WmzvMpSKPfqEc (9 November), https://edition.cnn.com/2018/11/09/business/american-express-china/index.html (last accessed 21 October 2022).

Pham, S. (2018). China gives American Express first shot at its huge payments market (9 November), https://edition.cnn.com/2018/11/09/business/american-express-china/index.html (last accessed 18 August 2022).

Porter, M.E. (1987). From competitive advantage to corporate strategy. *Harvard Business Review*, **65**(3), 43–59.

Reuters (2021). Mexico's Televisa says to merge content with Univision in new media company (14 April), https://www.reuters.com/business/media-telecom/mexicos-televisa-says-merge-content-with-univision-new-media-company-2021-04-13 (last accessed 18 August 2022).

Roll, R. (1986). The hubris hypothesis of corporate takeovers. *Journal of Business*, **59**(2), 197–216.

Rumelt, R. (1974). *Strategy, Structure and Economic Performance*. Cambridge, MA: Harvard University Press.

Rumelt, R. (1995). The evaluation of business strategy. In: Mintzberg, H., Quinn, B.J., and Ghoshal, S. (eds), *The Strategy Process*. Hemel Hempstead: Prentice Hall.

Shah, P. and Arora, P. (2014). M&A announcements and their effect on return to shareholders: An event study. *Accounting and Finance Research*, **3**(2), 170–90.

Shaoul, J., Shepherd, A., Stafford, A., and Stapleton, P. (2013). Losing control in joint ventures: The case of building schools for the future, https://www.icas.com/__data/assets/pdf_file/0006/7782/98-Losing-Control-in-Joint-Ventures-Building-Schools-for-the-Future-ICAS.pdf (last accessed 18 August 2022).

Søderberg, A.M. and Romani, L. (2017). Boundary spanners in global partnerships: A case study of an Indian vendor's collaboration with Western clients. *Group & Organization Management*, **42**(2), 237–78.

Statista (2021). Value of M&A transactions globally from 1985 to 2020 (2 March), https://www.statista.com/statistics/267369/volume-of-mergers-and-acquisitions-worldwide (last accessed 18 August 2022).

Statistica (2022). Annual net sales of Amazon in selected leading markets from 2014 to 2021 (14 February), https://www.statista.com/statistics/672782/net-sales-of-amazon-leading-markets (last accessed 18 August 2022).

Teece, D. (1980). Economies of scope and the scope of the enterprise. *Journal of Economic Behaviour & Organization*, **1**(3), 223–47.

The Telegraph (2017). Samsung heir Lee Jae-yong arrested amid bribery allegations (17 February), https://www.telegraph.co.uk/business/2017/02/16/south-korean-court-issues-warrant-arrest-samsung-heir (last accessed 18 August 2022).

Terwilliger, C. (2017). Interview: Blizzard Tecnica Marketing Manager Leslie Baker-Brown, https://sgbonline.com/one-on-one-with-blizzard-tecnica-marketing-manager-leslie-baker-brown (last accessed 22 October 2022).

Variety (2021). Univision and Televisa set merger deal to create Spanish-language content powerhouse (13 April), https://variety.com/2021/tv/news/univision-televisa-merger-spanish-deal-1234950743 (last accessed 18 August 2022).

The Wall Street Journal (2016). A presidential scandal transfixes South Korea (27 November), https://www.wsj.com/articles/a-presidential-scandal-transfixes-south-korea-1480112351?mod=article_inline (last accessed 18 August 2022).

Walter, J., Kellermanns, F.W., and Lechner, C. (2012). Decision making within and between organizations: Rationality, politics, and alliance performance. *Journal of Management*, **38**(5), 1582–1610.

10

CHAPTER ELEVEN

Innovation, Disruption, and Digitalization

CONTENTS

LEARNING OBJECTIVES

By the end of this chapter, you should be able to:

○ Evaluate the relevance and usefulness of innovation to organizational strategy

○ Explain how different types of innovation might influence organizational strategy

○ Explain how an organization can build strategically valuable innovation capabilities and assess the merits of different ways of developing an innovation strategy

○ Critically evaluate how digital transformation, digitalization, and data strategy might drive innovation in an organization

○ Identify and discuss future challenges for digital strategy

TOOLBOX

○ **Business model canvas**
A method to systematically map the components of a current business model in order to identify ways in which the business model might be changed.

○ **Blue ocean strategy**
An approach to innovation strategy that searches for uncontested market space; guides exploration of cost reduction and differentiation options, and identification of new value propositions that render the competition irrelevant.

○ **Innovation portfolio strategy**
A framework to identify the different ways in which innovation is being attempted by an organization; provides clarity around technical and commercial modes of innovating.

○ **Platform strategy**
An action-orientated framework for developing an innovation strategy that creates or develops an ecosystem. Organizations may direct this towards achieving platform leadership—a network position with maximum influence on the ecosystem.

○ **Data strategy orientation**
A checklist-based approach to align data strategy—data architecture, objectives, and activities—with broader organizational objectives; sets a platform for digital transformation which, in turn, enables organizational strategy.

 Access the online resources to watch a short video clip where Ned Phillips shares his top career tips.

11

OPENING CASE STUDY REINVENTING THE REINVENTOR: INNOVATION AT W.L. GORE

W.L. Gore & Associates Inc. is a manufacturer best known for Gore-Tex, the waterproof membrane used in high-end outerwear. The company also makes air filters, headlight vents, heart stents, guitar strings, and more. Gore has long been lauded less for 'what it makes' than for 'how it makes'—a workers' democracy with a thriving innovation culture. The company has grown steadily over the years to $3.8 billion revenue in 2020. Yet, in the past decade, the markets for Gore's most successful products have matured, and the company is seeking new directions.

Gore was founded by Wilbert Lee Gore, a DuPont research chemist, who became obsessed with a durable and inert substance called polytetrafluoroethylene (PTFE), commercialized by DuPont in 1945 under the brand name Teflon. DuPont was only interested in manufacturing PTFE, rather than innovating with it. In 1958, Gore quit his job and set up his own business applying PTFE to new product lines. W.L. Gore's earliest products were PTFE-insulated wires and cables, some of which were used in the first manned Moon landing in 1969.

Through extensive experimentation, Gore discovered a way to make expanded PTFE (ePTFE)—a lighter and stronger version of PTFE. Over time, Gore engineers perfected a set of techniques to refine the ePTFE molecular structure and product capabilities. ePTFE technical know-how now underpins diverse offerings from Gore, from hazmat suits to high-tension ropes for deep-water oil rigs to premium dental floss. Since 1976, Gore has allowed licensees to turn its membrane into garments for major brands such as The North Face and Patagonia under strict usage and branding agreements.

For all ePTFE's versatility, Gore's leaders and admirers tend to credit human, not molecular, structure with the company's success. Gore's founders organized the growing global business like a set of tribes, intending to optimize the human creative and social potential of its associates. From the 1970s onwards, the company opened a new plant whenever an existing one expanded past a couple of hundred workers, thus enabling direct communication between all associates who chose the projects on which they wished to work. As Gore employees followed their instinct to find new applications for PTFE in seemingly unconnected markets, the organization diversified and added new divisions and plants to organize production operations.

Although Gore now has over 11,000 associates across 68 sites, this approach still largely holds. Ideas live and die on collective enthusiasm; authority is temporary and contingent on the job at hand. Digital technologies are deployed to create collaboration opportunities and flow between projects. The company routinely finds itself on lists of the best places to work, and its highly trained, eminently employable employees rarely leave—turnover in its North American offices is 2%. But despite Gore's organizational flexibility, it is heavily reliant on its ePTFE-related technologies, and competition is growing. For example, eVent, NeoShell, and OutDry Extreme fabrics challenge the once supreme Gore-Tex brand. And today, an automobile firm or appliance maker looking for a basic ePTFE membrane for one of its products can choose from a plethora of suppliers who will sell it cheaper than Gore.

In 2015, the then CEO Terri Kelly commissioned support from Steve Blank, an innovation adviser known in Silicon Valley for the lean start-up concept in which companies are pushed to go to market early and often in order to let their customer feedback guide their product refinement. Lean start-up thinking has been introduced in Gore through a new innovation management approach. Its engineers can now pitch their ideas to investment committees of colleagues with relevant technical, financial, and market expertise. The process is 'survival of the fittest'. Concepts without clear market appeal are dropped, while those that show promise get additional funding rounds and more resources. So far so good for Gore's re-invention prospects—ideas are flowing into the investment process and new beta-products are already being sold in fabrics, electronics, and health-care markets. Gore is experimenting with aspects of its business model too, with the launch of a direct-to-consumer fashion brand called Vere.

Blank is already talking about Gore as a success story. 'The big idea that I see large companies getting wrong and Gore getting right', Blank says, 'is that innovation is not a point activity, it's an end-to-end process. You need a pipeline.' For W.L. Gore, a strategic refocusing on its innovation process is paying dividends.

Questions for discussion

1. Drawing on the definitions in the introduction, identify examples of technological, organizational, and strategic innovations in the W.L. Gore story.

2. The polymer PTFE arguably forms a technological platform upon which a wide range of further innovation activity occurs at Gore.

What are the apparent advantages and disadvantages of having such a platform?

3. To what extent will 'lean start-up' thinking and processes be part of how innovation is conducted in Gore in the long term? Explain your answer.

Sources

This example is based on an article by D. Bennett (2019). They're coming for your eyeballs. *Bloomberg Businessweek European Edition* (13 May), 38–45.

Palmieri, J. (2021). W.L. Gore creates incubator business (21 October), https://wwd.com/fashion-news/ready-to-wear/w-l-gore-creates-incubator-business-1234972858 (last accessed 31 October 2021).

WL Gore (2021). https://www.gore.com/about (last accessed 31 October 2021).

11.1 **Introduction**

Innovation—the successful exploitation of new ideas—refers to the process and outcomes of how new ideas are realized in practice (Dodgson et al. 2008). In this chapter, we consider the relationship between innovation and strategy. The strategic intent of innovation activity may be to improve operating efficiency, find new sources of value creation for stakeholders, or both. Furthermore, innovation within an industry changes the competitive landscape for rivals, customers, and suppliers. Innovation provides a means for organizations to cope with external disruption and refresh the value created from its resource base.

The scale and scope of innovation can vary from a small-scale change to holistic transformation. Innovation may occur within the closed confines of an organization or in a more open way through a network of collaborating stakeholders. The nature of innovation can also vary. **Technological innovation** involves conversion of new knowledge and technology into advances in products, services, operational processes, and infrastructure. **Organizational innovation** refers to new ways by which to organize firm activities, coordinate human resources, and facilitate management practices. **Open innovation** refers to the ways in which new ideas can be successfully exploited—to mutual gain—with external stakeholders and networks. **Strategic innovation** describes innovation in an organization's business model, creating value for customers in new ways and possibly creating uncontested new market space. And **platform innovation**—the creation or growth of an ecosystem of activity—increasingly features as a topic of strategic interest in a networked world.

In keeping with a process–practice perspective, we consider how an organization's situation will impact its capacity for innovation and how it might respond to the innovative activities of others. **Disruption** describes an event or trend which unsettles stable competitive or operating conditions. **Disruptive innovation** might arise from the activities of start-ups, existing firms, or new players entering a market from adjacent industries. We examine market-creating 'blue ocean', risk-managing 'portfolio', and ecosystem-defining 'platform-leader' strategies for disruptive innovation.

We also review the implications for the strategy of digital technology's increasing role as an enabler and outcome of innovation activity. We consider how digital transformation—a shift in how an individual, organization, institution, or system operates enabled by digital technologies—increasingly features in organizational strategy. Once a peripheral issue, how data is collected, stored, analysed, distributed, and deployed is now a central strategic concern for most organizations. We examine how organizations are responding to disruption from digital transformation and big data through innovation activity and strategy.

11.2 **Innovation and strategy**

In this section, we explain how innovation can be understood from a process–practice perspective, focusing on delivering enhanced value in an ever-changing world. We consider contemporary challenges that may trigger or inhibit innovative strategic initiatives before concluding with a discussion of how innovation strategy can be made and managed.

Process interpretation of innovation

Process–practice model of innovation

A widely used term, innovation is subject to multiple interpretations in practice. Innovation can mean a novel product, service, or way of organizing (i.e. an output), a way of preparing for the future, or a mindset focused on exploiting novelty. In keeping with a process–practice perspective, we focus on innovation as a continual process in which individuals or groups of individuals attempt to exploit new ideas successfully (Fagerberg 2006). Although the types of new ideas addressed by innovation activities can vary widely, innovation is broadly understood through several related activities, as shown in Figure 11.1.

Triggers for creative responses and innovation potential arise from continuing search and scanning activities (through the application of methods as detailed in Chapters 5 and 6). New ideas may arise from external factors such as customer feedback, competitor monitoring, or macro-trends (e.g. emerging digital technologies); purposeful internal exploratory activities such as R&D and design; or learning acquired from previous innovation activity. This learning may even be an unintended consequence of organizational activity directed towards an alternative target outcome (e.g. chewing gum being created during a search for a new type of adhesive).

Novel ideas and suggestions arising from search activities are then filtered through selection. This funneling of ideas from many options to a limited selection of active innovation interests (Wheelwright and Clark 1992) typically involves a combination of expert judgement and cost–benefit analysis such as through financial modelling methods. If an idea is selected, resource allocation activities are undertaken (e.g. assigning staff to work on implementation, allocating a budget, etc.). Selected ideas are then implemented as change projects, which embed the

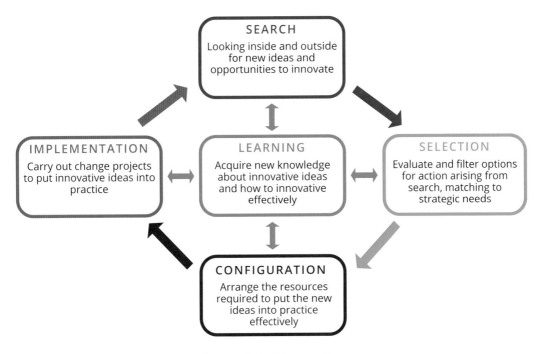

FIGURE 11.1 Process–practice model of innovation. *Source*: authors.

innovation into revised organizational practices in order that the innovation might be sustained as part of continuing organizational life.

Through all activities, practical learning occurs which influences current and future actions; for example, managers can decide whether to continue to support innovation ideas as actual rather than anticipated financial performance is revealed through innovation activity. Learning can also occur regarding how the innovation activities are conducted—using insights from 'doing' innovation to improve how future activities are planned and enacted.

Role of creativity in innovation

Innovation and creativity are two distinct but related concepts. Creativity describes a capacity for new ideas arising from original thinking and inventiveness. However, one can be creative without necessarily being innovative (von Stamm 2008) as innovation implies an attempt to put creative ideas into practice. Organizational potential to innovate arises from the capacity to creatively generate new ideas *multiplied* by the capacity to implement the associated change project (Govindarajan and Trimble 2010). If either capacity is lacking, the innovation potential of an organization is diminished. Collaborating with other organizations to tap into creative and/or implementation potential can help improve innovation results for an organization.

Diffusion of innovation: The role of time

Time—central to a process–practice understanding—plays a key role in the realization of value from innovations as 'new ideas of how to do things will usually spread via a "learning by observing" process' (Hall 2006: 459). The way in which innovation takes hold within an industrial sector was famously explored by Everett Rogers in 1962. Rogers noted that, by a process of diffusion, innovation is communicated through a range of channels over time by members of a social system such as a market or sector. The speed and scale of diffusion is influenced by:

- **relative advantage** of an innovation's value in comparison to the status quo;
- **compatibility** with the values, experiences, and current needs of potential adopters;
- **complexity** of use and comprehensibility of the innovation for adopters;
- **trialability**—the extent to which adopters can experiment with the innovation; and
- **observability**—the extent to which the effects of an innovation are apparent to others.

Rogers (2003: 17) also notes that the greater the perceived relative advantage, compatibility, trialability, and observability of an innovation, and the lower its perceived complexity, the faster and more widely it will diffuse within a social system.

Rogers noted how, over time, the process of diffusion is shaped by the preceding 'phase' of adoption. Rogers coined the phrase 'early adopters' to describe the influential opinion leaders who encourage or dissuade the majority of users to adopt an innovation. Winning over early adopters—whether for internal innovations such as new operating methods or externally facing innovations such as new products or services—is vital to an innovation being sustainable. Innovation strategy should address how 'early adopters' will be reached and influenced as part of planning for successful exploitation of new ideas.

Responding to creative destruction

Innovation as a continuing process helps to explain how organizations might contribute to, survive, and indeed thrive in the face of creative destruction. As articulated by the economist Joseph Schumpeter, creative destruction describes 'a process of industrial mutation that incessantly revolutionizes the economic structure from within, incessantly destroying the old one, incessantly creating a new one' (Schumpeter 1942). Schumpeter explained that continuing entrepreneurial actions and technological advances—probing for more effective ways of creating value, replacing old practices with new in pursuit of profit—will eventually render any technology, product, or organizational approach irrelevant (Gilbert et al. 2012).

Creative destruction can rapidly reconfigure a sectoral landscape or ecosystem but is easier to understand after it has occurred than whilst you are immersed in it (Bettis and Hitt 1995). As innovative organizational conduct is preferred by customers during creative destruction, the superior performance that follows changes the members and relationships within an ecosystem. Consider the evolution from video cassette players to DVDs to Blu-Ray to streaming technologies that occurred within the space of 30 years. JVC—the original 'winners' of the video cassette standards war—is one of many technology providers now in the media streaming technology industry. The consumer media industry is unrecognizable from its video tape origins, transformed several times over by creative destruction within a few decades.

Across organizational types, innovation provides a means of continuously refreshing products, services, and processes to keep pace with creative destruction. Public-sector organizations and governments must innovate services and policies as they compete with other nations to retain citizens, sustain economic activity, and attract new investment. Equally, third-sector organizations competing for funding, attention, and legitimacy need to be innovative in order to continue to deliver on their mandates. For leaders in all types of

11

organizations, creative destruction makes it imperative that innovation is addressed as a routine aspect of strategy work.

Dealing with disruption

Disruption refers to an event or shift in a context that unsettles the status quo. In competitive terms, disruption 'occurs when an innovation creates a new market and business model that cause established players to fall' (Kim and Mauborgne 2019: 46). Disruptive innovations typically 'challenge industry incumbents by offering simpler, good-enough alternatives to an underserved group of customers' (Christensen et al. 2006: 96).

For example, the streaming service Spotify disrupted the music industry, challenging long-established high-street music retailers such as HMV and Virgin Megastores, supermarket retailers, and even Apple's iTunes platform. All these incumbents had business models based on selling music. At a low monthly fee (no adverts) or no fee (with adverts), Spotify's launch offered consumers access to a massive library of streaming-quality music rather than ownership of high-quality music. This popular service has many imitators now (e.g. Apple Music), has changed the flow of revenues in the music industry, and boasted 165 million paying subscribers by February 2021 (Dean 2021).

Disruption can occur from start-ups, such as Spotify, from industry incumbents, such as First Direct (a division of HSBC that disrupted the UK banking sector in the late 1990s with the first internet banking offering), or from well-resourced competitors in adjacent industries—what Downes and Nunes (2013) refer to as 'Big Bang' disruption. As the name suggests, Big Bang disruption can be devastating for incumbents. For example, consider the speed with which sat-nav manufacturers (e.g. Tom-Tom, Garmin) were negatively impacted by the release of free high-performance navigational tools integrated into iOS and Android devices. Google and Apple had far larger resource bases than GPS mapping-sector incumbents and a flexible technical platform to distribute their services to a large user base. You may detect the possibility of disruption, or be disruptive, for an organization when applying the external analysis tools in Chapter 5. In developing a strategic response, specific modes of innovation can provide options for consideration. Acquiring capabilities in business model innovation will provide a means to respond to disruptive potential by (a) being the disruptor, (b) keeping pace with disrupting organizations, or (c) finding uncontested market space. Equally, platform innovation activity might provide some defence against Big Bang disruption. What these specific modes of innovation mean, and how they might be approached, will be discussed later in this chapter.

Disruption may also arise from unanticipated global events, such as the COVID-19 pandemic. Organizational responsiveness to global disruption might be enabled by using innovation methodologies such as 'lean thinking' approaches (see the Opening Case Study), agile product development, and digital prototyping to cut the cost and development time of new product, process, and platform development (Cooper 2021). In the face of a disrupted global environment, capabilities in agile and responsive innovation may confer a competitive advantage on an organization.

Understanding strategic capacity for innovation

As a mechanism for creating value, reducing costs, or preserving performance in a shifting external context, innovation is likely to be of continuing strategic interest to leaders. However, an organizational capacity to innovate is not a given. Being aware of general and specific innovation

11

capabilities, enduring innovation culture, and strategic resource constraints can help you gauge the potential for an organization to incorporate innovation initiatives into strategy work.

Possessing sufficient innovation capabilities

If an organization is described as having innovation capability, this broadly means it has formal or informal innovation processes, sufficiently knowledgeable staff, and a supportive environment in which innovation activities can be carried out. Bayley (2019) proposes that innovation capability can be nurtured by: constantly streamlining organizational processes; 'clearing out' non-value-adding activities in order to create capacity for change and free resources for new investments; investing in creating a work environment that encourages innovation at all levels of the organization; building process expertise for when it is required; and looking for ways in which to connect and integrate new innovative, even disruptive, business activities and technologies with the existing organization.

The extent to which innovation is possible is constrained by a number of factors. The organization's history and culture, its ever-changing operating environment, resource base, and focal activities, as well as the intended scope, scale, and focus of innovations under consideration all need to be understood in order to grasp the likelihood of innovation success in any situation.

Managing with a finite resource base

Awareness of available resource stocks (see Chapter 6) is important in understanding specific innovation capabilities in any situation (Burgelman and Doz 2001). Every organization has a finite resource base to support continuing operations and needs to plan around these limitations when considering any strategic initiatives or innovation activity (Kaplan and Norton 2008). Freeing resources for innovation that, in the short term, don't generate returns can be hard to justify for managers. Less resource-intensive, small-scale 'incremental' innovations are often attractive as they are easier to accommodate alongside operational demands. For lower possible returns, incremental innovations tend to be less complex than more ambitious 'radical' innovations that require the firm to develop new situation-specific competencies in technological, commercial, organizing, and project-managing domains (Vanhaverbeke and Peeters 2005). Considering resource scarcity, a series of incremental innovations rather than a radical innovation initiative can seem like a prudent low-risk way to improve the organization. However, an organization may become obsolete with this approach if more risk-seeking competitors succeed with game-changing radical innovation. Being able to balance short- and long-term innovation approaches is deemed crucial to an organization's survival prospects (Gurtner and Reinhardt 2016). As a means of addressing resource scarcity, innovating in collaboration with others in its network can enable an organization to achieve innovative outcomes which otherwise would have been too resource intensive for it to achieve on its own (Powell and Grodal 2006).

Nurturing an innovation culture

Innovation culture refers to patterns in the way innovation activity tends to be perceived and enacted in an organization. Manso (2017) observes that cultures that tolerate early failure and reward long-term performance will have higher rates of innovation. With the activity focus of the process–practice model of innovation (Figure 11.1), innovation culture will play a significant role in regulating what might be achieved through innovation in an organization.

In the Opening Case Study, we reviewed how W.L. Gore has a strong track record of innovation and is working hard to revise and sustain an innovation culture. Ex-CEO Teri Kelly suggested a need for organizational leaders to constantly focus on the question, 'How do we create the right environment where collaboration happens naturally—that people actually want to work together, that they actually like to be part of something greater than just the individual contribution?' (cited in Mangelsdorf 2009).

This view is echoed by IDEO, a world-leading design consultancy whose innovation successes range from creating the first mouse for Apple to redesigning complex health-care systems. However, IDEO and W.L. Gore are organizational outliers in how innovation is understood and enacted as part of their culture. For most organizations, innovation culture will present issues and development areas that inhibit the strategic exploration and exploitation of new ideas. According to Rao and Weintraub (2013), innovation culture will be shaped by the extent to which the six factors shown in Figure 11.2 are present.

Rao and Weintraub (2013: 30) comment that:

When it comes to fostering innovation, enterprises often give more attention to resources, processes and measuring success—the more easily quantified, tools-oriented innovation building blocks—but less to the harder-to-measure, people-oriented determinants of innovative culture—values, behaviors and climate.

Analysing the innovation culture, using the categories of influencing factors outlined in Figure 11.2 to organize data, can make a useful addition to resource base profiling (as described in Chapter 6). Insights into the nature of the innovation culture in an organization will be of value as an input into strategic decision-making.

 Access the online resources to watch a short video clip where Ned Phillips discusses organizational change and culture.

VALUES
Being entrepreneurial, promoting creativity, and fostering continuous learning

BEHAVIOURS
Willingness to change, communicate, and take action; tenacity and improvization

CLIMATE
Leadership attitude encourages engagement, experimentation, and independent thinking

INNOVATION CULTURE
How innovation activity is perceived, enacted, and reacted to in an organization

RESOURCES
Allocation of the right people to innovation, funding of projects, and supportive systems

PROCESSES
Capture and filter ideas, review and prioritize options, and implement initiatives

SUCCESS
Externally recognized success, positive business outcomes, and individual rewards

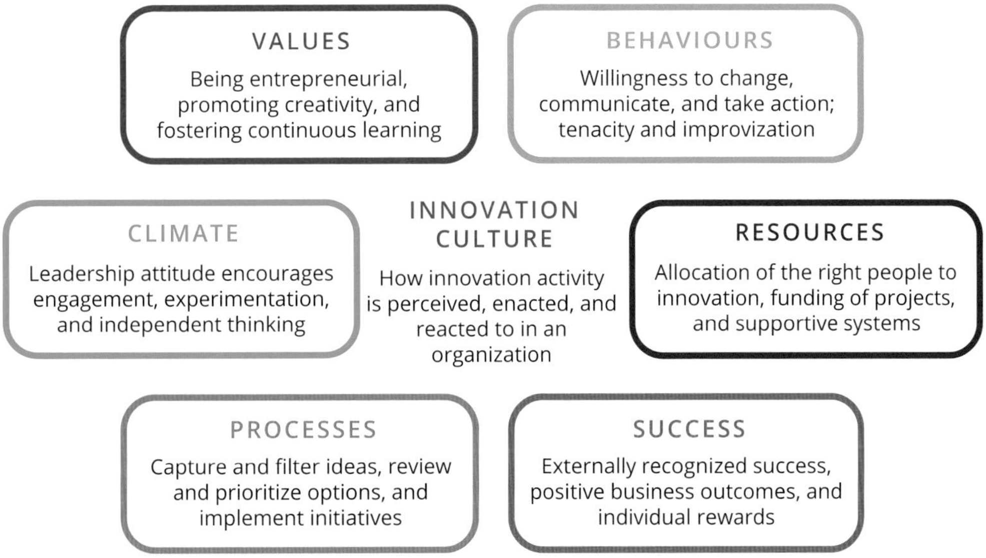

FIGURE 11.2 Factors shaping innovation culture. *Source*: authors.

11.3 Types of innovation

As you engage in strategy analysis, you will encounter different types of innovation. Each type has specific characteristics and strategic implications. Being aware of these types can help you understand your options in terms of instigating innovation through strategy and also the innovation activity of others to which you might have to respond. Having examined how innovation and strategy interact in contemporary organizations, in this section, we describe a range of innovation types and how they might feature in strategy.

Technological innovation

Technological innovation describes the application of new practical or scientific knowledge to exploit, extend, or create physical processes, products, services, or infrastructure. Technological innovation draws on learning by doing (such as experimentation) or learning by using (identifying gaps in existing product and process effectiveness) (Dosi et al. 2006). As an option for strategy, technological innovation might be used to improve efficiency or find new ways to compete (Dodgson et al. 2008). Henderson and Clark (1990) define a well-known typology of technological innovation, shown in Table 11.1. In Table 11.1, 'core concept' refers to the main technology used in a design, such as jet propulsion in aircraft engines, and 'components' are the peripherals (e.g. turbine housing) included in the design to allow the core technology to function. Linkages refer to how core concepts and components are configured as a system.

An **incremental innovation** is one which improves existing products, services, or ways of working by further exploiting existing capabilities or resources (Henderson and Clark 1990). For example, Netflix commissioning a new book series adaption into a mini-series is an incremental innovation—creating a new product offering valued by customers that draws on existing technical capabilities without transforming how the organization operates.

In contrast, a **radical innovation** is defined as 'highly revolutionary in nature, competence destroying, and induces major transformations of existing products, technologies, or services' (Obal et al. 2016: 137), based on introducing entirely novel thinking to an organization. For example, the introduction of a digital platform and services to local government processes in Singapore fits the radical innovation definition as it requires a new set of technical competences to operate and revolutionizes the way in which citizens are served.

TABLE 11.1 Types of technological innovation

		Core concepts	
		Reinforced	Replaced
Linkages between core concepts and components	Unchanged	Incremental innovation	Modular innovation
	Changed	Architectural innovation	Radical innovation

Source: based on Henderson and Clark (1990: 12).

Modular innovation refers to a change of a core design concept within a largely unchanged product architecture. For example, electric vehicles represent a modular innovation to internal combustion engine alternatives—requiring a new set of competences to deliver propulsion and drive train technology, whilst drawing on established competences for the remaining vehicle design.

Architectural innovation is 'the reconfiguration of an established system to link together existing components in a new way' (Henderson and Clark 1990: 12). This often involves a change in the scale of application of technology. Domestic wind turbines, for example, are an architectural innovation from industrial wind turbines—the underlying technology is the same, but the size and arrangement of the components differs to meet the different scale of use.

As you weigh up options for strategic initiatives, thinking about the technological innovation options available to your organization or currently being attempted by competitors will give you useful insights to feed into the decision-making process.

Organizational innovation

Organizational innovation, also known as managerial or administrative innovation, refers to:

Changes in the organization's structure and processes, administrative systems, knowledge used in performing the work of management, and managerial skills that enable an organization to function and succeed by using its resources effectively.

(Damanpour et al. 2009: 655)

New knowledge underpinning organizational innovation doesn't arise from R&D and therefore doesn't have a technological component (Edquist et al. 2001). Instead, it is a change in the social processes and configuration of an organization enabled by management insights (Damanpour 2014). Organizational innovation may involve shifting between organizational designs such as Toyota's restructuring as described in Chapter 7. It might mean allocating resource and focus in a different way, and it might involve introducing different management philosophies, as Gore attempted with a move to a lean start-up approach to innovating.

Organizational innovation may be undertaken to increase the potential for creativity, learning, and knowledge flows (Lam 2006). It may be triggered by changes in the external environment or as part of a broader strategic initiative (such as internationalizing). And organizational innovation might happen as a reflection of a new leader's own management philosophy and long-term vision for an organization, such as the widely-lauded organizational innovations at DBS, a Singaporean headquartered bank, towards a digital technological future following the appointment of CEO Piyush Gupta (Sia et al. 2021) (see case example 1.2).

11

Strategic innovation

Strategic innovation, also referred to as business model innovation, involves 'a fundamental reconceptualization of what the business is all about that, in turn, leads to a dramatically different way of playing the game' (Markides 1998: 32). In Chapter 8, we explained that a business model is the organization's guiding principle of how to make money or deliver value for money (if a non-profit organization). Amit and Zott (2012) propose that by reconfiguring or modifying the activity system of how an organization engages with customers, partners, and vendors, inexpensive ways in which to increase value created from the same or fewer resources might be identified.

The impact of strategic innovation can vary. Undertaking business model innovation might bring an organization into line with the business models of competitors (e.g. Apple launching Apple Music to compete with Spotify). Alternatively, strategic innovation might be disruptive to an existing market such as when the low-cost business model of Ryanair challenged established national carriers such as British Airways and Aer Lingus (Charitou and Markides 2003). Strategic innovation may also establish entirely new markets in a non-disruptive way; for example, the micro-finance business model of organizations such as the Grameen Bank emerged to address problems for customers who didn't use established banks anyway (Kim and Mauborgne 2019). We will explore how non-disruptive new market creation might be undertaken in the section on the **blue ocean strategy**.

A popular method for exploring strategic innovation is the **business model canvas** shown in Table 11.2. The elements of the canvas represent different aspects of the business model which, if adjusted, might represent a strategic innovation (Osterwalder and Pigneur 2010). The current business model for an organization can be described by answering the questions in each category (insights from the tools outlined in Chapters 5 and 6 will help you do this). Reviewing the output, options for changing elements of the business model can be identified, evaluated, and possibly enacted.

Open innovation

Open innovation is defined as 'the use of purposive inflows and outflows of knowledge to accelerate internal innovation, and expand the markets for external use of innovation, respectively' (Chesbrough 2008: 1). Open innovation implies two complementary kinds of openness: drawing in ideas and technologies from outside the organization or allowing an organization's ideas, technologies, and processes to be accessed externally by others such as customers, suppliers, or even competitors (Chesbrough 2011).

Intellectual property describes intangible resources—such as know-how, product designs, and brand assets—that can be shared, licensed, or sold. A traditional approach to managing new ideas and intellectual property has been to maintain secrecy and to retain exclusive ownership within the strict control of the organization. Collaborative communities—collections of individuals embracing open-innovation thinking—such as Wikipedia challenge this mindset by accepting the use of external ideas and the sharing of internally generated ideas with others for mutual advantage as a normal part of innovating (Kolbjørnsrud 2017). For all organizations, bringing outside ideas in might create new value through complementary combinations with existing organizational resources. And by taking ideas out from the organization, the potential of valuable internal resources might be exploited on a larger scale than the organization could achieve on its own. Attempts to capture such new sources of value from open innovation is referred to as 'open strategy' (Chesbrough and Appleyard 2007).

For example, LEGO has created highly successful new product ranges based on licensing intellectual property, such as the right to use Star Wars and Batman brand assets, for combination

TABLE 11.2 **Business model canvas**

Key partners	Key activities	Value propositions	Customer relationships	Customer segments
• Who are our key partners? • Who are our key suppliers? • Which key resources are we acquiring from our partners? • Which key activities do partners perform?	• What key activities do our value propositions require? • Our distribution channels? • Customer relationships? • Revenue streams?	• What value do we deliver to the customer? • Which one of our customers' problems are we helping to solve? • What bundles of products and services are we offering to each segment? • Which customer needs are we satisfying? • What is the minimum viable product?	• What key activities do our value propositions require? • Our distribution channels? • Customer relationships? • Revenue streams?	• For whom are we creating value? • Who are our most important customers? • What are the customer archetypes?

	Key resources		**Channels**	
	• What key resources do our value propositions require? • Our distribution channels? • Customer relationships? • Revenue streams?		• Through which channels do our customer segments want to be reached? • How do other companies reach them now? • Which ones work best? • Which ones are most cost efficient? • How are we integrating them with customer routines?	

Cost structure	Revenue streams
• What are the most important costs inherent in our business model? • Which key resources are most expensive? • Which key activities are most expensive?	• For what value are our customers really willing to pay? • For what do they currently pay? • What is the revenue model? • What are the pricing tactics?

Source: Strategyzer, https://www.strategyzer.com/canvas/business-model-canvas (last accessed 2 October 2022).

with its unique brand and play system manufacturing capabilities. Equally, LEGO has licensed its own brand to be used by others in creating a diverse range of products such as theme parks, clothing, and computer games. These examples of open strategy show how benefits can arise from managing knowledge flows across traditional organizational boundaries.

The possibilities of open innovation and open strategy can be explored through examining the resources, capabilities, needs, and activities of external parties such as customers, competitors, suppliers, and complementors. Where both the organization and the external party might benefit from a collaborative relationship (of any scope), there exists the possibility of open innovation. Supporting methodologies include the **value net** tool proposed by Brandenburger and Nalebuff (1996), or Chesbrough's (2011) **value web** method for open service innovation.

Platform innovation

Platform innovation, also referred to as ecosystems innovation, involves creating products, services, infrastructure, or technologies which become essential to a system of commercial activity whilst solving a strategic problem for many organizations and users in a sector (Gawer and Cusumano 2008). Organizations which provide rules and infrastructure that facilitate interactions between parties are known as **multi-sided platforms (MSPs)** (Hagiu and Altman 2017). For example, online platforms such as Expedia and Booking.com provide a marketplace in which all manner of travel organizations (accommodation, transport, currency, insurance, etc.) can efficiently compete to fulfil specific consumer needs, whilst consumers can easily search and compare rival offerings to quickly build travel experiences that meet their individual requirements. Without the online platform, higher transaction costs (in the form of greater expense and hassle) would be incurred for all involved.

Platforms change how value is created for and by an organization but are not a new concept. When first introduced, the shopping mall was a platform innovation, providing the physical and commercial infrastructure to bring together vendors and shoppers on an unprecedented scale. However, platform innovation has increased significantly in recent times through the possibilities of building scalable commercial networks using digital technologies. Accordingly, platform innovation is a topic of increasing focus and influence in organizational strategy. Adopting agile ways of operating and embracing a strategy as plasticity perspective (see Chapter 1) can help organizations capitalize on the potential of platform innovation (Denning 2018).

Van Alstyne et al. (2016: 57) note that 'with a platform, the critical asset is the community and the resources of its members. The focus of strategy shifts from controlling to orchestrating resources, from optimising internal processes to facilitating external interactions, and from increasing customer value to maximising ecosystem value.'

Platforms may have an internal focus, such as the Unreal Engine underpinning multiple product innovations for Epic Games or an organization's information management system allowing internal business processes to occur across functions (Gawer and Cusumano 2014). Many examples of digital platform innovation (e.g. Alibaba, Grab, Careem, etc.) are emerging in ecosystems where activity is reshaped, often in an overlapping way, with other industries. As Gawer and Cusumano observe:

Industry platforms and associated innovations, as well as platforms on top of or embedded within other platforms have become increasingly pervasive in our everyday lives (for example, microprocessors embedded within personal computers or smart phones that access the Internet, on top of which search engines such as Google and social media networks such as Facebook exist, and on top of which applications operate, etc.).

(Gawer and Cusumano 2014: 418)

Van Alstyne et al. (2016: 58) identify that all platforms have an ecosystem with the same basic structure, comprising four types of players. Owners control the platform intellectual property, infrastructure, and governance. Providers maintain the platforms' interface with those using it. Producers provide offerings through the platform, and consumers use those offerings. Complementary innovation by producers and providers is vital to the growth and health of the platform.

Whether as an owner, provider, producer, or consumer, platform innovation and its implications will be an essential consideration for organizational strategy on a continuing basis. We will explore platform innovation strategy in section 11.4.

11.4 Building an innovation strategy

An innovation strategy—akin to a functional strategy—describes the balance of ways, ends, and means for how innovation will contribute to broader organizational outcomes. Innovation strategy should guide the use of resources, time, and attention towards specific modes and intended outcomes from innovating. Further, innovation strategy should describe how to build capacity for innovation for future organizational advantage.

Innovation activity can vary in scale, scope, and approach, with equally variable consequences and potential for the organization. An innovation strategy can clarify the principles and intentions by which different types and foci of innovation are to be pursued. Whilst not guaranteeing success, having a coherent view in the senior team as to how innovation is to be approached increases the likelihood of a range of new ideas being successfully exploited. In this section, we examine three approaches to innovation strategy—blue ocean, **innovation portfolio**, and **platform leadership**—to illustrate different ways in which innovation might feature in organizational strategy.

Blue ocean strategy

A blue ocean strategy describes how an organization might achieve profitable growth by addressing the needs of currently unserved customers through strategic innovation. The term 'blue ocean strategy' was coined by Kim and Mauborgne (2004) as a metaphor for uncontested market space. The blue ocean stands in contrast to the typical 'red ocean' competitive environment (where red is the colour used to denote accounting losses). The concept of blue ocean strategy promises to make the competition 'irrelevant' by identifying and/or creating new markets.

Blue oceans arise when an organization either creates a new industry—such as the Nintendo Wii with family gaming consoles—or redefines the boundaries of an existing industry—such as Uber with the taxi and mini-cab industry. Incumbents and new entrants are equally as capable of being the blue ocean creators, regardless of the extent to which they are succeeding or failing in other endeavours at any given time. Through blue ocean strategy, organizations can draw in non-customers of the traditional industry and achieve fast, profitable growth without having to fight skilled competitors for a share of an existing market. Kim and Mauborgne (2019: 47) suggest that blue ocean strategy is an example of non-disruptive creation that 'taps into the immense potential for creating new markets where none existed before. This is creation without disruption or destruction. All the demand generated by this kind of innovation is new.'

Apply blue ocean

Blue ocean strategic initiatives focus on creating or re-imagining business models. A crucial framework for doing so is the Eliminate–Reduce–Raise–Create (ERRC) grid, shown in Table 11.3.

The ERRC grid breaks the Porterian view of competitive strategy requiring a choice between differentiation or low-cost focus (see Chapter 8). When making blue ocean strategy, using ERRC thinking forces you to consider how to do both simultaneously. New value is created through the provision of features not previously offered, and cost savings often arise from eliminating features or activities important to red ocean competition. As a non-competitive environment in which high growth is achieved, economies of scale quickly deliver further cost savings for the organization.

To illustrate this method, we consider how Cirque du Soleil created untapped market space (see Kim and Mauborgne (2004) for background information about this organization). Table 11.4 shows ERRC applied to the typical profile of organizations in the circus industry before Cirque du Soleil formed. The entries in the table describe how a new customer offering might be created.

TABLE 11.3 **ERRC grid**

Eliminate	Raise
Which of these factors that the industry takes for granted should be eliminated?	Which factors should be raised well above the industry's standard?
Reduce	**Create**
Which factors should be reduced well below the industry's standard?	Which factors should be created that the industry has never offered?

Source: Kim and Mauborgne (2004: 28).

TABLE 11.4 **ERRC applied to Cirque du Soleil**

Eliminate	Raise
Star performers	Unique venue
Animal shows	
Aisle concession sales	
Multiple show arenas	
Reduce	**Create**
Fun and humour	Theme
Thrill and danger	Refined environment
	Multiple productions
	Artistic music and dance

Source: Kim and Mauborgne (2004: 30).

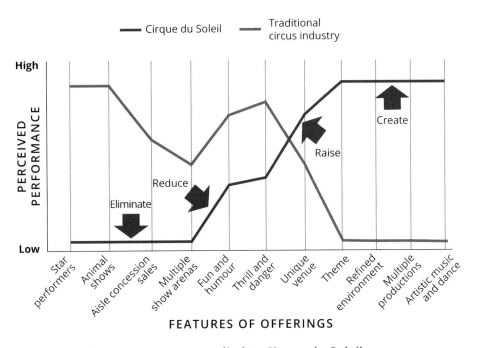

FIGURE 11.3 Blue ocean canvas applied to Cirque du Soleil. *Source*: authors.

The outcomes of completing the ERRC grid can then be transferred onto a blue ocean canvas (see Figure 11.3). The *x*-axis maps the features identified in ERRC against a *y*-axis showing how your organization competes against others in the industry; competitive analysis (Chapter 5) can inform this comparison. Alterations to the profile of your intended performance (known as the value curve) can be used to communicate and plan for the creation of a new offering to meet currently unserved customers.

According to Kim and Mauborgne (2015a), for a blue ocean strategy to be sustainable, it requires three new intertwined propositions to be developed in a coherent way:

- value proposition—provide an offering that attracts customers to pay for it;
- profit proposition—deploy a business model that allows revenues to exceed costs; and
- people proposition—motivate people working for or with the organization to execute it.

An organization might attempt a blue ocean strategy whilst continuing to service its core market through different competitive strategies. (See Case Example 11.1 for an illustration of how the International Olympic Committee is attempting to move into virtual games.) A blue ocean perspective as part of organizational strategy might help an organization break out of myopic thinking and play an active role in shaping industries of the future to its long-lasting benefit.

Innovation portfolio strategy

Pisano (2015) suggests that a lack of innovation strategy aligned with organizational strategic aims is the root cause of the failure of many organizations to benefit fully from innovation activity. In response, an innovation portfolio—comprising a deliberate mix of varying

CASE EXAMPLE 11.1 **TOWARDS THE VIRTUAL OLYMPICS**

In February 2021, the International Olympic Committee (IOC), best known for organizing the Olympic Games, published Olympic Agenda 2020+5, described as the new strategic roadmap of the IOC and the Olympic Movement through to 2025. This roadmap identifies a need for the organization to address a number of strategic concerns: (a) solidarity with athletes in difficult global conditions, (b) the impacts of digitalization on all walks of life, (c) sustainability in operations, (d) a requirement to retain credibility as a relevant force for good in the world, and (e) a need to achieve economic and financial stability.

To meet these challenges, the IOC's roadmap outlines a portfolio of 15 strategic initiatives, including 'Encourage the development of virtual sports and further engage with video gaming communities'. This initiative is intended to enable the IOC to 'leverage the growing popularity of virtual sport to promote the Olympic Movement, Olympic values, sports participation and grow direct relations with youth' (IOC 2021b: 21).

Enacting this initiative, in April 2021, the IOC announced that it would hold the Olympic Virtual Series (OVS), organizing virtual auto-racing, baseball, cycling, rowing, and sailing competitions ahead of the Summer Games in Tokyo 2021. At the launch, IOC President Thomas Bach commented:

The Olympic Virtual Series is a new, unique Olympic digital experience that aims to grow direct engagement with new audiences in the field of virtual sports. Its conception is in line with Olympic Agenda 2020+5 and the IOC's digital strategy. It encourages sports participation and promotes the Olympic values with a special focus on youth.

Whilst popular interest in e-sports is growing rapidly, organized video game competitions have been in existence since a SpaceWars tournament was held at Stanford University in 1972 (British Esports Association 2021). According to Statista.com (Gough 2021), e-sports is expected to grow to $2.89bn market size in 2025 from $0.97bn in 2020, with an expanding reach, scale, and legitimacy with formal institutions; for example, in 2013, the US government began offering sporting visas to e-sports professionals (*The Financial Times* 2021).

Source: Bryan Turner/Unsplash.com.

IOC publications show that their officials have been considering the inclusion of video games in Olympic proceedings at least as far back as 2017, arguably as a way of addressing falling viewing figures and engaging generations of audiences and participants (*The Washington Post* 2021a). The OVS might be considered an experiment testing compatibility of the e-sports format with the IOC's portfolio of Summer and Winter events. For example, to manage reputational risk, the IOC did not consider including the most popular game titles from e-sports competitions such as Dota 2 and Counterstrike: Global Offensive. The IOC also didn't hand out official Olympic medals to OVS winners, despite studies showing that e-sports can have comparable demands—in hours of practice, heartrate, and performance levels—to physical sports equivalents (Wolmarans 2016).

As plans are made to expand the OVS format and competitions, further challenges can be identified. The intellectual property for games held by developers means that the IOC is unable to control e-sports competitions or regulate participants and standards (concerning cheating or doping) to the same extent that it manages physical sports. Gender diversity and harassment also remain an issue in e-sports. To help address these issues, the IOC proposes to 'make available Olympic athlete-related online programmes and digital tools to the competitive video gaming community to support their physical and mental wellbeing'.

There seems to be a desire on behalf of the IOC to build on the OVS and expand its e-sports competitions. Perhaps, as observed by the *Financial*

Times (2021), this is a sign that as 'Esports is in the ascendance, the IOC is beginning to realise that it might need esports more than esports needs the Olympics'.

Questions for discussion

1. What do you think would be the impact on the value, profit, and people propositions of the IOC by launching an e-sports games format at the same level of prestige as the Summer and Winter Olympic Games?

2. Drawing on the concepts from this chapter, what types of innovation can you detect in this strategic initiative from the IOC?

3. Evaluate the importance of innovation in relation to e-sports to the 2020+5 strategic objectives of the IOC—how many of the five strategic concerns will be addressed by this initiative?

Sources

British Esports Association (2021). British Esports aim to promote esports in the UK, increase its level of awareness, improve standards, and inspire future talent, https://britishsports.org (last accessed 19 August 2022).

The Financial Times (2021). The Olympics need esports more than esports need the Olympics, https://www.ft.com/content/dbabdf17-2835-499e-890d-aa19a6b464e2 (last accessed 19 August 2022).

Gough, C. (2021). Esports market—statistics and facts. *Statista* (21 October), https://www.statista.com/topics/3121/esports-market/#dossierKeyfigures (last accessed 19 August 2022).

The Guardian (2021). Win a gold medal from your front room? IOC launches Olympic Virtual Series (27 April), https://www.theguardian.com/sport/2021/apr/22/virtual-olympic-series-launched-ioc-baseball-cycling-rowing (last accessed 19 August 2022).

IOC (2021a). IOC session approves Olympic Agenda 2020+5 as the strategic road map to 2025 (12 March), https://olympics.com/ioc/news/ioc-session-approves-olympic-agenda-2020-5-as-the-strategic-roadmap-to-2025 (last accessed 19 August 2022).

IOC (International Olympic Committee) (2021b) Olympic Agenda 2020+5: 15 recommendations, https://stillmedab.olympic.org/media/Document%20Library/OlympicOrg/IOC/What-We-Do/Olympic-agenda/Olympic-Agenda-2020-5-15-recommendations.pdf (last accessed 19 August 2022).

Palar, S. (2021). The Olympics Virtual Series (22 June). https://olympics.com/en/featured-news/olympic-virtual-series-everything-you-need-to-know (last accessed 19 August 2022).

TheSporting.blog (2021). A brief history of esports and competitive gaming (10 February), https://thesporting.blog/blog/a-brief-history-of-esports-and-competitive-gaming (last accessed 19 August 2022).

The Washington Post (2021a). IOC announces inaugural slate of Olympic-licensed esports events (22 April), https://www.washingtonpost.com/video-games/esports/2021/04/22/ioc-olympics-esports (last accessed 19 August 2022).

The Washington Post (2021b). Tokyo Olympics get a taste of esports, sort of (24 July), https://www.washingtonpost.com/video-games/2021/07/24/tokyo-olympics-esports (last accessed 19 August 2022).

Wolmarans, K. (2016). A German scientific study shows esports professionals are athletes. *Critical Hit Gaming* (16 May), https://www.criticalhit.net/gaming/german-scientific-study-shows-esports-professionals-athletes (last accessed 19 August 2022).

11

types of risk, reward, and resource requirements—might be defined. As shown in Figure 11.4, Pisano suggests that this strategy might create a portfolio across varying degrees of novelty in technical competences (the bodies of knowledge and operating capabilities that reside in the organization) and the business model approach (how the organization creates value for stakeholders).

Pisano's framework identifies four different modes of innovating that strategists might consider. Routine innovation—corresponding to incremental technological innovation—is the most common form of innovating that exploits existing technical competences to reach existing customers in a novel way (e.g. ever more powerful microprocessor chips from Intel). Radical innovation involves introducing new technical competences into the organization in order to serve existing customers in a transformational way (e.g. the introduction

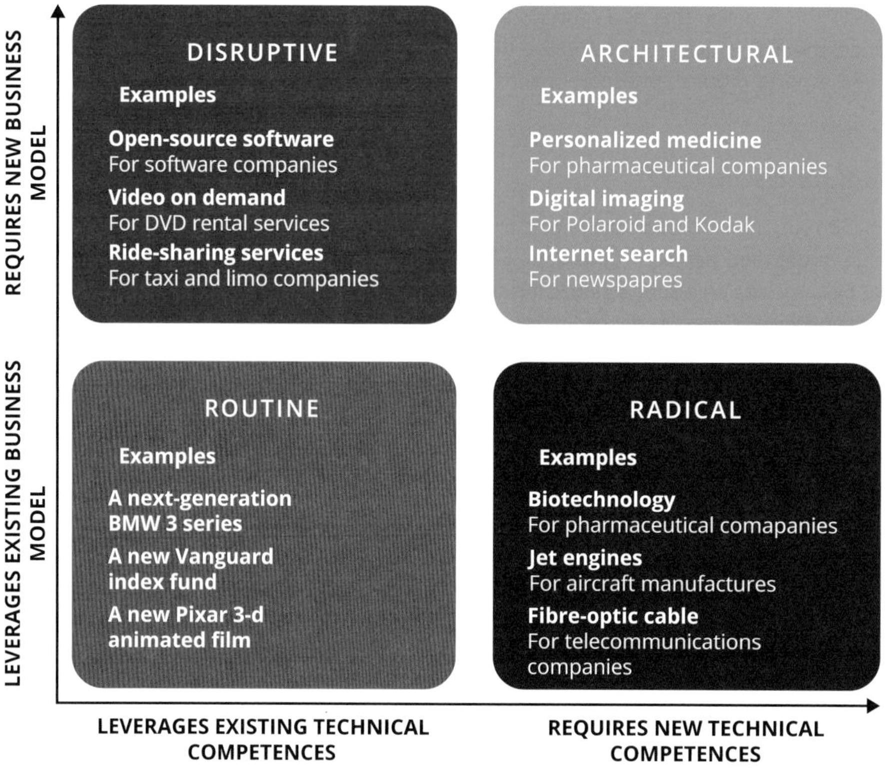

FIGURE 11.4 Innovation portfolio strategy. *Source*: reproduced with permission from Pisano, G. (2015). You need an innovation strategy. *Harvard Business Review*, **93**(6), 44–54. By permission of Harvard Business Publishing.

of enzyme technology to create a new category of biological washing powders by P&G). Disruptive innovation might draw on business model, open, or platform innovations to finding new ways to create value for new and/or existing customers using existing technical competences; for example, releasing Android for free disrupted the marketplace for mobile operating systems and created significant new value for a wide range of stakeholders. Architectural innovation (more comprehensive than technological architectural innovation) is new technical competences and business models reshaping an entire industry; for example, the introduction of the Kindle by Amazon required a new division of the organization to be launched, deployed a new commercial model for book purchase, and reshaped the nature of publishing.

Pisano (2015) challenges strategists to consider the question of 'How much resource should be dedicated to each of these categories?' Routine innovations will be the easiest and least risky projects to instigate. However, a routine approach leaves the organization exposed to radical, disruptive, or architectural changes from competitors. By clarifying how each of the 'portfolio' elements is to be explored, a guiding framework of innovation strategy can be prepared for an organization. The balance of the innovation portfolio can be evaluated using a risk matrix method, such as that proposed by George Day (2007).

Platform strategy

Platform strategy describes how an organization intends to create a new platform or grow an ecosystem in which the organization is embedded. Creation of a new platform involves developing a technology or service that acts as an essential foundation for an ecosystem of organizational activity. Platform ecosystems deliver benefits to all participants through network effects (see Chapter 5)—the more producers and consumers transacting through the platform, the greater the value of the platform to all involved. In platform innovation strategy, scale trumps differentiation as a target outcome (Van Alstyne et al. 2016).

Gawer and Cusumano (2008: 32) describe an action-orientated approach to delivering platform strategy as outlined in Table 11.5. Depending on whether the aim is to create or to grow a platform, an organization should develop a plan which considers how best to address these action points according to their specific context and broader organizational aims.

Platform leaders

When developing a platform strategy, an organization may target the establishment of a platform leadership position.

> *Platform leaders are organizations that successfully establish their product, service, or technology as an industry platform and rise to a position where they can influence the trajectory of the overall technological and business system of which the platform is a core element. When done properly, these firms can also derive an architectural advantage from their relatively central positions.*

> (Gawer and Cusumano 2014: 423)

TABLE 11.5 **Platform strategies**

Strategic option	Technology actions to consider	Business actions to consider
Coring strategy: how to create a new platform where none existed before	Solve an essential 'system' problem Facilitate external companies' provision of add-ons Keep intellectual property closed on the innards of your technology Maintain strong interdependencies between platform and complements	Solve an essential business problem for many industry players Create and preserve complementors' incentives to contribute and innovate Protect your main source of revenue and profit Maintain high switching costs to competing platforms
Tipping strategy: how to win platform wars by building market momentum	Try to develop unique compelling features that are hard to imitate and attract users Tip across markets, absorb and bundle technical features from an adjacent market	Provide more incentives for complementors than your competitors do Rally competitors to form a coalition Consider pricing or subsidy mechanisms that attract users to the platform

Source: Gawer and Cusumano (2008: 32).

This architectural advantage is synonymous with a keystone advantage in an ecosystem, as described in Chapter 5. This may be highly lucrative—an IBM study of 2,148 CEOs from around the world in 2018 found that platform business models were resulting in faster revenue growth and the generation of more profit than other strategies and that up to $1.2 trillion is planned to be invested in platform working by the surveyed firms over the next three years (Berman et al. 2018).

To become an effective platform leader, organizations need to address both the business and technology aspects of platform strategy. Platform leaders need to ensure that their innovation strategy allows them to balance generation of revenue (e.g. from transaction fees or supplying support services) with the ability of other players in the ecosystem to receive sufficient gains so as to stay part of the ecosystem (Gawer and Cusumano 2008). This will involve making decisions about the extent to which platform architecture will be open, allowing all involved access to platform resources (e.g. app developer tools). Further, the extent to which platform governance will be open, allowing non-owners to shape the rules of trade and reward sharing on the platform, also needs to be decided.

Cusumano and Gawer (2002) offer a set of practical advice for those making platform strategy based on research on how Intel sustains a platform leadership position. They list the following lessons from Intel's platform leadership:

- protect the core technology but share interface technology;
- sacrifice short-term interests in favour of the industry's common good;
- do not step carelessly onto partners' turf;
- when pushing the platform in a particular direction, test the waters in a low-key way;
- help complementors protect their intellectual property;
- separate internal groups that produce complements from those that assist complementors;
- leverage internal processes such as senior-management arbitration of conflicting goals; and
- communicate diligently with partners and internal stakeholders.

11.5 Strategic influence of digitalization

Contemporary innovation strategy and innovating activity are closely tied to the concept of digitalization. Incorporating concepts of digital transformation, big data, business intelligence, information, and data analytics, digitalization is a process that is of increasing relevance to organizational strategy.

Digitalization

Digital indicates a virtual electronic format for a platform, service, product, communication, or piece of data. **Digitization**—the process of converting physical or analogue assets into digital form—is occurring in all sectors, governments, and societies around the world (Parviainen et al. 2017). The phenomenon of *digitalization*—harnessing digitization for process improvement, innovation, and new business models—is transforming organizations worldwide at an increasing pace, particularly in this COVID-disrupted era (Amankwah-Amoah et al, 2021). As an example of the pace of change driven by digitalization, in a 2021 McKinsey survey of *c*. 1,140 global executives, 89% of respondents expected their business model to change—or it had changed already—by 2023 as a consequence of digitalization (McKinsey 2021).

Data and digital resources

Digital resources are assets owned or accessed by the organization which support 'virtual' electronic modes of working and creating value. The physical IT infrastructure in an organization, its website, a software product, an online 'bot' responding to customer queries, and a supplier database are all examples of digital resources. Digital resources can be classified according to the digitalization potential offered, for example, efficiencies technologies (e.g. 'cloud technologies'), connectivity technologies (e.g. 5G technologies and IoT), trust disintermediation technologies (e.g. Blockchain), or automation technologies (e.g. big data and artificial intelligence).

Digital resources are fuelled and controlled by data. Within an organization's digital resource base, data refers to discrete pieces of knowledge/things that are known. Data can be structured—organized into an easily searchable indexed form such as a customer relationship management system—or unstructured—such as images of failed components on a service engineer's phone. 'Data was once critical to only a few back-office processes, such as payroll and accounting. Today it is central to any business, and the importance of managing it strategically is only growing' (DalleMule and Davenport 2017: 121). Digital processes create, manipulate, distribute, or store data; for example, a customer making an online purchase of a train ticket will trigger digital processes in the banking system, the rail company, station ticketing operations, the intermediary seller, etc.

Strategic value of data science and *business analytics*

Data is distinct from information, where information is "data endowed with relevance and purpose" (Drucker 1988: 46). Raw data about individual transactions or physical process steps are of limited use until aggregated or combined with other data into an informational format that can aid decision-making. For example, sales figures combined with market trends are far more instructive to those making organizational strategy than individual customer purchase records. Data architecture describes how data is collected, stored, transformed, and deployed in an organization (DalleMule and Davenport 2017). Data architecture is an influential enabler of the extent to which an organization can generate value from its data.

As all manner of human interactions and activities convert to digital processes and systems, organizations can access vast new flows of data (McAfee and Byrnjolfsson 2012). This phenomenon is referred to as big data, which, according to the analytics firm SAS, 'is a term that describes the large volume of data—both structured and unstructured—that inundates a business on a day-to-day basis'. Big data sets are too voluminous, rapidly changing, or varied in format to be processed by conventional linear computational techniques. Instead, **data science** and analytics techniques are required.

Analytics refers to processes that convert big data into meaningful information known as business intelligence. Analytics uses a mix of machine learning, programming, communications, statistics, mathematics, and visualization methods in alignment with the data architecture and strategic objectives of the organization to create powerful insights from big data. Data science holds significant new potential for strategic decision-makers to address wicked problems too complex for conventional computational methods to unlock (Ketter et al. 2016).

Backward-looking descriptive analytics examines historical data to offer business intelligence about events that have happened in the past (e.g. to explore consumer responses to a new product launch). Forward-looking predictive analytics extrapolates from descriptive insights and experimental data to generate business intelligence anticipating what is likely to happen in the future. Descriptive and predictive analytics can form powerful aids to strategic decision-making.

As part of analytics processes, data science is the application of experimental methods and computational systems to generate new insights from big data sets. How an organization engages with digitalization, big data, data science, business intelligence, and the management of its digital resource base should be set out in a digital strategy.

Digital strategy

As introduced in Chapter 9, a digital strategy refers to the coherent set of decision-making principles, investments, and priorities that guide digitalization in line with broader organizational objectives. A digital strategy will address how data and digital technologies can solve customer problems, create new solutions that customers find valuable, and deliver discontinuous operational improvements (Ross 2018a).

If business models are how an organization creates value, digital business models are how they do so through the exploitation of digital technology. Transitioning to a digital business model involves rethinking what is possible and what is required from a customer's point of view, not just replicating the capabilities an organization currently has in a digital format (Anthony 2015).

Ross et al. (2017) suggest that an organization's digital strategy should push it towards either customer engagement or a digitized solution focused on business strategy. A customer engagement digital strategy focuses on customer needs first and foremost. Digital resources are harnessed to offer 'seamless, omnichannel customer experiences, rapid responses to new customer demands, and personalised relationship built upon deep customer insights [. . .] constantly identifying new opportunities to connect with their customers' (Ross et al. 2017: 8). As examined in Chapter 9, Kaiser Permanente, a Californian not-for-profit health-care firm, adopt this approach to facilitate the delivery of its patient-centred care services. Digital resources allow information to flow between patients and all organizations involved in care provision, analytics monitor patient behaviours, and social media engages families in patient care in carefully controlled way.

Alternatively, a digitized solution strategy prioritizes digital product development and the creation of integrated digital customer offerings. This approach delivers support for customers throughout the life cycle of the product, moving away from arms-length transactions to sophisticated offerings that generate recurring revenue in multiple ways. Schindler group, the manufacturer of elevators, escalators, and supporting services, has integrated real-time condition monitoring to reduce maintenance costs and increase the availability of its products to its clients around the world. For Schindler's clients, operating cost is reduced and product availability is enhanced. Alongside gains in revenue from increased customer loyalty, Schindler accumulates valuable product performance data that helps with the design of future products and services.

Digital strategies may differ between different divisions or geographical locations of an organization according to localized needs. Over time, digitized solutions and customer engagement approaches might converge (e.g. Schindler has developed a mobile app to communicate elevator status to facilities managers). Having a sense of the customer or product priorities for digital resource deployment sets an important platform for digital innovation activities.

Digital strategy also addresses the 'building of an operational backbone' in which efficient reliable transactions and processes are assured. This will typically require investment in open infrastructure capable of integrating new technologies, enterprise-wide capabilities and systems for customer and operation management, and a clear **data strategy**. The use of digital resources to improve operating efficiency is fast becoming a threshold capability within many industries (Ross et al. 2017). Without a digitalized operating approach, an organization may be unable to compete with others that have digitally transformed their organizations.

Bonnet and Westerman (2021: 85) propose a model of digital capabilities that can be developed over time as part of digital strategy work to create new sources of long-term value creation, operational efficiency, and renewal. As shown in Figure 11.5, business model outcomes can be achieved through re-imagining customer experience, operations design, and employee experience on a digital platform. This performance potential requires a digital strategy that leads to coherent investment over time, effective digital leadership to drive transformation, and a new approach to working with data in the organization.

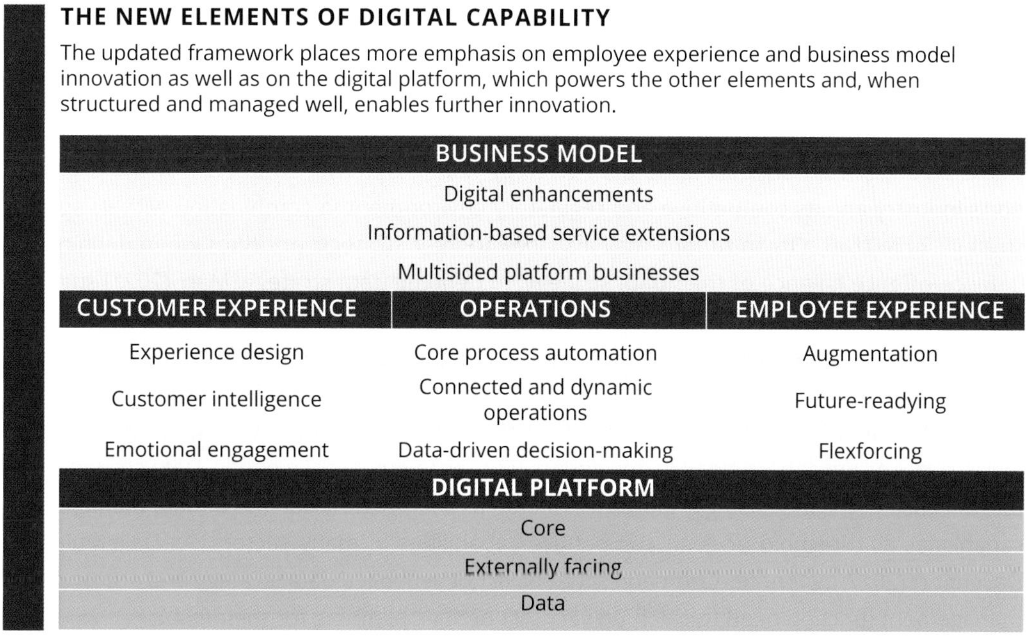

THE NEW ELEMENTS OF DIGITAL CAPABILITY

The updated framework places more emphasis on employee experience and business model innovation as well as on the digital platform, which powers the other elements and, when structured and managed well, enables further innovation.

BUSINESS MODEL		
Digital enhancements		
Information-based service extensions		
Multisided platform businesses		
CUSTOMER EXPERIENCE	**OPERATIONS**	**EMPLOYEE EXPERIENCE**
Experience design	Core process automation	Augmentation
Customer intelligence	Connected and dynamic operations	Future-readying
Emotional engagement	Data-driven decision-making	Flexforcing
DIGITAL PLATFORM		
Core		
Externally facing		
Data		

FIGURE 11.5 Bonnet and Westerman's (2021:85) model of digital capabilities.
Source: Bonnet, D. and Westerman, G. (2021). The new elements of digital transformation. *MIT Sloan Management Review*, **62**(2), 83–89.

Data strategy

It is common practice now for data to be treated as a class of economic asset akin to oil and gold, where 'an abundance of data is a valuable asset; a dearth of data is increasingly seen as a damning liability' (Farboodi 2018). Yet, cross-industry studies show that:

> on average, less than half of an organization's structured data is actively used in decision making—and less than 1% of its unstructured data is analysed or used at all. More than 70% of employees have access to data they should not, and 80% of analysts' time is spent simply discovering and preparing data. Data breaches are common, rogue data sets propagate in silos, and companies' data technology often isn't up to the demands put on it.

(DalleMule and Davenport 2017: 114)

As a component of digital strategy, a data strategy sets out the objectives, core activities, and orientation for how data—as a valuable strategic resource—is to be managed in an organization. DalleMule and Davenport (2017) identify two principal modes of strategically managing data—adopting a defensive orientation focused on data control or an offensive orientation targeting flexibility and creativity.

A defensive orientation deploys data management policies that ensure security and privacy, maintain compliance with regulations, and ensure that governance standards, data integrity, and quality are maintained. This approach places a premium on optimizing data extraction, standardization, storage and access activities, and building a single source of truth (SSOT) data set.

An offensive orientation seeks to use data to improve competitive position, revenue generation, and profitability, prioritizing flexibility of use over security. This approach emphasizes activities that optimize data analytics, modelling, prediction, visualization, and business intelligence as data-related outcomes. An offensive approach encourages multiple versions of the truth (MVOT) data sets to be created in the organization (where data sets are customized and mined for local applications).

The balance of an organization's data strategy will be determined in part by the organization's industry and its competitive and regulatory environment in combination with its specific strategic objectives. Organizations may also look to their strategic priorities when defining the defence/offence balance of their data strategy. In defining data strategy, Marr (2021) suggests that organizations start with considering three to five 'use cases'—possible applications of big data analytics that will yield new value for them if implemented—to better understand which orientation to adopt.

Data strategy will ensure that the needs of the organization are understood and systems, infrastructure, and capabilities are developed in order to meet those needs. Data strategy matters because of the increasing importance of data as a strategic asset and of data management capabilities as threshold or even competitive capabilities in many sectors. As DalleMule and Davenport (2017: 121) note: 'Companies that have not yet built a data strategy and a strong data management function need to catch up very fast or start planning for their exit.'

Further, there is increasing interest in how data can inform organizational strategy effectively through big data strategy initiatives to create actionable intelligence that feeds into strategic decision-making processes.

Digital transformation

Digitalization, strategy, and innovation concepts coincide in the concept of digital transformation. We define digital transformation as a step change in how an individual, organization, institution, or system operates enabled by digital technologies. Through this definition, digital transformation can be understood as a multilevel phenomenon. As a macro-level process of technological disruption, digital transformation of how we live and work is synonymous with the mega-trend of digitalization. At an organizational level, digital transformation might be considered a long-term process of change, where digital technologies are a core, every-day part of organizational life. And at a micro-level, a 'digital transformation' is a label that can be applied to projects or initiatives that use digital technology to change some aspect of an organization's processes.

As digitalization increasingly acts as a driving force in creative destruction across sectors and society, digital transformation might reasonably be assumed to be an inevitable part of the strategic plans of most organizations (Loonam et al. 2018), or even nations. (See Case Example 11.2 for an exploration of how digital transformation is occurring in Singapore.) As a strategic imperative, digital transformation can be viewed as the application of bundles of digital technologies to change the way the organizations operate, particularly around customer interactions, in the creation of new stakeholder value and in accordance with organizational objectives (Libert et al. 2016). However, an early study by McKinsey in 2016 found that only 16% of companies had embraced or prepared for digital transformation (Bughin and Catlin 2017: 2). A subsequent McKinsey (2021) survey noted that companies successfully engaging in digital transformation made more extensive investments in technology and in people capabilities—at all levels of the organization—than those struggling to find new ways of working with digital technologies.

Westerman et al. (2019) introduce the concept of digital maturity to explain why pace of digital transformation can vary between organizations. Figure 11.6 represents digital maturity as a combination of digital intensity—the level of investment in technology-enabled initiatives—and transformation management intensity—the level of investment in leadership capabilities for digital transformation. Palmié et al. (2016) note that, from an attention-based view, what organizations do in relation to digital transformation will be determined by how decision-makers direct attention to digitalization and digital strategy. This matters, as, according to the research by Westerman et al. (2014), 'digirati' organizations are already outperforming competitors in

11

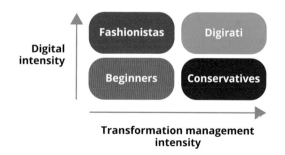

FIGURE 11.6 Model of digital maturity. *Source*: Westerman, G., Soule, D.L., and Eswaran, A. (2019). Building digital-ready culture in traditional organizations. *MIT Sloan Management Review*, May, https://sloanreview.mit.edu/article/building-digital-ready-culture-in-traditional-organizations (last accessed 21 July 2019).

CASE EXAMPLE 11.2 TRANSFORMING PUBLIC SERVICES IN SINGAPORE

Since the early 1980s, digital adoption and transformation at a national level has been an established priority for the Singaporean government. Achieving digital government outcomes has been a key part of this approach. On 5 March 2019, the government issued an update on its efforts to keep the public services relevant and agile in times of change. The update acknowledged the fact that Singapore's public services face a number of challenges such as 'an ageing population and shrinking workforce, fiscal constraints, rising citizenship expectations, and technological disruption'.

The update outlined four areas in which the government intended to focus on digital transformation efforts to the benefit of all stakeholders:

Improving service delivery: We will redesign services involving many agencies to be more customer-centric. One example is the Moments of Life project, which resulted in a digital application launched in June 2018. Citizens now have seamless interactions with the Public Service during key life moments, starting with families with young children.

Building a Digital Government as part of Singapore's vision to be a Smart Nation: We will better use data and new technologies and drive broader efforts to build a digital economy and digital society. The Digital Government Blueprint outlines how the Government will reorganise itself to deliver public services better through the use of technology.

Working with citizens closely: We will create more opportunities to partner with citizens, businesses and non-government organizations to improve our policy-making. For example, in 2017 the Ministry of Health organised a Citizens' Jury for the War on Diabetes, mobilising citizens to discuss and make recommendations on how to better manage and prevent diabetes as a nation.

Preparing every officer for the future: Every public officer will learn and reskill in how to adapt to changes. Every officer will pursue innovation and be open to new ways of working. The Civil Service College has launched LEARN, a mobile platform to enable officers to learn anytime, anywhere.

This long-term prioritization of digital transformation at a national level recently yielded additional benefits. The digital infrastructure, skills, and processes developed across the public and private sectors over many years significantly underpinned the

Who does a
Digital Government serve?

▸ Citizens
▸ Businesses
▸ Public Officers

What are the elements of
a Digital Government?

▸ Services that are easy to use, reliable and relevant
▸ Seamless digital transactions
▸ Systems and data that are secure
▸ A digitally confident public service workforce
▸ A digitally enabled public service workplace

How do we become
a Digital Government?

▸ Strengthening integration between policy, operations and technology
▸ Re-engineering the Government's ICT infrastructure
▸ Operating reliable, resilient and secure systems
▸ Raising our digital capabilities to pursue innovation
▸ Integrating services around citizen and business needs
▸ Co-creating with citizens and businesses, and facilitating adoption of technology

Source: GovTech Singapore (2020). Digital Government Blueprint, https://www.tech.gov.sg/digital-government-blueprint (last accessed 19 August 2022).

'circuit-breaker' measures enacted to contain the spread of COVID-19 (Lee, 2020). This was supplemented with government aid directed specifically to support businesses in digital initiatives to cope with pandemic-related challenges (Yu 2020). And high standards of digital infrastructure and capability continue to define Singapore as an attractive location for businesses.

In transforming Singaporean public services and influencing industries, a structured innovation process has been used that is inclusive, data-driven, and intended to shape future-proof outcomes (see Figure 11.7). By involving stakeholders widely (including citizens, business, and public officers), general digital capabilities have been raised and the national system as a whole has been transformed.

Digital Government is now an integral component of the national strategy for Singapore. Combining excellent national infrastructure and citizen capabilities, Digital Government is intended to set the global standard for government–citizen relations and enable smart nation development.

As outlined in the Digital Government Blueprint, the Singapore Government (Singapore Government 2020) intends to build on the foundations of previous national strategies. By 2023, the government intends to run 30–50 transformative digital projects that train all public officers in digital practice; exploit big data analytics and artificial intelligence; deliver 100% of government processes, transactions, and payments in a digital form; and drive high stakeholder satisfaction across citizens, businesses, and public life.

As 65% of global gross domestic product (GDP) is expected to be digitized by the end of 2022, and spending on digital transformation is anticipated to reach $6.8 trillion by 2023 (World Economic Forum 2021), the intensity of digital investment, development, and adoption in Singapore seems set only to increase.

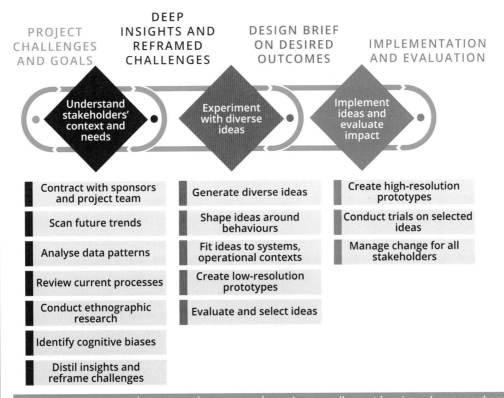

FIGURE 11.7 Public-sector innovation process deployed in Singapore. *Source*:

Innovation Lab, Public Sector Transformation Group, Public Service Division, Prime Minister's Office, Singapore.

Continued

Questions for discussion

1. With such strong existing national infrastructure, why does Singapore's national strategy urge public-sector transformation and the building of further digital and economic capabilities?

2. Critique the 'public sector innovation process' shown in Figure 11.7—how effective do you think it will be in supporting the Digital Government priorities of Singapore? Draw on any relevant insights from the whole of this chapter in explaining your answer.

3. What are the main challenges that you believe the Singapore Government will have to address as it progresses on its digital transformation journey over the next 5–10 years?

Sources

Centre for Public Impact (2016). Building a digital government in Singapore (12 April), https://www.centreforpublicimpact.org/case-study/building-digital-government-singapore (last accessed 19 August 2022).

GovTech Singapore (2020). Digital Government Blueprint, https://www.tech.gov.sg/digital-government-blueprint (last accessed 19 August 2022).

Lee, A. (2020). How COVID-19 spurred Singapore's digital transformation. *The Business Times* (13 July), https://www.businesstimes.com.sg/technology/how-covid-19-spurred-singapores-digital-transformation (last accessed 19 August 2022).

Singapore Government (2020). Digital Government Blueprint, https://www.smartnation.gov.sg/files/publications/dgb-public-document_30dec20.pdf (last accessed 19 August 2022).

World Economic Forum (2021). Bridging digital and environmental goals: A framework for business action (March), https://www3.weforum.org/docs/WEF_Bridging_Digital_and_Environmental_Goals_2021.pdf (last accessed 19 August 2022).

Yu, E. (2020). Singapore puts $352m focus on digital transformation to help firms cope with pandemic fallout. *ZDNet* (26 May), https://www.zdnet.com/article/singapore-puts-352m-focus-on-digital-transformation-to-help-firms-cope-with-pandemic-fallout/ (last accessed 19 August 2022).

all sectors, and organizations not building towards digital maturity risk being left behind. They suggest that it takes several years to build maturity and that it is transformation management capabilities that are constraining digital maturity more than digital intensity. Their advice is that digital transformation—with a focus on developing the required leadership capabilities—should be a prominent feature on any organization's strategic agenda.

Westerman et al.'s model is consistent with further findings from the field. Reflecting on a digital transformation process at a health-care provider (Carestream), Smith and Watson (2019: 96) observe that digital transformation is more of an organizational change process than a technical shift. For strategists, a crucial insight is that digital transformation requires organizational innovation capabilities and informed leadership to enable a fundamental rethink of processes, systems, capabilities, and ways of working (Parviainen et al. 2017; Svahn et al. 2017).

With digital transformation, there is a need to manage transformation tensions across organizational levels (Eden at al. 2019), and the limitations of **innovation culture** and organizational capabilities must be considered alongside technical concerns. For those involved in organizational strategy, the digital transformation imperative offers further justification for an investment in organizational innovation capability. It is important to note that, in keeping with a process–practice perspective, this transformation can occur through a process of discovery and strategic capability building over time rather than through a one-off, discontinuous change effort (McGrath and McManus 2020).

Access the online resources to watch a short video clip where Ned Phillips discusses digital transformation.

11.6 **Where next? Digital strategy challenges**

Despite widespread recognition of the need to adopt digital operating and business models (McKinsey 2021), between 66 and 84% of digital transformation efforts fail to deliver the desired results (Libert et al. 2016: 2). Digital innovation and transformation are fraught with challenges as legacy cultures and operating models struggle to accommodate new digital technologies and ways of working. Digital strategy needs to address a number of challenging factors including but not limited to human resource issues, increased operational complexity, limitations of maturity, cybersecurity, sustainability impacts, and remaining relevant.

Human resource challenges

The biggest employee concern raised by digitalization is a near-universal demand for **digital dexterity**—a set of beliefs, mindsets, and behaviours that help employees deliver faster and more valuable outcomes from digital initiatives (Gartner 2018). To maintain commitment from employees anxious about being left behind, digital strategy will need to allocate resources towards upskilling employees, modernizing work practices, and remaining inclusive in work design (Roth and Keller 2019).

More generally, digital transformation is often accompanied by workforce stress, fatigue, and the need to continually respond to unexpected events. Strategic investment is required to build a strong innovation culture foundation that enables the workforce to cope with the demands of digital transformation (Eden et al. 2019: 14). This approach to building digital skills should also preserve valuable components of traditional culture and seek to maintain the morale, integrity, and values of the organization (Westerman et al. 2019).

Organizational investment is also required in sourcing and nurturing skilled employees who are able to act as data translators—sufficiently skilled in data science, data analytics, and business intelligence but also with business management credentials that give them legitimacy in discussions with organizational leaders (Brady et al. 2017).

A further human resource challenge is the fatigue associated with customer expectations for constant connectivity and service. Siggelkow and Terwiesch (2019) report that continuous connectivity will quickly become the new normal to the extent that organizations should develop a **connected strategy**. For employees of organizations that remain under cost pressure, this may mean less downtime and increased demands to remain connected to work themselves.

Blended approaches and increased complexity

The rise of business intelligence has led to the rise of **data hubris**—'the often-implicit assumption that big data are a substitute for, rather than a supplement to, traditional data collection and analysis' (Lazer et al. 2014). Digital and data strategies must seek to balance the use of analytics and first-hand observations in a complementary way to form strategic decisions (Brady et al. 2017).

More generally, Vermeulen (2017) and Svahn et al. (2017) suggest that digitalization outputs will tend to supplement existing ways of working rather than replace them (except where there is direct substitution such as budget airlines using online booking portals only). This means that digital transformation may increase customer choice and business model complexity for an organization, for example, desktop computing existing alongside cloud computing for a company like Microsoft or online service capacity for a local council existing in parallel with a service desk at a council building.

The main counter to this view is the emergence of **cognitive technologies**—artificial intelligence and technological processes by which machines learn to embody the skills, knowledge, and capabilities that are performed in a cognate way by humans (Davenport and Mahidhar 2018). Very few organizations have a **cognitive strategy** (a plan to capitalize on or mitigate the possibilities of cognitive technologies), leaving themselves vulnerable to competitor activities in this technological space.

Need to start simply and build carefully

As a digitalization gap grows between organizations and their competitors, it is tempting to propose a radical digital **innovation strategy**. But digital transformation can't be rushed (Ross 2018b). Stephen Andriole (2017), former director of the Cybernetics Technology Office of the US Defense Advanced Research Projects Agency (DARPA), comments that many organizations lack the systems maturity and process knowledge to be able to transform digitally and that to attempt to do so would be ruinous to the organization. According to Andriole, digital transformation requires in-depth knowledge of current business processes in order to successfully model and enhance them in a digital format, which will typically employ conventional 'known' technology with proven capabilities. McGrath and McManus (2020) describe this as a discovery-driven process of digital transformation—always progressing but at a pace that ensures results are achieved in a sustainable way. Staying realistic but persevering with digital aspirations will be a key challenge for digital strategists. As Jeanne Ross, principal research scientist for MIT's Center for Information Systems Research, notes, 'digital is about speed, but it takes time' (Ross 2018b).

Cybersecurity

Cybersecurity is the preservation of the security of digital systems in the face of cybercrime. According to CyberSecurity Ventures, annual global cybercrime rose to $6 trillion in 2021. As digitalization unfolds, there is an increasing need to ensure the security of transactions, relationships, and systems. This is not just a technical challenge—where human interaction occurs, digital systems are vulnerable to scams such as phishing (Gartner 2018). Thus, investment in digital transformation brings with it a parallel obligation to invest in cybersecurity as part of the risk management obligations of any organization operating in a digital manner.

Environmental challenges

It is recognized that digitalization has the potential to deliver environmental benefits by displacing activities with a high carbon footprint and creating sustainable organizational practices (Unruh and Kiron 2019). For example, through secure video conferencing, an organization might reduce the degree of international travel undertaken by employees. However, digital transformation isn't guaranteed to deliver such effects. For example, the use of technologies such as cryptocurrency consume high levels of electricity—the BBC report that in 2021, global mining for Bitcoin used more electricity than the nation state of Argentina (Criddle 2021). Further, changes in consumer behaviour such as the increase in online retail is anticipated to have driven up to 36% more urban traffic from delivery vehicles (World Economic Forum 2021).

For strategists, achieving balance in sustainability and digitalization outcomes will increasingly demand attention and have consequences for the long-term performance of their organization. A report by Accenture (2021) suggests that companies able to drive digital transformation whilst improving sustainability outcomes will be 2.5 times more likely to be among tomorrow's strongest-performing businesses than others.

Remaining relevant

Ever-increasing digitalization and digital transformation organizational activity is creating permanent VUCA conditions in many sectors (Millar et al. 2018). As new waves of digital technology from fields such as artificial intelligence, machine learning, the Internet of Things, block chain, and autonomous vehicles progress towards mainstream adoption, a constant need for digital innovation will be required in order to remain relevant as an organization (Schoemaker et al. 2018).

For example, banking and financial services sectors around the world are being disrupted by fintech—digital financial technologies that deliver operational improvements, innovation, and new sources of customer value. The rise of fintech has created a situation where 'banks may freeze, fight, form alliances with challengers, or be forced into flight by the Big Tech companies' (Ashta and Biot-Pacquerot 2018: 301). Equally, regulators are faced with a continual challenge to renew legislation in the face of the digital transformation of the banking and finance sector.

For organizations, sectors, or even nations, embracing digitalization and digital transformation in a strategic way now seems an imperative for surviving and thriving in a digitally disrupted context.

11

PRACTITIONER INSIGHT **NED PHILLIPS, FOUNDER AND CEO, BAMBU**

Founded in March 2016, Bambu is a Singapore-headquartered financial technology (Fintech) company. Clients turn to Bambu for their digital innovation capability, financial technology expertise, and process knowledge of how to digitalize and digitally transform to create high-quality digital customer experiences.

Six years into its journey, Bambu has hired over 70 people, raised $5 million in funding, with $10 million more in the pipeline, and built a portfolio of 16 global financial institution clients including HSBC,

Standard Chartered, CIMB, and Franklin Templeton. Growing rapidly, Bambu now has offices in San Francisco, London, Kuala Lumpur, Hong Kong, and Jakarta, in addition to the head office in Singapore.

Bambu has already won seven awards, including the best Singapore start-up, best Hong Kong start-up,

Continued

and best Asian start-up, and has also reached the final of Alibaba's tech search.

Founder and CEO Ned Phillips shares his views on digitalization, disruption, growth, and innovation in banking and finance.

Digital-led creative destruction

Ten years ago, if you'd told a bank you have to have internet banking, they would have said 'Well, maybe.' But today, it's impossible to be a bank without internet banking. The same with e-payments in many countries. For example, in China, if you don't have an Ali-wallet or a TenCent wallet, you can't operate. And I think that in 10 years' time, the idea that your savings and investment are not digital will be crazy. People will marvel that it used to be normal to meet a financial advisor and have paperwork or multiple savings and investment accounts rather than an integrated digital portfolio. For financial institutions, FOMO—fear of missing out—is a significant driver of adoption of digital technologies as the sector evolves.

Big bang disruption and digital transformation

Banks are petrified that private wealth management and savings and investment will go to the likes of Amazon, Apple, Facebook, Alibaba—all of these e-commerce, e-wallet apps to which people are moving their wealth. And I think all financial institutions are trying to digitize, not because they think it will increase margin but because they realize customers want digital and if they don't react rapidly, they could lose out in a big way.

Responding to threats from big tech firms, financial institutions are asking 'What is the best and quickest way in which to digitally transform?' Quite often it is not building an in-house team but using external experts like us, accessing our technology platform and know-how. We can deliver a fully working digital solution in six months that would take a client two years to build themselves. Equally, companies like Apple represent a huge opportunity for banks as tech companies don't really want to manage money—they want to partner with financial institutions. The entrance of big tech companies is only a threat to financial institutions that don't think about it and don't partner up. The Apple credit card launch in partnership with Goldman's is an example of mutually beneficial partnering.

In our industry, I think that step-by-step digital transformation doesn't work as you will not even be changing at the speed of the environment. To digitally transform means building capability to radically alter what you are doing. Step-by-step for me is actually digital improvement—upgrading not transforming. If that's what you want, fine. But if you want to transform, you need to go for the home run.

On innovation culture

It is super-hard for a large corporate that is not a tech company to be disruptive or transform on their own as financial incentives and job security mean that employees don't want to get fired, and the easiest way not to get fired is not to do anything crazy or bold. That is why our sector lacked a disruptive presence until a few years ago—finance is a very well paid and conservative industry. People were tending to innovate just enough not to get fired. It was the work environment/culture that stifled innovation—if we go to a large bank, there are lots of people in there capable of being disruptive, clever people with good ideas. We operate in a different way—we also have clever people, but we remove negative outcomes for attempting to be innovative and disruptive and our physical space encourages great teamworking to achieve breakthroughs.

On strategy

I like the idea of strategy as process, influencing flow to build momentum. As the market is changing so quickly, if we take daily decisions to preserve our momentum, that is more valuable than any fixed plan. We formed this view from hard experience. Trying to work out what our long-term strategy should be, each time we tried we got it wrong. So we stopped and we just said, 'When opportunities come let's analyse them in real time and decide if we should pursue them. Yes or no.' For example, after setting up international offices in different ways, we realized, 'We've got a global operation now!' It is the planned way in reverse—we didn't try to build a global structure; it just happened as a result of our day-to-day decisions. It works for us, and we are going to keep growing like that.

Access the online resources to watch a short video clip where Ned Phillips talks more about his career.

CHAPTER SUMMARY

In this chapter, we addressed the following learning outcomes:

○ **Evaluate the relevance and usefulness of innovation to organizational strategy.**
Innovation—the successful exploitation of new ideas—is a process by which novelty is realized as a product of creativity and execution capabilities. As **creative destruction** and disruption incessantly replace old with new ways of working in an industry, innovation provides a mechanism through which organizations can keep pace with or instigate change in their operating environment. Innovation might enable lower operating costs, the creation of new customer value, and even new markets. Innovation is a crucial mechanism of renewal that all organizations need to consider as a routine aspect of their strategy work.

○ **Explain how different types of innovation might influence organizational strategy.**
Different types of innovation initiative offer different potential contributions that might be considered as part of organizational strategy. Technological innovations offer the potential to create or adapt products, services, operational processes, and infrastructure. Organizational innovations can alter how organizations are structured and managed. Open innovation enhances how knowledge-flows between the resource base and network of an organization can be used to create new value. Strategic innovation finds new ways for the organization to create value and platform innovation enables an organization to compete based on powerful network effects.

○ **Explain how an organization can build strategically valuable innovation capabilities and assess the merits of different ways of developing an innovation strategy.**
Organizational innovation capability describes the potential of an organization to successfully exploit new ideas. Innovation process capability can be nurtured by involving a relevant mix of people, setting effective parameters for activities, and creating a supportive environment according to the needs of the innovation. Innovation culture refers to the way innovation tends to be perceived and enacted in an organization. Innovation culture can be shaped by ensuring that resources, processes, values, behaviour, climate, and success are all invested in or managed according to organizational needs. Over time, organizational strategy might prioritize investment in addressing innovation capability gaps that build the capacity for innovation as a strategic resource. Technical competence (the bodies of knowledge and operating capabilities in an organization) and the business model (how the organization creates value for stakeholders) are two key strategic dimensions that can be used to understand innovation strategy. Without changing the business model, an organization can use existing technical competences for routine innovation or add new technical competence for radical innovation. With existing technical competences, changing the business model leads to disruptive innovation. Changing the business model whilst adding new technical competence is described as architectural innovation. The strategic value of each approach differs, as does the risk–reward profile. The challenge for the strategist is to instigate a portfolio of innovation approaches that matches the risk profile and broader ambitions of the organization.

11

○ Critically evaluate how digital transformation, digitalization, and data strategy might drive innovation in an organization.

Digitalization is the process of exploiting digital formats and technologies for operational improvement or new value creation. Digitalization is transforming how industries and sectors operate and serve customers around the world. Harnessing the potential of digitalization and data for innovation, transformation, and performance is a complex and challenging task which requires **strategic learning**, leadership, and vision if success is to be a possibility. Digital transformation refers to a step change in how an individual, organization, institution, or system operates enabled by digital technologies. Digital transformation can be a gradual process that is as much an organizational cultural change as it is a technical initiative. Forces of creative destruction suggest that non-participation in the digital revolution is not an option.

? END-OF-CHAPTER QUESTIONS

Recall questions

1. Describe innovation from a process–practice perspective. What are the key activities and how do they interface?

2. Explain why innovation might be considered a topic of high strategic importance to an organization, given the ongoing phenomena of creative destruction and disruption.

3. Describe what is meant by innovation culture and explain how it might influence organizational strategy.

4. Describe five different types of innovation and explain what potential each offers to those making strategy.

5. Define platform leadership and explain how it might be achieved through platform innovation strategy approaches.

6. Describe how digitalization is both a strategic threat and an opportunity for organizations.

Application questions

A) Pick an organization you know well and for which you can access product innovation launch data. Evaluate their product innovation successes and failures of the past 5–10 years. Use the innovation portfolio tool to map their approach and explain performance outcomes, and explain their attempted innovation portfolio with reference to their organizational strategy.

B) Apply the blue ocean method to an organization you are familiar with to identify possible uncontested market space. Take notes on how easy or not it is to deploy blue ocean thinking as you go. Reflecting on your experience, write a short critique of the possibilities and limitations of blue ocean strategy that you could use to advise a strategist considering using the method.

C) Deploy the **data strategy orientation** method to identify the required approach for three organizations—an environmental charity, an online retailer, and a government driving licence agency. Compare your findings, looking for common challenges and points of difference. What does your effort tell you about how data strategy should be made and managed in organizations?

ONLINE RESOURCES

www.oup.com/he/mackay2e

In addition to the video interviews already highlighted, the book's online resources include the following features for this chapter, specifically:

- *links to further reading material* to broaden your knowledge of key issues discussed in this chapter;
- *self-test multiple-choice questions* to test your understanding of the material covered in each section of the chapter; and
- *a flashcard glossary* to help you recall and test your understanding of key terms.

FURTHER READING

The Innovator's Dilemma: When New Technologies Cause Great Firms to Fail by Clay Christensen

Christensen, C. (2016). *The Innovator's Dilemma: When New Technologies Cause Great Firms to Fail*. Boston, MA: Harvard Business Review Press.

This latest edition of a seminal text by Clay Christensen examines the concepts of disruptive technology and innovation and proposes an up-to-date version of disruptive innovation theory. Not without its critics, this book provides many examples and a popular take on how disruption is both a problematic and potentially highly valuable feature of organizational strategy.

Blue Ocean Strategy, Expanded Edition: How to Create Uncontested Market Space and Make the Competition Irrelevant by W. Chan Kim and Renée Mauborgne

Chan Kim, W. and Mauborgne, R. (2015). *Blue Ocean Strategy, Expanded Edition: How to Create Uncontested Market Space and Make the Competition Irrelevant.* Boston, MA: Harvard Business Review Press.

This updated version of a famous business text explores how new sources of creation can drive business performance. Explaining in depth the value of exploring new ways to lower operating costs whilst pursuing differentiation, the authors provide many examples from their consulting work for students wishing to know how to apply blue ocean strategy in practice.

Big Data and Analytics by Bernard Marr

Bernard Marr & Co., https://bernardmarr.com/big-data-analytics (last accessed 19 August 2022).
Bernard Marr is a futurologist and strategist who writes extensively about the unfolding interface between business practice and technology. In his videos and content around data, analytics and business

performance, he explains the increasingly crucial role of data in driving value for organizations, and the need for data strategies. His website addresses further topics—with examples and practice guides—in relation to technology, strategy, and the future of business practice.

Value Proposition Design: How to Create Products and Services Customers Want by Alex Osterwalder, Yves Pigneur, Greg Bernarda, and Alan Smith

Osterwalder, A., Pigneur, Y., Bernarda, G., and Smith, A. (2014). *Value Proposition Design: How to Create Products and Services Customers Want*. Hoboken, NJ: John Wiley.
This book develops thinking about how the business model canvas and related ideas might be applied in organizational innovation and strategy. The business model canvas is extremely popular because of its simplicity and ease of use. Familiarizing yourself with how to lead a value proposition design session creates a useful employability skill that blends innovation, strategy, and business model capabilities.

REFERENCES

Accenture (2021). The European double-up (22 January), https://www.accenture.com/ch-en/insights/strategy/european-double-up (last accessed 1 November 2021).

Amankwah-Amoah, J., Khan, Z., Wood, G., and Knight, G. (2021). COVID-19 and digitalization: The great acceleration. *Journal of Business Research*, **136**, 602–11.

Amit, R. and Zott, C. (2012). Creating value through business model innovation. *MIT Sloan Management Review*, **53**(3), 41–9.

Andriole, S.J. (2017). Five myths about digital transformation. *MIT Sloan Management Review*, **58**(3), 20–2.

Anthony, S. (2015). How understanding disruption helps strategists. *Harvard Business Review Digital Articles*, 2–4, https://hbr.org/2015/11/how-understanding-disruption-helps-strategists (last accessed 22 October 2022).

Ashta, A. and Biot-Pacquerot, G. (2018). Fintech evolution: Strategic value management issues in a fast changing industry. *Strategic Change*, **27**(4), 301–11.

Bayley, N. (2019). Harnessing the power of disruption. *Rotman Management Magazine* (January), 112–14.

Bennett, D. (2019). They're coming for your eyeballs. *Bloomberg Businessweek European Edition* (13 May), 38–45.

Berman, S., Davidson, S., Ikeda, K., and Marshall, A. (2018). Navigating disruption with ecosystems, partners, and platforms. *Strategy & Leadership*, **46**(5), 26–35.

Bettis, R.A. and Hitt, M.A. (1995). The new competitive landscape. *Strategic Management Journal*, **16**, 7–19.

Bonnet, D., and Westerman, G. (2021). The new elements of digital transformation. *MIT Sloan Management Review*, **62**(2), 83–9.

Brady, C., Forde, M., and Chadwick, S. (2017). Why your company needs data translators. *MIT Sloan Management Review*, **58**(2), 14–16.

Brandenburger, A. and Nalebuff, B. (1996). *Coopetition*. New York: Doubleday Business.

British Esports Association (2021). British Esports aim to promote esports in the UK, increase its level of awareness, improve standards, and inspire future talent, https://britishesports.org (last accessed 19 August 2022).

Bughin, J. and Catlin, T. (2017). What successful digital transformations have in common. *Harvard Business Review Digital Articles*, 1–5, https://hbr.org/2017/12/what-successful-digital-transformations-have-in-common (last accessed 22 October 2022).

11

Burgelman, R.A. and Doz, Y.L. (2001). The power of strategic integration. *MIT Sloan Management Review*, **42**(3), 28–38.

Centre for Public Impact (2016). Building a digital government in Singapore (12 April), https://www.centreforpublicimpact.org/case-study/building-digital-government-singapore (last accessed 19 August 2022).

Charitou, C.D. and Markides, C.C. (2003). Responses to disruptive strategic innovation. *MIT Sloan Management Review*, **44**(2), 55–63.

Chesbrough, H. (2008). Open innovation: A new paradigm for understanding industrial innovation. In: Chesbrough, H.W., Vanhaverbeke, W., and West, J. (eds), *Open Innovation: Researching a New Paradigm*. Oxford: Oxford University Press, pp. 1–12.

Chesbrough, H. (2011). Bringing open innovation to services. *MIT Sloan Management Review*, **52**(2), 87.

Chesbrough, H.W., and Appleyard, M.M. (2007). Open innovation and strategy. *California Management Review*, **50**(1), 57–76.

Christensen, C.M., Baumann, H., Ruggles, R., and Sadtler, T.M. (2006). Disruptive innovation for social change. *Harvard Business Review*, **84**(12), 94–101.

Cooper, R. G (2021). Accelerating innovation: Some lessons from the pandemic. *Journal of Product Innovation Management*, **38**(2), 221–32.

Criddle, C. (2021). Bitcoin consumes 'more electricity than Argentina' (19 February), https://www.bbc.co.uk/news/technology-56012952 (last accessed 1 November 2021).

Cusumano, M.A. and Gawer, A. (2002). The elements of platform leadership. *MIT Sloan Management Review*, **43**(3), 51–8.

DalleMule, L. and Davenport, T.H. (2017). What's your data strategy? *Harvard Business Review*, **95**(3), 112–21.

Damanpour, F. (2014). Footnotes to research on management innovation. *Organization Studies*, **35**(9), 1265–85.

Damanpour, F., Walker, R.M., and Avellaneda, C.N. (2009). Combinative effects of innovation types and organizational performance: A longitudinal study of service organizations. *Journal of Management Studies*, **46**(4), 650–75.

Davenport, T.H. and Mahidhar, V. (2018). What's your cognitive strategy? *MIT Sloan Management Review*, **59**(4), 19–23.

Day, G.S. (2007). Is it real? Can we win? Is it worth doing? *Harvard Business Review*, **85**(12), 110–20.

Dean, B. (2021) Spotify user stats (14 October), https://backlinko.com/spotify-users (last accessed 31 October 2021).

Denning, S. (2018). The emergence of agile people management. *Strategy & Leadership*, **46**(4), 3–10.

Dodgson, M., Gann, D., and Salter, A. (2008). *The Management of Technological Innovation: Strategy and Practice*. Oxford: Oxford University Press

Dosi, G., Llerena, P., and Labini, M.S. (2006). The relationships between science, technologies, and their industrial exploitation: An illustration through the myths and realities of the so-called 'European Paradox'. *Research Policy*, **35**(10), 1450–64.

Downes, L. and Nunes, P.F. (2013). Big-bang disruption. *Harvard Business Review*, **91**(3), 44–56.

Drucker, P.F. (1988). The coming of the new organization. *Harvard Business Review*, **66**(1), 45–53.

Eden, R., Burton-Jones, A., Casey, V., and Draheim, M. (2019). Digital transformation requires workforce transformation. *MIS Quarterly Executive*, **18**(1), 1–17.

Edquist, C., Hommen, C.L., and McKelvey, M. (2001). *Innovation and Employment: Process Versus Product Innovation*. Cheltenham: Edward Elgar.

Fagerberg, J. (2006). Innovation: A guide to the literature. In: Fagerberg, J., Mowery, D.C., and Nelson, R.R. (eds), *Oxford Handbook of Innovation*. Oxford: Oxford University Press, pp. 1–26.

Farboodi, M. (2018). The problem with big data (21 December), https://sloanreview.mit.edu/article/the-problem-with-big-data (accessed 19 December 2019).

11

The Financial Times (2021). The Olympics need esports more than esports need the Olympics, https://www.ft.com/content/dbabdf17-2835-499e-890d-aa19a6b464e2 (last accessed 19 August 2022).

Gartner (2018). Every organizational function needs to work on digital transformation. *Harvard Business Review* (27 November), 6–9, https://hbr.org/sponsored/2018/11/every-organizational-function-needs-to-work-on-digital-transformation (last accessed 22 October 2022).

Gawer, A. and Cusumano, M.A. (2008). How companies become platform leaders. *MIT Sloan Management Review*, **49**(2), 28–35.

Gawer, A. and Cusumano, M.A. (2014). Industry platforms and ecosystem innovation. *Journal of Product Innovation Management*, **31**(3), 417–33.

Gilbert, C., Eyring, M., and Foster, R.N. (2012). Two routes to resilience. *Harvard Business Review*, **90**(12), 65–73.

Gough, C. (2021). Esports market—statistics and facts. *Statista* (21 October), https://www.statista.com/topics/3121/esports-market/#dossierKeyfigures (last accessed 19 August 2022).

Govindarajan, V. and Trimble, C. (2010). *The Other Side of Innovation: Solving the Execution Challenge*. Boston, MA: Harvard Business Review Press.

GovTech Singapore (2020). Digital Government Blueprint, https://www.tech.gov.sg/digital-government-blueprint (last accessed 19 August 2022).

The Guardian (2021). Win a gold medal from your front room? IOC launches Olympic Virtual Series (27 April), https://www.theguardian.com/sport/2021/apr/22/virtual-olympic-series-launched-ioc-baseball-cycling-rowing (last accessed 19 August 2022).

Gurtner, S., and Reinhardt, R. (2016). Ambidextrous idea generation—antecedents and outcomes. *Journal of Product Innovation Management*, **33**, 34–54.

Hagiu, A. and Altman, E.J. (2017). Finding the platform in your product: Four strategies that can reveal hidden value. *Harvard Business Review*, **95**(4), 94–100.

Hall, B.H. (2006). Innovation and diffusion. In: Fagerberg, J., Mowery, D.C., and Nelson, R.R. (eds), *Oxford Handbook of Innovation*. Oxford: Oxford University Press, pp. 459–85.

Henderson, R.M. and Clark, K.B. (1990). Architectural innovation: The reconfiguration of existing product technologies and the failure of established firms. *Administrative Science Quarterly*, **35**(1), 9–30.

IOC (International Olympic Committee) (2021a). IOC session approves Olympic Agenda 2020+5 as the strategic road map to 2025 (12 March), https://olympics.com/ioc/news/ioc-session-approves-olympic-agenda-2020-5-as-the-strategic-roadmap-to-2025 (last accessed 19 August 2022).

IOC (2021b). Olympic Agenda 2020+5: 15 recommendations, https://stillmedab.olympic.org/media/Document%20Library/OlympicOrg/IOC/What-We-Do/Olympic-agenda/Olympic-Agenda-2020-5-15-recommendations.pdf (last accessed 19 August 2022).

Kaplan, R.S. and Norton, D.P. (2008). Mastering the management system. *Harvard Business Review*, **86**(1), 62–77.

Ketter, W., Peters, M., Collins, J., and Gupta, A. (2016). Competitive benchmarking: An IS research approach to address wicked problems with big data and analytics. *MIS Quarterly*, **40**(4), 1057–89.

Kim, W.C. and Mauborgne, R. (2004). Blue ocean strategy. *Harvard Business Review*, **82**(10), 76–84.

Kim, W.C. and Mauborgne, R. (2007). How strategy shapes structure. *Harvard Business Review*, **87**(9), 72–80.

Kim, W.C. and Mauborgne, R. (2015a). Closing the gap between blue ocean strategy and execution. *Harvard Business Review Digital Articles*, 2–8.

Kim, W.C. and Mauborgne, R. (2019). Nondisruptive creation: Rethinking innovation and growth. *MIT Sloan Management Review*, **60**(3), 46–55.

Kolbjørnsrud, V. (2017). Agency problems and governance mechanisms in collaborative communities. *Strategic Organization*, **15**(2), 141–73.

11

Lam, A. (2006). Organizational innovation. In: Fagerberg, J., Mowery, D.C., and Nelson, R.R. (eds), *Oxford Handbook of Innovation*. Oxford: Oxford University Press, pp. 115–47.

Lazer, D., Kennedy, R., King, G., and Vespignani, A. (2014). The parable of Google flu: Traps in big data analysis. *Science*, **343**, 1203–5.

Lee, A. (2020). How COVID-19 spurred Singapore's digital transformation. *The Business Times* (13 July), https://www.businesstimes.com.sg/technology/how-covid-19-spurred-singapores-digital-transformation (last accessed 19 August 2022).

Libert, B., Beck, M., and Wind, Y. (2016). 7 questions to ask before your next digital transformation. *Harvard Business Review Digital Articles*, 2–5, https://hbr.org/2016/07/7-questions-to-ask-before-your-next-digital-transformation (last accessed 22 October 2022).

Loonam, J., Eaves, S., Kumar, V., and Parry, G. (2018). Towards digital transformation: Lessons learned from traditional organizations. *Strategic Change*, **27**(2), 101–9.

McAfee, A. and Brynjolfsson, E. (2012). Big data: The management revolution. *Harvard Business Review* (October), https://hbr.org/2012/10/big-data-the-management-revolution (last accessed 19 August 2022).

Mangelsdorf, M.E. (2009). Creating a culture of innovation (13 February), https://sloanreview.mit.edu/article/creating-a-culture-of-innovation (last accessed 19 August 2022).

Manso, G. (2017). Creating incentives for innovation. *California Management Review*, **60**(1), 18–32.

Markides, C.C. (1998). Strategic innovation in established companies. *Sloan Management Review*, **39**(3), 31–42.

Marr, B. (2021) What is a big data strategy?, https://bernardmarr.com/what-is-a-big-data-strategy (last accessed 16 October 2021).

McGrath, R., and McManus, R. (2020). Discovery-driven digital transformation. *Harvard Business Review*, **98**(3), 124–33.

McKinsey (2021) The new digital edge (26 May), https://www.mckinsey.com/business-functions/mckinsey-digital/our-insights/the-new-digital-edge-rethinking-strategy-for-the-postpandemic-era (last accessed 16 October 2021).

Millar, C.C.J.M., Groth, O., and Mahon, J.F. (2018). Management innovation in a VUCA world: Challenges and recommendations. *California Management Review*, **61**(1), 5–14.

Obal, M., Kannan-Narasimhan, R., and Ko, G. (2016). Whom should we talk to? Investigating the varying roles of internal and external relationship quality on radical and incremental innovation performance. *Journal of Product Innovation Management*, **33**, 136–47.

Osterwalder, A. and Pigneur, Y. (2010). *Business Model Generation: A Handbook for Visionaries, Game Changers, and Challengers*. Hoboken, NJ: John Wiley.

Osterwalder, A., Pigneur, Y., Bernarda, G., and Smith, A. (2014). *Value Proposition Design: How to Create Products and Services Customers Want*. Hoboken, NJ: John Wiley.

Palar, S. (2021). The Olympics Virtual Series (22 June). https://olympics.com/en/featured-news/olympic-virtual-series-everything-you-need-to-know (last accessed 19 August 2022).

Palmié, M., Lingens, B., and Gassmann, O. (2016). Towards an attention-based view of technology decisions. *R&D Management*, **46**(4), 781–96.

Palmieri, J. (2021). W.L. Gore creates incubator business (21 October), https://wwd.com/fashion-news/ready-to-wear/w-l-gore-creates-incubator-business-1234972858 (last accessed 31 October 2021).

Parviainen, P., Tihinen, M., Kääriäinen, J., and Teppola, S. (2017). Tackling the digitalization challenge: How to benefit from digitalization in practice. *International Journal of Information Systems and Project Management*, **5**(1), 63–77.

Pisano, G.P. (2015). You need an innovation strategy. *Harvard Business Review*, **93**(6), 44–54.

Powell, W.W. and Grodal, S. (2006). Innovation and diffusion. In: Fagerberg, J., Mowery, D.C., and Nelson, R.R. (eds), *Oxford Handbook of Innovation*. Oxford: Oxford University Press, pp. 56–85.

11

Rao, J. and Weintraub, J. (2013). How innovative is your company's culture? *MIT Sloan Management Review*, **54**(3), 29–37.

Rogers, E.M. (2003). *Diffusions of Innovation* (5th edn). New York: Free Press.

Ross, J. (2018a). Digital is about speed—but it takes a long time. *MIT Sloan Management Review* (April), https://sloanreview.mit.edu/article/digital-is-about-speed-but-it-takes-a-long-time (last accessed 19 August 2022).

Ross, J. (2018b). Let your digital strategy emerge. *MIT Sloan Management Review* (October), https://sloanreview.mit.edu/article/let-your-digital-strategy-emerge (last accessed 19 August 2022).

Ross, J.W., Sebastian, I.M., and Beath, C.M. (2017). How to develop a great digital strategy. *MIT Sloan Management Review*, **58**(2), 7–9.

Roth, M. and Keller, B. (2019). Modernization through digital transformation. *TD: Talent Development*, **73**(1), 32–7.

Schoemaker, P.J.H., Heaton, S., and Teece, D. (2018). Innovation, dynamic capabilities, and leadership. *California Management Review*, **61**(1), 15–42.

Schumpeter, J. (1942). *Capitalism, Socialism, and Democracy*. New York: Harper and Row.

Sia, S. K., Weill, P., and Zhang, N. (2021). Designing a future-ready enterprise: The digital transformation of DBS Bank. *California Management Review*, **63**(3), 35–57.

Siggelkow, N. and Terwiesch, C. (2019). The age of continuous connection. *Harvard Business Review*, **97**(3), 64–73.

Singapore Government (2020). Digital Government Blueprint, https://www.smartnation.gov.sg/files/publications/dgb-public-document_30dec20.pdf (last accessed 19 August 2022).

Smith, H.A. and Watson, R.T. (2019). Digital transformation at Carestream Health. *MIS Quarterly Executive*, **18**(1), 86–98.

TheSporting.blog (2021). A brief history of esports and competitive gaming (10 February), https://thesporting.blog/blog/a-brief-history-of-esports-and-competitive-gaming (last accessed 19 August 2022).

Svahn, F., Mathiassen, L., Lindgren, R., and Kane, G.C. (2017). Mastering the digital innovation challenge. *MIT Sloan Management Review*, **58**(3), 14–16.

Unruh, G. and Kiron, D. (2019) The environmental benefits of digital design (2 December), https://sloanreview.mit.edu/article/the-environmental-benefits-of-digital-design (last accessed 1 November 2021).

Van Alstyne, M.W., Parker, G.G., and Choudary, S.P. (2016). Pipelines, platforms, and the new rules of strategy. *Harvard Business Review* (April), **94**(4), 54–62.

Vanhaverbeke, W. and Peeters, M. (2005). Embracing innovation as strategy: Corporate venturing, competence building, and corporate strategy making. *Creativity and Innovation Management*, **14**(3), 262–73.

Vermeulen, F. (2017). What so many strategists get wrong about digital disruption. *Harvard Business Review Digital Articles*, 2–5, https://hbr.org/2017/01/what-so-many-strategists-get-wrong-about-digital-disruption (last accessed 22 October 2022).

von Stamm, B. (2008). *Managing Innovation, Design, and Creativity* (2nd edn). Chichester: John Wiley.

The Washington Post (2021a). IOC announces inaugural slate of Olympic-licensed esports events (22 April), https://www.washingtonpost.com/video-games/esports/2021/04/22/ioc-olympics-esports (last accessed 19 August 2022).

The Washington Post (2021b). Tokyo Olympics get a taste of esports, sort of (24 July), https://www.washingtonpost.com/video-games/2021/07/24/tokyo-olympics-esports (last accessed 19 August 2022).

Westerman, G., Bonnet., D, and McAfee, A. (2014). *Leading Digital*. Boston, MA: Harvard Business Press.

11

Westerman, G., Soule, D.L., and Eswaran, A. (2019). Building digital-ready culture in traditional organizations. *MIT Sloan Management Review* (21 May), https://sloanreview.mit.edu/article/building-digital-ready-culture-in-traditional-organizations (last accessed 19 August 2022).

Wheelwright, S.C. and Clark, K.B. (1992). *Revolutionizing Product Development*. New York: Free Press.

Wolmarans, K. (2016). A German scientific study shows esports professionals are athletes. *Critical Hit Gaming* (16 May), https://www.criticalhit.net/gaming/german-scientific-study-shows-esports-professionals-athletes (last accessed 19 August 2022).

World Economic Forum (2021). Bridging digital and environmental goals: A framework for business action (March), https://www3.weforum.org/docs/WEF_Bridging_Digital_and_Environmental_Goals_2021.pdf (last accessed 19 August 2022).

Yu, E. (2020). Singapore puts $352m focus on digital transformation to help firms cope with pandemic fallout. *ZDNet* (26 May), https://www.zdnet.com/article/singapore-puts-352m-focus-on-digital-transformation-to-help-firms-cope-with-pandemic-fallout/ (last accessed 19 August 2022).

11

CHAPTER TWELVE

Competing in a Globalized World

CONTENTS

By the end of this chapter, you should be able to:

○ Recognize the nature of globalization and examine how this influences strategy

○ Explore the drivers for globalization and their impact on organizations

○ Identify the cultural and practice challenges in global strategy implementation

○ Evaluate the motivations and models for internationalization

○ Examine the phenomenon of 'born global'

○ Compare and contrast the generic global strategy orientations

TOOLBOX

○ **Yip's industry globalization drivers**
Four sets of 'industry globalization drivers' which underlie conditions in each industry that create the potential for that industry to become more global and, as a consequence, for the potential viability of a global approach to strategy.

○ **Porter's diamond framework of national advantage**
A model that is designed to help understand the emergence of competitive advantage of nations or industry clusters because of certain factor conditions available to them and how strategists can apply the tool to identify attractive markets or locations to situate their production activities.

○ **CAGE distance framework**
A framework that identifies **c**ultural, **a**dministrative, **g**eographic, and **e**conomic differences or distances between countries that companies should address when crafting international strategies. It may also be used to understand patterns of trade, capital, information, and people flows.

○ **Foreign market entry modes**
These are the channels, ranging from export strategies to direct foreign investment, that an organization can employ to gain entry to a new international market.

○ **Three international strategy orientations**
The three main international strategy orientations are: (a) multidomestic, (b) global, and (c) transnational. Each strategy involves a different approach to trying to build efficiency across national markets, while remaining responsive to variations in foreign customer preferences and local market conditions.

○ **Born global firms**
A born global firm is an organization that, from its inception, seeks to derive significant competitive advantage from scaling up the use of resources and the sale of the firm's outputs in multiple countries. Born global firms are usually small, technology-orientated companies that operate in international markets from the very beginning.

Access the online resources to watch a short video clip where Fazeela Gopalani shares her top career tips.

12

OPENING CASE STUDY PHENOMENAL GROWTH OF ZOOM VIDEO COMMUNICATIONS, INC.

When COVID-19 spread to over 200 countries in 2020, Zoom, a relatively unknown company beyond corporate video conferencing, became a household name almost overnight. As the world locked down and started adjusting to the 'new normal' of social distancing and combating social isolation, people all over the world logged on to the Zoom platform for professional and personal activities. School classes and business meetings were conducted on Zoom, as were virtual dinner parties, weddings, religious services, games nights, and even virtual tourism and dating. The lockdown resulted in Zoom becoming the fifth most downloaded mobile app worldwide in 2020, with 477.3 million downloads.

Zoom was founded in 2011 by Eric Yuan, a former Cisco engineer, who had become frustrated by Cisco's Webex video conferencing functionality, the product development of which he was managing. Whenever a user logged on to Webex, the system had to identify which operating platform was being used (iPhone, Android, PC, or Mac), which slowed things down. According to Yuan, the platform simply wasn't good enough and the problem was compounded when too many people logged on to the system causing the line to slow down and the connection to become choppy. And the service lacked modern features such as screen-sharing for mobile devices. After pestering his Cisco bosses to let him to rebuild Webex, Yuan gave up and decided to leave Cisco and build his own video conferencing platform with a simple mission: 'to make video communications frictionless and secure'.

Yuan was able to attract only $3 million of seed money for his start-up. Venture capitalists thought that a new video conferencing platform was a terrible idea. The video conferencing industry already had entrenched incumbents: Microsoft's Skype and MS Teams, Google's Hangouts, GoToMeeting, and Cisco's Webex (still the market leader), as well as several well-funded start-ups. Undeterred, Yuan and his small team rented a rundown office space in Santa Clara in California and quietly worked on their product for almost two years. When Zoom was launched in 2013, it had several features that differentiated it from its competitors. Zoom didn't need

The COVID-19 pandemic led to the growth of online video conferencing platform Zoom.
Source: Surface/Unsplash.com.

different versions for different operating systems as the platform could almost immediately recognize the type of device that was being used to log in to the platform. It also contained a software layer that shielded Zoom from any bugs when browsers such as Chrome, Firefox, or Safari released updates, and the platform could operate even at 40% data loss, so it worked well over spotty or slow internet connections.

Zoom initially targeted small-to-medium-sized businesses using a 'freemium' business model that allowed up to 15 people to participate in video conference meetings capped at 40 minutes. Yuan explains how the 'freemium' model works for Zoom:

In our case, we really want to get the customers to test our product. This market is extremely crowded. It's really hard to tell customers, 'You've got to try Zoom.' Without a freemium product, I think you're going to lose the opportunity to let many users to test your products. We make our freemium product work so well. We give most of our features for free and one-to-one is no limitation. That's why almost every day there are so many users coming to our website, free users. If they like our product, very soon they are going to pay for the subscription.

12

By January 2017, the company had reached one million users across 450,000 business customers and the company was able to raise an additional $100 million of funding. Yuan stated that 'by addressing the huge market demand for cloud-based video conferencing, Zoom is seizing a leadership position and filling the void created by the industry's fading legacy providers'. With this additional funding, 'we will develop revolutionary products and features such as virtual reality, augmented reality, and the Zoom Developer Platform, expand internationally, and grow our sales and marketing teams'. The fast growth of Zoom culminated in the company becoming listed on the NAS-DAQ stock market in 2019 with a valuation of $9.4 billion and making Yuan a billionaire at age 49.

A year after Zoom's public listing, the world was hit by COVID-19. Yuan was quick to react to the challenges that businesses, academic institutions, and individuals faced as they tried to adapt to remote working and social isolation. In a series of blog articles, Yuan stated that 'we believe every business has the social responsibility to contribute back to the community and to society, and it's critically important during times of crisis'. With this tenet in mind, Zoom mobilized the organization to provide resources and support to those navigating the coronavirus outbreak. This support included the lifting of the 40-minute limit on meetings with more than two participants, providing unlimited time to collaborate, proactively monitoring servers to ensure maximum reliability amid any capacity increases, and scheduling information sessions and on-demand resources so anyone can learn how to use the Zoom platform with ease. These actions were aligned with Zoom's six key strategy elements that are articulated in the firm's 2022 Annual Report:

- **Keep our existing customers happy**. We provide happiness to our customers by giving them an experience that delights them. We respond to customer needs with action to drive positive user experiences.

- **Drive new customer acquisition**. Our platform is designed to make it easy to host meetings. By attracting free hosts to use our platform, we promote usage that allows hosts and their meeting attendees to experience the Zoom difference.

- **Expand within existing customers**. As organizations experience our platform and become familiar with its benefits, more teams and departments within these organizations adopt Zoom.

- **Innovate our platform continuously**. Our engineers aim to stay on the cutting edge of communication and collaboration technologies.

- **Accelerate international expansion**. With users, offices, and data centres strategically located around the world, we are poised to reach new customers globally. Our platform is intuitively designed such that localization requirements are minimal.

- **Grow our partnership ecosystem and continue to expand our platform**. Our platform integrates easily with other systems and tools. We enable developers to embed our platform into their own offerings through open application program interfaces and our cross-platform software development kits.
  https://investors.zoom.us/static-files/9a9d91bf-5c62-45fd-9573-fb03159c8a93 (last accessed 6 November 2022)

Yuan's quick response to the pandemic gave Zoom an unprecedented opportunity to scale up the firm's product globally. During the worst days of the pandemic, Zoom's stock price rose from $67 in January 2020 to $559 in October 2020 but it has since then settled to $105 in April 2022. The big strategic question is whether Zoom's global growth spurt was a temporary blip as a result of the pandemic or whether people will continue working remotely and integrate video conferencing as a 'new normal' in the way that they communicate both at work and in social interactions with family and friends.

Questions for discussion

1. How would you describe Zoom's business model?

2. What do you think are the similarities and differences, if any, between Zoom's business model and that of a more traditional global service company such as Hilton Hotels?

3. Besides the pandemic, what factors do you think have contributed to Zoom's rapid international expansion?

4. Compare and contrast Microsoft's MS Teams and Zoom or any other video conferencing platform that you are familiar with. Do you think that Zoom has a sustainable competitive advantage?

Continued

12

Sources

GlobalNewsWire (2017). Zoom partners with Sequoia in $100 million funding round (17 January), https://www.globenewswire.com/news-release/2017/01/17/1311117/0/en/Zoom-Partners-with-Sequoia-in-100-Million-Funding-Round.html (last accessed 19 August 2022).

Koetsier, J. (2021). Here are the 10 most downloaded apps of 2020. *Forbes* (7 January), https://www.forbes.com/sites/johnkoetsier/2021/01/07/here-are-the-10-most-downloaded-apps-of-2020/?sh=5882102a5d1a (last accessed 19 August 2022).

Sloan, M. (2020). The 3 secrets behind Zoom's triple-digit growth. *Drift* (10 April), https://www.drift.com/blog/how-zoom-grew (last accessed 19 August 2022).

Zoom Video Communications, Inc. Support during the COVID-19 pandemic, https://explore.zoom.us/en/covid19 (last accessed 19 August 2022).

Zoom Video Communications, Inc. (2022). Zoom for online learning updates (April), https://blog.zoom.us/how-to-use-zoom-for-online-learning (last accessed 19 August 2022).

Zoom Video Communications, Inc. (2022). Zoom's commitment to user support and business continuity during the coronavirus outbreak (26 February), https://blog.zoom.us/zoom-commitment-user-support-business-continuity-during-coronavirus-outbreak/ (last accessed 19 August 2022).

12.1 Introduction

Global strategy development has traditionally started with companies gradually building an international presence by taking their products and services to markets where foreign customers share similar needs and characteristics as the home market customers. With the increasing connectivity and digitization of business, some firms, both small and large, are beginning to explore new ways of launching international ventures. Although the traditional routes to foreign markets are unlikely to disappear anytime soon, we see a trend that will increasingly involve business-model-grounded globalization ('born global' businesses) compared with the more traditional product- and service-led global expansion.

Traditional **multinational enterprises (MNEs)** have become global entities, having evolved and developed their international operations over decades. Examples of MNEs include firms such as Siemens, Toyota, and Rolls-Royce Engines, among many other well-known enterprises. However, in our globally connected digital world, new innovative and entrepreneurial business models such as those of Alibaba, Airbnb, Meta, and Uber may challenge the dominance of the widely known and applied internationalization strategies. We are likely to see an increasing number of start-up companies that were 'born global'—firms that enter international markets from their inception or very early on after their founding—in contrast with the traditional MNEs.

In order to better understand international strategy and the challenges that organizations face when competing internationally, we start by exploring the changing landscape of global markets and businesses. We will consider globalization as a phenomenon that shapes the external context in which all organizations are embedded and take a critical look at its advantages and disadvantages on both economic and societal levels. Globalization has become an emotionally and politically charged concept that has made—and will continue to make—a significant impact on how global companies operate and conduct themselves in a whole host of areas, including employment and tax practices, corporate social responsibility, executive compensation and so on. Next, we will consider factors that may act as drivers for the globalization of industries, and, finally, we will assess the impact of these drivers at an organizational level.

12

As triggers for strategizing episodes, we will consider the challenges and decisions that organizations face when they evaluate opportunities for expanding their operations internationally. These sorts of strategic issues involve decisions such as how does the firm get its product to the foreign market and to what extent (if at all) does the product have to be adapted to meet local customer needs?

To help us explore these issues, we introduce analytical concepts and frameworks to develop our understanding of how and why organizations look to compete in a globalized world. More specifically, we will use Porter's diamond of national advantage to position an organization in the global economy within the context of its home nation and identify competitive advantage from that perspective. We will apply the **CAGE distance framework**, which will help us to evaluate cross-border challenges to consider when evaluating foreign market entry strategies. We will also analyse the mechanics of becoming international and the three main international strategic orientations (multidomestic, global, and transnational). Finally, we will evaluate the conditions for creating sustainable competitive advantage globally and consider the concept of 'born global' firms as an emerging strategic orientation.

12.2 **Globalization**

Globalization can be considered as an ongoing process of international integration that results from and supports the interchange of products, ideas, culture, and institutions. Many national economies today benefit from a form of globalization that is governed by both national laws and international agreements and treaties such as the trade rules of the World Trade Organization (WTO).

The term 'globalization' began to become more commonly used in the 1980s, reflecting technological advances that made it easier and quicker to complete international transactions, both trade and financial flows (Ashenfelter et al. 2018). More specifically, globalization encompasses economic globalization: the increasing integration of economies around the world, particularly through free trade in goods, services, and the movement of capital across borders. The term often includes the free movement of people (labour) and knowledge (technology), as well as broader cultural, political, and environmental dimensions (IMF 2008).

According to the IMF (2008), there is substantial evidence from countries of different sizes and regions to suggest that, as countries globalize, their citizens benefit in the form of access to a variety of goods and services, lower prices, increased numbers of better-paying jobs, improved health, and higher overall living standards. As the number of countries which have become more open to global economic forces increases, the percentage of the developing world living in extreme poverty has reduced dramatically.

In 1820, only a tiny elite enjoyed higher standards of living, while most people lived in conditions that we would call extreme poverty today. Subsequently, the share of extremely poor people has fallen continuously. More and more world regions industrialized and thereby increased productivity, which made it possible to lift more people out of poverty. In 1950, two-thirds of the world population were living in extreme poverty; in 1981 it was still 44%. Since then, the share of extremely poor people in the world has declined faster than ever before in world history.

In 32 years, the share of people living in extreme poverty was divided by 4, reaching levels below 10% in 2015 (Roser 2020).

A number of factors underpin the overall improvement in prosperity. One of the key factors has been greater foreign direct investment (FDI). This may include acquisitions, establishment of local manufacturing operations, or other forms of permanent investments made by foreign firms or individuals from one country into business interests located in another country. Other factors include the spread of technology, strong societal institutions, sound macroeconomic policies, an educated workforce, and the existence of a market economy (UN 2016). Fundamentally, however, all these advances are underpinned by what *The Economist* calls the 'competitive spirit of meritocracy', which has 'created extraordinary prosperity and wealth of new ideas'. In the name of efficiency and economic freedom, governments have opened up markets to competition and globalization has lifted hundreds of millions of people in emerging markets out of poverty (*The Economist* 2018).

Globalization has also opened unprecedented opportunities for firms to trade internationally. As a result of the removal of trade barriers, deregulation of financial transactions, and harmonization of product standards and legal frameworks, it is now relatively easy for companies to sell what they produce in their home countries to foreign markets, source raw materials and products globally, or even locate their value chain activities in one or more foreign countries. Globalized trading possibilities present a firm with strategic opportunities upon which it can build its competitive advantage.

De-globalization

While some countries have embraced globalization and experienced significant income increases, other countries that have rejected globalization, or only embraced it tepidly, have fallen behind (IMF 2008). A similar phenomenon is at work within individual countries, where some people have been bigger beneficiaries of globalization than others. In fact, rising incomes around the world have been accompanied by increasing inequality within individual countries across both developing and advanced economies (Kuttner 2018). However, there are regional variations in the degree of inequality. The southern part of Africa and Latin America stand out as regions with very high inequality. In contrast, South-East Asia and most rich countries have relatively low levels of inequality (Roser and Ortiz-Ospina 2016). It should be noted, however, that in the United States, income inequality has been rising over the past four decades, with incomes for the bottom 10% growing at a much slower rate than incomes for the top 10%. The poorest individuals in the United States have seen no real income growth in the period 1980–2014; while the ultra-rich have enjoyed an average annual growth of about 6% (Roser 2020). The United States is an exception when it comes to income inequality and different to the experience of other Organisation for Economic Co-operation and Development (OECD) countries. In contrast to the United States, top income levels in Europe and Japan have remained flat or increased only modestly; income inequality in Europe and Japan is much lower today than it was at the beginning of the twentieth century (Roser and Ortiz-Ospina 2016).

It is against this backdrop that protectionist trade policies, especially in the United States, have come to dominate the current discourse about the pros and cons of globalization. For workers in globalized industries in the United States who have experienced stagnating real wages, having been forced to compete for hourly wages with workers in Asia, a **de-globalization** trend is viewed as a relief (*The Economist* 2018). However, this is only one part of the story. The thinking of globalization where mainly US and European corporations shifted their supply chains to take advantage of cheaper Asian labour is coming to an end as wages in previously cheap labour cost countries are rising steadily. Hence, it will only make sense for global firms to relocate their manufacturing abroad if they save on tax or if such relocations bring the firm closer to the market that it is trying to sell to (*The Economist* 2018). In the twenty-first-century world, supply chains in Europe, North America, and Asia will be increasingly based on producing goods closer to the home of the customer. It is likely that this trend will accelerate because of the COVID-19 pandemic, which exposed the fragility of global supply chains. China's repeated lockdowns continue to play havoc on supply chains, and at the time of writing (2022), inflation rates in many Western economies have reached levels not seen for 40 years as there is a shortage of raw materials as well as semi-finished and finished goods. However, whatever form globalization will take in the post-pandemic world, global trade will not disappear. In fact, it will probably accelerate further with the digitization of trade and an increasing shift from manufacturing to service production. Digitization will make it easier for smaller firms and start-ups as 'born global' enterprises to participate in a global economy through e-commerce.

Digital data flows are already estimated to contribute as much as $450 billion to global growth annually (Pinkus et al. 2017). However, this also means that there are workers who will invariably be left behind by the onward march of globalization. It is suggested that retraining workers who have been affected by trade and globalization is not a solution on its own. In addition to retraining (where possible), policy responses will require a concerted effort by both governments and businesses to reinvest in dislocated communities, match smaller firms with foreign markets, match communities with foreign investors, ensure unfettered access for small firms and start-ups to cross-border digital platforms, and provide adequate safety net measures (Pinkus et al. 2017).

Finally, we should be clear that globalization is not the same thing as global strategy. Global strategy is effectively how a firm achieves its international expansion of their objectives and scope. However, economic globalization is a phenomenon that firms cannot ignore, and, in general terms, the larger the firm, the more extensive its global reach and the more the business must consider the impact of its operations on the local markets in which it operates. Case Example 12.1 demonstrates Walmart's global reach.

CASE EXAMPLE 12.1 **WORLD'S GLOBAL RETAILER**

Walmart, founded in 1969, is the world's largest bargain basement retailer, selling over 140,000 food and non-food items in its superstores and e-commerce sites. The retailer's promise of 'everyday low prices' certainly resonates with bargain hunters as, in 2021, the company served 230 million customers who visited more than 10,500 stores and numerous e-commerce sites under 46 different brand banners in 24 countries. This makes Walmart the world's largest retailer, both in person and online. In 2021, the firm's total revenue amounted to $572.8 billion with an operating cash flow of $24,2 billion (Walmart 2022).

Walmart's competitive advantage is based on its ability to consistently keep its cost base below that of its competitors. Walmart's economies of scale, its tight supply chain management processes, the purchasing power it exercises over its suppliers, and the sourcing of cheap manufactured goods for

Continued

sale in its stores have allowed the firm to become the world's largest retailer. Its revenues are only eclipsed by Alibaba, the Chinese online retailer.

Sam Walton, the founder of Walmart, thought that many US-produced goods were no longer competitive, and he began looking for opportunities to procure goods cheaper internationally. By 2004, Walmart had ordered $18 billion worth of goods from China, and it has been estimated that in the decade since then, Walmart's annual spending on Chinese manufactured goods has amounted to $50 billion (David 2018). Although Walmart is a significant retailer of Chinese electronics and other goods, its sales of Chinese-made goods only accounted for one in ten dollars spent by US consumers on Chinese-made products.

China was the United States' largest supplier of goods, with imports totalling $434.7 billion, accounting for 18.6% of total US imports in 2020. US goods exports totalled $124.5 billion, making China the country's third largest goods export market. The US goods trade deficit with China was $310.3 billion in 2020, although the United States maintains a services trade surplus of an estimated at $37.3 that is primarily composed of travel, intellectual property licences, and financial services (Office of the United States Trade Representative 2022).

Some studies (David 2018) estimate that Walmart has destroyed some 400,000 manufacturing jobs in the United States over the past 14 years. The company denies this and cites the benefits of the Chinese imports to the United States: creating new jobs in distribution and logistics and keeping bills down so that customers have money left over to spend on eating out or going to the cinema, thus boosting the takings elsewhere in the economy. However, it is argued that the new jobs that have been created

may not be manufacturing jobs or may not pay as well as the old manufacturing jobs. This was the justification for tariffs on Chinese imports that were levied by the Trump administration, which claimed that trade protection protects and creates jobs. Taxing foreign goods increases demand for domestic products, bolstering production and sending more Americans to work. However, we must note that any resulting trade war between the United States and China would have a detrimental effect on US export led jobs. According to the Office of the US Trade Representative (2022), the US exports of goods and services to China supported an estimated 758,000 jobs in 2019.

Questions for discussion

1. Why do you think it is imperative for Walmart to import goods from China to maintain its competitive advantage?

2. What impact would import tariffs on Chinese goods have on Walmart's business?

3. Do you think that the imposition of tariffs on Chinese imports would make a US consumer and worker better off? If so, why, and how? If not, why not?

Sources

David, D. (2018). *The Almighty Dollar*. London: Elliott & Thompson.

Office of the United States Trade Representative (2022). The People's Republic of China, https://ustr.gov/countries-regions/china-mongolia-taiwan/peoples-republic-china (last accessed 2 May 2022).

Walmart (2022). 2022 Annual Report,

https://s2.q4cdn.com/056532643/files/doc_financials/2022/ar/WMT-FY2022-Annual-Report.pdf (last accessed 2 May 2022).

 Access the online resources to watch a short video clip where Fazeela Gopalani describes the role of strategy in her organization.

12.3 Drivers of industry globalization

We have considered globalization as a phenomenon and taken a critical look at its advantages and disadvantages on both economic and societal levels. At the centre of economic globalization are businesses that have become increasingly global in their outlook and reach. However,

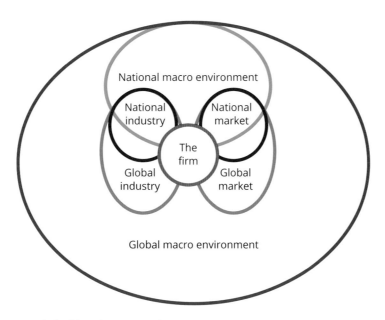

FIGURE 12.1 Global business environment. *Source*: authors.

global firms traditionally operate in several business environments, both national and global. The complexity of this operating environment is depicted in Figure 12.1, which incorporates both the macro- and industry-level environments that global firms must manage effectively when competing in multiple markets and even across traditional industry boundaries. Figure 12.1 shows that in a global business environment a firm is a participant not only in a domestic industry and market of a national economy but also in a global industry and market that is influenced by the global macro-environment. And even if one particular firm itself would not have cross-border operations, it is very likely that the firm would face competition in its domestic market from international competitors.

What factors act as drivers for the globalization of industries? And how do these drivers impact on firms at an organizational level? In this section, we consider how globalization affects firms' competitive activities. We begin our discussion by exploring the globalization of industries to identify whether there are any common factors that may act as enablers for an emergence of a global industry. We then develop a more specific understanding of why firms choose to compete in international markets, given the opportunities offered by the globalized nature of the industry in which the business operates.

Drivers of industry globalization and their effects on competitive activity

In his seminal book, *Total Global Strategy: Managing for Worldwide Competitive Advantage*, George Yip identified four generic sets of 'industry globalization drivers' (Yip 1995). According to Yip, these **industry globalization drivers** may create conditions for industries to globalize and, as a consequence, for the potential viability of adopting a global approach to a firm's

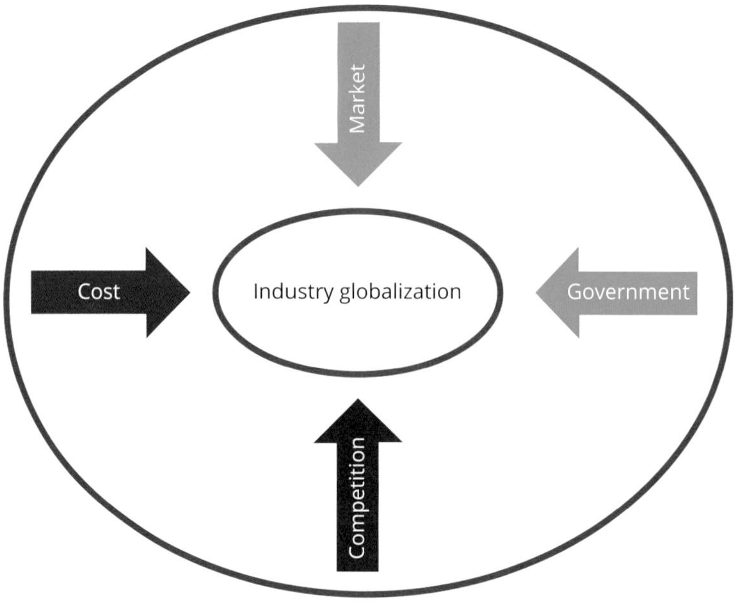

FIGURE 12.2 Industry globalization drivers. *Source*: authors.

strategy development. Yip's framework (see Figure 12.2) proposes four main drivers for industry globalization:

- market drivers;
- cost drivers;
- competition drivers;
- government drivers.

We will consider each of these drivers in turn.

Market drivers

One of the key drivers for industry globalization is a convergence of customer needs and tastes internationally. Think about how Coca-Cola is sold in 200 countries regardless of national culture or income levels, or think how many teenagers across the world, regardless of the language they speak, do not wish to use Apple or Samsung's smartphones to communicate with their friends. As customers across the world increasingly demand similar products and services, opportunities for economies of scale and scope arise through the production and marketing of more or less standardized offerings. How common needs, tastes, and preferences vary by product depend on such factors as the importance of cultural variables, disposable incomes, and the level of consistency of the conditions in which the product is consumed or used. This applies to consumer as well as industrial products and services. For example, McDonald's, while adapting to local tastes and preferences, has standardized many elements of its operations to ensure maximum operating efficiency and standardized the quality of its products across its global outlets. Increasingly, products such as software, oil and lubricants, and accounting services look alike, no matter where they are purchased.

Similarly, large corporations such as Airbus, DuPont, General Electric, HSBC, or Toyota demand the same level of quality in the products and services they buy, no matter where in the world they are procured. In many industries, global distribution channels are emerging to satisfy an increasingly global customer base, prompting a convergence of needs and tastes that results in further standardization of products and services. Finally, as consumption patterns become more consistent, global branding and marketing as a differentiating factor from competitor organizations, in the eyes of the consumer, will become increasingly important to global success. To further gain economies of scale and scope, many global companies (especially in consumer goods industries) run standardized advertising campaigns across their global markets, which are designed by advertising companies which themselves are increasingly global in their reach.

Figure 12.3 shows examples of an advertising campaign that was run by Ontario Maple Syrup Producers Association, advertising a standardized product. To take local tastes into consideration, the advertising hoardings were adapted to local market tastes and conditions in various international markets. However, the advertiser was able to earn economies of scope as the general theme of the campaign remained the same across the various markets.

Cost drivers

Economies of scale and scope, learning effects, and the exploitation of differences in factor costs for product development, manufacturing, and sourcing are important determinants in global strategy development and execution.

Global reach is vital for industries that are characterized by high research and development (R&D) costs, such as pharmaceutical and automotive industries. For such industries, a single domestic market will no longer be large enough to recapture the accruing development costs. Therefore, it is not surprising to see the global markets being dominated by relatively few global firms such as Pfizer and GlaxoSmithKline in pharmaceuticals and the Renault–Nissan–Mitsubishi alliance and the Volkswagen Group in automotive manufacturing.

The size of the national economy of the firm or industry can also act as a driver for globalization. For example, the mobile communications industry first emerged primarily in the Nordic region, spearheaded by Ericsson of Sweden and Nokia of Finland. Both countries are small: Sweden has a population of approximately ten million and Finland approximately five million. Given the small size of the domestic markets, which would not have been able to absorb the R&D costs, the emerging mobile telecommunications industry and firms had to think globally from the start to be able drive down the unit production costs through economies of scale to make the product affordable.

FIGURE 12.3 Ontario Maple Syrup Producers Association advertisements.
Source: © Trevor Neuman—Artist—driftwoodpensbc.com. Courtesy of the Ontario Maple Syrup Producers' Association 2019.

Many of the Scandinavian firms followed what is known as the Uppsala model of internationalization. Swedish researchers (Johanson and Wiedersheim-Paul 1975) from Uppsala University in Sweden found that companies normally start their expansion by selling to markets near their home base such as the trade between the Nordic countries. It is only after they become more knowledgeable about selling to a foreign market that they gradually expand to more 'distance markets'. Distance markets is a term used to refer to the cultural distance as well as the differences in language, politics, and geography and the difficulty in acquiring knowledge of and information about the market. The Uppsala model is in sharp contrast to a company, such as Airbnb, which became a global firm almost from the outset based on its 'born global' digital platform business model.

Competitive drivers

Industry characteristics, such as the diversity of competitors in terms of their national origin and the extent to which major players have globalized their operations, also affect the globalization potential of an industry. Consider a firm that operates in a globalized industry with a wide diversity of competitors. That firm risks being crowded out of the market by global competitors who may have achieved a lower cost structure, unless it enjoys such a strong position in its domestic market that it cannot be challenged. In reality, such a protected position in a free-trade environment is likely to be temporary at best. Therefore, if a nationally focused firm's competitors are global, the national firm is likely to be forced to become global in order to survive.

Government drivers

Government drivers, such as trade policies, technical standards, and other regulatory frameworks, are important drivers in shaping the global competitive environment. As the politics and economics of global competition become more closely intertwined, both national governmental and supranational regulations and policies will have an impact on firms' global strategies. (Supranational regulations are those that go beyond national boundaries.) Firms often engage with policymakers with the aim of shaping the global competitive environment to their advantage by lobbying local governments and international institutions. Examples of policy initiatives that attract lobbying by businesses are trade restrictions, investment subsidies, tax rebates, etc. This broadening of the scope of global strategy reflects a subtle but real change in the balance of power between national governments and global corporations, and it is likely to have important consequences for how differences in policies and regulations affecting global competitiveness will be settled in the years to come.

Additional globalization drivers

Yip's framework of industry globalization drivers (Yip 1995) is by no means an exhaustive list. In a review of literature on economic globalization, Bang and Markeset (2012) identified additional globalization drivers that may affect firms' competitive situation:

1. lower transportation costs;
2. lower communications costs;
3. ICT development;
4. technology development and penetration.

All these factors, especially information and communications technologies, enable firms to manage their global operations more efficiently and, with the reach of internet technology, almost in real time.

Reasons for organizations to enter international markets

We have seen that globalization drivers encourage and, in some cases (such as cost considerations), force organizations to expand outside their domestic markets. Table 12.1 highlights the six main reasons that may prompt firms to seek international expansion.

Given that globalization has become such a major phenomenon, a new orthodoxy has arisen which assumes that businesses of all types and sizes have to embrace it and the pressure to do so is likely to intensify further. Although the motivations for entering international markets listed in Table 12.1 make a compelling case for organizations to do so, we should be very clear that this is no mean feat. There are a number of very large and well-managed companies that have tried to take advantage of the opportunities and have failed in their globalization efforts. In the financial services industry, a Dutch banking group, ABN Amro, set out to create a global financial powerhouse by acquiring banks in numerous countries. However, the banking group failed to integrate the banking institutions acquired in order to generate value with its international network. ABN Amro was eventually broken up and parts of the group were acquired by the Royal Bank of Scotland, a bank that itself became a high-profile casualty and contributor to the financial crisis of 2008–09.

In the automotive industry, one of the largest mergers of recent times was that between Daimler–Benz and Chrysler in 1998. The two companies intended to create Welt AG, a world corporation. However, this ambition was never realized as the merged entity failed to acquire the power over the market and suppliers that the firms' global ambitions were supposed to deliver. The merger failed, and, in 2014, Chrysler became a part of the Fiat Group.

Many failures could be avoided if firms seriously addressed three seemingly simple questions (Alexander and Korine 2008):

1. **Are there potential benefits for our firm?**

Just because it makes sense for a firm's rival to globalize, does it make sense, given the firm's own market position and the resources and capabilities available to it, to do so as well? Perhaps most importantly, is the firm in a position to leverage its technology and know-how *beyond* the home market, or should it concentrate its efforts on developing and defending its position *within* the home market?

2. **Do we have the requisite management skills?**

Theoretical aspects such as economies of scale are very difficult to realize in practice. Realization of economies of scale is often one of the most common incentives for firms to pursue globalization strategies. However, firms often lack the managerial skills to deliver such an elusive benefit. Also, in many cases, making organizational and cultural change can become an insurmountable barrier. In order to succeed, the organization and its component parts should necessarily be able to achieve seamless coordination and collaboration across national boundaries. Both ABN Amro and Daimler–Chrysler made a failed attempt to unlock the prize of economies of scale.

3. Will the costs outweigh the benefits?

Going global is costly. Companies often underestimate the cost of globalization. Some of these costs are not direct costs but hidden opportunity costs. For example, would the effort to harmonize practices and products across the firm's global operating network drive existing customers away or distract national management teams from the local market needs?

TABLE 12.1 **Reasons for organizations to enter international markets**

Aim of entering an international market	Motivation or reason for entering an international market	Benefit or opportunity
To gain access to new customers	The firm's home market is mature, or nearing saturation	Opportunities for increased revenues and profits in markets at a growth stage of the firm's product life cycle
	The firm sits in an industry: with high R&D costs with products that can be quickly imitated by competitors where profits are dependent on high sales volumes	Opportunity to earn returns on investments more quickly or in higher volumes
To achieve lower costs through economies of scale, scope, learning effects, and increased purchasing power	The firm is not able to recapture development, manufacturing, and marketing costs through economies of scale offered in their domestic markets	Opportunity to gain experience, which enables the firm to move down the learning curve Producing and selling higher volumes may increase the organization's purchasing power
	The home market is too small to earn sufficient economies of scale	Achieving lower costs are a 'push' factor for firms in small countries to internationalize
To exploit core competencies	The firm has a competitive advantage in a given industry in one country	Opportunity to gain further leverage from their core competencies in another country
To gain access to global resources and capabilities	The firm needs access to resources that are not available in the firm's home market	Opportunity to access new expertise; expertise is often found in clusters and, by having a presence in one of the many clusters, companies can access the required expertise
To spread business risk across a wider operating base	The firm needs to reduce risk	Opportunity for organizations to spread their business risk by operating in multiple markets as opposed to a single market
To follow their customers abroad	The firm needs to secure loyalty and commitment from their own internationally operating clients that the business depends on	Companies that are suppliers to organizations that operate internationally will often need to follow their customers abroad, which builds two-way loyalty and commitment with the client

Source: authors.

Access the online resources to watch a short video clip where Fazeela Gopalani discusses her main strategic considerations when operating internationally.

12.4 **Complexity of cross-border strategy-making**

We have already seen that developing and implementing a competitive cross-border strategy is a complex undertaking. But what are the reasons for this complexity, and how do they differ between countries? There are a number of factors that increase the level of complexity as firms expand their international reach:

- differing competitive conditions between countries;
- differing availability of resources required for business operations;
- differing political and economic conditions;
- volatility of exchange rates;
- differing demographics, social norms and behaviours, cultures, and religions.

These factors are additional to the organization's internal capabilities in managing and coordinating a highly complex global operation. In this section, we consider the cross-border variation in factors that affect industry competitiveness and outline factors that govern decisions for locating value chain activities in different countries. We also consider the impact of variations in wider economic, social, and cultural conditions on the organization's cross-border strategy.

National variation in factors that affect industry competitiveness

Certain countries are often perceived to possess strengths in particular industries. Japan is known for its excellence in consumer electronics, with companies such as Sony and Canon, Switzerland for its precision watches, such as Swatch and Rolex, Australia for mining companies, such as the Anglo-Australian mining giant Rio Tinto, and Germany for its excellence in car manufacturing, including Volkswagen, one of the largest automotive manufacturing groups. These countries are said to possess a national advantage in these particular industries. Several factors may influence the likelihood of a country developing a competitive advantage. Porter (1990) developed a **theory of national advantage**, often referred to as **Porter's Diamond framework of national advantage**, which helps us understand the competitive advantage that nations possess due to certain factors available to them. It also helps us to explain how governments can act as catalysts to improve a country's competitive position in the global economy. The original model included only four factors:

- firm strategy, structure, and rivalry;
- related and support industries;
- demand conditions;
- factor conditions.

12

However, two additional forces can be considered to affect national competitiveness:

- the role of the government;
- the role of chance.

The Diamond model (with the two added factors) is depicted in Figure 12.4.

Porter's Diamond model is visually represented by a diagram that resembles the four points of a diamond. The four points represent four interrelated determinants that Porter considers to be the deciding factors of national competitive advantage. Porter defines these interrelated determinants as follows:

- **Firm strategy, structure, and rivalry** refers to the basic fact that competition leads to businesses finding ways to increase production and to the development of technological innovations.
- **Related supporting industries** refers to upstream and downstream industries that facilitate innovation through exchanging ideas.
- **Demand conditions** refer to the size and nature of the customer base for products, which also drives innovation and product improvement.
- **Factor conditions** are elements that Porter believes a country's economy can develop for itself, such as a large pool of skilled labour, technological innovation, infrastructure, and capital.

Factor conditions are the most important, according to Porter's theory. He argues that the elements of factor conditions are more important in determining a country's competitive advantage than naturally inherited factors such as land and natural resources. For example, Japan has developed a competitive global economic presence beyond the country's inherent natural

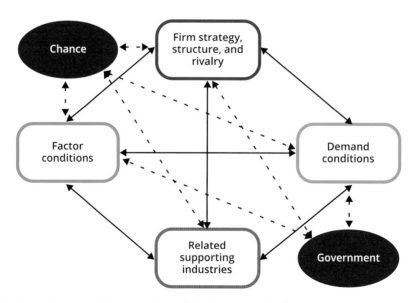

FIGURE 12.4 Porter's Diamond model of national advantage. *Source*: adapted from Porter, M. (1990). *The Competitive Advantage of Nations*. New York: Free Press. By permission of Harvard Business Publishing.

resources, in part by producing a very large number of engineers who have helped drive technological innovation by Japanese industries (Chappelow 2022).

Porter further suggests that the primary role of government in driving a nation's economy is to encourage and challenge businesses within the country to focus on creation and development of factor conditions. One way for government to accomplish that goal is to stimulate competition between domestic companies by establishing and enforcing anti-trust laws. However, it is important to note that government interventions must be considered in terms of their impact on domestic company activities because the underlying view in the Diamond model is that 'firms, not nations, compete in international markets' (Porter 1990: 33).

Finally, Porter also suggests that, in most markets, *chance* plays an important role. However, the influence of chance is, by its very nature, not predictable. For example, chance influences the creation of new ideas or new inventions. Additionally, international (or national) conflicts, significant shifts in world financial markets, discontinuities in input costs (e.g. oil price shocks), major technological breakthroughs, and major shifts in foreign market demand can all have a significant impact on a nation's competitive advantage. For example, as discussed in Chapter 8, it could be argued that the US automotive industry never recovered from the oil shock of 1973 when the Organization of the Petroleum Exporting Countries (OPEC) was formed. The US car industry was ill prepared to respond to sky-rocketing petrol prices by producing energy-efficient car engines, and the centre of gravity of car manufacturing excellence shifted to Europe and Japan.

Extending Porter's Diamond to understand industrial clustering

We can extend Porter's Diamond model to understand the emergence of industry clusters such as Silicon Valley or the Scottish wool industry. Industry clusters can be thought as groups of similar firms in a particular geographic area that share common markets, technologies, employee skills, and supporting industries such as financial, business, and legal services. In the absence of a natural national advantage, industrial clustering may occur as a result of a relative advantage that is created by the industry itself (Krugman 1993). Producers tend to locate manufacturing facilities close to their main customers. If transportation costs are not prohibitive and there are opportunities to earn economies of scale in manufacturing, a large geographic area can be served from a single location. This, in turn, will attract suppliers to the industry. In addition, a labour market is likely to develop, which begins to act like a magnet for 'like' industries that require similar skills. This locating together—clustering—of 'like' industries can lead to technological interdependencies, which will further encourage clustering. Therefore clustering is the natural outcome of economic forces and it is very closely the product of the factors detailed in Porter's Diamond model.

Another example of industrial clustering is the semiconductor industry. American and Asian firms supply most of the world's semiconductors needed to produce digital equipment from cameras to super-computers. The industry is capital intensive, R&D costs are high, and the manufacturing process is highly complex, but transportation costs are minimal, which means that semiconductors can be shipped globally relatively cheaply. Technology interdependencies encourage producers and suppliers to be located close together, whereas cost and learning curve effects can result in economies of scale efficiencies.

Only when transportation costs are prohibitive or scale economies are difficult to realize (i.e. when there are disincentives to clustering) do more decentralized patterns of industry location define the natural order. The appliance industry illustrates this. Companies such as General Electric and Whirlpool have globalized their operations in many respects, but the fundamental economics of the industry make clustering unattractive. For example, the production of certain value-added components, such as compressors or electronic parts, can be concentrated to some extent, but the bulky nature of the product and high transportation costs make further concentration economically unattractive.

Applying Porter's Diamond as a tool for strategy-making

Porter's Diamond model has been critiqued since it was first published in 1990. We highlight some of the criticisms but, despite the framework's shortcomings, it is important in your studies to understand the Diamond model as it can still be used by strategists as an effective strategy-making tool. Case Example 12.2 allows you to consider the value of the model in practice.

The most significant critique of Porter's Diamond model is that it has an almost exclusive focus on the home country. In Porter's model, the home country is perceived as the place from where the competitive advantages of a nation can be derived (Porter 1990). However, as Rugman and D'Cruz (1993) found, that was not the case for countries outside the United States, the European Union, and Japan. Cartwright (1993), in his research on New Zealand, concluded that Porter's Diamond model could not explain the success of export-dependent and resource-based industries. Porter's model failed to understand that for small open trading economies, where firms earn most of their revenues outside their home country, the diamond of their target markets is more relevant than their own home diamond (Rugman and D'Cruz 1993).

Another critical dimension that is missing in Porter's model is the influence of national culture, as pointed out by Van den Bosch and Van Prooijen (1992). Porter himself noted that many aspects of a nation, such as attitude towards authority, norms of interpersonal interaction, and attitude towards management and social norms, influence the way firms are organized and managed (Porter 1990). Many of these aspects of a nation originate from the national culture, whose influences on competitiveness through the Diamond model was a key issue which Porter did not explore. We will consider the impact of sociocultural factors in our discussion of the CAGE distance framework later in this section.

Despite these shortcomings, it is important for you to understand the model when studying strategy. Managers can apply the Diamond model to find answers to important questions for competing internationally.

1. The model can be used to predict where foreign entrants into a firm's industry are likely to come from. This information may enable managers to develop entry barriers for foreign competitor entry as the Diamond analysis will reveal some information about the foreign competitors' strengths and weaknesses.

2. The analysis may reveal the countries where international competitors are the weakest. This may help managers to decide which markets they should enter as competition is perceived to be weakest.

3. The Diamond model highlights countries where a certain industry has a competitive advantage or where a certain cluster of excellence is located. This signals that the country with world-leading industries or clusters of excellence has qualities that allow an industry

to flourish. This may help managers of international firms to decide where they could gain access to valuable knowledge and resource or even locate some of their firm's value chain activities in such countries.

CASE EXAMPLE 12.2 IDENTIFYING OPPORTUNITIES FOR MOBILE TECHNOLOGY-BASED RETAIL BANKING SERVICES

A European retail bank known for its mobile banking apps is considering opportunities for international expansion. The managers of the bank have identified a rapidly growing emerging economy with a large population and an emerging prosperous middle class. Porter's Diamond analysis reveals the following information:

Demand conditions

- Evolving mobile commerce possibilities;
- Growing number of smartphone owners;
- Data usage is becoming cheaper so smartphones will become available for most people in the country;
- Emerging prosperous middle class.

Factor endowments

- Technology workforce that is is developing and growing;
- High level of competence of using mobile and internet technology;
- Geographical technology advantages within the country;
- Upcoming online businesses, including app builders;
- Poor national fixed telephone line networks and lower usage of landlines;
- A limited number of physical bank branches that do not cover the country fully.

Related and supporting industry

- The country is the regional leader in the microchip market;

- The county is the regional leader in mobile network and technology;
- The banking system of the country is in need of new technology infrastructure.

Firm strategy and structure

- Emerging venture capital firms investing in technology start-ups;
- Small and medium-sized technology businesses;
- Market competition in mobile telecommunications;
- Continuous development and improvement of mobile technologies.

Government

- The government has stated that it will promote mobile communications technology over fixed-line communications;
- The government is planning to invest in mobile R&D and technology development;
- The government is in the process of developing mobile commerce regulatory frameworks;
- The government provides attractive tax incentives for foreign investors.

Questions for discussion

1. Does the information presented in this case study support a further investigation of mobile banking opportunities? Why/why not?
2. What additional information would you need before considering a decision to expand your operations to this market?

Source: authors.

12

CAGE distance framework

The CAGE distance framework (Ghemawat 2001, 2007; Ghemawat and Siegel 2011) identifies cultural, administrative, geographic, and economic (CAGE) distance or differences between countries that organizations should address when developing international strategies. The framework can also be used to understand patterns of trade, capital, information, and people flows. Unlike Porter's Diamond model, which makes an attempt to identify the sources of national advantage, the CAGE distance framework considers the distance between countries as the main contributing factors to the level of trade between countries. Approaching international trade and business relationships from different perspectives makes the Diamond model and the CAGE distance framework complementary analytical strategy tools.

The CAGE distance framework defines four major categories of 'distances' and considers that the differences along these dimensions generally have a negative effect on many cross-border interactions between countries and businesses (Ghemawat and Siegel 2011).

- Cultural distance includes differences in religious beliefs, race/ethnicity, language, and social norms and values. Countries can even differ in their social attitudes to the market power of firms and income inequality, which may have implications on the economic policies of the individual countries.

- Administrative distance covers historical and political associations between countries include colonial links, free trade agreements, and the length of bilateral relationships.

- Geographic distance encompasses more than how far two countries are from each other geographically. Other factors include a country's physical size, within-country distances to borders, access to ocean, topography, and even time zones.

- Economic distance includes consumer wealth and labour costs, but other factors that impact the economic distance include differences in availability of resources, infrastructure, and organizational capabilities.

The CAGE comparator, which covers 163 home countries and 65 industries and allows users to customize the impacts of 16 types of CAGE distance, is included in the **online resources**.

Some research quantifies the impact of these distances on bilateral trade (Ghemawat and Mallick 2003). Table 12.2 shows the effects of similarities versus differences on bilateral trade between two country pairs. Some of these factors probably make sense intuitively, such as the cultural factor of a common language. If there is a common language between two countries, communication channels are more straightforward and therefore trade is likely to be facilitated. This can be seen in the first row of Table 12.2, which shows a 42% increase in bilateral trade under these circumstances. However, not all factors are so straightforward. An example of a more surprising change in trade, according to the data in Table 12.2, is the magnitude of the impact of colonial ties. The data in the second row in Table 12.2 indicates that countries with colonial ties are almost three times as likely to trade as countries without them (188%). Ghemawat and Mallick (2003) state that such a relationship is even more pronounced if one considers the role of colonial ties in generating cultural similarities. This is especially significant as one considers that the impact of colonial ties on trade persists decades or even centuries after colonial relationships were dissolved.

TABLE 12.2 **Effects of similarities versus differences on bilateral trade**

Dimensions of distance/proximity	Determinant	Change in trade (%)
Cultural	Common language	+42
Administrative	Common regional trading block	+47
	Colony–colonizer links	+188
	Common currency	+114
	Differences in corruption	−11
Geographical	Physical distance	−1.1
	Physical size	−0.2
	Landlockedness	−48
	Common land border	+125
Economic	Economic size: GDP	+0.8
	Income level: GDP per capita	+0.7

Source: Ghemawat and Mallick (2003).

CAGE framework in strategy implementation

Ghemawat (2018) offers advice on how the CAGE framework can help managers to consider their options for international strategy development:

- It makes distance visible for managers.

- It helps to pinpoint the differences across countries that might handicap multinational companies relative to local competitors.

- It can shed light on the relative position of multinationals from different countries. For example, it can help to explain the strength of Spanish firms in many industries across Latin America compared with UK multinational firms operating in the same geographic market.

- It can be used to compare markets from the perspective of a particular company. One method to conduct quantitative analysis of this type is to discount (specifically, divide) raw measures of market size or potential with measures of distance, broadly defined.

Ghemawat emphasizes that different types of distance matter to different extents depending on the industry. For instance, because geographic distance affects the costs of transportation, it is of particular importance to companies dealing in heavy or bulky products. A cement manufacturer that is considering a globalization strategy would be ill advised to ship cement around the world from a central manufacturing location as the transportation costs relative to the value of a heavy shipment of cement would be uneconomical. Instead, the cement company should consider exporting its special technological know-how or open manufacturing operations in local markets (for further insights, see the example of Dangote Cement in Chapter 6). Conversely, high-value but low-weight items such as microchips can be shipped at low cost from one location across vast geographic distances. Cultural distance, on the other hand, affects consumers' product preferences. This should be a crucial consideration for a consumer goods or a media company as such a distance is more psychological than physical but by no means less important.

12

Access the online resources to watch a short video clip where Fazeela Gopalani discusses her involvement of stakeholders in strategy development.

12.5 Entering international markets

Once a business has decided to expand its operations beyond domestic markets, in what ways can it enter foreign markets? In this section, we consider six internationalization options available to existing organizations. But first we recognize that there are increasingly exceptions to the traditional idea that a firm starts in its domestic market and later on expands into foreign markets. These exceptions, often referred to as 'born global' firms, achieve international sales from an early stage in their development (Knight and Cavusgil 2005) without a gradual progression of their international activities.

Born global firms

Much of international strategy literature has focused on the evolutionary nature of firm internationalization, which has assumed an orderly expansion from exporting to strategic alliances and joint ventures to wholly owned foreign subsidiaries (Johanson and Vahlne 1977), which we discuss later in this section.

In contrast with the orderly development of international operations, from the outset **born global** firms consider opportunities that are present in international markets, and they develop their resources and capabilities accordingly to take advantage of such opportunities. Born global firms are not a new phenomenon, however. For example, the East India Company, which was founded in 1601, was a global firm from its inception as it was founded to trade with the East Indies. Today, the likely firms that can be viewed as born global will not be major domestic trading companies but digital enterprises. Many companies in the digital economy are, by their nature, born global from the outset. We have already seen the explosive international expansion of Zoom from a small start-up to a leading provider of video conferencing services. Other born global firms that are familiar to most of us are Meta, Uber, Amazon, and LinkedIn from the United States and Skype from Denmark, which was acquired by Microsoft in 2011 for $8.5 billion.

The 'born global' concept was first used by Rennie (1993) and describes the development that a firm does not need to evolve into a large organization in order to internationalize. In a digital economy, e-commerce companies can overcome barriers to internationalization and can do so quickly and cheaply.

In their review of the literature on born global companies, Rasmussen and Tanev (2015: 13) identify six characteristics and entrepreneurial challenges of early internationalization.

1. The decision of a born global firm to engage in a systematic internationalization process is usually determined by its nature—the type of technology that is being developed or the firm's specialization within the specific industry sector, value chain, or market (Jones et al. 2011).

2. Born global firms tend to be relatively small and have far fewer financial, human, and tangible resources compared with the large multinational enterprises that have been considered as dominant in global trade and investment.

3. Many born global firms are technology firms, although the born global phenomenon has spread widely beyond the technology sector (Moen 2002).

4. Born global firms have managers possessing a strong international outlook and international entrepreneurial orientation. The skills of top management teams have been found to be very important for the enablement of a more intense internationalization, particularly in the knowledge-based sectors (Andersson and Evangelista 2006; Johnson 2004; Loane et al. 2007).

5. Born global firms tend to adopt differentiation strategies focusing on unique designs and highly distinctive products targeting niche markets which may be too small for the tastes of larger firms (Cavusgil and Knight 2009).

6. Many born global firms leverage information and communication technologies to identify and segment customers into narrow global market niches and skilfully serve highly specialized buyer needs. Such technologies allow them to process information efficiently and communicate with partners and customers worldwide at practically zero cost (Maltby 2012; Servais et al. 2006).

By definition, born global firms are multinational enterprises that, from their founding, seek to derive a competitive advantage from the use of resources and sell their output in multiple countries (see Case Example 12.3). In the changing global landscape that is characterized by increasing digitization of products and services and e-commerce capabilities, we are likely to see an increasing number of born global firms. Some of them are likely to become household names. Further emergence of born global enterprises can be encouraged by universities and other knowledge clusters by channelling technology and business expertise to prospective entrepreneurs. This is especially important in countries with small domestic markets that force embryonic firms to think globally from the outset and for entrepreneurs in developing economies to reach out to global markets with innovative technologies and products that may be ahead of their time in their domestic markets.

Six internationalization options

In contrast with the born global firms just described, most traditional companies begin life as a domestic firm. If they choose to enter foreign markets, they have six options (adding an international dimension to the modes of diversification described in Chapter 10). These strategies, in order of their complexity and business risk, are as follows.

1. Maintain a domestic production base but export goods from the home market to foreign buyers and markets, either indirectly or directly.

2. Enter into a licence agreement with a foreign firm to manufacture and distribute the company's products in a foreign market.

CASE EXAMPLE 12.3 TIKTOK: BORN TO BE GLOBAL

TikTok needs little introduction as the 15-second video app is currently available in over 140 countries with one billion active monthly users who, on average, spend more than 850 minutes per month on the app; TikTok has considerably more social media engagement rates per post than Instagram and YouTube. TikTok is currently valued at close to $100 billion in the secondary market.

TikTok's origins are different from the many fairy-tale, world-conquering start-ups such as AirBnB. TikTok was not just an idea that was conceived and built by a couple of friends in a family garage, but it started life as two different apps. ByteDance, a Chinese company owned by a former Microsoft engineer and serial entrepreneur Zhang Yiming, launched a video-sharing social network app called Douyin in 2016 that is still used in China for local audiences. The international version of the app was renamed TikTok when it was released in 2017. Much of TikTok's Western audience initially followed another ByteDance app, Musical.ly, that was merged into TikTok in 2018. Although TikTok and Douyin share similar user interfaces and features, they are not identical, being customized for their respective local markets.

Another striking difference between many other global start-ups and ByteDance is that, for years, Zhang Yiming had aspired to make ByteDance the first Chinese firm to rival US internet mammoths on the global stage. Zhang speaks passionately of his vision of ByteDance as a fully global company in the image of Google and Meta.

The TikTok phenomenon was not just down to luck, say those who know Zhang. As early as 2013, when ByteDance was just a year old and barely generating any revenue, Zhang started planning its global expansion, according to Joan Wang, an early investor in ByteDance. Zhang had told Wang over numerous meetings that he believed his artificial intelligence (AI)-based recommendation algorithms that were used in Chinese-language news aggregators could be expanded to different languages and content formats. This AI algorithm is the engine that drives TikTok today. Although Zhang's resources at the time seemed far from enough for achieving his global goals, he kept pursuing his vision and he admits consciously emulating US internet giants' strategies.

TikTok has paid partnerships with celebrities to drive the app's popularity in different countries and regions. These partnerships have been the cornerstone to TikTok's geographical expansion strategy. The app uses celebrities to create buzz around the platform and generate viral content. In addition to these paid collaborations, the app also benefits from local social influencers and celebrities who use the platform. These celebrities help bring in their followers to TikTok, who are then targeted by the algorithm.

Another key success factor in the app's popularity is its strong focus on localized content. The app runs local contests and challenges and latches onto local trends using localized hashtags. TikTok runs the '1 million audition' contest across several countries and regions. For the contests, participants are given themes to create videos and the top video creators are awarded. These contests and challenges lead to the creation of thousands of local videos and it helps TikTok creators to gain recognition and followers. Using these techniques, TikTok has been able to pull off localization on a global scale.

Questions for discussion

1. What do you think are the sources of TikTok's success and why?

2. Undertake research on the early days of AirBnB. What are the similarities and differences between AirBnB's and TikTok's globalization strategy, if any?

3. TikTok AI recommendation algorithm originates from a news recommendation algorithm. Think creatively and brainstorm what other applications such an algorithm could be used for.

Sources

BBC (2020). TikTok: The story of a social media giant (5 August), https://www.bbc.co.uk/news/technology-53640724 (last accessed 12 May 2022).

Geyser, W. (2022). TikTok statistics—63 TikTok stats you need to know [2022 update]. Influencer Marketing Hub. TikTok (1 August), https://influencermarketing-hub.com/tiktok-stats (last accessed 12 May 2022).

McLachlan, S. (2022). What is TikTok? Best facts and tips for 2022. *Hootsuite.com* (6 April), https://blog.hoot-suite.com/what-is-tiktok (last accessed 12 May 2022).

Yang, Y. and Zhu, J. (2020). Zhang Yiming, founder of TikTok owner ByteDance, gears up for the global stage. *Reuters* (13 March), https://www.reuters.com/article/us-china-bytedance-ceo-idUSKBN21014Y (last accessed 12 May 2022).

3. Enter into a franchise agreement with a foreign franchisee to carry out specific production and/or sales activities for the company in the franchisee's own home market.

4. Enter into a cooperative agreement with a foreign partner through a joint venture or strategic alliance.

5. Enter a foreign market through an acquisition.

6. Enter a foreign market by establishing a presence through a wholly owned subsidiary.

The organization's choice of the foreign market entry strategy depends on factors such as the business potential offered by the foreign markets, the resources available for international expansion, and the previous experience of the firm in international business. For example, it is unlikely that a small to medium-sized firm operating in a national market will have the resources and expertise available to enter a foreign market immediately by establishing international operations unless the firm is acquired by a larger firm with resources and expertise in international markets. For example, the UK-based coffee chain, Costa Coffee, a medium-sized firm, was acquired in the summer of 2018 by Coca-Cola for £3.9 billion. It remains to be seen whether Coca-Cola will attempt to build Costa Coffee into a global brand to challenge the dominance of Starbucks.

The six strategies for international expansion can be arranged in terms of the degree of control the firm has over the internationalization process relative to the degree of risk and return from such activities. This degree of control–risk/reward relationship is depicted in Figure 12.5, where it can be seen that exporting either indirectly or directly to a foreign market represents the lowest level of risk/return but also the lowest level of control that an exporting firm has over how the product is positioned or represented in the foreign market. Conversely, having a wholly owned subsidiary in a foreign market affords the firm the highest level of control and return, but the firm also carries all the risk if the internationalization venture fails. The characteristics of each international expansion strategy and their advantages and disadvantages are detailed in Table 12.3.

When considering whether to internationalize, firms have to take into account not only the managerial and financial resources available to them but also factors that are beyond their control such as the globalization drivers which affect the industry that the business operates in. In addition, companies have to take into account geographical, national, cultural, and other legacy factors such as psychological distance between the firm's home country and the possible foreign markets.

12

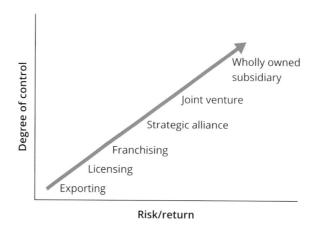

FIGURE 12.5 International expansion options. *Source*: authors.

Once a decision has been made to internationalize, companies are faced with a number of different foreign market entry strategies ranging from exporting to establishing wholly owned operations abroad. There is no single 'right' entry strategy. It will depend on the resources available to the firm and, in some cases, the foreign country regulations may dictate what type of operating presence is available for foreign company entrants. Most companies have to make trade-offs that are often based on the assessment of risk of the proposed entry strategy. As we have seen, different international expansion strategies have varying degrees of risk. The more control a firm has over its international operations, the more business risks are associated with such strategies. Hence, the managers have to make an honest appraisal of their own capabilities to manage complex international operations and choose an appropriate expansion strategy accordingly.

12.6 Three generic international strategy options

In section 12.5, we saw that companies may choose to expand internationally in a number of ways, ranging from export-driven strategies to establishing fully owned subsidiaries in foreign markets. Once a firm moves from just exporting its domestically produced products to more complex involvement in foreign markets, it will need to balance the conflicting pressures of product standardization with drivers for local responsiveness. The firm does this by adapting its products to local market conditions. Selling a fully standardized product across multiple markets will most likely allow the firm to earn efficiency gains in the form of economies of scale and scope (see the discussion in section 12.3 of the Ontario Maple Syrup Producers Association, which sells a standardized product across a number of markets with minimally adapted advertising campaigns). Should firms adapt their competitive approach in each market? And if so, how should they do this? In this section, we will consider three generic international strategy options that provide answers to these questions.

12

TABLE 12.3 **International expansion strategies**

Expansion strategy	Characteristics	Advantages	Disadvantages
Indirect exporting	• A firm sells its product to a foreign intermediary based in the company's home country • Requires little or no knowledge of foreign markets	• Particularly attractive for small-to-medium-sized companies as indirect exporting requires no international experience and no commitment of resources for foreign operations • Low risks as indirect exporting is a domestic transaction with a buyer located in the firm's home country • No foreign exchange risk, unlike in other international expansion strategies, as the firm is paid in its local home currency	• The firm has limited control over how the product is marketed and sold in the foreign market • The firm has limited knowledge of the foreign buyers of the product • Less profit is earned by the firm when a number of intermediaries are involved, which may include foreign buying agents, brokers, trading companies, and distributors
Direct exporting	• Unlike indirect exporting, the firm sells directly to a distributor or end-user located in a foreign market • Direct exporting is a suitable strategy for firms that expect foreign export markets to form a significant portion of the firm's total sales • In the United Kingdom, BP, Rio Tinto, and GlaxoSmithKline are the top three export companies	• Better control over the distribution, marketing, and sale of the firm's product to foreign buyers • Improved feedback from foreign customers that provides the firm with insight into the foreign market conditions and how the product is perceived by the foreign buyers • Low-cost strategy to build economies of scale • Better protection of trademarks and brand • Fewer intermediaries involved in direct exporting, which provides the firm with a larger share of the profit	• There is higher risk in terms of foreign counter-party risk as the firm is trading with intermediaries or buyers in a foreign market, which may involve both economic and political risks • There is limited knowledge of foreign market conditions based on arm's-length experience

Continued

12

TABLE 12.3 *Continued*

Expansion strategy	Characteristics	Advantages	Disadvantages
Licensing	• A firm may use licensing in the transfer of patented information and trademarks, information and know-how, including specifications, written documents, and computer programmes, as well as information needed to sell a product or service in a foreign market (Mottner and Johnson 2000) • Walt Disney is the world's largest licensor with the firm's portfolio of Star Wars and Mickey and Minnie Mouse characters	• Particularly attractive for small-to-medium-sized companies as licensing affords international expansion with very limited resource commitment in the foreign market • Allows speedy entry to a foreign market and can be used as a stepping stone for a more committed entry to the foreign market in the future	• The licensor may lose control of the quality of the product that is manufactured by the licensee • The licensor may lose control of the marketing and distribution of the product in the foreign market • Licensing may encourage opportunistic behaviour by a licensee copying the licensor's technology, know-how, or product • Licence agreements are based on royalty payments made to the licensor by the licensee and it may be difficult for the licensor to enforce agreements in some markets
Franchising	• Franchising is a 'contract-based organizational structure for entering new markets' (Teegen 2000) • The franchisor agrees to transfer to a franchisee a business concept that it has developed with corresponding product, technologies, and operational guidelines • The United Kingdom's BodyShop is probably one of the best known franchisors, which achieved quick global presence in the 1980s under the founders Anita and Gordon Roddick • 81% of MacDonald's outlets are franchises	• Requires moderate resources that are committed to a foreign market but allows speedy market entry • There is a steady cashflow of royalty payments and management fees made by a franchisee to the franchisor	• The main risk is that the franchisee does not follow the directives set by the franchisor, which can damage the overall reputation and brand of the franchisor • Requires detailed vetting and continuous monitoring of the franchisees

12

	Description	Advantages	Disadvantages
Strategic alliance/ joint venture	• A firm may enter into a strategic alliance that is a cooperative agreement between firms in different countries • A strategic alliance involves exchange, sharing, or co-development for achieving significant objectives that are mutually beneficial and beyond what a single firm could achieve alone (Frynas and Mellahi 2015) • A strategic alliance does not result in the creation of a separate corporate entity, but it may be a precursor to a joint venture • A joint venture is a cooperative agreement that has been created as a separate entity by two or more partners; a joint venture may result from a strategic alliance • Refer to Case Example 12.4 as an example of a complex alliance	• A strategic alliance may allow both partners to respond quickly to a changing business environment and contribute complementary knowledge and strengths to seize emerging opportunities quickly • A joint venture as a formalized agreement through the creation of a separate entity allows complementary strengths to be leveraged more permanently • In some markets, such as China, a joint venture with a local Chinese partner may be the only legal way to enter the market	• As strategic alliances and joint ventures are based on a shared risk, the profits are shared between the partners • Disagreements between partners may arise from disputes over management approaches, organizational cultures, differing levels of resource contribution to the partnership efforts, and lack of trust among the employees and managers of the partner firms
Wholly owned subsidiary	• Compared with other international expansion strategies, wholly owned subsidiaries involve the highest level of risk • A firm can either enter a market by building a wholly owned subsidiary in a foreign market from scratch (greenfield strategy) or establishing a presence through a merger or acquisition (M&A strategy) • For a firm to choose an acquisition rather than a greenfield entry strategy, the cost of constructing new facilities, installing equipment, and hiring a new labour force must exceed the cost of purchasing and recasting existing properties	• There is low risk to appropriation of the firm's know-how • There is full control of operations • There is the ability to appoint managers who are loyal to the parent firm • There is no need to share profits with outside partners	• High risk as all business risks are borne by the parent company • Could be perceived as a foreign firm by the local market, especially for greenfield strategy • There may be problems in recruiting qualified employees and managers from a local market • There may be problems in integrating management and operating systems in an M&A strategy

Source: Barkema and Vermeulen (1998).

12

CASE EXAMPLE 12.4 WILL THE WORLD'S LARGEST CAR MANUFACTURING ALLIANCE SURVIVE?

Fast-evolving technology of driverless cars and the sustainable manufacturing of electric vehicles are at the forefront of all car manufacturers' agendas looking to the future. However, despite the close alliance that has bound them together for over 20 years, Renault and Nissan, and—since 2016—Mitsubishi, not all is well. Some industry commentators have even stated that the three companies are barely talking to each other, despite launching a Common Roadmap 2030 that focuses on pure electric vehicles and connected mobility.

Renault, Nissan, and Mitsubishi Motors is a strategic alliance that is based on the rationale that, due to substantial cross-shareholdings, each company will act in the financial interests of the other alliance partners while still maintaining their individual brand identities and corporate cultures. Operationally, the three-member alliance is founded on the premise that cooperation will benefit all partners as automakers globally grapple with the expensive shift to electric and autonomous vehicles. The alliance partners are seeking to use common batteries and other key components to bring cost savings. In addition, the alliance partners have committed themselves for manufacturing electric vehicles that will make up 80% of the total production by 2026 and 100% by 2030.

The key deliverables of the 2030 Roadmap are stated as follows:

- To enhance usage of common platforms to reach 80% in 2026.

- Mitsubishi Motors to reinforce its presence in Europe with two new models based on Renault best-sellers.

- To invest 23 B€ in the next five years to support its offensive strategy in electrification.

- With 35 new electric vehicles in 2030, to propose the largest global electric vehicle offer, based on the five common vehicle platforms.

- Nissan to unveil an all-new electric vehicle platform to replace the Micra in Europe; vehicle planned to be manufactured at Renault

ElectriCity, the electric industrial centre in Northern France.

- To reinforce common battery strategy aiming to secure a global 220 GWh production capacity by 2030.

- Nissan to lead development of breakthrough all-solid-state battery technology to benefit all members.

- Renault to lead development on common centralized electrical and electronic architecture and launch the first full software-defined vehicle by 2025.

While the Roadmap is a well-argued and presented goal, shareholders are not easily convinced of the feasibility of the stated strategy. This is one of the reasons why the the members of the alliance (which was once thought to have the potential to become the largest carmaker in the world) are respectively valued at $10 billion (Renault), $20 billion (Nissan), and $4 billion (Mitsubishi Motors), taking it to a total of $34 billion. Electric car manufacturers such as Lucid Motors, Nio, and Rivian are all seen as being worth more than the combined value of the alliance and they've barely delivered a car. Tesla's market capitalization is $771 billion with an annual production of only 930,000 vehicles in 2020. In contrast, the alliance partners manufactured over 5 million vehicles in 2019 before the COVID-19 pandemic.

Additional tension is caused by conflict over control of the alliance. Nissan is a far larger and more profitable firm than Renault and has twice the market value of Renault. Renault holds a 43% stake in Nissan with voting rights, while Nissan owns 15% of Renault and has no voting rights. In addition, the single largest shareholder in Renault is the French government, which may have the effect of placing Nissan's operations under French government control and has contributed to resentment over the terms of the alliance within both Nissan and Japan. Were Renault to sell all or part of the stake in Nissan, it would generate as much as 7.2 billion euros for Renault, which is about equal to its current market value. Realizing this, Nissan halted dividend pay-outs in 2019, depriving Renault of a key source of cash.

Many automotive analysts are sceptical of the future success of the alliance. They suspect that these three car makers will still be standing, through a combination of government support and doggedness, come 2030, but they will almost certainly be substantially smaller and may no longer be in an alliance at all.

Questions for discussion

1. Identify key business drivers for the alliance.
2. What do you consider are the main difficulties for managing the alliance?
3. Critically consider the feasibility of continued future success of the alliance. What recommendations would you make to the management of the alliance?

Sources

Automotive News (2022). Renault–Nissan alliance leaders to meet amid new global business woes (7 April), https://www.autonews.com/executives/renault-nissan-alliance-leaders-meet-amid-new-global-business-woes (last accessed 19 August 2022).

The Economist (2018b). Renault Nissan Mitsubishi has become the world's biggest carmaker (17 March), https://www.economist.com/business/2018/03/17/renault-nissan-mitsubishi-has-become-the-worlds-biggest-carmaker (last accessed 2 August 2019).

The Financial Times (2019). Renault–Nissan: How long can the fractured alliance last? (7 July), https://www.ft.com/content/504e1682-9e76-11e9-9c06-a4640c9feebb (last accessed 19 August 2022).

Keown, C. (2020). The world's biggest car alliance just launched a reboot. Renault stock is soaring. *Barron's* (27 May), https://www.barrons.com/articles/the-worlds-biggest-car-alliance-just-launched-a-reboot-renault-stock-is-soaring-51590588589 (last accessed 12 May 2022).

Ma, J. and Horie, M. (2019). Divorce? Merger? Renault–Nissan alliance faces a crossroads. *BloombergUK* (11 June), https://www.bloomberg.com/news/articles/2019-06-11/what-may-happen-next-in-renault-s-20-year-alliance-with-nissan (last accessed 19 August 2022).

Renault Nissan Mitsubishi (2022). Alliance 2030: Best of three worlds for a new future, https://alliancernm.com (last accessed 12 May 2022).

White, P. (2022). Renault, Nissan, Mitsubishi—who will arrest the CEO this time? *Rethink Research* (2 February), https://rethinkresearch.biz/articles/renault-nissan-mitsubishi-who-will-arrest-the-ceo-this-time (last accessed 12 May 2022).

One of the key strategic decisions that firms who compete internationally must make is whether and how they have to adapt their competitive approach in each of the host countries to take into account the specific market conditions and customer preferences. Companies have three generic strategic options to solve this dilemma:

- a multidomestic strategy;
- a global strategy;
- a transnational strategy.

A multidomestic strategy is a strategy that is based on differentiating the firm's products on a country-by-country basis in an effort to be responsive to the local market conditions and customer tastes and preferences. A company that follows a multidomestic strategy takes the approach of thinking local and acting local. A high responsiveness to local market needs is appropriate when there are significant cross country differences in demographic, cultural, and market conditions and where opportunities for earning economies of scale and scope are limited. In order to be successful, local managers have to be given a significant degree of autonomy and decision-making power to address the local market needs and implement activities and policies accordingly. An example of multidomestic strategy is that white goods companies have to be highly responsive to local market conditions. In the United States, customers prefer large, two-door fridge-freezers as people tend to do their shopping weekly in bulk and homes are often bigger than in Europe. In contrast, Southern Europeans prefer small refrigerators as people tend to do their food shopping daily.

Global strategy is very different to multidomestic strategy. Companies that follow global strategy are said to 'think global, act global'. Such an organization employs the same competitive approach regardless of the markets where it operates. The firm attempts to sell the same product across all markets by developing a global brand with strong control from the company's headquarters in terms of product, marketing, and distribution standardization. A prerequisite for successful global strategy execution is that customer needs and preferences are relatively homogenous across markets. Examples of companies that follow a

TABLE 12.4 **Advantages and disadvantages of generic international strategy options**

International strategy option	Advantages	Disadvantages
Multidomestic strategy	• Ability to meet specific market needs and tastes • Ability to respond quickly to changes in local market conditions • Ability to respond better to local competitive opportunities and threats • Potential for a development of a market-specific competitive advantage	• Sharing of resources and knowledge across markets is difficult • Higher production, marketing, and distribution costs • Not conductive for development of a global brand and global competitive advantage
Global strategy	• Lower costs as a result of economies of scale and scope • Improved efficiency as knowledge is shared across markets • Global brand recognition and standardized promotion and distribution strategies • Potential for the development of a global competitive advantage	• Inability to meet specific market needs and tastes • Limited ability to respond to changes in local market conditions • Higher transportation costs than in multidomestic strategy • Possible exposure to import tariffs
Transnational strategy	• Benefits from being locally responsive but globally integrated • Ability to transfer and share some resources and knowledge across markets, such as manufacturing • Potential benefits from global coordination of activities, such as marketing and brand strategy • Potential for the development of a global competitive advantage	• Complex strategy that may be difficult to implement • High implementation costs due to the complexity of strategy • Difficult to assess the trade-off between conflicting goals of local responsiveness and global integration

Source: authors.

global strategy can be found in the pharmaceuticals industry as some human diseases are common across the world, or consider Apple Inc., which sells a standardized smartphone across the world.

In contrast, a **transnational strategy** is an approach that incorporates elements of both multidomestic and global strategy. This 'think global, act local' approach is often referred to as 'glocalization'. This hybrid strategy is appropriate when there is a relatively high need for local responsiveness but the firm can realize benefits from a degree of standardization. McDonald's is a good example of a firm that implemented a mass customization technique which allows it to address local market preferences in its menu selection in an efficient semi-standardized manner. Another example of semi-standardization is Disneyland Paris, although some Disney fans insist that the Paris amusement park failed to replicate the authentic Disney experience of their US parks.

As is the case in all strategy development, there is no one-size-fits-all approach. Table 12.4 highlights both the advantages and the disadvantages of each of the three strategy options.

PRACTITIONER INSIGHT **FAZEELA GOPALANI, HEAD OF MIDDLE EAST, ASSOCIATION OF CHARTERED CERTIFIED ACCOUNTANTS (ACCA)**

Fazeela Gopalani is Head of the Association of Chartered Certified Accountants (ACCA) in the Middle East, responsible for leading the operations in 11 countries and representing more than 20,000 students, affiliates, and members across the region. One of her fundamental roles is a thought-leader and conversation starter for all things 'accounting and finance profession' in the Middle East, with the purpose of growing the understanding of the value that professionally qualified accountants bring to businesses and economies across the region. Fazeela is an FCCA member and has over 18 years of experience in the field of accounting and finance. Fazeela has been the Head of Education for ACCA in the Middle East and she previously was a Senior Manager at PwC in Dubai. Prior to moving to the Emirates, Fazeela managed and owned an accounting practice in the United Kingdom.

'Can you describe the role of strategy in your organization?'

For me, strategy is a blueprint that helps us focus our energy and resources in an effective way and move with purpose and pace as one organization. Strategy helps us orient our work every day as to what we need to prioritize within our team, office, and organization. Part of my role is setting the strategy for ACCA in the Middle East (ME), working with colleagues in London to ensure coherence. By aligning to the strategy of ACCA centrally, it means we can be assured that we

Fazeela shares her views on strategy and purpose in an international organization

are focusing our efforts in an appropriate way. I ask all my team to put on their desks a copy of our strategic headlines—purpose, vision, values, top three strategic outcomes—so that's its always at the front of your mInd.

In terms of detail, in the ME, our strategy is the roadmap for personal contribution. Starting with the ME strategy, we then can develop plans of action for our territory which roll down to people's

Continued

objectives and commitments. Where required, we can (re-)align resources in the team to ensure that we are working towards the overall organizational aims effectively. Working in this way is so crucial for an organization of our scale and scope. We have 110 offices globally and this process based on central HQ developing the organizational strategy helps us work in a coherent way across the network. And central to all our strategy work is a sense of purpose. Our aim as an organization is to be a force for public good and lead the global accounting profession by creating opportunity.

'To what extent do you involve stakeholders—such as the UK.org, members, employees, local businesses etc.—in strategy development?'

In the ME, stakeholder engagement is crucial to our success. At any one time, we can be working with multiple national bodies and regulators. We seek to understand the priorities of governments, regulators, and the local national accounting bodies to understand how we can help deliver their strategies with impact.

We also have a team that focuses on members' and customers' feedback and insights to help us maintain our valuable services and position as thought leaders in the profession. From wide range of data sources, we use tools such as scenario planning to understand the implications of short- and medium-term change alongside generational shifts in service requirements. As we do so, we are always considering how best to stay true to our history and values. Like all organizations, evolving with the times is part of our strategic remit to ensure maximum relevance and effectiveness. And we are an organization with a tradition of being at the forefront of progressive change. For example, we were the first UK accountancy body to admit a woman in 1909. Through our purpose, we are driven to create equal opportunity and possibilities for all in the accounting profession. It is an approach that has provided an enduring strategic aim over the years.

'What are your main strategic considerations when operating internationally?'

Operating internationally, there are two main challenges we strive to address. First, we work hard to make sure that we have harmonious and respectful relationships with the accounting bodies wherever we operate. In many countries, there is a local accounting body that understandably might be concerned about an international entrant. So, through dialogue and engagement, we work hard to explain the uniqueness of our offering as a complement to existing in country provisions.

Second, there are additional complexities to operating internationally which you have to adequately plan for and resource. These include obtaining local licences, proving our right to operate, and defining mutually acceptable work policies. Each territory also views not-for-profit organizations differently, which makes a difference to registration, tax implications, etc.

Drawing on our experience, we address this complexity as part of our strategic planning and resourcing. Our adaptive strategic capabilities help us reach new territories as we serve our global membership. Through a combination of our regional headquarters in the United Arab Emirates and local teams within markets, we ensure that we develop organizational arrangements that comply with the laws of the land in which we operate, whilst serving the needs of our members effectively.

'How is the practice of strategy changing in your opinion? What would you advise strategic leaders to prioritize in the current climate?'

In my view, there has been a real shift in the expectations around strategy in recent years. In addition to the impact of the pandemic on how we live and work, geo-political events have disrupted organizational norms. As such, paying close attention to the external landscape and being able to react swiftly to local and global changes increases the value of frequent strategic analysis.

Further, the range of stakeholder voices expected to be represented in strategy has grown. This is a positive development, to everyone's benefit, but it means that, as strategy practitioners, there is a need to listen more, assume less, and regularly be asking more questions. For me, it is absolutely crucial that you don't ignore feedback received, particularly if you don't like it! Reaching out to your communities, such as our membership, has never been more important. It is also vital that we look after each other as part of being sustainable and responsible organizations. This means that strategy should now incorporate the potential of digital technologies for new ways of working, promoting colleague wellness, and

12

enabling people to use their talents fully to help you deliver your aims.

In short, we have to be adaptable as the world is moving so fast, placing an imperative on us being dynamic with our strategy work. Equally, in ACCA, our sense of purpose gives us continuity and stability even as we evolve our organization, as do our values of integrity, inclusivity, and innovation. I think this really matters as increasingly societal and membership views orient towards profit balanced with purpose. This is really important for us as we live out, every day, our purpose of being for the public good.

I see also the growing importance of partnering and collaboration for new opportunities. This is important to our mission and also implies a need for localization. Strategy gives you the overarching blueprint of what you are aiming to achieve. But how you do that, in an effective way, which meets local market needs aligned with your values and purpose, is where a collaborative mentality is required. Strategic leadership through people and partners can create a respectful and sustainable community to everyone's benefit.

Whilst the world is undoubtedly disrupted, for me, every challenge is an opportunity if you can stay true to your purpose. Because if you can consistently strategize and act in line with your purpose, everything else will follow!

 Access the online resources to watch a short video clip where Fazeela Gopalani talks more about her career.

Each of the three generic international strategy options involves distinct advantages and disadvantages. Which option is appropriate for the firm is dependent not only on the product attributes produced by the firm but also on the resources and capabilities of the firm and its management. Transnational strategy is probably the most difficult option to implement in practice. For such a strategy to succeed, not only should the firm be able to adapt to local market conditions by empowering local managers to make strategic decisions but also the firm's management should be able to ensure global coordination of activities in order to gain possible economies of scale and scope without restricting local responsiveness. As is often the case, theory is easy, but implementing it in practice is difficult. When evaluating opportunities for international expansion, in your future career as a strategist you should conduct an honest appraisal of what resources are available to the firm, including access to local management expertise and the ability of the top management team to manage a complex global organization effectively.

 ## CHAPTER SUMMARY

In this chapter, we addressed the following learning outcomes:

- ◯ Recognize the nature of globalization and examine how this influences strategy.
  Globalization is an ongoing process of international integration that results from, and supports, the interchange of products, ideas, culture, and institutions. The results of the removal of trade barriers, deregulation of financial transactions, harmonization of product standards, and legal frameworks present strategic opportunities upon which firms can build their competitive advantage by operating internationally. The shifting patterns in global trade, such as increasing regionalization of trade, require firms to anticipate

such macro-level shifts in their strategic decision-making over issues such as where to locate their value chain activities.

○ **Explore the drivers for globalization and their impact on organizations.**
There are four generic sets of 'industry globalization drivers': market, cost, competition, and government drivers. These industry globalization drivers may create conditions for industries to become global and, as a consequence, for the firms in such a global industry to adopt a global approach to their strategy development.

○ **Identify the cultural and practice challenges in global strategy implementation.**
When considering an internationalization strategy, a firm has to make a decision as to what extent its product or service can be standardized across multiple foreign markets or to what extent the firm has to adapt its offer to conform to local market, social, and cultural conditions. An ability to sell a standardized product across multiple markets will earn the firm economies of scale, but this has to be balanced with prevailing foreign market conditions and characteristics.

○ **Evaluate the motivations and models for internationalization.**
When considering whether to internationalize by adopting activities that range from exports to foreign direct investment, firms have to consider both the managerial and financial resources available to them and factors that are beyond their control such as the globalization drivers that affect the industry in which the business operates. In addition, organizations have to take into account geographical, national, cultural, and other legacy factors such as psychological distance between the firm's home country and the possible foreign markets. There is no single 'right' entry strategy. It will depend on the resources available to the firm, and, in some cases, the foreign country regulations may dictate what type of operating presence is available for foreign company entrants. Most companies have to make trade-offs that are often based on the assessment of risk of the proposed entry strategy.

○ **Examine the phenomenon of 'born global'.**
Born global firms are organizations that, from early in their founding, seek superior international performance from the application of knowledge-based resources to the sale of outputs in multiple foreign markets. From the outset, such firms consider opportunities that are present in international markets, and they develop their resources and capabilities accordingly to take an advantage of these opportunities. Today, the firms that are most likely to be viewed as born global are digital enterprises.

○ **Compare and contrast the generic global strategy orientations.**
The three generic global strategy orientations are multidomestic, global, and transnational. Each of the three generic options involve distinct advantages and disadvantages. Which option is appropriate for a firm depends not only on the product attributes produced by the firm but also on the resources and capabilities of the firm and its management. When evaluating opportunities for international expansion, strategists should conduct an honest appraisal of what resources are available to the firm, including access to local management expertise and the ability of the top management team to manage a complex global organization effectively.

END-OF-CHAPTER QUESTIONS

Recall questions

1. What is the difference between globalization and the firm's global strategy?
2. Identify **Yip's industry globalization drivers**.
3. What are the different internationalization options available to firms?
4. What is understood by the concept born global?

Application questions

A) What do you consider to be the advantages and disadvantages of globalization?
B) Conduct an analysis of an industry of your choice using Yip's globalization drivers. Does your analysis support the globalization of your choice of industry? Why/why not?
C) Identify companies that followed multidomestic, global, and transnational strategies. Why do you think that the firms adopted such a strategy?
D) It is often assumed that firms internationalize gradually. Identify firms that became global almost from the start. Why do you think that these firms were born global?

ONLINE RESOURCES

www.oup.com/he/mackay2e

In addition to the video interviews already highlighted, the book's **online resources** include the following features for this chapter, specifically:

- *links to further reading material* to broaden your knowledge of key issues discussed in this chapter;
- *self-test multiple-choice questions* to test your understanding of the material covered in each section of the chapter; and
- *a flashcard glossary* to help you recall and test your understanding of key terms.

12

FURTHER READING

'Observations of deglobalization against globalization and impacts on global business' by Hag-Min Kim et al.

Kim, H.M., Li, P., and Lee, Y.R. (2020) Observations of deglobalization against globalization and impacts on global business. *International Trade, Politics and Development*, **4**(2), 83–103.

This article investigates the drivers of deglobalization trends against globalization. Applying an empirical model, the paper posits that deglobalization has emerged since the global financial crisis of 2008. This is evidenced by a decreasing trend of import share in a country's GDP, and it is influenced by manufacturing imports, country's income divide, and political globalization. Deglobalization is more apparent in developed countries than in developing countries and this trend is predicted to continue in future.

'Viewing global strategy through a microfoundations lens' by Farok Contractor et al.

Contractor, F., Foss, N.J., Kundu, S., and Lahiri, S. (2019). Viewing global strategy through a microfoundations lens. *Global Strategy Journal*, **9**(1), 3–18.

Studies of corporate strategies have focused on the firm as a unit of analysis, as if the firm could decide or think on its own, neglecting the fact that it is practitioners who think, decide, and act. The underlying motivations, interactions, and characteristics of individual managers of companies have often been missing in explanations of global strategy formulation. This introductory article refines and enunciates strategic practice theory in its application to global business.

Global Strategic Management by Jedrzej George Frynas and Kamel Mellahi

Frynas, J.G. and Mellahi, K. (2014). *Global Strategic Management*. Oxford: Oxford University Press.

This specialized textbook on global strategic management provides insight into the corporate strategies of organizations operating on a global scale and explains the analysis, decision-making, and development processes behind securing competitive advantage.

'Systematic literature review on born global firms' by Sinan Nardali

Nardali, S. (2017). Systematic literature review on born global firms. *Journal of Management & Economics*, **24**(2), 563–78.

Born global firms enter the global marketplace soon after their inception, bypassing the domestic market in many cases. Sometimes, these firms grow largely in their home markets before they rapidly reach high percentages of international revenues. This article offers a systematic literature review on born global firms.

'The nature of service characteristics and their impact on internationalization: A multiple case study of born global firms' by Murray Taylor et al.

Taylor, M, et al. (2021) The nature of service characteristics and their impact on internationalization: A multiple case study of born global firms. *Journal of Business Research* **132**, 517–29.

Literature on born global firms often assumes a uniform pattern of internationalization across manufacturing and service industry sectors. The literature pays scant attention to the different characteristics of service-based born global firms and how they shape these firms' internationalization process. The article reveals that service-based born global firms have different internationalization drivers, target different foreign markets, and have distinct **foreign market entry modes**.

The Competitive Advantage of Nations by Michael E. Porter

Porter, M.E. (1998). *The Competitive Advantage of Nations* (11th edn). New York: Free Press.

This seminal book presents a theory of competitiveness based on the causes of the productivity with which companies compete. The author shows how traditional comparative advantages, such as natural resources and pools of labour, have been superseded as sources of prosperity and how broad macroeconomic accounts of competitiveness are insufficient. The concept of 'industry clusters' outlines a new way for companies and governments to think about economies, assess the competitive advantage of locations, and set public policy.

12

REFERENCES

Alexander, M. and Korine, H. (2008). When you shouldn't go global. *Harvard Business Review* (December).

Andersson, S. and Evangelista, F. (2006). The entrepreneur in the born global firm in Australia and Sweden. *Journal of Small Business and Enterprise Development*, **13**(4), 642–59.

Ashenfelter, O., Engle, R.F., McFadden, D.L., and Schmidt-Hebbel, K. (2018). Globalization: Contents and discontents. *Contemporary Economic Policy*, **36**, 29–43.

Automotive News (2022). Renault–Nissan alliance leaders to meet amid new global business woes (7 April), https://www.autonews.com/executives/renault-nissan-alliance-leaders-meet-amid-new-global-business-woes (last accessed 19 August 2022).

Bang, K.E. and Markeset, T. (2012). Identifying the drivers of economic globalization and the effects on companies' competitive situation. In: Frick, J. and Laugen, B.T. (eds), *Advances in Production Management Systems. Value Networks: Innovation, Technologies, and Management*. Berlin: Springer.

Barkema, H. and Vermeulen, F. (1998). International expansion through start-up or through acquisition: A learning perspective. *Academy of Management Journal*, **41**, 7–26.

BBC (2020). TikTok: The story of a social media giant (5 August), https://www.bbc.co.uk/news/technology-53640724 (last accessed 12 May 2022).

Cartwright, W.R. (1993). Multiple linked 'diamonds' and the international competitiveness of export-dependent industries: The New Zealand experience. *Management International Review*, **33**(2), 55–70.

Cavusgil, S.T. and Knight, G. (2009). *Born Global Firms: New International Enterprise*. New York: Business Expert Press.

Chappelow, J. (2022). Porter Diamond (11 March), https://www.investopedia.com/terms/p/porter-diamond.asp (last accessed 19 August 2022).

David, D. (2018). *The Almighty Dollar*. London: Elliott & Thompson.

D'Urbino, L. (2019) The steam has gone out of globalisation. *The Economist*, 24 January.

The Economist (2018a). A manifesto for renewing liberalism (13 September), https://www.economist.com/leaders/2018/09/13/a-manifesto-for-renewing-liberalism (last accessed 19 August 2022).

The Economist (2018b). Renault Nissan Mitsubishi has become the world's biggest carmaker (17 March), https://www.economist.com/business/2018/03/17/renault-nissan-mitsubishi-has-become-the-worlds-biggest-carmaker (last accessed 2 August 2019).

The Financial Times (2019). Renault–Nissan: How long can the fractured alliance last? (7 July), https://www.ft.com/content/504e1682-9e76-11e9-9c06-a4640c9feebb (last accessed 19 August 2022).

Frynas, J.G. and Mellahi, K. (2015). *Global Strategic Management* (3rd edn). Oxford: Oxford University Press.

Geyser, W. (2022). TikTok statistics—63 TikTok stats you need to know [2022 update]. Influencer Marketing Hub. TikTok (1 August), https://influencermarketinghub.com/tiktok-stats (last accessed 12 May 2022).

Ghemawat, P. (2001). Distance still matters: The hard reality of global expansion. *Harvard Business Review* (September).

Ghemawat, P. (2007). Managing differences: The central challenge of global strategy. *Harvard Business Review* (March).

Ghemawat, P. (2018). *The New Global Road Map: Enduring Strategies for Turbulent Times*. Boston, MA: Harvard Business Review Press.

Ghemawat, P. and Mallick, R. (2003). The industry-level structure of international trade networks: A gravity-based approach. Working paper. Harvard Business School.

Ghemawat, P. and Siegel, J. (2011). *Redefining Global Strategy: Crossing Borders in a World Where Differences Still Matter*. Boston, MA: Harvard Business School Press.

GlobalNewsWire (2017). Zoom partners with Sequoia in $100 million funding round (17 January), https://www.globenewswire.com/news-release/2017/01/17/1311117/0/en/Zoom-Partners-with-Sequoia-in-100-Million-Funding-Round.html (last accessed 19 August 2022).

IMF (International Monetary Fund) (2008). Issues Brief, Globalization: A brief overview. 02/08 (May), https://www.imf.org/external/np/exr/ib/2008/pdf/053008.pdf (last accessed 19 August 2022).

Johanson, J. and Vahlne, J. (1977). The internationalization process of the firm: A model of knowledge development and increasing foreign market commitments. *Journal of International Business Studies*, 8(1): 23–32.

Johanson, J. and Wiedersheim-Paul, F. (1975). The internationalization of the firm: Four Swedish cases. *Journal of Management Studies*, **12**, 305–23.

Johnson, J.E. (2004). Factors influencing the early internationalization of high technology start-ups: US and UK evidence. *Journal of International Entrepreneurship*, **2**, 139–54.

Jones, M.V., Coviello, N.E., and Tang, Y.K. (2011). International entrepreneurship research (1989–2009): A domain ontology and thematic analysis. *Journal of Business Venturing*, **26**(6), 632–59.

Keown, C. (2020). The world's biggest car alliance just launched a reboot. Renault stock is soaring. *Barron's* (27 May), https://www.barrons.com/articles/the-worlds-biggest-car-alliance-just-launched-a-reboot-renault-stock-is-soaring-51590588589 (last accessed 12 May 2022).

Knight, G.A. and Cavusgil, S.T. (2005). A taxonomy of born global firms. *Management International Review*, **45**, 15–35.

Koetsier, J. (2021). Here are the 10 most downloaded apps of 2020. *Forbes* (7 January), https://www.forbes.com/sites/johnkoetsier/2021/01/07/here-are-the-10-most-downloaded-apps-of-2020/?sh=5882102a5d1a (last accessed 19 August 2022).

Krugman, P.R. (1993). On the relationship between trade theory and location theory. *Review of International Economics*, **1**, 110–22.

Kuttner, R. (2018). *Can Democracy Survive Global Capitalism*. London: W.W. Norton.

Loane, S., Bell, J.D., and McNaughton, R. (2007). A cross-national study on the impact of management teams on the rapid internationalization of small firms. *Journal of World Business,* **42**(4), 489–504.

Ma, J. and Horie, M. (2019). Divorce? Merger? Renault–Nissan alliance faces a crossroads. *BloombergUK* (11 June), https://www.bloomberg.com/news/articles/2019-06-11/what-may-happen-next-in-renault-s-20-year-alliance-with-nissan (last accessed 19 August 2022).

Maltby, T. (2012). Using social media to accelerate the internationalization of start-ups from inception. *Technology Innovation Management Review*, **2**(10), 22–6.

McLachlan, S. (2022). What is TikTok? Best facts and tips for 2022. *Hootsuite.com* (6 April), https://blog.hootsuite.com/what-is-tiktok (last accessed 12 May 2022).

Moen, O. (2002). The born globals. *International Marketing Review*, **19**(2), 156–75.

Mottner, S. and Johnson, P.J. (2000). Motivations and risks in international licensing, a review and implications for licensing to transitional and emerging economies. *Journal of World Business* **35**(2): 171–88.

Office of the United States Trade Representative (2022). The People's Republic of China, https://ustr.gov/countries-regions/china-mongolia-taiwan/peoples-republic-china (last accessed 2 May 2022).

Pinkus, G., Manyika, J., and Ramaswamy, S. (2017). We can't undo globalization, but we can improve it. *Harvard Business Review* (10 January).

Porter, M. (1990). *The Competitive Advantage of Nations*. New York: Free Press.

Rasmussen, E.S. and Tanev, S. (2015). The emergence of the lean global start-up as a new type of firm. *Technology Innovation Management Review*, **5**(11), 12–19.

Renault Nissan Mitsubishi (2022). Alliance 2030: Best of three worlds for a new future, https://alliancernm.com (last accessed 12 May 2022).

Rennie, M.W. (1993). Global competitiveness: Born global. *McKinsey Quarterly*, **4**(1), 45–52.

12

Roser, M. (2020). The short history of global living conditions and why it matters that we know it. *Our World in Data*, https://ourworldindata.org/a-history-of-global-living-conditions-in-5-charts (last accessed 19 August 2022).

Roser, M. and Ortiz-Ospina, E. (2016). Income Inequality. *OurWorldInData.org*, https://ourworldindata.org/income-inequality (last accessed 19 August 2022).

Rugman, A.M. and D'Cruz, J.R. (1993). The 'double diamond' model of international competitiveness: the Canadian experience. *Management International Review*, **33**(2), 17–32.

Servais, P., Madsen, T.K., and Rasmussen, E.S. (2006). Small manufacturing firms' involvement in international e-business activities. In: *Advances in International Marketing, Vol. 17. International Marketing Research.* Bingley: Emerald Publishing, pp. 297–317.

Sloan, M. (2020). The 3 secrets behind Zoom's triple-digit growth. *Drift* (10 April), https://www.drift.com/blog/how-zoom-grew (last accessed 19 August 2022).

Strategy+Business (2008). 26 February.

Teegen, H. (2000). Examining strategic and economic development implications of globalising through franchising. *International Business Review*, **9**(4), 497–521.

UN (United Nations) (2016). Human Development Report, 2016: Human Development for Everyone, United Nations Development Programme, https://sustainabledevelopment.un.org/content/documents/25212016_human_development_report.pdf (last accessed 19 August 2022).

Van Den Bosch, F.A.J. and Van Prooijen, A.A. (1992). European management: An emerging competitive advantage of European nations. *European Management Journal*, **10**(4), 445–8.

Walmart (2018). Annual Report 2018, http://www.corporatereport.com/walmart/2018/ar/Walmart_2018_Annual%20Report.pdf (last accessed 19 August 2022).

Walmart (2022). Annual Report 2022, https://s2.q4cdn.com/056532643/files/doc_financials/2022/ar/WMT-FY2022-Annual-Report.pdf (last accessed 2 May 2022).

White, P. (2022). Renault, Nissan, Mitsubishi—who will arrest the CEO this time? *Rethink Research* (2 February), https://rethinkresearch.biz/articles/renault-nissan-mitsubishi-who-will-arrest-the-ceo-this-time (last accessed 12 May 2022).

Yang, Y. and Zhu, J. (2020). Zhang Yiming, founder of TikTok owner ByteDance, gears up for the global stage. *Reuters* (13 March), https://www.reuters.com/article/us-china-bytedance-ceo-idUSKBN21014Y (last accessed 12 May 2022).

Yip, G. (1995). *Total Global Strategy: Managing for Worldwide Competitive Advantage*. Upper Saddle River, NJ: Prentice Hall.

Zoom Video Communications, Inc. Support during the COVID-19 pandemic, https://explore.zoom.us/en/covid19 (last accessed 19 August 2022).

Zoom Video Communications, Inc. (2022). Zoom for online learning updates (April), https://blog.zoom.us/how-to-use-zoom-for-online-learning (last accessed 19 August 2022).

Zoom Video Communications, Inc. (2022). Zoom's commitment to user support and business continuity during the coronavirus outbreak (26 February), https://blog.zoom.us/zoom-commitment-user-support-business-continuity-during-coronavirus-outbreak/ (last accessed 19 August 2022).

12

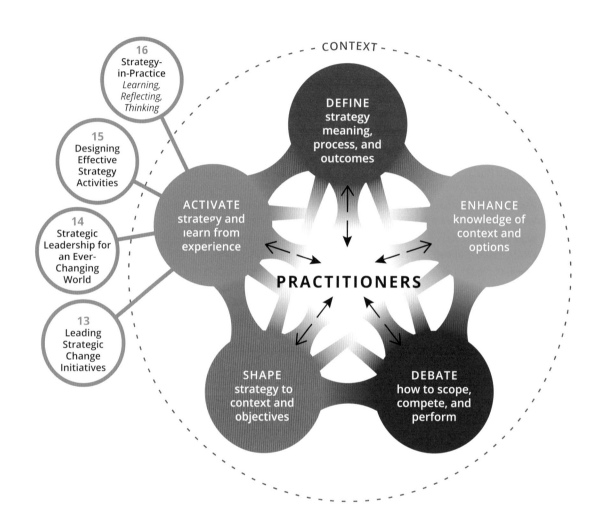

16
Strategy-
in-Practice
*Learning,
Reflecting,
Thinking*

15
Designing
Effective
Strategy
Activities

14
Strategic
Leadership for
an Ever-
Changing
World

13
Leading
Strategic
Change
Initiatives

CONTEXT

DEFINE
strategy
meaning,
process, and
outcomes

ENHANCE
knowledge of
context and
options

ACTIVATE
strategy and
learn from
experience

PRACTITIONERS

SHAPE
strategy to
context and
objectives

DEBATE
how to scope,
compete, and
perform

PART FIVE

Activate strategy and learn from experience

In this concluding section, we examine how strategic decisions can be activated through change initiatives, strategic leadership activities, and insights gained from multiple learning experiences.

To enhance your understanding and vocabulary, in Chapter 13, we introduce the concepts of path dependency, organization culture, and models of strategic change that can meet a wide range of strategy implementation needs and, in Chapter 14, we examine ways in which the concept of strategic leadership can guide activation of strategy on a continuing basis in a responsive and inclusive way.

We supplement these chapters with two further online chapters examining how practitioners can approach developing blueprints for highly effective strategy activities, and theories of strategic learning and reflection that enable continuous improvement of strategy practice.

To support your capacity to apply these insights, in Chapter 13, we review methods to plan and implement strategic change initiatives, complemented, in Chapter 14, by a framework to support development of effective strategic leadership practice. In the online Chapters 15 and 16, we show how you can develop effective strategy activities and describe techniques for undertaking individual or group reflective activity that drives experiential learning and practical impact during strategy work.

By the end of Part 5, you should have enhanced abilities to think, talk, and act like a practitioner, activating strategy and learning from experience.

CHAPTER THIRTEEN

Leading Strategic Change Initiatives

CONTENTS

By the end of this chapter, you should be able to:

○ Recognize the importance of the organization's history as a creator of path dependence and its role in both formal and informal organization culture

○ Evaluate the importance of organizations' ability to manage in the present while simultaneously preparing for the future

○ Define the concept of strategic change and distinguish the types of strategic change

○ Examine the processes and tools available for managers to effectively manage and implement strategic change in various contexts

○ Recognize the role of sense-making and sense-giving in leading change

TOOLBOX

○ **Cultural Web of the organization**
An analytical framework to identify the components of the organization's culture.

○ **Strategic drift**
A framework that can be applied to understand the consequences of the organization failing to keep pace with changes in the external environment.

○ **Forcefield analysis**
An analytical tool to identify forces in the organization that may drive and restrain change.

○ **Step-based models for managing strategic change**
Models that have been developed to enable managers to approach the task of strategic change as a logical step-by-step process. This includes forcefield analysis, Lewin's model of change, Kotter's eight-step Accelerate model.

○ **Sense-making and sense-giving**
A cognitive process that individuals use to make sense of complex situations and influence others to share their perceived world view.

🎧 Access the online resources to watch a short video clip where Kathryn Kerle shares her top career tips.

13

OPENING CASE STUDY HORIZON SCANDAL AT THE POST OFFICE

The Post Office Horizon affair has become known as one of the United Kingdom's most 'widespread miscarriages of justice'. Over 700 sub-postmasters had their contracts suspended, terminated, and wrongfully prosecuted between 2000 and 2015 based on data generated by Horizon, a deeply flawed Post Office accounting system. Many sub-postmasters were convicted and imprisoned for theft, false accounting, and fraud. In his judgment (16 December 2019), the Honourable Mr Justice Fraser described the Post Office as demonstrating:

> a simple institutional obstinacy or refusal to consider any possible alternatives to their view of Horizon, which was maintained regardless of the weight of factual evidence to the contrary. [. . .] This approach by the Post Office has amounted, in reality, to bare assertions and denials that ignore what has actually occurred [. . .] It amounts to the 21st century equivalent of maintaining that the earth is flat.

The Post Office, established by Charles II in 1660, is a limited liability company fully owned by the UK Government, but the Post Office Ltd (POL) board of directors has the responsibility for its day-to-day operations. The POL is required to maintain at least 11,500 branches; the majority (99%) of post office branches are operated by franchise partners, sub-postmasters, who are independent businesspeople. At the time when the Horizon scandal unfolded, the franchise contract stipulated that 'the subpostmaster is responsible for all losses caused through his own negligence, carelessness, or error, and also for losses of all kinds caused by his Assistants. Deficiencies due to such losses must be made good without delay.'

In 1999, the POL rolled out a new IT system developed by the Japanese company Fujitsu for use in accounting, stock-taking, and transactions across POL's branch network. Horizon was hailed at the time as the largest non-military IT project in Europe that was totally bullet-proof and secure. However, from the very beginning of the Horizon rollout,

sub-postmasters started complaining about defects after the system reported shortfalls in account reconciliations, some of which amounted to thousands of pounds. Some sub-postmasters attempted to plug the gap with their own money, even re-mortgaging their homes as the franchise agreement held them individually liable for any loss as evidenced by the Horizon account reconciliation. The POL held a defensive position that there was nothing wrong with Horizon and that the problems experienced by sub-postmasters were due to their incompetence or were simply theft. The only evidence that the POL criminal investigators offered was a Horizon printout, which sub-postmasters had to accept as totally accurate.

During the trial brought against POL by sub-postmasters, it became evident that numerous people and connected organizations, including Fujitsu, knew something very serious was going wrong, although this was never made public. When Paula Vennells was appointed the POL CEO in 2012, she seemed to be the perfect choice to affect transformational change in the underperforming POL as she had had an impressive track record in the private sector. Prime Minister David Cameron's government tasked her to make the POL operationally profitable by 2020. Unfortunately for Vennells, many of the POL's employees had started as postal delivery people or counter clerks and worked their way up into middle management. By keeping their heads down for 20 or 30 years, they were rewarded for their loyalty with jobs for which they didn't have capacity. Vennells recognized this and tried to recruit new staff and introduced training events in an attempt to improve the performance of existing staff. But for the old-timers, who considered the POL the 'nations most trusted brand', any criticism of it was a direct attack on their own personal integrity. Furthermore, anything that could get in the way of PM David Cameron's 2020 financial performance target was considered a risk to be minimized.

Vennells brought in a team of independent forensic accountants, Second Sight, to audit the POL's

13

IT and business processes. The accountants detected a culture of bureaucratic intransigence and organizational inertia: 'We asked for short, easy-to-understand, honest and complete answers to our questions and what we get are highly technical, multi-page responses that appear to have been crafted so as to avoid actually giving any answers.' When Second Sight tried to criticize the POL's training, support, investigation, and basic treatment of sub-postmasters, the accountants came under direct pressure to water down their criticisms and language.

The accountants' report was particularly critical of the way the emphasis of the POL investigators was on 'asset recovery solutions' of getting its money back rather than identifying and fixing the underlying problems which were causing the deficits to appear in sub-postmasters' accounts. But the POL held its position—Horizon contained no systemic errors.

Due to increasing concerns, a Select Committee of Members of Parliament (MPs) was set up to question the POL's top team and seek for more evidence of corporate dysfunctionality. The select committee meetings developed a circular rhythm. The MPs would ask a question, which Vennells would answer with something that was not directly relevant. The MPs would press her to give the answer to the actual question, and it would transpire that she either didn't know or decided she needed to take some offline advice before answering. Towards the end of one session, Ian Henderson of Second Sight publicly stated his concerns about the POL's woeful investigation function. He was 'very concerned' about many of the prosecution cases brought by the POL against sub-postmasters. The POL denied this claim, but pressure on Vennells was mounting. In an interview for a TV documentary, Panorama, a former Tory MP, now Lord James Arbuthnot, called for her to resign and said that the POL's behaviour had been 'one of the most shocking things that I came across while I was a member of parliament'. Meanwhile, in 2018, Vennells was awarded a CBE for her services to the POL. Within weeks, Vennells announced that she would be leaving the POL to take up a board position at the Cabinet Office and chairmanship of Imperial College Healthcare NHS Trust. Neither job lasted long as questions about her time

at the POL mounted. The Communication Workers Union called for Vennells to be stripped of her CBE and demanded a criminal investigation into those at the Post Office 'who put these loyal postmasters in this situation'.

In December 2019, the judgment of the Horizon trial was handed down. The findings by the Court determined that bugs, errors, and defects did in fact exist in the Horizon and on numerous occasions they had caused financial discrepancies in sub-postmasters' branch accounts, issues that had been vigorously denied by the POL ever since the Horizon system was introduced, which had been used to prosecute and convict sub-postmasters.

Questions for discussion

1. What do you think were the reasons behind the Post Office's corporate misconduct?

2. Paula Vennells had all good intentions trying to solve the problem with Horizon. Why do you think she became complicit with the cover-up?

3. Visit the Post Office Corporate website at https://corporate.postoffice.co.uk and read the statements made under the 'Historical Matters' tab on the Horizon scandal. Consider whether the policies and actions put in place in the aftermath of the scandal will change the culture of the Post Office.

Sources

Flinders, K. (2021). Fujitsu escaped huge lawsuit because Post Office behaved so badly in Horizon scandal. *Computer Weekly* (4 November 2021), https://www.computerweekly.com/news/252509066/Fujitsu-escaped-huge-lawsuit-because-Post-Office-behaved-so-badly-in-Horizon-scandal (last accessed 24 May 2022).

Justice for Sub-postmasters Alliance, https://www.jsfa.org.uk (last accessed 24 May 2022).

The Post Office (2021). Commons library research briefing. House of Commons Library, 18 October.

The Post Office Group Litigation Case No: HQ16X01238, HQ17X02637 and HQ17X04248

https://www.judiciary.uk/wp-content/uploads/2019/12/bates-v-post-office-judgment.pdf (last accessed 24 May 2022).

Wallis, N. (2021). *The Great Post Office Scandal*. Bath: Bath Publishing Limited.

13

13.1 **Introduction**

Managing strategic change is not easy. Within an ever-changing environment, organizations need to be able to manage and reconcile their current activities to protect their current market position while simultaneously adapting to the future. Any adaptation of the way the organization operates currently, governed by its prevailing culture, will entail change, and any change is bound to encounter resistance. Organizations are composed of people and embedded processes that have emerged over long periods of time. People are highly resistant to any change in their routines and day-to-day processes, while being protective of their positions, spheres of influence, and power. Therefore, change is perceived as disruptive, uncomfortable, and costly. Moreover, managers must consult a multitude of stakeholders and often convince them to change their behaviours and attitudes, not to mention changing and realigning organizational processes and routines to new organizational realities. Additionally, with conflicting priorities and objectives among the various stakeholder groups, change management can become a socio-political process that strategists need to navigate. Considering these difficulties, Balogun et al. (2016) estimate that approximately 70% of organizational change programmes fail to achieve their stated aims and outcomes.

In this chapter, our focus is on exploring how strategists can approach the strategic change management process in organizations. We open the chapter by introducing the concept of path dependency and its relationship with organization culture and consider whether culture can be managed effectively. Next, we discuss the need for organizations to develop ambidexterity, an ability to manage the tension between operating in the short term within the current competitive environment while developing longer-term organizational capabilities to be able to compete successfully in the future. We then offer a definition of what constitutes strategic change, discuss the types of change, and outline the sources of organizational inertia that makes strategic change difficult. We then turn our attention to the change process and evaluate various prescriptive models of how strategic change can be managed and implemented. An integral part of this discussion is the role that practitioners play in effectively managing strategic change, and we consider sense-making and sense-giving as fundamental skills in leading change.

13.2 **Culture: History and path dependency**

In Chapter 4, we discussed the purpose and values of organizations. But how do the purpose and values of an organization provide a framework for its culture? Organizational values and the ways that a business operates are greatly influenced by its past. Many organizations have long histories, and the values of the founders are often deeply embedded in the psyche of the organization. Both an organization's history and its well-established processes can shape strategy successfully or can act as a barrier for change, which can, in turn, negatively impact the organization. In this section, we will explore the influence of history, path dependency, and culture, and the impact they may have on strategy.

The history and cultural heritage of an organization can be a source of advantage because it cannot easily be replicated by competitors. For example, Tesco, a British multinational groceries and general merchandise retailer, was founded in 1919 by Jack Cohen as a group of market stalls. The Tesco name first appeared in 1924, after Cohen purchased a shipment of tea from T.E. Stockwell and combined those initials with the first two letters of his surname. The firm still carries the founder's name, and his ethos of 'pile it high and sell it cheap' is embedded in the operating principles of the firm. For many years, Tesco was the leading discount chain.

However, it can be argued that Tesco's leading position as a high-value discount retailer has become challenged by Aldi and Lidl. As relatively new entrants to the UK market, Aldi and Lidl seem to have created a business proposition that delivers higher value at a lower price to the UK consumer, and this has eaten into Tesco's dominance. Hence, the organization's history and heritage can also be problematic as they can act as barriers for change. Either way, managers cannot ignore the role of the organization's heritage and culture in understanding the firm's strategy or in trying to change the culture or develop new capabilities.

Path dependency

Path dependency is a useful concept for thinking about the influence of history on a business and is integral to shaping a business's culture. Path dependency stresses the importance of past events for future action or, more precisely, the role of foregone decisions for current and future decision-making in an organization (Schreyogg and Sydow 2010). This means that current and future decisions are historically conditioned: 'bygones are rarely bygones' (Teece et al. 1997: 522). This is because an organization's decisions are often made within and with reference to the cultural and operating framework and processes that have evolved over its history and are unique to that organization.

Path dependency can be used to explain the development of strategic resources and organizational capabilities. As we explored in **Chapter 6**, an organization's existing capabilities are the sum total of past decisions taken by managers in accruing resources and developing the organization's strategy and position in a competitive marketplace. For example, as discussed in Case Example 12.1, the competitive advantage of the world's largest retailer, Walmart Inc., is based on its supply chain logistics capabilities and low prices. However, the firm's super-efficient warehousing operations, distribution, and supplier network was not a result of careful strategic planning; it evolved gradually over time from the trading conditions that the firm faced during its early years in rural Arkansas. Sam Walton, the founder of Walmart, could not afford to locate his stores in expensive in-town retail locations with high footfall. Instead, he had to accept locations in small, rural towns that were deemed unattractive by other retailers. However, these locations became strategic assets as they provided enough space for parking for shoppers and very large hypermarkets. Moreover, as Walmart was the first to establish a presence in these rural locations, it became evident that the locations chosen by Sam Walton could not support more than one hypermarket.

As suppliers were not keen to deliver merchandise to Walton's out-of-town locations, he was forced to develop his own distribution system, and in order to attract customers to these locations from major towns, he had to find ways to make his prices so low that customers deemed

13

them worthy of a journey to the Walmart store. This example illustrates how path dependency can support a successful strategy by creating a set of processes and development of strategic assets that are unique to the firm and difficult, if not impossible, for the competitors to copy, which may serve as the basis of competitive advantage.

However, path dependency can be a double-edged sword. Whilst an organization's competitive advantage may be based on culture and/or capabilities that have evolved from the very early stages of its life, is it possible for a business to develop radically new capabilities or adapt to new competitive realities? The prevailing culture and existing capabilities can become barriers to change, especially in fast-moving competitive environments where the continuous renewal of capabilities is a prerequisite for sustaining a competitive advantage. Leonard-Barton (1992) posits that if an organization is unable to develop new capabilities in response to future competitive developments, its existing core capabilities are simultaneously core rigidities that limit the organization's ability to respond to competitive changes. For example, Dell Computers' direct sales business model was so highly developed and recognized that the firm had difficulties in developing a complementary business model of selling its computers through retailers. Customers associated Dell with low-cost, built-to-order systems, rather than computers that they could see and feel at retail outlets.

We next consider the strategic importance of the culture of the organization which is a product of the environment in which the organization is embedded, its history, and the sum total of the processes and competencies that have evolved throughout its past activities. The key point to remember is that while the organization's past may give it a competitive advantage, if the organization is not able to renew itself in an evolving competitive marketplace, it may lose the advantage by attempting to rely on its past competencies.

Organization culture

Organizations can be considered as complex cultural systems which interact with the environments in which they are embedded and from which they recruit their employees. Multinational corporations such as Unilever or Sony Corporation may operate differently from country to country, but they also have their own distinctive characteristics and styles which do not vary from one geographical location or national culture to another.

For example, Chase Manhattan Bank (JPMorgan Chase of today), one of the pathfinders of global banking, understood the importance of corporate and national cultures to the bank's business operations in the 1980s, ahead of its closest competitors, which made Chase the leading global corporate bank. The bank recruited employees from different cultures to their local international offices. Because Chase realized that their employees had been socialized in their own native cultures, management recruits had to attend a year-long management training programme at the bank's headquarters in New York and London, where they were instilled with the 'Chase way of doing business', including how to dress and interact with corporate clients. Moreover, the bank employed facilities managers who travelled to Chase's international locations to ensure that the office furniture, artwork, and even the managers' desk name plates were compliant with corporate standards. This meant that the bank's global clients, such as General Motors, would receive the same level of customer service regardless of the international location.

13

Culture can be perceived to be strategically important as a possible source of competitive advantage. It is worth emphasizing that what makes a particular culture successful for an organization is that the values are widely shared and acted on by all organizational participants (see Table 4.1 regarding our discussion of forward-looking statements). When organizational values are fully aligned with participants' personal values, drives, and needs, culture can unleash tremendous amounts of energy towards a shared purpose and foster the organization's capacity to thrive (Groysberg et al. 2018).

However, in large and diverse companies with complex operations, cultures can give rise to subcultures. Subcultures can be thought of as a subset of the organization's members who identify themselves as a distinct group with their own values and norms that may be separate from the overall corporate culture of the organization. Subcultures may form around shared interests within the organization, or they may reflect similar professional, gender, ethnic, or national cultural identities. If an organization has a number of subcultures with values that are not commonly shared, this may result in a fragmented culture, and these subcultures may evolve into behaviours and attitudes that are in conflict with the overall values and purpose of an organization. A fractured or fragmented culture may hinder the organization from reaching its goals or cause serious damage to the business and its reputation.

Schein's three dimensions of culture

Edgar Schein (1997) defines culture as deeply embedded fundamental assumptions and beliefs that are shared by the members of the organization. Culture represents the basic assumptions and frameworks that organizational actors use to make sense of challenges and opportunities, both internally and externally, and how they deal with them. These 'taken for granted assumptions' may have a physical and visual manifestation in artefacts such as logos, dress codes, or corporate colours. The assumptions and frameworks that make up culture are grounded on the purpose and the values of the organization that guide its mission and on the activities conducted to realize the organization's mission (Deal and Kennedy 1982; Schein 1997).

Schein classifies culture in three dimensions:

1. The first dimension of culture is built around **artefacts** that represent the visible organizational features such as logos, uniforms, buildings, architecture, and workplace designs. The organization's customers may interact with some of the artefacts, such as a customer placing a hamburger order at a MacDonald's self-service kiosks before being served by a uniformed employee. Inside the organization, the way workspace is configured may have a significant impact on the way that employees interact with each other. Apple's Campus2 in Cupertino, California, houses 12,000 employees, and the circular building is divided into modular sections, known as pods, which are used for office work, teamwork, and social activities. Everyone, from the CEO to summer interns, will be placed into these pods, helping employees build connections, collaborate, and discover mentorship opportunities, as employees of all levels of experience and seniority frequently come into contact with each other.

2. Schein's second dimension of culture encompasses the organization's **articulated values**. These values are made explicit in the purpose, value, and mission statements that we studied at the beginning of this chapter. The objective of these statements is to get the whole organization to work towards common shared goals and objectives.

13

3. The third dimension of Schein's culture classification includes the **deeply held beliefs and assumptions** that are not explicitly articulated in artefacts or statements. Often, this level is hidden as mental (or cognitive) maps of organizational actors that provide them with the implicit means of interpreting the world and making decisions (Weick 2001, 2009; Huff 1990). An example of this sort of cognitive mapping is known as causal mapping, which is used by strategists as a means of improving the quality of managerial decision-making processes by making decision-makers' assumptions of a strategic problem more explicit. (You can develop your understanding of causal mapping in Chapter 3.)

These deep cognitive structures of culture have emerged over a long period of time throughout the history of the organization, and if they are not visible, they will be difficult to manage and change. However, cognitive maps are vitally important in managerial practice as they implicitly guide thinking and decision-making in organizations.

Cultural web

As you study strategy, it is important to understand not just the different aspects of organizational culture but also how, in your future career, you might analyse organizational culture. The **cultural web** (Johnson 1992) has become the most commonly used tool to analyse organizational culture. (There are also a number of different frameworks for assessing organizational cultures, such as Groysberg's Eight Distinct Culture Styles, which is included in the **online resources** (Groysberg et al. 2018).) The cultural web is an attempt to incorporate Schein's dimensions of culture which depict the behavioural, physical, and symbolic manifestations of culture forming the 'paradigm' of an organization (see Figure 13.1).

The Cultural Web identifies six interlinked elements that make the 'paradigm' of an organization. The paradigm (e.g. 'the way we do things around here': Johnson 1992) at the centre of the Cultural Web is the set of assumptions that is shared and taken for granted in the organization. It is likely that the assumptions of the paradigm are very basic. For example, the paradigm of the UK National Health Service (NHS) is to treat the sick. It is often difficult to identify the elements that constitute the paradigm, especially for those who work inside the organization. The six elements of the Cultural Web are a means of guiding strategic conversations about organizational culture:

1. **Stories:** the past events that people talk about inside and outside the organization, including stories about employee and manager behaviours. Who and what the company chooses to immortalize says a great deal about what the organization values and what is perceived as exemplary behaviour. For example, does the organization revere stories about successful sales deals or about innovations by factory-level workers that reduced the organization's production costs? 'Stories capture organizational life in a way that no compilation of facts ever can. This is because they are carriers of life itself, not just reports on it' (Czarniawska 1997: 21).

2. **Rituals and routines:** the daily organizational behaviours and actions of people that are deemed acceptable, determining what is expected in certain situations, and what is valued by management. Rituals and routines can be both formal and informal. Examples

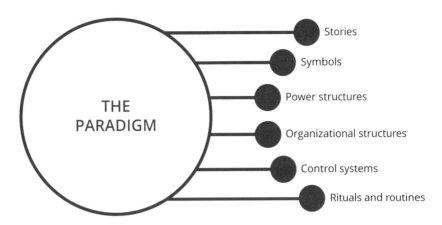

FIGURE 13.1 Cultural web of organization. *Source*: reproduced with permission from Johnson, G. (1992). Managing strategic change—strategy, culture and action. *Long Range Planning*, **25**(1), 28–36, https://doi.org/10.1016/0024-6301(92)90307-N. Copyright © 1992 Published by Elsevier Ltd.

of formal rituals and routines include events such as annual performance appraisals, promotion or disciplinary processes, sales conferences, and so on. Impromptu birthday celebrations with cake, drinks after work, or gossiping around the water cooler are examples of informal rituals or routines.

3. **Symbols:** the visual representations of the company including logos, how upmarket the offices are, size and location of offices for different levels of staff, formal or informal dress codes, etc. Job titles have a functional purpose in an organization, but they also have a symbolic meaning in communicating status or power. Consider the symbolic meaning of two different office layouts: some organizations may have separate dining facilities and private elevators that are reserved for exclusive use by the senior managers to take them to their offices at the top of the building; in contrast, some organizations design their senior management offices to be modest with 'lots of glass walls for the executives who have offices, and most people working in open plan' (Bulkin 2015: 134). Although symbols are depicted as a separate element in the Cultural Web, it should be noted that many other elements of the Web also have a symbolic meaning.

4. **Organizational structure:** this includes the roles, responsibilities, and reporting relationships that are defined by the organization chart as well as the unwritten lines of power and influence that indicate whose contributions are most valued. Fewer formal reporting lines may be a manifestation of a less hierarchical organization, which may indicate that the organization culture is more collaborative than an organization with deep and rigid reporting relationships.

5. **Control systems:** the formal and informal ways that the organization and people are monitored and supported. These include financial, product, and service quality control and assurance and employee reward systems. The nature and design of the systems indicate what is important to the organization. An expenditure approval process that requires a number of signatories up the organizational structure may be representative of a company that is focused on financial control, and therefore may be indicative of the lack of trust in the organization.

13

6. **Power structures:** power is an ability for groups or individuals to persuade, induce, or force others to behave in a certain way. Power structures identify the pockets of real power in an organization. This may involve one or two key senior executives, a whole group of executives, or even a department. The key is that these people have the greatest amount of influence on the decisions, operations, and strategic direction of the organization. They are the ones most closely associated with the organizational paradigm and the established way of doing things.

Many organizations conduct culture surveys of their staff to understand how the existing culture is perceived by organizational members and how it relates to an ideal culture that organization members would prefer. Such surveys resemble student satisfaction surveys that you may have taken. A number of culture analysis tools are employed by change management consultants, but many of them are built around the Cultural Web framework, or a variation thereof, such as the Organizational Culture Inventory® by Human Synergistics (https://www.humansynergistics.com). A wide gap between the perceived and the ideal culture may signal a need for cultural change.

CASE EXAMPLE 13.1 EXERCISE: CONSTRUCTING A CULTURAL WEB

A starting point for organizations to understand their culture is to construct a cultural web. This can be accomplished for the organization as a whole or for independent subsidiaries and divisions. As a strategist would do, start by looking at each element of the cultural web separately and asking questions that help to determine the dominant factors in each element.

Choose an organization that you are familiar with, such as your university, and construct a cultural web for it in your study group. Develop the cultural web by considering the following questions as they relate to the individual elements of the web.

Stories

- How do people currently describe the organization?

- What is the reputation of the organization among its customers and other stakeholders?

- How do these stories describe what the organization believes in?

- How do employees think about and describe the history of the organization?

- What stories do employees tell new recruits who join the company?

- Who are the heroes, villains, mavericks, or rebels in these stories?

Rituals and routines

- What rituals and routines do customers experience when dealing with the organization?

- What are the daily and special occasion routines among the employees in the organization?

- Would a change in rituals and routines be immediately obvious if they were changed?

- What behaviours are embedded in the organization's rituals and routines?

- What core beliefs of the organization are embedded in its rituals and routines?

- When confronted with a new problem, what rules do employees apply when trying to solve it?

Symbols

- Does the organization use specific jargon or language that is often only understood by the people in the organization?
- Are there specific status symbols that are used to connote seniority or special positions in the organization?
- What imagery, including logos, trademarks, and photos, are associated with the organization and how are they perceived by employees, customers, and other stakeholders?

Organizational structure

- Is the organization structure flat or hierarchical?
- Does the organization operate using formal or informal communication practices?
- Does the organization rely on formal or informal lines of authority?

Control systems

- Which of the organization's processes or procedures have the strictest levels of control? Which processes and procedures have the loosest levels of control?
- Are employees rewarded for doing good work or following set procedures?
- What reports are produced, and to whom are they circulated, to keep control of operations, finance, etc.?

Power structures

- Is there a concentration of power in the organization and who exercises it?
- What do those in power believe in and champion in the organization?
- Who are the decision-makers in the organization and who is able to influence decision-making?
- How do employees perceive those in power? Is power being used for the good of the organization or abused for personal gain?

As you answer these questions, a picture of organizational culture should begin to emerge, allowing you to describe the culture and identify the dominant factors across the cultural web.

After completing the existing organizational cultural web, repeat the process with the aim of understanding what an ideal culture would look like if everything was correctly aligned. This allows you to make a direct comparison between the perceived and ideal cultures of the organization and understand the differences between the two cultural webs.

After comparing and identifying the differences between the existing and ideal cultural webs of the organization, next consider the organization's strategic aims and objectives and develop a programme to align the organization's culture with these aims and objectives.

- What cultural strengths and weaknesses have been highlighted by the analysis of the current culture?
- What factors are hindering strategy or are misaligned with one another?
- What factors are detrimental to the health and productivity of the workplace?
- What factors should be encouraged and reinforced?
- Which elements need to change?
- What new beliefs and behaviours are needed?

Questions for discussion

Having completed this exercise, compare and contrast the cultural webs developed by the members of the other study groups.

1. How similar or different are the cultural webs enacted by the various study groups?
2. What are the main similarities and differences in the cultural webs?
3. Why do you think there are differences in the enacted cultural webs and how would you develop a shared understanding between the cultural webs enacted by the different study groups?
4. How easy or difficult do you think it is to change the culture of the organization and how would you go about effecting change?

Source: authors.

13

Can culture be managed?

The steps you took in constructing the Cultural Web for your organization show that culture is clearly an important element in any organization. However, if culture is such an important element (and possibly a source of competitive advantage), can it be effectively managed?

Two McKinsey & Co consultants, Peters and Waterman, in their book, *In Search of Excellence* (Peters and Waterman 1982) argued that the answer to this question was 'Yes'. They stated that truly great companies have excellent cultures, which are the sources of their financial success. Such successful cultures are built around core values that are widely shared and acted on by organizational participants. Peters and Waterman's book and other works by academics, such as Deal and Kennedy (1982) and Schein (1997), elevated organizational culture to the forefront of academic minds as well as the minds of managers and consultants. This led to the emergence of a group of strategy culture theorists and academic studies that argued for a link between culture and competitive advantage (Hall 1993).

This view came under scrutiny not only because some of the organizations that Peters and Waterman had listed as truly excellent lost their leading competitive positions shortly after publication of their book but also because questions were raised over Peters and Waterman's data integrity and analysis. Early on in the debate, Jay Barney, in a seminal article (Barney 1986), questioned whether culture could be a source of competitive advantage. Basing his argument on the tenets of the resource-based view (RBV), which is explored in depth in Chapter 6, Barney argued that if organization culture could be a source of sustainable competitive advantage, it would have to meet the criteria of being valuable, rare, inimitable, and non-substitutable (VRIN).

Barney (1986) identified three requirements for culture to form the basis of competitive advantage. The first is that an organization's culture must enable it to do things and behave in ways that add economic **value** to the organization. If an organization's culture enables it to behave in ways that are inconsistent with an organization's competitive situation, that culture cannot be a source of superior financial performance, sustained or otherwise.

The second requirement is that valuable cultures must be rare. If many organizations have similar cultures that allow them to behave and compete in approximately the same way, none will possess a culturally based competitive advantage, and above-normal economic performance cannot be expected.

Finally, even if these conditions are met, it is still necessary for an organization's culture to be inimitable for it to generate sustained superior financial performance. Imitable cultures, even if they are valuable, and even if they are currently rare, remove any competitive advantages they may provide. The culture-driven success of one organization creates an incentive for other organizations to modify their cultures to duplicate that success.

Barney questioned whether culture could be created intentionally by strategists because if culture could be designed and implemented as a result of managerial intervention, it would not be inimitable (meaning that it could be copied by competitors) and therefore would not be a source of sustainable advantage. Barney concluded his argument by stating that, while culture was important, it was beyond the reach of strategists to create because if a superior culture could be engineered, it could be replicated by the organization's competitors. We should also remember that culture is a product of path dependency and to change it radically will require the dismantling of deeply embedded beliefs, values, and processes.

13

13.3 **Organizational ambidexterity**

Given the constraints of culture, one of the biggest challenges that strategists face is how to develop an organizational capability to explore future opportunities while simultaneously working on exploiting their organization's current competencies and capabilities in existing markets. Essentially, strategists must consider future opportunities and current activities and performance together, so it is important for students of strategy to understand how this might be done. Abell (1993) states that running a successful business requires a clear strategy in terms of defining target markets, paying attention to those factors that are critical to the organization's success, and changing the business in anticipation of the future. This requires a vision of how the future will unfold and a strategy for how the organization will have to adapt or anticipate future challenges. In this section, we explore the idea of being adaptable to this challenge (a concept known as organizational ambidexterity) and consider how strategic leadership is needed to deal with this challenge successfully.

Most successful businesses are better at refining their current offerings than at pioneering radically new future products and services (O'Reilly and Tushman 2004). Several theories have been put forward to explain this conundrum—for example, that established companies simply lack the flexibility to explore new opportunities and that organizations find it difficult to reconcile 'mastering the present' with 'pre-empting the future'. However, in turbulent markets, organizations must be able to move quickly towards new opportunities, adjust to volatile markets, and avoid complacency (Birkinshaw and Gibson 2004). O'Reilly and Tushman (2004) have termed such adaptability '**organizational ambidexterity**', which can be defined as a capability of the organization to simultaneously exploit existing competencies (exploitation) and explore new opportunities (exploration). As we explored in the Case Example 1.2, DBS has developed as a strategic 'ambidextrous' organization that has been able to deliver excellent business results, coping with the operational challenges of the pandemic, whilst continuing to transform the business in order to secure its position as a digital leader in banking.

O'Reilly and Tushman (2004, 2011) argue that the ability of an organization to be ambidextrous is at the core of dynamic capabilities. Ambidexterity requires senior managers to accomplish two critical tasks. First, they must be able to accurately sense changes in their competitive environment, including potential shifts in technology, competition, customers, and regulation. Second, they must be able to act on these opportunities and threats—to be able to seize them by reconfiguring both **tangible and intangible assets** to meet new challenges. As a dynamic capability, ambidexterity combines a complex set of routines, including decentralization, differentiation, and integration, with the ability of senior leadership to coordinate the complex trade-offs required when pursuing exploitation and exploration at the same time. Developing these dynamic capabilities is a central task of executive leadership.

Birkinshaw and Gibson (2004) have identified two forms of organizational ambidexterity: **structural ambidexterity** and **contextual ambidexterity**. In structural ambidexterity, exploitation and exploration are undertaken in separate organizational units with different types of activity. For example, business units have the responsibility for exploiting current market opportunities, while research and development (R&D) and business development units have the responsibility for exploring new markets, developing new products and services, and keeping

13

abreast of the emerging market trends. In contrast, contextual ambidexterity entails the same organizational units with their members pursuing both exploratory and exploitative activities. Contextual ambidexterity requires individuals to take the initiative and remain alert to opportunities beyond the boundaries of their own jobs. This could mean working collaboratively with a colleague from another area of the organization to combine their skills and efforts.

In Chapter 14, we will explore further how approaches to 'strategic leadership' might impact on organizational ambidexterity and the balancing of operational delivery and organisational performance with strategic change needs.

13.4 **What is strategic change?**

Having considered the importance and the constraints of culture and the need for organizational ambidexterity in continually changing environments, we now turn our discussion to what constitutes strategic change before going on to identify organizational factors that make change difficult to manage and implement.

How do we decide whether change is strategic or not? At any given point, an organization may have a number of change initiatives under way. For example, the organization's finance department may be in the process of installing a new invoicing system, while the marketing department is considering outsourcing some of its marketing material development to a specialist content development organization. However, the litmus test of what constitutes strategic change is whether the changes will have an impact on the overall direction, competitive position, and scope of the organization's activities. As we saw in Chapter 4, organizations are a collection of stakeholder groups that may have conflicting interests, objectives, and even their own organization cultural norms, which may constitute a series of subcultures within the organization. Hence, the kind of change which is deemed to be strategic is a result of a political process in organizations. This is not the only indication of a strategic change. For example, we can consider change to be strategic if it results in:

- changes to the competitive position of the organization;
- changes to the organization's overarching business model;
- changes to the organization's product and service offer;
- development of new organizational capabilities;
- changes to the geographic scope of the organization through international expansion;
- outsourcing of activities or bringing activities in-house that have previously been carried out by outside suppliers;
- changes to the nature and overall structure of the organization through the formation of strategic alliances, mergers and acquisitions, divestments, etc.

While this level of impact may feel significant to those experiencing the strategic changes, it is worth understanding that not all strategic change is disruptive or revolutionary. Incremental changes that take place gradually in the organization may have a strategic impact on the organization's competitive position over an extended period of time. As we saw in the previous

13

section, employees may simultaneously engage in exploitation and exploration, meaning that changes might be implemented either gradually or more suddenly as a result of breakthrough discoveries.

Why is change difficult?

All approaches to change management are based on the recognition that change and its implementation are difficult due to organizational inertia or resistance to change. Five common barriers to change are presented in Table 13.1.

TABLE 13.1 **Barriers to change**

Common barriers to change	Why this factor is a barrier to change
Social and political structures	Organizations are both social and political constructs. As social systems, organizations develop shared practices and processes that make change disruptive and stressful for organizational participants. As political systems, organizations have concentrations of power and authority. Any change that may threaten the position of those in power will meet resistance.
Organizational routines	Routines and processes that have been developed over a long period of time and become embedded in the way the organization operates are difficult to change. Organizations fall into competency traps where exiting core competencies become core rigidities (see Chapter 4, section on path dependency).
Institutional isomorphism	**Isomorphism** is a similarity of the processes or structures of one organization to those of another. It can result from competitive imitation or independent development under similar competitive conditions. It can also emerge from external pressures by investors, lenders, or regulators that encourage organizations in a particular industry to develop similar strategies and structures. Change under institutional isomorphism will be difficult as managers may be concerned that, by moving away from the processes and structures of their competitors, they may lose their competitive position in the industry.
Bounded rationality and satisficing	Decision-makers engage in a limited information search due to the concepts of bounded rationality and satisficing. These behaviours lead decision-makers to find solutions to problems from their existing knowledge and competencies. This is also a reason why organizations have a bias towards exploitation over exploration when doing things in a new way or seeking new opportunities (see Chapter 3 on strategic decision-making in organizations).
Equilibrium-seeking behaviour	Organizations develop a fit between their strategy, structure, management systems, culture, and competencies and their external competitive environment. If the environment changes, it might not be sufficient to change only some of the elements of the organization in response (see Chapter 4 on organizational culture). Hence, organizations tend to operate in an equilibrium state until such time as the gap between the external environment and the organization grows to a stage where a complete realignment of the organization and its environment is required (as explored in the opening case study on Blockbuster).

Source: authors.

13

Given these common barriers to change, it is not surprising that the majority of organizational change programmes fail to deliver their aims (Balogun et al. 2016). Research by Schwartz (2018) found that 85% of companies have undertaken a transformation during the past decade, but nearly 75% of those transformations failed to improve business performance.

Most managers have a rational understanding that change is an ever-present phenomenon and is essential if organizations are to survive in an environment that is characterized by technological innovation, globalization, and new business models such as 'born global' (Chapter 12). However, few organizations are capable of successfully managing change, and the consequences of this failure to deliver and manage change means that organizations will eventually lose their competitive position.

There are countless examples of once leading companies that have completely vanished. Goh (2017) identifies two well-known firms that were not able move with the times: Kodak and Toys 'R' Us. Kodak (1889–2012) failed to keep up with the digital revolution for fear of cannibalizing its strongest product lines in film. The company was blindsided by its core business of selling silver halide film. Kodak, as the leader of design, production, and marketing of photographic equipment, had a number of opportunities to renew itself, but the firm's hesitation to fully embrace the transition to digital led to its demise. For example, Kodak invested billions of US dollars into developing technology for taking pictures using mobile phones and other digital devices. However, it held back from developing digital cameras for the mass market for fear of eradicating its all-important film business. Competitors, such as the Japanese firm Canon, jumped at this opportunity. Kodak filed for bankruptcy in 2012 and, after exiting most of its product streams, re-emerged in 2013 as a much smaller consolidated company focused on serving commercial customers.

Toys 'R' Us (1948–2018) was once one of the world's largest toy store chains. With the benefit of hindsight, Toys 'R' Us may have been the architect of its own downfall when it signed a 10-year contract to be the exclusive vendor of toys on Amazon in 2000. Amazon began to allow other toy vendors to sell on its site in spite of the deal, and Toys 'R' Us sued Amazon to end the agreement in 2004. As a result, Toys 'R' Us missed the opportunity to develop its own e-commerce presence early on. Far too late to the e-commerce retail revolution, Toys 'R' Us announced in May 2017 its plan to revamp its website as part of a $100 million, three-year investment to jump-start its e-commerce business. However, under pressure from its debt and fierce online retail competition, the company ceased trading in 2018.

Strategic change is a result of an organization's socio-political processes, and there are a number of factors that make the management of change very difficult. Moreover, if organizations are not able to manage change and stay relevant in the changing environment, they will ultimately fail regardless of their current position in the industry. This idea is reinforced by Jeff Bezos, CEO of Amazon, who famously said that he is under no illusion that at some point in time Amazon's business model will be disrupted by a new competitor; it is inevitable, but he will fight to make sure that that day will not be soon (https://www.youtube.com/watch?v=32rCNumOu4E).

13.5 **Types of change**

We have discussed what strategic change is and why it is difficult. But how might strategists realize that they need to implement change? And how can we categorize different sorts of change? In this section, we discuss how the need for change emerges and will identify four main types of change.

How the need for change emerges

Rational decision-making models (see Chapter 3) assume that change is a rational outcome in organizations. Such a perspective attempts to explain change as a process where strategists adjust the organization's strategy as a result of continuous **environmental scanning**, which detects changes in the organization's competitive environment, changes in customer tastes, emerging new technologies, etc. Analytical tools such as PESTEL and Five Forces analysis (see Chapter 5) provide managers with the ability to engage in environmental scanning and adjust the organization's strategy based on the results of such analysis through the application of change management tools and techniques.

However, in practice, strategic change does not always occur in such a measured way. The concept of **strategic drift** lies at the core of organizational change management. Often, the environment changes gradually without any detectable revolutionary shocks. Political and economic changes do not generally occur overnight, nor do new technologies, and changes in customer preferences do not emerge without some warning. However, if the organization is not able to keep pace with such incremental evolutionary changes, strategic drift occurs. This is because the organization's strategy becomes detached from the changes happening in the external competitive environment. Figure 13.2 illustrates the concept of strategic drift.

Figure 13.2 illustrates how the organization is initially able to keep up with the changing environment (shown by the blue line) by implementing incremental change (shown by the orange line). However, as environmental change accelerates (in the middle section of the graph), the organization is beginning to fall behind the changing environment, resulting in strategic drift. This is demonstrated in the graph by the widening gap between the red and blue lines in the middle section of the graph. Over a period of time, it becomes clear that incremental change is no longer sufficient, but more transformational revolutionary change is required if the organization is to recover its competitive position in a changing competitive environment. If successful, the organization is able to make a step change where the orange line closes the gap with the blue line as the organization catches up with the environmental change.

A classic example is how Blockbuster lost its leadership position in the video rental industry by failing to change its strategy in light of the emerging digital download and streaming technology. The company tried to adapt to change, but this change was made within Blockbuster's main business paradigm based on charging customers late return fees by replacing them with high membership subscription fees, cost-cutting programmes, and adding additional services that were offered to customers from the firm's retail outlets. In a fairly short period of time, Blockbuster's strategic drift had become so severe that radical revolutionary change was the only

13

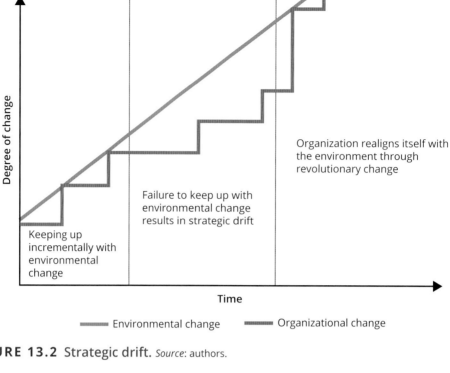

FIGURE 13.2 Strategic drift. *Source*: authors.

option for the firm's survival. Unfortunately, by this time, Blockbuster had been overtaken by rivals such as Netflix and the organization's attempt to launch its own online service and divest itself of extensive physical retail outlets came too late. The change that was required of Blockbuster was too big for the firm to close the gap with their competitors, and the environment had evolved beyond Blockbuster's reach, given the resources and capabilities available to it.

Speed and extent of change

Balogun et al. (2016) identify two dimensions of organizational change: the speed and the extent of change that is required. These two dimensions give rise to four main types of strategic change: adaption, evolution, reconstruction, and revolution. The nature of these types of change is explored in Table 13.2.

We should keep in mind that if the approach of incremental change in the organization is taken, there still remains a danger of strategic drift, especially in adaptive change strategies. This is because this type of change is based on the existing culture and strategy of the organization, and it might be that environmental or competitive pressures require more fundamental transformative (reconstructive or revolutionary) change than the organization is making.

When selecting an approach to strategic change, managers struggle with the question of how extensive and how fast a change programme should be. On the one hand, to fundamentally transform the organization, a break with the past is required. On the other hand, managers recognize the value of continuity through incremental change that builds on the organization's past experiences, existing resources and capabilities, and employee loyalty.

TABLE 13.2 **Types of strategic change**

Speed of change	Extent of change	
	Realignment	**Transformation**
Incremental	Adaptation is the most common form of organizational change. Change is undertaken incrementally within the existing cultural norms and strategy to realign the organization to the changes in the competitive environment. It builds on the existing strategy rather than fundamentally changing the existing strategy. It may include changes that are made to the current methods of production, new product introductions, or related diversification of activities.	Evolution is perhaps the most challenging form of strategic change. It involves exploiting and building on the organization's existing strategic capabilities, while also exploring new opportunities and developing new capabilities (organizational ambidexterity, as we discussed earlier in this chapter).
Big bang/ transformative	Reconstruction is rapid change. It may involve major structural changes and cost-cutting programmes to address a decline in the organization's financial performance or difficult market conditions. Reconstruction does not fundamentally change the culture or the prevailing strategy. Reconstruction is often referred to as turnaround, which is discussed later in this chapter.	Revolution is urgent transformational change. It requires a change in both culture and strategy. The pressure for change is often extreme as the future viability of the organization is at stake. For example, a hostile takeover may threaten the very existence of the organization. Revolution differs from reconstruction as in revolutionary change it is often necessary to change both the culture and the strategy of the organization (as in the case of Blockbuster).

Source: adapted from Balogun et al. (2016).

In contrast with incremental change, big bang/transformative change disrupts the existing paradigm of the organization and often the 'window of opportunity' for such extensive strategic change can be narrow, as witnessed in the case of Blockbuster. Some of the most common triggers that necessitate big bang/transformative change are as follows:

- **Competitive pressure:** when an organization comes under intense competitive pressure and its market position begins to deteriorate quickly, a rapid response might be the only approach possible, especially when the organization is threatened by insolvency.

- **Regulatory pressure:** when an organization comes under pressure from the government or regulatory agencies to push through major changes within a short period of time. Such externally imposed revolutions can be witnessed in public-sector organizations, such as hospitals and schools that fail official quality inspections, and highly regulated industries such as utilities and telecommunications that may come under scrutiny for exercising too much monopolistic market power.

13

- **First mover advantage:** when a organization adopts a more proactive reason for instigating revolutionary change. The organization places itself under pressure to be the first organization to introduce a new product or technology to build up barriers to entry for competitors who may follow the first mover with competing products or technologies.

13.6 Models for managing change

In section 13.5, we explored four main types of change. What processes and tools can managers use in practice when confronted by a need for change? The most common change management frameworks consider change as a series of rational steps and processes that the organization takes to pivot from one state into another. In this section, we consider two examples of such models—Lewin's change model and Kotter's eight-step accelerator model.

Lewin's model of change management

Lewin's model is one of the best known and most widely applied models of change management. Lewin (1947) was a social psychologist who was interested in group dynamics and how individuals relate to and become influenced by others. As a social psychologist, his primary interest was to understand how social groups changed for the worse and what could be done to effect recovery and improve group interaction and performance. The fundamental assumptions of Lewin's theory of change are as follows:

- Change is the result of dissatisfaction with the current state of the organization (e.g. financial performance, deteriorating market position).

- Change does not happen by itself. It is critical for the organization to develop a vision of a better future.

- Management needs to formulate strategies to implement change.

- Any change will inevitably meet resistance, but this is not impossible to overcome.

Based on these assumptions, what does Lewin's model actually entail? We will go through it step by step, starting with **forcefield analysis**.

Forcefield analysis

The first stage of Lewin's model is to conduct a forcefield analysis which provides an overview of the problems that need to be tackled by the organization, splitting factors into forces that act for and against change. The cultural web (Chapter 4) or causal mapping (Chapter 3) could be useful frameworks to conduct the analysis.

Lewin's forcefield model in Figure 13.3 identifies driving and restraining forces for change. Where there is an equilibrium between the two sets of forces, no change takes place. In order for change to occur, the driving forces must be stronger than the restraining forces and can then be leveraged to overcome the restraining forces. In undertaking forcefield analysis, all forces for change and forces resisting change should be identified. Each force should then be

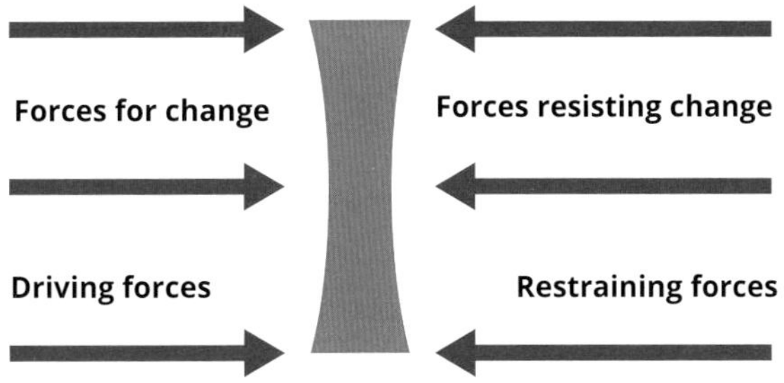

FIGURE 13.3 Forcefield analysis. *Source*: Lewin, K. (1951). *Field Theory in Social Science*. New York: Harper and Row.

assigned a relative weighting. Based on the relative weighting of the forces, a strategist can identify the critical forces that can be leveraged for maximum effect and the restraining forces that must be eliminated for change to take place.

Examples of forces for change are:

- new management and/or employees;
- changing market and customer tastes;
- new technology;
- competition;
- changing regulatory environment;
- public opinion.

Examples of forces resisting change are:

- individuals' fear of failure;
- organizational politics and turf wars;
- organizational apathy and inertia;
- hostility to management;
- change fatigue.

Lewin's change as three steps (CATS)

Having conducted the forcefield analysis and identified the critical forces to be addressed, the next stage in Lewin's change model is to effect 'change as three steps' (CATS): unfreezing, moving, and refreezing (adapted from Burnes 2004).

Step 1. Unfreezing

As we have seen from the forcefield analysis, Lewin believed that the stability of human behaviour is based on an equilibrium (or state of balance), supported by a complex field of driving and restraining forces. He argued that the equilibrium needs to be destabilized (unfrozen) before old behaviour can be discarded (unlearnt) and new behaviour successfully adopted (refreezing).

The key to 'unfreezing' is to recognize that change, whether at individual or group level, is a psychological dynamic process. In fact, three simultaneous actions are necessary to achieve unfreezing:

- statement that the current state of affairs or behaviours is no longer acceptable (disconfirmation of the validity of the status quo);
- the introduction of a sense of survival anxiety, should the change not succeed;
- the creation of a sense of psychological safety to institute a shared belief that the group is safe from negative consequences that may arise from interpersonal and group risk-taking.

Unless sufficient psychological safety is created among the organization members, the disconfirming information will be denied or in other ways defended against. If so, no survival anxiety will be felt and, consequently, no change will take place. Those organization members who are most affected by change have to feel safe from potential loss and humiliation before they can accept the desired new state of affairs and reject old behaviours.

Step 2. Moving

Unfreezing creates motivation to learn, but it does not generate change. Any attempt to predict or identify a specific outcome from planned change is very difficult because of the complexity of the driving and restraining forces. Instead, strategists should seek to take into account all the forces at work and identify and evaluate, on a trial-and-error basis, all the available options to pivot the organization from its existing state to a new state of affairs. Using an iterative approach of developing viable options and testing them enables groups and individuals to move from a less acceptable to a more acceptable set of behaviours.

Step 3. Refreezing

Without continuous reinforcement, change could be short-lived. Refreezing seeks to position the group at a new state of balance in order to ensure that the new behaviours are relatively stable. The main point about refreezing is that new behaviours must be somewhat consistent with the rest of the behaviours, personality, and environment of the members of the organization. If not, it will simply lead to a new round of disconfirmation. To avoid this happening, Lewin saw successful change as a group activity, as individual behaviours will not be sustained without the transformation of group norms and routines. Therefore, in organizational terms, refreezing often requires changes to organizational culture, norms, policies, and practices.

Critiques of Lewin's CATS model

In recent years, some scholars have critiqued Lewin's CATS model as being too simplistic (Cummings et al. 2016). Kanter et al. (1992) suggest that Lewin's CATS model is too linear and treats an organization as an 'ice cube' and therefore is 'so wildly inappropriate that it is difficult to see why it has not only survived but prospered' (Kanter et al. 1992: 10). Child (2005: 293) also critiques Lewin's rigid idea of 'refreezing' as inappropriate in today's complex environments as organizations change constantly, which requires flexibility and adaptation. Furthermore, Clegg et al. (2005) critique the way in which Lewin's framework of unfreezing, moving, and refreezing has become the template for most change programmes. For them, it would just be a matter of repackaging the Taylorian concept of scientific management that is based on mechanistic analysis of workflows to identify and implement optimum performance and maximization of efficiency.

Despite the critiques, these scholars acknowledge that Lewin's CATS model, as well as other step-based change management models, have an enduring appeal to managers. This popularity can be explained by the perception of certainty that such models offer that there is one 'correct way' to manage change, however simplified the models are in real life.

Kotter's eight-step process to accelerate change

An influential step-based model is based on John Kotter's work *Leading Change* (Kotter 1996), *Leading Change: Why Transformation Efforts Fail* (Kotter 2007) and *Accelerate: Building Strategic Agility for a Faster-Moving World* (Kotter 2014). Kotter's change process models are inspired by Lewin's work, but instead of effecting change in three steps, change is described as an eight-step process with associated guidance for effective implementation.

Kotter's eight accelerators

Kotter's Accelerate model (2014) proposes a way to activate strategic change as a managed process, addressing the increasing complexity and dynamism of today's fast-moving competitive environments with organizational agility and a propensity to innovate. The accelerators are an evolution of Kotter's (1996) seminal eight-step change process, which had a major impact on the strategic change consulting industry (see Chapter 1).

The premise of Kotter's Accelerate model is that although traditional organizational hierarchies and processes that form a company's 'operating system' are optimized for day-to-day business, they are too rigid to adjust to the quick shifts in today's complex and rapidly changing competitive environments. Therefore, a second transient 'operating system', built on a fluid network-like structure, is needed to continually implement strategic initiatives (Kotter 2012). This 'dual operating system'—attending to business as usual in parallel with change—is designed to bridge the gap between evolutionary and revolutionary innovation (see Chapter 11). The stabilized, hierarchical component delivers efficiencies in the fulfilment of known customer needs. The fluid, network component is dynamic and free from bureaucratic layers, enabling creativity and responsive change. At its core is a guiding coalition that represents each level and department in the hierarchy, and its drivers are a 'volunteer army' of people energized by and committed to the coalition's vision and strategy.

Kotter suggests that instead of focusing on the problem to be solved, practitioners should focus on 'the big opportunity' to create new value. That feeds into a 'change vision' which, in turn, informs the required 'strategic initiatives'. The key to making the dual operating system work is alignment, with the big opportunity providing an anchor round which to rally stakeholders in both systems concurrently. This should not be an either/or choice between the hierarchy and the network. If the organization only manages the day-to-day hierarchy, it has no hope of seeing revolutionary innovations. On the other hand, if all the focus is on the network, revolutionary innovations will never see the light of day as a hierarchy is needed to realize the innovations in practice. Therefore, this justifies the dual operating system in Kotter's model.

13

Five principles

Kotter's eight accelerators are based on five principles for the successful activation of strategic change:

1. Get buy-in from more than 50% of the organization for the initiative.

2. Create a 'get-to' environment that generates an army of volunteers for the initiative.

3. Involve people's hearts (not just their heads). Their passion brings more power to the initiative.

4. Invite, encourage, and promote many small acts of leadership.

5. Ensure that all those involved are in alignment.

Eight accelerators

The eight accelerators are as follows (adapted from Kotterinc.com and Kotter 2012):

Step 1. Create a sense of urgency around a single big opportunity: heighten the organization's awareness that it needs continual strategic adjustments that should be aligned with the biggest perceived opportunity.

Step 2. Build and maintain a guiding coalition: create a group of volunteers whom the leadership trusts and is able to see inside and outside the organization. These volunteers know the detail and the big picture and use information to make good organization-wide decisions about what strategic initiatives to launch and implement.

Step 3. formulate a strategic vision and develop change initiatives designed to capitalize on the big opportunity: develop a well-formulated vision that is focused on taking advantage of the big make-or-break opportunity.

Step 4. Communicate the vision and the strategy to create buy-in and attract a growing volunteer army: develop a communications strategy that can go viral and attract employees to buy in to the ambition of the message and begin to share commitment to it.

Step 5. Accelerate movement toward the vision and the opportunity by ensuring that the network removes barriers: as design and implementation of the big opportunity occur in the network but are instituted in the hierarchy, ensure that the network and the hierarchy truly operate closely together.

Step 6. Celebrate visible significant short-term wins: to ensure success, the best short-term wins should be obvious, unambiguous, and clearly related to the vision. Celebrating the wins of the volunteer army will prompt more employee volunteers to join the effort.

Step 7. Never let up—keep learning from experience and don't declare victory too soon: carry through on strategic initiatives and create new ones to adapt to shifting business environments to enhance the organization's competitive position. Be aware that when an organization lets up, cultural and political resistance arise.

Step 8. Integrate changes in the organization culture: institutionalize the new direction, processes, and methods into the organization culture. This can be done as long as the initiative produces visible results and sends the organization into a strategically better future.

See kotterinc.com for a workbook and a discussion guide on how to improve organizational agility through the development of the dual operating system (https://www.kotterinc.com/research-and-perspectives/8-steps-accelerating-change-ebook).

13

Step-based models for managing strategic change have an enduring appeal to managers as such frameworks maintain that there is a universal approach to the management of change using an orderly process. In reality, however, managerial practice differs from theoretical abstractions. Research by Pettigrew (1985) found that formal change management plans bore little relationship to what actually happened in the organization as the way that change unfolded was influenced by complex interplay between organizational history, culture, and politics. Mintzberg (1987) observed that planned change is not always implemented, and some strategies emerge without formal planning. And relatedly, Dunphy and Stace (1988, 1993) and Balogun et al. (2016) argue that there are no universal 'one-size-fits-all' models for managing change.

Instead, these authors propose that the management of change should be contingent on the context, such as the type of change needed and the nature of the organization, including social, cultural, and political considerations as well as its operating environment. Depending on the context of change, strategists have to decide to what extent the change has to be incremental or transformational and to what extent it is necessary to hold consultation with employees. A more consultative approach to managing change may be more appropriate in the context of incremental change where the organization is adopting or evolving with the environment and its survival is not an issue. In contrast, where radical change is the only option for corporate survival, the change effort will most likely require a directive approach set by the management. In practice, however, many change programmes involve both managerial approaches of consultation and direction.

Research by Dunphy and Stace (1993) suggests that a comprehensive approach to managing change should incorporate transformational change, as well as incrementalism, but also that change management should accommodate both directive and consultative means for achieving change. Rather than evolution and transformation being incompatible strategies, and collaboration, consultation, and more directive approaches being incompatible modes, they are, in fact, complementary.

Dunphy and Stace's research findings suggest that for most organizations undergoing transformational change at the corporate level, a directive management style is required to begin the process of repositioning the organization. However, these scholars go on to suggest that once the basis for organizational renewal is in place, there is a choice to be made at the corporate level in terms of mixing the directive and consultative management approaches that are needed to keep up the momentum of change. If the change programme is to be successful, while it may be started with a directive, there must also be a predominance of consultative practices at the business unit level in order to win commitment to the implementation of change. Essentially, if people at the business level do not feel properly consulted, they may find it more difficult to get on board with the changes that have been imposed on them. Hence, effective organizational change necessitates that strategists design organizational change programmes with flexibility, rather than relying on rigid change management models. In Chapter 14, we will explore how strategic leadership approaches can build engagement as an enabler of effective strategy activation.

 Access the online resources to watch a short video clip where Kathryn Kerle discusses change management.

13

CASE EXAMPLE 13.2 **FROM AN IDEA TO A PRODUCT LAUNCH IN SIX MONTHS**

Sometimes, a light-bulb moment brings a new idea to an employee for a new opportunity or product that should be shared with their manager. However, sometimes it takes particular perseverance to demonstrate the potential of the opportunity and get the backing (and funding) to pursue it.

A first step to get this managerial backing might be to present the opportunity to a general manager. However, no matter what the opportunity is, the general manager might focus on current business rather than look to expanding into new areas. As a response to this rejection, an employee might choose to go away and prepare evidence to support the case put forward for the new product or opportunity.

Once a supportive case has been collated, the employee might present the idea to their manager a second time, using financial projections that would substantiate their idea within a business context. However, this still might not necessarily convince a manager that the idea is a lucrative business opportunity. In fact, it might even convince a manager to refuse the idea a second time in favour of concentrating on current business.

Using some real tenacity by this point, as well as some willing team resources, the employee might look for ways to strengthen the support for their idea beyond financial projections. This might involve mocking up a campaign for the opportunity or product, perhaps involving branding, advertising material, and samples. At this point, a manager might accept the potential of the opportunity but only so far as to allow the employee financial support, rather than any further team support, in order to pursue the idea.

This would be enough to launch a product. This process, from idea to launch, could take as little as six months. But why would the manager push back if they could see the opportunity was so worthwhile for their business? Essentially, the manager might seek to set up a dual operating system. This would involve focusing one side of their team on managing the core business, continuing to grow business steadily with safe evolutionary innovation, and simultaneously allowing the other side of the team to work in an opportunity-driven mindset, with opportunity-driven volunteers who wouldn't take no for an answer and were freed up to experiment and try completely new things and new ways of taking them to market.

Questions for discussion

1. What are the two Kotter's operating systems in the case?

2. How did the operating systems interact in this case?

3. How would you describe the elements of the culture of the organization in this case? (See the discussions about culture in Chapter 4 and innovation in Chapter 11.)

Source

Bradt, G. (2014). Leverage John Kotter's 'dual operating system' to accelerate change in large organizations. *Forbes* (14 May), https://www.forbes.com/sites/georgebradt/2014/05/14/leverage-john-kotters-dual-operating-system-to-accelerate-change-in-large-organizations/#66fadda1aef8 (last accessed 19 August 2022).

13

13.7 **Leading change through sense-making and sense-giving**

In section 13.6, we considered change management models which assumed that the management of change was a rational, step-by-step process. However, we concluded that there was no universally 'correct' way of managing change. Change is context dependent, and managers have to deal with organizational complexity that is compounded by the uncertainty and ambiguity of the information they have to rely on in their decision-making (see Chapter 3 for a more detailed discussion). Given this complexity, how can strategists make sense of the situation they find themselves and the organization in? In this section, we will consider how strategists try to gain an understanding of the organization's resources and capabilities, the dynamics of the competitive environment, and the urgency of the change that is needed. Rouleau and Balogun (2011) refer to this as sense-making (an individual's understanding of the world filled with uncertainty and ambiguity) and sense-giving (an individual influencing others' perspectives). Research by Balogun et al. (2015) highlights that managerial sense-making and sense-giving are critically important leadership skills in the management of change.

Sense-making and sense-giving in managing change

It is generally accepted that organizations find it difficult to respond to changes in their environment, be they technical innovations, regulatory changes, or market crises (Kaplan 2008). Although some organizations are more adaptable, many are subject to strong forces that restrain change. It is not necessarily the environmental changes themselves that make change hard to manage but rather the ambiguity that makes it difficult for managers to assess what the changes mean. This creates a challenge for strategy-making and the management of change, which require managers to match strategic choices to their understanding of the external environment (Bower 1970).

Research in managerial cognition has suggested that cognitive frames, or mental maps, are the means by which managers try to deal with these uncertainties and ambiguities (Walsh 1995). This psychological perspective is based on the view that strategic action is influenced by how managers make sense of and interpret change, and how they translate these perspectives into strategic choices (Daft and Weick 1984).

Sense-making is a process through which individuals try to understand novel, unexpected, or confusing events, and it has recently become a critically important topic in the study of organizations (Maitlis and Christianson 2014). When organizational members are faced with moments of ambiguity or uncertainty, they seek to understand what is going on by interpreting signals from their internal and external environment. They then use these signals as the basis for constructing a plausible account that provides order and 'makes sense' of what has occurred and through which they continue to enact or construct their understanding of these environments (Brown 2000; Maitlis 2005; Weick 1995; Weick et al. 2005). Sense-making is not a passive activity but an active interpretation and construction of events and frameworks for understanding as people play a role in constructing the very situations they attempt to comprehend (Weick 1995; Weick et al. 2005).

Sense-giving is an opposite activity to sense-making. In sense-giving, the person who is trying to give sense is making an attempt to influence other people to perceive and interpret certain actions and events in a particular way. In their work on strategic change processes, Gioia and Chittipeddi (1991) found that sense-giving was concerned with the process of managers attempting to influence the sense-making and meaning construction of others towards a preferred definition of organizational reality. The sense-giving process bridges the top and middle manager levels as well as the gap between managers and employees.

13

CASE EXAMPLE 13.3 **SUCCESSFUL STRATEGIC CHANGE AT MULCO**

In 2005, a new president was recruited to MulCo, a family-owned 100-year-old global firm operating in construction and the construction technology industry. The new president came from a global telecommunications company, where he had been the executive director of strategy development.

In the mid-2000s, MulCo employed about 27,000 people with €4 billion in net sales. Although MulCo's business was cyclical, reflecting global trends in the construction industry, the company had successfully balanced this by growing its servicing business, which accounted for more than 50% of the company's net sales. MulCo was recognized as a technology developer in the industry and its employees took a lot of pride from its leadership position in innovation. MulCo ranked fourth in its industry globally, although it struggled to rise from this position. The new president observed:

> At the turn of 2004 and 2005, MulCo was a good company and it had a healthy culture in many ways. However, its profitability was lagging behind its competitors and its global market share was not strengthening anymore. Therefore, it was easy to arrive at the conclusion that that firm needed to get onto a new path of growth—profitable growth in particular. The first task was, hence, to create a shared understanding of the existing situation, the need for change, and to define the new strategy.

The president wanted to refocus the employees' perceptions to become more customer-orientated and pursue profitable growth by becoming more globally inclusive. He was also determined to restructure MulCo from functional departments to cross-functional collaboration. Moreover, the president wished the company to become more agile.

The president's first task was to create a sense of urgency for change through communication. He observed the importance of communication in ensuring that the employees maintained their sense of pride in their work and the company, following this change. For the first time in MulCo's history, the new strategy was communicated to the entire global workforce. The president's dedication to involve and engage everyone in the strategic change placed his communication efforts in centre stage at MulCo. He stated that 'the way we put strategy into practice was [. . .] through the entire organization. It was essential [. . .] to mobilize the entire company [. . .] In this respect, the must-win battles [. . .] connected every employee to the change at least in some way.'

However, MulCo's historical growth through acquisitions and its decentralized management structure did not fit well with the firm's goal of global alignment, which was at the base of the new strategy. Previously acquired companies had been allowed to keep their own local processes, cultures, and languages until the beginning of the strategic change process. This posed challenges for top management. A large gap was identified between global and local functions in the firm, and the business processes were fragmented. A new process architecture was required to improve global alignment. In addition, the company's corporate values, which originated from the family-firm background and its entrepreneurial culture, presented a challenge in the face of change.

As a result, the strategic change process called for an extensive global communication programme involving both direct top-down communication and local communication efforts between managers, supervisors, and employees in the form of a dialogue. The president had to find his own 'voice', and he did so mainly through letters which he sent directly to all organization members in English. These letters were meant to support two-way strategy dialogue between all managers and supervisors and their teams on a personal level. This personal communication provided opportunities to discuss new change-related topics, such as asking: 'What's in it for me?' In order to support the communication within the organization, the president chose strategy facilitators—experts from the middle of the organization, often energized and highly motivated early adaptors—to support local management to facilitate open conversations.

MulCo proved a challenging environment to communicate the new strategic direction towards global alignment. The history of the company as a multi-domestic federation of autonomous subsidiaries

13

had led to fragmented processes with little communication across these units. Additionally, the very contextual engineering language in the firm meant that conveying meanings from the top of the organization was cumbersome, especially early on in the change process. In addition, the lack of urgency for change shaped the way the president's sense-giving efforts unfolded.

Questions for discussion

1. Using forcefield analysis, identify the driving and restraining forces of change in MulCo.

2. Why do you think that the new president adopted a consultative approach to the management of change?

3. How was language used to create a frame for change?

4. What evidence of sense-making and sense-giving does the case offer?

5. If anything, what would you have done differently, and why?

Source

Adapted from Logemann et al. (2019).

Sense-giving initiatives to explain change at the organizational level might be approached through corporate storytelling. This provides a narrative framing of the current state of the organization, and the preferred future position, by sense-giving. Essentially, this develops shared values among organization members in understandable and evocative terms. Hence, strategists leading change processes have to have strong communication skills in order to convince others of the necessity of change and to shape the interpretations of the employees of the preferred future direction and state of the organization (Logemann et al. 2019). Therefore, language provides a frame for change. Framing is a process through which people construct a meaning or experience through the use of symbolic constructs, metaphors, and images.

It is important for the student of strategy to understand that sense-making and sense-giving are critical skills for leading and implementing strategic change. While the development of strong verbal and non-verbal communication skills requires holistic professional and personal growth, they are a powerful combination when applied along with the prescriptive change management models. For example, the cultural web can be used as a framework for making sense of the existing and the future desired culture of an organization. In addition, the cultural web of the future paradigm of the organization can be used as a framework for creating a sense-giving narrative.

13.8 Turnaround and crisis management

13

We have considered the important leadership skills of sense-making and sense-giving in the management of change. Before we close this chapter, we will consider two special change management situations: turnaround and crisis management. How can strategists approach particularly complex situations that deal with troubled organizations and managerial practice? There are strategists and consultants who specialize in crisis and turnaround management, and we will discuss the techniques they apply in these difficult situations. We conclude the chapter with a Practitioner Insight featuring one such professional strategist.

Turnaround management

Turnaround management is a process dedicated to organizational renewal. It uses analysis and planning to save troubled organizations and often seeks to return businesses to financial solvency. It identifies the reasons for failing performance and tries to rectify the problems identified. Turnaround management can involve a management review, including a root analysis of the causes of organizational failure, and strategic analysis to determine why an organization is failing based on internal and external factors. Once an analysis is completed, long-term strategic plans and short-term restructuring plans can be created and implemented.

Turnaround managers

Turnaround managers are also called turnaround practitioners. They are often interim managers (either freelance or in permanent positions) who stay with the organization for as long as it takes to achieve the turnaround. Assignments typically last from 3 to 24 months, depending on the size of the organization and the complexity of the situation.

Turnaround management not only applies to distressed companies but may also help in any situation where a new direction, strategy, or general change in the ways of working needs to be implemented. Therefore, turnaround management is closely related to change management and post-merger integration management. Turnaround management may also help in high growth situations, for example, where an organization needs to adopt a new approach in order to make the most of some emerging opportunities.

Techniques for repositioning during a turnaround

Seminal work by Mayes, McKiernan, and Grinyer (1988), amongst other researchers, has shown that the four main stages/techniques adopted when seeking to create a turnaround are typically known as:

- retrenchment;
- repositioning;
- replacement; and
- renewal.

We will discuss each of these stages in turn.

Stage 1. Retrenchment

The **retrenchment** stage of turnaround management comprises wide-ranging short-term actions intended to reduce any financial losses, stabilize the organization, and, where possible, solve any immediate problems that are causing poor performance. The essential content of the retrenchment stage is often to reduce the scope and size of the organization by selectively shrinking it. This can be done by selling assets, abandoning difficult markets, halting unprofitable lines of production, downsizing, outsourcing, and so forth. These actions can generate resources with the intention of redirecting the organization's attention towards more productive activities and preventing or reducing further financial losses. Retrenchment is often orientated towards efficiency and a refocusing of the organization on its core business(es).

Stage 2. Repositioning

The **repositioning** stage attempts to generate revenue by introducing innovations and making changes in product portfolios and market positioning. This may include the development of new products, entry into new markets, exploring alternative sources of revenue, and/or modifying the image or the mission of a company. Therefore, it is a very different phase from the previous (retrenchment) phase, which typically focuses on efficiency. In the repositioning phase, the leadership is focused on more positive and entrepreneurial strategic thinking.

Stage 3. Replacement

During a turnaround, a decision may be made to replace the chief executive officer (CEO) and/or other senior managers. The thinking behind the **replacement** stage of a turnaround is typically that new managers will help to introduce strategic change, and resulting recovery, based on their different experiences and backgrounds. Top teams, such as the board of directors, may also be concerned that the current CEO and/or other senior managers will have an entrenched view of the organization and its situation, meaning that they cannot view the organization's problems with fresh eyes. If they rely too heavily on their past experience of running the organization, the current leadership may fail to recognize that significant change is necessary to turn the organization around. However, introducing a change of CEO can clearly bring new problems, such as the potential resignation of other well-qualified and experienced employees that the organization would have preferred to retain.

Stage 4. Reorganization/renewal

Within the **reorganization/renewal** stage of a turnaround, the leadership team should begin to pursue long-term actions that are intended to return the organization to a more successful level of performance. The first step may be to analyse the existing strategies and structures within the organization. This examination may end with a closure of some divisions, a development of new markets or business areas, and an expansion into new initiatives and projects. A reorganization/renewal stage may lead the organization to remove inefficient routines or make better use of existing resources. If core competencies are identified and more widely implemented, this may lead to an increase in knowledge-sharing and a stabilization of the organization's value.

This stage is sometimes merged into the first two, leaving a '3Rs' strategy of retrenchment, repositioning, and reorganization. It is important for the student of strategy to understand that these stages do not address the costs or impact of a turnaround strategy on the organization's employees. Neither do they address the potential impact on the culture of the organization.

Turnaround management in the public sector

Much has been written about turnaround management in the private sector—but what about public-sector organizations? Problems of public service 'failure' are high on the political agenda (Boyne 2004, 2006) in the United Kingdoms and other countries, and national policymakers and local service managers in the public sector also need strategies to improve the performance of organizations that are struggling or failing.

Boyne (2006) developed a model of the turnaround process (Figure 13.4) and reviews evidence on the effectiveness of different turnaround strategies. There are a substantial number of studies of decline and recovery in private firms—and fewer studies on public-sector organizations. The private-sector evidence suggests that recovery from failure is associated with

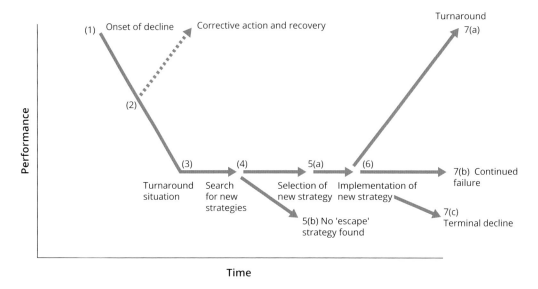

FIGURE 13.4 Stages of organizational turnaround. *Source*: reproduced with permission from Boyne, G.A. (2006). Strategies for public service turnaround: Lessons from the private sector? *Administration & Society*, **38**(3), 365–88.

strategies of retrenchment, repositioning, and reorganization, as already outlined. In fact, it appears that turnaround is more likely in companies that pursue these approaches. Boyne (2004, 2006) analyses the relevance of this '3Rs' strategy to the public sector, and broadly supports the approach. However, he notes that the replacement stage can be particularly sensitive in the public sector for the following reasons.

- A new senior management team may revive a private-sector company through the comprehensive implementation of strategies of retrenchment and repositioning. However, the scope for the pursuit of these strategies is likely to be more limited in the public sector.

- New executives in the private sector may be able to achieve turnaround through financial incentive schemes for staff and more flexible approaches to human resource management. However, these options are less likely to be available to new senior managers in a public-sector organization.

- Leadership in the public sector is political as well as managerial (e.g. in local government). To identify whether executive succession is likely to lead to turnaround, it is first necessary to discover whether any weakness of leadership is attributable to appointed officials or elected politicians. Service improvement may hinge on democratic as much as managerial processes.

Crisis management

Crisis management is the process by which an organization deals with disruptive and unexpected events that threaten to harm the organization or its stakeholders. The study of crisis management originated with large-scale industrial and environmental disasters in the 1980s. A crisis mindset requires the ability to think of the worst-case scenario while simultaneously suggesting a range of feasible solutions. There are many types of crisis, but some that are important to consider and prepare for include the following:

- **Natural disaster:** including environmental phenomena such as earthquakes and tsunamis;
- **Technological crisis:** caused by human applications of science and technology, including systems failure or human error;
- **Confrontation crisis:** such as boycotts and strikes;
- **Crisis of malevolence:** use of criminal means or other extreme tactics by opponents of the organization (e.g. product tampering or kidnapping);
- **Crisis of deception:** when management conceals or misrepresents information about itself and its products when dealing with consumers and others;
- **Crisis of organizational misdeeds or skewed management values:** when management takes action it knows will harm or place stakeholders at risk of harm or when management favours short-term economic gain and neglects broader social values and stakeholders other than investors.

We can categorize these crises into three common elements:

- a threat to the organization;
- the element of surprise;
- a short decision time.

Within an organization, crisis can also be viewed as a process of transformation, where the 'old system' can no longer be maintained. Therefore, it has been argued that there is a fourth defining quality of a crisis—the need for change. If change is not needed, the event could perhaps be described as a failure or incident, rather than a crisis. In contrast with risk management, which involves assessing potential threats and finding the best ways to manage and avoid them, crisis management involves dealing with threats before, during, and after they have occurred.

Crisis management is often viewed as a situation-based management system that includes clear roles, responsibilities, and process-related requirements across an organization. The set of responses within the crisis management system will often include actions in the areas of crisis prevention, crisis assessment, crisis handling, and crisis termination. The aim of crisis management is to be well prepared for any crisis situation: to ensure a rapid and adequate response to the crisis; to maintain clear lines of reporting and communication when a crisis occurs; and to agree rules for crisis termination.

Crisis management techniques

But how does a strategist manage a crisis? A strategist should implement the following techniques of crisis management:

- Design and adopt strategies for preventing, alleviating, and overcoming different types of crisis.
- Maintain up-to-date lists of contingency plans; always remain on the alert for potential crisis situations.

13

- Assess a potential crisis situation and gain an understanding of its influence on the organization.

- Establish metrics to define what scenarios constitute a crisis and consequently trigger the necessary response mechanisms.

- Deploy a set of methods used to respond to both the reality and the perception of crisis.

- Establish clear communication throughout the response phase of crisis management scenarios.

Crisis management is considered to be a very important process in public relations as organizations must seek to communicate effectively, as well as taking effective action, during periods of crisis. The credibility and reputation of organizations is strongly influenced by the internal and external perceptions of their responses during crisis situations. The ability to communicate effectively while responding to a crisis in a timely fashion often presents organizations with a significant challenge. There must be open and consistent communication throughout the hierarchy to contribute to a successful crisis communication process.

Crisis management in the public sector

Comfort (2007) argues that 'cognition' is central to performance when seeking to manage crises and emergencies by public administrative agencies. Comfort writes that 'cognition' is defined as the capacity to recognize the degree of emerging risk to which a community is exposed and to act on that information. Using the case of Hurricane Katrina and how the public agencies and crisis responders managed the environmental crisis, Comfort proposes a dynamic system with four main decision points:

- **awareness stage:** detection of risk;

- **cognition stage:** recognition and interpretation of risk for the immediate context;

- **communication stage:** communication of risk to multiple organizations in a wider region;

- **engagement stage:** self-organization and mobilization of a collective community response system to reduce risk and respond to danger.

In practice, it is at these four main decision points, with escalating requirements for action, that human cognitive, communicative, and coordinating skills frequently fail—and this means that organizations are likely to lose control of the situation. In particular, if the first three steps are not successfully completed, the fourth—engagement—is unlikely to succeed.

Crisis management across sectors

Crisis management should also be considered in the particular context of different industries. For example, the hospitality and tourism industry is highly susceptible to crises and disasters of different kinds, so it is particularly important for that industry to have a good understanding of crisis management. The sector is relatively fragmented and often impacted by a range of external factors. However, an improved analysis of the nature of crises provides insights into how

13

they can be managed, while adopting a more strategic, holistic, and proactive approach (Ritchie 2004). For example, the strategist in this industry should:

- develop proactive scanning and planning;
- implement strategies when crises or disasters occur;
- evaluate the effectiveness of these strategies to ensure continual refinement of crisis management strategies.

Flexibility and continual monitoring is required by organizations and destinations to design and implement effective strategies to deal with crises. Organizations should take a holistic approach to managing crises and may have to reconfigure their management structure and consider aspects related to resource allocation and organizational culture, all of which may influence the effectiveness of crisis management. Furthermore, there is a need for cooperation between a wide number of stakeholders, both internal and external to the organization, to effectively plan and manage crises and disasters. Leadership is required to provide direction to the industry in times of crisis and to bring stakeholders together at an organizational and destination level for integrated crisis/disaster management (Ritchie 2004).

Coombs and Holladay (2006) point out that crisis managers believe in the value of a favourable pre-crisis reputation. The prior reputation of the organization can create a 'halo' effect that protects it during a crisis. Coombs and Holladay (2006) undertook two studies—one based on an amusement park, and another on a major retailer—to test whether the halo effect seemed to occur in practice. Their study suggests that the 'halo' effect for prior reputation can indeed be a valuable attribute for organizations in crisis and that the 'halo' may operate within a limited range for organizations with very favourable prior reputations, acting as a shield that deflects the potential reputational damage from a crisis.

PRACTITIONER INSIGHT KATHRYN KERLE, INDEPENDENT NON-EXECUTIVE DIRECTOR

Kathryn Kerle is an independent non-executive director. She is currently Chair of the Audit & Risk Committee of Planet Smart City, a company that designs and builds affordable smart cities. She is also Chair of the Audit & Risk Committee of Newcleo, a company that is working towards the generation of safe, clean, and sustainable nuclear energy. Prior to these appointments, Ms Kerle was an independent non-executive director of Al Rayan Bank and Greater London Mutual. She spent much of her executive career in financial services, working at Moody's Investor Services credit rating agency and the Royal Bank of Scotland, where she was Head of Enterprise Risk Reporting and Chair of the Decision-Making Committee responsible for adjudicating loan cases in a high-profile  strategic remediation project at the bank. Ms Kerle discusses the types of change in organizations but, more specifically, the role of strategists as leaders in transformational change and crisis situations.

Continued

Drawing on her experience in global financial services, Ms Kerle says that change in organizations is about doing new things, such as Goldman Sachs, a Wall Street investment bank, becoming a commercial bank and launching Marcus, a banking service targeted at individual retail customers, or doing things in a new way, such as replacing organizations' legacy IT systems with new systems.

> *Given the rate of change in financial services, one of my favourite questions to ask executives is: what business are you in? Unless organizations understand what exactly customers buy from them, you may be confronted with potentially the most dangerous type of competitors: those who look at the problem in a different way. If one were to ask banks in the UK who their competitors were, Royal Bank of Scotland would probably say Lloyds, HSBC, Santander, etc., but until recently they wouldn't necessarily have thought that iTunes might be a competitor through Apple Pay: iTunes could conceivably just exchange payments between people who are already connected because they're all customers of Apple. Companies such as Apple think of payments as a technical problem, not a banking problem, and therefore they bring tech expertise to it. And who knows, it might turn out to be a technological as opposed to a banking problem. So, I think dealing with a new competitor might make us think we've looked at this in the wrong way. And do we have the wherewithal to look at it and compete on an entirely different basis?*

Organizational crisis presents its own challenges, but, as Ms Kerle says, 'Never allow a good crisis go to waste.' The key thing in the management of radical change is for the leader to 'provide a vision, move forward, and not dwell in the past'.

The traditional approach to change management in crisis has been to adapt very much of a dictatorial style of management. However, if we rely only on diktat and coercion, change management won't work. Ms Kerle refers to a conversation she had with an executive coach about this. She had asked the coach if she had ever worked with a company where an individual was put into an executive role because they were good at managing people.

> *She thought about that long and hard. And she said, no, I can't think of a single one. So, we often think that the dictator is the leader. And the person who has a strong ego, loud voice, can command a room, or whatever, is best placed to make things happen. I would really challenge this—if you want lasting change where people are happy to be part of it, and bring their skills and knowledge, that is precisely the wrong way to do it.*

This is quite possibly the case, especially in crisis:

> *You may need someone to point out that the house is on fire. Not that people don't already know it, but people very often need to have a focal point. And I think having someone articulate what the issue is is absolutely useful. But then to actually mobilize people to solve the problem, I don't think that has to be done by diktat at all.*

In terms of senior management teams, 'the most effective company boards and the most effective chairs will typically be people who facilitate the arrival at a good decision by the members of the board, not those who inform the board of what their view is'. To be an effective change leader is a difficult skill that requires a:

> *need to hear all the voices in the room and arrive at a solution; there's an art to arriving at a plan. But what is being decided and what the plan for change is should be something that everyone can at least live with because you can't do it yourself. Change is implemented through people and if they're not sold on it, it's just not going to happen.*

Finally, management style has to be flexible and listening. As for the leader, one has to remain calm. 'Different people respond to crisis in different ways. But if you can remain calm, or if you're a naturally calm person, and certainly not reacting in a negative way, then that calms everybody else down.'

 Access the online resources to watch a short video clip where Kathryn Kerle talks more about her career.

CHAPTER SUMMARY

In this chapter, we addressed the following learning outcomes:

○ **Recognize the importance of an organization's history as a creator of path dependence and its role in both formal and informal organization culture.**
An organization's values and the ways that the organization operates are, to a great extent, influenced by its history. History and its cultural heritage can be a source of advantage for the organization because it cannot easily be replicated by competitors. The way the organization operates is said to be path dependent on its history and practices that have evolved and accumulated over time. However, we must remember that while the organization's past may give it a competitive advantage, if the organization is not able to renew itself in an evolving competitive marketplace, it may lose this advantage by attempting to rely solely on its past competencies and activities.

○ **Evaluate the importance of organizations to be able to manage in the present while simultaneously preparing for the future.**
The only constant in our twenty-first-century world is change, and no organization is immune to it. We considered the dual task of exploiting the organization's existing resources and capabilities while simultaneously exploring future opportunities and developing new capabilities. Organizational ambidexterity and agility are crucial competencies if an organization is going to survive in highly dynamic competitive environments. This requires strategists to possess a vision of how the future will unfold and a strategy for how the organization can adapt or anticipate future challenges while continuing to manage for the present.

○ **Define the concept of strategic change and distinguish the types of strategic change.**
Change can be considered to be strategic if it has an impact on:
- the competitive position of the organization;
- changes to the organization's overarching business model;
- changes to the organization's product and service offer;
- development of new organizational capabilities;
- changes to the geographic scope of the organization through international expansion;
- outsourcing of activities or bringing activities in-house that have previously been carried out by outside suppliers;
- changes to the nature and overall structure of the organization through the formation of strategic alliances, mergers and acquisitions, divestments, etc.

Organizations can approach implementing change incrementally and consultatively over a period of time or radically through more directive big bang/transformational means. However, recent research has shown that most successful change management initiatives apply both consultative and directive approaches regardless of the type of change effected.

13

○ Examine the processes and tools available for managers to effectively manage and implement strategic change.

Using the prescriptive rational process approach to change management, we considered how forcefield analysis can be used to identify forces that either drive or constrain chance. Once these forces have been identified, there are a number of step-by-step process tools available to strategists to implement change in organizations. These are useful tools for strategists, but we need to bear in mind that change is always context specific.

○ Recognize the role of sense-making and sense-giving in leading change.

Successful change management requires skills of sense-making and sense-giving through which change is conceived and implemented. However, sense-making and sense-giving skills require strong verbal and non-verbal communication that do not come pre-packaged in frameworks. The development of these skills requires holistic professional and personal growth, but they are a powerful combination when applied along with the prescriptive rational change management models.

? END-OF-CHAPTER QUESTIONS

Recall questions

1. What is the relationship between path dependency and organization culture?

2. What is understood by organizational ambidexterity?

3. What are the most common barriers to change?

4. What is the purpose of forcefield analysis?

5. What is the difference between sense-making and sense-giving?

6. What is the difference between turnaround and crisis management?

Application questions

A) What do you consider to be the biggest obstacles for successful change management and why?

B) What are the different types of change and how would you approach each change situation with the models outlined in this chapter?

C) What do you consider to the key leadership qualities in managing strategic change?

D) Based on the work you undertook in enacting a cultural web of an organization in Case Example 13.1, create a sense-giving narrative for the future paradigm of the organization that you analysed.

ONLINE RESOURCES

www.oup.com/he/mackay2e

In addition to the video interviews already highlighted, the book's online resources include the following features for this chapter, specifically:

- *links to further reading material* to broaden your knowledge of key issues discussed in this chapter;

- *self-test multiple-choice questions* to test your understanding of the material covered in each section of the chapter; and

- *a flashcard glossary* to help you recall and test your understanding of key terms.

FURTHER READING

'Organizational culture: Can it be a source of sustained competitive advantage?' by Jay Barney

Barney, J.B. (1986). Organizational culture: Can it be a source of sustained competitive advantage? *Academy of Management Review*, **11**(3), 656–65.

This seminal article explains Barney's argument that if organization culture could be a source of sustainable competitive advantage, it would have to meet the criteria of being valuable, rare, and inimitable.

'An agile approach to change management' by Sarah Jensen Clayton

Clayton, S.J. (2021) An agile approach to change management. *hbr.org.* (11 January), *https://hbr.org/2021/01/an-agile-approach-to-change-management* (last accessed 24 May 2022).

The article proposes to rewrite change management interventions by using lessons learned from agile software development processes. This is particularly relevant as organizations emerge from the COVID-19 pandemic and having to rethink their product portfolios, restructure their supply chains, and manage digital transformation initiatives.

'Unfreezing change as three steps: Rethinking Kurt Lewin's legacy for change management' by Stephen Cummings, Todd Bridgman, and Kenneth G. Brown

Cummings, S., Bridgman, T., and Brown, K.G. (2016). Unfreezing change as three steps: Rethinking Kurt Lewin's legacy for change management. *Human Relations*, **69**(1), 33–60.

Lewin's model is regarded by many as the fundamental approach to managing change. Lewin has been criticized by scholars for oversimplifying the change process and has been defended by others against such charges. However, what has remained unquestioned is the model's foundational significance. Based on a comparison of what Lewin wrote about change as three steps (CATS) with how this is presented in later works, the article argues that he never developed such a model and it took form after his death. The authors investigate how and why CATS came to be understood as the foundation of change management and to influence change theory and practice to this day.

13

Accelerate: Building Strategic Agility for a Faster Moving World by John P. Kotter

Kotter, J. (2014). *Accelerate: Building Strategic Agility for a Faster Moving World*. Boston, MA: Harvard Business Review Press.

Kotter explains how traditional organizational hierarchies have evolved to meet the daily demands of running an enterprise. For most companies, the hierarchy is the singular operating system at the heart of the organization. In practice, however, this system is not built for an environment where change has become the norm. Kotter advocates a more agile, network-like structure that operates in concert with the hierarchy to create what he calls a 'dual operating system' for change.

'Sensemaking in organizations: Taking stock and moving forward' by Sally Maitlis and Marlys Christianson

Maitlis, S. and Christianson, M. (2014). Sensemaking in organizations: Taking stock and moving forward. *Academy of Management Annals*, **8**(1), 57–125.

This article develops a definition of sense-making that is rooted in recurrent themes from the literature and integrates existing theory and research, focusing on two key bodies of work. The first explores how sense-making is accomplished, unpacking the sense-making process by examining how events become triggers for sense-making, how meaning is created, and the role of action in sense-making. The second body considers how sense-making enables the accomplishment of other key organizational processes such as organizational change, learning, and creativity and innovation.

'Organizational ambidexterity in action: How managers explore and exploit' by Charles A. O'Reilly III and Michael L. Tushman

O'Reilly, C.A. III and Tushman, M.L. (2011). Organizational ambidexterity in action: How managers explore and exploit. *California Management Review*, **53**(4), 5–21.

Conceptually, the need for organizations to both explore and exploit is convincing, but how do managers and organizations actually do this? The focus of this article is to gain a deeper understanding of the challenges of ambidexterity for managers and organizations and what, in practice, differentiates the more successful attempts at ambidexterity from the less successful organizational efforts in developing ambidexterity.

REFERENCES

Abell, D.F. (1993). *Managing with Dual Strategies*. New York: Free Press.

Balogun, J., Bartunek, J.M., and Do, B. (2015). Senior managers' sensemaking and responses to strategic change. *Organization Science*, **26**(4), 960–79.

Balogun, J., Hailey, V.H., and Gustafson, S. (2016). *Exploring Strategic Change* (4th edn). Harlow: Pearson.

Barney, J.B. (1986). Organizational culture: Can it be a source of sustained competitive advantage? *Academy of Management Review*, **11**(3), 656–65.

Birkinshaw, J. and Gibson, C. (2004). Building ambidexterity into an organization. *MIT Sloan Management Review*. **45**(4), 47–55.

Bower, J.L. (1970). *Managing the Resource Allocation Process: A Study of Corporate Planning and Investment* (2nd edn). Boston, MA: Harvard Business School Press.

13

Boyne, G.A. (2004). A '3Rs' strategy for public service turnaround: Retrenchment, repositioning, and reorganization. *Public Money and Management*, **24**(2), 97–103.

Boyne, G.A. (2006). Strategies for public service turnaround: Lessons from the private sector? *Administration & Society*, **38**(3), 365–88.

Bradt, G. (2014). Leverage John Kotter's 'dual operating system' to accelerate change in large organizations (14 May), https://www.forbes.com/sites/georgebradt/2014/05/14/leverage-john-kotters-dual-operating-system-to-accelerate-change-in-large-organizations/#23096fffaef8 (last accessed 19 August 2022).

Brown A.D. (2000). Making sense of inquiry sensemaking. *Journal of Management Studies*, **37**(1), 45–75.

Burnes, B. (2004). Kurt Lewin and the planned approach to change: A reappraisal. *Journal of Management Studies*, **41**(6), 977–1002.

Bulkin, B. (2015). *Crash Course: One Year to Become a Great Leader of a Great Company*. London: Whitefox Publishing.

Chathoth, P.K., Ching-Yick Tse, E., and Olsen, M.D. (2006). Turnaround strategy: A study of restaurant firms. *International Journal of Hospitality Management*, **25**(4), 602–22.

Child, J. (2005). *Organization: Contemporary Principles and Practice*. Oxford: Blackwell.

Clegg, S.R., Kornberger, M., and Pitsis, T. (2005). *Managing & Organizations: An Introduction to Theory and Practice*. London: Sage.

Comfort, L.K. (2007). Crisis management in hindsight: Cognition, communication, coordination, and control. *Public Administration Review*, **67**, 189–97.

Coombs, W.T. and Holladay, S.J. (2006). Unpacking the halo effect: Reputation and crisis management. *Journal of Communication Management*, **10**(20), 123–37.

Cummings, S., Bridgman, T., and Brown, K.G. (2016). Unfreezing change as three steps: Rethinking Kurt Lewin's legacy for change management. *Human Relations*, **69**(1), 33–60.

Czarniawska, B. (1997). *Narrating the Organization*. Chicago, IL: Chicago University Press.

Daft, R.L. and Weick, K.E. (1984). Toward a model of organizations as interpretation systems. *Academy of Management Review*, **9**(2), 284–95.

Deal, T.E. and Kennedy, A.A. (1982). *Corporate Cultures: The Rites and Rituals of Corporate Life*. Reading, MA: Addison-Wesley.

Dunphy, D. and Stace, D. (1988). Transformational and coercive strategies for planned organizational change: Beyond the OD model. *Organization Studies*, **9**(3), 317–34.

Dunphy, D. and Stace, D. (1993) The strategic management of corporate change. *Human Relations*, **46**(8), 905–20.

Flinders, K. (2021). Fujitsu escaped huge lawsuit because Post Office behaved so badly in Horizon scandal. *Computer Weekly* (4 November 2021), https://www.computerweekly.com/news/252509066/Fujitsu-escaped-huge-lawsuit-because-Post-Office-behaved-so-badly-in-Horizon-scandal (last accessed 24 May 2022).

Gioia, D.A. and Chittipeddi K. (1991). Sensemaking and sensegiving in strategic change initiation. *Strategic Management Journal*, **12**(6), 433–48.

Goh, F. (2017). 10 companies that failed to innovate, resulting in business failure, *Collective Campus*, https://www.collectivecampus.com.au/blog/10-companies-that-were-too-slow-to-respond-to-change (last accessed 19 August 2022).

Groysberg, B., Lee, J., Price, J., and Cheng, J. (2018). The leader's guide to corporate culture: How to manage the eight critical elements of organizational life. *Harvard Business Review* (January–February).

Hall, S. (1993). Culture, community, nation. *Cultural Studies*, **7**(3), 349–636.

Huff, A.S. (eds) (1990). *Mapping Strategic Thought*. London: John Wiley and Sons.

Johnson, G. (1992). Managing strategic change—strategy, culture, and action. *Long Range Planning*, **25**(1), 28–36.

Kanter, R.M., Stein, B., and Jick, T. (1992). *The Challenge of Organizational Change*. New York: Free Press.

Kaplan, S. (2008). Framing contests: Strategy making under uncertainty. *Organization Science*, **19**(5), 729–52.

Kotter, J. (1996). *Leading Change*. Boston, MA: Harvard Business Press.

Kotter, J. (2007). Leading change: Why transformation efforts fail. *Harvard Business Review* (January).

Kotter, J. (2012). Accelerate: How the most innovative companies capitalize on today's rapid-fire challenges—and still make their numbers. *Harvard Business Review* (November).

Kotter, J. (2014). *Accelerate: Building Strategic Agility for a Faster Moving World*. Boston, MA: Harvard Business Review Press.

Leonard-Barton, D. (1992). Core capabilities and core rigidities. *Strategic Management Journal*, **13**, 111–26.

Lewin, K. (1947). Frontiers in group dynamics. In: Cartwright, D. (ed.), *Field Theory in Social Science.* London: Social Science Paperbacks.

Lewin, K. (1951). *Field Theory in Social Science*. New York: Harper and Row.

Logemann, M., Piekkari, R., and Cornelissen, J. (2019). *Long Range Planning*, **52**(5), 101, 852.

Maitlis, S. (2005). The social processes of organizational sensemaking. *Academy of Management Journal*, **48**, 21–49.

Maitlis, S. and Christianson, M. (2014). Sensemaking in organizations: Taking stock and moving forward. *Academy of Management Annals*, **8**(1), 57–125.

Mayes, D., McKiernan, P., and Grinyer, P.H. (1988). *Sharpbenders: The Secrets of Unleashing Corporate Potential*. Oxford: Blackwells.

Mintzberg, H. (1987). *Crafting Strategy*. Boston, MA: Harvard Business School Press.

O'Reilly, C.A. and Tushman, M.L. (2004). The ambidextrous organization. *Harvard Business Review* (April).

O'Reilly, C.A. and Tushman, M.L. (2011). Organizational ambidexterity in action: How managers explore and exploit. *California Management Review*, **53**(4), 5–21.

Peters, T. and Waterman, R. (1982). *In Search of Excellence: Lessons from America's Best Run Companies*. New York: Harper & Row.

Pettigrew, A. (1985). *The Awakening Giant: Continuity and Change at ICI*. New York: Basil Blackwell.

The Post Office (2021). Commons library research briefing. House of Commons Library, 18 October.

Ritchie, B.W. (2004). Chaos, crises, and disasters: A strategic approach to crisis management in the tourism industry. *Tourism Management*, **25**(6), 669–83.

Rouleau, L. and Balogun, J. (2011). Middle managers, strategic sensemaking, and discursive competence. *Journal of Management Studies*, **38**(5), 953–83.

Schein, E.H. (1997). *Organizational Culture and Leadership* (2nd edn). San Francisco, CA: Jossey Bass.

Schreyogg, G. and Sydow, J. (2010). *The Hidden Dynamics of Path Dependence: Institutions and Organizations*. Basingstoke: Palgrave Macmillan.

Schwartz, T. (2018) Leaders focus too much on changing policies, and not enough on changing minds. *HBR.org* (25 June), https://hbr.org/2018/06/leaders-focus-too-much-on-changing-policies-and-not-enough-on-changing-minds (last accessed 24 May 2022).

13

Teece, D.J., Pisano, G., and Shuen, A. (1997). Dynamic capabilities and strategic management. *Strategic Management Journal*, **18**, 509–33.

Wallis, N. (2021). *The Great Post Office Scandal.* Bath: Bath Publishing Limited.

Walsh, J.P. (1995). Managerial and organizational cognition: Notes from a trip down memory lane. *Organization Science*, **6**(3), 280–321.

Weick K.E. (1995). *Sensemaking in Organizations*. London: Sage.

Weick, K.E. (2001). *Making Sense of the Organization*. Oxford: Blackwell.

Weick, K.E. (2009). *Making Sense of the Organization*, Vol. 2 *The Impermanent Organization*. Chichester: John Wiley.

Weick, K.E., Sutcliffe, K.M., and Obstfeld, D. (2005). Organizing and the process of sensemaking. *Organization Science*, **16**(4), 409–21.

13

CHAPTER FOURTEEN

Strategic Leadership for an Ever-Changing World

CONTENTS

By the end of this chapter, you should be able to:

- ◯ Describe the evolution of the concept of leadership with reference to individual, relational, and processual interpretations

- ◯ Explain how strategic leadership can be considered a subset of leadership studies

- ◯ Compare the scope and implications for strategizing of apex stakeholder, managerial system, and practice interpretations of strategic leadership

- ◯ Explain how strategic leadership interpretations can be integrated through a process-practice perspective of high value to strategy practitioners

- ◯ Evaluate the usefulness of strategic leadership to individuals and organizations strategizing in an ever-changing world

TOOLBOX

- ◯ **Strategic Leadership Practices Framework**
  Based on Schoemaker et al.'s (2013) analysis of effective strategic leadership approaches, this model advocates anticipating, challenging, interpreting, deciding, aligning, and learning practices that individuals or collectives might deploy towards being effective strategy practitioners.

- ◯ **Integrated Process–Practice Perspective of Strategic Leadership**
  A process–practice framework proposing adaptive, engaging, interdependent, pluralistic, purpose-driven and responsible practitioners, practices, and processes of strategic leadership as a contributor to organizations surviving and thriving in a volatility, uncertainty, complexity, and ambiguity (VUCA) world.

Access the online resources to watch a short video clip where Nada Khorchid shares her top career tips.

14

OPENING CASE STUDY PROFIT AND PURPOSE AT NATURA

Natura Cosméticos SA is a Brazilian multinational enterprise with a global reach in the cosmetics, hygiene, and beauty products markets. It was founded in 1969 by 27-year-old Antonio Luiz da Cunha Seabra as a small lab and cosmetics shop in São Paulo. The name Natura—Portuguese for nature—reflects the organization's deep commitment to environmental sustainability. As long-time employee and ex-CEO of 10 years, Alessandro Carlucci notes, Natura's origin in Brazil, two-fifths of which is covered by the Amazon, means 'being committed to the Amazon is in our strategy, our capacity and our mission in some way'. Further, Natura's founders wanted to foster a company ethos and operating model based on 'healthier relationships'—between the company and its customers, its customers and its million-plus sales consultants, the company and its suppliers, and, more broadly, society and the environment.

Natura has expressed a public commitment to sustainable development since its creation. As an integral part of its operating approach, the organization runs initiatives intended to preserve the Amazon and Atlantic Forest ecosystems and ways of life, work towards 100% carbon neutral products, use mainly recyclable materials, fund education for 500K children annually in developing countries, and advocate on behalf of women's rights and well-being.

On its website, Natura comments: 'Thanks to its commitment to sustainable development since its creation and its objective by 2020 to generate a positive environmental, social and economic impact, Natura has become the world's largest certified B Corp company and the first publicly traded company to receive this certification in December 2014.'

B-Corp is a corporate form which builds sustainable commitments into an organization's legal constitution (see Chapter 4 for more information). The B-Corp register listing for Natura describes it as 'a cosmetics company that is conscious about well-being and sustainable development by cultivating better relationship within the community as well as with nature. They work with sustainable practices in their operations, bringing awareness to better choices for a better future [. . .] [and seek to] attract other companies interested in sustainable business development.'

Natura has a track record as a leading proponent of environmental responsibility recognized by the Corporate Knights awards (a global business sustainability monitoring body). Natura was the first in its sector to adopt integrated environmental, social, and governance (ESG) reporting practices, treating financial, social, and environmental prosperity as all part of the same organizational concern—'the company saw integrated reporting as the best way to signal its management's focus on environmental and social stewardship and to ensure leadership's commitment to those goals'.

Natura has long drawn on the Amazon for inspiration, and *c.* 75% of its raw ingredients, in its product portfolio. For example, since 2000, Natura's Ekos line of cosmetics has been made from raw materials gathered through sustainable methods from the Amazon. The company uses the rainforest's biodiversity as a 'technological platform' for research and development, having realized early in its development that it 'could not be able to compete with the big players in the cosmetic industry by trying to find the right molecule in a lab'. To avoid abuse of its proximity and reliance on the rainforest, Natura established agreements with all its many thousands of small suppliers to guard against 'biopiracy'—the unethical commercialization of the region's genetic and cultural heritage. This way of operating positions the company as the leading, authentic player in the market for natural cosmetics and skincare.

The leadership team in Natura emphasizes the importance of sustainability credentials in reaching increasingly ethics- and purpose-motivated consumers. For example, the co-chair of Natura's board, Guilherme Leal, is a board member of the Brazilian Fund for Biodiversity, the World Wildlife Foundation in Brazil, and the United Nations Global Compact, a sustainability initiative. He also founded the Instituto Arapyaú, which is focused on promoting the 'green economy'.

In addition to environmental considerations, Natura has a distinctive 'social' strand to its way of operating that mirrors the community-orientated culture of the indigenous people of the Amazon. This is reflected in the organization's distinctive network of consultants. Inspired by Avon's approach but adapted to Brazilian culture, in the early 1970s,

14

Natura began building a network of direct sales consultants across the country. This network has steadily grown over the past 50 years to c.1.4 million in 2022. Although initially costly, once established, direct sales networks are efficient to operate and expand. With a commitment to relationships and shared prosperity that resonated with company and community values, Natura created jobs, brand evangelists, and rich flows of communication with the consumer base across Brazil. The sales network also imbued Natura with a competitive advantage, in comparison to department stores and pharmacies selling competitors' products, as a way of operating better able to adjust to the economic hardships of the 1980s.

In harmony with its ecological credentials, Natura developed products meeting consumer wellness needs before ideals of beauty. This was a natural direction for the organization in alignment with national attitudes in Brazil and customer insights flowing from the direct sales network. Consumers responded by rewarding Natura with a 43% compound annual rate of revenue growth from 1979 to 1989. As global attitudes have shifted in recent decades towards a similar view, Natura has emerged as an authentic and credible proponent of wellness with consumers around the world. This has enabled Natura to expand into overseas markets and to acquire firms such as Avon and the Body Shop (that once would have been considered giants in comparison to Natura).

Social impact is also evident in Natura's investment in education and local employment initiatives for rainforest communities. Taking an ecological view of how to create a wellspring of indigenous talent, Natura notes, 'When you have local leadership in the communities, they develop, they grow. The challenge is persuading talented individuals to stay and not head to the cities. [So as we] invest in education and leadership development we also invest in the production chain to allow them to have some business there too.'

Looking to the future, Natura describes an ongoing commitment to open innovation, powered by communication and collaboration with its partners and in harmony with its natural surroundings. Innovation leaders in the organization connect open innovation with the local cultivation practices and environmentally focused culture of the organization. They also note that innovation strategies emerge from the engrained 'operating mode' of the organization.

Natura is supporting the evolution of capabilities in daily operations, including in the skills of its door-to-door associates, providing payment machines and helping them open web stores. In keeping with the times, an industry consultant observes, 'This powerful sales network that gets into consumers' homes already existed offline, and now it's converting itself into an online network.'

Natura leadership continues to emphasize the importance of its relationship with and concern for the Amazon as it has done since 1969. Commenting on globally recognized challenges they note—'We don't think that we have the solution. It's a complex issue, the Amazon. But we believe we can be one of the actors to mobilize other companies and also the local society to help the Amazon be developed in a sustainable way.' And as a business with a global footprint, ambition, and sense of responsibility, Natura seems to extend this care for sustainability to every aspect of its operation and activities.

Questions for discussion

1. Describe how a strategic focus on sustainability has shaped the development of Natura since it was founded. How have sustainability initiatives impacted on long-term business performance?

2. How important has consistent top management team activity been to developing an organization focused on sustainability? To what extent have other stakeholders played a part?

3. If you were part of the top management team at Natura, what would be your approach to global expansion? What would be your concerns, priorities, and objectives? Explain your answers.

Sources

Balch, O. (2013). Natura commits to sourcing sustainably from the Amazon (13 March), https://www.theguardian.com/sustainable-business/natura-sourcing-sustainably-from-amazon (last accessed 19 June 2022).

B-Corp website (2022). Natura & Co, https://www.bcorporation.net/en-us/find-a-b-corp/company/natura-co (last accessed 19 June 2022).

Butler, S. (2017). L'Oréal to sell Body Shop to Brazil's Natura in 1 bn euro deal (9 June), https://www.theguardian.com/business/2017/jun/09/loreal-body-shop-natura-aesop (last accessed 19 June 2022).

BusinessWeek (2019). Selling the rainforest door-to-door, https://www.bloomberg.com/news/articles/2019-07-31/brazil-s-natura-wants-to-take-rainforest-chic-global-with-avon (last accessed 19 June 2022).

Eccles, R.G. and Serafeim, G. (2013). The performance frontier. *Harvard Business Review*, **91**(5), 50–60.

Jones, G. (2012). The growth opportunity that lies next door. *Harvard Business Review*, **90**(7/8), 141–5.

14

14.1 Introduction

Strategy happens through the actions and interactions of practitioners and stakeholders as part of ongoing social and political processes in organizational life (Ackermann and Eden 2011). In these processes, stakeholders' histories, skills, relationships, and motivations shape strategy outcomes to the extent that they are included and engaged. In Chapter 13, we examined how strategic change might be activated from a range of perspectives, including organizational, cultural, and communication considerations. Building on Chapter 13's tools and insights, we now examine the topic of **strategic leadership** as a further important influence on organizational processes of strategy activation.

We will explore how strategic leadership has conventionally focused on the attributes and activities of the practitioners at the top—or apex—of the organization's hierarchy in alignment with what is known as 'upper echelon theory' (Hambrick and Mason 1984). **Upper echelon theory** posits that the nature of an organization will reflect what its 'top' managers say, think and do. As we consider this traditional view, we introduce common terms that you will encounter when discussing strategic leadership—such as the board of directors and the executive team. Knowing what these mean and the role these types of stakeholders are typically expected to play in most organizations will help you interpret strategy theory and practice.

We'll then consider the value in alternative perspectives of strategic leadership that go beyond upper echelon theory—namely, strategic leadership as a managerial system of relationships and interactions and strategic leadership as distributed practices and processes. We consolidate these views, using the process–practice framework as a point of reference, to describe ways in which strategic leadership might play a key role in activating strategy.

Reflecting on mega-trends such as sustainability, globalization, and digitalization as introduced in earlier chapters, we consider contemporary demands on strategic leadership in organizations. We build awareness of how different views of strategic leadership can help explain strategizing activities and outcomes in uncertain and dynamic contexts. We make the case for a contemporary emphasis on strategic leadership approaches characterized by adaptive, engaging, interdependent, pluralistic, purpose-driven and responsible practitioners, practices, and processes.

We conclude by reflecting on how you can build strategic leadership insights and nurture capacities for strategic leadership that are fit for an ever-changing world. In summary, this chapter aims to equip you to discuss strategic leadership as an important aspect of how strategy might be activated and the personal insights required to build and deploy effective strategic leadership capacities on a continuing basis.

 Access the online resources to watch a short video clip where Nada Khorchid discusses the greatest strategic challenges she has faced.

14

14.2 What is strategic leadership?

In this section, we explore interpretations of what strategic leadership might mean. We start by offering insights into how leadership might be understood. We then examine strategic leadership in relation to a focus on the top team in an organization—who they are, what they do, and how they engage with strategy. We then offer complementary perspectives on strategic leadership as a system of relationships and interactions within the management team, and as collective processes and practices distributed across organizations.

Exploring the concept of leadership

Leadership has been a long-term topic of interest in business and organization studies. As described by Northouse (2011), leadership is a contested term with multiple possible interpretations. The 'traditional' view of leadership is expressed through trait—or great man—theory which focuses on the leader and their natural attributes that set them apart as appropriate for positions of responsibility and authority. This perspective was the original take on leadership popular in the early twentieth century and remains a popular view in the 'showmen' articles of the popular media and business press (Gill 2010).

By examining inherited traits, the **'great man' theory** doesn't account for how individuals are able to learn and grow as leaders, nor the influence of context on leadership potential. From the 1930s onwards, alternative views of leadership were proposed such as **'leadership as a behaviour'**—an observable pattern of conduct as part of everyday work life; **'leadership as a skill'** that can be developed through training, mentoring, and experience; or **'leadership as an ability'**, a capacity to act from a combination of natural potential and learned approaches. Whilst retaining trait theory's focus on individual leaders, these views provide explanations of how leaders might develop over time.

Since the 1960s, further interpretations of leadership have been proposed that avoid a focus on individual leaders, instead viewing 'leadership' as what occurs between leaders and followers—both of whom affect outcomes achieved; or **'leadership as practice'**- where, rather than a leader, there is a dynamic process between stakeholders, and through interaction and cooperation, decisions and actions are taken as a collective. As more recent additions, these views are less developed in the literature but provide promising ways in which to further explain how activities, relationships, and practices of individuals and groups lead to organizational outcomes.

It is generally accepted that leadership means different things to different people (Gill 2010) and how we understand leadership will influence our personal practice and understanding of how to work effectively. In relation to strategy, as Iszatt-White and Saunders (2014: 159) observe, leadership's 'natural habitat'—in which stakeholders expect formal leaders to be identified and corresponding decisions and communication to occur—is in strategic change processes, such as Kotter's Accelerate process described in Chapter 13. Considering how we can recruit, develop, and engage leaders into formal positions, encourage positive leadership relationships and interactions, and nurture effective moments of 'leading' is a key concern in strategic change.

In the following section, we explore the concept of strategic leadership as subset of leadership and what interpretations of strategic leadership might mean to strategy activation.

Strategic leadership as leadership of organizations

Strategic leadership refers specifically to the leadership *of* organizations and thus sits within the broader interests of leadership studies concerning all aspects of **supervisory leadership** *in* organisations (Fernandes et al. 2022).

Strategic leadership is a concept of high interest when exploring how strategy activation occurs. Strategic leadership guru, John Adair (2010), defines the value of strategic leadership as providing direction, strategic thinking and planning, activating change, encouraging cohesive work as a whole organization, defining and harnessing corporate purpose, and nurturing the leaders of tomorrow. Adair (2010: 1) further notes that 'an effective strategic leader is one who delivers the goods in terms of what an organisation naturally expects from its leadership in times of change'.

As a field of academic interest, strategic leadership has potential to shed light on how strategy is activated from a process–practice view, given its relevance to strategizing and the 'perennially unfinished project' of strategy work (Iszatt-White and Saunders 2014). Mirroring varied possible perspectives of leadership in organizations, there are a number of ways in which strategic leadership can be understood.

There is a long-established view that strategic leaders own 'whole organizational planning' (e.g. Pink's (1988) example of how strategic leadership happened in ICI, a British chemical manufacturer). In these sorts of activities, what is known as upper echelon theory (UET) addresses questions of executive accountability and 'Why do organizations act as they do?'. The main premise of UET is that by studying how those at the top of the organization think and act, we gain new insights into how the rest of the organization responds (Van Doorn et al. 2022). Reflecting thinking from trait theory, the seminal work of Hambrick and Mason (1984: 193) notes that, according to UET, 'organizational outcomes—strategic choices and performance levels—are partially predicted by managerial background characteristics'.

Alternatively, a number of popular strategic leadership theories focus on the practice of leadership by individuals, mirroring a more general 'leadership as an ability' perspective. Examples include **charismatic leadership**—the use of effective interpersonal skills to influence others, **transformational leadership**—delivering systems-level change that impacts on social as well as organizational outcomes, and **visionary leadership**—being able to explain how the world could be and compelling others to work towards that vision. These strategic leadership concepts suggest alternative ways in which the practices of leaders are able to deliver strategic change (as per Adair's challenge).

Prescriptive strategic leadership theories zoom in on the impact of the top team or senior leaders' practices on organizational outcomes and strategy activation. With this narrow focus, prescriptive strategic leadership theories necessarily offer high-level and generic explanations of how strategic leadership occurs in practice, 'bearing little resemblance to the day-to-day lived experience of doing leadership work or developing and enacting strategy' (Iszatt-White and Saunders 2014: 207). Therefore, when examining how strategy activation might be led from a process–practice perspective, there is valuable complementary understanding to be gained from considering the activities, relationships, interactions, and dynamics of practitioners involved in strategizing processes.

In the following subsections, we'll unpack aspects of prescriptive, relational, and processual interpretations of strategic leadership, seeking to clarify terminology and access new insights as to how leaders and acts of leading impact on strategy activation.

14

Strategic leadership as a synonym for the attributes and responsibilities of apex practitioners

Who are apex practitioners and what are they expected to do?

A common usage of the term 'strategic leadership' is to refer to a type of practitioner at the top—or apex—of an organization, namely, the chief executive officer, top management teams, and boards of directors (Cortes and Herrmann 2021) (see also the Chapter 7 review of 'apex' considerations as part of organizational structuring). In this approach, apex leaders—as depicted in Figure 14.1—are synonymous with strategic leadership. These 'strategic leaders' are responsible for the 'efficient management of an organization's resource portfolio' (Fernandes et al 2022: 647).

The **top management team**—sometimes known as 'the executive'—of an organization are the most senior managers accountable for short- and long-term performance outcomes, with the power to allocate resources and set strategy. The top management team are headed by a **chief executive officer (CEO)**, who typically reports to a board of directors. Directors are independent, knowledgeable individuals that—as a collective known as 'the board'—monitor and govern the activities of the top management team. The board is led by a chairperson, who has the power to hire, fire, and manage the CEO, but otherwise doesn't take part directly in running operations. The **chairperson**'s role is to ensure, through the board and executive team, that the organization's obligations to its stakeholders are met in an appropriate way.

In profit-seeking organizations, directors are elected by shareholders to oversee the maximization of the value of the firm. In not-for-profit organizations, the board of directors (also known as trustees) oversee the achievement of the organization's mandate, such as providing a charitable service.

Top management teams and boards of directors sit at the top, or 'apex', of the organization. Their activities and decisions individually and collectively have high visibility to all organizational

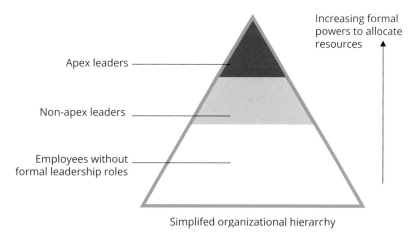

FIGURE 14.1 Apex leaders' hierarchical position. *Source*: authors.

stakeholders, and upper echelons logic examines how what they do impacts on organizational performance outcomes (Luciano et al. 2020). This might be during periods of relative stability in operating conditions. But, as we examined at the end of Chapter 13, strategic leaders, as the apex of the organization, are expected to play a crucial role in a crisis by detecting major issues, acting swiftly and effectively under pressure, and communicating with stakeholders (Schaedler 2022).

The constitution of the top management team can evolve over time, influenced by emergent organizational needs and external pressures. For example, strategic leadership—as a descriptor of the top team—has now been expanded to include chief digital officers as a standard expectation (Kunisch et al. 2022). Installing new top managers typically has to be accompanied by 'bureaucratic machinery' of direct reports, teams, and resources to support whatever new contribution to organizational performance they are intended to deliver. Equally, Strand (2014) notes that once a so-called special interest—such as sustainability—becomes embedded across an organization and diffused into general leadership responsibilities, corresponding top team roles—in this case Chief Sustainability Officer—might be removed from the top management team.

How might the top management team influence strategy activation?

In Chapter 1, we defined organizational strategy in terms of an ongoing balance of 'ways, means and ends'. In the face of competing and often contradictory pressures from shifting organizational and environmental circumstances, the formal responsibilities of strategic leaders mean that they play a crucial role in finding and preserving such balance for the whole organization through selection and activation of strategizing activities.

Crossan et al. (2008) propose that leaders at the top of the organization have three main types of responsibility—to themselves (being proactive and developing strengths); to others (influencing and guiding stakeholders effectively); and to the organization (acting to align organization, strategy, and environment for sustainability). In so doing, strategic leaders 'embody the ability to anticipate and manage changes that can help develop a competitive future for the organization' (Fernandes et al. 2022: 647).

Because of their resource allocation powers, the characteristics and mentality of the top team members are highly influential in shaping the way in which strategic initiatives occur and how strategy activity takes place. Aligned with the ideas of the attention-based view (see Chapter 2), strategic leaders influence how strategy occurs in an organization according to their personal preferences and focus of attention. This is known as *discretionary influence* on strategizing. Further, through their behaviours and investment of resources, strategic leaders create an organizational context in which other types of activity, such as innovation or responsible practice, are more or less likely. This is known as *architectural influence* on strategizing (Cortes and Hermann 2021).

With a range of stakeholders, the influence of strategic leaders applies to specific episodes of strategic change and also to the ideals of strategy as purpose (see Chapter 1). From the apex of the organization, it can be considered the role of strategic leaders to define an appropriate shared purpose that is accepted and used across stakeholder groups (Kaufman 2017). When strategic leaders become overly focused on the internal context and local issues, to the exclusion of longer-term scanning, planning, and exploration, they can be said to be acting in a myopic way. **Strategic myopia** may give a short-term boost to strategy activation efforts;

14

it creates a potential blind-spot, as insufficient attention is paid to external trends and future needs (Levinthal and March 1993).

The external context also influences how strategic leadership attention is directed, according to the munificence, complexity, and dynamism that the organization is facing (Luciano et al. 2020). Monitoring and navigating the trends and trajectories of the external environment is a key concern for strategic leaders. Potentially beneficial external environmental change—such as new markets opening up—may catch strategic leaders' interest and become a focus of their strategizing to deliver business performance. In Chapter 13, we also examined how strategic change to addresses crises—such as responding to the COVID-19 pandemic—can dominate strategic leaders' attention. When strategic leaders become overly focused on the external context and distant issues, to the exclusion of organizational performance, they can be said to be acting in a hyperopic way (Mackay and Burt 2014). **Strategic hyperopia** might help organizations prepare to meet future needs but in so doing will diminish strategy activation efforts which deal with local issues in the here and now, leading to substandard organizational performance.

To provide effective formal strategic leadership outcomes, the top management team needs to be able to balance the demands of managing in the present whilst preparing for the future (Mckay 2020). Strategic leadership approaches therefore have a significant impact on the extent to which organizational ambidexterity, introduced in Chapter 13, might be achieved. As discussed in Chapter 13, research by O'Reilly and Tushman (2011) indicates that ambidextrous organizations have strategic leaders able to establish and work with organizational systems that balance 'exploration' and 'exploitation' activity in a dynamic and productive way. As the intensity and magnitude of change requirements varies over time, the role of the top management team is to actively lead changes in initiative planning, organization structures, systems, and processes of the organization as well as to create an environment that embeds organizational agility in the culture and activities of the business.

Distinctiveness of individual strategic leaders

Whilst it can be helpful to consider the implications for all strategic leaders operating as a collective at the 'apex' of the organization, it is also crucial to consider the impact that individual strategic leaders might make to processes of strategy activation on account of their unique **mental models**, biases, experiences, skills, and motivations (Cummings et al. 2022). From a process–practice perspective, as circumstances change and new situational demands arise, each strategic leader may interpret needs and attempt to emphasize a distinctive profile of outcomes through the influence of their position. (See Case Example 14.1 for an illustration of the individual reflections from the CEO of Lego on responding to challenging strategic circumstances.) A study by Fernandes et al. (2022: 650) identifies a range of possible strategic leadership emphases—'Transformational' 'Performance', 'Innovation', 'Dynamic', 'Creative', and 'Reorganization'—each of which, when adopted, will influence strategizing and the type of strategic change enabled within the organization.

The capabilities of individual strategic leadership practitioners will define how they respond to situations and the nature of the organizational responses that follows. Ireland and Hitt (2005) suggest that the effectiveness of strategic leaders will depend in part on their ability to balance rationality and intuition in their approaches and persuade others within and outwith the top management team that they are making effective decisions (see Chapter 3 for further

14

CASE EXAMPLE 14.1 **CEO REFLECTIONS ON STRATEGIC LEADERSHIP AT LEGO**

Source: Xavi Cabrera/Unsplash.com.

Between 2003 and 2012, Lego was transformed from a business on the point of bankruptcy to the global leader in the toy market. Consider the following comments from an interview with 'the man who saved Lego', ex-CEO, Jorgen Vig Knudstorp.

'What have been your key lessons in adapting the enterprise?'

I think it was obvious that the strategy was wrong but we didn't know what it should be. It looked like it was the right strategy on paper. So, for the first two years of this new transformation, we said, 'We don't have a strategy—we just have a plan of detailed actions that we intend to carry through' and by doing that we could start to build confidence again. Only then did we develop a new strategy for Lego as a second phase of adaptation.

And I think the major distinction we made—and maybe we could do it because we were a family-owned business—many companies in this situation will say, 'Let's grow. Once we get growing, we'll get profitability.' We said:

for the next three years, there is going to be no growth but productivity will be many-fold increased. It's kind of like if you look at a national economy, and the Government goes out and says, 'there's not going to be any growth in the economy but we're going to make this country far more competitive than it is today.'

That's what we did with the Lego group.

'That clear plan was yours?'

People said, 'that must be the Knudstrop survival plan'. I said:

No, its super-generic—Leadership is not about these conceptual ideas. The difference between the good and the bad leadership is that you actually do it! And its like your New Year's Resolutions, too many leaders think the idea 'I must lose weight' is the insight. That's not the insight [. . .] the insight is actually knowing how to make it happen through 8000 people.

'How did you coalesce your executive team at the time around your insights?'

The major thing I learned is that too often you believe you need to think your way into a new way of acting, but actually what you do is you act your way into a new way of thinking. This was a challenge for me as I think a lot [. . .] for us it was about less talk and more action. We closed offices, we sold off businesses, we shut down activities, we started introducing measures. For instance, in the factories where we weren't in control, rather than introducing an IT system and elaborate reporting, we put the reporting up on a white board, and we created something we still use to this day called 'the visual factory'. Every Friday morning, we get together as a management team, and each manager writes down how their bit of the factory is performing in front of us all. Green numbers for good outcomes, red numbers for bad outcomes. And people look at that and say, 'When are you going to put that in an IT system?' And I say, 'Its never going to go into the IT system!' Because it is all in the doing. The sharing of data and how are we doing is a social mechanism that starts driving change. Because once you have written that red number up there, you don't need to be told you need to change it, you start changing it.

My favourite motto is that the CEO needs any avenue to the truth that he or she can find. And some of those avenues are candid dialogue with employees, which means nine out of ten times they may tell you something you know or consider vaguely relevant. But if you dismiss those nine times, you don't get

14

the tenth time where they tell you something that is crucial. You were never aware of it, and if they didn't tell you, you'd only learn later, once it is too late.

'We live in a 24/7, always-connected world. But if you don't make time for yourself to plan change, then your leadership is only a reaction to change. How do you make time for yourself to plan?'

Well what you do, which is harder to do than to just say it, is that you have to build your defences. I have periods where I don't get disturbed by phone calls or e-mails. And that means sometimes there is a long log of things that are fairly important or urgent that I'm not touching as I want to make sure that I have room for the not urgent but extremely important stuff. At times, I turn off my mobile—absolutely! Leave it in the car, it's a great solution! But you may also have a day where you tell your staff, 'I'm not reachable. I'm going to spend some time reflecting today.' You need to carve out that time. And it is hard as you will say no to things where you are thinking 'Shoot! I really ought to do this.' But you don't.

Questions for discussion

1. In what ways did the context of the organisation shape how the CEO responded to the strategic challenges facing Lego?

2. What actions, interactions and processes did the CEO draw on during the strategic transformation of the business?

3. How open does the CEO seem to be to having his thinking challenged? Why do you think he has this attitude?

4. Why might it be important for the CEO of a firm like Lego to take time out from the business on a regular basis, in which they can't be contacted?

Sources

Ashcroft, J. (2014). The man who rescued Lego—meet the Boss TV, https://www.youtube.com/watch?v=JlVy-iFqIg0w (last accessed 10 October 2022).

commentary on decision-making approaches). Similarly, Gavetti (2011: 120) observes that strategic leaders need to be good economists and organizational psychologists—able to spot opportunities and threats in emerging trends whilst understanding how to influence stakeholders and build commitment to required change. It is generally assumed that individual strategic leaders will be motivated to act for the benefit of the organization, but, equally, they may also take actions that maximize outcomes for their function or directorate (Lin et al. 2019).

An important task for any CEO is to maintain sufficient diversity of capabilities in its top management team so as to be able to respond effectively to the diversity of challenges that might face an organization over time. In so doing, differences between individual strategic leaders' outlooks can be a useful source of creative tension and adaptive response, enabling balance and effectiveness in organizational strategizing.

Strategic leadership as a system of interactions and relationships

Extending beyond 'apex'-only focused views, an alternative perspective on strategic leadership is that it might be considered a system of interactions and relationships through which the technology, media, and telecom (TMT) sector continually connects with leaders throughout the organization in strategizing activities. In this system, strategic leadership influence depends not just on the attributes and actions of the CEO and top team but also on their relationship with leadership across levels of the organization. This can be referred to as the **'strategic leadership interface' perspective** (Cummings et al. 2022).

This perspective draws attention to a **'strategic leadership system'** in which the TMT and board are part of a strategizing 'multiteam system' across organization leadership levels and the external networks in which the organization is embedded (Luciano et al. 2020: 675). Viewing strategic leadership as a system emphasizes the importance of the connectedness and agility of those at the 'apex' of the organization in leading effective strategizing activity in a networked world. Van Doorn et al. (2022) highlight that in a strategic leadership system, strategic leaders require capabilities in addressing 'ecological complexities' of working with networks of internal and external actors.

Examining dynamics and relationships within a strategic leadership system can help us understand how strategy activation occurs in practice. This might be within the traditional realms of strategic leadership study. For example, Srour et al. (2022) note that the extent to which a CEO and chairman can collaborate effectively will have a profound impact on what an organization might achieve. Further, Kurzhals et al. (2020) demonstrate that the way in which exchange of experiences and knowledge between the board and the TMT happens has an impact on the strategic initiatives an organization might realize.

Equally, 'strategic leadership as a system' supports a view that decision-making of relevance to strategizing outcomes might be distributed amongst top management and leaders throughout the organization (Fernandes et al. 2022). If appropriate authority to take and act on decisions is delegated throughout the organization (what is known also as a decentralized organizational structure), then the organizational responsiveness to change needs can be increased, nurturing organizational dynamic capability (Gilbert 2006).

This broad involvement of organizational leaders might matter in strategizing for, as Gavetti (2011: 120) comments, 'in the real world, strategic leaders are not omniscient'. As there are always opportunities to improve competitive or internal performance beyond the capabilities of any individual or top management team, the broader the system of strategic leadership that can be nurtured and synchronized, the greater the potential for effective strategic performance in an organization.

Building an effective strategic leadership system will be an increasingly important competitive consideration for organizations. Digitalization is opening up new possibilities for strategic leadership systems to draw in participants across stakeholder groups beyond the top management team and board (Kurzhals et al. 2020). Luciano et al. (2020) propose that in the context of an ever-changing world, strategic leadership systems in which practitioners can deliver effective independent and interdependent contributions will have a beneficial effect on strategic organizational performance. Increasing stakeholder involvement increases the diversity of ideas under consideration in strategic decision-making and thus increases the potential for creative and effective responses to organizational needs to be initiated (Ackermann and Eden 2011). Stronger relationships, information flows, and frequency of interaction across levels of leadership also increases the possibilities for shared meaning-making, motivation, and capability-building, which, over time, engenders responsiveness and agility at an organizational level.

The risk of not building such strategic leadership systems is that competitors will, leaving an organization with a relatively diminished set of strategizing capabilities. To understand how to develop strategic leadership systems, we can turn our attention to strategic leadership as a distributed practice, exploring the individual actions, interactions, and practices that help cultivate higher-level processes and outcomes (Srour et al. 2022).

14

Strategic leadership as practice

As an alternative to an exclusive focus on 'apex' stakeholders, such as board and top management team members, or even systems of formal leaders distributed in an organization, a 'strategic leadership as practice' perspective draws attention to the processes and practices occurring throughout the whole organizational ecosystem on a daily basis that have a bearing on how strategy is activated (Carroll et al. 2008).

According to Coghlan and Holian (2021: 15), 'leadership-as-practice is less about what one person thinks or does and more about what people may accomplish together. It focuses on the social interactions in defining shared goals, taking collaborative action, engaging in joint reflection and sense-making, and articulating shared learning in the pursuit of a practical outcome.'

If we overlay our definition of strategic leadership being about leadership of organizations, we can build new insights into strategic leadership as practice by examining practices that contribute to achieving specific 'strategizing' outcomes and effective strategizing.

Strategic leadership as practice towards specific strategizing outcomes

We can identify practices within ongoing strategy activity that are within the scope of strategic leadership, as expressed by Adair (2010). In most settings, these practices would typically expect to be undertaken by the top management team and their direct reports, such as 'goal and objective setting, resourcing and development of capabilities, market-orientation and commercialization choices, fostering innovation, setting the cultural and values climate for the organization, and workforce engagement' (O'Shannassy 2021: 235). These are the types of strategy practices that we have examined in the rest of this book, addressing *what* might be done through strategic leadership activity. As we build our understanding of strategic leadership as practice, there is value in examining how the top team and those they interact with engage with these sorts of practices on a daily basis.

Strategic leadership as practice towards effective strategizing

We can identify a further class of strategic leadership practices which relate more to *how* strategizing processes might occur effectively within an organization. These practices need not be associated with specific leaders and instead can describe collectively enacted processes that achieve leadership outcomes. This can help to explain organizational leadership responses to common challenges, such as coping with COVID-19 disruption (Ford et al. 2021).

For example, drawing on analysis of the federal level response to the COVID-19 pandemic in Canada, Farhan (2021: 3) proposes four strategic leadership practices that defined the ongoing process of strategic leadership response—*gathering* practices motivate stakeholders to engage in strategy work; *protecting* practices enable collaboration between stakeholders to overcome shared issues; *challenging* practices encourage creativity, entrepreneurship, and questioning of the status quo; and *integrating* practices convert collective outputs into strategic change results. Without excluding the involvement of TMT/senior government officials, these practices don't necessarily require apex stakeholder involvement to be undertaken. Within the

TABLE 14.1 **Practices of strategic leadership**

Practices	Scope of activity
Anticipating	Displaying constant vigilance and scanning for signals of change in the organization and the environment; being aware of peripheral developments as well as current main organizational concerns
Challenging	Questioning the status quo in and through strategizing; challenging self and others' assumptions and encouraging divergent points of view
Interpreting	Absorbing complex and conflicting information, identifying patterns, pushing through ambiguity, and generating new insights and implications
Deciding	Making tough calls with speed and often incomplete information, considering trade-offs, and taking short- and long-term aims into account
Aligning	Finding common ground and achieving buy-in among stakeholders who have disparate views and agendas; actively reaching out to others through multiple channels of communication, engagement, and trust-building
Learning	Promoting a culture of inquiry and searching for lessons in successful and failed initiatives in an open constructive way to find hidden learning and ideas for improvement

Source: adapted from Schoemaker et al. (2013).

overall response of the Federal Government, these practices—where present and accepted—encourage coordinated, coherent movement of mixed-stakeholder groups towards the common beneficial aim of coping effectively with COVID-19 disruption.

In a similar way, Schoemaker et al. (2013: 131) suggest six inter-related practices of strategic leadership—anticipating, challenging, interpreting, deciding, aligning, and learning (see Table 14.1 for more details). Consistent with strategic leadership as a synonym for TMT practitioners, these strategic leadership practices might be associated with adaptive individuals that are 'both resolute and flexible, persistent in the face of setbacks but also able to react strategically to environmental shifts'. Equally, these six strategic leadership practices can be associated with collective processes in which—according to circumstances—different stakeholders might become involved.

Strategic leadership practices that enable effective strategizing processes play a key role in defining the dynamic managerial capability of an organization (see Chapter 6 for further discussion). By considering the ways in which strategic leadership practices influence how strategizing occurs, we can add depth to our understanding of strategy from a process–practice perspective.

 Access the online resources to watch a short video clip where Nada Khorchid discusses whether the practice of strategy is changing or enduring.

14.3 **An integrated process–practice perspective of strategic leadership**

So far in this chapter, we have defined strategic leadership as the leadership of organizations. In unpacking what this might mean, we have considered three strategic leadership perspectives—as a synonym for attributes and activities of practitioners at an organization's

14

apex, as a broader system of managerial relationships and interactions, and as practices in which dynamic group processes rather than individuals are the focus and which may or may not include **apex practitioners**.

We can integrate these views from a process–practice perspective (as described in Chapter 2), to understand how each interpretation of strategic leadership can add to understanding of organizational strategy and how it is 'activated'. For example, we can use different perspectives of strategic leadership to help explain how the development journey of Rex Bionics, an innovative technology start-up, unfolded over time as illustrated in Case Example 14.2.

Examining the attributes and activities of 'apex' practitioners can help us understand how those expected to spend most of their efforts—individually and collectively—on leading the organization actually shape resource allocation, prioritization, and strategizing activity on a continuing basis. According to the attention-based view, how the top management team focus their limited attention will determine what is prioritized in strategizing activities. Further, the experiences, capabilities, and tendencies of apex practitioners will influence how they attempt to shape strategizing in any given situation. Relating these ideas to the process–practice framework (Figure 2.5), by virtue of their formal positions, apex practitioners have the power to include and exclude stakeholders from involvement, direct focus to internal and external trigger issues, and define the tools, practices, and activities of strategizing that are considered acceptable.

The dynamics of how apex practitioners act and interact will constitute at least part of how strategizing occurs in an organization. Further, through their relationships and interactions, it is possible for a wide range of stakeholder groups to be drawn into strategizing activities to varying degrees. This notion aligns with Hughes's (1998: 7) comment that 'strategic leadership is an interpersonal process, not an administrative procedure' that arises from the efforts of groups within the organization working together to deliver initiatives and achieve aims, while 'building healthy and constructive norms, systems, climate and an agenda for the whole organisation' (Hughes 1998: 4). The process–practice framework (Chapter 2) identifies five types of strategy practices which might be used to lead others towards this type of continuing collective accomplishment.

Whilst lacking the organizational-level resource allocation powers of apex practitioners, those in leadership positions elsewhere in the organization help to bridge the gap between operational and strategizing processes in a number of ways. Their interpretation of strategic priorities, based on messaging and interactions from the top team, will determine the influence non-apex leaders exert over stakeholder activity within their domain—contributing to how strategic initiatives are activated and realized in practice. Furthermore, based on their observations and interpretations of events occurring in the operational domain, the information non-apex leaders attempt to share with the TMT will contribute to potential triggering of strategizing episodes, the (re-)focusing of TMT attention, and consideration of new methods and tools of strategizing. Thus, examining the system of managerial relationships and interactions—including but extending beyond apex practitioners—helps to explain how strategy occurs from a process–practice perspective.

Finally, how strategizing activities occur can be understood through examining 'daily' strategic leadership practices and 'micro-processes' of interaction distributed across the organization. In part, this involves exploring the ways in which apex practitioners engage independently in activities with organizational-level consequences and work with others across levels of the

14

managerial system to deliver the expected outcomes of effective strategic leadership. Further, it will involve exploring the everyday practices of strategic leadership—social interactions, decision-making, and collaborative actions occurring within stakeholder groups that impact on how strategizing happens. These practices need not include an apex practitioner—for example, members of a customer engagement team may interact with each other in a manner consistent with the strategic leadership practice framework shown in Table 14.1 and, based on their shared operational experiences, generate new strategic market insights that, through the managerial system, trigger a strategizing episode. In this way, examining how the experiences, activities, and interactions across all organizational stakeholders—even in a minor way—contribute to strategizing might enrich our understanding of strategy from a process–practice perspective.

From an integrated process–practice perspective, strategic leadership provides a useful focus for examining how strategy is activated through the activities and interactions of apex and non-apex stakeholders in the organization. By considering the practitioners, practices, and processes of strategic leadership, we can develop understanding of how individuals or organizations cope in complex and demanding situations where 'there is no right answer—just the best response at the time' (Mckay 2020: 15).

CASE EXAMPLE 14.2 **THE JOURNEY SO FAR FOR REX BIONICS**

Rex Bionics is a company engaged in the research, development, manufacture, and commercialization of advanced robotic devices. Rex Bionics was founded in Auckland, New Zealand in 2007 by Richard Little and Robbie Irving, two robotics engineers with first-hand experience of wheelchair users and their needs. Rex Bionics is the pioneer of the REX robot, 'the world's first hands-free, self-supporting, independently-controlled robotic walking device'. The Rex robot is a wearable exoskeleton that does not require crutches or a walking frame to provide stability. This leaves the user's hands free and can be used by people with a complete spinal cord injury who are paralysed from the waist downwards.

Rex Bionics has been in the vanguard of robot-assisted physiotherapy (RAP), in collaboration with a range of medical institutes distributed globally. RAP involves the exoskeleton supporting the user to variously sit, stand, or move as part of a physiotherapy regime. Applications have been trialled for users with spinal cord injuries, traumatic brain injury, stroke, and multiple sclerosis. In addition to mobility gains, by stimulating the user's muscles and joints, REX provides further health benefits,

including improved sleep and range of movement and a reduction in spasm and pain.

As described in Woods et al. (2021: 252), Little and Irving committed many years of their lives to 'commercialising their vision of an exoskeleton that would enable wheelchair-bound people to walk tall [. . .] pursuing what they believe will make a difference'. The venture started in 2003, when Irving informed his friend Little that he had been diagnosed with multiple sclerosis and would, in time, likely need a wheelchair. From family members' experiences, both were familiar with the physical, physiological, and social challenges encountered by many wheelchair users. They resolved to build a robotic device to give people in wheelchairs the ability to walk.

The initial concept, sketched on a beermat, was inspired by the power-loader exoskeleton used by the hero Ripley in the movie Alien. Little and Irving decided to develop a prototype in their spare time and in secrecy whilst they continued full-time employment as engineers. Development took place in an Auckland garage over the course of four years, until, in 2007, a working prototype that could sit, stand, and walk was ready. At this point, Little and

Irving formed Rex Bionics and sought venture capital funding from a trusted investor, Jen Morel, to build an organization that might tap into what they felt could be a global market.

Over the following three years, Rex Bionics continued development work, adding investors, staff, and government funders within the boundaries of confidentiality to protect the nascent intellectual property. Paul Dyson, an authority in the medical devices industry and Paul Sackier, the inventor of the world's first surgical robot, joined as directors. A team of highly skilled engineers drove on Rex's development, and sales and commercial staff were employed. To limit the time available to potential competitors to imitate their innovation, patent protection was filed in 2010 as their first model was revealed to the world.

Little and Irvine knew they needed to change the strategic leadership structure to enable Rex Bionics to move from a tech start-up to a commercially viable business. They also resolved to stay closely involved in order to protect the vision of the venture. By 2012, they had assembled a board of directors and a separate advisory board. The board of directors was to provide strategic guidance and direction and monitor progress in the commercialization journey. It also had to access further investment, and it was expected that board members—including Little—would seek funding from within their respective networks. In contrast, the advisory board members were from the medical sector, tasked with providing product development insights based on knowledge of user clinical needs, compliance standards, and medical customer expectations.

As a founder–owner–director, Little commented that he found himself 'outnumbered and frustrated' by the boards. He noted that extensive operational and developmental efforts might be made by him and colleagues in the business which, after a short discussion at board level, might be rejected or delayed. He observed that the personality of board members was more influential on decision-making than he'd anticipated and that 'company boards are a lot less difficult when you have money in the bank'.

From its New Zealand base, REX Bionics started to build operational capability to explore international markets and build presence in selected locations by investing in dedicated in-country resources. Point-of-sale and distribution sites were created in the United States, mainland Europe, and the United Kingdom. To access funding to support this growth, Rex Bionics listed on the AIM Stock Exchange in London in 2014, raising *c.* £10 million.

To manage this growing business, two boards of directors were established—one in London and one in New Zealand. A new CEO was hired, with Little assuming a chief technology officer role. International colleagues in sales and development were added to the 30 staff in New Zealand. Work accelerated to develop the US market as a massive potential user base but with a challenging regulatory approval process. Trialling was ramped up to build the evidence base, educate clinicians, and accelerate adoption by potential users. The complexity of manufacturing operations necessarily increased to support international reach whilst retaining perfect traceability in compliance with medical device legislation. New competitors started to flood the market as the concept of exoskeletons became accepted by consumers, regulators, and clinicians. In 2016, Rex Bionics announced it was starting work on a remodelled, lower-cost unit to address some of these challenges.

Despite promising tests, longer-than-expected trials impacted commercial potential and losses started to mount up. Rex Bionics' share price dropped £138 to £0.70 on news of delays in its commercial sales and, as issues continued, in 2017, the company exited the AIM stock exchange with a share price of £0.065.

To continue trading, urgent intervention was required. In May 2017, Rex Bionics was bought out by BioScience Managers, an international health-care investment firm. Of this acquisition, the Rex Bionics CEO said, 'The restructuring enables the continued development of the REX technology and allows Rex to continue to work towards its vision—that every day, thousands of people get relief with REX, from the pain, discomfort and inconvenience of severe neurological conditions.'

Rex Bionics continues to develop its competitive offerings in the global wearable robotic exoskeleton market, which is now predicted to grow from USD 953 million in 2022 to USD 11,996 million by 2029. Whether Rex Bionics emerges as a key player in the market the company initiated in 2010 remains to be seen. After many years of nurturing the exoskeleton business ecosystem, Irving and Little will be interested observers, whilst they dedicate their energies to growing their new start-up, Exsurgo, which uses brain monitoring and medication technology to help people manage chronic pain.

Continued

14

Questions for discussion

1. Describe how strategic leadership roles have evolved in Rex Bionics from when it was founded to the present day. Explain why the roles evolved in this way.

2. Describe the evolving relationships in the 'strategic leadership system' over the course of the organization's journey. Comment on the tensions and benefits that seem to have arisen from evolving relationships.

3. To what extent did the practices and priorities of the founders change over the years? How did the strategic leadership approach of the founders' impact on the business?

4. What would you expect to be the focus of the strategic leadership of Rex Bionics now, given the anticipated exponential growth of the global wearable exoskeleton market?

Sources

Ashton Legal Services (2018). Rex Bionics . . . the robot that enhances the mobility of wheelchair users (17 December), https://www.ashtonslegal.co.uk/insights/legal-news/rex-bionicsthe-robot-that-enhances-the-mobility-of-wheelchair-users (last accessed 18 June 2022).

Bioscience Managers (2022). https://biosciencemanagers.com/about-us (last accessed 18 June 2022).

TheExpressWire (2022). Global wearable robotic exoskeleton market to hit USD 11,995.7 million by 2029 (17 June), https://www.digitaljournal.com/pr/global-wearable-robotic-exoskeleton-market-size-to-hit-usd-11995-7-million-by-2029 (last accessed 18 June 2022).

Hall, M. (2022). Headset games target brain and pain. *New Zealand Doctor* (29 April), https://www.nzdoctor.co.nz/article/news/business/headset-games-target-brain-and-pain (last accessed 18 June 2022).

NZ Herald (2021). Australian government fund under fire for investment in NZ's Rex Bionics (23 May), https://www.nzherald.co.nz/business/australian-government-fund-under-fire-for-investment-in-nzs-rex-bionics/TGV2G64JQ2FIJXLBX45TUZJPNY (last accessed 18 June 2022).

Rex Bionics (2022). https://www.rexbionics.com (last accessed 18 June 2022).

Simmons + Simmons (2017). Advising Rex Bionics on restructuring and new investment (30 May), https://www.simmons-simmons.com/en/about-us/news/ck0f6t8ndwyik0b36uz8nmae0/advising-rex-bionics-on-its-restructuring-and-new-investment (last accessed 18 June 2022).

Woods, C., Callagher, L., and Jaffray, T. (2021). Walk tall: The story of Rex Bionics. *Journal of Management & Organization*, **27**(2), 239–52, https://doi.org/10.1017/jmo.2018.68.

 Access the online resources to watch a short video clip where Nada Khorchid advises strategic leaders on what to prioritize in a VUCA world.

14.4 **Strategic leadership for an ever-changing world**

14

In this closing section, we consider how process–practice understanding of strategic leadership can meet the unfolding challenges of strategizing in dynamic conditions. We start by recapping on some of the key examples, issues, and implications of global challenges highlighted throughout the book. We then consider emerging strategic leadership practices—what practitioners might have to do through interactions, activity, and practices, in context and over time, to guide strategizing in an effective and impactful way. We conclude by considering how we might play our part in building capacities for impactful and responsible strategic leadership that readies our organizations to meet the challenges of an ever-changing world.

Global challenges for strategic leadership

In Chapter 4, we introduced the concept of megatrends—disruptive global processes changing the way we live and do business. Across preceding sections, we have highlighted three inter-related 'megatrends' of globalization, digitalization, and sustainability that are defining the operating contexts for most organizations around the world. To set the scene for discussing applied strategic leadership, we reflect on case examples covered in this book that illustrate how strategic leadership practitioners, practices, and processes have faced into the challenges and opportunities posed by an ever-changing context.

Globalization

We defined globalization as a continuing process of integration and movement of people, companies, goods and services, and finance, and harmonization of rules and regulations between governments globally. We noted also the reverse process, deglobalization, which refers to situations where interdependence and integration between nations reduces, possibly for political reasons.

We've seen how globalization has created opportunities for 'born global' start-ups to expand rapidly into international markets, such as Castore in sportswear, Happy Socks in fashion, Zoom in video conferencing, and TikTok in social media. We've also seen the perils that this can bring, depending on the product market, as illustrated by the challenges facing Rex Bionics.

Responding to globalization potential, we've also seen how established organizations have been able to restructure their operations and supply chains for cross-border cost advantage (e.g. Primark, Walmart); access to new suppliers or customers (e.g. Arcelik and Dangote, Starbucks, Amazon); and new partnering opportunities (e.g. Audi, FAW, and Volkswagen; Univision and Televisa). Equally, we've analysed new risks presented by globalization such as Amazon and Alibaba's intense competition; collaborative issues for Renault, Nissan, and Mitsubishi; and the sorts of cultural challenges which impacted StarTV.

We've noted the increased complexity that international operations and globalization have rendered on industries (e.g. Automotive & Energy); prompting organizations (e.g. Shell) and governments (e.g. Singapore; UAE) to engage in long-term planning and capability building initiatives.

Digitalization

We defined digitalization as the disruptive spread of technologies at a global level and the process of exploiting digital technologies and resources for operational improvement, innovation, or new value creation in organizations.

We noted how, in recent decades, digitalization has generated new business creation opportunities such as for Alibaba and Amazon in online retail, Relativity Space in the space industry, Delivery Hero in takeaway food, Zoom in video conferencing, TikTok in social media, and Rex Bionics in robotic medical devices.

We've seen how digitalization has enabled operational changes (e.g. Vail Resorts), new customer channels (e.g. Walmart), and product offerings (e.g. International Olympic Committee, mobile banking), and strategic transformation of organizations (e.g. DBS in banking).

14

We've also examined how digitalization has focused strategic attention on capability renewal (e.g. Google) and national capability development and competitiveness (Underline; Singapore Gov; UAE Gov).

Sustainability

We introduced sustainability as the focus in the international community on finding ways to live that meet the needs of the present without compromising the ability of future generations to meet their own needs. The concept of sustainability, expressed in the United Nations Sustainable Development goals, is focusing attention of leaders in all walks of life on achieving social and environmental impacts, in addition to economic aims.

We examined how strategic initiatives have led to organizations delivering enhanced environmental performance (e.g. Vail resorts) and social outreach and community impacts (e.g. Zoom, Underline). We considered new organizations launching with a socially progressive but profit-seeking agenda (e.g. Angel City; Happy Socks), with others prioritizing positive environmental impact too (e.g. Natura).

We've noted established organizations adopting objective setting and strategic reporting approaches that drive sustainable outcomes (e.g. Gap and Iberdrola, AB-Inbev). And we've observed national-level developments that deliver economic, social, and environmental outcomes (e.g. Smart Sustainable Cities).

Impacts of globalization, digitalization, and sustainability on strategic leaders

Throughout this book, we have referred often to VUCA—volatile, uncertain, complex and ambiguous—as a descriptor of the environment in which many organizations are operating. Reflecting across the organizational challenges and initiatives described in the case examples, we can see evidence of how strategic leaders should now expect to deal continuously with VUCA conditions underpinned by the megatrends of globalization, digitalization and sustainability.

Volatile: globalization is creating new sources of volatility for organizations in the competitive environment as markets become increasingly connected, spurred on by digitalization of commercial platforms and increasing connectivity to customers. Further, the global flow of people and goods has increased vulnerability to systemic shocks such as witnessed in the global pandemic. Sustainability-related volatility can be observed in the impact of extreme weather and climate change on global activity and the fallout for civilian populations and continuity of business operations.

Uncertain: the rapid pace of digital disruption of nations, industries, and organizations is creating a 'normal' condition of high uncertainty for strategic leaders. How sustainability challenges of social impact and environmental performance will be met remain largely unknown too, and the policy environment is unfolding rapidly as climate and global political emergencies continue to escalate. Recovery from globalization-related challenges of the COVID-19 pandemic and emerging global energy and cost-of-living crises are creating high levels of uncertainty about future operating conditions.

Complexity: globalization has increased the networks, relationships, and possibilities availability to organizations. As they are embraced, the complexity of managing operations equally increases. Sustainability has added complexity to the strategic intent of organizations,

14

with multi-layered goals and a wide variety of stakeholders now requiring attention. And digitalization—and associated trends for operating in a networked way—has increased the technological complexity of organizations alongside their social embeddedness through increased technology-partnering.

Ambiguity: the inter-related challenges, processes, and mechanisms of globalization, digitalization, and sustainability have created a 'new-normal' operating environment for organizations that aligns with the definition of 'wicked problems' as described in Chapter 1. This means that strategic leaders are regularly facing intractable, original challenges for which there is no precedent to evaluate responses and high ambiguity about what might constitute effective long-term solutions.

Contemporary strategic leadership concerns

Despite the demands created by perpetual VUCA conditions, we recognize enduring expectations that those in apex practitioner roles will fulfil traditional strategic leadership responsibilities and practices to delivering organizational-level strategic initiatives such as 'changes in organization structure, corporate culture, business process re-engineering and human resource management' (Taylor 1995: 78).

However, a more nuanced process–practice view of strategic leadership as a dispersed, complex, collaborative, and multimodal endeavour (Drath 2008) appears to offer further potential for coping in an ever-changing world. As noted by Mckay (2020: 15), strategic leadership practitioners 'understand that they exist within context, culture, time, and audience. They focus their energy on adapting to change, competition, debate, and conflict. They focus on grappling with paradox, challenge and uncertainty and on responding to their shifting environment, mobilising their supporters and stepping towards a bigger vision.'

In this section, we summarize a range of contemporary opinions for how strategic leadership might enable organizations to adapt, survive, and thrive in an unrelenting VUCA context. In short, we make the case for strategic leadership to be characterized by *adaptive, engaging, interdependent, pluralistic, purpose-driven, and responsible* practitioners, practices, and processes.

Adaptive

It has long been proposed that strategic leadership is 'key to survival in a chaotic or turbulent business environment' (Taylor 1995: 72). This is partly through the role that strategic leadership practices and practitioners play in nurturing organizational ambidexterity (as described in Chapter 13). Through creating an environment where learning and experimentation are encouraged alongside delivery of commitments, a balance of entrepreneurial and operational capabilities can be nurtured, creating adaptive potential within complex leadership challenges of ambidexterity (Uhl-Bein 2021).

Strategic leadership sense-making approaches (addressed in Chapter 13) are also key to effective adapting activities. In novel or disrupted situations, sense-making can be undertaken effectively through swift, experimental actions to generate new insights. 'Learning to learn' in changing circumstances provides a valuable source of adaptive insights that nurture organizational resilience, or 'elasticity under pressure', outcomes (Sarkar and Clegg 2021).

14

Engaging

The benefits of engaging and communicating extensively with stakeholders is a recurring theme in contemporary strategic leadership commentaries. Beer (2021) emphasizes that high-quality meaning-making and information-flows—in terms of authenticity, freshness, and accuracy—are associated with conversations and dialogue undertaken in open forums for which 'apex' practitioners are accountable. Through such transparent and legitimized processes of engagement, collective learning is enabled that supports responsiveness and adaptability across the whole organization. This view echoes Srour et al.'s (2022) finding that strategic leadership approaches which create an engaging, supportive communication climate will enhance organizational resilience.

The more that diverse voices and plurality of opinions are engaged in strategizing, the more likely that strategic leadership as a system will operate effectively (Sergi et al. 2021). Engaging people-centric approaches to strategic leadership communication processes will tap the potential of a wider group of stakeholders than top-down approaches, respecting and empowering strategic activity across organizational levels in a distributed and responsive way (de Sousa and van Dierendonk 2021).

Interdependent

By increasing the emphasis on interdependent as opposed to independent ways of working, the power of networks can be tapped to mutual benefit (Crevani et al. 2021). Strategic leadership approaches can enhance scope and scale of responsiveness to challenges of VUCA conditions by nurturing collaboration potential and finding new ways to relate effectively with others. This is particularly the case in addressing the grand challenges of globalization and sustainability (Bryson et al. 2021).

The importance of relating to stakeholders in an ethical way is emphasized in current debates about how to build capacities for reacting with speed and efficacy to sustainability issues (Maak 2021). Similarly, nurturing collaborative capabilities and encouraging partnering are valuable strategic leadership contributions that will help organizations respond to societal challenges (By 2021).

How this is achieved may include harnessing upsides of digitalization by using collaborative platform technologies to enact strategic leadership processes with scale across stakeholder groups in a transparent and efficient way (see online Chapter 15 for an example of how this has been done in IBM). Digital platforms can enable senior leadership stakeholders to retain their authority whilst operating more at the centre of a network than the apex of a hierarchy. Increasing digital flows of information and increasing the number connected collaborators will reduce response times to challenges whilst increasing empowerment of what is effectively a distributed strategic leadership system. As Oliveira and Cunha (2021: 215) note, through multi-sided digital platforms (see Chapter 11), 'centre' leadership can 'both distribute leadership and retain leadership' power.

Pluralistic

Building a diverse network of engaged strategic leadership practitioners, practices, and capabilities is a proposition emphasized in contemporary leadership debates as valuable for organizational strategy and coping. As proposed by Ford et al. (2021), the COVID-19 pandemic demonstrates that leadership as a combination of many leadership practitioners distributed

14

in an organizational system can better meet the needs of a disrupted situation than a small number of apex-position leaders. In addition to the intellectual benefits of increased diversity in the leadership practitioner population, considering leadership as embedded in a system of practitioners, dispersed among the members of an organization, is likely to increase the resilience and responsiveness of the organization (Oliveira and Cunha 2021).

Systematic approaches to building a managerial network of strategic leadership doesn't mean that there is no need for traditional apex-leadership roles. Instead, robust strategic leadership systems can include apex and networked leadership practitioners in pluralistic arrangement. Effective organizing and respectful relationships are required, though, to make this system function advantageously (Crevani et al. 2021).

Purpose-driven

A sense of purpose is knowing what you stand for and how you will meet the needs of stakeholders. When strategic leadership is understood as the responsibility of many stakeholders, the collective pursuit of purpose can provide a navigational aid with which to direct and cohere efforts for mutual benefit (By 2021).

Being purpose-driven is increasingly important in an environment characterized by stakeholder sustainability concerns. As Clegg et al. (2021: 7) comment, 'foregrounding purpose enables us to explore the pursuit of worthy ideas and activities, in particular to connect doing leadership with working for sustainable development, extending the reach of leadership processes beyond the individual and the individual organization'.

Responsible

O'Shannassy (2021: 235) argues that strategic leaders need to contribute to sustainability outcomes and social impact as part of the price of operating in an ever-changing world. More generally, as part of balancing profit and purpose motives, a hallmark of contemporary strategic leadership is a sense of responsibility to stakeholders such as employees, communities, societies, the environment, and humanity (Kempster and Jackson 2021). This means that strategic leadership practitioners, practices, and processes might incorporate awareness and acceptance of the consequence of actions taken by an organization, seeking ethical outcomes at all times (Clegg et al. 2021). The more plural and engaged the composition of a strategic leadership system, the more likely that diverse views and perspectives will be able to engender a nuanced approach to responsible strategic leadership practice.

Building strategic leadership capacities

To conclude this section, and chapter, on strategic leadership, we consider how we all might build our insights into strategic leadership from a process–practice perspective and the steps we might take to nurture strategic leadership capacities.

Building insights

To develop insights about strategic leadership, we can focus our attention on how processes, practices, and interactions of strategy occur in organizations. By thinking about leadership in a processual way, akin to strategizing as the ongoing processes of strategy, we can start to build insights into leadership which aren't limited to explanations linked to the attributes and activities of senior individuals (Crevani et al. 2021).

Clegg et al. (2021: 6) encourage us to examine 'the networks of actions, relations, language, practices, configurations and assemblages interacting in time and space' that drive strategy outcomes as we seek to deepen understanding of strategic leadership.

In so doing, we might stop treating strategic leadership as an elite, heroic concept but rather as a normal part of everyday life across an organization to which we can all contribute (Sergi et al. 2021). Further, by making leadership a less sanitized and romanticized topic, we can learn from failings as well as success in mundane as well as prominent situations that are relatable and understandable to a wide range of stakeholders.

From a process–practice perspective, these views encourage us to consider the interactions and dynamics of a wide range of stakeholders contributing to how strategizing is directed and enacted. Reflecting on examples or experiences of engaging with strategizing will help us generate insights into what might constitute effective strategic leadership in a given situation.

Developing strategic leadership capacities

Adopting a traditional competence model focus, Norzailan et al. (2016: 396–8) suggest that any practitioner can develop strategic leadership competences through deliberate practice, regular experience, reflective learning, and mentoring. This aligns with Saiti's (2021: 130) views that 'Strategic leadership is primarily an action [. . .] how the strategy will be implemented in order to achieve goals.' From this point of view, through practice, reflection, and feedback, practitioners can hone their understanding of 'how' to engage in strategizing in effective ways.

From a competence perspective, the temptation is to focus on building traditional strategic leadership capabilities, such as towards transformational or charismatic leadership. If we can broaden our thinking about what leadership is, however, we can start to think more about how to encourage capabilities, practices, and processes across an organization that might address matters such as emergence, holism, dynamism, and boundary issues that characterize a VUCA world. Adopting such a perspective may drive different approaches to strategic initiatives, such as the Sustainable Smart Cities work occurring in the United Arab Emirates (UAE) (see Case Example 14.3).

With an emphasis on networks, relationships, and interactions, capabilities in complexity management, emotional intelligence, and influencing will be crucial in contemporary strategic leadership. Capacities to harness technologies, such as online platforms and digital devices, towards strategic leadership outcomes will also be crucial (Fernandes et al. 2022).

Crevani et al. (2021: 140) encourage us all to play our part in renewing leadership approaches through 'questioning taken-for-granted assumptions, adopting new vocabularies, recognizing tension and embracing emergence'. As we think about the role we all can play in activating strategy, it feels important to have the courage to try to build our capacities—individually and in organizations—for strategic leadership that is fit for purpose in an ever-changing world.

14

CASE EXAMPLE 14.3 TOWARDS SMART SUSTAINABLE CITIES IN THE UNITED ARAB EMIRATES

A smart sustainable city (SSC) is an urban area that incorporates digital technologies and infrastructure to improve quality of life, efficiency of urban operation and services, and competitiveness, while ensuring that it meets the needs of present and future generations with respect to economic, social, and environmental aspects. In other words, SSCs add a focus on sustainability outcomes to the use of digital technologies to improve the lives of citizens that characterize the smart cities (SC) concept deployed in cities around the world (for a worked example of Amsterdam as a smart city, see Fitzgerald 2016).

SSCs are of interest to governments around the world as a possible strategic response to demographic, digitalization, and sustainability trends. According to a study by the International Telecommunications Union, over 50% of the world's population live in an urban environment, a trend that is set to continue towards 70% by 2050. Between 1950 and 2010, half of this urban migration was to 'small cities' of less than 100k population, creating congestion and complex demand-and-supply issues for energy, water, sanitation, education, and healthcare services. United for Smart Sustainable Cities (U4SSC)—a global UN initiative to support cities and communities adopt technology towards sustainability outcomes—highlights that in addressing the implications of urbanization, SSCs will be crucial to the attainment of the United Nations (UN) sustainable development goals.

Further, according to Bruno Lanvin, President of IMD's Smart City Observatory, 'the pandemic has seen an acceleration of digital and ecological transformations in smart cities'. 'This acceleration is redefining resilience, which is increasingly becoming a local objective. And cities that have been seen as handling COVID challenges in an efficient and effective way rank highly in the index, e.g. Singapore (1st) and Taipei City (4th).'

In 2021, Abu Dhabi and Dubai were identified as the highest ranked smart cities in the Middle East and North Africa in the Global Smart City Index. The index uses citizen, economic, and social data to rank 118 cities based on relative sustainability, quality of life, urban operations, and digital intelligence (or smartness) impacts on the population.

A commitment to establishing smart cities in the UAE has been a long-standing feature of strategic visions at national and emirate levels. Going further, in 2006, the government of Abu Dhabi initiated the planning of Masdar City, the first attempt in the Middle East to build a smart sustainable city using a combination of digital technology, sustainable architectural designs, and solar power to run. The subsequent Dubai Sustainable City initiative, completed in 2016, saw a sustained period of investment in technology infrastructure and policy advancement for the city to provide, amongst other outcomes, open and easy access to data, smart transport, optimized use of energy resources, and adaptive public amenities such as smart parks and beaches.

Establishing an SSC is a major programme of transformation, or 'megaproject', characterized by high complexity in planning and budgeting, major investment, timelines measured in years, multiple public and private stakeholders, and impact on many citizens. The latest such SSC mega-project is the Sharjah Sustainable City initiative that aims to create a first-of-its-kind, fully integrated, net zero energy community.

Yousif Ahmed Al-Mutawa, CEO of Sharjah Sustainable City, describes the initiative as:

making sustainability widely accessible. It offers modern, smart homes, that use sustainable materials, sustainable design and renewable energy production, which reduces utility bills and operational costs. There is 100% recycling of waste and water on site as well as environmentally friendly mobility options such as electric vehicles and an autonomous shuttle bus. Leafy green vegetables and herbs are produced in bio-domes and with vertical farming and there is an emphasis on wellbeing with shared sporting facilities and open areas.

Factoring sustainability considerations into designs from the outset, sustainable communities are not more costly to build than conventional ones and ongoing savings are made on water and energy for

Continued

14

Source: Sharjah Sustainable City (2021). Sharjah Sustainable City builds on green concept (26 October), https://www.sharjahsustainablecity.ae/sharjah-sustainable-city-builds-on-green-concept (last accessed 19 August 2022).

homeowners. Working with many of the supply chain partners for the Dubai 2016 initiative, Mr Al-Mutawa highlights the importance of embracing technology developments whilst learning from others, observing that 'we are building Sharjah Sustainable City with the highest standards of sustainable products and materials, following the footsteps of The Sustainable City in Dubai but with the latest best practices'.

In explaining the strategic rationale, Mr Al-Mutawa notes:

projects like Sharjah Sustainable City will act as pioneers for the industry to showcase how you can build sustainably without compromising on lifestyle. A sustainable city improves the environment, ensures rich biodiversity, reduces air pollution, helps water storage, dampens noise and help cooling down in warm periods. All real estate developments can benefit from these best practices even if they are not fully sustainable, as they can still have sustainable elements within them.

In addition, the UAE government has been keen to encourage opportunities for investment in green projects by creating an attractive investment environment, legislation, regulation, and management, as well as by promoting partnership initiatives between the public and private sectors and relevant international organizations.

That support from the top level means the future is definitely promising for the sector.

Questions for discussion

1. Why would a national government consider investing in smart sustainable cities?

2. Considering a location in a country you know well, describe the strategic leadership approach that would be effective in your view in delivering a megaproject such as a smart sustainable city.

3. What do you think are the long-term risks of not pursuing a smart sustainable city initiative for the strategic leadership teams of a local or regional government?

Sources

Atallah, C. (2022) A clear message is key to the success of sustainable developments, by Sharjah Sustainable City's Carl Atallah. *Middle East Campaign* (14 August), https://campaignme.com/a-clear-message-is-key-to-the-success-of-sustainable-developments-by-sharjah-sustainable-citys-carl-atallah (last accessed 18 June 2022).

Mr Al-Mutawa's comments are taken from an interview with Gavin Davids reported in Davids, G. (2021). Sharjah Sustainable City: Green living. *ME Construction News* (10 June), https://meconstructionnews.com/47946/sharjah-sustainable-city-green-living (last accessed 18 June 2022).

Fitzgerald, M. (2016). Data-driven city management. *MIT Sloan Management Review*, **57**(4), 3–10.

Flyvbjerg, B. (2021). What you should know about megaprojects and why. *From Academia*, https://www.pmi.org/-/media/pmi/documents/public/pdf/research/

14

research-summaries/flyvbjerg_megaprojects.pdf (last accessed 18 June 2022).

Quantum (2021). 2021 Global Smart City Index, https://www.quantumesco.it/en/2021-global-smart-city-index (last accessed 18 June 2022).

UAE Gov (2022). Smart sustainable cities, https://u.ae/en/about-the-uae/digital-uae/smart-sustainable-cities (last accessed 18 June 2022).

United for Smart Sustainable Cities (2021). https://u4ssc.itu.int (last accessed 10 October 2022).

PRACTITIONER INSIGHT **NADA KHORCHID, CEO, LEAD FOR IMPACT**

Nada Khorchid is a leadership and organization culture coach and advisor, a seasoned executive, an active board member, a technologist, and a passionate mentor. Nada is the founder and CEO of Lead for Impact, a coaching and consulting company based in California. Through Lead for Impact, she aspires to influence leaders and organizations to create inclusive, purposeful, and value-driven cultures where people can co-create, co-own, innovate, and achieve their full potential while positively impacting all their stockholders and humanity. Nada has over 25 years of experience in the tech industry with various executive roles. Part of her journey was building and leading a tech start-up—ArabiaGIS—to become a regional player.

'What have been the greatest strategic challenges you've faced and how did you respond?'

Well, there have been so many of them! The first one is about redefining the core of who we were as a company. After toying with the idea for a year, ArabiaGIS was established in 2001 as an e-mapping commerce company. These were the days before Google Maps. We wanted to launch a series of online portals/websites, similar to Google Maps of today, to serve the Middle East and North Africa (MENA) region offering sophisticated services for the public, businesses, and government. We found the company in Lebanon, but after two years, we encountered a series of technology issues, connectivity limitations, a realization of the niche nature of the geo-mapping sector, and a lack of consumer readiness. In response, we pivoted the company's focus to become a solutions-orientated entity to meet niche customer needs. We focused on customers and industries not served by the traditional mapping service providers. ArabiaGIS was envisioned as a pioneer in a 'blue ocean'. This continued to be embedded in our culture and formed part of our shared strategic direction. We would continue to seek out areas with very little competition and develop our products/services there.

Nada shares her thoughts about strategic leadership

Another strategic challenge came from the environment we operated in. Our headquarters were in Lebanon, with constant political, economic, and security challenges. This also applied to some of our markets. Reflecting on that time, we managed to grow the company in what is now identified as a VUCA context, a level of disruption similar to that experienced globally with COVID. That, along with being part of the fast-moving tech industry, forced us to be very agile operationally and in our strategic thinking. To ensure our growth and sustainability, we had to continuously review our strategy, using annually agreed-on goals as a guideline for activity but treating any more detailed strategy as a work in progress.

Finally, a critical strategic challenge in growing the business was an ongoing need to diversify our market geographically. Our profile expanded from Lebanon to Iraq, UAE, Oman, Yemen, and Sudan. We were simultaneously addressing highly sophisticated and competitive stable markets with low margins alongside less mature markets with higher margins and a higher risk of instability. The needs were very different. It was a period of constant,

Continued

14

rapid learning—where we continuously re-invented our products, services, and delivery methods to fit the customers' needs. And to maximize the impact of learning, we decided not to split our teams based on geographical territories but rather to keep the products and services teams unified and diversify the implementation teams. We needed as many people as possible to see the bigger picture. We also empowered teams to make local adaptations based on specific market needs.

We had a learning organization—everyone was continuously learning, which became a strength for us as part of our organizational culture. People weren't put off by this—on the contrary, it gave them meaning, and they co-owned the creation process. This culture sustained our resilience and agility in the face of adversity. Our people were growing individually and collectively—and we were doing it with joy!

'How is the practice of strategy changing or enduring, in your opinion?'

We used to develop strategies for a long time frame: three to five years. Today, with our VUCA world, this seems less practical as it is becoming more challenging to predict the future. Recent strategic leadership experiences from the impacts of shocks like COVID, supply chain issues, and the war in Ukraine are resetting our understanding of strategy to that of a working document or a set of guidelines that are less rigid and can change frequently.

Further, though this is happening more slowly, 'who' is working on creating strategy is changing. It used to be the people in suits! But now, it needs to be sensed and opened up across stakeholders. In my view, there is much to be gained from involving those at the frontlines and fringes of the organization. Part of our success in our entrepreneurial journey was to do just that. We constantly reached out to the 'frontliners' as they knew more than us executives in many ways!

Also, the disruption of the pandemic has raised the strategic challenge of thinking global *and* local to balance reach and resilience. We cannot stop thinking global because of our customers, but we must look at local and regional solutions for business continuity and supply chains. Though this might be difficult in practice initially, it can solve other strategic problems in addition to continuity issues. Traditionally, many of the key decisions were made very far away from where decisions are enacted. Localized decisions can improve the quality and speed of responsiveness.

A fundamental change we are seeing is the understanding that organizational culture can be a strategic edge, especially for resilience and agility. Therefore, culture needs to be a key focus in strategy working. Human-centric approaches need to feature more prominently in the leadership styles and strategy processes and practices we adopt.

Another change we are seeing is the pressure to think about people and planet goals alongside profit—this is now an increasingly felt pressure across organizations. That pressure comes from consumers and younger generations wanting to know what organizations are doing for the planet and communities. Strategies can no longer be driven by short-term profit at the expense of people and natural resources.

'What would you advise strategic leaders to prioritize in a VUCA world?'

I would advise strategic leaders to focus on people, people, people! In ever-changing environments, your strength is your people. Aim to create an environment and culture in which people feel **psychologically safe**, can experiment, learn quickly/fail fast, and find meaning. Exemplify this through your leadership style, and work with them to shape and bring alive strategy as a framework for cohesive action.

Strategic alliances and collaborations are other areas to bring to your strategic thinking. In my view, co-creation rather than competition will become the norm for organizations as we move into the future. So, start preparing for this now through practice and look for increasingly more collaborative opportunities with other players in your ecosystem.

Finally, develop a sense of purpose. For me, this means knowing how you serve all of your stakeholders—shareholders, employees, customers, communities, and the planet. Today, organizations can be a force for good. They haven't necessarily been so in the past, but it is now time to change that. Organizations should review their social contract; without serving all stakeholders in the ecosystem, organizations won't be able to survive. Consumers/clients are becoming more conscious. If you want to sustain your business, retain your employees, and attract the right talent, then investing in creating a purpose-driven entity is essential.

 Access the online resources to watch a short video clip where Nada Khorchid talks more about her career.

14

CHAPTER SUMMARY

In this chapter, we addressed the following learning outcomes:

○ **Describe the evolution of the concept of leadership with reference to individual, relational, and processual interpretations.**

We examined leadership as a contested term that means different things to different people. Traditional views of leadership focus on individuals—their inherited traits, learned skills, behaviours, and abilities. Each of these views can help explain how those identified as leaders act in any given circumstance. This includes how leadership styles such as transformational, charismatic, and visionary leadership will impact on situational outcomes. Further, relational views examine the impact of 'followers' and those with whom leaders have relationships and interactions. Considering the relational and systemic perspectives of leadership provide further insights into how leaders influence outcomes in context. Finally, we considered an alternative processual view of leadership as practice, in which a focus on individual leaders is replaced by attention to dynamic processes and practices through which stakeholders interact, collectively take decisions, and work towards realizing outcomes.

○ **Explain how strategic leadership can be considered a subset of leadership studies.**

We made a high-level distinction between general leadership in organizations—including supervisory arrangements—and the leadership of organizations, which we identify as strategic leadership. Strategic leadership can thus be thought of as a subset of leadership studies. Strategic leadership is concerned with providing direction, strategic thinking and planning, activating change, encouraging cohesive work as a whole organization, defining and harnessing corporate purpose, and nurturing the leaders of tomorrow.

○ **Compare the scope and implications for strategizing of apex stakeholder, managerial system, and practice interpretations of strategic leadership.**

Mirroring a traditional leadership focus on individuals, considering strategic leadership as synonymous with apex stakeholders informs us about how the attributes, actions, and arrangements of senior leaders in the organization influence strategy work. This might be as a collective or as distinctive individuals. Because of their resource allocation powers, these 'apex stakeholders' are observed to have a high degree of impact on how formal strategizing approaches occur and what is decided and initiated in strategy processes. We consider a second managerial systems view, which emphasizes the importance and impact of relationships and interactions between leaders as a vehicle for making and managing strategy. This includes but isn't limited to apex stakeholders, thus potentially drawing in the activities and attributes of leaders throughout the organization in explaining strategizing effects. Finally, we examine strategic leadership as a practice, where daily interactions between stakeholders define collective agreements and actions that contribute to strategic leadership outcome. This non-heroic, non-individual perspective emphasizes how micro-processes and practices involving a wide range of stakeholders can shape strategy.

14

○ Explain how strategic leadership interpretations can be integrated through a process–practice perspective of high value to strategy practitioners.

We propose a process–practice integration of the different strategic leadership perspectives that focuses on practitioners, practices, and processes. Based on a summary of existing debates and reflection on the cases and megatrends of digitalization, globalization, and sustainability addressed in this book, we make the case for this integrated perspective to be defined by adaptive, engaging, interdependent, pluralistic, purpose-driven, and responsible practitioners, practices, and processes. If this profile of characteristics can be distributed across activities of individual leaders, leadership systems, and everyday dynamic processes involving a diverse range of stakeholders, then arguably we will have an effective organizational approach to strategic leaders.

○ Evaluate the usefulness of strategic leadership to individuals and organizations strategizing in an ever-changing world.

We examined the implications of a VUCA context for strategic leadership, with an emphasis on the impacts of digitalization, globalization, and sustainability to the operating environment for organizations. We noted that the interlocking challenges of these megatrends are likely to continue, and the sense of existing in a dynamic and 'ever-changing' world will be the new normal for most organizations. In this setting, we argue that a process–practice perspective of strategic leadership offers a valuable coping approach through which 'apex practitioners', distributed leadership practitioners, and a diverse range of stakeholders can co-create strategizing outcomes. By loosening our views from individual-centric interpretations of strategic leadership, we can open the potential for greater collective performance of strategic leadership that allows all in an organization to contribute to strategic survival and success in an ever-changing world.

(?) END-OF-CHAPTER QUESTIONS

Recall questions

1. How has the concept of leadership developed over the twentieth century, and what are the implications for how leadership is understood today?

2. What might we mean by strategic leadership, and what function might it play in organizational life?

3. What are the main differences between apex practitioners, systemic, and practice foci of strategic leadership?

4. Describe an integrated, process–practice interpretation of strategic leadership—what it means and what are arguably relevant characteristics for modern organizations?

5. What might be the implications of megatrends in digitalization, sustainability, and globalization on what constitutes effective contemporary strategic leadership?

Application questions

A) Think of a practitioner in a formal strategic leadership position whom you admire. Explain why you admire them with reference to their attributes, activities, and attitudes.

B) Think of an organization you know well and list the strategic challenges it is currently facing. Describe what you believe would be an effective strategic leadership approach to addressing these challenges. Make reference to individual 'apex stakeholders' and distributed leaders and to daily processes, practices, and interactions across stakeholders in your response.

C) Based on your appraisal of global megatrends, identify three alternative descriptors of characteristics you believe would be valuable for strategic leadership practitioners, practices, and processes to exhibit. Explain your choices.

 ONLINE RESOURCES

www.oup.com/he/mackay2e

In addition to the video interviews already highlighted, the book's online resources include the following features for this chapter, specifically:

- *links to further reading material* to broaden your knowledge of key issues discussed in this chapter;

- *self-test multiple-choice questions* to test your understanding of the material covered in each section of the chapter; and

- *a flashcard glossary* to help you recall and test your understanding of key terms.

 FURTHER READING

Strategic Leadership by John Adair (2010).

Adair, J. (2010). *Strategic Leadership*. Kogan Page.

Students can gain an insight into how strategic leadership is widely understood in practice from this book by a 'guru'. John Adair is considered a key authority on strategic leadership following a career in the military and a series of academic roles, including appointment to the UN Chair of Strategic Leadership in 2009. This book unpacks each of the strategic leadership functions highlighted in this chapter—providing direction, strategic thinking, and planning and activating change, encouraging cohesive work as a whole organization, defining and harnessing corporate purpose, and nurturing the leaders of tomorrow.

Double-Edition Special Issue—Reframing Leadership and Organizational Practice (2021)—Journal of Change Management

Editorials

Clegg, S., Crevani, L., Uhl-Bien, M., and By, R.T. (2021). Changing leadership in changing times. *Journal of Change Management*, **21**(1), 1–13.

Crevani, L., Uhl-Bien, M., Clegg, S., and By, R.T. (2021). Changing leadership in changing times II. *Journal of Change Management*, **21**(2), 133–43.

This special issue double edition of the Journal of Change Management highlights a wide range of new leadership perspectives that have informed this chapter. It incorporates contributions from a wide range of leadership thinkers who examine in detail many process–practice concepts and considerations. It makes an excellent point of departure for readers looking to explore an integrated process–practice interpretation of (strategic) leadership. Further, the authors aim to address contemporary organizational, societal, and global challenges, including new ways of leading towards attainment of the Sustainable Development Goals in the face of globalization and digitalization disruption.

14

REFERENCES

Ackermann, F. and Eden, C. (2011). *Making Strategy: Mapping Out Strategic Success*. London: Sage.

Adair, J. (2010). *Strategic Leadership*. London: Kogan Page.

Ashcroft, J. (2014). The man who rescued Lego—meet the Boss TV, https://www.youtube.com/watch?v=JlVyiFqIg0w (last accessed 10 October 2022).

Ashton Legal Services (2018). Rex Bionics . . . the robot that enhances the mobility of wheelchair users (17 December), https://www.ashtonslegal.co.uk/insights/legal-news/rex-bionicsthe-robot-that-enhances-the-mobility-of-wheelchair-users (last accessed 18 June 2022).

Atallah, C. (2022) A clear message is key to the success of sustainable developments, by Sharjah Sustainable City's Carl Atallah. Middle East Campaign (14 August), https://campaignme.com/a-clear-message-is-key-to-the-success-of-sustainable-developments-by-sharjah-sustainable-citys-carl-atallah (last accessed 18 June 2022).

Balch, O. (2013). Natura commits to sourcing sustainably from the Amazon (13 March), https://www.theguardian.com/sustainable-business/natura-sourcing-sustainably-from-amazon (last accessed 19 June 2022).

B-Corp (2022). Natura & Co, https://www.bcorporation.net/en-us/find-a-b-corp/company/natura-co (last accessed 19 June 2022).

Beer, M. (2021). Reflections: Towards a normative and actionable theory of planned organizational change and development. *Journal of Change Management*, **21**(1), 14–29.

Bryson, J.M., Barberg, B., Crosby, B.C., and Patton, M.Q. (2021). Leading social transformations: Creating public value and advancing the common good. *Journal of Change Management*, **21**(2), 180–202, https://doi.org/10.1080/14697017.2021.1917492.

BusinessWeek (2019). Selling the rainforest door-to-door, https://www.bloomberg.com/news/articles/2019-07-31/brazil-s-natura-wants-to-take-rainforest-chic-global-with-avon (last accessed 19 June 2022).

Butler, S. (2017). L'Oréal to sell Body Shop to Brazil's Natura in 1 bn euro deal (9 June), https://www.theguardian.com/business/2017/jun/09/loreal-body-shop-natura-aesop (last accessed 19 June 2022).

By, R.T. (2021). Leadership: In pursuit of purpose. *Journal of Change Management*, **21**(1), 30–44, https://doi.org/10.1080/14697017.2021.1861698.

Carroll, B., Levy, L., and Richmond, D. (2008). Leadership as practice: Challenging the competency paradigm. *Leadership*, **4**(4), 363–79.

Clegg, S., Crevani, L., Uhl-Bien, M., and By, R.T. (2021). Changing leadership in changing times. *Journal of Change Management*, **21**(1), 1–13, https://doi.org/10.1080/14697017.2021.1880092.

Coghlan, D. and Holian, R. (2021). Insider action research as leadership-as-practice: A methodological reflection for OD scholar-practitioners. *Organization Development Review*, **53**(5), 13–17.

Cortes, A.F. and Herrmann, P. (2021). Strategic leadership of innovation: A framework for future research. *International Journal of Management Reviews*, **23**(2), 224–43.

Crevani, L., Uhl-Bien, M., Clegg, S., and By, R.T. (2021). Changing leadership in changing times II. *Journal of Change Management*, **21**(2), 133–43, https://doi.org/10.1080/14697017.2021.1917489.

Crossan, M., Vera, D., and Nanjad, L. (2008). Transcendent leadership: Strategic leadership in dynamic environments. *Leadership Quarterly*, **19**(5), 569–81.

Cummings, M.E., Eggers, J.P., and Wang, R.D. (2022). Monitoring the monitor: Enabling strategic change when the former CEO stays on the board. *Long Range Planning*, **55**(3), https://doi.org/10.1016/j.lrp.2021.102130.

Davids, G. (2021). Sharjah Sustainable City: Green living. ME Construction News (10 June), https://meconstructionnews.com/47946/sharjah-sustainable-city-green-living (last accessed 18 June 2022).

14

De Sousa, M. and van Dierendonck, D. (2021). Serving the need of people: The case for servant leadership against populism. *Journal of Change Management*, **21**(2), 222–41, https://doi.org/10.1080/14697017.2021.1917494.

Drath, W.H., McCauley, C.D., Palus, C.J., Van Velsor, E., O'Connor, P.M.G., and McGuire, J.B. (2008). Direction, alignment, commitment: Toward a more integrative ontology of leadership. *Leadership Quarterly*, **19**(6), 635–53, https://doi.org/https://doi.org/10.1016/j.leaqua.2008.09.003.

Eccles, R.G. and Serafeim, G. (2013). The performance frontier. Harvard Business Review, 91(5), 50–60.

TheExpressWire (2022). Global wearable robotic exoskeleton market to hit USD 11,995.7 million by 2029 (17 June), https://www.digitaljournal.com/pr/global-wearable-robotic-exoskeleton-market-size-to-hit-usd-11995-7-million-by-2029 (last accessed 18 June 2022).

Farhan, B. (2021). A new strategic leadership model for surviving and coping: Lessons from Canada's leadership approach to COVID-19. *Cogent Business & Management*, **8**(1), 1–13.

Fernandes, C.I., Veiga, P.M., Ferreira, J.J., Rammal, H.G., and Pereira, V. (2022). Assessing strategic leadership in organizations: Using bibliometric data to develop a holistic model. *Journal of Business Research,* **141**, 646–55.

Fitzgerald, M. (2016). Data-driven city management. MIT Sloan Management Review, **57**(4), 3–10.

Flyvbjerg, B. (2021). What you should know about megaprojects and why. From Academia, https://www.pmi.org/-/media/pmi/documents/public/pdf/research/research-summaries/flyvbjerg_megaprojects.pdf (last accessed 18 June 2022).

Ford, J., Ford, L., and Polin, B. (2021). Leadership in the implementation of change: Functions, sources, and requisite variety. *Journal of Change Management*, **21**(1), 87–119, https://doi.org/10.1080/14697017.2021.1861697.

Gavetti, G. (2011). The new psychology of strategic leadership. *Harvard Business Review*, **89**(7/8), 118–25.

Gilbert, C.G. (2006). Change in the presence of residual fit: Can competing frames coexist? *Organization Science*, **17**(1), 150–67.

Gill, R. (2010). *Theory and Practice of Leadership*. London: Sage.

Hall, M. (2022). Headset games target brain and pain. New Zealand Doctor (29 April), https://www.nzdoctor.co.nz/article/news/business/headset-games-target-brain-and-pain (last accessed 18 June 2022).

Hambrick, D.C. and Mason, P.A. (1984). Upper echelons: The organization as a reflection of its top managers. *Academy of Management Review*, **9**(2), 193–206.

Hughes, R.I. (1998). Strategic leadership. *Leadership in Action*, **18**(4), 1–8.

Ireland, R.D. and Hitt, M.A. (2005). Achieving and maintaining strategic competitiveness in the 21st century: The role of strategic leadership. *Academy of Management Executive*, **19**(4), 63–77.

Iszatt-White, M. and Saunders, C. (2014). *Leadership*. Oxford: Oxford University Press.

Jones, G. (2012). The growth opportunity that lies next door. Harvard Business Review, 90(7/8), 141–5.

Kaufman, R. (2017). Practical strategic leadership: Aligning human performance development with organizational contribution. *Performance Improvement*, **56**(2), 16–21.

Kempster, S. and Jackson, B. (2021). Leadership for what, why, for whom and where? A responsibility perspective. *Journal of Change Management*, **21**(1), 45–65.

Kunisch, S., Menz, M., and Langan, R. (2022). Chief digital officers: An exploratory analysis of their emergence, nature, and determinants. *Long Range Planning*, **55**(2), https://doi.org/10.1016/j.lrp.2020.101999.

Kurzhals, C., Graf-Vlachy, L., and König, A. (2020). Strategic leadership and technological innovation: A comprehensive review and research agenda. *Corporate Governance: An International Review*, **28**(6), 437–64.

Levinthal, D.A. and March, J.G. (1993). The myopia of learning. *Strategic Management Journal*, **14**, 95–112.

14

Lin, S.-H., Scott, B.A., and Matta, F.K. (2019). The dark side of transformational leader behaviors for leaders themselves: A conservation of resources perspective. *Academy of Management Journal*, **62**(5), 1556–1582, https://doi.org/10.5465/amj.2016.1255.

Luciano, M.M., Nahrgang, J.D., and Shropshire, C. (2020). Strategic leadership systems: Viewing top management teams and boards of directors from a multiteam systems perspective. *Academy of Management Review*, **45**(3), 675–701.

Maak, T., Pless, N.M., and Wohlgezogen, F. (2021). The fault lines of leadership: Lessons from the global COVID-19 crisis. *Journal of Change Management*, **21**(1), 66–86.

Mackay, D. and Burt, G. (2015). Strategic learning, foresight and hyperopia. *Management Learning*, **46**(5), 546–64.

McKay, A. (2020). What exactly is strategic leadership? *Human Resources Magazine*, **25**(3), 14–17.

Northouse, P.J. (2011). *Introduction to Leadership* (5th edn). London: Sage.

Norzailan, Z., Othman, R.B., and Ishizaki, H. (2016). Strategic leadership competencies: What is it and how to develop it? *Industrial & Commercial Training*, **48**(8), 394–9.

NZ Herald (2021). Australian government fund under fire for investment in NZ's Rex Bionics (23 May), https://www.nzherald.co.nz/business/australian-government-fund-under-fire-for-investment-in-nzs-rex-bionics/TGV2G64JQ2FIJXLBX45TUZJPNY (last accessed 18 June 2022).

Oliveira, P and Cunha, M.P. (2021). Centralized decentralization, or distributed leadership as paradox: The case of the patient innovation's COVID-19 portal. *Journal of Change Management*, **21**(2), 203–21.

O'Reilly, C.A. and Tushman, M.L. (2011). Organizational ambidexterity in action: How managers explore and exploit. *California Management Review*, **53**(4), 5–21.

O'Shannassy, T. (2021). The challenges of strategic leadership in organizations. *Journal of Management & Organization*, **27**(2), 235–8, https://doi.org/10.1017/jmo.2021.36.

Pink, A.I.H. (1988). Strategic leadership through corporate planning at ICI. *Long Range Planning*, **21**(1), 18–25.

Quantum (2021). 2021 Global Smart City Index, https://www.quantumesco.it/en/2021-global-smart-city-index (last accessed 18 June 2022).

Saiti, A. (2021). Is strategic and sustainable leadership synonymous with effective leadership? *Journal of Leadership, Accountability & Ethics*, **18**(1), 126–36, https://doi.org/10.33423/jlae.v18i1.4009.

Sarkar, S. and Clegg, S.R. (2021). Resilience in a time of contagion: Lessons from small businesses during the COVID-19 pandemic. *Journal of Change Management*, **21**(2), 242–67, https://doi.org/10.1080/14697017.2021.1917495.

Schaedler, L., Graf-Vlachy, L., and König, A. (2022). Strategic leadership in organizational crises: A review and research agenda. *Long Range Planning*, **55**(2), https://doi.org/10.1016/j.lrp.2021.102156.

Schoemaker, P.J.H., Krupp, S., and Howland, S. (2013). Strategic leadership: The essential skills. *Harvard Business Review*, **91**(1/2), 131–4.

Sergi, V., Lusiani, M., and Langley, A. (2021). Highlighting the plural: Leading amidst romance(s). *Journal of Change Management*, **21**(2), 163–79, https://doi.org/10.1080/14697017.2021.1917491.

Sharjah Sustainable City (2021). Sharjah Sustainable City builds on green concept (26 October), https://www.sharjahsustainablecity.ae/sharjah-sustainable-city-builds-on-green-concept (last accessed 19 August 2022).

Simmons + Simmons (2017). Advising Rex Bionics on restructuring and new investment (30 May), https://www.simmons-simmons.com/en/about-us/news/ck0f6t8ndwyik0b36uz8nmae0/advising-rex-bionics-on-its-restructuring-and-new-investment (last accessed 18 June 2022).

Srour, Y., Shefer, N., and Carmeli, A. (2022). Positive chair–CEO work relationships: Micro-relational foundations of organizational capabilities. *Long Range Planning*, **55**(3), https://doi.org/10.1016/j.lrp.2021.102124.

Strand, R. (2014). Strategic leadership of corporate sustainability. *Journal of Business Ethics*, **123**(4), 687–706, https://doi.org/10.1007/s10551-013-2017-3.

14

Taylor, B. (1995). The new strategic leadership—driving change, getting results. *Long Range Planning*, **28**(5), 71–81, https://doi.org/10.1016/0024-6301(95)00039-L.

UAE Gov (2022). Smart sustainable cities, https://u.ae/en/about-the-uae/digital-uae/smart-sustainable-cities (last accessed 18 June 2022).

Uhl-Bien, M. (2021). Complexity and COVID-19: Leadership and followership in a complex world. *Journal of Management Studies*, **58**(5), 1400–4, https://doi.org/10.1111/joms.12696.

Van Doorn, S., Heyden, M.L.M., Reimer, M., Buyl, T., and Volberda, H.W. (2022). Internal and external interfaces of the executive suite: Advancing research on the porous bounds of strategic leadership. *Long Range Planning*, **55**(3), 102214, https://doi.org/10.1016/j.lrp.2022.102214.

Woods, C., Callagher, L., and Jaffray, T. (2021). Walk tall: The story of Rex Bionics. *Journal of Management & Organization*, **27**(2), 239–52, https://doi.org/10.1017/jmo.2018.68.

14

GLOSSARY

Acceptability Test of a proposed strategy which addresses how stakeholders might feel about the expected outcomes of the strategy.

Accountability test One of a number of possible tests of good organizational design, this test stresses the importance of clear lines of accountability, aiming to ensure that managers are committed to achieving the organization's goals and that they are accountable for delivery against its strategy.

Acquisition A transaction when one company purchases most or all of another company's shares to gain control of that company.

Activity That which is actually done by practitioners, individually or collectively.

Activity outcomes The consequences of individual or organizational activities.

Activity system The ongoing system of resource stocks and flows through which the organizational resource base changes shape as activity outcomes are realized through the deployment of capabilities grounded in existing resources.

Adhocracy A form of organization that is flexible, informal, and adaptable, lacking a formal structure and operating in a manner that contrasts with a traditional bureaucracy.

Advantage This test of a proposed strategy is about competitive advantage or whether the organization can capture enough of the value it creates.

Affective conflict Concerns interpersonal relationships or incompatible personalities; arises from emotions and frustration in conflict situations that may have a detrimental impact on group decision-making and the acceptability of the group decision outcome.

Affordances All the possible ways in which a user might use a tool or object in everyday strategy activity.

Agency The ability of humans to be creative and exhibit independently minded choices.

Agility Being able to organize and respond to situations quickly and nimbly.

Analytical methods Procedures which, focusing on a limited aspect of the organization's situation, provide a framework for organizing external data and/or capturing participant views and uncovering deeper understanding of trends and implications through structured conversations.

Ansoff matrix (Ansoff growth vectors) A strategy tool that can help managers devise strategies for future growth.

Apex practitioner A practitioner in the upper echelons of an organization with a formal position that enables them to have influence over strategy process and content.

Architectural innovation Innovation involving the reconfiguration of an established system to link together existing components in a new way.

Artefact An object, such as a piece of media, drawing, or other physical construct made by human activity; in the case of strategy, an object arising from strategic activities (e.g. a causal map can be considered an artefact built by a decision-making group).

Articulated values Organizational values that have been made explicit.

Attentional design Using tools and procedures to deliberately channel the attention of decision makers to consider a broad and representative set of information in order that they can better understand the context in which they are operating.

Attentional structures Communication channels, knowledge flows, organizational procedures, and opportunities for interaction with others that influence how information reaches the attention of decision-makers.

Attention-based view (ABV) A set of concepts and theoretical contributions that help explain how organizations behave, adapt to changing environments, develop capabilities, and strategize according to how the attention of decision-makers is informed and directed.

Balanced scorecard A set of measures that give managers a fast but fairly comprehensive view of key aspects of an organization.

Benefit Corporation (B-Corp) A type of for-profit corporate entity which includes in its constitution positive impacts on society, workers, the community, and the environment as legally defined goals alongside profit aims.

Beyond compliance An emerging managerial perspective in which the full environmental and social costs of operating are considered alongside creating shared value during the development of sustainable organizational strategy.

Big data The vast information flows available to organizations from multiple sources on a daily basis.

Biodiversity The variety and variation in the species of life on the planet.

Blue ocean strategy An approach to innovation strategy that searches for uncontested market space; it guides exploration of cost reduction and differentiation options and identification of new value propositions that render the competition irrelevant.

Born global A term used to describe companies that from very early on pursue a vision of becoming global and globalize rapidly without any preceding gradual internationalization of activities; born global companies are usually small technology-orientated companies that operate in international markets from the earliest days of their founding.

Bounded rationality An idea that when individuals make decisions, their rationality is limited by the availability of information, their capability to understand the decision problem, the cognitive limitations of their minds, and the time available for decision-making.

Budgeting Development of a plan for deploying financial resources.

Bundles (of resources) A term used to describe the use of resources in combination during organizational activities.

Business analytics Processes that convert big data into meaningful information which can inform strategic and operational decision-making.

Business ecosystem A complex network of relationships, interactions, and influences within which a business is embedded and in which the prosperity of the ecosystem affects the prosperity of the business.

Business model The overarching logic and rationale of how an organization creates, delivers, and captures value in a competitive environment.

Business model canvas A method to systematically map the components of a current business model in order to identify ways in which it might be changed.

Business performance The financial and non-financial results achieved by an organization against a set of standards or expectations within a given time frame.

Business strategy Answering the question, 'How to meet customer needs?', this strategy addresses how to gain an advantage over competitors in selected geographies and sectors.

Buyer power The bargaining power that the entity purchasing a good or service has over the supplier.

CAGE distance framework An analytical framework that identifies Cultural, Administrative, Geographic, and Economic differences or distances between countries which companies should address when developing international strategies.

Capabilities What an individual or organization is able to do to a threshold level of performance based on the potential inherent in accumulated resources.

Capabilities audit A method for identifying the capabilities currently being used by the organization to undertake activities and deliver outcomes.

Causal ambiguity Where the causes of a phenomenon are unknown or unknowable; for example, the relationship between the firm's resources and capabilities and competitive advantage may be causally ambiguous, which makes the management of resources difficult.

Causal map Provides a visual explanation of why an incident occurred or what the consequences of a decision would be; it contains a visualization of individual cause-and-effect relationships to reveal the system of causes within a given issue or decision problem (sometimes referred to as a concept or cognitive map).

Chaebol A large industrial conglomerate in South Korea that is run and controlled by an owner or family.

Chairperson A senior officer of an organization whose role is to ensure, through the board and executive team, that the organization's obligations to its stakeholders are met in an appropriate way.

Change management A collective term for all management approaches to prepare, support, and help individuals, teams, and organizations in effecting organizational change through deliberate planned efforts.

Charismatic leadership The use of effective interpersonal skills to influencing other.

Chief Executive Officer (CEO) The head of the top management team, or executive team, who typically reports to a board of directors.

Circular economy An alternative to a traditional linear economy (make, use, dispose) in which resources are kept in use for as long as possible, extracting the maximum value from them whilst they are in use, and then recovering and regenerating products and materials at the end of their service life.

Climate The patterns in weather conditions in any given area.

Climate change A shift in weather conditions in an area over time, often with consequences for natural environmental conditions.

Cognitive bias A systematic pattern of deviation from the norm or rationality in judgement; inferences about other people, situations, or problems may be made in an illogical fashion. Individuals create their own mental map of 'subjective social reality' based on their perception of the situation.

Cognitive conflict Arises when a group focuses on a task or a problem and debate to come to a solution. Group members might argue and exchange views vigorously, yet there is two-way communication and an openness to hearing each other. The goal is to find the best possible solution rather than to win the argument. Alternative solutions to the problem are seen as valuable rather than threatening (see definition of 'affective conflict').

Cognitive strategy A plan to capitalize on or mitigate the possibilities of cognitive technologies.

Cognitive technologies Artificial intelligence and technological processes by which machines learn to embody the skills, knowledge, and capabilities that are performed in a cognate way by humans.

Collaboration The act of cooperating with one or more other parties in order to achieve a shared outcome.

Communication practices Approaches to giving or receiving information within an organization.

Competence Individual or collective potential to take action to a superior level of performance.

Competitive advantage The capacity of an individual, organization, or nation to outperform competitors in attaining some outcome of interest (often financial performance).

Competitive strategy Describes how a company seeks to compete; sometimes known as 'domain navigation' (compare with corporate strategy, which focuses on where to compete).

Competitor profiling A method that guides evaluation of how competitors operate and how they might act/react to future strategic initiatives by your own organization.

Complementarity When two separate resources, products, or services enhance the qualities and usefulness of each other when present together; for example, the gaming and console markets are complementarities.

Complex structure In contrast with a simple structure, the term 'complex structure' refers to a set of more complex organizational forms such as multidivisional, holding, matrix, network, and transnational structures.

Configuration The way in which an organization arranges its activities to create a particular organizational structure; configurations are the result of grouping the key elements of a structure and combining them in a particular manner.

Connected strategy A plan to deal with the new normal of customer expectations for continuous connectivity to service providers.

Consensus decision-making A group decision-making process in which group members develop and agree to support a decision in the best interest of the whole group or organization. Consensus decision can be defined as an acceptable and satisfactory solution to a problem that is acceptable to all group members, even if is not the favourite solution of each individual decision-making group member.

Consistency This test of a proposed strategy points out that the strategy must not present goals and policies that lack consistency.

Consonance This test of a proposed strategy is focused on the creation of social value.

Consortium An association of two or more organizations created with the objective of participating in a common activity or pooling their resources for achieving a common goal (often a large and complex project) for a fixed short term.

Consultancy Provision of expert advice on a given topic, typically on a commercial basis as an external party to an organization.

Consumer activism A process by which activists seek to influence the way in which goods or services are produced or delivered by spending money on goods, services, or organizations that align with the purchaser's values.

Consumer surplus The difference between what the customer would be willing to pay for a product less the price charged by the organization.

Context The circumstances which form the setting for strategy activity to occur.

Contextual ambidexterity When individuals are able to make choices between either exploitation-orientated or exploration-orientated activities in their work. To enable this, it is necessary for the organization to be more flexible, permitting employees to use their own judgement in pursuing both exploratory and exploitative activities.

Control limits The levels of performance that will trigger a corrective action in an organization.

Control system A system that manages or directs the behaviour of other parties; it aims to ensure that individuals, locations, and activities are governed by strategic decisions and are accountable for their performance.

Cooperative strategies Strategies where two or more organizations choose to work together (e.g. in a strategic alliance or joint venture), while remaining separate entities, that is, not engaging in mergers, acquisitions, or other strategies that create a single entity.

Core competences Competences that recur throughout an organization, underpinning value creation and strategy across all aspects of operations.

Core dynamic capabilities Capabilities to create, extend, or modify the resource base which are continually engaged in an organization.

Core rigidities Resources which were once valuable, and are still considered so in strategy work, but in actuality are a hindrance to organizational performance.

Corporate parent/parenting Looks at the relationship between 'head office' (i.e. the corporate parent) and the strategic business units that report to head office; it explores how the head office can add value to the individual business units.

Corporate relatedness Considers the potential offered by a strategy of diversification to combine capabilities and pursue asset creation or improvement across two or more organizations.

Corporate social responsibility (CSR) A management philosophy in which an organization's obligations to society at large are prioritized over other business objectives to varying degrees.

Corporate strategy Sets out where a company seeks to compete; sometimes known as 'domain selection' (compare with competitive strategy, which focuses on how to compete and operate).

Corporate value The present value of the expected returns from a combination of the current business strategies and future invesetment programmes of an organization.

Costs An outlay or deployment of resources (often financial) towards some specific end or activity.

Creating shared value (CSV) A management philosophy focused on growing the total value created for an organization and its stakeholders and splitting the benefits fairly.

Creative destruction A process of industrial mutation which incessantly revolutionizes the economic structure from within—incessantly destroying the old one and incessantly creating a new one.

Creativity Original thinking and inventiveness that generates new ideas.

Crisis management A process by which an organization deals with a major event that threatens to harm the organization, its stakeholders, or the general public—often considered to be one of the most important processes in public relations.

Critical reflection In-depth focused attention given to questions of how political and social context shape values, assumptions, judgements, and beliefs.

Cultural web An analytical framework to identify the components of an organization's culture. Cultural web is a power tool in change management (see definition of 'change management').

Culture The habitual and patterned ways in which activity is done in a social setting, such as how work is carried out in an organization.

Customer matrix See 'strategy clock'.

623

Customer perspective One of the four perspectives of the balanced scorecard;it asks, 'How do you customers see us?'

Customer value proposition The way an organization satisfies customer needs.

Cyber-security The preservation of the security of digital systems in the face of cyber-crime.

Data Discrete pieces of knowledge/things that are known.

Data hubris The often implicit assumption that big data is a substitute for rather than a supplement to traditional data collection and analysis.

Data science The application of experimental methods and computational systems to generate new insights and business analytics from big data sets.

Data strategy Sets out the objectives, core activities, and orientation for how data, as a valuable strategic resource, is to be managed in an organization.

Data strategy orientation A checklist-based approach to align data strategy—data architecture, objectives, and activities—with broader organizational objectives; sets a platform for digital transformation which, in turn, enables organizational strategy.

De-globalization A process of reducing interdependence and integration between certain units around the world, typically nation states; it is often used to describe periods of history when economic trade and investment between countries decline.

Deeply held beliefs and assumptions Beliefs and values held by organization's members that have not been articulated explicitly. They have a tacit dimension that they nevertheless are important parts of the organization culture that underpin behaviours, processes, and beliefs.

Design thinking A human-centred set of methods and attitudes for creating products, services, solutions, and experiences based on the needs of stakeholders that is increasingly used to design strategizing episodes and strategy activities.

Devil's advocacy A group decision-making method where, for the sake of debate, one or more members of the decision-making group take a position they do not necessarily agree with (or simply an alternative position from the rest of the group) to explore the decision problem further

by using a valid reasoning that disagrees with the proposed solution to the problem.

Dialectical enquiry A group decision-making method that attempts to eliminate groupthink, attributed to Plato, who insisted that his students consider both the thesis and antithesis to any idea. Groups using this technique divide into two camps: those advocating for an idea and those advocating against it.

Difficult links test One of a number of possible tests of good organizational design, this test asks us to consider whether a proposed structure will set up links between parts of the organization where good relationships are important but such relationships are also likely to be strained.

Diffusion The process by which innovation is communicated through a range of channels over time by members of a social system such as a market or sector.

Digital A virtual electronic format for a platform, service, product, communication, or piece of data.

Digital dexterity A set of beliefs, mindsets, and behaviours that help employees deliver faster and more valuable outcomes from digital initiatives.

Digital resources Assets owned or accessed by the organization which support 'virtual' electronic modes of working and creating value.

Digital strategy A coherent set of decision-making principles, investments, and priorities which guide digitalization in line with broader organizational objectives.

Digital transformation The use of bundles of digital technologies to change the way the organization operates, particularly around customer interactions, in the creation of new stakeholder value and in accordance with organizational objectives.

Digitalization The process of exploiting digital technologies and resources for operational improvement, innovation, or new value creation.

Digitization The process of converting physical or analogue assets into a digital form.

Disruption An event or trend which unsettles stable competitive or operating conditions.

Disruptive change This type of change is required when the fundamental technologies, processes, or products of an industry or a firm begin to shift. In such situations, small, incremental changes are no longer adequate and a high-level response from the company's leadership is needed to ensure that the firm can survive in the long term.

Disruptive innovation Drawing on business model, open, or platform innovation to finding new ways to create value for new and/or existing customers using existing technical competences.

Distinctive capabilities The potential to take value-creating actions that are not available to all competitors.

Distinctive competences The potential to act in unique ways to superior performance levels compared with what competitors can do.

Distinctiveness The quality or attribute of a resource which indicates its degree of difference from other resources and thus the extent to which it might be a source of resource-based competitive advantage.

Diversification Ansoff uses the term 'diversification' to refer to strategies where both products and markets are new to the firm.

Divestment The sale or disposal of one of an organization's activities, such as a strategic business unit.

Divisionalized A divisionalized organization is typically organized around a number of different products or services, markets, or geographies.

Double-loop learning A framework that aids evaluation of the likely impact of learning activities on future organizational performance by altering strategies and tactics whilst casting new light on our values, assumptions, and beliefs.

Dynamic capabilities The subset of organizational capabilities associated with managing or manipulating the resource base.

Dynamic capability analysis A method for figuring out how new resource configurations might be created to develop a capability profile that is fit for the future.

Dynamic capability view (DCV) A set of concepts and theoretical contributions that helps explain how organizations can purposefully create, extend, or modify their resource base over time; an extension of the resource based view.

Dynamic control systems Robert Simons argues that, for a control system to be effective in a fast-changing context, it must be dynamic, that

is, it must promote the strategic flexibility and innovative capabilities that the organization needs to adapt to change in a controlled manner.

Eco-innovation All forms of innovation that create business opportunities and benefits to the environment by preventing or reducing their impact or by optimizing the use of resources.

Economic value The financial measure of the benefit of a good, service, or course of action to interested parties.

Economies of scale The cost advantages that an organization can achieve when it increases the scale of its operations; economies of scale occur when the cost per unit of output decreases as output increases.

Economies of scope The cost benefits resulting from using the same resource across a range of outputs.

Ecosystem A complex network of relationships, interactions, and influences in which an individual or organization is embedded.

Ecosystems perspective A theoretical perspective that considers organizations as embedded in a complex network of relationships, the prosperity of which directly affects the prosperity of the organization.

Efficacy A gauge of effectiveness—the extent to which an activity (one off or continuing) achieves desired outcomes.

Efficiency The extent to which organizational activity can achieve target outcomes with minimal use of resources; often described as a rate measured by 'output divided by input'.

Embedded approach An approach to strategic thinking in which the organization's strategic options are influenced by but also have the potential to influence the environment in which the organization is embedded.

Emergence The process of activities, events, or outcomes happening in a non-planned way, arising through the natural course of events.

Emotional commitment A willingness to advocate on behalf of ideas or decision outcomes based on positive feelings of ownership to the ideas.

Engagement Involvement as an active participant in a process with a stake and interest in process outcomes.

Entrepreneurial Showing initiative, a sense of opportunity, and a capacity to access and organize resources in order to exploit situations profitably.

Environmental scanning A process that detects changes in the organization's competitive environment, changes in customer tastes, emerging new technologies, etc.

Episode A period of time, with a defined start and end-point, within which a set of activities involving practitioners, practices, context, and outcomes can be examined.

Espoused theories The narratives we use to justify the logic behind our behaviours and decisions.

Experiential learning cycle A model of learning that highlights how concrete experience can be transformed into learning, which, in turn, can drive experimental action and new experiences.

External context All aspects of an organization's situation which exist beyond the boundaries of its direct control.

Facilitation Creation of conditions in which activities, interactions, decisions, or a flow of events can occur in an effective and/or efficient manner.

Feasibility This test of a proposed strategy considers how well the strategy will work in practice and how difficult it might be to achieve.

Feelings, Facts, Proposals (FFP) A reflective writing tool from practice that is intended to guide an individual to collect their thoughts and feelings on a matter, seek external perspectives and data on the same matter, and uncover new insights to guide future actions.

Financial control systems Financial control systems are based on hard data ('numbers') as key metrics used to define budgetary activities and financial targets and support financial planning and budgetary review to control organizational performance.

Financial perspective One of the four perspectives of the balanced scorecard; it asks, 'How do we look to shareholders?'

Financial strategy Includes the organization's approach to both raising the funds it needs and managing the employment of those funds within the organization.

Fintech Digital financial technologies that deliver operational improvements, innovation, and new sources of customer value.

First-mover advantage Circumstances when the first firm to market with a new product, process, technology, business model, or platform is able to gain such a solid foothold by earning customer loyalty, economies of scale, or learning benefits that subsequent entrants are unable to successfully challenge the first mover's dominant position.

Five Forces A framework for evaluating the profit potential of an industrial sector or market through analysis of its structure, considering buyer, supplier, and competitor factors, alongside the threats of new entrants and substitutes.

Flexibility test One of a number of possible tests of good organizational design, this test considers the extent to which that design will allow for change in the future, perhaps in response to shifts in a fast-moving external environment.

Flow A continuous stream of activity or movement.

Forcefield analysis An analytical tool to identify forces in the organization that may drive and restrain change.

Foreign direct investment (FDI) The activities of multinational corporations are based on FDI, that is, locating part of the firm's activities in countries other than the firm's domestic market.

Foreign market entry modes The channels ranging from export strategies to direct foreign investment that an organization can employ to gain entry to a new international market.

Formulation Activity or effort dedicated to generating new strategy ideas, plans, and initiatives.

Four Es Particularly in public and not-for-profit organizations, a proposed strategy may be tested against objectives that are founded on the 'four Es': efficiency, effectiveness, economy, and equity.

Functional strategy Addresses the question, 'How to operate?', in order to deliver an optimal contribution to corporate and business strategy from functions such as human resources, finance, and operations.

Functional structure The simplest form of organizational structure which typically divides responsibilities according to the organization's primary functions, such as operations, finance, marketing, human resources, and IT.

Generic strategies An explanation of strategies (differentiation, cost-leadership, and focus strategies) which describe how a company pursues competitive advantage across its chosen market scope.

Glide path A visual representation of anticipated progress against meeting a target based on knowledge of organizational activity and context. It is used to enable more nuanced management of key performance indicators and targets. Glide paths should be derived from a knowledgeable evaluation of possible progress against a target.

Global strategy The opposite of a multidomestic strategy—it sacrifices responsiveness to local requirements within each of its markets in favour of emphasizing efficiency. Some minor modifications to products and services may be made in various markets, but a global strategy stresses the need to gain economies of scale by offering essentially the same products or services in each market.

Globalization A continuing process of integration and movement of people, companies, goods and services, and finance, and harmonization of rules and regulations between governments globally.

'Great man' theory A traditional view of leadership as a trait, meaning some people are naturally born to be leaders or hold positions of authority.

Greenwashing The act of deliberately misleading consumers about the environmental practices of a company or the environmental traits or benefits of a product or service.

Groupthink A cognitive phenomenon that occurs within a group of people in which the desire for harmony or conformity in the group results in an irrational or dysfunctional decision-making outcome. Group members try to minimize conflict and reach a consensus decision without critical evaluation of alternative viewpoints.

Growth An organization seeking growth may be aiming to increase profits or serve more clients. Strategies for growth may be driven by new opportunities present in the external environment or by the financial ambitions of the owner of a firm.

Heuristics An approach to problem solving that uses a practical method not guaranteed to be optimal, perfect, or rational, but instead sufficient for reaching an immediate goal. Heuristics can be speedy mental shortcuts that ease the cognitive burden of deciding, such as a gut feeling or extrapolating from previous experience.

Holding structure This structure brings together a number of diverse businesses under a central head office; these diverse businesses may have come together through diversification activities such as mergers or acquisitions.

Horizontal integration This strategy involves the combination of two businesses operating in the same industry and at the same stage of the supply chain.

Horizontal keiretsu An alliance of cross-shareholding companies, led by a Japanese bank, which provides a range of services.

HRM strategy This aspect of functional strategy typically includes an organization's plans for managing its people, their performance, and their training and development. It may also cover the organization's culture and its approach to determining how people and culture fit into the organization's future growth strategies and plans.

Human-centred design An approach to design activities that puts the user–product interaction at the centre of the process rather than the capabilities or preferences of the designer.

Implementation Activity and effort directed towards turning strategy ideas into reality.

Inclusive design A set of principles that can be used to guide design choices towards maximum inclusivity of participants within the practical constraint of the situation.

Inclusive strategizing An approach to designing strategizing activity in which the methods, timescale, location, tasks, etc. meet all stakeholder needs as an enabler of inclusion and participation.

Incremental innovation An innovation that improves existing products, services, or ways of working by better or further exploiting existing capabilities or resources.

Industry A group of organizations engaged in a particular type of commercial or economic activity (e.g. the smartphone industry)—potentially related markets which can be grouped together according to similarity in products and/or geographies.

Industry forces analysis A method of examining the organizational implications of how a market is structured and interacts now and in the future.

Industry globalization drivers This is a framework that identifies four set of drivers (market, cost, competition, government) that underlie conditions in each industry that create the potential for that industry to become more global and hence warrant a global approach to strategy.

Industry life cycle The historical development of an industry from birth through growth to maturity and then decline.

Industry structure The number of entities and their transactional relationships within a sector.

Information asymmetry Where one party has more or better information than the other.

Innovation The process and outcome of the successful exploitation of new ideas.

Innovation and learning perspective One of the four perspectives of the balanced scorecard; it asks, 'Can we continue to improve and create value?'

Innovation capability Capacity to innovate arising from adequate formal or informal innovation processes, sufficiently knowledgeable staff, and a supportive environment in which innovation activities can be carried out.

Innovation culture Patterns in the way innovation activity tends to be perceived and enacted in an organization.

Innovation-orientated structures Flexible and dynamic structures, such as project-based structures and adhocracies, associated with an intention to innovate.

Innovation portfolio strategy A framework to identify the different ways in which innovation is being attempted by an organization; provides clarity around technical and commercial modes of innovating.

Innovation strategy Akin to functional strategy, it describes the balance of ways, ends, and means in which innovation will contribute to broader organizational outcomes.

Integration methods Procedures which can be used to organize data and insights into a framework for further analysis, development, or decision-making.

Integrative review A method for consolidating and improving initial insights and options generated by external analysis techniques.

Intergovernmental Panel on Climate Change (IPCC) An organization comprised of global scientists who compile the latest research on climate change and make the aggregated findings freely available.

Internal business perspective One of the four perspectives of the balanced scorecard; it asks, 'What must we excel at?'

International community Collaboration between nations, typically brokered through intergovernmental organizations.

Internationalization The process by which an organization interacts across national borders through import or export trade or the flow of capital/investment in other geographical locations.

Interpretation A way of understanding or assigning meaning—in relation to strategy, part of the way in which a stakeholder comprehends what strategy means or should involve.

Investor value A valuation of a company which reflects the required returns of the capital markets and the financial value placed on the company's securities by the markets.

Isolated interpretation An approach to strategic thinking in which the organization is considered separately from its external environment, which acts as a constraint of strategic choice.

Isolating mechanism The impediments to immediate imitation of a firm's resource position, equivalent to entry barriers to an industry; can include privileged access to scarce resources, time lag for competitive resource acquisition, and information asymmetries.

Isomorphism A similarity of the processes or structures of one organization to those of another.

IT maturity models A set of models which can help an organization to assess the current effectiveness of its IT capabilities and which capabilities it should aim to acquire next in order to improve its performance.

IT strategy This aspect of functional strategy includes the total pattern of decisions relating to the use of technology within an organization.

Joint venture A new organization created by two separate organizations, perhaps for a specific purpose such as entering a new market or exploiting complementary capabilities.

Keiretsu This structure, traditionally seen in many major companies in Japan, results in a grouping of organizations which take equity stakes in one another and sometimes collaborate and share projects.

Key performance indicators (KPIs) A type of performance measurement used to evaluate the success of an organization or a particular activity in which it engages.

Key processes Operational and managerial activities and processes that enable the organization to deliver value to its customers in a unique way.

Key resources All value-creating tangible and intangible resources to deliver the organization's value proposition and generate profit for the company.

Keystone advantage The position of a leading firm that provides a stable and predictable set of common assets to an ecosystem and therefore is in a position of influence over all others in the ecosystem.

Knowledge loop An inclusive design method that tests prototypes of planned approaches with a wide range of users in order to refine activity designs for inclusivity.

Leadership Concerns the systems, practitioners, processes, practices, and activities of leading, guiding, or influencing others—a contested term with multiple meanings.

Leadership as an ability A view that leadership is a capacity to act from a combination of natural potential and learned approaches.

Leadership as a behaviour A view that leadership is an observable pattern of conduct in everyday work life.

Leadership as a skill A view that leadership is competence that can be developed through training, mentoring, and experience.

Leadership as practice Rather then having a leader, there is a dynamic process between stakeholders and, through interaction and cooperation, decisions and actions are taken as a collective.

Learning Acquisition of knowledge or skills through study, experience, or being taught.

Licensing A business arrangement involving a firm authorizing another firm to temporarily access its intellectual property rights, such as a manufacturing process or a brand name; for example, Coca-Cola and Pepsi are globally produced and sold by local bottlers in different countries under licence.

M&A A general term used to describe the consolidation of organizations and their assets through a financial transaction such as a merger or an acquisition.

McFarlan's strategic grid A model developed to assist managers to analyse the portfolio of IT projects that their organization might be pursuing.

Market The individuals, organizations, and activities involved in the provision or consumption of a product or service within a defined geography.

Market advantage test One of a number of important tests of good organizational design, this test questions the fit between an organization's structure and its market strategy.

Market development A growth strategy based on an organization identifying new markets for its existing products.

Market penetration A growth strategy based on an organization increasing its market share in its present market(s).

Market position How the organization compares with rivals on key performance dimensions (such as price and product features) in the minds of customers.

Market segmentation The process of dividing a market of potential customers into groups or segments based on different customer characteristics.

Market-based view (MBV) A collection of concepts and theoretical contributions intended to explain how an organization can effectively gain and sustain competitive advantage by adopting strategies for organizational conduct appropriate to its external environment—also known as the 'outside-in' approach to strategy.

Marketing mix (4Ps or 7Ps) A model for exploring the components of the organization's marketing options, such as price, product, promotion, place and other key dimensions.

Marketing strategy This aspect of functional strategy typically sets out the firm's overall approach to reaching people and turning them into customers of the product or service that it offers as well as its approach to retaining existing customers.

Matrix structure This structure sets up reporting relationships as a grid or matrix rather than a traditional hierarchy. Employees are likely to have dual reporting relationships—for example, to both a functional manager and a product manager.

Mediating assessment protocol (MAP) This is a structured approach to reducing errors in strategic decision-making. There are three core elements to MAP: identification of mediating assessments that are key attributes to decision evaluation, independent assessments grounded on available evidence, and final evaluation after all key attributes have been identified and assessed.

Megatrend A global shift, such as globalization or digital technologies, that is reshaping the world and changing the way we live and do business.

Mental models Deeply ingrained assumptions, generalizations, or even pictures or images that influence how we understand the world and how we take action.

Merger An agreement that unites two existing organizations into one new organization.

Method A technique or approach to undertaking activity designed to achieve an outcome in an effective manner.

M-forms or multidivisional forms or multidivisional structure See 'multidivisional form or multidivisional structure (M-form)'.

Mission The current main focus of organizational effort towards a set of coherent goals and objectives.

Mission statement A short and memorable statement defining why an organization exists, its overall goal, and the extent of its operations—what kind of product or service is provided, to whom, and in what markets.

Modular innovation An innovation that involve changing a core design concept within a largely unchanged product architecture.

Monopoly A situation in which a single individual or organization is the exclusive supplier of a product or service.

Monopsony A situation in which a single individual or organization is the exclusive buyer of a product or service.

Multi-business organization A diversified organization where no single business unit is responsible for the majority of the revenue.

Multi-criteria decision analysis A highly structured, rational approach to evaluating and prioritizing strategy options which can aid the resolution of contentious issues or support groups learning to work together through a strategy activity.

Multidivisional form or multidivisional structure (M-form) An organizational structure separating an organization into several discrete units which are guided and controlled by targets from the corporate centre.

Multidomestic strategy A strategy by which companies try to achieve maximum local responsiveness by customizing both their product offer and marketing strategy to match different national conditions. This strategy sacrifices efficiency in favour of emphasizing responsiveness to local requirements within each of its markets.

Multimodality The use of multiple means, in parallel, of achieving the same user utility or outcome, such as in the communication of information.

Multinational company/corporation (MNC) A business that operates in more than one country; that is, it has business operations in two or more countries. This goes beyond selling goods and services in more than one country and involves FDI.

Multinational enterprise (MNE) An alternative term for MNC—MNC and MNE are interchangeable terms.

Multi-sided platform (MSP) An organization that provides rules and infrastructure that facilitate interactions between parties.

Network structure A flexible and non-hierarchical organizational structure that brings together a number of strategic business units (SBUs) or even independent organizations, linked together by formal or informal relationships which change over time.

Noise Unwanted variability in professional judgements. For example, if two judges pass a different judgment for the same crime, at least one of them is wrong. That is a judgement where variability is not desirable. When you don't have the same answer to something where the same answer is needed is knowns as 'noise'.

Non-governmental organization (NGO) A non-profit group organized at a local, national, or international level around a common purpose, providing advocacy and information on an issue of societal or environmental importance.

Objectives Desirable outcomes targeted by an organization or individual for attainment in the future.

Open innovation The flow of ideas to and fro between an organization and its network to be exploited in novel collaborative ways to the benefit of all involved.

Open strategy Strategy processes and activities designed on principles of inclusivity and transparency.

Operational relatedness If two organizations have a high level of operational relatedness, there may be the opportunity to share assets at the business unit level.

Operational systems Mechanisms, working practices, or routines that underlie the efficient use and deployment of resources and capabilities, for example, the order fulfilment system in a warehouse where customer orders that have been placed online are picked and prepared for distribution.

Operations strategy This aspect of functional strategy addresses the efficient and effective allocation of resources to ensure that the organization's infrastructure and activities like production or distribution are properly supported.

Opportunism Reacting swiftly and effectively—often in an unplanned way in response to emerging circumstances—in order to achieve desirable outcomes as situations unfold and opportunities are presented.

Ordinary capabilities Capabilities that have a direct impact on the production of goods or provision of services.

Organization charts A useful way of depicting formal relations, charts that represent the different 'levels' within larger organizations and typically indicate reporting lines.

Organizational ambidexterity An organization's ability to be efficient in its management of current business activities whilst adapting to changing operating conditions; requires the use of exploration and exploitation techniques in parallel.

Organizational change A process that focuses on the stages that organizations go through as they evolve or attempt renewal. The principles of organizational change theory apply to both short- and long-term changes as well as the speed and urgency of change in adverse business operating conditions.

Organizational conduct The choices taken and activities attempted by an organization out of the many options available to it.

Organizational culture A set of the underlying beliefs, assumptions, values, and ways of interacting that contribute to the unique social and psychological environment of an organization.

Organizational design The purposeful design of how work is conducted in an organization through structures, systems, and procedures, including reporting lines and allocation of responsibilities to employees and teams.

Organizational innovation New processes by which we can organize firm activities, coordinate human resources, and revise management approaches—also known as managerial or administrative innovation.

Organizational learning The continuing process of generating, retaining, flowing, and deploying knowledge within an organization, as opposed to the same effect in individuals.

Organizational strategy Organizational effort, initiative, and attention towards maintaining a balance between ends, ways, and means of surviving and thriving—providing a framework for making choices and trade-offs and identifying resources, methods, actions, and value-creating objectives that sustain the organization over time within an ever-changing context.

Organizational structure The particular structure adopted by a given organization.

Organizational survival An organization remains financially viable in the long term and can continue in its current form without merging, being taken over, or having to shut down.

Outsourcing The practice of hiring a party outside an organization to perform activities that were traditionally performed in-house by the organization's own employees.

Parenting advantage test One of a number of possible tests of good organizational design, this tests reminds us that there should be a good fit between the organization's structure and the parenting role of the corporate centre.

Patent A type of intellectual property that provides the patent owner legal protection to prevent others from using, making, or selling a product or service based on the patent. Patents can be considered as a means of providing the patent holder competitive advantage for the duration of the patent.

Path dependency Refers to the effect that what an organization is capable of doing in the present is a function of what has happened in the past; for example, a firm may gain competitive advantage today based on past acquisition and development of resources and capabilities.

Paths, positions, processes framework Associated with the dynamic capability view—a framework for understanding what an organization can do today based on its historical paths and what it might do today in order to create future options.

People focus Goals and activities directed towards improving the impact of an organization on its stakeholders, such as employees, shareholders, owners, customers, and suppliers.

People test One of a number of possible tests of good organizational design, this tests reminds us that there must be a good fit between the organization's structure and the people available to fill key roles.

Performance management A system for managing employees, teams, and aspects of an organization towards the attainment of quantified targets.

PESTEL A framework for describing the state and trajectory of the non-market macro-environmental context in which strategy is made, addressing Political, Economic, Social, Technological, Environmental, and Legislative factors.

Plan A deliberate course of action towards desired objectives.

Planet focus Goals and activities directed towards improving the relationship between an organization and the natural environment—how finite resources and energy are used, how waste is created and managed, and how climate change is impacted by organizational activities.

Plasticity The characteristic of being able to adapt or be moulded to meet changing needs or circumstances.

Platform A product, service, infrastructure, or technology that becomes essential to a system of commercial activity whilst solving a strategic problem for many organizations and users in a sector.

Platform innovation The creation or growth of a foundation for an ecosystem of activity—increasingly features as a topic of strategic interest in a networked world; also referred to as ecosystems innovation.

Platform leadership An organization's position in a network from which it can exert maximum influence on the ecosystem—relates to keystone advantage.

Platform strategy The deliberate innovative actions an organization can make to either create a new platform or grow an ecosystem in which the organization is embedded.

Policy Formal principles or rules which are to be followed by an organization through its decisions and activities.

Political process Strategy as a political process means that decisions and interactions reflect the use of formal and informal power and the vested interests of individuals and groups.

Porter's Diamond framework of national advantage A theoretical model that is designed to help understand the emergence of competitive advantage of nations or industry clusters as a result of certain factor conditions available to them and how strategists can apply the tool to identify attractive markets or locations to situate their production activities.

Positioning map See 'strategy clock'.

Practical acceptability Perception of the feasibility and cost effectiveness of a strategy activity within given practical constraints (time, cost, effort, etc.).

Practice An ongoing stream of activity occurring over time; that which is actually done.

Practices The ways of working adopted by practitioners when trying to accomplish a type of task.

Practitioners Those who 'do' or are involved in the 'doing' of strategy work—either employed by the organization or external parties contracted or included on a temporary basis.

Prescriptive models Step-by-step guides to strategy work that indicate exactly how strategy activity and processes should take place.

Prioritization methods Approaches for determining the relative importance of individual ideas within a broader set of ideas.

Private sector The part of the economy that is owned by private individuals, rather than the government, comprising organizations that need to make profit to endure.

Procedural justice Perception of the fairness of the way a strategy activity is conducted.

Procedural rationality Perception that a strategy activity and its outcome is sensible and based on well-articulated reasoning.

Process A flow of events, experiences, and activities occurring over time and in context.

Process studies Research that addresses how human factors such as errors, learning, culture, habit, power, and politics play a role in how strategy happens over time and in context.

Product development A growth strategy based on an organization creating new products to replace or add to current ones in its existing markets.

Profit The difference between the financial income received by an organization and its operating costs.

Profit focus Goals and activities directed towards generating profit or financial performance for an organization.

Profit formula A quantifiable analysis that reveals how a company creates value (profit) for itself while providing value to customers.

Project-based structure An organizational structure where teams are created, undertake their work (usually for a fixed timespan), and are then dissolved.

Prospect theory A foundational concept in behavioural economics—describes the way people choose between alternatives that involve risk, where the probabilities of decision outcomes are known. The theory states that people make decisions based on the potential value of losses and gains rather than the final outcome and that people evaluate these losses and gains using certain heuristics.

Psychic distance The perceived distance between an organization's home market and a foreign market. It results from perceptions of both business and cultural differences, such as language, religion, legislation, and business practices.

Psychological safety A context for social activity in which participants feel able to give their candid views on a subject without fear of retribution or negative outcomes.

Public sector Organizations and aspects of an economy which are funded and controlled by local or central government.

Purpose An enduring sense of meaning and intended impact of an individual or organization that reflects vision, mission, and values.

Question burst A method for encouraging a group to creatively and positively engage in a discussion task by framing all contributions in the form of questions.

Radical innovation Innovation that involves the introduction of entirely new thinking into an organization.

Rational decision-making A process or sequence of activities that involves the stages of problem recognition, information search, definition of alternatives, and selection of an optimal outcome from two or more alternatives that are consistent with the decision-maker's ranked preferences.

Rational plans Plans developed based on data-based analysis of a situation, where the situation is modelled, options identified, and an optimal option selected as the logical way forward.

Redundant hierarchy test One of a number of possible tests of good organizational design, this test reminds us that a proposed structure should not have too many layers of management.

Reflection A learning mechanism which gives in-depth focused attention to the examination of an episode in life to better understand the flow of events, how outcomes emerged, and our role in proceedings.

Reflection-in-action Reflection that occurs during the moment of activity.

Reflection-on-action Reflection that occurs after an event.

Reflective practice Development of insight and practice through critical attention to practical values, theories, principles, assumptions, and the relationship between theory and practice which inform everyday actions.

Reflexivity Focused, in-depth reflection on one's own perspective, values, and assumptions—also known as critical self-reflection.

Regulation The act of controlling the flow of strategy activities in order to best meet perceived organizational needs.

Related diversification The process that takes place when an organization expands its activities into products/services that are similar to those it currently offers.

Relatedness The commonality between any two products, companies, or industries (see also 'corporate relatedness' and 'operational relatedness').

Reorganization/renewal In the reorganization/renewal stage of turnaround management, the leadership team should begin to pursue long-term actions that are intended to return the organization to a more successful level of performance.

Replacement In the replacement stage of turnaround management, senior managers may be replaced by new managers, who will help to introduce strategic change, and resulting recovery, based on their different experiences and backgrounds.

Repositioning The repositioning stage of turnaround management attempts to generate revenue by introducing innovations and making changes in product portfolios and market positioning.

Resource base The total set of resources that an organization has or has access to on a preferential basis.

Resource base profiling A method of building up a clear shared picture of what an organization currently has available in terms of resources.

Resource deployment The allocation of organizational resources towards a specific activity or long-term aim.

Resource flows The incremental changes in resource stocks that occur over time.

Resource heterogeneity Acknowledging that different firms, even in the same industry, possess different bundles of resources (where firms are thought of as bundles of value-creating resources).

Resource stocks The current level of resources available to the organization.

Resource-based view (RBV) A collection of concepts and theoretical contributions intended to explain how an organization can effectively gain and sustain competitive advantage by adopting strategies to identify and organize around value-creating distinctive resources.

Resources What an organization has or has access to that it can use to undertake activities or attempt to achieve objectives—synonymous with assets.

Retrenchment Stage of turnaround management comprising wide-ranging short-term actions intended to reduce any financial losses, stabilize the organization, and solve any immediate problems.

Risk management The process of identifying and evaluating risks, as well as procedures, to avoid or minimize their negative impact.

Routines Semi-patterned ways of working in which activity is undertaken in a predictable way, embedding learning from previous activities, in order to improve effectiveness and efficiency of effort.

Satisficing A combination of the words 'satisfy' and 'suffice'—a decision-making process that entails searching for available alternatives until an acceptable solution to a problem is found. Satisficing can explain the behaviour of decision-makers under circumstances in which an optimal solution cannot be determined.

Scenario planning A method of modelling alternative plausible futures, deriving learning about the nature of those futures, and undertaking initiatives today in order to be ready to meet the challenges of multiple possible future scenarios.

Scenario thinking A method of exploring the possible future implications of current trends and trajectories for an organization.

Scope The range of activities, geographical territories, products, and services that an organization attempts to address.

SCP The structure–conduct–performance framework of the market-based view that explains how the external environment and firm strategies interact.

Sector A part or subdivision of an economy or industry (such as the public sector, private sector, etc.) that it is useful to analyse separately from the whole.

Sense-giving The process of attempting to influence a target audience's perception of meaning. It can be used as a powerful process to set forth a desired future state of an organization and motivate people to deliver that vision.

Sense-making A process by which people give meaning to their individual or collective experiences;

often used to describe individuals' ongoing retrospective development of plausible mental frames to rationalize what they are doing.

Servitization Involves organizations developing the capabilities they need to provide services and solutions that supplement their traditional product offerings.

Shareholder An individual or organization that owns some or all of an organization.

Shareholder value maximization A management philosophy which implies that the ultimate measure of a company's success is the extent to which it enriches shareholders.

Simple structure At an early stage in its development, an organization is likely to have a simple structure that reflects how work is divided between a number of sections or departments according to function (also known as a functional structure).

Single business unit An organization that operates in a single industry.

Single-loop learning Learning in which our strategy and methods are enhanced without challenging our assumptions and beliefs.

Situated activity Activity that occurs within and is influenced by context at a certain moment in time.

Situated attention The influence of context on the direction of attention.

Situated learning perspective A framework to help us understand how contextual, environmental, and social factors influence learning.

Situation The set of circumstances which provide the context for the activity of an individual or organization at any given moment in time.

Social Occurring between individuals or groups of individuals—strategy as a social process is enacted through multiple interactions between individuals and groups.

Social acceptability Perception that a strategy activity is attuned to the social needs of stakeholders in a trustworthy way.

Social complexity Resources and capabilities that have evolved over time as a result of social interaction within the organization, for example,

interpersonal relationships among managers, the firm's culture, and its reputation among customers and suppliers.

Social enterprise An entity that pursues a social mission while relying on a commercial business model—also known as a hybrid organization.

Specialized cultures test One of a number of important tests of good organizational design, this test reminds us that a good organizational design brings together specialist staff, allowing them to develop their expertise in close collaboration with each other.

Sponsor An individual or group of individuals who purposefully initiate a strategizing activity based on their formal position and allocated ownership of the outcomes.

Stakeholder mapping An analytical framework and process to identify and prioritize the stakeholders in the organization.

Stakeholders Those individuals or groups affected by and with the power to influence the outcomes of organizational activities.

Stakeholder value maximization A management philosophy that regards maximization of the interests of all its stakeholders (customers, employees, shareholders, and the community) as its highest objective.

Step-based models for managing strategic change Popular frameworks in managerial practice that have been developed to help managers approach the task of strategic change as a logical, step-by-step process.

Strategic activity Work done by practitioners towards attaining some sort of strategy-related outcome.

Strategic alliance An agreement by two or more organizations to cooperate in the development, manufacture, or sale of products or services without becoming a single entity.

Strategic business unit (SBU) A fully functional unit of a business that has its own vision and direction.

Strategic drift A concept in change management that can be applied to understand the consequences of the organization failing to keep pace with changes in the external environment.

Strategic group A collection of organizations adopting broadly the same strategy to service the needs of the same group of customers.

Strategic group analysis A method of identifying clusters of competitors in a market that are following broadly similar strategies to serve similar groups of customers.

Strategic hyperopia When strategic leaders become overly focused on the external context and distant issues to the exclusion of organizational performance.

Strategic innovation Innovation in an organization's business model, altering how it creates value whilst possibly disrupting how a current market operates or creating uncontested new market space.

Strategic leader An organizational leader who is resilient and flexible, capable of drawing on talents in anticipating, challenging, interpreting, deciding, aligning, and learning to lead an organization successfully regardless of contextual events.

Strategic leadership The leadership of organizations arising from an individual or group's ability to articulate a strategic vision for the organization and to motivate and persuade others to buy into and execute that vision.

'Strategic leadership interface' perspective The view that strategic leadership influence depends not just on the attributes and actions of the CEO and top team but also on their relationship with leadership across levels of the organization.

Strategic leadership system A strategizing 'multiteam system' across organization leadership levels and the external networks in which the organization is embedded.

Strategic learning Learning which informs and influences the identification and enactment of strategic initiatives intended to deliver future capacity for organizational growth and survival.

Strategic myopia When strategic leaders become overly focused on the internal context and local issues to the exclusion of longer-term scanning, planning, and exploration.

Strategic perspective Capacity of an individual or group to be able to think about and perceive holistically a system of events or activities and how they interrelate over time rather than just understanding individual components of that system.

Strategic thinking A holistic approach to framing and interpreting an aspect of the world, such as the current and future state of an organization.

Strategizing The enactment of activity relating to strategy.

Strategy The best word we have to describe how we maintain a balance between ends, ways, and means; identifying objectives and the resources and methods available for meeting such objectives within the context of the drama and challenge of the inherent unpredictability of human affairs.

Strategy-as-practice (SAP) A collection of concepts and theoretical contributions intended to explain how strategy can be considered a continuing achievement, the outcomes of which are influenced by who is involved, when they are involved, and which tools and practices they use.

Strategy clock A theoretical model that explores the options for the organization to strategically position its products and services in a competitive market, that is, how a firm can position its product in a marketplace to give it a competitive advantage.

Strategy map A diagram intended to illustrate the organization's strategy and performance, identify relationships between key strategic concepts, and communicate the organization's objectives and where employees contribute and fit in.

Structural ambidexterity The creation of separate organizations or structures for different types of activities. Such organizations or structures are either fully explorative or exploitative. In these organizations or structures, employees have clearly defined responsibilities.

Structuralist approach An approach to strategic thinking in which the organization's strategic options are bounded by the environment.

Structures The enduring physical, social, and institutional settings in which an organization's activity occurs.

Substitute In terms of market strategy, an alternative product or service that provides equivalent utility through very different means (e.g. an encyclopaedia compared with a Google search).

Suitability The suitability of a proposed strategy can be assessed by the extent to which it matches the needs identified from a strategic analysis.

Sunk cost fallacy When we continue an action or behaviour because of our past decisions (time, investments, resource allocations) rather than attempting to make a rational choice that would maximize our utility or improved performance at this present time.

Supervisory leadership All aspects of leadership occurring in organizations.

Supplier power The bargaining power that the entity selling a good or service has over the purchaser.

Supply chain The network of organizations involved in the creation and sale of a product, from the delivery of source materials from the supplier to the manufacturer through to the delivery of the product to the end-user.

Sustainability The capacity of a system to continue over time at a global level, defined by the United Nations as meeting the needs of the present without compromising the ability of future generations to meet their own needs.

Sustainable development Human progress that doesn't harm future generations or the planet.

Sustainable development goals (SDGs) Proposed by the United Nations, the SDGs are a framework of interrelated goals and objectives intended to influence national, local, and organizational strategies for driving sustainable development.

Sustainable investment Also known as ethical investment or green investment, an approach to managing an investment portfolio where the stocks and shares owned reflect the investor's sustainability, moral, and ethical concerns.

SWOT A framework for describing and comparing the internal strengths and weaknesses of an organization with the external opportunities and threats presenting in its environmental context.

Synergy The idea that the whole is greater than the sum of the parts or that the value created by business units working together can exceed the value of those units create working independently.

Systems The micro-structures that make organizations work; they tell people and machines what to do, monitor performance, and provide the basis for an overall evaluation of the organization's performance.

Tangible and intangible assets The two main asset classes of an organization: tangible assets include both fixed resources (such as machinery, buildings, and land) and current assets, such as inventory; intangible assets are non-physical resources, such as patents, trademarks, copyrights, goodwill, and brand recognition.

Technological change Possibilities for new ways of working and interacting driven by advances in technical know-how, products, and equipment.

Technological innovation New knowledge and technology being converted into advances in products, services, operational processes, and infrastructure.

Theory A set of ideas that helps explain something—often set out in a format that can be tested through field research.

Theory of national advantage See 'Porter's Diamond framework of national advantage'.

Theories-in-use The thought processes that actually drive our behaviours and decisions, regardless of how we make explanations to others.

Third sector Organizations fulfilling a social purpose that are not exclusively profit focused or controlled by government, such as charities, voluntary organizations, social enterprises, and community groups.

Threshold capabilities Capabilities that an organization is required to maintain to a minimum performance level in order to compete in an industry.

Time compression diseconomies The time and space needed to acquire or develop resources by an organization. Once time and space pass, firms that do not possess the same or similar time- and space-dependent resources may face significant cost disadvantages in acquiring and developing matching resources because doing so would require these disadvantaged firms to recreate history.

Tools The techniques, methods, models, and frameworks which support interactions and decision-making in strategy activity.

Tools-in-use How strategy tools are deployed— exploiting the potential of affordances—in an effort to effectively meet the needs of strategy activity in any given situation.

Top management team The most senior managers in an organization, accountable for short- and long-term performance outcomes and with the power to allocate resources and set strategy.

TOWS An integrating method for collating contextual insights and strategy options arising from the use of analytical methods; serves as a platform for creative development of options and as an input to evaluative methods.

Transformational leadership Delivering systems-level change that impacts on social as well as organizational outcomes.

Transnational strategy A middle ground between a multidomestic strategy and a global strategy. A firm that pursues transnational strategy seeks to balance the desire for efficiency with the need to adjust to local preferences within the various countries in which it operates.

Transnational structure This configuration is a means of managing internationally, which can be effective in making good use of knowledge spread across geographic borders (see 'transnational strategy').

Triangulation A method for combining different data sources in order to establish a richer understanding of a matter of interest.

Triple bottom line (TBL) A model of sustainable performance in which a balance is achieved within a system of objectives addressing people, profit, and planet-related outcomes.

Turnaround management A process of corporate renewal using analysis and planning to save troubled companies and return them to solvency and to identify the reasons for failing performance in the firm's markets and rectify them.

United Nations (UN) A global organization comprising representatives from the nations of the world which seeks to addressed shared challenges with policies, initiatives, and cooperative action.

Unrelated diversification The process of entering a new industry that lacks any important similarities with the firm's existing businesses; often accomplished through a merger or acquisition.

Upper echelon theory Posits that the nature of an organization will reflect what its 'top' managers say, think, and do.

Utility The usefulness or advantage of a product or service to a user in providing a function or experience.

Value Relative worth—often the extent to which an individual is willing to pay for a good or a service.

Value chain analysis A method which models an organization's direct activities that create value and indirect activities that shape the environment for value creation.

Value creating The quality or attribute of a resource that describes the extent to which it can be used to achieve outcomes which a customer is willing to pay for.

Value net A method that helps identify opportunities for enhanced collaboration with other players—competitors, customers, suppliers, and complementors—within an organization's network.

Value web A map of the network of interactions and relationships between an organization, suppliers, customers, and complementors through which open innovation may occur.

Values Characteristics which describe how behaviour and conduct of individuals and teams should be consistently carried out, in compliance with ethical and moral codes of the organization.

Vertical integration This strategy involves a firm extending its operations within its value chain, for example, acquiring businesses in its supply chain.

Vertical keiretsu A partnership of manufacturers, suppliers, and distributors that work cooperatively to increase efficiency and reduce costs.

Vision A loose description of where an organization should aspire to be in a (typically far-off) future time that can be used to motivate, guide, and include organizational stakeholders in a collective effort to move in a certain direction.

Visionary leadership Being able to explain how the world could be and compelling others to work towards that vision.

VRIO A framework for identifying resources which might act as a source of competitive advantage for an organization, by the extent to which they are Valued by the customer, Rare, Imperfectly imitable, and can be used within the Organization.

VUCA An acronym for Volatile, Uncertain, Complex and Ambiguous circumstances that describe the challenging conditions facing many strategists.

Wicked problem A problematic situation which is so complex and interwoven with influential factors that it is impossible to 'solve it' fully; instead, the challenge is to try to mitigate or deal with the situation in a better way.

Yip's industry globalization drivers Four sets of 'industry globalization drivers' which underlie the conditions in each industry that create the potential for that industry to become more global and, as a consequence, for the potential viability of a global approach to strategy.

Zero-order capabilities The operational capabilities of an organization that provide the potential to produce goods or provide services.

NAME INDEX

SUBJECT INDEX